Images from the Holocaust
A LITERATURE ANTHOLOGY

Jean E. Brown
Saginaw Valley State University

Elaine C. Stephens
Saginaw Valley State University

Janet E. Rubin
Saginaw Valley State University

National Textbook Company
a division of NTC/CONTEMPORARY PUBLISHING GROUP
Lincolnwood, Illinois USA

Acknowledgments for literary selections can be found beginning on page 569, which should be considered an extension of this copyright page.

ISBN 0-8442-5920-9 (student text)
ISBN 0-8442-5921-7 (instructor's edition)

Sponsoring Editor: Marisa L. L'Heureux
Associate Editor: Nancy Liskar
Cover design: Ophelia M. Chambliss
Interior design: Matthew Doherty
Production Manager: Rosemary Dolinski

Library of Congress Cataloging-in-Publication Data

Images from the Holocaust: a literature anthology / [compiled by]
    Jean E. Brown, Elaine C. Stephens, Janet E. Rubin.
        p.   cm.
    Includes index.
    ISBN 0-8442-5920-9 (pbk .)
        1. Holocaust, Jewish (1939–1945)—Personal narratives.
    2. Holocaust, Jewish (1939–1945)—Literary collections.   I. Brown,
    Jean E.   II. Stephen, Elaine C.   III. Rubin,
    Janet.
    D804. 195. I43   1996   96-21319
    940 . 53' 18—dc20   CIP

Published by NTC Publishing Group,
a division of NTC/Contemporary Publishing Group, Inc.,
4255 West Touhy Avenue,
Lincolnwood (Chicago), Illinois 60646-1975 U.S.A.
©1997 by NTC/Contemporary Publishing Group, Inc.
Manufactured in the United States of America.

11 12 13 14 15 16 DOC/DOC 0 9 8

ISBN: 978-0-8442-5920-8
MHID: 0-8442-5920-9
ISBN: 978-0-8442-5921-5
MHID: 0-8442-5921-7

Dedication

To my aunt and uncle, Vesta and Elmer Mitchell, with my love and gratitude for the richness they bring to me.

Jean E. Brown

To my lovely daughter, Melinda, who is a source of great joy in my life.

Elaine C. Stephens

To my brother, sister, niece, and nephews for the love and the memories we share.

Janet E. Rubin

Contents

chapter 3

Fleeing for Their Lives　　73

chapter 4

Surrounded by Ghetto Walls　　115

---

chapter 5

Imprisoned in the Camps 201

---

chapter 6

Resisting Evil 293

chapter 7

Liberation   335

chapter 8

The Days After   375

c h a p t e r   9

A Mosaic of Courage   445

c h a p t e r   10

Echoing Reflections   513

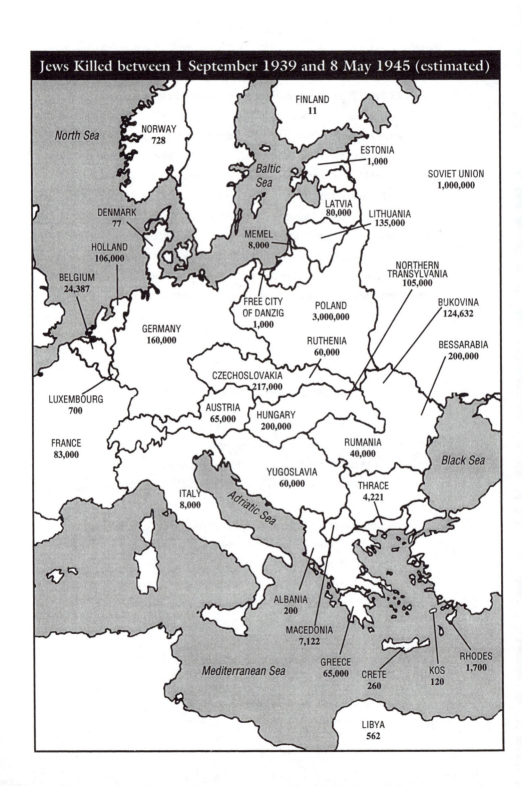

Jews Killed between 1 September 1939 and 8 May 1945 (estimated)

Preface

The fiftieth anniversary of the end of World War II (celebrated in 1995) provided opportunities for both remembrance and reflection. Aged veterans of the Allied forces re-enacted the D-Day landings at Normandy. Citizens of Dresden recalled the horrific bombing campaigns that nearly destroyed their city. And survivors of the Nazi Holocaust recalled the terror of the war years and the incomprehensible magnitude of the death and devastation that resulted from Hitler's attempt at a "final solution."

It is on the Holocaust that this anthology focuses. Selecting literature to convey the essence of the Holocaust is difficult because there was no standard Holocaust experience. Each person who experienced the Holocaust—whether victim, witness, rescuer, or descendant—has a unique story to tell. In this book you will find stories that tell of acts of unspeakable cruelty juxtaposed with stories of courage and dignity. We have included representative examples of a very wide range of experiences.

Selections for this anthology include fiction (both short stories and excerpts from novels), poetry, historical accounts, biographical sketches, and drama. Each entry is preceded by a brief biographical note about the author and an introduction. In addition, each chapter opens with material that provides historical context for the selections that follow.

The book is constructed around ten powerful metaphors. In Chapter 1, "Rumblings of Danger," we have chosen selections that explore Hitler's rise to power and the roots of anti-Semitism in Germany. Chapter 2, "In Hiding," chronicles the experiences of those who tried to escape from the Nazis by going into hiding and of those who hid them. The selections in Chapter 3, "Fleeing for Their Lives," describe the terrifying existence of life on the run from the Nazis. In Chapter 4, "Surrounded by Ghetto Walls," we provide a variety of voices describing what life was like inside the Polish ghettos in which the Jews were forced to live. Chapter 5, "Imprisoned in the Camps," relates the stories of those who died in and those who survived the concentration camps. Chapter 6, "Resisting Evil," explores the acts of courage by individuals and groups who endangered their own lives to save the lives of those who were in peril. In Chapter 7, "Liberation," the readings describe the liberation of the camps and the restoration of freedom for those imprisoned therein. Chapter 8, "The Days After," describes the efforts of survivors to find their relatives and rebuild their lives. Chapter 9, "A Mosaic of Courage," focuses on those who made a difference in the lives of others affected by the Holocaust. Finally, the selections in Chapter 10, "Echoing Reflections," explore the ongoing impact of the Holocaust.

Acknowledgments

We are grateful to a number of people for their encouragement and support. Professors Richard Prystowsky, Charles Fishman, and Sid Bolkosky were graciously responsive to our queries and generous with their assistance. Nadine Burke lent us materials, reacted to our efforts, and shared our interest and enthusiasm. Kristy L. Brosius, Resource Center Coordinator at the United States Holocaust Memorial Museum, helped us locate materials and gave us advice. Additionally, we thank Joanna H. Krause and Mary Hardy of the Bret Adams Limited Artists' Agency. We are also grateful to Sari Grossman and Jeff Schiff for their thoughtful reviews of the manuscript.

We have been fortunate to work with outstanding editors at NTC. John Nolan helped us with the initial conceptualizing of the project. Marisa L. L'Heureux has been the guiding force whose insights helped craft and refine this book. And, finally, we thank Nancy Liskar for her care in helping to bring this book to completion.

chapter 1

Rumblings of Danger

Though the twentieth century has witnessed the carnage of several wars and a host of smaller regional conflicts, perhaps no period of modern history is so rife with acts of unspeakable cruelty as the years of the Third Reich in Germany (1933–1945). In those twelve years, Adolf Hitler's grandiose sense of German nationalism plunged the world into a catastrophic war, resulting in the deaths of nearly ten million people.

While the rise of the Third Reich can be dated from Adolf Hitler's appointment as chancellor of Germany in 1933, discontent in Germany was deeply rooted and growing. The German people were still reeling from a demoralizing defeat in World War I, and the worldwide depression of the late 1920s and early 1930s brought further economic hardship. It was against this background of psychological and economic woes that Hitler came to power. Germans wanted a leader who could rally their hopes and restore their pride; they found such a leader in Hitler, with his fervent nationalism and his plans for Germany's rejuvenation.

More lethal even than Hitler's nationalism, yet directly related to it, was his virulent hatred of Jews. In them, Hitler found a handy scapegoat for Germany's woes. German Jews, however, accounted for less than 1 percent of Germany's population.

Hitler first attempted to seize power in a failed revolution with a small band of storm troopers in 1923. He was jailed for his actions, but there he found a captive audience for his messages of Aryan supremacy. He also met another prisoner, Rudolf Hess, who assisted Hitler in writing his book entitled *Mein Kampf* ("My Struggle"), which became a guidebook for the growing legion of Nazis (the name for members of the National Socialist Party). After his release from prison, Hitler traveled throughout Germany spreading his nationalistic views. In addition to the Jews, Hitler identified secondary targets for his campaign of purification, including communists, homosexuals, the handicapped, Gypsies, Jehovah's Witnesses, and political opponents of the Nazi doctrine.

In the elections of 1930, the National Socialist Party emerged as the second most powerful party, making Hitler a political force who could not be ignored. Hitler steadily gained power over the next three years. After the 1933 elections, German President Paul von Hindenburg felt that he had no choice but to appoint Hitler to be German chancellor. Once he was appointed chancellor, Hitler began to dismantle democratic practices in Germany, thus beginning the reign of devastation that would flow from Germany throughout Europe until the end of World War II.

One of his first acts as chancellor was to have the concentration camp at Dachau built, beginning in March 1933. Jews, communists, and homosexuals were among the first to be incarcerated there. On April 1, 1933, Hitler's government directed a boycott of Jewish-owned stores and businesses. Later that month, the Civil Service Law of April 7, 1933, forced Jews and others defined as non-Aryans out of civil service jobs or other positions with public visibility. This act was the first of over two hundred pieces of legislation passed in Germany from 1933 to 1939 that were designed primarily to segregate, isolate, and demoralize German Jews. On May 10, 1933, a government-organized book burning took place in thirty German cities. The works of authors who were disapproved of by the Hitler regime were burned. Ironically, one hundred years before this event, poet Heinrich Heine, a German Jew, had said of book burning, "Where one burns books, one will, in the end, burn people." These words were sadly prophetic of events that would take place in Germany and Eastern Europe.

Conditions for Jews in Germany continued to deteriorate as new laws banning them from participating in German cultural life and from owning property were enacted in September 1933. Hitler declared himself *führer* (leader) after the death of President Hindenburg on August 2, 1934. In 1935, attacks against Jews escalated. On September 15, the Nuremberg Race Laws were enacted, stripping German Jews of their citizenship and depriving them of all of their political rights. Marriage or sexual relations between Jews and non-Jews were forbidden. The *Mischling* laws specified that anyone with even one Jewish grandparent was considered to be Jewish, regardless of his or her religion. The Nuremberg Laws fueled public ostracism of Jews. Businesses bore signs saying Jews were not welcome. The Nazis were squeezing the Jews from the social and economic mainstream of German life.

Acts of discrimination diminished during 1936 when the eyes of the world turned to Germany as the host nation of the Olympic Games. Though Hitler's views of Aryan superiority were well known, overt campaigns against Jews were hidden from the public and the foreign press during the Olympics. Thus, while the world was aware of the anti-Semitic posturing of the German Reich, it had no idea of the magnitude of Hitler's plans.

Nazi attacks against the Jews escalated after the Olympics. The erection of the concentration camp at Buchenwald in 1937 was followed by a number of significant actions in 1938 that created further problems for European Jews. In Germany, all Jewish property had to be registered, and 80 percent of Jewish businesses were either seized or sold at ridiculously cheap prices. Jewish lawyers were denied the right to practice; Jewish doctors could treat only Jewish patients. As German Jews sought to escape Germany, their passports were stamped with the letter *J* for *Jude* (Jew). In Austria and Hungary, discriminatory acts, modeled on Germany's, were also established against Jews.

The events of November 9–10, 1938, marked a further deterioration of the already difficult conditions for German Jews. A seventeen-year-old Jewish man living in Paris, enraged that his parents, Polish-born Jews, were among the 17,000 people who were expelled from Germany, shot and killed a low-ranking German official in the Paris office of the German embassy. In a violent rampage, people in Germany, Austria, and the Sudetenland used the assassination as the justification for a public assault on Jewish people and their synagogues. This night of violence, known as *Kristallnacht* (crystal night or night of broken glass), saw the murder of ninety-six Jews, the destruction of over one thousand synagogues, and the looting of over seven thousand Jewish businesses. Also, thirty thousand Jews, mostly men, were arrested, while numerous Jewish cemeteries, hospitals, and residences were destroyed. As the first wave of systematic arrests of Austrian and German Jews began, the concentration camps at Dachau and Buchenwald were expanded to accommodate the newly incarcerated.

All of these events provide the background for the selections in Chapter 1, which explores the roots of the Holocaust. The campaign of terror began slowly in the 1930s with arrests, the confiscation of Jewish property, and the establishment of discriminatory laws, but it did not escalate into a full-blown assault on European Jews until 1940, when the major round-ups of all Jews in occupied German territories began. The readings in this section explore the early signs of Nazi tyranny that, by 1939, with Germany's invasion of Poland and the start of World War II, would become a ruthless campaign of murder against the enemies of the Reich, especially the Jews.

Why Remember?

Milton Meltzer

A noted writer of nonfiction for children and young
adults, Milton Meltzer is the author of two highly
respected works about the Holocaust: *Never to
Forget: The Jews of the Holocaust*, from which this
excerpt is taken, and *Rescue: The Story of How Gentiles
Saved Jews in the Holocaust*. Born in 1915, Meltzer
grew up in Worcester, Massachusetts, and attended
Columbia University. Before becoming a full-time
writer, he worked as a reporter and editor. He also
served in the Army Air Force from 1942 to 1946. He
lives and works in New York City.

In the following commentary, which serves as
the introduction to *Never to Forget*, Meltzer relates his
experience as a young Jewish American becoming
aware of the growing Nazi presence in Europe.

I was fifteen years old when I first noticed the
strange words "Nazi" and "Hitler" in the newspaper. I lived in Worcester, a city
in the center of Massachusetts. It was September 1930, and I was just starting my
junior year in high school. I used to read the papers, but not very thoroughly.
Sports, the funnies, stories about local people, rarely any foreign news.

But on this day something caught my eye in a report datelined from Germany.
A hundred-odd members of Adolf Hitler's Nazi party had just been elected to
the German legislature—the Reichstag they called it—and they had shown up
for the first session wearing brown uniforms and shouting, "*Deutschland erwache!
Jude verrecke!*"

The paper obligingly explained what those foreign words meant: Germany awake! Jew perish!

Who was Hitler? What was a Nazi? Did the Germans take that slogan seriously—"Jew perish!"

It was those words that had leaped out at me from the small print. I wasn't looking for them; I didn't know they would be there. Still, I saw them as with a special sense, attuned to those three letters, J-E-W. The same sudden alarm would go off in a busy place—the school gym, the Y swimming pool, the corner hangout—if the word "Jew" were spoken by someone in the crowd. Through the confusion of noise the sound would arrow straight into my brain.

I was Jewish, of course, but a feeble kind of Jew, as I think of it now. I mean I had no religious training and almost no knowledge of Jewish life, history, or language. Our neighborhood was very mixed, and so were the schools I went to. I thought of myself as an American. If someone said yes, but what *kind* of American, then I'd say Jewish. Once on a Saturday morning an old Jewish widow who had just moved into the neighborhood saw me on the street and asked me to come into her house and light the stove. I wondered why she couldn't light it herself, but I did it, and she gave me a cookie. When I told my mother about it, she laughed and said, "She took you for a *Shabbos goy.*" She explained that religious Jews could not light a fire on the Sabbath. If they needed it, they'd ask a non-Jew, a goy, to do it.

I thought it was funny, too.

Then why did my skin prickle when I saw those words in the newspaper? Whatever kind of Jew I was, I had somehow absorbed the knowledge that Jews lived under threat. I had heard of the Jews of Egypt, enslaved under Pharaoh, and of how Haman's plan to annihilate the Jews of Persia had been foiled by Queen Esther. I knew vaguely about the persecution of the Jews during the Crusades and that the Inquisition had driven the Jews from Spain. Somewhere I had seen the word "pogrom" in print, knew it meant bloody riots against the Jews, and linked it to the immigrants who, like my mother and father, had fled Eastern Europe. On the street I had heard Jewish boys called "kike" and seen them fling themselves upon their tormentors.

But for politicians to stand up now in public and shout that the Jews must die?

I shuddered. "That could never happen here, could it, Pa?" He looked up, then smiled to reassure me. "Don't worry about it," he said. "Hitler and those Nazis of his—they won't last long."

They didn't. Not in the long perspective of time. They took power in 1933; they lost power in 1945. Twelve years. It's the length of time most of us spend in grade school and high school. That's only about a sixth of the average life span.

But how do you measure the cost of those dozen years of Nazi rule over Germany and most of Europe? By the time Hitler's power was smashed, 29 million people were dead. They were from many different countries, including Hitler's Germany and our United States.

Among the myriad slaughtered were the Jews. Six million of them. Two out of every three in Europe. One-third of the world's Jews. Statistics. But each was a man, a woman, or a child. Each had a name. Each suffered his or her own death.

Historians now speak of Hitler's extermination of the Jews as the Holocaust. The word derives from the word *olah* in the Hebrew Bible. It had the religious meaning of a burnt sacrifice. In the Greek translation of the Old Testament the word became *holokauston*. The English definition made it "an offering wholly consumed by fire." In our century it has acquired the secular meaning of a general disaster. But what Hitler did added another meaning to the dictionary definition: "a complete or thorough sacrifice or destruction, especially by fire, as of large numbers of human beings." (The Hebrew noun the Israelis use for it is *Shoa*. In Yiddish the word is *Khurbn*.)

The Holocaust was one of innumerable crimes committed by the Nazis. Then why single out the extermination of the Jews? Is it necessary to remember? Is it good? Can it even be understood by those who have come after?

No one would claim that the Nazi extermination of the Jews was greater or more tragic than what has been done to other persecuted peoples. Such comparisons are unfeeling and fruitless. What is historically significant is its uniqueness. There is no precedent for it in Jewish history. Nor in the history of any other people.

Civilians in the past have been massacred for what men called "reasonable" goals, utilitarian goals—to extend power, to acquire wealth, to increase territory, to stamp out opposition, to force conversion. What some power conceived to be in its self-interest was the reason behind the persecution.

But Hitler and the Nazis wanted to murder all Jews *because* they were Jews. Not because of their faith, not despite their faith. But because of what Hitler called their "race." He did not believe this "inferior" people had any right to share the earth with their superiors," the Germans. So Jews—religious and unreligious—were exterminated. They were killed even when their deaths proved harmful, militarily or economically, to the Nazis. It was a crime against all humanity, committed upon the body of the Jewish people. That the Jews were the victim this time derives from the long history of anti-Semitism.

How could it have happened?

It did not occur in a vacuum. It was the logical outcome of certain conditions of life. Given the antihuman nature of Nazi beliefs, the crime of the Holocaust could be expected. We see that now. That it happened once, unbelievable as it seems, means it could happen again. Hitler made it a possibility for anyone. Neither the Jews nor any other group on earth can feel safe from that crime in the future.

I do not believe that the world of Hitler was totally alien to the world we know. Still, before we can compare Hitler's Germany to anything else, we need to find out what it was like and how it came to be. And just as important, we need to expand our knowledge of our own human nature to understand why people were infected by Nazism, how the poison spread, and what its effects were. The question has to do with good and evil, with our inner being, with our power to make moral choices.

No one of us can know the whole truth. It is not made up merely of facts and figures. We have an abundance of that kind of evidence now, for the hell of Nazi Europe has become one of the most fully documented crimes in history. One can read the cold record for endless hours. The better path to the truth is through the eyewitness accounts—the letters, diaries, journals, and memoirs of those who experienced the terror and grief. This book will rely upon them. However inadequate words are, human language is all we have to reach across barriers to understanding.

The Roots

Barbara Rogasky

Barbara Rogasky was born in 1933 and raised in
Wilmington, Delaware. After attending the
University of Delaware, she moved to New York City,
where she worked for a time in the New York Public
Library system before making a career in publishing.
She now lives in Vermont, where she works as a free-
lance writer and editor. She is the author of several
books, including *Smoke and Ashes: The Story of the
Holocaust*, from which the following excerpt is taken,
and *The Golem*. It was only after the publication of
Smoke and Ashes that Rogasky learned that twenty
of her family members perished in the Holocaust.

In this excerpt from *Smoke and Ashes*, Rogasky
provides a concise historical overview of anti-
Semitism beginning with the early years of
Christianity. She then focuses specifically on its roots
in Germany and describes the rise of Adolf Hitler.
This historical perspective provides a context in
which to place the events of the Holocaust.

Their synagogues should be set on fire. . . . Their homes should likewise be
broken down and destroyed. . . . Let us drive them out of the country for all time.

Martin Luther, 1542

When Jewish blood spurts from the knife, then things go twice as well.

From the Horst Wessel Song, a Nazi anthem

The seeds of misunderstanding, ignorance and hate were sown long before Hitler. The Nazis would not have been able to succeed in their work of destruction if the foundation had not been formed centuries earlier.

In the early years of Christianity, Jews were called Christ killers, murderers of God. That crime was so basic and horrible that they were believed capable of anything and everything evil. Martin Luther, the founder of Protestantism, declared they were the Christian's most vicious enemy, second only to Satan himself. In the Middle Ages they were said to have poisoned the wells and caused the years of the plague that killed millions in Europe. Jews were believed to murder Christians, especially innocent children, in order to use their blood during religious ceremonies. This was the infamous Blood Libel, which the Nazis made good use of again hundreds of years later.

Thus the Jews rarely lived in peace for long. Whole communities were raided, ransacked and destroyed. Jewish children were taken from their parents to be raised as Christians. Jews were burned at the stake because they refused to give up their religion.

Strict limits were placed on what they could and could not do. At one time or another they were forbidden to be doctors, lawyers or teachers of non-Jews. They were not permitted to sell food to Christians or hire Christians to work for them. They could not be cared for by Christian nurses. They were not allowed to live in the same houses as non-Jews. They were forced to wear a special article of clothing or a cloth badge so that all would know they were Jews and could more easily avoid them.

Christians believed that lending money and charging interest—usury—was a sin. Jews came to fill an important need by taking on that job and making money available to non-Jews who requested it. The role expanded over the years, and Jews were used by those in power to collect taxes, supervise the peasant farmers of large estates, and act as a bridge between the ruling nobility and the people in matters of money and finance. It is probably the basis in history for such ideas as "All Jews are rich" and "The Jews control all the money."

Jews were expelled from country after country, among them England, France, Spain, Portugal, Italy and Germany. When they were not expelled, they often had to live in limited special areas—the ghettos. In Russia during the 1700s, they were restricted to a land area in the west of the country called the Pale of Jewish Settlement. The restriction was not lifted until almost two hundred years later, in the twentieth century.

Things did not improve very much, even closer to modern times. In Russia, the Ukraine and Romania, hundreds of Jews died in pogroms in which organized groups attacked defenseless Jewish communities, looted and destroyed them, and killed or maimed their inhabitants. Between 1900 and 1904, at least 50,000 Jewish lives were lost in such incidents.

Anti-Semitism in Germany

The roots of anti-Semitism in Germany go back a very long time. In the eleventh century, when the Christian knights went on their crusades to convert or kill—mostly kill—the Moslems of the Middle East, they found easier victims closer to home. Thousands of Jews in German towns were massacred at the hands of German Christian Crusaders. In the years of the plague, over two hundred Jewish communities were partly or completely destroyed. Throughout their history in that country, Jews found their homes attacked, their cemeteries desecrated and their synagogues burned. Their lives were made miserable even in small ways—in country villages it was the custom to stone Jews during the Holy Week before Easter.

In the 1800s signs of what would become the building blocks of Nazism began to appear. Anti-Semitic incidents grew in number and violence, including anti-Jewish riots led by a group that had as their slogan, "Death and destruction to all Jews!"

But one of the most important events was the invention of the word "anti-Semitism" itself in 1873. It was used for the first time in a small book—which became very popular—called *The Triumph of Jewry Over Germanism*, by Wilhelm Marr. That marked an important change in the history of Jewish persecution.

Before then, Jews were considered dangerous because of their religion: they were capable of all things evil because of what they believed, not because of what they were. That meant it was possible for them to change for the better. The best way to show that change was to give up their religion and convert to Christianity. In other words, they could choose not to be Jews.

But after 1873 things began to be different. Now called Semites, not only Jews, they were thought of as a race for the first time. The "Jewish question" became one of birth and blood, not belief. If the Jews were a race by birth, then they could not change. From the beginning, they were basically and deeply different from everyone else. That single idea was the cornerstone of Nazi anti-Semitism.

In 1881 an "Anti-Semites' Petition" was sent to the leader of the country demanding that Jews be removed from government, that no more Jews be allowed to come to Germany and in general urging "the liberation of Germany from the exploitation of the Jews." The demands were not met, but the chancellor sympathized.

Anti-Semitic politicians were elected to the Reichstag, Germany's ruling body. One of them gave a speech to much applause that said such things as "The Jews are indeed beasts of prey. . . . The Jews operate like parasites. . . . The Jews are cholera germs." Anti-Semitism was called "the greatest national progress of this century."

Anti-Jewish books and pamphlets appeared by the dozen and were read by everyone. *The Handbook of Antisemitism*, for example, went into thirty-six printings and had thousands of readers. The thousand-page *Foundations of the Nineteenth Century*, which came out in 1899, proclaimed that all the good in civilization came from the Aryans. The best true living examples of this blond and blue-eyed master race were the Germans. Most of what was bad came from their enemy, the Jews. Obviously, Hitler was influenced by these ideas, as were millions of others.

In 1903 *The Protocols of the Elders of Zion* made its appearance in Russia. It was supposed to be the secret plans of the "international Jewish conspiracy" to take over the world. Translated into many languages, it reached millions of readers everywhere. The German version appeared in 1920. By the end of the year, 120,000 copies had been sold—a huge number for that time—and classes and evening lectures were held to enlighten the public about its true meaning.

In 1921 it was proved a forgery—lies from start to finish—but that made no difference. Its popularity kept on growing, and it continued to be used as proof of the Jews' true intentions. Hitler was so impressed by the *Protocols* that he declared the Nazis could learn a lot about gaining power from its contents.

Adolf Hilter and Mein Kampf

Adolf Hitler was born in 1889 in Austria and went to Germany in 1913. He served in the German army in the First World War and was wounded twice. When Germany lost the war, Hitler returned to find his adopted country in turmoil.

Unemployment was extremely high. There were bloody street fights and revolutions. The government seemed unable to govern, and the country could not find its balance. Bitter, poor, hungry and angry, the people tried to find answers and fix blame for the world that seemed to be falling apart around them.

Dozens of new political organizations and parties appeared, each claiming to know the answers and to offer solutions. Most of these groups were extremely patriotic, antidemocratic, antigovernment and anti-Semitic.

Hitler was among their members. He joined a small group called the German Workers' Party that eventually became the National Socialist German Workers' Party—the Nazis.

Helped by Hitler's magnetic personality and his amazing ability as a speaker, the party grew. Its program promised jobs, food and education to all Germans. It demanded that Germany be allowed to take its rightful strong place among the nations of the world. It "explained" that Germany had lost World War I through a "stab in the back" from its own government, which had allied itself with Jews. The Jews had so weakened the government that it had lost the will and the strength to fight.

Point Four of the Nazi party program said plainly: "Only a racial comrade can be a citizen. Only a person of German blood can be a racial comrade. No Jew, therefore, can be a racial comrade." In other words, because a Jew was a member of a different race from the Germans, he could not be a citizen of Germany. The Nazis made good on that statement a few years later.

In 1923, just five years after the country lost the war, an inflation hit that was the worst the world had ever seen. Millions of people were without work, but even if they had jobs there was little they could afford to buy. The German reichsmark, their unit of money, had almost no value. A loaf of bread cost five million reichsmarks. That was in the morning. The inflation grew so fast it might cost twice that in the evening. One American cent was worth 1.66 million reichsmarks. Money was carried in boxes and wheelbarrows; it was not worth the paper it was printed on. Germany was simply falling apart.

Hitler and the young Nazi party tried to take over the government during this period. They failed, and Hitler was arrested. Given a five-year sentence, he spent only nine months in jail. He used that time to write the book that would become a bible of the Nazi movement—*Mein Kampf*, My Struggle. It is the story of his early years, his political development and the growth of the Nazi party.

Mein Kampf is deadly dull; it is almost impossible to read. That may explain why almost no one bothered to find out what it said. It very clearly states Nazi theories and plans for the future that would become all too real a few years later. The ideas that gave rise to the Holocaust are spelled out in no uncertain terms.

Hitler was possessed by the idea of race. He believed that all that was worthwhile in the world, even civilization itself, was the product of one race—the Aryan. There is no such thing as an Aryan race, but that made no difference to Hitler or his followers.

He insisted that every government and state has the sacred right and duty to protect the race and "to see to it that the blood is preserved pure." Because, he said, "All that is not race is trash."

The Jew is mentioned again and again in *Mein Kampf*.

"The Jew forms the strongest contrast to the Aryan."

"The Jewish people is without a true culture."

"The fake culture the Jew possesses is the property of other people."

The Jew is a "maggot," "parasite," "vermin," "plague," "spider sucking blood," "vampire," "pimp," "snake"—and that is far from all he said.

The Jew is everyone's enemy. He desires the "lowering of the racial level of the noblest." He wants to dominate "through extermination" of the best in the nation, and replace them with "members of his own nation."

Jews disguise their true purpose by pretending to be a religion, which is "the first and greatest lie." They were "always a people with definite racial qualities, never a religion."

If the Jew is victorious, "then his crown will be the wreath on the grave of mankind, then this planet will, as it did millions of years ago, move empty through space."

Small wonder he could then say, "In fighting off the Jew, I am fighting the Lord's work."

The country had lost the war, he reminded his readers, because Germany had been weakened by not keeping herself pure; the people had been betrayed. "World War I might not have been lost," he said, "if some twelve or fifteen thousand of the Hebrew corrupters of the people had been poisoned by gas before or during the war."

The Holocaust stands as history's evidence that he meant every word he said.

They Wanted Everyone to Know
Who the Jews Were

David A. Adler

David A. Adler is a prolific author of both fiction and
nonfiction. Born shortly after the end of World War
II, he grew up surrounded by Holocaust survivors,
hearing stories of their experiences. His mother, born
in Germany and raised in Austria, escaped from the
Nazis shortly after they entered Austria. Adler wrote
We Remember the Holocaust because he wanted his
own children to learn more than just the dates,
names, and places of the Holocaust. Adler's books
have won numerous awards.

In the following excerpt from *We Remember the
Holocaust*, Adler describes the rapid deterioration of
Jewish life as a result of a systematic campaign of
legislation and humiliation that Jews were subjected
to in Germany after Hitler's rise to power in 1933. He
relates the experiences of several Jews as anti-
Semitism became overt in Germany and as it spread
to other European countries.

Sidney Adler traveled to Germany with his father
in 1929 and again in 1930. "People don't realize how strong Jewish life was in
Germany before Hitler. In 1929 we traveled from New York to Bremen, Germany,
on the *Stuttgart*, a German boat. There was an extra chef on board to prepare
kosher meals for whoever wanted them. When we were seated near the captain,
my father told the head steward that as religious Jews we wore yarmulkes on

our heads when we ate, and he asked for a less prominent table. The steward was a German. The whole crew was German. He told my father to stay where we were. 'People should respect you for your religion,' he said.

"We went to visit relatives and we traveled throughout Germany. There were many beautiful synagogues and kosher hotels and restaurants. Even in America, many of the kosher foods we bought for Passover were prepared in Germany."

But Jewish life in Germany deteriorated quickly. During 1933, the first year of the Nazi regime, Jewish judges and lawyers were shut out of German courts. Jewish doctors could no longer work in certain German hospitals. Jewish teachers, bankers, and railroad workers were fired. Jews were removed from service in the army and navy. And the number of Jewish students in high schools and colleges was severely limited.

Henni Prager Sonneberg lived in Wenings, Germany. She remembers spring 1933: "My father was a member of the town council. He had been a first lieutenant in the German Army in the First World War. When the town wanted to build a memorial to the war dead, he got them the steel. He helped with the casting. And he was the first Jew in Wenings to be beaten, the first to be locked up."

Henni Prager Sonneberg's father and brother were beaten in March 1933. "We had a large picture window in our house. Hoodlums, members of the *Arbeitslager* [government work crew] broke the window with two by fours. They found my brother sleeping downstairs and beat him. He fought back. They didn't know a Jew could fight back. And they got pleasure from beating my father, a quiet, middle-aged Jew."

Clara Wachter Feldman lived in a small German town during the early years of Nazi rule. "In the middle of the school year of 1933, our class was given a new teacher, a Nazi party member. The first day he came in, he said, 'I understand we have a Jew pig in our classroom.' Then he said, 'Now we will see how much pain a Jewish pig can endure.' He had me put out my hand, and he hit me with a stick. I don't know how many times he hit me. I don't remember the pain. But I do remember the laughter of the other children."

Henriette Kaplan remembers: "I was told by Jewish friends who lived near Nuremberg that they were taken by the Nazis to a park and forced to pull weeds out with their teeth. This happened soon after Hitler came to power." And she remembers what happened to her several years later in Frankfurt am Main: "I was out mailing letters, and a small boy of seven carrying a stick told me, 'Don't you know that Jews must be beaten?' and he struck me on the back several times. I was furious because I knew I couldn't do anything."

The Nazis issued orders that a general boycott be carried out on April 1, 1933, against Jewish shops, Jewish-made goods, and Jewish doctors and lawyers. The orders urged that the boycott be carried out in "complete calm and with absolute discipline," that Germans "not harm a hair on a Jew's head." The orders stressed the need for Nazi party members "to stand in blind obedience, as one man, behind our leadership."

There were worldwide protests and a boycott of German goods. On March 31, 1933, Dr. Joseph Goebbels told a large crowd of Nazi supporters, "Jewish trade throughout Germany will be paralyzed tomorrow." And he declared that if the anti-German protests did not stop, the boycott would be resumed "until German Jewry has been annihilated." His speech was interrupted by shouts from the audience: "Hang them! Hang them!"

On April 1, 1933, SS and SA soldiers stood outside Jewish-owned stores, carrying signs urging Germans not to go in. Signs posted throughout the country instructed Germans, "Defend yourselves! Do not buy from Jews." The word *Jude* (Jew) and Jewish stars were painted on the doors and windows of the stores. Jewish chidren were not allowed in class.

Fred Erlebacher worked in an iron-and-wood supply house in Baisingen, Germany, a small village near Lahr. He remembers the boycott: "Some people we knew, and were friends the day before, came in wearing brown uniforms. They no longer recognized us. They only knew we were Jews. They yelled at us and insulted us. When a few brave people walked into our store, they were yelled at and called 'Friends of the Jews.' "

Netti Golde Dessau remembers: "There was a young Jewish doctor I knew. She worked in a very poor, non-Jewish section of the city, mostly for free. Before the boycott she said, 'If the people I'm helping here are standing in front of my door with pickets, I'm not staying one day longer.' And they were there." A short while later her friend left Germany and moved to Palestine, the small Middle Eastern country that later became the Jewish state of Israel.

Hilda Bondi remembers the boycott: "My class was on a trip of a few days in the mountains. We all had to return home. The Nazis wanted people to see which children were taken out of the class. They wanted everyone to know who the Jews were."

During the next few years, many Germans refused to buy from Jewish-owned stores. There were anti-Jewish riots. Books written by Jews were thrown into the streets and burned. Jews Not Wanted signs were posted along roads and in stores and restaurants.

Officials throughout the country, eager to show their support of Nazi policy, made their own decrees against Jews. They tried to force Jews out, so their towns could be made *judenrein*, free of Jews. More and more Jews moved to the large cities.

Tirzah Rothschild lived in Hamburg, Germany. She remembers when she saw *Juden Unerwünscht*—Jews Not Wanted—signs: "They appeared all over, in food stores, clothing stores, and department stores. It wasn't the law yet that Jews be forbidden to enter these stores. The owners put up such signs to impress others that they were good Nazis. I remember when I saw those signs I felt sad, scared, and angry."

There were some protests outside Germany, and in July 1933, during an interview, Hitler responded, "I would be only too glad if the countries which take such a great interest in Jews would open their gates to them. It is true we have made discriminatory laws, but they are directed not so much against the Jews, but for the German people, to give economic opportunity to the majority."

Nazi discrimination against the Jews was not reserved only for the living. Any street named after a Jew was renamed. A monument to Heinrich Heine, a Jew and one of Germany's most popular writers, was removed. The monument to Jacob Herz, a great doctor who had served Germany during two wars, was destroyed. A hundred thousand Jewish soldiers had fought in the German Army in the Great War, less than twenty years earlier. Thirty-five thousand had died. Now the names of the Jewish soldiers who died were scratched off German memorials to the war dead.

Jewish children were no longer allowed in public schools. And in public schools a course in "scientific anti-Semitism," the "scientific" hatred of Jews, was taught to every student.

According to the Nuremberg Laws of September 1935, Jews were no longer citizens of Germany. They were not even allowed to fly a German flag. Jews were not allowed to marry non-Jews nor have any non-Jewish woman under the age of forty-five work in their homes.

Fred Erlebacher was arrested for violating the Nuremberg Laws. "I was accused of being with a German girl. The Gestapo came to my place of business and arrested me. It's true, she looked German. She had long blond braids. But she was a Jewish girl, and I told them that. They checked it out. When they found out it was true, they released me. That girl is my wife now."

Lena Mandelbaum was a young child in Germany at the time. She remembers: "My father was in the wholesale fruit business. His partner was not Jewish. He took over the business. Then he lied and said my father stole from him, and he took our apartment. My parents were taken to jail. Soon after that my sisters, brothers, and I were thrown out of school."

Helga Lowenthal Greenbaum remembers: "My brother's bar mitzvah was in 1937. That Friday I was working for my father, and a registered letter came to the office. The letter withdrew permission for my father to have a business. Of course, I didn't show it to my parents until after the bar mitzvah. I didn't want to ruin the celebration. After that my father just wasn't the same. He was still a young man, and he had no work."

The effects of Nazi anti-Jewish policy were felt far beyond Germany. Anti-Semites throughout the world were encouraged by the Nazis. Anti-Jewish laws were passed in Hungary. Jews there lost their jobs, their homes, their rights as citizens. In Romania there were anti-Jewish student riots. Jewish students were kept out of colleges. High taxes were imposed on Jewish businesses. Jews were attacked. In Poland there were anti-Jewish boycotts and riots in the large cities, including such centers of Jewish life as Vilna and Warsaw. In small Polish towns and villages, peasants carrying clubs and rocks attacked Jews.

Thousands of Jews left Poland for British-controlled Palestine. But the Arabs there protested the arrival of the Jews. They became violent and destroyed Jewish property. They attacked and killed Jews.

Arthur Rubin lived in Derecske, Hungary, in the 1930s. "I remember at the young age of five or six years walking to school or to synagogue, and all of a sudden kids in the courtyard would say, 'Hey, you're a Jew.' I remember being beaten and coming home with a bloody nose. It was particularly unwise to walk on the streets during Easter and Christmas holidays. On those holidays the name-calling and the Jew-beatings were carried out with more zeal, with more passion than at other times. This hatred and hostility was a reflection, a mirror image, of the adult population."

Cecilia Bernstein was a young child in the 1930s and lived in a small town in Hungary. She remembers: "Police with long black feathers in their hats rode on horses through the streets. We ran from them. They beat us, and no one could stop them."

Alfred Lipson lived in Radom, in central Poland, during the mid 1930s. He remembers: "There were roving gangs in the streets. We were beaten many times. Once, I was in a movie theater with my mother. She was wearing a fur coat. When we left the theater, we found that anti-Semitic hoodlums sitting behind us in the theater had slit my mother's coat with razor blades."

Leah Goldberg remembers growing up in Poland: "Before Passover my gentile friends weren't allowed to play with us. Their parents said Jews kill gentile children and use their blood to make matzos. 'No,' I told them. 'I saw them bake matzo. They use just flour and water. If they used blood, the matzo would be red.' "

Abraham J. Goldberg remembers being a young boy in Poland: "I was once surrounded by six fellows, and one of them said, 'We're going to kill a Jew today.' I ran for my life."

Anti-Semitism was on the rise in Austria, Greece, Yugoslavia, Italy, and France. Even in the United States.

Cantor Moshe Ehrlich was born in Vienna, Austria. He remembers: "Anti-Semitism was rampant. Just as an example of it, on Good Friday, Holy Thursday, and Easter Sunday I was warned by my parents, 'Don't go out, because Jews will be beaten up.' This was before Hitler marched into Austria. The people would come home from church, and any Jew they could find, they would beat up."

In the United States many anti-Jewish groups were formed, including the German-American Bund, the Silver Shirts, and the Christian Front. They publicized their views on radio and in leaflets and magazines.

In the United States and elsewhere only a small minority of the people declared themselves to be anti-Semites. But they were a loud minority. Almost everyone else was quiet.

39 Casimir-the-Great Street

Yala Korwin

Yala Korwin was born and educated in Lvov, Poland. During the occupation, her family lived in the ghetto until her father fled to hide on the Aryan side. The family was denounced, and her father, mother, and older sister were killed. Korwin and her younger sister survived for three years (1942–1945) by working in a German labor camp, using forged identity papers obtained by Polish Christians. After the war, she lived in France until 1956, when she moved to the United States. Her poems have been published in a number of journals and collected in *To Tell the Story*, from which the following poem was taken.

In this poem, Korwin relates the confusion of being a child in a society that is out of control.

1. The Courtyard

The image of my childhood paled
like the old photos Mother kept
in her chest of drawers.
The image of our courtyard grew faint,
but never quite vanished.

Cobblestone-heads scampered round
an old chestnut tree spreading
its deep, refreshing shadows
where I and my friend Jancia
played games of hide-and-seek
and a bridge falling down.

When we grew tired, we just sat
and watched the flocks of clouds
blown helter-skelter across the sky
framed by outlines of chimneys.
The air was balmy, the sun stood high,
laughter glowed in our eyes.

My peasant nanny and my friend's mother
came down to fetch us for our midday meal.
They stopped to chatter. "Look at them,"
the neighbor said pointing at us,
"Next to that damned Jewish brat,
Mine is a darling lamb.

Her skin milk-white, her eyes two
    cornflowers,
hair like palest wheat in the fields,"
Too young to comprehend, numb I stood,
sparks of gold in my hair, fair was my skin,
my eyes blue, pretty my dress,
and Mama said she loved me.

20

2. The Street

Dressed in cotton with printed flowers,
I waited impatiently in our yard
for Mom and Dad to take me along
for a visit with the auntie.
The landlord's servant, Olga, arrived.
"Look who's here! Come with me, dolly,
I'll buy you a candy."
She took my hand and out we ventured.
The candy she got me was long, thin,
with white and pink stripes.

In front of our house stood Mom and Dad
surrounded by a crowd of people.
"Our little girl is lost," wailed Mom.
Dad said nothing, just stood very pale.
The crowd was silent. Then, they saw us.
Mom quickly grabbed me and held tight.
Olga escaped into the dark hall
as fast as she could, without a word.
Dad said only: "Thank God. Let's go."

"Good people, stop them," a fat man shouted,
"don't let them take her, she's mine!
See how fair she is! Her eyes are blue!
She can't belong to these Jews!"
The crowd grew restless.
"They'll slay the poor child and use
her innocent blood in matzos
for Passover, their damned feast!"
"Save her, good people!"
The crowd began to threaten.

Police appeared. "What's all this about?
Why screams? Why that commotion?"
The fat man turned away in a blink
and disappeared in the midst of the crowd.
The crowd dispersed. We went home.

Other Victims

Ina R. Friedman

Ina R. Friedman was born in Chester, Pennsylvania, and educated at Pennsylvania State University. She is the author of several books, including *The Other Victims: First-Person Stories of Non-Jews Persecuted by the Nazis*, from which the following excerpt is taken, and *Escape or Die: True Stories of Young People Who Survived the Holocaust*.

While the fate of European Jews during the reign of the Third Reich is well-known, they were not the only victims of a systematic process of discrimination. The physically handicapped, Gypsies, political dissidents, and homosexuals were also targets for persecution. In this selection, Friedman relates the experience of a young hearing-impaired girl, Franziska Schwarz, who faced sterilization because of her deafness.

I never saw anything wrong with being deaf. My younger sister, Theresa, and most of my friends were deaf. Though my parents were hard of hearing, my younger brother, Theo, had normal hearing. My father was one of six brothers. Four of them were hearing. When they came to visit, every hand was busy sharing news of the deaf community or giving advice. Our eyes were glued to the hands and faces of the signers. Everyone had so much to say.

In deaf school, the teachers got mad if I signed. They wanted me to read lips and to use my voice. I got so tired of watching the teacher's lips. I couldn't look away for a minute. It was even harder when she tried to teach me to say the letters correctly. The teacher put a strip of paper in front of my lips. "To make the *B* sound, purse your lips and blow just enough to make the paper quiver. To make a *P*, blow a little harder and make the paper shake." Day after day, the teacher drilled me.

I felt like a bellows. I liked it better after school when the teachers weren't around. My friends and I would make signs and chat with our fingers.

When I was fourteen, Hitler took over Germany. Theo, my eleven-year-old hearing brother, liked to go to the Munich Stadium to the rallies. Once Theo came home all excited because he had shaken Hitler's hand. My favorite uncle, Karl, who could hear, got mad.

He shouted at my brother and signed at the same time. "Hitler is a disgrace to Germany. Don't waste your time and hearing listening to him."

My father put his fingers on my brother's lips. "Don't ever repeat what you have just heard. Swear by the Holy Father!"

Theo looked scared. "But in school, they tell us to report anything bad people say about Hitler."

"If you don't repeat it, no one will know your uncle said it."

I couldn't hear the radio so I never got excited about Hitler. The year 1933 was hard for me. I had just begun my apprenticeship at the convent. The sisters were teaching me how to sew, and I found it hard to understand them. On Saturdays I enjoyed going to a special Catholic club for deaf girls. Later, Hitler turned it into a branch of the *Bund Deutscher Maedel*, the Nazi club for girls. We went hiking, and once we went on a camping trip to Koenigsburg. That was enjoyable.

The rest of Hitler was horrible. For me, the trouble started in 1935. I came home from the convent and found Mother crying. "What's the matter?" I signed.

She handed me the letter that read, "Frau Schwarz and her daughter Franziska are to come to the health office to arrange for their sterilization. Heil Hitler." I couldn't make out the signature at the bottom.

The whole family got upset. Uncle Karl started to sputter, as he always did when he was excited. "We'll protest. The Nazis can't do this to Franziska. She's perfectly healthy. I'll appeal to the administrative court and ask them to over-turn the order."

The day of the hearing, my mother, my father, and all my uncles accompanied me to court. "She's only sixteen years." Uncle Karl talked and signed at the same time so I could understand. "Deafness is not always inherited. I'm her uncle, and I can hear perfectly well. As for her mother, she is going through the menopause. Though she is a good Catholic, she promises not to have any more children."

The two men on the judges' bench whispered to each other. They frowned and shook their heads. After a few minutes, the one with the big nose and bald head stood up. "Petition denied for the minor, Franziska Schwarz. Since the mother promises not to have any more children, she will not have to be sterilized."

I started to cry. The previous year, I had met a boy I liked, Christian Mikus. As a child, he had had scarlet fever and lost his hearing in one ear. Christian and I liked to walk in the park. We'd sign for hours. Whenever he saw children playing, he'd smile and sign, "One day, we will have children, too." Of course we couldn't get married then. He didn't make much money working in a clothing factory. Whatever deaf people made, it was always less than other people. We used to get angry. We'd do just as good work as others, but the employers would always give us less. If I were sterilized, I didn't think Christian would want to go with me anymore.

When my uncle walked out of the courtroom, his face was almost purple. "Franziska, Germany is no place for either of us. We'll run away to Switzerland. I won't let them sterilize you."

Before we could run off, he was arrested by the Gestapo. He had shouted at his secretary, "Turn off the radio whenever Hitler talks. It's not healthy to listen to a madman." The secretary's father was a storm trooper. She reported Uncle Karl to the Gestapo. The Gestapo sentenced him to death for "spreading slander."

I don't know how, but his brothers got him released. "For God's sake. Keep your opinions to yourself. Hitler can't last," my father said. "Why take chances?"

At the same time my uncle was in prison, a letter came from the department of health. "Franziska Schwarz is to report to the Women's Hospital in Munich for the sterilization."

"I won't go," I cried. "I want to be able to have babies."

Father looked sad. "If you don't go, the police will drag you to the hospital."

I screamed all the way to the hospital. The nurse locked me in a room with two other deaf teenagers. The three of us cried all night. When the nurse came to give us tranquilizers, I tried to fight her off. She held me down and gave me the injection. In the morning, I woke up in a room full of beds. My stomach hurt. I touched the bandages and started to cry. The nurse who brought me water was crying, too. "I'm sorry, there's nothing I could do to help you. With Hitler, you have to be quiet." Her finger pointed to the portrait of Hitler hanging over the bed. She tapped her temple with her finger, to indicate, "He's crazy."

I had so much pain, I couldn't go to the convent. I asked the public health insurance office for the standard sick pay.

"Why should you get sick pay?" the social worker sneered. "You can have all the fun you want. You don't have to worry about getting pregnant."

When Christian came to the house, I started to cry. "The doctors sterilized me. I guess you won't want to be my boyfriend anymore."

Christian made the sign for love. "Whatever happens, we'll be together. As soon as you're twenty-one, we'll get married."

Before the Storm

Richard Plant

Richard Plant was born in Germany in 1910. He
graduated from the University of Basel before
immigrating to the United States in 1938. He has
published numerous articles and a novel in addition
to *The Pink Triangle: The Nazi War against
Homosexuals*, from which the following excerpt is
taken. He taught at the New School for Social
Research in New York City until 1993.

In addition to the Jews, other groups were
labeled by the Nazis as "undesirables." These groups
were targeted for discrimination and eventually
arrested and sent to the camps. Among these were
homosexuals, who had previously experienced some
degree of tolerance in Germany. In this selection,
Plant describes the social conditions in Germany
after its demoralizing defeat in World War I and
traces their influence as factors in the rise of Hitler
and his brutal regime.

The anxiety and insecurity that would come to
grip all social classes by 1933 began with the shock of military defeat at the end of
World War I. It was a war that had left 1.7 million German soldiers dead and
another four million wounded. The returning veterans, convinced that they
had been betrayed, claimed to have been "stabbed in the back." Most Germans
agreed. How was it possible for the Kaiser's mighty army to have been defeated?
Only days before the end, hadn't the army's own press releases promised the

certain victory of the "sacred German cause"? What the man in the street suspected, what the popular press trumpeted, was that traitors at home had caused the great catastrophe. War profiteers, foreigners from the East, Communists and Socialists, the Jews—all were to blame for Germany's humiliation.

A tidal wave of shame and resentment, experienced even by younger men who had not seen military service, swept the nation. Many people tried to digest the bitter defeat by searching furiously for scapegoats. The belief that internal enemies had brought down the Empire, the Kaiser, and the "Golden Age of German Power" was widespread. Enraged ex-soldiers and younger men formed violent bands that roamed Germany. A palpable yearning could be felt on all levels of society, from farm and factory workers to middle-class businessmen and big-city intellectuals, for security and vengeance. The old guard of the Empire had never given up their positions of privilege and power, and no truly democratic government ever really grew strong enough to dislodge them. Archconservatives still held most of the leading positions in the army and navy, the universities, the civil service, and especially the courts. Long before Adolf Hitler entered politics, long before anti-Semitism and antiliberalism had become battle cries for the Nazis, the Weimar Republic's experiment in democracy and social tolerance was steadily undermined by distrust, injustice, and violence. One is almost tempted to say that Hitler did not bring the Republic down; he merely saved it from suicide by murdering it himself. It was bankrupt long before he appointed himself as Germany's savior.

The social hurricane at the heart of the Weimar Republic was prompted and complicated by five factors: (1) fear of revolution; (2) racist and xenophobic paramilitary groups; (3) unprecedented inflation; (4) extreme unemployment; and (5) the Nazi Party.

First, directly after World War I, many older people were frightened by the specter of revolution. The Bolsheviks had accomplished it in Russia, and they had counted on the spreading of revolution in Europe to ensure their survival. The revolt in Munich in 1918 seemed to many to be but the opening shot in a class war. German newspapers were soon filled with hysterical reports of famine in the Ukraine. Many people feared that a Socialist triumph in Germany would doom the country to Russia's plight.

Second, dozens of racist and virulently nationalistic groups began to flourish in this climate, each more fanatical than the other. Many participated in the civil strife that began to break out sporadically all over the country. These guerrilla skirmishes especially alienated those Germans (the majority, it is safe to say) who wanted an orderly society in which to live and work.

A third factor cracked open the thin walls of stability and did more than any other to destroy trust and hope: the mammoth inflation of 1922–23. In just sixteen months the German mark soared from 192 marks to the American dollar to a staggering 4.2 *trillion* marks to the dollar. The financial faith of the country was shattered beyond repair. The middle class lost its savings and its confidence in government. Persons on fixed incomes, such as pensions, war bonds, and annuities, found their dreams drowned in monetary quicksand. An incomprehensible economic sickness infected everyone, diminishing all salaries and gobbling up savings. Everywhere, pawnshops were packed, and relief rolls lengthened. The labor unions, too, in which many had put their trust, failed. Since the unions' funds were gone, they could no longer resist the demands of employers: the ten-hour day returned to many industries. Unions began to lose members. Death and suicide rates rose; many children suffered from malnutrition. Those who had left the unions—and there were hundreds upon hundreds of thousands— found themselves politically adrift. Neither the left-wing Social Democratic Party (to which most labor unions belonged) nor the liberal or right-wing parties offered any prescriptions to cure this epidemic.

That the middle classes and the workers lost faith in both the state and the economy is not surprising. When money loses its value, then government is robbed of its authority. As Alan Bullock, the distinguished British historian and biographer of Hitler, has observed, the "result of the inflation was to undermine the foundations of German society in a way that neither the war nor the revolution of 1918 nor the Treaty of Versailles had ever done. The real revolution in Germany was the inflation." Berlin, the capital of the country, became the object of hatred for many Germans. A wave of anti-Berlin sentiment, always dormant on many levels of German society, swept through the provinces. Berlin, it was said, was different; it was evil, dominated by Jews, homosexuals, Communists.

A fourth factor compounding the deepening crisis was the rapid rise in unemployment, especially after the 1929 New York Stock Exchange crash, which toppled half of the financial institutions of Central Europe. Austrian banks collapsed first, then a number of leading German banks. In January 1930, the number of unemployed workers rose from 1.5 million to 3.2 million. Some economists estimate the actual number to have been more than six million by 1933. Many of the unemployed were teenagers or in their early twenties; they waited in endless lines before the welfare agencies to receive their meager welfare stamps worth less than twenty dollars a month. On every corner, peddlers offered trinkets nobody wanted; street singers and itinerant musicians played endlessly in courtyards for people who could not afford to drop a few pennies into their empty caps. Many young men, without hope, sullen and bewildered, were filled with a rage that knew no release. Many began to join the extremist parties of both the left and the right; many joined first the left, then the right. The promise of dramatic change suddenly made sense. Men were hungry too long, and now they were angry and desperate.

Into this social cauldron was added the fifth and most poisonous ingredient: the Nazi Party. As the numbers of unemployed rose, the Nazi membership rolls grew. To be sure, just before Franz von Papen maneuvered Hitler into the chancellorship in 1933, the Nazis had lost quite a few members. Still, the rise in unemployment and the growing strength of the Nazis were indissolubly linked. The Nazi Party not only provided food, weapons, and a splendid uniform, it proclaimed a new purpose, a new faith, and a new prophet. Inflation and unemployment catapulted into power a man who promised rebirth to all "Aryan" Germans, regardless of status. Hitler vowed to avenge the injustices of the Treaty of Versailles, and to punish the culprits who had been responsible for Germany's defeat. As was so often the case, Hitler's rhetoric was littered with sexual metaphors. Jews and other minorities, for example, were guilty of the "syphilitization of our people." In 1935, Nazi lawyer Hans Frank would warn that the "epidemic of homosexuality" was threatening the new Reich. America, too, was an enemy, a "niggerized Jewish country" where women painted their faces—a practice that enraged Nazi moralists. Heinrich Himmler, head of the SS, would later boast that no Aryan woman he knew ever used lipstick. It was Himmler who would mastermind the attacks on homosexuals, whom he endowed with the same subhuman, dangerous qualities as were ascribed to Jews, Communists and Gypsies.

During the Weimar Republic, the homosexual subculture had managed an uneasy coexistence with the larger heterosexual society surrounding it. Of course, those in the spotlight—famous actors, designers, dancers, doctors, politicians, directors, and lawyers—had to live with a certain amount of abuse. But many had acquired power, money, and even connections to the Weimar government, which served as protection. The average gay man could live unnoticed and undisturbed unless he fell victim to police entrapment or blackmail. The average lesbian enjoyed a kind of legal immunity. During the Weimar years, organized lesbian costume balls were held; luxurious lesbian bars and nightclubs flourished. Their owners never feared a police raid. The reason: neither the Second German Empire nor the Weimar Republic had ever promulgated laws forbidding or punishing sexual acts between women. Lesbian magazines enjoyed healthy circulations, some even featuring personal ads, and a few lesbian plays achieved widespread popularity.

But the sexual tolerance so often associated with the Weimar Republic began to disappear as rapidly as Germany's economy began to crumble. (The unemployed are generally less tolerant of contragenics.) Germany, it must be remembered, had never been an ethnically pluralistic society. Almost all German churches were state churches. There were no large ethnic groups or religious sects other than the Jews, the Gypsies, and the Jehovah's Witnesses—the latter relatively small in number. Homosexuals were an obvious, if largely invisible, scapegoat.

The years from 1929 to the end of the Weimar Republic were years of mounting tension. The Brown Shirts, or SA, under the leadership of Ernst Roehm, who was himself homosexual and would later be the target of Hitler's wrath, became even more brutal and more repressively efficient. Hitler had promised Germany's youth life as an endless military parade, replete with dashing insignia, badges, and banners. He invented special ranks for SA recruits and later for the SS. He proffered the vision of a brave, sunny world of soldiering for those who had given up hope. His enemies he threatened with war and extinction. They would be eliminated "ruthlessly" (his favorite word), and "heads would roll." His various adversaries were united in nothing but blindness. Only when it was too late did some grasp that Hitler's program of wholesale destruction would indeed be carried out, its scope widening year after year. The initial misreading of the implications of the Nazis' policy of systematic violence was shared by almost all of those who were their victims: union leaders, shrewd politicians of the center and the right, Marxists, Jewish scientists, writers, lawyers, and, of course, homosexuals of all professions and educational levels. To be sure, a small minority did read the omens correctly and managed to leave Germany before it was too late; but many stayed behind to face their doom uncomprehendingly.

We Were Jehovah's Witnesses

Ina R. Friedman

Ina R. Friedman is the author of several books, including *The Other Victims: First-Person Stories of Non-Jews Persecuted by the Nazis*, from which the following excerpt is taken. For additional biographical information on Friedman, see page 22.

In this selection, Friedman recounts the story of discrimination against the family of Franz and Hilda Kusserow, whose only crime was their devotion to their faith as Jehovah's Witnesses.

"Quick, Elisabeth," Annemarie shouted, "the Gestapo!" In Paderborn, very few people besides the Gestapo had cars. The clouds of dust raised by a car coming down the road signaled danger.

Before the Mercedes stopped, I scooped up the *Watchtower* pamphlets and put them in my knapsack. Magdalena stuffed the books into hers. We ran outside and hid the literature behind the bushes. At eight, I knew to walk over to the coops and feed the chickens. Magdalena, who was nine, picked up a bottle to feed the baby lamb.

We were Jehovah's Witnesses. Our parents, Franz and Hilda Kusserow, had taught their eleven children to hide the books and pamphlets of the International Society of Bible Students if anyone spotted the men from the Gestapo coming toward the house. Anyone found with literature from our Watchtower Society could be arrested.

What a happy family we were before Hitler. Our parents had been sent by the Watchtower Society from Bochum, Germany, to Paderborn to set up a congregation of Jehovah's Witnesses. The house sat on three acres of land. Father organized our daily chores. One week the boys took care of the chickens and ducks and lamb. That week, the girls worked in the garden. Then the following week we switched chores. When the apple and pear trees were ripe, everyone helped to pick the fruit.

But it wasn't all work. Before we went to school in the morning, and in the evening, we sat around the table talking about the Bible and what the passages meant. Mother had graduated from teachers' school, and Father made time for her to teach us music and painting. The house was filled with musical instruments: five violins, a piano, a reed organ, two accordions, a guitar, and several flutes. What joyful music we made as we played from the book *Hymns to Jehovah's Praise*.

My father sensed that some of the faithful would be persecuted by Hitler. He talked to us about what it meant to be a Jehovah's Witness. Sometimes he quoted from Matthew and Revelations. "Fear none of those things which thou shalt suffer; . . . be thou faithful unto death, and I will give thee a crown of life."

In 1936, the Nazis tried to get Jehovah's Witnesses to renounce their faith. When the Gestapo knocked on our door, one of them waved a piece of paper in Father's face and shouted, "Franz Kusserow, you must sign this document promising never to have anything to do with the International Society of Bible Students. If you don't, you will be sent to prison."

The whole family stood, dumbfounded. Promise not to be Jehovah's Witnesses? Hitler was truly Satan.

Father read aloud the first paragraph. " 'I have recognized that the International Society of Bible Students spreads a false doctrine and pursues goals entirely hostile to the state under the cover of religious activity.' " Father shook his head. "This is ridiculous. I can't sign."

The S.S. man, who was about the same age as my oldest brother, became angry. "Stubborn fool!"

I was shocked; no one ever talked to Father that way. He was one of the most respected people in Paderborn.

The S.S. man turned to Mother. "And you? If you don't, your children will be without parents."

Mother removed her apron and placed it over the chair. "No, I cannot sign. Annemarie"—Mother turned to my oldest sister—"take care of the children."

The agent shoved my parents outside and into the car.

Paul-Gerhard, who was five, began to cry. Hans-Werner, who was six, put his arms around his little brother. Fifi, our dachshund, began to growl. I bent down to calm her and to hide my tears.

After a few days the Nazis released Mother from prison. They kept Father. Why was it a crime to be a Jehovah's Witness? Mother couldn't understand why they released her, because she still refused to sign the paper. Mother and my oldest brother, Wilhelm, made sure we followed Father's schedule and always did our chores. But how we missed Father and his talks about the Bible! What a joyful reunion we had when he was released a year later. All thirteen of us took up our instruments, and the house resounded with hymns of praise. A few months later, our family was shattered. Our brother, Siegfried, who was 21, was killed in an accident.

It was difficult enough losing a brother, but as the years passed, the situation in school became more and more painful. Every day, the teacher reprimanded me for not saluting the Nazi flag. The big black swastika on the red banner flew over the schoolhouse and hung on a pole in every classroom. My stomach churned as I tried to think of how I could avoid saluting it or saying "Heil Hitler." My parents had taught me to salute only Jehovah God. To salute a flag or a person was the same as worshiping idols. I wouldn't sing the horrible Nazi songs, either. I kept my lips together.

The teacher always watched me. "So, Elisabeth, you do not want to join in praise of our leader. Come to the front of the classroom." She turned to the others. "Children, Elisabeth thinks it is all right to insult our leader. Tell us why, Elisabeth."

"Acts 4:12 of the New Testament says, 'There is no salvation in anyone else except Jesus Christ.' "

"Imagine, Elisabeth Kusserow believes in that ridiculous New Testament."

The children laughed. I couldn't understand why. All of them went to church. On the way home from school, they pushed me and threw my books to the ground. It got worse when Hans-Werner and then Paul-Gerhard were old enough to go to school. Now I had to worry about the children tormenting them.

Our troubles grew. It wasn't just the terror of going to school. The Nazis cut off Father's pension from World War I because he still refused to say "Heil Hitler." It was hard doing without the money, even though my older brothers and sisters had jobs. We planted more vegetables and canned as much as we could. In 1938, the Gestapo arrested Father for a second time. What could be wrong in obeying Jehovah God?

In the spring of 1939, the principal came into my class. "Elisabeth, since you refuse to salute our flag and say 'Heil Hitler,' it is obvious that your parents are neglecting your spiritual and moral development. I have taken it upon myself to obtain a court order to remove you and your two younger brothers from your home. The three of you will be sent to a place where you will get proper instruction." He pulled me into his office. Paul-Gerhard, who was then eight, and Hans-Werner, who was nine, stood there trembling.

At thirteen, the words made no sense to me. "Our parents raised us according to the teachings of Jehovah God," I protested.

"Quiet! This policeman will take you to your new home."

I was so upset, I hadn't noticed the policeman standing next to the window.

"Please, please, let me call my mother." I begged. "She'll be frantic when we don't come home."

"Traitors are not to know what happens to their children."

For several months Mother tried to find out where we were. She went to the police, called orphanages, hospitals, and prisons. Finally, she reached the clerk at the reform school in Dorsten who admitted we were there. Secretly, Mother sent us letters. "Always know that we love you. Be steadfast in your faith to Jehovah God. One day we will be together in heaven or on earth."

The director of the reform school couldn't understand why we were there. "You are the best behaved children I have ever seen. It's ridiculous to have you here with these delinquents." He sent a letter to Mother, "Your children will be arriving in Paderborn on Friday at two P.M."

As we started to climb the steps of the train, two men stopped us. "The director was guilty of misconduct. You are coming with us." They drove us to Nettelstadt, a Nazi training school.

"Don't cry," I told the boys. "Jehovah God will one day rule the earth. We will see our family, either here or in heaven." I didn't feel as brave as I sounded.

At the training school, the teachers became furious when we still refused to salute the flag or say "Heil Hitler." In punishment, the three of us were sent to different places. I kept worrying about Paul-Gerhard and Hans-Werner. They were just little boys.

For six years I remained in the custody of the Nazis, praying that all of my family would survive the war.

Kristallnacht

Werner Weinberg

Born in a small rural town in Westphalia, Germany,
Werner Weinberg graduated with honors from
Hebrew Teachers Seminary in Würzburg in 1936,
earning the title judischer Lehrer, or Jewish teacher.
He and his wife were survivors of the camps. Now a
professor in the United States, Weinberg lectures
and writes extensively about the Holocaust. One of
his best-known works is *Self-Portrait of a Holocaust
Survivor*, from which the following selection is taken.

On November 9, 1938, the Nazis led a night-long
campaign of terror and violence against the Jews in
Germany that has come to be known as *Kristallnacht*
(crystal night or night of broken glass). At the time,
Weinberg and his fiancée were teachers living in the
city of Hannover. In this selection, he describes their
harrowing experiences.

At the time of the Crystal Night, Lisl, my fiancée,
and I were teachers at the Jewish elementary school of Hannover.

Among the Jews with Polish citizenship deported from the city two weeks
before the event had been the family Grynszpan. One of their sons, Herschel, 17
years old, had earlier fled to Paris. Upon learning about the desperate situation
of his family through a smuggled-out postcard, he bought a pistol, entered the
German embassy on a pretext, and shot the official who received him. The fatally
wounded victim was Ernst Freiherr vom Rath, third secretary of the embassy—
the date of this act: November 7, 1938.

34

Headlines screamed it out, the radio shouted bloodcurdling threats, Göbbels himself was heard: "Woe to you Jews—if he dies." Vom Rath succumbed to his wounds on November 9. We were paralyzed by fear. It was not just a normal fear of reprisals. The year 1938 had been the worst so far, one anti-Jewish decree had followed on the heel of the other. Everything pointed toward a cataclysmic event.

But there was something else behind the realistic apprehension of a looming catastrophe. It had to do with the date. The date of November 9 had assumed an almost mythical character. Hitler had given this day a solemn and—for us Jews—ominous significance on the Nazi calendar. It was the anniversary of the German revolution of 1918, the "dagger thrust into Germany's back" (by Jews, of course) which ended World War I so ignominiously for Germany. On the same date, in 1923, Hitler staged his abortive *coup d'état* in Munich, and since then, November 9 had become a memorial day for the Nazi party. It was the day for promotions in the party ranks and for consecration of new banners by touching them with the "blood standard" of Munich. Every November 9 Hitler assembled his old guard, carriers of the "blood order," in the Munich *Bürgerbräukeller*, and reminisced with them. It was at these occasions that he would emit his vilest threats against the Jews.

And now vom Rath had died on November 9, from the bullets of a Jewish assassin. Fate itself had turned against us!

At that time my fiancée and I roomed with Jewish families. In my case it was a Polish-Jewish family, and the last two weeks I had lived alone in their large apartment. That evening I went to be with my fiancée. Together with her land-lords, an elderly couple, we sat in the living room, listening to the radio for news. Much shouting was going on about the murdered German diplomat, about his Jewish murderer, about the world-wide Jewish conspiracy, and about the intoler-able situation of Jews still residing on German soil, gloating, no doubt, over the successful assassination. But no concrete threat was uttered, no new anti-Jewish decree announced. The expected speech by the *Führer* from Munich did not materialize. Everything that we heard and did not hear made our vigil more terrifying. Our guesses concerning the fate awaiting us included: total removal of Jews from business and other sources of income; deportation of all remaining Jews (—but where to?); transportation of all able-bodied men to concentration camps; street riots with beatings, possibly killings. Actually, our fantasies moved along comparatively conservative lines; even the idea of concentration camps meant "only" maltreatment, hard labor, starvation, cruel punishment, and death sentences for small transgressions (at that time ash-urns were still being sent to next-of-kin from Dachau, Buchenwald and Sachsenhausen). Yet the general dread of "the Ninth of November" and the apprehension of the "lesson" Göbbels and his consorts promised to teach us weighed more heavily upon us than any definite fear.

The association of that calendar date with calamity was so strong that, as the evening progressed and nothing happened, our mood grew cautiously optimistic. Still, when I kissed Lisl good night at about eleven o'clock, both our hearts were heavy. On my way home I avoided the light circles of the street lamps. Individual SA and SS men in uniform were on their way to places of assembly.

I lay on my bed, fully dressed, without even removing my shoes. This precaution was essential; it was a rare storm trooper who, during nightly arrests, gave you a few seconds to finish dressing: their *"raus, raus!"* (out, out!) calls made the element of utter haste a part of the terror. That night I discovered that the cliché of "being bathed in cold sweat" can have a very literal meaning. I thought of packing a few belongings, but I could not summon the energy. The light was out; all my senses strained to detect the first signs of danger in the street. Being alone in the rambling apartment made the situation even more sinister.

About 1 a.m. it started: the thud of hobnailed boots on the pavement to the staccato rhythm of their marching songs. Most of the SA and SS songs were drawn from the rich well of old German folk songs. *"Im Wald, im grünen Walde,"* they sang, "in the forest, the green forest." Soon there followed the sounds of breaking windows, of banging on doors, of yelling and shouting. This continuous noise was punctuated by occasional pistol or rifle shots. After a while the strip of sky visible between the heavy draperies turned a flickering orange.

I discerned that the events outside happened in different parts of the city at the same time. Some of the shattering of glass, splintering of wood, shouting of orders, came from far away, but it also went on around the next corner. I could even hear the crackling of fire. I lay on my bed, motionless, waiting. The pogrom sounds drew closer, moved away again, came from right under my window, and once more echoed from a distance. It was as though someone was playing a cat-and-mouse game with me. My fiancée, I knew, was comparatively safe: women and the elderly were, as a rule, not included in Nazi terror actions.

Between four and five o'clock in the morning a tremendous explosion occurred. I did not doubt for a second that it was the synagogue. The Central Synagogue was a vast, imposing building. Said to be the largest church building in Hannover, it was built as for eternity, and its lower walls were many feet thick. Preparations to blow it up took the Party demolition teams all night. My apartment was far away from the synagogue, yet my windows clattered. When morning dawned, flocks of crows circled low over the city, their plaintive caw-caw filling the air—the birds' nests had been in the synagogue spires.

I got up, put my head under the faucet, and then ventured a look through the slit between the window drapes. November 9 had come and gone, yet the pogrom noise continued in the distance. Then my doorbell rang.

A great calm came over me. (How often have I later experienced such moments of dignity—reward for presuffering, for sustained expectation of the worst!) I opened the door. It was my fiancée! On her way she had seen smashed Jewish store fronts, the merchandise scattered over the pavement. She had steered around large pieces of furniture thrown from windows of Jewish apartments, and she had witnessed a group of Jewish men being treated with clubs and rifle butts, as they were being marched to the police station.

For a while her report and our being together loosened the rigidity of the night, giving way to a spate of activity. First of all, we wondered about whether or not to report to school. After all, it was not officially closed or suspended, as far as we knew. The apartment had no telephone; but we probably would not have dared to make the call anyhow. The idea of holding classes seemed ludicrous; still we felt uneasy about simply ignoring our duty. I packed a suitcase. Lisl made sandwiches for me and wrapped them in paper. I put the two packages into the pockets of my overcoat. This accomplished, we continued waiting together. We left the drapes in the living room closed and moved into the kitchen, away from the street. We sat down at the table; the suitcase stood at my side; my hat and overcoat laid out on a chair. The kitchen was closest to the apartment door. Both Lisl and I would be ready the moment they came for me!

On that Tenth of November we sat in the kitchen of the rambling apartment for over twelve hours and waited. We talked little and ate nothing. Now there were two of us listening to the street sounds, and once in a while, one or the other went to the living room and peeped through the curtain slit. The noises were the same as those of the night; also, the pattern of the din, drawing nearer and wandering off, had not changed. The radio was much less communicative, though, than the day before. It briefly mentioned isolated incidents here and there in Germany, where the infuriated population had vented their grief on Jewish property. A troop of Hitler Youth marched through our street. After each stanza, they interrupted their sprightly marching songs by shouting in chorus slogans like: "Death to the Jews!" "The Jews are our misfortune!" *"Juda verrecke!"* ("Perish, Judah").

We tried to formulate a plan. It entailed seeking refuge in a Jewish household that in all probability was omitted from the list of the present action: households of women and children only, or those in which the men were 65 or older. For a moment we considered my fiancée's landlords, but dismissed the idea immediately since, according to the *mores* of the time, an engaged couple did not live in the same household. Not even an emergency could break that moral code! Another elderly couple came to mind, who probably would take me in; but when it came to actually leaving the apartment, our courage forsook us. So we stayed in the kitchen. From time to time the flock of crows passed the window and their call seemed to express criticism of this "spontaneous outburst of the seething soul of the people." But what could one expect of birds whose home had been a synagogue?

In the late morning the doorbell rang. There had been no noise of hobnailed boots and the ring was not followed by banging on the door. We waited for the second ring, and Lisl opened the door. It was the Christian cleaning woman of the household. She sat down with us in the kitchen without taking off her coat or hat. Hastily and in a hushed voice she announced that she had come at great personal risk. Then she talked about the synagogue. The explosion, she said, had been caused by a large amount of dynamite which the Jewish community had stored in the basement of the synagogue, together with a large assortment of firearms. She was sorry, though, for the innocent among the Jewish men, whom she had seen being led to the railway depot. She lamented the destruction of the fine downtown stores, complaining that the merchandise had been thrown into the streets rather than being distributed among the needy.

Eventually she came to the real purpose of her visit. Surely we had heard of the new decree that forbade Jews to possess any money (we had heard nothing of the sort). A Jew found with money on him would be shot. She was willing to take for safekeeping any money we might have on us; she even volunteered to cash in our savings accounts if we gave her our passbooks. As to the future, we could count on her not to leave us without means. We had to be cautious warding off her attempt at blackmail, as she might tell the nearest storm troopers about my apartment that had—so far—been overlooked. During the hour after her departure our waiting for the boots and the banging was at its keenest. Then we sank back into a stupor, each submerged in private musings. There was little to be said anymore. When we talked, it was in short remarks and retorts, such as expressing our astonishment at the long duration of this action against the few thousand Jews of Hannover, or wondering how many other places were going through the same experience (Hannover, after all, being the hometown of Herschel Grynszpan). In case the action was widespread, was it better or worse in small towns like Rheda, where I was due the next day for my weekend visit to conduct services and hold religious school?

In the afternoon the noises grew more sporadic and moved farther away. Dusk fell early, and a long evening began. Our restlessness became unbearable. At about nine o'clock—not having heard any special activity in the street for over an hour—we could stand it no longer. We put on our overcoats, left the apartment, locked the door, and went down the stairs. We decided to look up a relative who had apprenticed himself to an upholsterer and lived with a Christian family. (It was common then, even for middle-aged Jews, former businessmen, professionals or officials, to start anew, learning a trade as an "emigration skill.") The people let us in, but not without anxiety. Yes, the Gestapo had been there earlier in the day, asking for my relative. But he had left the house at daybreak, saying that he was taking a train out of town. However, the Gestapo might come back, searching for him in earnest. Their original search had been perfunctory—"after all, we are Aryans." We understood their nervousness. I only asked permission to use their telephone to call my congregation in Rheda. A woman answered. She told me, for God's sake to stay where I was, and hung up.

Back in the street, we deliberated whether we should, after all, walk to the Jewish couple who were safe by virtue of their age. But we were too unnerved by the visit at the upholsterer; we also heard anew ominous noises from the direction of downtown. In the absence of any better idea, we went back to the apartment. We had been gone for less than half an hour.

The apartment door was broken open, the lock torn out. We checked our impulse to run back down the stairs. No sound came from the apartment, and lying in wait for Jews did not fit the pattern the storm troopers followed this day. We entered. Most of the furniture had been smashed, apparently with axes; even the grand piano sloped precariously, held up by only one leg. Tables and chairs were overturned, pictures and mirrors broken. We looked for my suitcase under the debris in the kitchen; it was gone!

There was no saying whether they would come back for me. So we hurried outside and did go to our acquaintances, who agreed to put me up until it was safe again. My fiancée left to return to her room.

I spent only a few days with our friends. Although Hannover was one of those cities where groups of Nazis staged sporadic anti-Jewish raids even after November 10, the "action" was officially at an end. It was so announced over the radio. I received the notice in my hiding place to report to school on Monday morning. It had been decided on high that Jewish life had to go on "normally," but at the same time decrees such as the billion marks penalty for the Jews and their "expulsion from the German economy" (both promulgated on November 12) put the finishing touch to the happening of November 10. Another decree annulled all exceptions for Jewish children still attending public schools. These children had to be immediately absorbed by our school.

There was an inconsequential sequel to what happened to us in the Crystal Night in Hannover. I will relate it here because I think it is typical for the Nazi mind in which order and chaos were neatly compartmentalized. My fiancée suggested that we should try to retrieve my suitcase. The idea appalled me. Extraordinarily lucky, we had weathered the pogrom with no greater loss than a suitcase and the repair bill for the apartment door. Should I go to Gestapo Headquarters to claim the suitcase and thereby admit having evaded the storm troopers? But Lisl never intended for me to do the claiming. Men were endangered, women were not. The "teaching of a lesson" to the Jews was completed and, as it turned out, petty theft had not been on the official program. In short, she did go to Gestapo Headquarters. I waited "inconspicuously" across the street around a corner. Later Lisl told that there had been a waiting room filled with Jewish women, all wanting to inquire to which concentration camp their husband, son or father had been taken. Just as in a doctor's office, one at a time they were called in. It seemed that they got a straight, even polite, answer concerning the whereabouts of their men. At that time people were still being released from concentration camps. All that was required were valid papers which assured a person's immediate emigration. When such papers could be supplied, the prisoner was freed—after signing an affidavit that he had not been mistreated. Unfortunately, for some it was too late; they had died of one of the two admissible causes of death: "weakness of circulation" or "shot in an attempt to escape."

When Lisl's turn came, she had to describe the "lost" object. Thereupon she was led to a room full of property, where she identified my suitcase. It had been opened and searched but the contents were complete and undamaged. She signed a receipt, and the SS man apologized for the incident ("after all, we are not thieves"). She left Gestapo Headquarters carrying my Crystal Night suitcase. When she had crossed the street and turned the corner, I took it. We walked together through the cold November drizzle. The crows were still circling low over the roofs.

They Had a System

Yala Korwin

Yala Korwin's poems
have been published in a
number of journals and
collected in *To Tell the
Story*, from which the
following poem was
taken. For additional
biographical information
on Korwin, see page 20.

Korwin's poem,
written in memory of a
young girl whose name
has long been forgotten,
depicts the irony of
attempting to anticipate
and make sense out of
the senseless acts of the
Nazis.

In memory of the Girl whose name vanished with her

She went to the bakery
just around the corner
to get rations of bread
for them all.
She didn't let her mother go.
She said: stay home.
Yesterday
they took old people away.
Where to?
No one knows.
Stay. I'll go.
She went and didn't return.
That day
they took the young ones away.
They had a system. They were
thorough.

Her mother worried. The girl
had nothing warm on.
Winter was near and winds
were quite strong already.
How will she work in the cold
wherever they had sent her?
Then, a postcard arrived.
Just a few words scribbled
with the girl's hand:
Dear Mama. I'm well.
Work isn't hard.
Don't worry.

Her mother worried.
She put the girl's warm coat
in a box,
made a neat package
and waited.
She waited for another postcard
with an address on it.
It never came.

They had a system.

chapter 2

In Hiding

To go into hiding is to choose to become invisible, to suspend one's identity, and to turn away from a life of certainty to one of danger. When we think about people in hiding, we generally envision secret closets, cramped quarters, and extreme danger. Such were the conditions faced by many who went into hiding to escape Nazi tyranny.

Initially, the Nazis and their collaborators selectively carried out arrests and deportations. As Hitler's campaign to eradicate European Jewry escalated, Jews sought escape routes. In many cases, they attempted to escape by going into hiding. For many Jews, especially those with long-standing ties to their communities, hiding seemed a less drastic alternative than emigration. Others who waited too long found the exit routes closed to them when they sought to escape. Hiding became their most feasible means of avoiding Nazi round-ups.

Many people first learn of the Holocaust when they read *The Diary of Anne Frank*. The story of Anne and her family reflects the experiences of thousands of Jews who gave up everything and went into hiding in an attempt to escape the Nazis. Life in hiding was a difficult experience. The circumstances for people who chose to hide were varied, yet those in hiding all shared a fear of discovery and a sense of isolation. In some cases, whole families and perhaps even friends hid together in basements, attics, and other more horrible places. In other cases, strangers were hidden together, their fates interwoven.

Another kind of hiding was experienced by those Jewish children whose parents felt compelled to send them away to safety, never knowing if they would be reunited. For others, hiding involved taking on a false identity, while still others altered their appearance to look "more Aryan" so that they could live openly, yet hiding their true identities. Hiding was part of life even within the ghettos and concentration camps, as prisoners hid young children, the handicapped, or the ill, all of whom would be certain targets for death.

Throughout Germany and the occupied countries, there were individuals who chose to help the Jews. These individuals risked their own lives to provide Jews with refuge, sustain them with food and supplies, and keep their secrets.

The selections in Chapter 2 reflect the painful conditions those in hiding endured and the determination and will to live that sustained them while the fear of discovery haunted their daily lives. The lives of those who hid and protected the Jews were also in constant danger. Discovery would often result in the same fate for the protectors as for the Jews.

Singing in the Sun

Yala Korwin

A Holocaust survivor,
Yala Korwin has
published poems in a
number of journals; in
addition, her poems have
been collected in *To Tell
the Story*, from which the
following poem was
taken. For additional
biographical information
on Korwin, see page 20.

For those who hid,
the threat of betrayal was
a minute-to-minute
reality. In this poem,
Korwin captures a young
girl's yearning to be free
to do simple things like
singing in the sun.

*For the Italians, friends of the Jews, stationed in 1942
in Lwow*

Be still as a mouse, warned my gentile friends.
So I sat there, half-holding my breath,
in a dark corner of the hiding place,
an empty garage. Till I heard her sing.

If only I could catch but a glimpse
of her who among such sorrows and pains
can remain so joyful, so spry.
I glued my face to a cleft in the door.

Hanging out her freshly washed linen
on a thick rope stretched across
two trees in her garden,
she was humming a merry, lively tune.

The sun gilded the crown of her hair,
air tinted the skin of her cheeks,
sky brightened the glow in her eyes,
she was free to sing and rejoice.

Piercing envy filled me to the brim
as I moved my face a bit closer,
much too close. Sudden screech of old planks.
Too late to recede. She approached. I froze.

She stood there watchful, anxious, keen.
Let me live, my frightened eyes implored,
don't denounce me. I'm young as you are.
Let me sing a carefree song once more.

Did she notice my dispirited gaze?
Did she guess my silent, ardent prayer?
She just stood there, then she turned away
and slowly went back to her chore.

The Hidden Children

Kristine Keren
(as told to Jane Marks)

Kristine Keren was a child in Lvov, Poland, when the
Nazis began rounding up Jews for deportation to
concentration camps. Her story is one of a family so
determined to stay together that they endured, with
the help of a Gentile contact, in the sewers beneath
the Lvov ghetto for fourteen months. Keren now
shares a dental practice with a son and lives on Long
Island. Her story is excerpted from Jane Marks's *The
Hidden Children: The Secret Survivors of the Holocaust*.

Keren's memoir illustrates both the fear that her
family experienced before going into hiding and the
terrible conditions they suffered through while in
hiding.

We lived in Poland, in the ghetto of Lvov. My
father was always looking for places to hide my little brother, Pavel, and me
because the Germans were intent on getting rid of all the Jewish children. One
hiding place was a small, empty space, three feet long and one foot deep, below
the window, which my father had camouflaged to look like the wall. I remember
having to sit in there with Pavel for hours, struggling for air and being so scared!
Tears were running down my cheeks, but I didn't dare make a sound for fear the
Germans would find us. But silently I'd pray for my father to come and let us
out. Each time he came back, I begged him, "Daddy, *please* let this be the last
time." I didn't think I could take it anymore.

My parents had to work in the labor camp, so I was often left alone with my
brother. Several times when the Germans came, I had to hide Pavel in a suitcase
under the bed while I hid in the closet, behind my mother's long, rust-colored

satin robe. I was only seven or eight years old at the time, but I could recognize the German footsteps. I had to hide myself and then wait a few more minutes for fear they'd come back again. Then I ran back to let my brother out of the suitcase so he could breathe again.

He was good! He was only three and a half years old, but he never made a fuss. He understood, as I did, that we just had to be quiet and do what we were told. Life was getting scarier by the day.

One day I heard a noise—like somebody gasping for air—and I looked out the back window. There I saw some Polish teenagers swinging bats and hitting a Jewish man, who was begging them to stop. But they kept it up until he lay there dead. I'll never forget that choking sound he made. I was just stunned.

It was only a few days later that we fled—not through the gates of the ghetto but straight down! My father had been digging a tunnel from the basement of a house near us, right into the sewer. When he broke through, he found himself face-to-face with a sewer worker. Instead of reporting my father, the man said, "I can help you, but you'll have to pay me—a lot." My father agreed, and the next day he brought the man all the money we had. It was a risk, but the only real chance we had.

The next night my father saw some cars with soldiers coming close. He came down to where my brother and I were hidden in the basement, and he whispered, "This is it!" I cried when he explained that we'd have to go down this very narrow tunnel. He would go first, then me. Then Pavel and my mother.

I could hear the sound of water in the tunnel down below, and I knew I couldn't do it. I sobbed, "I don't want to go." My father said gently but urgently, "You have to go. Trust me, don't worry." I watched him go down, and then somebody pushed me. I felt myself falling through the blackness, and then my father caught me and put me on his back. He said, "Hold tight."

I grabbed his neck, and I held on to his hips with my feet. He kept telling me to hold tight. I was shaking. My teeth were chattering so hard, I couldn't talk. Then my mother was behind us, holding Pavel. The walkway was narrow, and we had to be careful not to fall into the water. It seemed like we had to walk forever! I kept asking my father how much longer. He said, "Don't worry, a few minutes more, a few minutes more." It was especially frightening when we had to cross from one side of the river to the other.

Meanwhile, all around us people were dropping down into the sewer through manholes. It was terrifying! Then my father's contact, whose name was Leopold Socha, appeared and took us and several other people to a special tunnel where we wouldn't be seen. He told my father where to find boards we could put across the flowing water, and on which we could sleep. By then I was so tired, I fell asleep leaning on a strange man, who said to me, "You're little, but you're so heavy."

We all stayed there for a few days. Some people couldn't take the stench and the darkness, so they left, but ten of us remained in that sewer—for fourteen months! During that time we never went outside or saw daylight. We lived with webs and moss hanging on the wall. The river not only smelled terrible, but also it was full of diseases. We got dysentery, and I remember Pavel and I were sick with unrelenting diarrhea. There was only enough clean water for each of us to have half a cup a day. My parents didn't even drink theirs; they gave it to Pavel and me so that we wouldn't die from dehydration.

Mr. Socha and two of his friends very faithfully brought us food. But there were dangers. A few times other sewer workers found us because they had seen our wet shoes hanging up. We had to run to try to escape. I would get so scared, I stopped breathing. But we got away! Another time our little lamp started a fire. We thought we'd be burned, but we survived that too.

Then there was a heavy rainstorm, and the sewer swelled so that the water was almost up to the ceiling, which was less than five feet high. My parents, who were constantly bent, had to hold us children up high so we could breathe. We were frequently soaking wet.

The rats were all over us—each one was about a foot long. But we weren't afraid of them; we played with them. We fed them, and they grew even bigger from eating our bread. But they always wanted more, and my father had to stay awake at night to keep them from eating it all.

All this time nobody had to tell us to be quiet. I felt like an animal, ruled by instinct. I never spoke above a whisper. But after a few months of this life I was very, very depressed, and I didn't want to eat or talk to anybody.

That was when Leopold Socha picked me up and took me through the tunnels and said, "Look up." I saw the daylight, and he said to me, "You have to be very strong, and one day you will go up there and live a life like other children." At my father's suggestion Mr. Socha brought books so my father could teach me to read and count. This way, they said, I'd be ready for school when the war was finally over.

From then on I'd always watch for Mr. Socha when he would come every other day with our food. Always the first thing I'd see was his smile: a radiant smile with perfect teeth. He was such a cheerful man—and thoughtful too! He managed to get my mother candles for the Sabbath, and he'd always share his own lunch with Pavel and me.

When liberation came, Mr. Socha was the one who came to tell us. We'd heard plenty of Russian bombs exploding nearby, but we didn't know we were free until Mr. Socha banged on the pipe. We all stayed very quiet, unsure of what the banging meant. Then he called our names. He said, "You can come out now!"

The Survivor of Babi Yar

Othniel J. Seiden

Born in Vienna, Austria, Othniel J. Seiden escaped
from Nazi Europe shortly before the Holocaust
began. His family had been active in smuggling Jews
out of Europe as conditions steadily deteriorated.
Living in the United States, he graduated from the
University of Missouri School of Journalism and
worked in advertising for newspapers, magazines,
radio, and television. A prolific writer, he later
graduated from medical school and entered private
practice. *The Survivor of Babi Yar*, from which the
following excerpt was taken, was his first novel.

In the fall of 1941, German SS troops and their
allies in the Ukrainian militia slaughtered over 30,000
Jews and Gypsies in a gorge at Babi Yar, near Kiev in
the Soviet Union. The victims were dumped in mass
pits for burial. Seiden has created a fictionalized
account of a victim who survived by hiding and then
fleeing. In this excerpt, he is rescued and hidden by a
non-Jew. In the aftermath, he is faced with questions
about why this could have happened.

Solomon awoke in a small enclosure—the space
under a stairway—dimly lit by a lantern. He felt weak. Any movement was
painful.

Where am I? How did I get here?

He was lying on a cot, naked to the waist, under a clean sheet. He felt under
the sheet and found the undershorts, not his own, unfamiliar. Above, what

appeared to be the underside of a landing, the stairs angling down to his feet; at his head, a high wall about a meter from the end of the cot; to the right, the cot stood against another of the walls, an outside wall of cold stone, like a foundation. The undersides of the stairs were wooden, the wall at his head and the one to his left, an arm's length from his cot, stucco or plaster. The floor was dirt.

Am I a prisoner?

He looked around for an exit. He was able to make out a small door at the base of the tall wall beyond the head of his cot, not more than a meter high and no wider than a man's shoulders. It was not made to enter or exit conveniently.

He remembered a massive crowd of people. Fleeting, confusing . . . he was terrified.

"What is this place?" The words barely escaped his throat. His mind was a blank.

From somewhere beyond the walls, he heard the sound of a door opening. Then footsteps on the landing and stairs above him—heavy, bold steps. The lantern swung. Eerie shadows moved on the walls.

They're coming for me.

Again, that image of crowds. Fierce pain tore through his whole body as he tried to move toward the foot of his cot. He didn't have the strength to move to the end of the chamber away from the door. He felt resigned. His eyes followed the invisible footsteps from the bottom of the stairs to where the closed door stood, half hidden in shadow. He heard something being dragged along the floor, but he didn't hear the door swing open. Quietly, a figure maneuvered, with some difficulty, through the low entrance. Its features remained obscured. Solomon lay frozen as the figure waited in darkness.

He's not in uniform, Solomon thought with relief. He has no weapon.

The figure turned toward him. "It's about time. You've been sleeping like the dead since I found you."

What does he mean? Where am I? Why can't I remember?

"Don't be afraid. My name is Ivan. Ivan Igonovich. Do you feel anything?"

Solomon shook his head feebly.

"I found you two days ago, in a ditch along the road. I've never seen such a mess. Mud, blood, filth caked all over you." The figure was animated now, gesturing with his arms and massive hands as much as the small chamber would allow. "I thought you were dead. But, when I jogged you, you mumbled. Then you fainted again. You've been mostly unconscious ever since."

Solomon managed, "I don't understand. Where am I?" Some of Solomon's fear melted. The lantern light in the small room was too weak for Solomon to make out Ivan's features clearly, but the deep voice was gentle. Though the man looked powerful enough to crush him with one hug, Solomon's terror faded to a nagging anxiety.

"You are safe," the stranger reassured him. "We have you hidden. We've gotten some broth into you, but you've been delirious. Do you remember anything at all?"

Solomon tried. He couldn't seem to focus.

"You spoke of a pit of death. German gunners. Piles of death. What does it all mean?"

Solomon nearly cried out, "The Germans were shooting us. All of us. Shooting us in the ravine."

"What is your name?" Ivan asked. "What do they call you?"

"Solomon Shalensky. I am called Sol by my friends—if any of my friends are still alive."

"How old are you, Solomon?" Ivan asked, calmly.

"Eighteen. Eighteen on September the third."

"Tell me more. Where did all this take place? You spoke of a ravine."

"At Babi Yar, near Kiev. The Germans killed all of us in the ravine."

Ivan stared in astonishment. "What do you mean they killed *all* of you? And how did you get here? Kiev is over ten kilometers to the south."

"I don't know how I got here. I must have crawled. . . . I think I crawled at night." Solomon's voice dropped and his speech slowed. His mouth became dry and his heart started to pound. "They thought I was dead. I was buried. They killed us all."

"Who?"

"All of us. All the Jews."

"A pogrom?"

"No. They just took us to the ravine and shot us down with machine guns."

"Were you and your friends . . . a resistance group?" Ivan's voice was suspicious.

"No. They took all of us from Kiev and shot us in the ravine. All of the Jews from Kiev. They shot us."

Ivan shook his head. "You must be mistaken. There are thousands of Jews in Kiev!"

"All of us," Solomon repeated. "Thirty thousand in two days. I was among the last. I was buried with the rest."

Ivan stared a long time. "You're tired." He gestured toward the cot. "Rest, Solomon. You're safe here. I'll come back later with more broth, and we'll talk."

Ivan left Solomon alone under the stairs.

*　*　*

Solomon tried to put things in order. Where must I start? Suddenly he was crying. Mama, Papa, my sister and brothers—they must all be dead. And Grandpa. All dead. His tears came in a torrent now. He cried until it hurt. "Oh, God," he whimpered. "Why me?"

His face was still damp when Ivan returned an hour later with some broth. There was black bread, too. Broth and bread. Solomon was amazed that he was hungry.

★　★　★

Ivan watched Solomon eat. His eyes gazed at the boy's face. Could it be true what he has told me? What part is exaggeration? He was a mess when I found him. He's truly been through something horrible.

"How is it that you've hidden me in your home?" Solomon asked. "It's not usual for a Russian or a Ukrainian to hide a Jew."

Ivan felt a moment of hostility. "Not all of us are like that!" Then he realized that Solomon had reason to be curious. "When I was younger, I saw the aftermath of a pogrom. I saw the organized slaughter of Jews in their village. Sixty-three Jews were killed in their shtetl one Easter. I don't know how many were maimed and injured. Their homes were burned and their shops looted. The so-called Christians claimed it was vengeance for the Crucifixion." Ivan's gaze fell to the floor as a frown of disgust wrinkled his forehead. His eyes closed.

"Since that day I have never placed foot inside a church. Once I worked for a Jew, too. I was treated fairly and decently. But I had no idea you were Jewish when I found you. I thought perhaps . . ."

"What?" said Solomon.

"I thought you were a resistance fighter. I had no idea that the Jews were special enemies of the Germans. But, if I had known, it would not have made any difference."

"How is it that you have a secret place like this in your home?"

"It was the home of the Jew I worked for—a Zionist. He built this secret room to hide his family, should a pogrom have come this way. He was always afraid of a pogrom. He had survived one as a child and had never gotten over it. Several years ago, he decided to leave Russia for Palestine. One night, he and his family stole out of Russia. They took only what they could carry. He left me all of this for my loyalty during the years I worked for him." Ivan looked about the little chamber. "It will probably get some more use now."

After a short silence, Solomon asked, "How will I ever be able to repay you?"

"Never mind that. Tell me, do you remember any more now than you did before?"

"A little has come back to me." A distant frown crossed Ivan's face. "It is all so unreal, like a horrible dream."

Ivan waited for Solomon to continue.

"It all seems so impossible. We actually thought we were being liberated by the Germans. We thought that the cultured Europeans were going to liberate us from the tyranny of the Ukrainians and Russians. No more pogroms, no more poverty, no more anti-Semitism, that is what we thought. We welcomed the Germans. I don't understand how it happened."

Noemi

Yala Korwin

Yala Korwin's poems
have been published in a
number of journals and
collected in *To Tell the
Story*, from which the
following poem was
taken. For additional
biographical information
on Korwin, see page 20.

In this poem,
dedicated to the memory
of Noemi "Stefania"
Meisels, Korwin explores
the ironic doom of one
who tried to hide by
altering her appearance.

In memory of Noemi "Stefania" Meisels

You hid behind a borrowed name,
bleached your raven crown,
but there was no dye
to cover the pigment of doom
in your eyes.

Night after night I see you
alone in that place
guarded by a killer-fence.
Night after night I am dying
all your deaths.

I didn't follow you, sister.
Can I be ever forgiven
the blueness of my iris,
the paleness of hair—hues of
Slavic fields?

I escaped to be your witness,
to testify: you were.
I live to carve your name
in all the silent stones
of the world.

Hiding to Survive

Andy Sterling
(as told to Maxine B. Rosenberg)

Andy Sterling was born in Hungary shortly before
the outbreak of World War II. Although Hungary
was a German ally in the war, Hungarian Jews were
not exempt from the Nazi roundups. Sterling's
family finally sent him to safety in a Catholic
orphanage in Budapest. His story is excerpted from
*Hiding to Survive: Stories of Jewish Children Rescued
from the Holocaust* by Maxine B. Rosenberg.

In this personal narrative, Sterling relates his
experiences as a Jewish boy being hidden in a
Catholic orphanage, where he could never reveal his
true identity to anyone.

In 1941 Hungary, where I was born, entered the
war as a German ally. A year later, when I was six and a half, my father and other
Jewish men in our village were sent away to do forced labor. For the next eighteen months I didn't know where he was.

When he came back in late 1943, he told my family stories about Jews being
rounded up throughout Europe and said that we were no longer safe. He thought
we should leave our small village of Nagykata where everyone knew we were
Jewish and go to Budapest, the capital city, where we might blend in more.

First my parents left and moved in with my aunt. For the next few months
they tried to get things in order. Suddenly, in March 1944, the Germans occupied
Hungary, and Jews living in and near my village were relocated to a ghetto. My
grandmother, my younger sister, Judith, and I went there along with my grandmother's brother and his wife.

Every day Jews from this ghetto were being sent to the camps. We knew that our time was running out. Luckily my uncle's daughter knew a Christian who had connections and helped us to escape. A few weeks later we learned that all the Jews in our ghetto had been shipped to Auschwitz.

Now I was with my parents again. My father had already gotten false identity papers for himself and had become an ambulance driver. I, though, had to wear a star and abide by the curfew.

That September the Germans, with the Hungarian SS as their helpers, began deporting Jews in huge numbers and shooting Jews on the street. At the same time, the Russians were bombing the city. Things got so bad, my parents forbade me to leave the apartment and said I could play only in the garden within the building.

One day I disobeyed and went across the street with a little mirror to see how the sun's rays reflected off it. Out of nowhere, an SS man holding a leashed German shepherd appeared and grabbed me by the collar. He accused me of giving signals to American flyers and was about to take me away when the superintendent of my apartment house came to my rescue. He convinced the SS man to let me go.

At this point my parents realized how much danger we were in and said that my sister and I had to be hidden. When I heard that I'd be separated from my parents, I was very upset.

My parents said I'd be going to a Catholic orphanage in Budapest with Paul, their friend's child, who was two years older than I. Paul's parents had found the place, and the priest in charge was willing to hide us. Judith, now five, was being sent to a convent, and my mother was going to live with a Catholic family in town. My father said he'd be moving around in his ambulance trying to get false papers for my aunt and grandmother.

Before I left, my parents warned me not to tell anyone at the orphanage I was Jewish. Because I was circumcised, they said I had to be extra careful not to be seen when I undressed or urinated.

In October 1944 my father drove Paul and me to the orphanage. We left at night in the middle of an air raid, when only emergency vehicles were allowed on the street.

As soon as we got to the door, my father said good-bye and promised to visit whenever he could. As he drove away, I felt abandoned. It was the first time I was on my own.

The priest and his assistant took Paul and me into an office and told us never to talk about being Jewish, not even to each other. If the orphanage boys asked why we had come a month after school had started, we were to say that our fathers had been killed on the front and that our mothers were too ill to take care of us.

After the priest coached us on some of the morning prayers, he showed us to the dormitory. I lay in bed terrified. Everything was strange. I wanted my parents.

The next morning the priest introduced us to the boys. There were sixty of them, and most had been in the orphanage for years and years and knew one another. I had only met Paul twice before.

That morning I went to services and carefully watched what the others did. When they stood up, I stood up. When they knelt, I knelt. But when they crossed themselves, I got uncomfortable. I had been brought up in a Jewish home and gone to Hebrew school, and I felt awkward. In the end I crossed myself like the rest of the boys, and from then on I did what I was told. I was too afraid to do anything else.

My father visited from time to time. He could only stay for a few minutes, but at least I knew he was alive. Once in a while he came when I wasn't around, and the priest would give me the message. The priest tried to look after me and make sure I was okay, but with so many boys to take care of he didn't always have the time. Mostly I fended for myself.

In November, one month after I arrived, the bombing increased and the air raid sirens went off night and day. In a hurry we'd all rush down into the bunker, where the priest would lead us in prayer. In between the bombings the priest and his assistant tried to conduct classes, but when the air raids became too frequent, they gave up.

After that we moved into the bunker full time, running upstairs only to use the bathroom. We'd go in shifts of four or five, with just twenty-five seconds each. For emergencies we kept some buckets downstairs.

By then it was winter, and it was very cold. We had no heat or electricity, and there was a water shortage. That meant we couldn't bathe or change our clothes. For me it was easier not having to undress in front of the others. But soon we all were infested with lice.

At this time the Russians invaded Budapest, arriving in tanks. They destroyed one building after another until the Germans and the Hungarian SS were trapped and resorted to street fighting. It got so dangerous, my father was afraid to drive his ambulance and stopped coming to see me. Now I felt totally alone.

Worse, we were running out of food. Except for some corn left in the pantry, there was nothing to eat. In desperation the priest ran out on the street to scrounge up something. Once he found a dead horse that had been shot in front of the orphanage and asked me and some other boys to help chop it up. That night he grilled the meat over some wood, and everyone had a couple of bites. The meat tasted sweet. After not eating for so long, I thought it was an incredible meal.

By late December the bombing had worsened, and fires were spreading throughout the city. When a building to the right of ours was shelled, the priest got scared. He thought the Russians were probably targeting the Hungarian Gestapo's headquarters, which were next to the orphanage. To protect us, he decided to break through the wall of our cellar and tunnel into the adjacent building where it would be safer.

With only a pickax, he and his assistant chipped away at the bunker's stone wall, shoveling out the debris. Meanwhile bombs and shells whistled overhead. We kids watched, petrified. Eventually they dug out a large enough space for us to crawl through one at a time.

By then I hadn't seen my father in a month and a half. I didn't know where he or my mother were or if they were alive or dead. It was tough not having any word from them.

At the same time the firing outside was getting more severe. The older boys in the orphanage tried to act brave, but the younger ones, like Paul and me, couldn't stop crying. He and I clung to each other while the priest kept telling us to pray.

"The war is almost over," the priest said to everyone. With the bombing overhead, it was hard to believe, especially since the priest himself seemed scared. Only when he said I'd soon be with my parents did I have some hope.

Finally, on January 15, 1945, the Russians liberated Pest, the part of the city where I was hiding. With the priest leading us, we all went into the street to witness the events. Except for some distant shelling in the hills, it was deadly silent. I looked around and saw one building after another in rubble. Suddenly my whole body started shaking. Instead of feeling joy, I felt weak. More than ever I wanted my parents.

Six days later my father drove up in his ambulance. When I saw him, I ran into his arms and couldn't stop crying. He had brought bread for everyone, which we quickly grabbed. We were very hungry.

Now, I thought, I'll finally be with my parents. But Buda, the part of the city where my mother was hiding, hadn't yet been liberated. My father didn't even know if she was safe. Also, there were still pockets of Germans around who were shooting at whim, so I had to stay in the orphanage for another two months.

During that time my father visited and brought everyone food. Then in March he came for me, taking me to my aunt's apartment, where once again the family was together. The four of us and my aunt and grandmother had survived the war.

Now we had to figure out how to get food and clothing to keep us alive. Since my father had to give the ambulance back to the government, we had no transportation. Besides, there was nothing to be bought in the city. So my parents walked forty miles back to our old village to see what they could find there. A week later they returned in a donkey cart filled with enough food for us and extra to sell. Not long after, we all left Budapest and returned to our home in Nagykata.

Of the 628 Jews who had lived in and around our village, very few had survived the war. When the villagers saw us, they acted as if we had returned from the dead.

In school, my sister and I were the only Jewish children in our classes, which made us feel strange. My parents too were uncomfortable with no other Jews nearby. So in 1949 we moved back to Budapest. Until the year before, my father had been sending donations to the orphanage. But then in 1948 the Communists banned religious schools in the country, and the orphanage ceased to exist. The building was standing, but the priest, his assistant, and the children were gone.

I never saw the priest again, but I learned from my father that there were eight other Jewish boys in the orphanage besides Paul and me. Paul and I had suspected certain kids were Jewish, but we had been afraid to ask. It's too bad, because it would have been comforting to know we weren't the only ones.

In Hiding

Helen Degan Cohen

As a child, Helen Degan
Cohen fled with her
family from their native
Poland to Byelorussia at
the beginning of World
War II. The family was
held in a ghetto before
they escaped. After her
parents became involved
in the resistance
movement, Cohen was
sent into the country,
where she was hidden by
a Catholic woman.
Although reunited after
the war, the family found
that there was nothing
left of their home in
Warsaw, so they had to
begin a new life. Cohen's
poem first appeared in
Spoon River Quarterly in
1985 and was reprinted in
*Blood to Remember:
American Poets on the
Holocaust*, edited by
Charles Fishman.

In this poem, Cohen
evokes the image of a
young girl's all too brief
escape from the terror of
living in hiding.

Poem about the many days in hiding
with a Catholic woman in a countryside
beside a place called War.

Once, in hiding, we went open-
riding in a lenient sleigh
buoyant on the lack of sound and motion
full-away from war
sleepweaving through a back country
my white-haired "lady saint" and I
our frozen faces craning
out of homespun colors:
one soft hour the sound of bells was all.
We were missed by the storm
in its silent eye:
mounds of forest meandered past us
and nearer, more intricate intrusions
fled like calendars behind
their knowledge of our presence—
nature had to wait, we folded leaves
to dream in our escape, the sleigh
was like a god-crib carried by
some fabled beast across her snowy haven
and it hazed the deep green to a waiting green
where animals we knew of kindly
slept unblessed. Our war went still
and deep, around the weightless sleigh.
And now, in a trembling present,
tense with the lunacy of peace
such as it is—a masquerade in blooming
shades of sacrifice, of comfort jaws
and love-drops like the red of war—
I crane my turtle-head for frozen air,
then burrowing
into the soft escape, the easy ride,
I hear, beside the child I was,
those solitary bells of joy
pulling her lonely sleigh.

I Shall Live

Henry Orenstein

Henry Orenstein was born in 1923, one of five
children and the youngest of four sons. Along with
his parents, brothers, and younger sister, Orenstein
hid for three years during the Nazi occupation of his
hometown of Hrubieszow, Poland. When his
parents were killed, Henry and his siblings were part
of the roundup of thousands of Jews as the ghetto
was closed and the residents sent to probable death
in the gas chambers of Sobibor. Orenstein is the
author of *I Shall Live: Surviving against All Odds, 1939–
1945*, from which the following excerpt is taken.

Based upon his personal experiences when he
was a teenager, Orenstein creates a vivid portrayal of
his family's attempt to survive the liquidation of
their small village in Poland. The purpose of these
"actions," as they were called by the Germans, was
to rid the area of Jews through murder or
deportation to the camps. Not knowing whom they
can trust and who will betray them, his family and a
few others flee from one hiding place to another in a
desperate attempt to elude capture.

T hat very day, the Germans ordered that all Jews
were to gather in the town square the next morning, Tuesday, September 1, at
nine. Sam gave the Pole half of all the money we had left, promising him the
other half after he had taken us to Hrubieszów. Our lives were in his hands, Sam

told him. He promised he would not let us down. He was to meet us at three in the morning. We were to wait for him in a World War I ditch not far from the Bug bridge.

After packing a few belongings we tried to get some sleep, but I couldn't even close my eyes from nervous excitement. So it had come—the final extermination action. I was worried about this Pole. He seemed altogether too reassuring, almost too friendly, but what good did it do to think about it? We had no choice but to trust him.

At one o'clock we left the house and started walking toward the ditch, watching out for the Ukrainian patrols. In a few minutes we had reached the ditch. So far, so good. Now we had only to wait. The time crept by; we waited patiently. Three o'clock passed, and he hadn't come. Fear seized our hearts; he had betrayed us. But maybe he was just a few minutes late. By three-thirty we were losing hope. The bastard had taken our money and betrayed us. Still we tried to reassure each other. Maybe he was having trouble with the truck. Maybe he would still come. At four-thirty a woman and a little girl came into the ditch, and a few minutes later a middle-aged man and his wife joined us. So did a young man, a locksmith. A few more Jews came, all desperate people who had nowhere else to go. By five-thirty there were thirteen of us in the ditch.

Slowly the sun rose. It was going to be a glorious day, not a cloud in the sky. It was September 1, the day of the action, and we were trapped. The ditch was long and narrow, its top covered with long grass and weeds growing across it from either side, so that from a distance it was almost invisible. We decided to hide all that day and try to get to the river at night, if the Germans didn't find us first.

From time to time we heard machine-gun and rifle fire. It was hard to believe time could drag so slowly. Twelve o'clock came, then three o'clock, four o'clock. I would never have believed a day could last so long. At five minutes to five I decided to stop looking at my watch, hoping that would make the time pass more quickly. After what seemed at least an hour later I allowed myself to look again. It was just five o'clock—only five minutes had elapsed! I really thought my watch must have stopped, and checked it against Sam's. It was correct. I shall never forget that experience; it was as though we had entered some new dimension outside the normal movement of time. Five-thirty came. We began to hope. Maybe we would make it to nightfall without being discovered. At six o'clock we began a whispered discussion about the best route to take to the river.

It was six-thirty when suddenly we heard a harsh German voice bark: *"Juden-raus!"* (Jews—out!) At the sound my brain seemed to explode. This was it. They had us. Slowly we climbed out of the ditch. The sun was still very bright. There were two Germans with machine guns and a Ukrainian policeman with a rifle. Both Germans were of medium height. I still remember the eyes of one of them: they were shiny, almost glazed, like mirrors. Neither of them hit or cursed us;

they were merely efficient, impersonal professionals who wanted to get their job done without delay.

Quickly they herded us into a group. The two Germans led the way, fingers on their gun triggers, and we followed. The Ukrainian, tall and lanky, his rifle at the ready, walked right behind us. We walked in silence. No one wept, no one pleaded for mercy.

Soon we turned into the main street of town. A strange calm came over me. The day was still beautiful, the sky still blue, even bluer against the orange red of the setting sun. The colors pierced me with their vividness. I remember my thoughts very clearly. I knew this was the last day of my life. I looked at the sun and thought, "I will never see the sun again." I looked at the trees, and thought, "I will never see trees again." I felt no bitterness, but there was a great sadness in my heart. I was not yet nineteen. I had never slept with a girl. My mouth felt very dry, and I couldn't swallow. My tongue seemed swollen to twice its normal size. I had to hold my mouth open.

As we walked down the street, I watched the reaction of the Ukrainian towns-people. They seemed undisturbed at the sight of Jews being led to their deaths. A few even laughed and joked about us. I can never forget a young woman who, seeing us from a window on the second floor of her house, turned and called to her little girl, whom she held up to see us as we passed. That there was a little girl among us seemed not to trouble her at all. I remember thinking: "How can these people be so merciless, don't they have any hearts?"

We were now three or four blocks from the end of the street and only a few hundred yards from the execution pits. Father said to us, "One should not have children." He didn't care what happened to him, but he was in despair at the prospect of having to watch us die.

We were now approaching a narrow street that led to the tile shop where Felek and I had worked. Sam suggested that we shove our money and our watches into the hands of the Ukrainian policeman and run for it.

In a few feverish seconds we took off our watches, wrapped them and the paper money in a handkerchief, pushed it into his hand, and started running to our right, toward the narrow street. I expected the shooting to start imme-diately, so I ran the six or seven steps before we reached the corner with my head turned toward the Germans and the Ukrainian, to see what they would do. The two Germans weren't even aware of what had happened, and continued walking on in front of the group. The other Jews stopped and looked in our direction, confused. The locksmith reacted quickly enough to follow us, a step or two behind. The Ukrainian stood still, holding the handkerchief.

Everything was in a whirl. In about thirty seconds we had reached the back of the tile workshop. Through the windows we could see that there was no one inside. We tried the door, but it was locked and the windows were closed. To this day I don't know how I found the strength, but I managed to grab the window frame and pull it out with my bare hands, along with the two or three nails that held it. We climbed inside the room where Felek and I had worked before the action started. There were large windows all around it, and empty tile racks and a few pieces of equipment, but no place to hide. Behind the door was a storage room for cement and other materials, but it was locked. Several bursts of machine-gun fire erupted outside. They were shooting the rest of the people from our group.

Our position was desperate; at the moment the narrow street was empty, but anyone who happened to pass could see us. We couldn't understand why the door, which was usually open, was now locked. Suddenly we realized: There were Jews hiding in the other room, and they had locked the door from the inside. "We are Jews, open the door!" we called. No answer came, but we heard a noise like the shuffle of feet. We tried to frighten them. "We know you are there. If they catch us, we'll tell them where you are." After a few seconds we heard the click of the turning lock and the door opened. Two old Jews stood there, shivering with fear. We went into the storage room and locked the door behind us. There was an attic above with straw and bags of cement. We climbed up the ladder and lay down on the straw.

We tried to think what to do. It would be too dangerous to try to reach the river during the first day or two of the action, so we decided to stay where we were until the hunt and the shooting had slowed down. It continued sporadically for another couple of hours, until nightfall, when it stopped. Exhausted, I fell asleep at last and slept for seven or eight hours.

Early in the morning we were awakened by the renewed clatter of machine-gun and rifle fire. The action was in full swing once again, and the hunt was on. It was Wednesday morning, September 2. At about eight o'clock we heard a voice outside that we recognized. My heart was pounding hard. It was the voice of the Ukrainian supervisor of the shop, who was knocking at the storage room door. "I know you are there," he called out. "Don't worry. I'm your friend." In a quick, whispered consultation, we decided we had to take the risk and let him in. We unlocked the door. He came in and told us the Germans were shooting every Jew they could find. "You'd better stay right here," he said.

The only possession of any value that we had left was Felek's coat, a fine English brown herringbone tweed. "Give him the coat," I whispered. Maybe with such a gift he would not betray us. After hesitating a moment, Felek handed his coat to the Ukrainian, saying, "Here, take it. If we don't make it you'll have something to remember us by." The Ukrainian made a dismissive gesture, but he didn't need much persuasion. He took the coat, saying, "I will be back," and left.

New discussions ensued. "Is he going to betray us?" The Polish engineer had made us skeptical about trusting people, but we had no choice in the matter.

Machine-gun and rifle fire continued throughout the day. It would have been suicidal to go out. Once again night fell. We decided against going out as SS patrols were everywhere. I was in a state of nervous exhaustion, and that night slept fitfully.

The morning came, Thursday, September 3. Although we had eaten nothing in two days, we were not hungry. Thirst, however, was becoming hard to bear. My mouth and throat were very dry. Late in the afternoon a Russian who was a friend of our Ukrainian supervisor came to the door. He was not a local man but a Soviet citizen who had come with the Russians in 1939 and had been unwilling or unable to escape with the Russian army. He came into the storage room half drunk. His speech was slurred as he assured us that we had nothing to fear from him; he was a friend. On and on he kept assuring us of his friendly feeling. We couldn't figure out at first what he was getting at, until it occurred to us that he wanted something from us, money or a gift. But we had nothing left. Half of our money had gone to the Pole, the other half and our watches to the Ukrainian policeman. Felek now had no coat, and the coats of the rest of us were old and valueless. We didn't know what to do. Felek had a straight razor that we all used to shave with, but should we offer it to the Russian? Perhaps he would be offended by such an insignificant gift. We were reluctant, too, to give it up because we had talked about using it to cut our wrists. Better that than to be shot by the Germans. Giving the razor away would mean losing the chance to take our own lives.

The Russian kept gabbling away. Finally Felek said, "We have nothing left but this razor." He handed it to the Russian, who examined it, opened the blade, tested its sharpness, closed it, put it in his pocket, and staggered out of the room, as we tried to assure him of our sincerity. "Really, we have nothing else left. Please believe us."

It was night again, but I could scarcely sleep. My mouth was very dry and there was not a drop of water anywhere. Friday morning came, and the shooting still continued, although now it was less frequent. We decided we couldn't stay any longer where we were. At least two people knew we were there, and they might have told others. And our thirst was becoming unbearable. We decided to leave that night—if only we weren't betrayed in the meantime.

Late in the afternoon the Russian returned, even drunker, and rambling still more incoherently. He became abusive, calling us *Nadoedlivye Yevrei.* There is no exact English equivalent for *nadoedlivye*, but it means people who are a nuisance to others. *Yevrei* means Jews. We knew it was just a matter of time before he betrayed us, and could only hope he was too drunk to do it before nightfall. When he left he was reeling, so drunk he couldn't walk without holding on to something. After he had gone, we counted the minutes.

It finally got dark outside. We decided to go first to Mietka, who had been Sam's friend and lover during the Soviet occupation. She lived in her father's house on the outskirts of Uściług, and we were hoping to get from her water and food, and then go to the river Bug.

At about midnight the locksmith wished us luck and went out. Then the four of us stepped out into the dark. (The two old Jews had decided to stay.) We dashed from one dark spot to another, hiding whenever we saw a guard until he passed. When we arrived at Mietka's house, Sam called out her name in a low voice. A wave of joy swept over me when I saw the tall, blond girl come to the door. I'll never forget her face—a sweet face with a strong nose— and her long, straight blond hair. She was surprised to see us, and glad that we were alive.

Nor will I ever forget the sensation of drinking the milk she brought us. That milk was an elixir of life, filling every dry cell of my body. It was heaven. We drank and drank and drank. Only after we finished the milk did we realize how hungry we were, and we wolfed down the bread.

The girl warned us to be quiet. Her father was asleep, and she was afraid that he might not want us there. Evidently he was not so brave and humane as his daughter; I had the feeling too that he didn't approve of her friendship with a Jew. She led us out to the barn so we could get some rest. I lay down on the straw enjoying the bliss of a full stomach, and promptly fell asleep.

Just before dawn we were awakened by a loud man's voice. It was the girl's father, and he was not in the least friendly. "Out, out you go," he ordered. We pleaded with him: "It's almost day, please let us stay here just until night. It would be very dangerous to go out in the street now." But he was adamant. "If you don't leave immediately, I will get the police."

We came out of the barn and started walking toward the river. The sun was not up yet, but soon it would be daylight. Suddenly we heard a voice say, "Stop!" There was a Ukrainian carrying a rifle, but not wearing a uniform, only an armband—he was one of the auxiliary militiamen who had been enlisted for the duration of the action. We knew right away that he was no danger to us—he even showed us which way to go to avoid the SS patrols. We thanked him, and walked on a few more blocks.

Soon we realized that we were near Lipińska's, whose son I used to tutor; Sam and Felek knew Mrs. Lipińska, too. It was almost daybreak. We had to find a place to hide for that day, and so we cautiously entered the Lipiński yard. The house was on the edge of a property of about two and a half acres, with vegetable and flower gardens in front. Farther down was a barn with a cow, and a stall where Mr. Lipiński kept a horse. On the opposite side of the path, facing the stall, was a haystack. Behind it was a fruit garden with raspberry bushes and other fruit trees and bushes. The hay was packed tightly between four poles about twelve or thirteen feet high, which formed a square, each side seven or eight feet long. A tile roof rested on top of the four poles, and a ladder leaning against the hay led to the top of the haystack. It had been made from the trunks of two young trees, with small branches for rungs. We climbed the ladder to the top of the stack and wearily lay down on the hay.

Soon we saw Mrs. Lipińska come out of the house and walk toward us. She was a woman of about forty with blue eyes, light brown hair, and a round, pleasant face. Cautiously I called out, "Mrs. Lipińska!" She was startled but calm. "How many of you are there?" she asked. Father, Sam, and Felek raised their heads so that she could see the four of us. She nodded, and told us to be very quiet and not come down, because the SS and the Ukrainian police were searching all over town for Jews. She said she would come back later, and went into the barn.

At least she hadn't thrown us out; probably she would let us stay until night-fall. But we were worried about her husband, whom the Germans had appointed mayor of Uściług; to what extent was he cooperating with them?

In mid-morning Mrs. Lipińska left the house. A few hours later she returned, went into the house, and came out to us carrying a bag full of food: potatoes, soup, bread, butter, and milk. This we had not expected; what a wonderful woman! At least for the moment the pressure was off, and we enjoyed every bite. She came back to collect the dishes and warned us again to be very careful. Her husband and children must not see us, she said. Her children might say something to their friends, and her husband might not be willing to run the frightful risk of having Jews found on his property.

No wonder. In the afternoon a sound truck drove by, blaring out a warning: Anyone caught hiding Jews, or helping them in any way, would be summarily shot. If he or she had a family, they also would be killed. It took a very special person to run this kind of risk. Mrs. Lipińska knew very well that she was en-dangering not only her own life, but also the lives of her son, daughter, and husband.

Those were wild times, savage, merciless. It meant nothing to the SS to take a life, Jewish or gentile. The order was "Kill all Jews," and anybody who stood in the way was eliminated as a matter of course. Nevertheless, Mrs. Lipińska never hesitated. It was clear to us that she was prepared to do whatever was necessary to save us, regardless of the risk.

On our second day there we heard a woman's voice humming a little tune as she approached the Lipińskis' house. We recognized the voice as that of an elderly woman known for her anti-Semitism even before the arrival of the Ger-mans. She was always very solemn; Felek and Sam, who knew her well, had never before heard her laugh or sing. "Can you hear her now?" Sam said. "Happy as a lark. She's delighted to see Jews being killed."

Later that afternoon we suddenly heard the voices of men nearby. As they drew closer, we realized that they were Ukrainian police searching for Jews in the bushes nearby. Suddenly there was a commotion, and a female voice, pleading. Then we heard a shot, and a loud scream, a full-throated cry of terror. It was cut short by another shot. The voices of the Ukrainians grew louder, until we could hear their every word. There were two of them, and they were directly beneath us.

One of the two poles of the ladder leading to the top of the haystack was longer than the other, and from our perch we could see the end of it. Suddenly it shook a little. My heart stopped. Then one of the voices said, "Oh, there's nobody here. Let's look in the stall." We heard steps move away and the creak of a door. After a moment we heard them close the door of the stall and move off toward the house. We went limp with relief. But how much longer could we live with such tension?

The Last Jews in Berlin

Leonard Gross

Leonard Gross is the recipient of numerous awards, including the National Headliners Club Award, the Columbia University Graduate School of Journalism Outstanding Alumnus Award, and Overseas Press Club citations for foreign reporting. He has had a long and distinguished career in journalism, including twelve years with *Look*. Gross is the author of several books of nonfiction. He researched and wrote *The Last Jews in Berlin*, from which the following excerpt is taken, over a four-year period.

During the 1940s, Jews who were unfortunate enough still to be in Germany were in extreme danger. They feared for their lives as they attempted to avoid discovery either by hiding or trying to pass as Aryan with disguises and false identities. In this selection, Gross tells of Willy Glaser, who secures a temporary hiding place from a Christian friend but finds the isolation almost unbearable.

The Jews who went underground in Germany in the 1940s to escape the Nazis called themselves "U-boats," a self-mocking reference to the country's efficient and effective fleet of submarines. But the comparison was as apt as it was sardonic, because to remain underground required much the same degree of wile, stealth and courage as that employed by the crews of the submarines. Some of the Jews who had gone underground were able to remain sequestered until the end of the war. But the majority, like the submarines, had constantly to surface and prowl about. They worried about whether the Gestapo and the S.S. were on their trail or whether neighbors had reported their presence. The Germans who sheltered them became nervous as well. Either or both circumstances required them to find new hiding places every few days or weeks; only infrequently were the majority of Jewish "U-boats" able to remain in their safe harbors for months. Then there was the matter of money for food; it was up to the Jews to find it somehow. They had to secure the ration cards that would enable them to buy food, or develop black market contacts.

Every Jew not permanently hidden had to leave his residence each day as though going to work, and return home each night. During the day he had no alternative but to walk the streets, ever on the alert for Wehrmacht patrols and S.S. plainclothesmen demanding to know why he wasn't in uniform, or for former friends, neighbors, and business and professional associates who might wittingly or unwittingly give him away. He had to constantly remind himself to stay away from old haunts and neighborhoods, lest he unconsciously drift toward them. Prowling the streets of Berlin in this manner for twelve hours each week-day took its toll not just on the body but on clothes and shoes, which had to be repaired or replaced, a process requiring as much stealth, at times, as the daily purchase of food. Even personal hygiene was as necessary as it was desirable, for an unwashed pedestrian would surely attract attention. But soap too was rationed, and even after it was acquired it was difficult for those Jews constantly on the move to use it. If they washed themselves or their clothing in public rest rooms they increased their visibility.

Like the submariners, many Jewish "U-boats" were efficient and effective. They went underground only after elaborate planning, the hoarding of re-sources, the identification of safe houses and the acquisition of false papers. But Willy Glaser, the middle-aged enthusiast of the arts, had failed to make such preparations. Where more efficient Jews had slipped carefully under the surface of life in Berlin, Willy's descent into hiding had been a sudden plunge down a flight of tenement stairs. He hadn't thought about resources because he had none to hoard. False papers were luxuries for others than the likes of him; even if he had had the money for bribes, he wouldn't have known how to go about acquiring the papers. As to a safe house, he'd had no promises, only hopes.

But for once in Willy's life the hopes had been realized.

Fortunate people in fortunate times had known nothing but happiness in the garden house in which he now found himself, Willy reckoned. It was a wooden house situated on a huge piece of land in the middle of a forest a mile from Müggelheim, a village near Köpenick, on the southeast fringe of Berlin. The house had once belonged to a Jewish family named Schwerin that had had the good sense to emigrate in time to England. It was a summer house, without electricity or inside plumbing, and Willy was occupying it during a miserable winter. Yet it had been his salvation, that house, exactly the place he had had in mind as he ran away from the Gestapo on the morning of January 31, 1943. He knew the house, because it now belonged to a Christian friend, George Meier. It was to Meier's home in Berlin that Willy had gone on his first night as a fugitive.

Meier had sent him to the country house the following night. He had given Willy the keys, a small petroleum lamp and a supply of food and water. But Willy wasn't supposed to light the lamp except in a dire emergency, because the neighbors might see the light. Willy had risked the S-Bahn to Köpenick and then a bus to Müggelheim and then walked through the forest in the middle of the night until he found the house. The bed was damp, the water pump wasn't working, and the cold permeated his bones. But he couldn't light a fire, lest the neighbors see the smoke.

For three days he lived in the house without light or heat; when his supplies ran out he did without food and water. He tried desperately to control his urges until nightfall, when he could make the trip to the privy under cover of darkness. By the fourth day, when Meier came with a fresh supply of food and water, Willy was near despair. "It's like living in a dungeon," he said. And yet they both knew that there was no alternative.

For weeks the isolation continued. One day, at last, Willy opened the door a crack. Outside the sun was shining. He crept out and walked around the property. The next day he repeated the excursion, and the day after that, each time venturing a little farther from the house. With success came boldness. One day he went out the garden gate and walked for twenty-five minutes until he was in the small village of Müggelheim. There he sat in a cafe and drank a cup of coffee. The next day he walked to Müggelheim and took a bus to Köpenick, a suburb-size community. Finally the day came when he ventured into Berlin itself. It was foolish, and he knew it, but he preferred the risk to the isolation.

His greatest fear was being caught in an air raid and having to go to a shelter. Berlin was like a ghost town during air raids. Everyone was required to be off the streets; there was no vehicular traffic. It was the best of all times for the police patrols to tour the shelters in their constant search for criminals, deserters and underground Jews. Thus far, however, his luck had held; he hadn't been caught in a raid, no one had questioned him, and he was beginning to believe divine Providence was guarding him.

And then one day, just as the weather was warming up and the cottage was beginning to seem hospitable, Meier came to tell Willy that it was time for him to leave. The neighbors would be coming soon to use their country homes, and there was no way that he could be explained, particularly since many of them had known him from another time and knew that he was Jewish.

It was a bitter moment for Willy Glaser, but since he had already survived for three months as an illegal, he couldn't help but believe that he could survive still longer. All he needed was another place to go.

The trouble was that there was no other place to go.

1980

Abraham Sutzkever

Abraham Sutzkever was born in Smorogon, Lithuania, in 1913. During World War II, he and his wife spent two years in the ghetto at Vilna. He spent time both in hiding and working in forced labor groups. His infant son was killed by the Nazis. In 1943, Sutzkever and his wife escaped to join a Jewish resistance group. They returned to Vilna when it was liberated. After the war, in 1947, they went to Palestine (now Israel), where they still reside. Sutzkever's poem, as translated from the Yiddish by Cynthia Ozick, originally appeared in *The Penguin Book of Modern Yiddish Verse*.

In this poem, Sutzkever pays tribute to Yanova Bartoszewicz, a Polish woman who hid him during a period of mass killings.

And when I go up as a pilgrim in winter, to recover
the place I was born, and the twin to self I am in my mind,
then I'll go in black snow as a pilgrim to find
the grave of my savior, Yanova.

She'll hear what I whisper, under my breath:
Thank you. You saved my tears from the flame.
Thank you. Children and grandchildren you rescued from death.
I planted a sapling (it doesn't suffice) in your name.

Time in its gyre spins back down the flue
faster than nightmares of nooses can ride,
quicker than nails. And you, my savior,
    in your cellar you'll hide
me, ascending in dreams as a pilgrim to you.

You'll come from the yard in your slippers, crunching the snow
so I'll know. Again I'm there in the cellar, degraded and low,
you're bringing me milk and bread sliced thick at the edge.
You're making the sign of the cross. I'm making my pencil its pledge.

chapter 3

Fleeing for Their Lives

A frequently asked question about the Holocaust is why the Jews stayed in Germany and the occupied countries. While this appears to be a simple question, it is one without a simple answer. In retrospect, the scope of the crimes of the Third Reich seems immense. For those who were living through it, however, it was impossible to know the full scope of what was happening. Mass communication was far more primitive than it is today. Further, emigrating was not easy, because many countries, including the United States, had annual immigration quotas that prevented large numbers of people from any one country from entering at the same time.

For many German Jews, the reason for staying was even more fundamental: they considered themselves to be Germans. Many German Jewish families had been in Germany for generations; they had businesses, homes, and places of distinction in their communities. Many of the men had served with honor and distinction in the German army during World War I. Furthermore, they had experienced anti-Semitism before and had survived. Also contributing to the reluctance of many to leave were the restrictions that the Nazis placed on them. In order to leave, Jews had to sign their property over to the government and pay a "security tax," which left them with few resources with which to make a new beginning in another country. For every Jew who chose to stay, there were many tangible and intangible reasons and feelings that contributed to the decision.

In the early days of the Third Reich, the Nazis sanctioned the emigration of Jews from Germany. In August 1933, the German Ministry of Economics forged an agreement with a Zionist organization to allow and promote the immigration of large numbers of German Jews to Palestine; however, like other countries, Palestine, under British rule, had quotas. From 1933 to 1938, only 38,000 of the half million German Jews were able to emigrate to Palestine. While quotas were a factor in this, it should also be noted that many German Jews were not Zionists and did not long to move to Palestine to help establish a Jewish state.

Many of the Jews who fled in the early days of the Third Reich were prominent members of the community who would have been obvious targets, including writers, artists, business owners, and scientists. For those Jews who emigrated to other European countries to wait for Hitler to lose power, escape was only temporary. Those who wanted to find refuge in the United States faced particularly stiff quotas because of an immigration law passed in 1924. By 1939, the waiting period for German Jews to enter the United States was between four and five years. Reconsideration of the regulations was foiled by a vocal anti-Semitic faction in the United States, and there was fear that some immigrants from Germany might be Nazi spies. By 1939, western Europe and the United States had essentially closed their doors to these refugees.

Flight from the Nazi threat took many forms. Until November 1937, when Jewish passports were invalidated for foreign travel, families would plan "vacations" abroad, vacations from which they were never to return. Often these plans required such absolute secrecy that there could be no farewells to family and friends left behind. Children were, at times, uninformed that they would not be returning home. Depending on the circumstances, parents were sometimes compelled to split up their families. Some parents who were unable or unwilling to leave sent their children to safety in other countries. These parents made what must have been the most difficult decision of their lives—to send their children away with the knowledge that they might never be reunited.

Perhaps one of the most significant examples of flight occurred in Denmark where, as a nation, the Danes stood up to their Nazi invaders and helped the Danish Jews to flee. Fewer Jewish lives were lost in Denmark than in any other occupied country because of the national effort to help Jews. Many fled on fishing boats to neutral Sweden, where they found safety.

This chapter relates the experiences of some of those who fled Nazi tyranny, including those who were fortunate enough to escape from the Nazis before it was too late and those for whom life became a nomadic experience of fleeing and hiding only to have to flee again and again. It also tells the stories of those who helped Jews escape.

Cast Out

Karen Gershon

Karen Gershon is the
pseudonym for Karen
Loewenthal Tripp, who
was born in 1923 in
Bielefeld, Germany. At
the age of sixteen, her
family sent her to
England. Her parents
died in the Holocaust.
After the war, she
remained in England,
where she married and
had four children. Her
career as a poet and
prose writer evolved
from her experiences as a
refugee who had fled the
Nazis. An award-winning
author, she is the editor
of *We Came as Children: A
Collective Autobiography*,
from which the following
poem is taken. Gershon
died in 1993.
   This poem describes a
child's feeling of being
sent (or cast) away.

Sometimes I think it would have been
easier for me to die
together with my parents than
to have been surrendered by
them to survive alone

Sometimes it does not seem that they
spared me the hardest Jewish fate
since by sending me away
they burdened me and cast me out
and none suggested I should stay

When the Jews were branded there
was one number meant for me
that another had to bear
my perennial agony
is the brunt of my despair

Sometimes I feel I am a ghost
adrift without identity
what as a child I valued most
for ever has escaped from me
I have been cast out and am lost

We Came as Children

Karen Gershon

In *We Came as Children: A Collective Autobiography*,
Karen Gershon compiled the words and memories
of numerous children who were sent to England as
part of the Kindertransports. She edited and
compiled the accounts of 234 of her fellow child
refugees as well as comments from those who
helped them. For additional biographical
information on Gershon, see page 75.

In the following selection, we read the stories of
several refugee children through a combination of
commentaries, letters, and personal conversations.
Each of the accounts is like a snapshot, focusing on a
single aspect of the British rescue movement. Taken
together, these "snapshots" present a collage of the
refugee experience of children in Great Britain.

One Case

Vienna, 15th February, 1939.

Dear Miss Anny!

My Brother Kurt and Ma wrote me, that I shall bestow on you, about a permit
to come to England. I am thirteen years old and I am alone at my parents at home,
who are banished, and therefore I must seek a home for me. My parents can't take
me along with, and so I pleased you to help me to spend my childhood in
England. I should like to come into a Jewish house and I will endeavour me to
make you always honour and joy. My dear parents would be very thankfully you
would be so kind to help me.

Thank you in advance for your kind help.

Hoping to receive a letter from you I remain yours faithfully,

Paul.

From an undated letter from Anna, a refugee servant, to the Worthing Refugee Committee:

> Paul is a German Refugee living since about 3 years in Vienna. His father has been a long time in Dachau concentration camp—is now released and must leave Austria by the end of this month. Parents want to try to get illegal somewhere and Paul must be saved, as his parents cannot take him with them. Paul can't attend school now in Vienna—because he is afraid to go on the street as he was beaten several times already by young Nazi youth. Paul is very intelligent and learns at home from books. His English is quite good. Parents had lost all their fortune at first in Germany and since November they have lost their livelihood in Vienna.

From a letter from the Secretary of the Worthing Refugee Committee to the Secretary of the Movement for the Care of Children from Germany:

> June 13th 1939.
> I ask you to consider whether you could possibly give a formal guarantee for this child if my committee will promise maintenance and education? We have a promise of two years' hospitality and he could attend the local school; we also have £100 that could be earmarked for him in case the hospitality were not extended.

From a translation of a letter from the boy's father to the Secretary of the Worthing Refugee Committee (Mr. O. Thorneycroft, O.B.E.):

> June 30th 1939.
> We received a communication from the Kultusgemeinde telling us of your application for our son Paul, and he was put down for a transport which leaves on July 18th. We cannot describe in words the joy of our boy at this knowledge. . . . The expulsion order against me expired on June 28th. . . . We do not know yet where we are to go after the departure of the child.

*　*　*

The World Movement for the Care of Children from Germany was the response of the British people to the pogrom of 10th November 1938. The first transport of 320 children arrived at Harwich on 2nd December; when the war broke out 9,354 children had come, of whom 7,482 were Jewish.

Those who had relations or friends and were therefore individually sponsored were classified as "guaranteed." The "non-guaranteed" were those whose maintenance was undertaken by the organisation itself or by local committees. Jewish children who had no friends or relations in Britain were selected in Germany by the Central Jewish Organisation, the Reichsvertretung, and in Austria by the Kultusgemeinde. The Christian, "non-Aryan" children were selected in Berlin by the Christian body, Paulusbund, and in Vienna by the Society of Friends.

Lists with particulars and photographs of the children were sent to the Movement in London, and travel arrangements were made on the continent after permits had been issued by the British Home Office and passed by the German police. Priority was given to those whose emigration was specially urgent because their fathers were in concentration camps or at least no longer able to support them, or because they were homeless, or orphaned, or old enough to be in danger themselves. During the first few months several large transports of these children, Jewish and non-Jewish together, reached England. From April 1939, however, individual guarantors had to deposit £50 per head to cover the expenses of future emigration; also, it became difficult to find hospitality for the older boys. The rate at which children could be brought to England therefore decreased.

Trevor Chadwick's Account:

In 1938 I was teaching at our family prep school. Rumours of the many distressed children in Central Europe reached us, and it was decided to adopt two, according to Home Office regulations, which required a full guarantee of care and maintenance until the age of 18; strict personal references covering the guarantor's character and solvency were also demanded.

Another master at the school and I set off for Prague to select our pair. We did not know where to begin, and had interviews with various people. . . . Within a few days we had found a couple of small boys of about eight and ten.

We got a clear impression of the enormity of the task. We so often saw halls full of confused refugees and batches of lost children, mostly Jewish, and we saw only the fringe of it all.

Soon after our return I felt that I had to do more about it. I went to Friends House, and later to the Movement for the Care of Children from Germany. They were busy finding guarantors, and I flew back to Prague to find children who would fit in with the guarantors' wishes.

I took my first air transport rather proudly, on a twenty-seater plane. They were all cheerfully sick, enticed by the little paper bags, except a baby of one who slept peacefully in my lap the whole time. The Customs Officers were a little puzzled and began to open some of the suitcases, which contained the kids' worldly treasures. But when I explained the position they were completely cooperative. Then there was the meeting with the guarantors—my baby was cooed over and hustled off, and the other nineteen were shyly summing up their new parents, faces alive with hope for the love they were obviously going to be given. I felt depressed as I returned to Prague. Only twenty! This was late that winter, early in 1939.

But on March 15 the air transports came to an end when the Nazis came in. By then I had a hundred or so children waiting to be sent to England, most of them in odd accommodation in Prague schools, a score in Bratislava, and so on. On March 13 I had a telegram from home —"advise return immediately"—and thinking one of my sons was ill flew back at once. It appeared that war was feared, but it was only the Einmarsch. I made all haste to fly back, as, while my Prague children were being vaguely fed by Jewish organisations, the Bratislava bunch's rations were rather dubious.

On the morning of the 15th I got no further than Rotterdam. No flights to Prague. Thwarted and angry I flew to Berlin and began to hammer on tables, except at the British Embassy, where I asked politely for help and was politely refused. Goebbels' office coldly explained that no foreigners could travel to Prague that day (except Germans!). But early the next morning, at the Alexander Platz police station, I was given a special pass enabling me to travel to Prague by train.

A member of the Czech cabinet lent me an office, and I had two young helpers. The whole days, from 7 until 7, with twenty minutes for lunch, were taken up with interviewing, filing and writing letters to the guarantors, which perforce could not be scrappy. I can't say how many children were on my books, but it must have been in the thousands. Nor can I say how many I eventually got away, but it was only hundreds, alas.

Attention had primarily to be paid to the wishes of the guarantors. The majority stipulated girls seven–ten and if possible fair. Boys of twelve and upwards were hard to place. Girls were in the majority on the transports.

I tried to find the most urgent, helpless cases. This was not easy. Many were already refugees from Germany and Austria; many parents had "disappeared."

I had contacted a Prague travel agency, because special trains were needed. Now money was getting difficult, and my only hope of financing the thing seemed to be to allow the Movement to pay the travel agency in London, and to ask the connections of the little travellers to pay cash in Prague, or as much as they could afford. Many, of course, were penniless.

The Nazis had arrived. But Kriminalrat Boemmelburg was an elderly, smiling gentleman, far from sinister, who eventually proved to be a great help, sometimes unwittingly. He was really interested in my project, and his only Nazi-ish remark was a polite query why England wanted so many Jewish children.

He happily gave his stamp to the first train transport, even though I had included half a dozen adult "leaders" on it. I went to the station accompanied by a Gestapo clerk, and all the children were there, with labels prepared by my helpers tied round their necks. The train took them off, cheering, through Germany to the Hook of Holland, a hundred or more.

Soon Boemmelburg sent for me. (He insisted that we spoke in French, not German or English—French is the diplomatic language, he explained. We were both appalling at it.) He said people were throwing dust in my eyes. It was now absolutely forbidden for any adult to leave the country without a special *Ausreisebewilligung* and the "leaders" of my transport had really escaped illegally. I expressed my deepest sorrow and grovelled. I was a blue-eyed boy again, and thereafter he agreed to stamp my lists of children for transport without delay. A kindly Jewess with an American passport was good enough to go with them. I sealed my friendship with Boemmelburg by "confessing" after the second transport that I had discovered later that one child was not Jewish. (There were several "Aryans" in all transports.) He praised my honesty and begged me to be careful, because of course the Nazis would look after "Aryan" children.

The second train transport was illegal—from the British point of view. Each child on the transport had to be accompanied by a Home Office document, a large stiff affair, foolscap size, perforated across the middle, with a photograph and all sorts of details on each half. These took a long time to arrive. They just didn't realise. If only the Home Secretary could have spent a few days with me, seeing brutality, listening to, not arguing with, young Nazis, as I often did, he would doubtlessly have pushed the whole thing along fast. If he had realised that the regulations were for so many children the first nudge along the wretched road to Auschwitz, he would, of course, have immediately imported the lot. But that is too much wisdom after the event.

I could wait no longer. Letters explaining urgency bore no fruit. I had my guarantors lined up and the children waiting. The next transport was taking shape. There had to be documents, so I had some made, as near as possible like the Home Office ones, and away the train went. I informed everybody and awaited the Home Office telegram in reply. I betted myself that it would contain the word "irregular" and I won. It also contained a threat to send them back, but I figured the mob of legally accepted guarantors would stop that one.

Boemmelburg remained friendly, and things were going as smoothly as possible. But in the evenings there were other fish to fry which did not have anything to do with children. It became obvious to me as summer developed that certain of my movements were at least suspect, and that B. and his boys might turn sour. This would jeopardize the children, so I explained these things to London and they arranged a replacement. I shall always have a feeling of shame that I didn't get more out.

★   ★   ★

The two girls were sent to England by their father when they were eleven and twelve years old, in the winter of 1938–39; he had made an arrangement with an English friend of his to act as their guardian. They were to be at an independent boarding school; he had plenty of money and there was no question of their being a liability to anyone. However, when war broke out it became impossible for him to send any more money and the following winter their English guardian dropped dead, having, naturally enough, made no mention of the girls in her will. So there they were, completely cut off from home and financial aid, in a very expensive school and with no one whatever to look after them and their interests in any way. In September 1939 I had become headmistress of the school—a rather strange appointment as I was then a young girl in my twenties—and I found the girls there, destitute and friendless. The Governors of the school felt that they could not stay there indefinitely without paying and with nobody to be responsible for them in the holidays and to act as a parent. I, young, idealistic and compassionate, felt they could not possibly be turned out and sent to an orphanage; they were just beginning to feel at home and the staff and the girls there represented the only "family" they could now be said to have got. After endless arguments and discussions (complicated by the fact that I was engaged to be married and had my future husband, as well as the School Governors to convince) I was allowed to adopt the children by means of a special war-time adoption order. It was a temporary measure and remained in force only until (if ever) the children could be restored to their real parents. The Governors allowed the girls to stay in the school without paying as long as I acted as their mother (which I was much too young, in fact, to be) and arranged for their holidays etc. They were certainly most unattractive children, poor little things, and it was very hard to love them. They were very plain, quarrelled unceasingly and found it very difficult to become integrated into the community. Margaret was determined from the very first to become English; she pretended to have forgotten the German language, as soon as she had learned English, and resolutely refused ever to speak a word of German or to help with translating it or anything like that. She clamoured to be baptised and confirmed into the Church of England for this reason alone, I am sure. She ceased to be called "Grete" by which name she was always known at school and insisted on her full name of Margaret, which is also an English name. She made every conceivable effort to disguise her markedly foreign appearance. As soon as it was legally possible she became a naturalised British subject, and she soon succeeded in her determination to find a British husband and produce some English children! Anne showed none of this repudiation of her own nationality; she did eventually become naturalised, but not in any frantic hurry and not without much thought. Gradually the children calmed down; they were no longer "the two Austrians" to be pointed out to visitors as if they were a pair of wild animals. They were accepted as two ordinary members of the school, no more or less interesting than any others, and as the community forgot their differences, so these differences disappeared.

Bunce Court:

Anna Essinger started Bunce Court in Kent in 1933, with 75 children between the ages of six and sixteen from her school in Germany. In 1938–39 she took about a hundred of those who came with the children's transports. The first ten she brought from Dovercourt, chosen on the basis of her private feelings; she thought they would fit in and she would like them and she could give them something. The oldest we got were thirteen. Anna wanted young ones she would have for some time. One boy's sister was fourteen and she was too old to come. But some who came were only three because they had an older brother or sister.

Sometimes nobody paid for them, sometimes English people did. In the beginning everybody had 200 Marks, and money could still be sent from Germany. After that stopped we got money through the committee, and from America or Africa or wherever relations lived. One night we had no money any more—that was at the beginning of the war. Anna went to London, and we all waited and waited and kept the children singing so that they would not notice that there was no supper.

She often went to London to raise funds, she went to the committee and wherever she was invited to speak about the school. Once somebody asked her to come to tea, to meet Iris Origo; she didn't want to go, she said: "I never go to tea, my time is too precious." The friend said: "I beg you to come, it will help the school," and we all said: "Go, go, go." Iris Origo is English, married to an Italian Count. She said: "How can I help you?" And Anna said there were many ways, to invite a child for the holidays or to pay his school fees and keep for a year, or we had a building fund—just money, we always needed money. And she said: "I think I'll pay school fees for ten children." That meant that ten children could be brought out of Germany because there was a guarantor for them. She said: "Pick ten children to bring out and I will pay for them. Pick small children, so they will be with you a long time." And then she gave us a thousand pounds for the building fund.

To prepare the children for life in England, as they were so cut off in the country, Anna always tried to find families who would take them for holidays, so that they would see English life and only hear and speak English. She did not choose only Jewish families, but whoever was humanly nice and invited children. Quaker families invited many. When people asked: "What can we do for the school?" Anna always said: "If you like and have children of your own you can invite a child for holidays," and when it worked the first time the people invited them again, and it became an institution that they always went there. Even before the war she already had an English family for every child.

When the children came they were very disturbed and very restless and very unhappy, because they had lost their homes and their parents; first they had their loss and then they settled here and took it for granted and enjoyed their daily life. And only when they left school and had to go out on their own, then it came again, the realisation that they were alone in the world and had no one. They settled here or in another school, where they lived and loved and were loved, and afterwards they were again lost, and had again unsettled experiences. And then, only then, they settled and became English.

Whittingehame House:

This Farm School was part of the English Youth Aliyah Movement, which provided training for hundreds of boys and girls waiting to migrate to Palestine. I became matron there when the school opened on 15th February 1939.

The local Scottish Committee of School Governors devoted an enormous amount of time and effort to the school and they were generous and helpful even if they did not understand the children's point of view. There was, for instance, the question of pooling all the pocket money decided on in one of the school meetings. That smacked too much of communism to please Edinburgh business men. Or of less importance—I ordered cake for the Sabbath breakfast. "Cake for breakfast?" It seemed awful to the Edinburgh people (including the baker). But it came punctually every Friday.

Less understanding was shown by the London Committee. I hardly believed my eyes when I unpacked some sample clothes for the children: they all were khaki coloured. So I sat down and wrote in my best—not very good—English that design and quality of the garments were excellent and very acceptable but that I could not ask continental children to wear brown uniforms, after their experiences with the Brownshirts from whom they had just escaped. Navy blue was decided upon instead.

There were numerous visitors to the school. The children hated to be kept waiting for them and to be talked down to. They resented being told to be grateful for the refuge they had found. Most of them cold-shouldered the journalists who beleaguered the grounds in the first few weeks out for sensational stories. What should have been an attentive, reverent audience at pious stories and exhortations was often a giggling crowd—on the other hand nobody laughed at one woman's valiant attempt to speak to them in their own language.

For some of the English teachers these foreign children were as strange as beings from another world; they had never seen such a lack of conformity, which resulted from the fact that they not only came from very varied social backgrounds and every part of Middle Europe but had also not undergone the levelling training of an English school.

The attempt of one headmaster to run Whittingehame as a Jewish Eton was not appreciated by the children; their ideal was a Kibbutz, not an English public school. But the same headmaster was intelligent and great-hearted enough to participate in the pervading ideological spirit, even as far as learning and performing a large part in a Hebrew play.

There was laziness and indifference amongst the children, especially in the first year of their stay, most probably aggravated by long times spent waiting in reception camps with hardly any work or tuition or leadership. So it was not a rare sight to see a group of boys playing football when they should have been in class learning English or arithmetic—there was much less absenteeism from practical work.

Lord Balfour's house had to withstand considerable wear and tear; during a short stay in the sickroom one boy dismantled the electrical fittings so thoroughly that not even the electrician could put them together again. The problems proper seem not to have originated in the school but might have become severer through the shock of emigration: the bedwetting boys were probably afflicted before they came. Insecurity became manifest in overbearing as well as cringing attitudes— the latter much more among the girls.

Later work improved, even in school, when the youngsters realised how much teaching they had missed by being excluded from their German schools at the age of twelve or thirteen. The same girls who at first followed only reluctantly, if at all, expert advice when doing domestic chores, were now eager to learn the correct way of doing things; standards of gracious middle-class living deliberately suppressed and rejected at the beginning came to the surface when they hankered for the jobs in the headmaster's flat, where a less institutional way of life prevailed.

That boys and girls were on the right road to a healthy development of their personalities was borne out by the test put upon the school by outside events; in June 1940 a great number of boys were interned as "enemy aliens," and the girls took over heavy work and greater responsibilities.

When the school was closed about two years later—it had never been intended as a permanent establishment—the boys began to earn their living as agricultural labourers and the girls as domestic servants.

The Children's Exodus

Karen Gershon

A child refugee herself,
Karen Gershon compiled
the stories of hundreds of
children with similar
experiences in *We Came
as Children: A Collective
Autobiography*. For
additional biographical
information cn Gershon,
see page 75.

This poem expresses
the children's confused
and troubling emotions
as they began their lives
as refugees.

I

It was an ordinary train
travelling across Germany
which gathered and took us away
those who saw it may have thought
that it was for a holiday
not being exiled being taught
to hate what we had loved in vain
brought us lasting injury

II

Our parents let us go
knowing that who stayed must die
but kept the truth from us although
they gave us to reality
did they consider what it meant
to become orphaned and not know
to be emotionally freed
when our childhood seeds were spent

III

When we went out of Germany
carrying six million lives
that was Jewish history
but each child was one refugee
we unlike the Egyptian slaves
were exiled individually
and each in desolation has
created his own wilderness

IV

This race-hatred was personal
we were condemned for what we were
no one escaped the ritual
from which we rose inferior
the blood-guilt entered every home
till daily life was a pogrom
we who were there are not the same
as those who have no wreck to share

V

Home is where some know who you are
the rescue was impersonal
it was no one's concern what use
we made of the years given us
one should not ask of children who
find their survival natural
gratitude for being where
ten thousand others have come too

VI

At Dovercourt the winter sea
was like God's mercy vast and wild
a fever to a land-locked child
it seemed fire and cloud to me
the world's blood and my blood were cold
the exiled Jew in me was old
and thoughts of death appalled me less
than knowledge of my loneliness

VII

My mother sold my bed and chair
while I expected to return
yet she had kept me close to her
till I saw our temple burn
it was not for her sake but mine
she knew that I was unripe fruit
and that exile was a blight
against which one prepared in vain

VIII

People at Dovercourt were gay
as if they thought we could forget
our homes in alien play
as if we were not German Jews
but mealtimes were a market-place
when sudden visitors could choose
although we were not orphaned yet
a son or daughter by their face

IX

My childhood smoulders in the name
of the town which was my home
all we were became no more
than answers on each questionnaire
at Dovercourt we were taught that
our share of the Jewish fate
had not been left behind but was
the refugee life facing us

The Return

Arnost Lustig

Arnost Lustig was born in 1926 in Prague, where he lived with his parents until they were sent to the concentration camp at Terezin. Eventually, they were sent to Auschwitz, where his father died. In 1945, Lustig was among the survivors when the United States Army liberated Buchenwald. After the war Lustig returned to Prague, where he began his career as a screenwriter and journalist and established himself as a leading chronicler of life under Nazi oppression. When the Soviets invaded Prague in 1968, he fled and went into exile. Two years later, he arrived in the United States. He is now a naturalized U.S. citizen who teaches literature and writing at American University in Washington, D.C. Lustig is the author of several books, including *Night and Hope*, from which the following short story is taken, *Diamonds of the Night*, *A Prayer for Katerina Horovitzova*, and *Street of Lost Brothers*.

The protagonist in this short story, Hynek Tausig, is one of thousands of ghetto residents awaiting the inevitable transport to a camp and almost certain death. The increasingly dehumanizing impact of fear is his daily companion until he makes a life-changing decision.

He walked across the ghetto.

He had grown still leaner. His roaming eyes had sunk deep and they had an unpleasant, expectant gleam. They resembled a membrane. He had learned to register the slightest vibrations and pulsations of the town. It had become a subconscious process that went on incessantly. Yes, something was happening. Be careful, Hynek Tausig, he commanded himself. Something was in the air.

At ten in the morning the car from the German *Kommandatur* drove up to the house of the Council of Elders. Nobody was any longer in doubt as to what was in preparation. A transport. Invisible mouths passed the information on to sixty thousand ears.

The information reached him too. He gave a start, but then he thought perhaps he would not be in it. Another piece of news: "Half the ghetto is to go." Why should he, of all people, be left out? He had no one here who would remove his card from the index of the records department, according to which the transport was to be compiled. And even if he had—would that alter anything if half the ghetto was to be sent away? He had long felt hostility towards the big fortress. He had an antipathy to this town, did not like the stone beak, bent six times, which pecked at the streets and houses, and which let people see that they used to look different. He had lost the sensation of having returned, that relaxing satisfaction he had felt when Mönderling had beaten him, and again when the muster was over.

He walked between the ramparts, from one corner to the other. The well outside the church was finished and he was now working on the railway line, on the Terezín-Bohušovice track. When you have finished the railway line, he told himself, you will ride on it to Poland. Why did he not go back to the barracks and sleep? He had spent the whole night removing the last projecting rock with a pneumatic drill. What was it he was looking for anyway?

The ghetto was narrow, but you could not traverse it from end to end even in four hours. Now he had reached the Kavalír barracks. Nothing about them was in keeping with the noble name. Inside, behind the bars, were mental patients. Someone in there was just raising his right arm in the Nazi salute. A nurse came running and took him away to a cell. Something forced Hynek Tausig to give a nasty laugh. What was the difference between that woman and the lunatic, he reflected. She drew attention to herself even more than he did. Whose attention, though, came the disappointing thought. Theirs—the Jews. What did it matter to him, Hynek Tausig? He pressed his forehead against the cool bars. He did not feel like going to the barracks. In his heart of hearts he knew why. He was afraid that on his cot he would find a card with the summons to join the transport. But let him not think about that. He reached the sappers' barracks which had been turned into a hospital. Hospital? Was it not funny, to heal people so that they would be able to go with the transport? In the yard next to the barracks he could see old men praying. They were leaning against the latrine wall, white papers and black prayer books in their hands. The rabbis had come to the conclusion that the ghetto was a stone preserve. If nothing else, they thought, ancient religious customs would at least be maintained here. But the preserve was to become a museum, reflected Hynek Tausig. Nothing living would remain here.

He walked faster. Again that unseen whip cracking in his ears. Transport. And somewhere in the background bigger doses of beating. And then the end. A very different end to that which the boys were in the habit of conjuring up after returning from work—according to which a neighbour would one day turn up, saying: "Go on, run along home, you idiots, the war is over." The hope of this kind of end slumbered on in them in spite of everything, despite the fact that they postponed the date of Germany's defeat from day to day and from year to year. The hope lived in him, too, even in moments when he was not actually thinking of it, yes even when he deliberately tried to avoid it in his thoughts. In spite of it all he was encouraged by this faint, indistinct mirage. Somewhere something was waiting. And now it was to be spoiled.

The nearer he came to the barracks, the greater his fear that he would be among those included in the transport. He was again hurrying with his head bent forward. You have been like this before, Hynek Tausig, in Prague, on your way between the alcove and Wenceslas Square—should he not stop and straighten up? But he did not slacken speed and he did not turn round. The corners of his narrow mouth drooped. His face was a dark ashen colour, distorted by a wild grimace. Suddenly he stopped, as though he had run up against an invisible wall. Why was he rushing so? In order to hold the summons card in his hand twenty seconds earlier? He was almost certain that the white card lay on his cot. But how could he be certain, was he clairvoyant or what? Why cross his bridges before he came to them? He understood then that if man was ever in his life a beast, then it was fear that made him so. Why was he standing here foolishly like this? He realized that he was standing still and people were treading on his toes. Yes, it was fear that did it, every child knew that. Only he did not know it, not he. He started walking again. He was afraid that he would be included in the transport, was he not? But he had been through this before. Nevertheless, in spite of the knowledge he had just gained, fear again predominated. He could only think of the transport, and whether he would be in it. Something told him it was different, but a second voice said, no it wasn't, it was the same. He too. One did not change at forty-one. He had remained the same. A coward, he added in disgust. He had been born only to tremble for his mousy little life.

In the faces of the passers-by he saw himself. All of them were cowards, once and for all, he consoled himself, not only he. They trembled for their own sake and concealed it by pretending to be afraid for someone else. But then he thought that even if he did get left out of it, he would go and beg to be taken along.

He was in front of the barracks. He entered, full of the reserve and excitement of fear. His cot . . . his cot was empty. He felt better. Oh yes, the life of a mouse, but at least it was not over yet. He was not going. He sank wearily on to the cot.

"When did they come with the cards?" he asked the room orderly.

"As soon as you left."

"And what about you?"

"Not me, but my mother is in it."

He nodded, but felt at the same time that this gesture lacked true sympathy. The orderly was thirty. He had been digging on various building sites since the "AK" transport, which had been the first to arrive here and had had most of the hard work. So his mother was going. They would be separated. No, nothing stayed together in this place. At home it was all different, a mother was everything, she had respect, and a quiet old age. Not so here. The mother would go and the son would be glad he had been left behind. In a week's time he would go with another transport and would reproach himself that each of them had gone off to die on his own.

"Mother is seventy," said the digger. "I shan't let her go alone. I'm going to report with her."

I am a swine, Hynek Tausig said to himself. That is how things are: some men are human beings and some are beasts. And some a little of both, and that's me. But most of all I am a swine.

"I guess you're doing the right thing," he said quietly, adding: "I'd do the same myself." This time he was quite sure he really would. This time he was not lying. Still, he was glad he did not have to do it, and he went out again.

It was evening. He returned to the room, which was different from yesterday. It looked like a military camp. The boys were packing their stuff. The gloom of the first moments had gone. His eyes lighted on the digger and he went over to help him. Then he helped his neighbour. He did not say a word the whole time. Finished.

"Lights out, chaps," the digger called out when they had all finished.

Time to sleep.

But Hynek Tausig could not sleep. He kept thinking that there were a great many things in a human being, something of the beast too, but that it was up to him to choose; maybe nobody was going to ask him about it after the war. Perhaps he would not have to answer the question: were you in a blue funk, old fellow, or did you not give a damn? After the war, if only he lived to see it, life would be completely different. No one would need to know anything, either about himself or anyone else. One could live without that, just as one did before. Everything would be plain sailing. Good morning and good-bye. Without being kicked and called names. No, he had never imagined that he would carry out a revolution in his life. It was not to be recommended at his age.

Sleep stayed away from him as the night advanced. Bitter thoughts pinned him down on his cot. He could smell the pungent odour of human bodies. He was sure not to sleep any more now. Well then, Hynek Tausig, you are going to live through it all, obedient as ever, helping your pals to the trucks. And if by chance you should stumble under someone's foot, or even into one of the trucks, you will not say a word. No, he would not sleep now, but just lying there was also difficult. He got up, put on his coat, and went to the door. He was not allowed out, but he could look out of the door, could he not?

It was a clear night. The silky blue of the sky was illuminated by the glow of immensely distant diamonds. When you were small, Hynek Tausig, you thought everything was like the stars, pure and beautiful. What would become of man? He could not tear himself away. He stood there for hours, hours and minutes.

The transport left in the morning.

The ashen-looking little man did not move from his place.

Evening came again, and with it night. He would not go to bed. He would remain there, by the door. Today it would be different.

The ghetto lay at his feet. A strange prison, he thought sleepily. Every part of a man was imprisoned separately, broken in pieces. One transport had left. There now remained an invisible time limit for the next. When that ran out, it would all begin anew.

Someone was calling to him: "Don't stand there gaping, man! You'll be as weak as a fly in the morning."

He felt a sudden chill and pulled his coat more closely around him. He forgot to reply.

A moment later he came back to his cot and bent down to look under it. There he had the suitcase he had borrowed. He tore away the paper and pulled out Alfred Janota's identity card. It seemed to him all of a sudden that a man of that name really lived somewhere. He had to find him and give him his life.

Slowly he pushed the identity card into his pocket. He still had some money left. The world seemed huge and free to him now. But that was a deceptive impression, everyone had to find himself a narrow little street. A street of his own. And to walk that street and not turn left or right. Once you did that, you would not be able to go straight again. He could not go to the north-west, where the mountains were. What about the south? No, he must not start doubting, otherwise he would never do it. He went to the door, feeling the snores, the sweaty odours and the breathed-up air behind his back. He stood there, looking at the sky. The clouds were thick and dark and there were no stars.

A look at his watch. A little after twelve. He looked back at the room he was leaving. They were all asleep now. Should he perhaps stay? He might not be in the next transport either. He was safely hidden in a crowd. He must not behave recklessly . . . the echo of the last word did not have time to reverberate through him. No, he must not stop now. He must not undress and get back in bed like a cowardly mouse. By morning he could walk at least twenty kilometres. But if he went to bed now, he would be stronger tomorrow. Take it easy, he admonished himself, take it easy. And don't try to fool yourself! His chin trembled. They might catch him. But wasn't he as good as caught now, this very minute that he was thinking it? That was how it was that time in Prague. He need not look for a gap in the fence. Why not climb into some empty truck at the station and let himself be taken away, far from the ghetto. And then—no, he must not lie to himself.

He stood there a moment longer. Then he left the doorway. But not to return inside.

A little later, concealed by the night, Hynek Tausig stopped on the northern rampart of the ghetto. He caught hold of the bough of a tall cherry tree whose thin trunk grew less than a yard away from the reddish slopes of the ramparts. He clambered down rather clumsily—he was afraid and that hampered him. He scratched his face and hands and coat on the bark of the tree, but at last he felt the damp yielding earth beneath his feet. He glanced up, murmuring to himself: "I'm leaving." It sounded inside him, however, as if he were trying to convince himself.

And then, slightly bent forward, he ran through the night and the mud, past the gendarmes' post.

Phimosis Is Not Circumcision

Joseph Joffo

Joseph Joffo was ten years old when his father sent
him and his brother Maurice (age twelve) away from
Paris to Vichy, France, to escape the increasing
danger for Jews in Paris. Joffo related their
dangerous and frightening journey in "A Bag of
Marbles," which appeared in *The Lost Generation:
Children in the Holocaust* (edited by Azriel Eisenberg)
and from which the following excerpt is taken.

In this personal narrative, Joffo relates how he
and his brother, fleeing without any identification
papers and armed with only a knapsack and their
wits, were told by their father never to admit that
they were Jewish. In this selection, Joffo tells of
being stopped for questioning by the Gestapo. The
brothers could bluff everything else except the
physical evidence that every Jewish male carried
with him: the mark of circumcision.

Maurice looks at me. He speaks through teeth
that he can hardly unclench.

"You going to be all right, Joseph?"

"I'll be all right."

The door in front of us opens. The two women come out. Both of them are
crying. I know they haven't been beaten—that makes me feel better.

The women go back downstairs, and we go on waiting. It reminds me of the
dentist's office on the *rue* Ramey, when Mama used to take me there after school.

The interpreter appears. This time it's our turn. All three of us go in.

94

It used to be a hotel room, but the bed isn't there anymore; instead there's a table with an SS man behind it. He's in his forties, with glasses; he seems tired and yawns several times.

He's holding Ferdinand's identity card and looking at it. He says nothing and motions to the interpreter.

"You're Jewish?"

"No."

The interpreter has a childish voice and a Provençal accent. He's certainly from Nice.

"If you aren't a Jew, why do you have a forged identity card?"

I don't look at Ferdinand; I know that if I look at him, I won't be brave when my time comes.

"But . . . that is my identity card."

There's a brief exchange in German. The SS man speaks, and the interpreter translates.

"We can easily find out if you're a Jew or not, so start talking and don't give us any trouble—otherwise you're going to annoy people around here and get yourself a beating. That would be stupid, so let's have the truth right away, and we'll forget the whole thing."

He gives the impression that we need only talk, and everything will be all right—we'll be set free.

"No," says Ferdinand. "I am not Jewish."

There's no need for translation. The SS man gets to his feet, removes his hornrimmed glasses, goes around to the front of his desk, and plants himself squarely before Ferdinand.

A ringing slap on Ferdinand's sickly cheek sets his head wobbling; a second crack sends him reeling back a couple of steps. Tears stream down his face.

"Stop," says Ferdinand.

The SS man waits. The interpreter encourages Ferdinand.

"Go ahead, talk. Where are you from?"

In a voice that can scarcely be heard, Ferdinand speaks.

"I left Poland in 1940. My parents were arrested. I went through Switzerland and—"

"Fine. We'll see about all that later. But you do admit that you're a Jew?"

"Yes."

The interpreter goes up to him and gives him a friendly pat on the shoulder.

"There, you see? Don't you think you should have talked sooner? All right, you can go downstairs. Show that to the clerk at the foot of the stairs."

He holds out a green ticket, which Ferdinand takes. I'm soon going to learn what the green ticket means.

"It's your turn now, you two. Are you brothers?"

"Yes, he's Joseph, and I'm Maurice."

"Joseph and Maurice what?"

"Joffo."

"And you're Jews."

This is no question: this guy is stating a fact. I want to help Maurice.

"Oh no, you've got it all wrong."

He's surprised by my vehemence. Maurice doesn't give him a chance to get a word in edgewise.

"No, we aren't Jewish. We're from Algiers. If you want, I can tell you all about it."

He knits up his brows and speaks to the SS man, who now has his glasses on and is looking us over. The German asks us a question. I understand him better and better; it's really very close to Yiddish, but I musn't show him that I understand.

"What were you doing on the *rue de Russie?*"

"We came from New Harvest, the camp of the *Compagnons de France.* We went along with Ferdinand and were waiting for him—that's all. He told us that he was going in to see a pal."

The SS man rolls a pencil between his fingers.

Maurice gains confidence. I can sense that he's in perfect control of himself. He begins to give him our story right away: Papa, a barber in Algiers; the school; the vacation; and then the landing in North Africa that kept us from going back. It all goes like clockwork until—the only thing we hadn't planned.

"And you're Catholic?"

"That's right."

"Then you've been baptized?"

"Yes, we've also made our communion."

"What church?"

Rotten luck! But Maurice's voice is loud and clear, even clearer than before. "La Buffa. In Nice."

The interpreter strokes his belly. "Why not in Algiers?"

"Mama wanted us to make our communion in France; she had a cousin in this part of the country."

He looks at us, writes a few lines in a notebook, and closes it.

"All right, we're going to check and see if everything you've said is true. First, you go for physicals. We're going to see if you've been circumcised."

Maurice doesn't flinch. I try to remain absolutely calm.

The interpreter looks at us. "You understand?"

"No. What does that mean—*circumcised?*"

Both men look at us. Maybe you've gone a little too far, Maurice, a little too far. In a few minutes they may make us pay for that confidence. In any case, our pretty house of cards is about to go tumbling down.

A soldier pushes us up the stairs. They'll find out everything. I don't give a damn—I'll jump from the train while it's moving. They won't take me to Germany.

Then I'm in another room; this one is empty. There isn't any desk—just three men in white smocks.

The oldest one stares when we come in. "Oh, no, we're not staying here all night. I went off duty half an hour ago."

The other two grumble and slip out of their smocks. One of them is German.

"What are these two?"

The soldier accompanying us hands him a slip of paper. Meanwhile the two others put on their jackets. The old one reads. He has very black eyebrows that contrast with his iron-gray hair.

"Take off your shorts and drop your underpants."

The two other men are still gabbing; I hear words, street names, the first names of women. They shake hands with the doctor who's going to examine us, and they leave.

The doctor sits on a chair and motions us to come closer. The German who led us in is behind us, near the door. Our backs are to him.

With his right hand, the doctor lifts the shirttail covering Maurice's penis. He says nothing.

Then it's my turn. He looks.

"So you aren't Jewish, eh?"

I pull up my underpants. "No, we aren't Jewish."

He sighs and, without looking at the soldier, who's still waiting, he says, "Don't pay attention to him. He doesn't understand French. We're alone here—you can tell me the truth and it won't go out of this office. You're Jewish."

"No," says Maurice. "Our parents had us operated on when we were little—because we had adhesions; that's all."

He nods. "A phimosis, that's called. Do you know that every guy who comes in here says he had a phimosis in his childhood?"

"It wasn't a—what you said—it was an adhesion."

"Where was the operation performed?"

"In Algiers, in a hospital."

"What hospital?"

"I don't know—we were very small."

He turns to me.

"Yes, Mama came to see me. She brought me candy and a book."

"What book?"

"Robin Hood—it had pictures."

Silence. He leans back in his chair and studies each of us in turn. I don't know what he sees in our eyes, but there's something that makes him try a new tack. With a wave, he has the soldier leave the room.

He walks to the window, looks at the street that's all yellow from the setting sun. His hands toy with the curtains. Slowly he begins to speak.

"My name is Rosen," he says. "Do you know what it means when your name is Rosen?"

We look at each other. "No."

I add politely, "No, doctor."

He comes near and places both his hands on my shoulders.

"Well, it just means that I'm Jewish."

He gives us a chance to take in this fact and, after glancing at the door, adds, "It also means that you can talk with me."

I am still silent, but Maurice reacts quickly.

"All right," he says. "You're Jewish—but *we aren't!*"

The doctor doesn't answer. He walks to the coatrack, fishes around in his jacket pocket, takes out a cigarette, and lights it. He goes on studying us through the smoke.

It's impossible to guess what's going through the man's mind. All of a sudden as if he were talking to himself, he murmurs, "Well done!" The door opens, and there in the doorway stands the SS man with the glasses who interrogated us. He asks one brief question. I catch only a single word of the doctor's reply, but it's the one that counts; it has saved our lives. *"Das ist chirurgisch gemacht worden"* (This was a surgical operation).

The Bitter Years

Richard Petrow

A native of New York, Richard Petrow has taught
journalism at New York University and worked as a
news p. oducer for both NBC and CBS. He is the
author of *The Bitter Years: The Invasion and Occupation
of Denmark and Norway, April 1940–May 1945,* from
which the following excerpt is taken.

When Germany invaded and conquered
Denmark in 1940, the Nazis attempted to force the
Danes to adopt anti-Jewish laws and other measures
of discrimination. Because the Jews were a respected
part of Danish society, the Danes refused to be
accomplices to Germany's anti-Semitism. In October
1943, the Nazis decided to round up the Danish Jews
to transport them to Germany and the concentration
camps. This selection describes the Danish response.

Late at night on Wednesday, September 29, two
German freighters sailed quietly into Copenhagen harbor and tied up at
Langelinie Pier. The vessels, including the large *Wartheland,* unloaded no cargo,
nor was any cargo in evidence on the pier. The ships had come on a different
mission: they were scheduled to transport back to Germany the Jews who would
be arrested during the evening of October 1 and the morning of October 2.

During that whole uncertain and confused Wednesday, the news of what
Germany planned spread by word of mouth throughout the Jewish community:
relative warned relative; friend warned friend; Jew warned Jew; non-Jewish
Danes warned their Jewish acquaintances. Warning by warning, one by one, the
dread news of the impending German roundup reached the Jewish population
of Denmark.

A Copenhagen woman heard the news from a friend on the newspaper *Politiken*. After the war she related how she was called and asked with some urgency to stop by at the newspaper's office.

I went up to *Politiken* and was at once received by my friend whom I had known for many years and asked "Would you like to go to Sweden?"

"No, certainly not," I replied, "I too have heard certain rumors—"

"They are no longer rumors but extremely grave facts," he broke in, "and in any case you must promise me not to be at home on the night of October 1."

"I am not accustomed to giving promises of that sort," I replied.

"Well," he said, "you will not leave here until you have promised me."

Only then did I think that I understood. "But if things are like that," I continued, "then there are lots of people I must warn."

"You should only think about your nearest relatives," was his reply, "since measures will be taken to have everybody informed."

I promised to leave my house, and, shaken to the core, I left my acquaintance, whom I was not to meet again until May, 1945.

I had only just returned to my apartment from the newspaper office when one of my colleagues, also a Jewess, who lived nearby, came to warn me. Alsing Andersen had visited her personally to inform her of the danger and had requested she also inform me; otherwise he would do it himself—but there were so many he had to go round to.

The Sompolinsky family heard the news that night at religious services organized in their home to mark the eve of the Jewish New Year. The elder Sompolinsky, owner of a secondhand clothing store in Copenhagen, conducted the services for his wife and their eight children. Theirs was a close-knit orthodox family. Toward the end of the service a young Dane entered the room unannounced and warned them to leave the apartment and go into hiding. His voice tense and hushed, the visitor urged the family to heed his warning, explaining that he had been instructed by the local branch of the Social Democrats to warn all Jews in his district. He left the apartment with tears in his eyes, begging the Jews to believe him. One of the Sompolinskys' teen-age children, David, who had just started studies in veterinary medicine, was the first to act. That evening, despite his orthodox religion's prohibition against work on holy days, a prohibition which covered use of the telephone, David Sompolinsky telephoned his Jewish friends throughout the city, warning them of the coming German raid. Those who received his call realized with what urgency David viewed the news, for they knew he would break the laws of his religion only in a very grave emergency.

Professor Richard Ege, a non-Jewish biochemist attached to the Rockefeller Institute in Copenhagen and a highly respected member of the medical faculty of the University of Copenhagen, heard the news from an associate. When he got home that evening, Ege and his wife, Vibeke, began calling their Jewish friends to invite them to a "social gathering" at their home which, they stressed, was being held for a "special reason." Those they called detected the urgency in their voices. When the Jews arrived, the Eges warned them of the German plans. Some asked where they could hide, and Professor Ege sent them to his apartment above the laboratory in the Rockefeller Institute. That could serve as a temporary haven.

Many Jews refused to heed the warnings, however. One of Professor Ege's colleagues, Dr. L. S. Fridericai, refused to go into hiding, explaining that he was scheduled to sit in on the oral examinations of some of his students who were working for advanced degrees and he would not think of disappointing them no matter how pressing the danger to himself personally. Not until Professor Ege volunteered to fill in for him during the oral examinations did Dr. Fridericai agree to go into hiding.

A Jewish judge who lived in the town of Assens, on the island of Fyn, also refused to heed the warning. The judge was notified by a newspaper acquaintance who called from Copenhagen urging him to leave his home because "something is wrong."

"Do you know what I mean?" the caller asked.

The judge understood all too well, but still he refused to flee. "I am a Dane and I am going to stay at home where I have a right to live," he replied. When the arrests took place, the judge was among those captured.

Other Danish Jews refused to act on the warnings to flee because they did not believe the news when they were told. The Danish resistance worker Mogens Staffeldt personally visited his Jewish acquaintances and found that many scoffed at his news, "because it could not happen in Denmark." Emil Abrahamsen, a shopkeeper friend, thought Staffeldt's news was "just another silly rumor." He too refused to flee and was among those arrested in the sweep, committing suicide by poison on the German steamer carrying him to Germany.

Even Wolfgang Bardfeld, Inga's husband, had difficulty convincing the group of *chaluzim* with whom he was staying that the news in his wife's letter was urgent. "You worry too much," they told him. Only one man agreed to seek shelter with him with Danish friends. The rest stayed on the farm; all were arrested.

As zero hour approached, however, the majority of the Jews had heard the news and had fled from their houses and apartments. Rabbi Melchior's first warning, followed by warnings from other sources, sent the Jews of Denmark scattering throughout the country seeking temporary safety with non-Jewish friends or in out-of-the-way rural cottages where they hoped the Germans would not find them.

Rabbi Melchior, his wife, and their four children fled southward to the town of Ørslev, forty miles from Copenhagen, where Melchior planned to appeal for help to the Lutheran pastor there, the Reverend Hans Kildeby. Rabbi Melchior had often stayed at the Reverend Kildeby's home, but always when he was traveling alone, and always when his visits had been planned in advance. Now as he traveled south with his family, Melchior wondered what Kildeby's reaction would be. When the two men met, Melchior explained his plight and asked Kildeby if he could help find rooms for all six in his family. The rabbi said that he understood that any family would be reluctant to provide a hiding place for six fleeing Jews, because of the danger of detection, but possibly six different households could be found which would accept single members of his family. Kildeby, who had listened quietly while Rabbi Melchior explained his plan, rejected it out of hand. "Ridiculous," he barked, "you will all stay with us." The entire Melchior family soon found themselves comfortably settled in three private rooms in the Kildeby home.

Jews without non-Jewish friends often found refuge through chance encounters. In Copenhagen, ambulance driver Jorgen Knudsen pored over telephone directories seeking addresses of families with "Jewish-sounding names." Knudsen made up long lists of "possible victims" and then, using his ambulance for transportation, systematically visited the homes to warn the occupants of the coming danger. When some Jews insisted that they had no place to go, Knudsen drove them to Bispebjerg Hospital, where, he knew, a member of the medical staff, Dr. Karl Henry Koster, was active in resistance work. (Koster's laboratory had already been used for radio transmissions to England.) Koster accepted all the Jews whom Knudsen brought to the hospital, hiding them in private quarters or dispersing them as patients in the wards. During the last days of September, as the Jews of Denmark fled their homes, Bispebjerg Hospital became a central collection point for the escapees.

Knudsen's activities on behalf of the Danish Jews, most of whom were strangers to him, were not unique. Many Jews, walking the streets of Copenhagen or riding the city's trams, were startled at the approach of strangers who offered them keys to their apartments or cottages, "where you can hide until it's safe." For Mendel Katlev, a Jewish foreman in a leather-goods factory, help came from the conductor of the suburban commuter train he usually rode to and from work. Although both men had seen each other regularly on the train, they had never spoken personally. On the afternoon of September 29, when Katlev heard the news of the impending German roundup while at work in the factory, he immediately reported to his superior that he had to leave because of an emergency. He hurried to the nearby railway station and caught an early train home. His regular conductor, surprised to see Katlev on a train during working hours, commented that Katlev was "off schedule today." Katlev told him why, remarking almost in passing that he and his family would have to find a place to hide.

Without a moment's hesitation, the conductor offered Katlev, his wife, and children refuge in his own house.

So widespread was the willingness of the average Dane to help that by the evening of October 1 most Jews had found safety somewhere. One Dane wrote of his feelings: "In the midst of all the tragedy we underwent a great experience, for we saw how that same population which had hitherto said to itself, in awe of German power, 'What can we do?'—how this same population suddenly rose as one man against the Germans and rendered active help to their innocent brethren."

* * *

For the Jews of Denmark, their mass escape during the night of the persecutions marked not the end but the beginning of a period of peril. They were still in Denmark, and the Germans were still hunting them—a German order dated October 2 instructed all Jews in the country to report to the nearest Wehrmacht headquarters and all non-Jews housing Jews to turn them over to authorities. To remain in Denmark under these conditions was no longer possible. They must think of escaping.

When the Jews looked around them, only one avenue of escape appeared open—eastward to Sweden. To the south lay Germany, the land of *Nacht und Nebel* (night and fog) and beyond Germany the rest of occupied Europe. Norway too was under German occupation and had experienced its own Jewish persecution. To the west was England, but escape by boat was impossible; German vessels patrolled the straits and major sea routes. Far to the east lay the Soviet Union, itself battered by German armies and certainly no haven, even if accessible, to the Jews of Denmark. Only Sweden was open, tantalizingly close, separated from Denmark at the closest point by only two-and-a-half miles of water—the Øresund. On a clear day the Jews of Denmark could see safety with their own eyes.

But how could the Jews reach Sweden? Every normal route of travel was closed to them. Escape from Denmark would have to be made by illegal underground routes. But the Jews of Denmark, cut off from their friends, torn from their familiar surroundings, and hunted by the Germans, were unable to arrange their own mass escape. Terrified of what the immediate future might hold, the Jews struck out on their own, without foresight or planning. Erling Kiaer, a Danish bookbinder who lived in the Swedish city of Hälsingborg, found himself in the Danish town of Helsingør on the night of October 1, when Jews from Copenhagen swarmed into town hoping to find some means of reaching Sweden. As Kiaer later recalled, the Jews "were despondent and deeply afraid and their attempts to cross the straits were panicky and unplanned. They tried to contact fishermen or sail across by themselves. By day and night they fled in all sorts of craft which they had bought, borrowed or rented."

Kiaer was so touched by the plight of the Jews that within a few days he organized an escape route of his own, transporting groups of Jews from Denmark to Sweden in a small powerboat that he purchased with his own funds. Danish police cooperated. As Kiaer later wrote:

> I was in constant touch with Denmark through a young policeman who guarded the ferry. From him I received instructions about when to anchor off the Danish shore and when to arrive. . . . I always sailed to bathing jetties. . . . We used about 50 of them, with or without the owner's permission. Some people were even kind enough to lend us their houses so we could hide people there prior to sailing.

Kiaer's associates in Denmark included a doctor, a journalist, a police official, and a lawyer, all of whom had been active in underground work before. This small group, which called itself "the Sewing Circle" and its rescue service "the Kiaer Line," found hiding places for Jews and arranged their transportation to the waterfront. By the end of October the Kiaer Line had carried hundreds of Jewish refugees to safety in Sweden.

Although the Kiaer Line was one of the first rescue routes to go into operation, others sprang up quickly, for the Jewish persecution proved a turning point for the Danish resistance. Thousands of law-abiding Danes who had previously shrunk from overt acts of resistance eagerly joined the movement. By October, Denmark's underground press was posing the question of resistance versus collaboration in terms the Danes could respond to as human beings. The question no longer was whether Denmark should resist the Germans or collaborate with them, but whether individual Danes would help the Danish Jews or stand idly by and watch them plucked into captivity and transported to Germany. To this question, Denmark answered with its heart, thereby setting into motion the greatest mass rescue operation of World War II.

How could the refugees be hidden from German arrest squads and how could they be safely transported to Sweden? Resistance leaders thought immediately of the large fleet of fishing boats that plied the waters off Denmark, sailing from scores of small ports along Denmark's eastern shore. If pressed into service, these vessels could carry the bulk of the Jews to Sweden, but the resistance leaders realized that underground organizations of some sophistication were needed to select those fishing captains who would cooperate in the rescue and to coordinate the sailings by bringing refugees to selected ports at specific times. Organizations were needed also in Copenhagen and the other major cities to handle matters before the Jews could be dispersed to the coastal areas.

In Copenhagen, where the great majority of Jewish refugees could be found, the medical profession threw itself into the task of hiding the Jews during the first few days of their flight. Under the city's normal hospital-admittance procedures, all patients except emergency cases were required to report to a central classification office, *Visitationen*, located in the Kommunehospital, where medical histories were taken and preliminary evaluations made. From *Visitationen*, patients were distributed to various hospitals in the city, depending on the nature of their ailments and the beds available. When the first Jewish refugees began to seek refuge, they were adroitly slipped into this normal stream of hospital patients. On instructions from underground workers who sought out Jews in the city, refugees made their way to *Visitationen*, where they were given fictitious names and fictitious illnesses and assigned to hospital beds in various institutions, there to become lost in the general hospital population, often without their presence being known to most of the hospital staff. As the number of Jews seeking safe hiding places increased, however, this system broke down, and the Jews went directly to the hospitals, often in large groups whose identity could not be camouflaged.

At Bispebjerg Hospital a twenty-five-year-old medical student, Ole Secher, worked closely with Dr. Karl Henry Koster in harboring Jewish refugees. When Secher heard that a group of Jews was hiding in the woods outside Copenhagen, he consulted with Dr. Koster, then sought out the Jews and brought them to the hospital, where they were housed in the funeral chapel. Later these Jews, as well as those brought to the hospital by ambulance-driver Jorgen Knudsen, and those who arrived on their own initiative, moved to the nurses' quarters in a building adjacent to the hospital. After the war Dr. Koster wrote of those trying days:

> Many an elderly Miss who would usually get terribly upset if anyone put a finger on her polished mahogany table now found it completely natural that an entire family whom she didn't know occupied her flat.

Secher also arranged the departure of Jewish refugees from Bispebjerg Hospital. As a member of the Danish Students' Rowing Club, Secher had friends in many coastal towns, including the city of Nykøbing on the island of Falster, where an active resistance group had made arrangements with some friendly fishing boat captains. Secher sent the Jewish refugees to Nykøbing by train. Local underground workers picked them up and housed them in small inns and private homes until they could be placed on board boats for the voyage to Sweden. To help the Nykøbing resistance workers spot the Jews at the railroad station, Secher gave each refugee a small blue flag—the symbol of the Danish Students' Rowing Club—to wear as a means of quick identification.

The movement of Jews into and out of Bispebjerg Hospital did not escape the notice of German officials, however. One week after the abortive German roundup, troops surrounded the hospital in the evening, examined all ambulances that left and entered the hospital grounds, and set up checkpoints at entrances and exits. Dr. Stephen Lund, who was in charge of the distribution of Jews to hospitals throughout all of Denmark, described what happened next:

> Since there were two hundred refugees in the hospital that night, it cannot be said that the situation was particularly encouraging. . . . Only a higher authority had the power to order a large-scale action such as searching the hospital. We knew that the authorities in *Dagmarhus* [The Gestapo headquarters] would only come to their offices in the morning and that we had to move the people quickly, before anything happened. Thus it was that at nine o'clock in the morning a funeral cortege left the chapel. The procession consisted of twenty to thirty taxis all filled with refugees. The operation succeeded and the refugees, who knew nothing of the danger they were in, had all slept well in the nurses' apartments placed at their disposal.

Before the Jewish rescue was over, approximately eight hundred Jews had moved through Bispebjerg Hospital alone.

In the Copenhagen suburb of Lyngby, a group led by the pacifist school-teacher Aage Bertelsen also participated in the Jewish rescue. At the time of the German invasion of Denmark in 1940, Bertelsen fully supported his country's quick surrender: he saw no reason for a "hopeless fight." Throughout the early years of the occupation, he supported the policy of collaboration that most Danes adopted toward the German occupation forces. By the summer of 1943, his views began to change and he began to understand the ideology of sabotage, even if he was not himself ready to desert his pacifist background and become active himself. The Jewish persecution changed his posture. "In the face of these open acts of atrocity, insanely meaningless, it was not a question of one's view-point," he wrote later. "Action was the word. . . . No honest man could possibly refrain from action after this raid, when the persecuted cried for help."

Bertelsen's home became a receiving-and-dispatching center for Jews, operating almost in the open. It was Bertelsen's policy that his home should become known as a place where anyone seeking to flee to Sweden could get aid. During the first half of October, "the house with the blue curtains," as it was described by those who passed through it, teemed with movement. The schoolmaster's wife handled the telephone and all internal arrangements, while Bertelsen did most of the outside "contact" work. They were aware of the risks they ran by operating in the open, but hoped nevertheless that they could "finish a useful piece of work" before they were closed down. By the end of October, the Lyngby group had rescued approximately five hundred persons.

The *Holger Danske* sabotage group, which had been forced to disband during the August crackdown, resumed its activities in October under the leadership of Jens Lillilund, concentrating solely on the rescue of the Danish Jews. Its central meeting point was Mogens Staffeldt's *Nordiske Boghandel* (Scandinavian Book-store), located in a building on the Kongens Nytorv, opposite Copenhagen's best hotel, the D'Angleterre. The rear room of the *Nordiske Boghandel* became another collection point for Jewish refugees, who remained hidden inside until other hiding places could be found for them in homes near the docks—the Kongens Nytorv site being close to Copenhagen's busy port district. At the height of the rescue operation, *Holger Danske* had under its control as many as twelve fishing vessels, which by the end of October had transported approximately one thousand Jews to Sweden.

Special organizations came into existence to coordinate the activities of the field rescue groups. University students in Copenhagen created an informal *Studenternes Efferretningstjeneste* (Student Intelligence Service), which concentrated on gathering information on German activities along the escape routes; while newspapermen at *National Tidende* took over the job of maintaining contact with the various underground rescue groups. The newspapermen pooled all information, from whatever source, and made it available to those field groups in need of up-to-the-minute intelligence. The word "potatoes" came to be used as a code word for Jewish refugees. One of the newspapermen, Borge Outze, described how the calls would sound to any German who might listen in:

> Eighteen sacks of potatoes have been sold today to Mrs. Ege. . . . Twenty sacks were sold through the middleman at Lyngby. . . . It would be a good idea for the potatoes to be transferred to another place.

By these references, clearly understood by those involved, groups of Jews would be moved along their way from one rescue group to another until they boarded the escape vessels ready for sea.

For non-Jewish Danes, October, 1943, marked a rebirth of hope and dignity through action. Every boatload of Jewish refugees that sailed from Danish shores meant another victory for the underground workers who had planned the trip. With victory came confidence, and a desire for further victories. Its efforts to rescue the Danish Jews gave the Danish underground an impetus that continued until final victory.

For the Jews, however, it was a time of uncertainty and fear. By necessity they were forced to entrust their lives to strangers who they could only hope would not betray them. The results of failure were known to all: arrest, deportation, imprisonment, and possibly death. What the Danish resistance workers later remembered as the "happy Jew time" was, for the Danish Jews, a period of darkest despair. Some committed suicide before arrest. All feared what would happen to them and their families if they did not escape from Denmark. Even when the escape was successful, the experience was harrowing. One Jewish woman survivor related the story of her escape:

We were taken by taxi to the beach near a little fishing harbor. Each of the four passengers and the organizer were then hidden under a bush by the shore. The plan was that at a certain time we were to crawl along the beach to the harbor, where there was a watchtower manned by Germans. We lay a whole day waiting for darkness. Up on the road we could hear cars drive by and we shivered with fright. . . . As far as we knew, the Germans in the watchtower had been bribed to turn a blind eye. At seven o'clock in the evening, a strange sight revealed itself. From the bushes along the beach human forms crawled out on their stomachs. We discovered that these were other passengers of whose presence we had been completely unaware. After awhile we reached the fishing boat without mishap and were herded into the hold, like herrings in a barrel. As there was not enough space down below, a few passengers were wrapped in fishing nets and in sacks on the deck. . . . Shortly after our sailing, a wind blew up and many became seasick and were forced to come up on deck and retch, as they could not bear to be in the smelly hold. Then we saw the searchlight of the German patrol boat. The engine was immediately stopped and we were ordered to stand stiff and still around the wheelhouse, whose weak light could have given us away. Everyone thought his last hour had come and was ready to jump overboard and drown, rather than be taken by the Germans. . . . Tension on board was extreme. . . . However, the passengers calmed down after the initial danger had passed and made every effort to stay calm, although every muscle was tense for fear of discovery. The little boat had in the meantime gone off course because of the gale. . . . Gradually it began to grow light, but we had no idea of the boat's position. . . . Would we ever be saved? At seven in the morning, land was sighted, but what land? . . . The boat approached the coast; we hoped that liberty was at hand. We were really in Swedish territorial waters. The Danish flag was raised and people threw their arms around one another and cried for joy. We were saved at last. The harbor we had sailed into was full of Swedish warships on whose decks sailors waved and shouted "Valkommen."

Escape from Sobibor

Richard Rashke

A professional writer, Richard Rashke was born in
1936 in Milwaukee, Wisconsin. He interviewed
eighteen of the thirty survivors of Sobibor, an
extermination camp in eastern Poland where a
quarter of a million Jews were murdered. Sobibor
was the site of the biggest prisoner escape of World
War II. All of the physical evidence and documents
of Sobibor were destroyed except for three
documents. From the oral and written accounts of
the survivors, Rashke wrote *Escape from Sobibor*,
from which the following excerpt is taken.

In October 1943, Jewish prisoners revolted against
the guards in Sobibor and broke through the walls.
Several hundred survived and fled into the nearby
forest. This selection describes the experiences of
Esther and her small band as they attempted to find
a safe haven.

Sobibor, Poland
October 14–19, 1943

SS Sergeant Karl Frenzel waited until most of the shooting was over, then tried
to call Security Police headquarters in Lublin, twenty-five miles away. But the
phones were dead, and the officer in charge of Sobibor was missing.

Frenzel walked through the main gate, crossed the tracks to the small pub-
lic railway station, and handed a message to the Polish telegraph operator:
JEWS REVOLTED . . . SOME ESCAPED . . . SOME SS OFFICERS, NON-COMS, FOREIGN GUARDS
DEAD . . . SOME JEWS STILL INSIDE THE CAMP . . . SEND HELP.

The Security Police dispatched SS and police task forces to Sobibor to round up the Jews still trapped behind the fences; they also ordered the army to chase those who had escaped and the Luftwaffe to buzz the pine forests. The next day, October 15, the Security Police sent the following report to Berlin:

On October 14, 1943, at about 5:00 P.M., a revolt of Jews in the SS camp Sobibor, twenty-five miles north of Chelm. They overpowered the guards, seized the armory, and, after an exchange of shots with the camp garrison, fled in unknown directions. Nine SS men murdered, one SS man missing, two foreign guards shot to death.

Approximately 300 Jews escaped. The remainder were shot to death or are now in camp. Military police and armed forces were notified immediately and took over security of the camp at about 1:00 A.M. The area south and southwest of Sobibor is now being searched by police and armed forces.

The SS ferreted out the 159 Jews still inside Sobibor. A few had pistols and fought back; the others hid wherever they could. When the Jews were executed in the woods and buried, the SS dismantled the gas chambers, razed the buildings they didn't want to move, and planted pine saplings where the barracks had once stood.

The Nazis left Sobibor—the forest of the owls—as they had found it. In the center of what had been the camp stood the foresters' tower, reaching a hundred feet above the pines. And across the tracks from the public train station sat the old post office, where the Sobibor Kommandant had lived.

On October 19—five days after the Jews of Sobibor had escaped—SS chief Heinrich Himmler halted Operation Reinhard. The Red Army was less than three hundred miles from Sobibor, and the evidence had to be destroyed before they found it. Besides, Operation Reinhard had been a complete success. In twenty months, it alone had killed almost two million Jews. (Not even the Nazis knew the exact number; they did not keep records.) And there were no more Jews left to murder in the ghettos of eastern Poland, Latvia, Estonia, Lithuania, White Russia, and the Ukraine.

But Himmler couldn't destroy all the evidence. When the Russians crossed the Bug River into Poland and pushed past Sobibor, a few miles away, the evidence, hidden in the barns and fields, or fighting with the partisans, was among the first to hug them.

★   ★   ★

When the Jew cried "Hurrah! Hurrah!" and Camp I exploded, Esther had to make a quick decision. Should she follow the mob toward the main gate or head for the south fence behind the carpenter shop?

She chose the carpenter shop. Someone—Esther wasn't sure who—flung the ladder against the fence. She scampered up like a squirrel and jumped. Her close friend Samuel followed. She crossed the ditch on a plank and squeezed through the second fence. Samuel followed. The mines in front of her began to explode, and she prayed that God would help her step in the right spot.

The Ukrainians opened fire on the crouched figures in the field. Most of the Jews did not zigzag like soldiers. They headed for the woods like arrows. Esther felt pain sear through her hair just above her right ear. Blood began to trickle down her neck. She didn't know how badly she'd been hit, only that the pain disappeared quickly and that the warm sticky blood kept flowing.

Esther began to feel sick and weak. She reached to hold on to the girl running next to her. "Leave me alone!" the girl screamed as she pushed Esther away. Esther stumbled forward. "Leave me—" As bullets tore into her, the girl fell on the field.

Esther kept running until she broke into the woods. Samuel looked at her wound. The bullet had just grazed her, leaving a little ridge above her ear like a furrow in a newly ploughed field.

Nine other Jews, all trying to decide what to do, where to go, how to foil the Nazi chase, joined Esther and Samuel. The others who had made it over the fence behind the carpenter shop had scattered. Esther told them she didn't care what *they* were going to do, but she intended to go to Janow, where a friend owned a large farm. That's what her mother had told her to do in a dream, she said. That's where her mother had promised she'd be safe.

It was irrational to stake her life on a dream, Esther knew. But this was no time for logic. She had followed her instincts ever since the Germans invaded Poland four years ago, and she was still alive. She would follow her instincts now.

The other ten Jews—all men, including Samuel—couldn't come up with a better plan, so they tagged along. Esther had told them that if they made it to Janow, which was close to the Staw work camp, the farmer would hide them. At least they had a definite place to go and the name of a farmer who would not betray them to the Germans. What more could they ask?

They began running, walking, resting. When they felt lost or discouraged, the men would complain. "You're going to get us all killed, looking for that farmer," they'd say. But they followed her anyway. Once they met what appeared to be friendly partisans. Some of the men wanted to join them, but Esther refused. Her mother had told her to go to the farm, she said, and to the farm she would go. They tagged along.

After three nights of wandering and two days of sleeping, they found an isolated farm at the edge of Novosiolki. It was Sunday morning, October 17. The eleven Jews caucused in the forest. Should they ask for food? Should they ask the farmer to hide them? They decided that only three should approach the house. If the farmer saw eleven, he surely would send them away. And if he betrayed or killed the three, the other eight would be free.

Esther, Samuel and Avram knocked on the door. The farmer made the sign of the cross and invited them inside—quickly, so that no one would see them. He knew about the escape from Sobibor, he said. He was just on his way to Sunday Mass. Would Esther like hot water to wash her bullet wound? He'd be back soon.

Esther cleaned the scab matted with hair. Samuel cut her pigtails and clipped the hair around her ear. Then they waited. Was the farmer looking for the Germans or the Polish Blue Police? Was he selling them for a kilo of sugar? Or would he really help them? They waited.

When the farmer returned, he dabbed Esther's wound with salve and invited the Jews to join his family for a huge Sunday morning breakfast.

"Will you hide us?" Esther asked after they had eaten. "We have money."

"Yes." The man did not hesitate. It was as if he had expected the question.

"First," Esther said, stubbornly, "I have to go to Janow to a farmer. He's a friend. Can you show us the way?"

"My son will take you to the main road," the farmer said. "If that farmer doesn't want you, you come back here. I'll hide you."

Esther offered him money, but he shook his head. He made the sign of the cross over them again before they left so that God's power would protect them against the Germans they both hated. On the way to the main road, they stopped in the woods to pick up the other eight men, but they were gone. Esther figured that they had thought that she, Samuel, and Avram were dead or had deserted them, and that they had struck out on their own. She hoped they'd find friendly partisans. As for her, it was Janow. Esther thanked the farmer's son, and the three Jews waited in the woods for nightfall.

It took them eleven nights to walk to the farm owned by Stefan Marcyniuk. After World War I, he had escaped from a Communist prison and, almost penniless, had lived in the attic above the flour mill owned by Esther's father.

"How are you going to make it?" Esther's father had asked him one day. "You live in an attic. You don't have a job. Your wife is expecting a child."

"I don't know," Marcyniuk had said. "I'm a baker by trade. If only I had half a sack of flour, I could bake bread and sell it."

"I'll give it to you. Pay me back when you can," her father had offered.

In a few years Stefan Marcyniuk had become one of the richest men in Chelm. The farm in Janow was one of his investments. He and Esther's father had become as close as brothers. To the two religious men, it made no difference that one was a Jew and the other a Christian. They respected each other's religious beliefs, their children played together, and their families celebrated religious and secular holidays together. Esther knew Marcyniuk would welcome her as if she were a lost daughter.

When Esther found that no one was home at the Marcyniuk farmhouse, she knocked on the caretaker's door. The man thought they were partisans. "Take anything you want," he told them. "Just don't shoot me."

Esther caught on quickly. It was better that he believe they were partisans than Jews. "I'm not looking for you," she said. "I'm looking for the owner. I'm going to kill him."

"Why? What did he do?"

"None of your business. Where is he?" Esther demanded. "We have something to settle."

"He doesn't live here. He just comes once or twice a week."

"All right, then give us some bread and we'll be off."

It was a beautiful farm, huge by Polish standards. A wooden fence enclosed the farm itself, which opened onto a tree-lined dirt road. The farmhouse had two stories, with a single dormer poking out the roof. Surrounding the house were a large barn filled with straw, a cattle barn, and two chicken coops. In the square that made up the barnyard sat two haystacks. And beyond the barns and yard were the well and two ponds and a string of other buildings.

Esther suggested that they hide in the large straw barn. From there, they could see the yard, house, gate, and road. "We'll wait for him," she said.

For three days and nights, they watched and waited. They saw partisans creep into the yard to steal chickens and eggs. Samuel was getting edgy. "Let's go with them," he suggested. "At least we'll have a chance to make it."

"Go if you want," Esther said. "I'm waiting here." Samuel stayed, for Esther was his rabbit's foot. In Sobibor, she had saved his life twice in one day.

Surrounded by Ghetto Walls

In the late 1930s, as the conditions for Jews in Germany continued to deteriorate, the spread of Nazism signaled new levels of persecution in occupied territories. In 1939, when Germany invaded Poland, the war on the Jews also escalated. Eastern European Jews became the targets of some of the most violent Nazi attacks, especially in Poland. These two factors seemed to fuel a German policy that was already out of control. In the first two months of German occupation, five thousand Polish Jews were killed. The Nazis then ordered that all Jews be taken to major cities and detained as a group. To this end, the Nazis barricaded run-down sections of major cities in Eastern European countries, making ghettos to imprison the Jews. At first, the ghettos' chief function was to provide slave labor for the Nazi war effort, but, as time passed, the ghettos became a temporary holding place for the Jews until the Nazis could deport them to the concentration camps, where they faced an almost certain death.

Hundreds of thousands of Jews were forced into ghettos, where day-to-day life meant scarce food, rampant diseases, limited sanitation, restricted privacy, and constant danger. While food rations were small, the lack of fuel was an even more significant problem. The winter's cold combined with hunger and disease to pose a major threat to the prisoners' survival. As time went on, conditions worsened. Those living in ghettos were often reduced to begging, smuggling, and fighting for every scrap of food. Once malnutrition and disease had rendered ghetto residents defenseless and demoralized, they were unfit for forced labor and were deported to death camps.

Among the largest of the ghettos were those in Lodz and Warsaw, Poland. Each of these ghettos was only one-and-a-half square miles in size and housed hundreds of thousands of people. In Lodz, 150,000 to 200,000 Jews were crammed into twenty city blocks, where they lived with seven or eight people to a room. The Warsaw ghetto enclosed between 400,000 and 600,000 people, most of them living in quarters with eight to fourteen people to a room. It is estimated that, during the worst period, as many as five hundred people starved to death each week in the Warsaw ghetto. Additionally, in 1941, a reported sixteen thousand died there from typhus. Anyone discovered to have typhus was taken from the ghetto and either killed or left to die untreated.

Travel into and out of the ghettos was restricted. Often the only Jews who were allowed to leave were those on work assignments to assist the German war effort. While the workload was difficult and the hours long, the workers did have a place to go each day, and they earned a small wage and a little extra in food rations.

While the Nazis ultimately controlled the ghettos, they established in each ghetto a Jewish Council (*Judenrat*) of twelve leading male members of the community. It was the task of the *Judenrat* to ensure that the directives of the Nazis were enforced and to oversee the daily operations of the ghetto. The *Judenrat* distributed food, ran hospitals, and tried to keep order by establishing Jewish police forces. The role of the *Judenrat* was painful, trying, and complex. Even today, the debate continues about whether the *Judenrats* provided strength and made life more bearable or were guilty of complicity.

Chapter 4 explores the experiences of some of those who were forced into ghettos and the dehumanizing effect of life in the ghetto.

Lodz Ghetto

Dawid Sierakowiak

Dawid Sierakowiak was a fifteen-year-old Polish Jew when the Germans invaded his homeland in 1939. He regularly chronicled his daily life in his diary. He graduated from the Lodz Ghetto Gymnasium (the equivalent of high school in the United States) in 1941. He was active in politics in the ghetto, as a communist and as a member of the underground. Sierakowiak died in the Lodz ghetto of tuberculosis at age nineteen.

Lodz, Poland, was a textile center with the second largest Jewish population in Europe. In 1940, the Nazis forced 150,000 to 200,000 Polish Jews into a sealed ghetto. In 1941, these were joined by 20,000 more Jews who had been displaced and relocated by the Germans from other European countries. While the Lodz ghetto served as a huge work camp for the German war effort, it also was the scene of transports to the death camps. By the end of the war, almost all of the ghetto inhabitants were dead, either from the unbearable conditions in the ghetto or as a result of having perished in the camps. Left behind, however, were diaries, journals, notebooks, and poems that provide a chronicle of ghetto life. These excerpts from Sierakowiak's diary begin with entries from 1939, when the Germans invaded Poland.

LODZ, AUGUST 24, 1939

Mobilization! We don't know if this is the real thing or not, but nearly every recruit is reporting. Many of our neighbors have already gone. . . . There's not the least hint of defeatism.

LODZ, AUGUST 26, 1939

Today I read Mayor [Jan] Kwapinski's appeal for volunteers to dig anti-aircraft ditches. Having gotten my parents' permission, I signed up immediately at the police station, as did all my schoolmates, and tomorrow morning I go to work. There are tens of thousands of volunteers. . . . Old Jews, young women, Chassidim, all citizens (except the Germans) are rushing to volunteer. The bloody Hun will not pass!

LODZ, AUGUST 28, 1939

My bones ache like everyone else's from yesterday's work. Fifty thousand people were out digging.

AUGUST 30, 1939

General mobilization! All reservists up to age 40 have been called.

LODZ, SEPTEMBER 1, 1939

The German army has crossed the Polish border in several places. Air raids on Polish towns such as Cracow, Czestochowa, Katowice, Grodno, etc., have begun. Things are boiling around the world. We're waiting for France and England to join the war; maybe even the United States. Meanwhile, we're repelling German attacks quite well. We had 3 alerts today, during which enemy planes were kept from approaching our town. I go to bed half dressed.

WEDNESDAY, SEPTEMBER 6, 1939—LODZ

Oh, God, what's going on here? Panic, departures en masse, defeatism. The city, abandoned by its institutions and by the police, awaits the imminent arrival of the German army in terror. What's happened? People are running nervously from place to place, anxiously carrying around their worn-out possessions. An aimless confusion. I was on duty till 1:00 a.m. I go to wake Rysio Wojcikowski for his turn. He is quite pessimistic, and he tells me that some kind of evacuation of the city is contemplated. He tells me that in his father's office everything is packed, and that they're getting ready to leave Lodz at any minute. I'm astonished. How? Where? I hear that the Germans are going to occupy Lodz any hour now. At home I meet our neighbor Mr. Grabinski, who has just returned from the city. He tells me of the great panic and frenzy seizing people. Throngs are leaving their homes on a dangerous migration to an uncertain future. There is crying and lamenting in the streets.

I go to bed, but at 5 a.m. loud voices in the apartment wake me. Our neighbor Mr. Grodzenski, with his crying wife, is urging us to leave. Where? What for? Nobody knows. Run, run, run away as far as possible; move with care, stumble, forget everything—as long as you run from danger. My mother, my beloved, everlastingly sensitive mother, shows unusual composure as she consoles Mrs. Grodzenski, dissuading her from her ridiculous plans. Slowly, the contagion of mass hysteria, as well as the psychosis of crowds heading for slaughter, is eliminated. Father loses his head; he doesn't know what to do. Other neighbors come in, Jews, to seek counsel. They say that it's recommended that everyone able to bear arms leave the city, since the enemy will send them to work camps. They don't know what to do. The matter is considered and the decision is made to stay put. Whatever will be will be.

People are constantly on the move. Groups of men are heading toward Brzeziny to report for duty, while at the same time reservists and recruits are running away. Following them are women carrying bundles on their backs, filled with clothes, bedding and food. Even small children are running. All the leaders have left, so, for fun, we acted like we were the leaders, playing that role till noon.

Meanwhile, the situation is becoming ever more tense. Everyone has a different story to tell. Someone said that 150 English airplanes are waiting in Sieradz, another that the Germans have already occupied Zdunska Wola and are heading toward Lodz. The news gets stranger and more fantastic all the time.

Aunt Estera came to us with her children, and the house is filled with crying. Abek and Jankus ran away to Brzeziny. What is to be done? What can be accomplished? At 5 p.m. a kind of potato soup materialized: that's today's dinner. Other people might not even have that much. My father runs to our uncle, uncle back to father, but the decision remains the same: we will stay put and not run. In the afternoon a civilian patrol is organized in our neighborhood. My father signs up for it. In the evening Rysio Wojcikowski returns with his father. They've bought bicycles and are leaving once again. The roads are impossible.

I go to bed, expecting, for the first time, a good night's sleep. Unfortunately, there is no fear of air raids now. When you want to take over something, you don't destroy it. In the evening a column of Polish soldiers began arriving in town. They march quietly, in formation. It's hard to tell whether they're advancing or retreating. A little later some armored tanks left the city heading for the front. . . . What will tomorrow bring?

THURSDAY, SEPTEMBER 7, 1939

Today there was nothing new. Like everyone else I went outside this morning, did nothing but talk about what will happen. Will they, or won't they come? We dragged ourselves to Pabianicka Highway to watch the approaching Polish military column. So that's how a retreating army looks, rather like a regular army passing by. Can it be hoped that they won't come? Will there be another "Miracle on the Vistula River"? Will we live to see another Marne? We sit together, boys and girls, trying to chase our worst thoughts away. It's no use. What will happen?

Our neighbor's brother came on horseback. He says the Germans are being pushed back and our columns are holding fast. The afternoon newspaper claims that the French are marching into Germany and that the Poles are holding fast. A militia is being organized. My father has signed up. Maybe now he'll regain his composure and calm down.

In the evening we could hear the cannons boom and see a fiery glow in the south. Can it be so near? Some fellow claims that Lodz will be taken any moment now. I'm going home to bed, so I won't hear or see anything. Come what may! Maybe there'll be a miracle . . . Marne, oh Marne, if only it could happen again. Maybe a miracle is possible.

FRIDAY, SEPTEMBER 8, 1939—LODZ

Lodz is occupied. It's been quiet all day, too quiet. As I sit in the park in the afternoon, drawing a portrait of a girl I know, the frightening news reaches us: Lodz has surrendered. German patrols are on Piotrkowska Street. Fear, surprise . . . surrendered without a fight? Maybe it's just a tactical maneuver. We'll see. Meanwhile, conversations cease, the streets empty.

Mr. Grabinski returned from town and told everyone how the local Germans greeted their countrymen. The Grand Hotel, where the General Staff is to be headquartered, is decked with flowers. Civilians, including boys and girls, are jumping into passing military cars with a happy "Heil Hitler." One can hear loud German conversations on the streets. Whatever was hidden in the past, under the pretext of patriotism and civic-mindedness, now shows its true face.

SATURDAY, SEPTEMBER 9, 1939—LODZ

An announcement in Polish and German (German first) was posted this morning, advising calm while German units enter the city. It was signed "Civic Committee for the City of Lodz." A little later I went over to Pabianicka Highway to see the arriving army. A great number of vehicles, but the soldiers are nothing out of the ordinary. They differ from Polish soldiers only by the uniforms they wear, which are steel grey. Their expressions are boisterous—after all, they are the conquerors! A car of officers with Martian-like faces speeds by like lightning. The street is quiet, watching the passing army with indifference. It's quiet, all quiet. We get back to our neighborhood, sit on benches, talk, and joke. What the hell! Damn them.

SUNDAY, SEPTEMBER 10, 1939—LODZ

The first manifestation of the German presence: Jews were being seized to do digging. An elderly retired professor, a Christian who lives in no. 11, warned me about going into town. A decent man. What should I do now? Tomorrow is the first day of school; who knows what's happening to our beloved school. My friends are all going to attend, just to see what's going on. But I have to stay home. I must. My parents feel they don't want to lose me yet. Oh, my beloved school! Curse the times I complained about getting up early or about tests. If only those times could return!

LODZ, SEPTEMBER 12, 1939

Jews are being seized again, and beaten and robbed. The store where my father works was robbed, as the local Germans freely indulge their whims. People speak about the way Jews are treated at work: some are treated decently, but others are sadistically abused. Some Jews were ordered to stop working, to remove their clothes and stand facing the wall, at which point they were told they'd be shot. Shots were fired in their direction, and though nobody was killed, this was repeated a few times.

LODZ, SEPTEMBER 13, 1939

Erev Rosh Hashanah [Rosh Hashanah eve]. I haven't gone out and won't now that the sad holiday is approaching. It's no different from a sad ordinary day, when all one has is bread and (occasionally) herring. According to an order issued today, stores are to remain open tomorrow. What a blow to the Jews on Rosh Hashanah, the worst in ages! However, the synagogues are to be closed. There is no possibility of communal prayer for mercy. All basic personal freedoms are cancelled. Though I'm not old-fashioned (I've considered it my freedom to avoid prayer every year), this prohibition is painful, for I understand what faith means to the devout. It's an irreparable crime to take away someone's only happiness, his belief. The Jews will not forgive Hitler for this. Our vengeance will be awesome.

LODZ, SEPTEMBER 15, 1939

German agents remove Jews from all food lines, so that a poor Jew who has no maid is condemned to die of hunger.

LODZ, SEPTEMBER 16, 1939

Store-robbing continues. They get everything they can. Epsztajn's jewelry [and] watch store was completely emptied, and they scarcely got away alive.

SEPTEMBER 19, 1939

. . . listened to Hitler's speech about Danzig, ranting, raving, insulting, begging, ingratiating himself, but above all lying and lying. He lied that Poland started the war, he lied about the barbaric persecution of Germans in Poland and lied about his own, always peaceful, intentions.

LODZ, SEPTEMBER 20, 1939

The Germans have introduced the German mark alongside the Polish zloty (2 zlotys per mark) and the civic committee scrip. And a few anti-Semitic orders have been issued, namely that Jews cannot have more than 1000 marks and can draw only 250 marks per week from the bank. Stores are being robbed less often, but grabbing people for work continues.

LODZ, OCTOBER 3, 1939

People are gradually getting used to the new conditions and are returning to their jobs.

WEDNESDAY, OCTOBER 4, 1939—LODZ

I have not escaped the sad fate of my compatriots being seized to do work. Yesterday I took a shortcut to school, passing buildings covered with swastikas, many German cars, a lot of soldiers, and Lodz Germans wearing swastikas. I managed to evade them and, emboldened, took the same road today. A youth holding a big stick ran over, yelling in German: "Come, let's get to work! You're not allowed to go to school." I didn't resist, for no identification card would have been of any use there. He took me to a certain square where several Jews were already working, clearing the ground of leaves. He wanted me to jump over a high fence, but when he saw I wouldn't do it, he left me. The work on the square was supervised by a soldier, also with a big stick, who told me to fill some puddles with sand.

I've never been more humiliated than when I saw those passersby smiling and laughing at someone else's misfortune. Oh, you stupid, ignorant oafs, you simpletons! We don't need to feel ashamed; only our tormentors should. Enforced humiliation isn't humiliation. But the anger, the helpless fury of being forced to do this stupid, disgraceful task filled with provocation tore me apart. One thing is left: revenge!

After about a half hour of work, the soldier gathered all the Jews, some with their hats turned the wrong way (for the sport of it), lined us up, told one of us to put away the shovels, and dismissed the rest of us. It was supposed to be a show of magnanimity. I got to school halfway through the first class, my first lateness ever. The teachers can do nothing. "For reasons beyond the Jews' control."

This evening we found out that one of the Germans who live in our neighborhood is "eyeing" the Jews, "keeping watch" over them. This completely unnerved my poor anguished parents. Meanwhile, it was announced in school that students who do not pay at least some tuition will be barred from classes. What will happen to me? We will see.

LODZ, OCTOBER 6, 1939

Hitler called a meeting of the Reichstag, where he laughed at the former Polish government, rightly so, and where he gave his "final" offer for peace. His terms, given on the radio earlier this week, are unacceptable. He said that he is even ready to resolve the Jewish question, and ridiculed the British rule in Palestine. At any rate, the speech brought nothing new.

LODZ, OCTOBER 8, 1939

Today the Jewish community council announced that it will provide 700 Jews for work. Will they now stop grabbing people on the street?

LODZ, OCTOBER 18, 1939

The Germans have set up a police station in our area and are going through apartments belonging to Jews, taking away radios, carpets, quilts, etc. They'll probably throw us out of our apartment soon.

LODZ, OCTOBER 19, 1939

No bread, no coal to be had.

LODZ, OCTOBER 20, 1939

An order was issued today forbidding Jews from trading in textiles, leather, and clothing. A Jew is not allowed to buy any of these, and he can sell these goods only to Christians. A shoemaker can buy leather for repairing heels and soles but not for making new shoes. It's true that this order hurts the black market in clothing; still, thousands of Jewish families are being brought to ruin.

LODZ, OCTOBER 22, 1939

Sunday, 11 a.m. A knock at the door. In comes a German officer, two policemen, and the super. The officer asks how many people live in the apartment, looks over the beds, asks about bedbugs, then if we have a radio—and finally leaves disappointed. He took radios from our neighbors (of course, they only go to Jews), as well as mattresses, quilts, carpets, etc. He found nothing of value in our place. Father was very frightened because he was praying in a *tallis* [prayer shawl], but the officer didn't notice. It's lucky, because people say that in such cases the Germans drive the Jews into the street and make them run until their *tallis* and *tefillin* [phylacteries] fall off. They took our neighbor Mr. Grabinski's only down quilt. Now it's 100% sure that they'll throw us out of our buildings.

OCTOBER 28, 1939

They ordered Mrs. Heller out of her apartment by 4 p.m. tomorrow; the administration gave her an empty apartment but only until she finds another one. Now we are all endangered.

LODZ, NOVEMBER 7, 1939

And so it's happened. Today's *Deutsche Lodscher Zeitung* announces the annexation of Lodz to Wartheland [the western part of Poland, annexed into the Reich] and, thus, to the Greater Reich. Of course, the appropriate orders have been issued, namely: Jews are not allowed to walk on Piotrkowska Street, since it's the main street; Jews and Poles are to yield always and everywhere to uniformed Germans; wearing four-cornered hats, uniforms, army coats, shiny buttons, and military belts is forbidden. Jewish bakeries are permitted to bake only bread. Jewish stores are to be marked *"Jüdisches Geschaft"* [Ger: Jewish business] next to a yellow Star of David inscribed with the word *"Jude"* [Ger: Jew]. It's a return to the yellow patches of the Middle Ages.

LODZ, NOVEMBER 8, 1939

Terrible things are going on in town. Jews are grabbed and ordered to report tomorrow to a designated area, to bring a shovel, food for 2 days, and 20 zlotys. What new idea is this? What kind of agony? Posters on street corners announce the annexation of Lodz to the Reich. A Nazi Youth Party was formed in the city: marching, singing, parades—one wants to stay home to keep from seeing all of this.

A meeting of "The Jewish Elders of Lodz" with the authorities was called for tomorrow. We'll see what comes of it.

LODZ, NOVEMBER 9, 1939

The Germans came to school yesterday and ordered that its Polish-Hebrew sign be taken down and the library made orderly.

The Jews who were grabbed for work and told to bring food and money were released after one day and their money taken from them. Those living on Piotrkowska Street can buy a pass for 5 zlotys per person. Everything is done for money. The community elders meeting with the authorities have not yet returned.

LODZ, NOVEMBER 10, 1939

There is talk that the Jewish elders were jailed and also that they were released. We were advised in school not to venture out tomorrow, the 11th of November, the traditional Polish national holiday. They hanged 3 criminals in Balut Market today—2 Poles for murder and a Jew for blackmarketeering, so it's rumored—

to scare us. They're afraid of provocation. I am sure nothing will happen; nobody would dare attempt anything.

LODZ, NOVEMBER 11, 1939

It's quiet in town, though yesterday and today they arrested a lot of teachers, activists who fought for Polish independence (in 1918), policemen, etc. The daily *Dziennik Lodzki* is discontinued as of today. An order was issued that all signs must be written in German, correctly, since we are now part of the Reich! As of the 15th all Poles and Jews must give up their radios. We'll have no news after that. The Germans do whatever they want.

WEDNESDAY, NOVEMBER 15, 1939—LODZ

The synagogue was burned down. Barbaric methods for annihilating the world are being activated. They demanded 25 million zlotys in exchange for stopping the terror. The community didn't have it, so it didn't deliver. Something is wrong with the Germans. Since yesterday they've been engaged in terrible plunder, robbing wantonly, whatever they can: furniture, clothes, underwear, food. All Lodz German males, 18 to 45, are being mobilized today for *selbstschutz* [Ger: self-defense]. Since the regular army is leaving, someone has to stay and guard the city. We'll get the brunt of it. It's worse dealing with one Lodz German than a whole regiment from Germany.

THURSDAY, NOVEMBER 16, 1939—LODZ

We're returning to the Middle Ages. The yellow star is again part of the Jew's garb. An order was issued today that all Jews, regardless of age or gender, must wear a 10-centimeter armband—of "Jewish-yellow" color—on the right arm, directly below the armpit. In addition, Jews are to observe a curfew from 5 p.m. to 8 a.m.

FRIDAY, NOVEMBER 17, 1939—LODZ

The mood in town is depressed. It's hard getting used to the idea of being persecuted. The Germans are on the lookout for provocations from "yellow-armbanded Jews." There's a lot of opportunity now to ridicule and provoke. It'll be interesting to see how the Poles react. Will they join the German rabble?

The required armbands were prepared at home.

SATURDAY, NOVEMBER 18, 1939—LODZ

The Poles lower their eyes when they see Jews wearing yellow stars. Acquaintances console us that it will not be for long. Meanwhile, the Germans show complete indifference. The curfew for Poles and Germans has been changed: they may go out at 6 a.m. (it was 5 a.m. before), but now they can stay out till

8:30 p.m. (it was 8 before). We can stay locked in our homes from 5 p.m. It doesn't matter. There will be better times!

LODZ, DECEMBER 6, 1939

The first Chanukah candle was lit. Father made a hole in a potato, poured in some oil, inserted a wick of braided cotton, and lit it. All our Jewish neighbors are waiting for a new Chanukah miracle. Maybe the fervent prayers of millions of Jews to be liberated will be answered! We have a buyer for our wardrobe and couch, who will give us 130 zlotys for both pieces. (They cost us 350 zlotys.) He is a German, a very decent man, known for his kindness toward Jews. Father is trying to secure a permit from the authorities allowing him to make the sale so that he can pay the rent.

THURSDAY, DECEMBER 7, 1939—LODZ

The ZUS administration gave its permission to sell the furniture. Father is still worried constantly; he gets upset very easily. I wish everything could finally be taken care of. Everyone is surprised that nothing's been heard about Hitler lately. There is speculation that he is dead or removed from power. There is news that Germany has suffered heavy defeats in the air and at sea.

LODZ, DECEMBER 8, 1939

The cupboard-wardrobe was finally sold and rent paid till Dec. 31. There are new rumors of all kinds, probably just gossip.

LODZ, DECEMBER 9, 1939

Today we heard about Jews being badly beaten on Reymont Square yesterday; even 3-year-old children were kicked. Jews are now living on messianic prophesies. A rabbi has said that on the 6th day of Chanukah a judgment, and liberation, will occur. Uncle says there are few Germans and not many soldiers on the streets. I'm annoyed by such talk, would prefer to hear nothing.

LODZ, DECEMBER 10, 1939

A great many of the large buildings in the city center have been "cleared" of Jews, and there's talk of sending a large number of Jews from Lodz to the Protectorate—not a pleasant prospect.

LODZ, DECEMBER 11, 1939

Father came home with the news that starting today at 6 p.m. Jews will be deported from Lodz. All the neighbors packed bags, bundles, etc., and we did also, but nothing happened, and everyone eventually went to bed.

LODZ, DECEMBER 12, 1939

I saw a frightful sight. A Jew was being hit with a huge pole by a German. The Jew kept bending lower and lower without turning around, so as not to be hit from the front.

A new order was issued today: The yellow patches are to be removed, and 10 cm. yellow Stars of David are to be worn on the right chest and on the right side of the back.

LODZ, DECEMBER 13, 1939

There was more fear and anxiety when Dadek Hamer came to tell us that Jews are being driven into the empty market halls in Nowo-Zarzewska Street, to be sent into the Lublin district.

This evening we heard that the Jewish community administration has announced that the Jews must leave Lodz. Apparently, during the next four days, anyone can leave for any destination, except the Reich, and after that mass deportations will begin. The community administration will give the poor 50 zl. each and has started sending them out as of today. There is terrible panic in town, everyone has lost his head, but knapsacks and bundles are being packed.

LODZ, DECEMBER 14, 1939

Mass arrests continue into the third day: thousands of teachers, doctors, engineers with families (babies included) are driven into the empty market halls and then to German prisons. The same happens to old activists, former legionnaires, even ordinary rich men. Quite often, groups of important people are dispatched to their death.

It seems that Lodz is really going to be cleared of Jews. For the time being, only the poor are registering. They get 50 zl. per person and are literally thrown out of town: first transported by rail to Koluszki and from there let go.

LODZ, DECEMBER 15, 1939

It gets worse all the time. Last night some Jews were evicted from a few places in Baluty and sent to the Reich. It's not known where they are, or what happened to them. Everywhere people have their bags packed with essentials. Everyone is very nervous.

LODZ, DECEMBER 17, 1939

The Jews are to remain in town till March 1, and then—out! They say that 80 frozen babies from Koluszki were sent to Lodz today. These babies belong to deported Jews.

LODZ, DECEMBER 31, 1939

The last day of 1939, a year that began with tension and ended with war. Let's hope next year will be better, for no one knows what awaits us.

*   *   *

MARCH 21, 1942

This evening there was suddenly news that another 15,000 are to be deported immediately, in groups of a thousand a day. Everyone is saying that now all the ghetto's inhabitants will go.

MARCH 25, 1942

I feel very sick. I read but can't study at all, so I'm working on English vocabulary. Among other things, I was studying Schopenhauer. Philosophy and hunger, some combination.

MARCH 26, 1942

Again, total confusion. The deportations are continuing, while at the same time the shops are receiving huge orders and there's enough work for a few months.

MARCH 28, 1942

Today we bought an étagère (my pre-war dream) and a kitchen table with drawers from our neighbors who are being deported. These—and some other household items—all for two packs of local cigarettes.

MARCH 30, 1942

Aside from the deported, a number of people have left in the last few days, taken out by relatives (for big money).

APRIL 9, 1942

Rumkowski made a long speech today but said nothing of importance. It's the demagoguery of a megalomaniac.

APRIL 19, 1942

Mother cried when I came home today. She's the only one in our family who [as unemployed] is in danger. Father, whose rage intensifies all the time, revealed his true nature today. He wants to get rid of Mother, as he has not even lifted a finger to do anything for her. All he does is scream at her and annoy her on purpose.

Oh, if only things with Mother were different: the poor, weak, beloved, broken, unhappy being! As if she didn't have enough trouble, she has to put up with these noisy quarrels (which according to Father are due to my "indifference" toward the family, or rather toward him). If we could only save her. We'll settle with Father after the war.

Since Mother isn't feeling well, she's decided to give my father only 25 dkg. of bread from her loaf (rather than the 50 dkg. she used to). He doesn't like it, but he's probably figured out that if she were not around he'd have even less.

APRIL 20, 1942

The ghetto is going crazy. Thousands of those at risk are struggling every which way to get jobs, mostly through influence. Meanwhile, the German commission started its work. All those examined by the commission get an indelible letter stamped on their chests, a letter whose significance nobody knows.

APRIL 23, 1942

Last night the police went through apartments. Those who have not reported to the commission and could offer no excuse had to give up their bread and food ration cards. Today there were round-ups in the streets. There's talk that soon the entire population of the ghetto will be stamped.

Another group of people left today by bus, to join relatives in Warsaw. They say that things in Warsaw are wonderful. The ghetto is open, and one can buy anything for money; work is paid for, and it's easy to get. Meanwhile we perish here.

APRIL 24, 1942

A commission came to our shop today, and they stopped by our room. These people come from another world—these rulers, these masters of life and death. Their look doesn't in the least suggest a quick end to the war.

APRIL 29, 1942

Again I have no desire, actually no strength to study. Time is passing, as is my youth, my energy and enthusiasm. The devil knows what will be rescued from this pogrom. I'm gradually losing hope that I shall come back to life, or be able to hold on to the one I am now living.

MAY 7, 1942

Things in the ghetto are ever more scandalous, but we are now in such a state of exhaustion that I truly understand what it means to lack the strength to complain, let alone protest.

MAY 18, 1942

In the last few days, with frightening speed, my legs have become weak. I almost cannot walk because it tires me so. Still I can't avoid it, since my unit works on the third floor.

MAY 21, 1942

Again, life has been extended for a time: on, from day to day, from one food ration to the next, more deportations and more new arrivals into the ghetto, until . . .

SATURDAY, MAY 30, 1942

Our situation at home is again getting extremely tense and awful. Father, who for the last two weeks was relatively peaceful and divided his bread into equal daily portions, lost his self-control again on Thursday and ate my entire loaf yesterday and today finished the extra half kilo of bread he gets from Mother and Nadzia. He also stole another 10 dkg. from them when he weighed the bread. I don't know why he hoards all the money, or why he takes Mother's and Nadzia's wages. He doesn't want to give us any money to buy rations. Today he went to get the sausage ration and ate over 5 dkg. on the street (Nadzia saw him), so that we were all short-changed. He has also managed to borrow 10 dkg. of bread from Nadzia. (Foolish girl!) I took tomorrow's portion of bread and half of Monday's with me to the shop. I'll do so every day from now on.

Father bought meat today, and with the liter of whey he got for the whole family, he cooked and guzzled it all up. Now there is nothing left for us, so we'll go to bed without supper. Mother looks like a cadaver, and the worrying is finishing her off.

MAY 31, 1942

In the evening when I returned from the shop I was missing a few teaspoons of honey (which we received instead of marmalade), and Mother was missing even more honey.

JUNE 11, 1942

The days pass imperceptibly, and no change is visible. The food supply has improved; however, the specter of next winter is confronting everybody. Everyone realizes all too well that he won't last through the winter (I'm not talking about those who gorge themselves, of course)—and pessimism is getting worse all around. "Either the war will end before the winter, or we will." It's true: we're pushing on with our last strength.

JUNE 26, 1942

Today I heard that two people went to Warsaw. Apparently, one of them ate so much the day he got there that he was in bed with a high fever for a week. At least he felt full, something I haven't experienced in two years.

MONDAY, JULY 14, 1942

It seems that last year Rumkowski said that he couldn't save everyone and, therefore, instead of having the entire population die a slow death, he would save the "top ten thousand."

JULY 27, 1942

Apparently, they're deporting a huge number of Jews (ten thousand a day) from Warsaw. Accompanying this, of course, were pogroms, and those being deported were shot. The Eldest there committed suicide. However, they didn't go through the kind of extreme suffering we have had, and there is no end for us yet.

TUESDAY, SEPTEMBER 1

The first day in this new, fourth year of the war has brought the terrible news that the Germans have emptied all the ghetto's hospitals.

In the morning, the areas around the hospitals were surrounded by guards. All the sick, without exception, were loaded on trucks and taken out of the ghetto. There was a terrible panic, because it's no secret, thanks to people who've recently come from the provinces, how the Germans "take care" of such evacuees. Hellish scenes occurred during the moving of the sick. People knew that they were going to their death! They fought the Germans, and were thrown onto the trucks by force. In the meantime, a good many of the sick escaped from the hospitals which the Germans got to a little later. It's said that even the sick in the Marysin preventorium were shipped out. In our office nobody could think about work (I'm now in an office which distributes payments to the families of people working in Germany). It seems no work was done in other offices and factories, either. People are fearing for their children and for the elderly who aren't working.

WEDNESDAY, SEPTEMBER 2

Having discovered that many of the sick escaped, the Germans are demanding they be brought back. On the basis of hospital records, the homes of the escapees' relatives have been searched and the sick captured. On this occasion, the Jewish police committed a crime unlike anything, it seems to me, committed previously in the ghetto.

The Germans demanded a full complement of all those on the hospital registers. The police found a novel way of doing the job, following instructions from people with influence to spare any of their relatives who escaped. They went to the homes of other sick people, namely those already deported, and asked where the sick could be found. When the unfortunate families answered that the sick were most probably deported, since they had never come back, the police detained some of these relatives as hostages, until the "escapees" were turned in. And when the Germans sent in vehicles today to fetch the rest of the sick, some of these hostages were included among them, as substitutes for sick people with influential relatives.

The mood is still panicky, though things progress their normal way. It feels as though something is hanging in the air.

THURSDAY, SEPTEMBER 3

It seems the Germans have asked that all children up to the age of 10 be delivered, most probably to be murdered. The situation resembles what happened in all the surrounding small towns prior to deportations and differs only in the precision and subtlety which prevails here. There, everything was sudden and unexpected.

FRIDAY, SEPTEMBER 4

There is terrible panic. No work is being done anywhere. Everyone is trying to get jobs for those not working. Parents are trying everything possible to save their children. The registrar's office was sealed after the lists were completed. Now any attempt at falsifying birth certificates, registry books or other documents is for naught. Today in our office job assignments were given out in great haste, even though there is talk that they're meaningless, because there will be orders confining everyone indoors. That way medical teams can decide who is fit for work.

As an office worker, I was able, despite great difficulty, to get a job in the furniture factory for my mother. In spite of this, I'm terribly worried about her, because she is emaciated and weak. She's not sick though and has worked in the vegetable gardens on the outskirts of the ghetto all along, and she cooks, cleans and does laundry at home.

In the morning, children between 8 and 10 were registered at the school office for work, but at 12 o'clock it was announced that these registration lists would be void. At 2 o'clock our office was closed, and we were all told to go home until further notice. All factories, offices and agencies were closed, except for food supply, sanitation wagons, police, firemen and various guards. Panic is increasing by the minute.

At 4 o'clock Rumkowski and Warszawski, the head of many factories, spoke at 13 Lutomierska. They said: Sacrificing the children and the elderly is necessary, since nothing can be done to prevent it. Therefore, please do not hinder our effort to carry out this action of deporting them from here.

It's easy for them, since they're able to get the Germans to agree not to take the children of factory heads, firemen, police, doctors, instructors, bureaucrats, and the devil knows who else. All kinds of favoritism will also be set in motion, and the Germans will get entirely different people than the 25,000 they've demanded, people who are fit for work but who'll be sacrificed for the elderly and children with pull.

In the evening, my father's cousin came to us with her 3-year-old girl, trying to save her. We agreed they could stay and later took in her whole family as well, because they're afraid to stay home, in case they're taken as hostages for the child.

Later there was an air raid; a few bombs were dropped, producing sounds that were bliss for every Jew in the ghetto.

SATURDAY, SEPTEMBER 5

My saintly, beloved, worn-out, blessed MOTHER has fallen prey to the bloodthirsty Nazi beast!!!!

In the morning fright enveloped the town, as news spread that last night some children and elderly were taken from their homes and placed in empty hospitals, from which they'll be deported beginning Monday, at a rate of 3,000 a day.

After 2 p.m., vehicles with medical examiners, police, firemen and nurses drove into our street, and the raid began. The house across from us was surrounded and after an hour and a half three children were brought out. The cries, screams and struggles of the mothers and everybody else on our street was indescribable. The children's parents were completely frantic.

While all of this was going on, two doctors, two nurses, a few firemen and policemen quite unexpectedly came to our house. They had a list of the tenants in every apartment. The doctors, sour and angry, from Prague, began examining everyone very thoroughly, despite objections from the police and nurses. They fished out many "sick and unfit" people, as well as those they described as "reserve." My unlucky, dearest mother was among the latter, which is no consolation, since they were all taken together to the hospital at 34 Lagiewnicka.

Our neighbor, 70-year-old Mr. Miller, the uncle of the ghetto's chief doctor, was spared, and my healthy though exhausted mother took his place!! The doctor who examined her, an old geezer, looked and looked for some ailment, and when he was surprised he couldn't find any, said to his companion, in Czech, "Very weak, very weak." He wrote down those two wretched words, despite protests from the police and nurses present. These doctors apparently didn't know what they were doing, because they also took David Hammer, a 20-year-old who has never been sick in his life. Thanks to his cousin, who's an official, he was re-examined and released, and the two doctors were denounced to the Chairman and not allowed to examine anyone else. But what good is this to me? My mother fell into the trap, and I very much doubt anything will save her.

After my mother's examination and while she was frantically running around the house, begging the doctors to save her life, my father was eating soup. True, he was a bit bewildered and approached the police and the doctors, but he didn't run outside to beg people he knew in power to intercede on her behalf. In short, he was glad to be rid of a wife with whom life was lately getting too hard, a fact which Mother had to struggle with. I swear on all that is holy that if I knew Mother would not be sent to her death, that she'd survive after all, I'd be very pleased with things the way they are.

My little, exhausted mother, who has suffered so much misfortune and whose life has been one long sacrifice for family and others, would probably not have been taken because of weakness had she not been robbed of food by my father and Nadzia. My poor mother, who always believed in God and accepted everything that came her way, kept her clarity of mind even now, in spite of her great agitation. With a certain resignation and a heart-rending logic, she spoke to us about her fate. She agreed when I said that she'd given her life by lending and giving away so much food, but she said it in such a way that I knew she had no regrets, for even though she loved life dearly, there were things to value greater than life itself—such as God and family. She kissed each one of us goodbye, took a bag with some bread and potatoes in it, because I forced her to, and left quickly to meet her terrible fate.

I could not muster the strength to look at her through the window, or to cry. I was like a stone. Every now and then nervous spasms gripped my heart, my mouth and my hands. I thought my heart would break, but it did not. It allowed me to eat, think, talk and go to bed.

Up till now I've considered myself an egoist where life was concerned. However, I'm not sure that it would make that much difference to me if I went to death together with my mother.

It exceeds human endurance to have heard the words Mother said before she was taken and to know that she is an innocent victim. It's true she was designated for the reserve contingent, but our officials will give away the healthiest reserve for the infirm whom they protect. Cursed capitalistic world!

Hala Wolman came to see us in the evening. She works as a nurse in the hospital Mother was taken to. She consoles us that Mother is scheduled for a reexamination and that she'll be released. But nothing can make me happy now, because I know what it means when thousands of condemned have pull—and reserve victims are put in their place.

Nadzia cried, screamed and carried on, but that hardly moves anyone now. I am silent and near insanity.

SUNDAY, SEPTEMBER 6

Yesterday afternoon notices were posted that from 5 p.m. until further notice no one may leave his apartment without a pass from the police. Excepting, of course, these, those, the others, and so on! Apparently, there is going to be a serious raid. At night a great many people were taken in other neighborhoods, but ours was relatively quiet. So far, all this is being done without the Germans and without slaughter—the one thing everyone fears. But let it happen—if only Mother could be returned to me!

Today, at 6:30 I went to Hala Wolman and took a towel, some soap and clean underwear for Mother—articles she requested yesterday through Hala, who promised she'll do everything she can to have Mother re-examined and released. Father, apparently moved by his conscience overnight, went to two or three acquaintances in the morning, seeking help—to no avail, of course.

Tonight there was no air raid and little said about miracles coming to us from the outside.

The heat is still extraordinary. In spite of the ban, people are running around the streets, everyone seeking help in his adversity. Now there is talk that the Germans are accompanying the medical teams, and they are deciding who should go and who should stay. All children previously exempted have now been told to report to one hospital, and though Rumkowski insists that the children's registers are iron-clad, no one believes him. Even policemen, instructors and managers are despairing. The cries, mad screaming and wailing are now so common that not much attention is paid to them. Why should I be moved by some other mother's cries, when they've taken my own mother away? No revenge would be enough for this deed!

On Bazarna Street huge gallows have been erected to hang some people from Pabianice who ran away before it was cleared of Jews. The devil knows why they need these gallows.

People who are hiding children in attics, lavatories and other holes are losing their heads in despair. Our street, which is very near the hospital, is filled all day with the wails of passing funeral processions, which follow the wagons of victims.

In the evening my father was able to get to Mother. He said the hospital is real hell—everyone is in terrible condition, everything is confused. Mother, apparently, is changed beyond recognition, which narrows her slim chance for release.

At times I get such jitters and heart spasms that I think I'm going insane or entering delirium. In spite of this, I cannot stop thinking of Mother, and suddenly I find myself, as though I were split in two, inside her mind and body. The hour of her deportation is approaching with no rescue in sight.

It rained a bit this evening, with some thunder and lightning, which did not lessen our suffering any. Even a torrential rain could not renew a torn heart.

The Sunflower

Simon Wiesenthal

Simon Wiesenthal, the most famous Nazi hunter, was born in 1908 near Lvov, Poland. He was educated as an architect and was working in a firm in Lvov when the Soviet army occupied the territory and began its reign of anti-Semitism. When the Soviets were replaced by the Nazis, conditions for Jews became even more difficult. Wiesenthal arranged for his wife to obtain falsified papers and pass as Aryan. He, however, was sent to a series of concentration camps and barely survived his experiences. Once the war ended, Wiesenthal assisted the U.S. Army's efforts to identify and bring to trial Nazi war criminals. He has continued his quest to bring former Nazis and their collaborators to justice. Currently, Wiesenthal runs the Jewish Documentation Center in Vienna, which serves as the nerve center for the identification and tracking of former Nazis. He is the author of numerous books, including *The Murders among Us, Krystyna: The Tragedy of the Polish Resistance*, and *The Sunflower*, a collection of personal narratives about the Holocaust from which the following excerpt is taken.

In this powerful excerpt, Wiesenthal provides a glimpse of a child's precarious existence in a ghetto.

The children in the Ghetto grew up quickly, they seemed to realise how short their existence would be. For them days were months, and months were years. When I saw them with toys in their hands, they looked unfamiliar, uncanny, like old men playing with childish things.

When had I first seen Eli? When did I talk to him for the first time? I could not remember. He lived in a house near the Ghetto gate. Sometimes he wandered right up to the gate. On one occasion I heard a Jewish policeman talking to him and that is how I knew his name—Eli. It was rarely that a child dared to approach the Ghetto gate. Eli knew that. He knew it from instinct without understanding why.

"Eli" is a pet name for Elijah—Eljahu Hanavi, the prophet.

Recalling the very name awoke memories in me of the time when I too was a child. At the Passover Seder, there stood on the table among the dishes a large, ornate bowl of wine which nobody was allowed to touch. The wine was meant for Eljahu Hanavi. After a special prayer one of us children was sent to open the door: the Prophet was supposed to come into the room and drink the wine reserved for him. We children watched the door with eyes large with wonder. But, of course, nobody came. But my grandmother always assured me that the Prophet actually drank from the cup and when I looked into the cup and found that it was still full, she said: "He doesn't drink more than a tear!"

Why did she say that? Was a tear all that we could offer the Prophet Elijah? For countless generations since the exodus from Egypt we had been celebrating the Passover in its memory. And from that great event arose the custom of reserving a cup of wine for Eljahu Hanavi.

We children looked on Eljahu as our protector, and in our fancy he took every possible form. My grandmother told us that he was rarely recognisable; he might appear in the form of a village peasant, a shopkeeper, a beggar or even as a child. And in gratitude for the protection that he afforded us he was given the finest cup in the house at the Seder service filled with the best wine—but he drank no more than a single tear from it.

Little Eli in the Ghetto survived miraculously the many raids on the children, who were looked upon as "non-working, useless mouths." The adults worked all day outside the Ghetto, and it was during their absence that the SS usually rounded up the children and took them away. A few always escaped the body-snatchers for the children learnt how to hide themselves. Their parents built hiding holes under the floors, in the stoves or in cupboards with false walls, and in time they developed a sort of sixth sense for danger, no matter how small they were.

But gradually the SS discovered the cleverest hiding places and they came out the winners in this game of hide-and-seek with death.

Eli was one of the last children that I saw in the Ghetto. Each time I left the camp for the Ghetto—for a period I had an entry permit for it—I looked for Eli. If I saw him I could be sure that for the moment there was no danger. There was already famine at that time in the Ghetto, and the streets were littered with people dying of hunger. The Jewish policemen constantly warned Eli's parents to keep him away from the gate, but in vain. The German policeman at the Ghetto gate often gave him something to eat.

One day when I entered the Ghetto Eli was not by the gate but I saw him later. He was standing by a window and his tiny hand was sweeping up something from the sill. Then his fingers went to his mouth. As I came closer I realised what he was doing, and my eyes filled with tears: he was collecting the crumbs which somebody had put out for the birds. No doubt he figured that the birds would find some nourishment outside the Ghetto, from friendly people in the city who dare not give a hungry Jewish child a piece of bread.

Outside the Ghetto gate there were often women with sacks of bread or flour trying to barter with the inmates of the Ghetto, food for clothes, silver plate or carpets. But there were few Jews left who possessed anything they could barter with.

Eli's parents certainly had nothing to offer in exchange for even a loaf of bread.

SS Group Leader Katzmann—the notorious Katzmann—knew that there must still be children in the Ghetto in spite of repeated searches so his brutish brain conceived a devilish plan: he would start a kindergarten! He told the Jewish Council that he would set up a kindergarten if they could find accommodation for it and a woman to run it. Then the children would be looked after while the grown-ups were out at work. The Jews, eternal and incorrigible optimists, took this as a sign of a more humane attitude. They even told each other that there was now a regulation against shooting. Somebody said that he had heard on the American radio that Roosevelt had threatened the Germans with reprisals if any more Jews were killed. That was why the Germans were going to be more humane in future.

Others talked of an International Commission which was going to visit the Ghetto. The Germans wanted to show them a kindergarten—as proof of their considerate treatment of the Jews.

An official from the Gestapo named Engels, a greyhaired man, came with a member of the Jewish Council to see for himself that the kindergarten was actually set up in suitable rooms. He said he was sure there were still enough children in the Ghetto who would like to use the kindergarten, and he promised an extra ration of food. And the Gestapo did actually send tins of cocoa and milk.

Thus the parents of the hungry children still left were gradually persuaded to send them to the kindergarten. A committee from the Red Cross was anxiously awaited. But it never came. Instead, one morning three SS trucks arrived and took all the children away to the gas chambers. And that night, when the parents came back from work, there were heart-rending scenes in the deserted kindergarten.

Nevertheless, a few weeks later I saw Eli again. His instinct had made him stay at home on that particular morning.

In the Ghetto

Harry Gordon

Harry Gordon was born in 1925 in Lithuania, where
his education was limited to five years of elementary
school. After the war, he immigrated to the United
States, settling in Wisconsin, where he started a
recycling business in 1955. Gordon's memoirs,
written in Yiddish in the 1950s and published in *The
Shadow of Death: The Holocaust in Lithuania*,
represent the type of literature that reflects the
recollections of ordinary people who were often
described as humble members of the community.

This excerpt from *The Shadow of Death* describes
the early days in the ghettos, when the inhabitants
had to become accustomed to restricted movement
and constant danger.

The ghetto fences were locked and no one could
leave at all. There were a lot of people who didn't have any rooms to move into,
so many people were lying in the streets and many families were living all together in one room. But the Jews didn't lose hope. Everybody thought this was
not for long, that we would be left alive over our murderers. All our Jewish politicians (everybody became a politician) became colossal optimists. Everyone
would tell you what you wanted to hear. Each was trying to cheer you up and to
cheer himself up.

There were two ghettos behind the fences, a little one and a big one, connected by a bridge, and about 30,000 Jews. On the bridge was a Lithuanian with
a gun. We could walk from the big to the little ghetto only between 6:00 AM and
8:00 PM. If anyone was seen after 9:00 P.M. outside his house, he was shot to

death on the spot. The fence surrounding the ghetto had electric wiring so that if anybody tried to run he would be electrocuted. On the other side of the ghetto fence there were Lithuanian partisans and German guards every five meters with big searchlights.

We lived in the little ghetto at 27 Paneriu Street, which was close to the fence. Every morning Lithuanian partisans and Germans came into the ghetto to catch people to work. After work they would bring them back, some still able to walk, others beaten up and bloody. The catching of men to work took several hours. This we knew because we were close to the fence. In these hours we would hide in the attic. When we saw that they had gotten enough people, we would come down from the attic and wait for night.

Nearly every night, around 1:00 AM, the guards would start shooting. They kept pounding and shooting just to keep us in panic, to keep us scared so we wouldn't know what to think or be able to get together and organize to rebel, to make a stand against the Germans. And so it was; all this fear kept us disoriented—it didn't even occur to us to fight back. The only thing we could feel was the terror that we would soon be dead.

The Germans came to the conclusion that they shouldn't have to run every day to catch Jews to work. They decided they would create a Jewish government, a Jewish Presidium of elders and Jewish police who would be responsible to the Germans. They would tell them that they wanted 500 Jews to work and the Jewish government would be responsible for delivering 500 people. The man chosen as chairman was Dr. Elkes, a very intelligent, a very honorable man. He was assisted by five others. Yakov Goldberg was head of the labor office and Pavel Margolis was in charge of recruiting workers. The better positions went to the family and friends of these officials.

This group started the Jewish police for the ghetto. The Germans knew that if they gave these particular people a little more food they would be able to get anything out of them, whether information or getting them to do whatever they wanted them to do. And that was the way it was.

The Germans also began to organize stores in the ghetto—not places where you could buy anything, but more like factories where things were made and distributed. Each Jew got a ration card. We went to the stores, showed our card, and got our rations for the week: a four pound loaf of bread, two and a half ounces of salad, a pound of horsemeat, and, once a month, a little marmalade. They would bring in the dead horses shot at the front line and prepare them in the ghetto.

In short, the Germans built a little Jewish state. Nobody believed, even the Jewish government and police, that the Germans would leave it to them to rule the whole ghetto. The Germans, however, understood what they were doing.

All over the ghetto, the police went from one house to another to register everyone. All of the lists with names and numbers of people were given to the Germans. Using those lists the Germans would send in just enough food and decide how many Jews they wanted delivered to work. The Jewish police delivered to the Germans exactly the number of people needed, rounding them up any way they could, beating and kicking those who didn't want to go. They were living well while the rest of us were either running around confused or trying to hide ourselves to stay out of the way of the work patrols. It wasn't long before the Jewish police had an opportunity to profit even more from our misery.

The Collection of Valuables

Harry Gordon

Harry Gordon's memoirs were written in Yiddish in
the 1950s and published in *The Shadow of Death: The
Holocaust in Lithuania*, from which the following
excerpt is taken. For additional biographical
information on Gordon, see page 139.

In this recollection, Gordon describes how
ghetto residents were forced by the Nazis to hand
over anything of monetary value.

We had hoped to hold onto what little property
we had, but at the beginning of September an order appeared that all valuables
must be delivered to the Jewish council on September 4, under an order from
the Germans. After that the Gestapo would come with bloodhounds and go
from house to house looking for any hidden valuables. If they found any at all,
they would shoot not only everyone in the household but everyone on the whole
block. It was the middle of the week. The sky was covered with dark clouds and
that was how everyone felt at the time. Everyone was scared, not so much about
himself as that maybe his brother or neighbor would try to hide something.

The Jewish police went all over the ghetto trying to tell everyone not to hide
anything but to give it up voluntarily. Each block had a depository and everyone
went to it to give up everything he had. There were long lines with each person
holding something in his hands—his wife's diamond or a gold watch, or carrying
a fur coat on his shoulder. On everyone's face one could read, "Maybe this is
going to help. We have given up everything we have. Maybe this will buy our
lives." On the other hand, everyone was thinking, "Look at these things, at the
fur coat I have worked hard for, and now I have to give it to the murderers. But if
I could buy my life. . . ." It really meant nothing. Today the valuables, tomorrow
our lives.

When we moved to the ghetto, my uncles and aunts buried all their valuables in the garage. They took a sheet metal bathtub and dug a hole under the pile of firewood, placed all their furs and valuables in the tub, and buried it, covering it with the firewood. When the order came, we had to take all the firewood off again, uncover the tub, and take it all to the murderers. My aunts were screaming and crying, not so much because of the worth of the gold and diamonds as because of the sentimental value. When Aunt Ettel had married, Uncle Abraham had given her a brooch, earrings, and a diamond wedding ring; but my uncle said to her, "If you are going to be alive you will have other jewels and fur coats, but if you are not going to be alive, what good are the diamonds and furs?" His words didn't help, for she was still crying.

The aunts discussed the situation, saying, "Why did we even dig it up? The Germans were not going to find it anyway." For a while it seemed that we were going to bury it again, but the uncles said no, that we were going to give it all to the Germans, and that's the way it was done.

I went to the depository carrying a box that held my aunts' diamond rings or some other valuables. I didn't know what was in it for sure, but it seemed to weigh a few pounds. Uncle Abraham was carrying the fur coats. As we came to the depository, we got in line and from the side saw Jewish police standing to keep order. I kept staring at the box; it was bothering me that I would soon have to give the box to the Germans. We saw that the Jewish police took some things from people standing in line, saying that they would take it to the depository, but instead of turning it in, as they went through the back door of the depository they would put it in their pockets. They took the valuables from their brothers to their own homes and hid them. Their homes were not searched by the Germans.

We were surprised that there were no German guards, only Jews. As we approached the depository, there was a thin older Jewish man sitting by a little table who wrote down whatever was turned in and gave each person a receipt. Inside the depository Jewish police walked around whispering to each other. For them it was just like Christmas in the United States. As Uncle Abraham and I left the depository with a piece of paper in our hands, we did not say a word to each other; we just looked at each other and went home.

When we came into the house, the aunts gave us resentful looks, but they were quiet. They wanted us to talk, but we didn't say anything either. That silence must have held for at least a half an hour, until Aunt Golda jumped up with a question: "Well, did the Germans search you in the depository?" Uncle Abraham answered, "In the depository there were no Germans, only our own Jews who took our gold and everything away from us. Here is the piece of paper they gave us."

Aunt Golda spoke with a harsh voice, "You see? I told you before—I hope that I am lying—that that was only to scare us so we would give everything up right away. The Jewish police wanted our valuables. I'll bet you the Germans won't even come to search our houses and I'll bet you that the one who hides his valuables will have a lot easier life in the ghetto, not like us, the stupid ones. We went and dug it up from the ground and gave it right to the devil in his hands. Even if the Germans do come, they wouldn't ever have found it. But now it is too late. Why should I eat my heart out? It's too late. It is all done."

Everybody sat very quietly with a hangdog look, heads down. Nobody had any words to answer. I could tell that the uncles felt sorry and knew they had made a mistake. Later on it really showed; those who had all their valuables hidden lived pretty well because they could bribe their way out of being sent to work outside the ghetto.

After three days, German SS men came with bloodhounds, looking for valuables. Half the ghetto had hidden their valuables but only a few families were found out. Those families were executed in their homes. While the Germans were looking for valuables, if they saw nice furniture, they would tell people to put it onto the street. Then big trucks pulled up and took it to the houses where the Germans lived.

When my uncles heard that the dogs were running around searching for valuables, they felt better, but my Aunt Golda didn't talk about valuables any more. We knew that she felt in her heart that we had made a mistake.

When the collection was over, life in the ghetto became again as before, with the Jewish police catching people to work. But this didn't last long. The Germans wanted to see how the Jews would react if they tried to pull people out of the ghetto and kill them. They wanted to see if the Jews would fight or just go like sheep to the slaughter.

Volunteers

Vladka Meed

Vladka Meed was the "Aryan" name that Feigel
Peltel-Miedzyrzecki took when she left the Warsaw
ghetto. Born in Poland in 1922, she was an active
member of the Polish underground throughout the
Nazi occupation, although she was only seventeen
when the Nazis first arrived. Her Aryan appearance
and ability to speak fluent Polish helped her to be an
effective member of the underground. She served as
a courier, helping Jews to escape and smuggling
guns into the ghetto. She is the author of *On Both
Sides of the Wall: Memoirs from the Warsaw Ghetto*,
which was originally published in Yiddish in 1948
and from which the following excerpt is taken.

The following excerpt from Meed's memoirs
presents an ironic view of volunteering.

Ten days since the deportations had begun—
could it have been so short a time? We had been through so much . . .

Thousands upon thousands of Jews had already been deported and there was
no reliable knowledge of their whereabouts. Some still thought the deportees
had been assigned to some kind of work. One rumor was that they had been
dispatched to the city of Smolensk, close to the Russo-German front, to dig
trenches. But by now an ever-growing number of Jews tended to believe the
horrible new rumors that all the German promises were false and that the so-
called "resettlement" actually meant only one thing—death! We fought against
accepting that grisly thought. Our loved ones were among the deportees. No,
they must be alive; they surely must be alive . . . somewhere . . .

Throughout each day, while the raids continued, individuals and small groups of Jews, parents and children, trudged through the comparatively deserted streets, weighed down by bundles, baskets, and battered valises, their last pitiful belongings, towards the *Umschlagplatz*. Some walked slowly with heads bowed; others hurried along, as if pressed for time. No one detained them or barred their way; they were the "volunteers." The ghetto watched their mute, resigned march without surprise. In hiding places and workshops, hearts ached with silent admiration for the strength that had enabled these people to take at least this decisive step. My sister and I could summon no such courage.

Gloom pervaded the ghetto. There was no security whatsoever. Exhausted by privation, emaciated or bloated by hunger, crushed by the incessant fear of being trapped, many simply gave up the struggle. The Germans' diabolic tactics reaped their harvest. Hunger drove famished Jews to the bread line, where each received his three kilograms of bread—before being pushed into the waiting railroad cars. Three kilos of bread loomed very large in the eyes of a starving man. The temptation, even for once, to still that gnawing hunger eclipsed all other considerations, including the dread of the unknown, the destination of the railroad cars. In his tragic helplessness, the victim let himself be lulled by the Germans' soothing promises of an end to his daily struggle for survival. Perhaps it was true, after all, that there would be jobs waiting for them.

Yakub Katz, a barber from Kalisz, an intelligent man whom I knew from my work in the underground, had been driven in 1940, together with his wife and two daughters, from his home to Warsaw, where his family languished in the refugee compound at Leszno 14 for some time. Katz had worked hard, enduring hunger and cold, barely making ends meet, hoping that he and his family would weather the storm. I met him during the early days of the German roundups. Unnerved and starved, he informed me that his wife was ready to surrender to the Germans. "And you?" I asked, astonished. After all, Katz was familiar with the underground press. He knew better than to have any faith in the German promises. What had come over him?

"One can't go on starving forever," he answered gloomily. "We have no strength left to go on. We'll perish here anyway." His sallow, emaciated face and sad, sunken eyes underscored his words. The very next day I learned that he had left the ghetto.

The widow Chaveleh, whose husband had died in the war, came often to our home. She lived at Mila 48, gladly accepting a bowl of soup and a piece of bread in payment for her services as a seamstress. The evening after my mother and brother had been taken away, Chaveleh came to my mother's apartment while I happened to be there. A small, wizened old woman carrying a basket, she halted timidly at the threshold, inquiring after my mother. She had come to beg a few *zloty*—for the last time, she said, adding, "You see, I am about to go to the *Umschlagplatz* to get three kilograms of bread, and perhaps I'll find odd sewing jobs in some other town."

When she learned of our misfortune, her deadened eyes suddenly showed a strange gleam; she seemed jubilant. She had better hurry along, she said, if she wanted to catch up with my mother. It was easier to travel with friends.

Hunger was not the only reason for voluntary surrender. There were Jews who could have remained safely in the ghetto, who had bona fide employment cards, as well as jobs at German factories. They were not crushed by the trying conditions around them. On the contrary, they still harbored a strong will to live, to resist, yet they proceeded voluntarily to the waiting railroad cars. They did this for only one reason: they did not want to be separated from their families.

Abramek Bortenstein had been well aware of the fate that awaited the deportees. He worked at Roerich's factory at Nowolipki 74. He could have obtained an employment card and remained in Warsaw. But during the roundup on Mila Street, when his wife and year-old daughter were threatened with eviction, he had abandoned his job—the only secure place then—and had gone into hiding with his family. Together with a group of other Jews, they had hidden in a loft. The atmosphere in the attic was stifling and the baby whined. The others in the group, fearing that the baby's cries would give them away, forced Abramek and his family to leave the hideout. Meanwhile, out in the street, the Germans continued to "select" the inhabitants of the ghetto: idle Jews to the left, employed to the right. Abramek did not present his employment card, but silently followed his family to the left, rather than forsake them even in the face of death.

Yurek Blones, a classmate of mine, who was to be a participant in the ultimate uprising, was also taken to the *Umschlagplatz* along with his younger brother Lusiek. While some were being loaded into the railroad cars, other young men were singled out and sent back to work. Twenty-two years old and an able auto mechanic, Yurek would have been saved. But his little brother would not have been permitted to remain. Just then Yurek was spotted by a German fellow worker, who motioned him to step aside. "Your services could still be utilized in the factory," he said.

"But what about my little brother?" Yurek countered.

"He has to be deported," was the reply.

"In that case, I'm staying with him; he wouldn't be able to take care of himself."

Yurek and his brother were shoved into a freight car destined for Treblinka. Somehow, Yurek cut a hole in the wall of the car and the two brothers jumped off the speeding train.

Miraculously, they survived and reached Warsaw. I met them shortly after they had smuggled themselves back into the ghetto. Eventually, the two brothers joined the ranks of the resistance organization and distinguished themselves in the Warsaw ghetto uprising.

My sister and I made a similar choice. Learning that the public kitchen on Nowolipki Street, where she was working, was scheduled for a raid, I rushed there to warn her of the imminent danger and pleaded with her to go into hiding with me. We were the only two survivors of our family, I said; we should at least stick together. Either both of us would escape or else we would go down the last road together. She listened attentively, then replied in a trembling voice: "I'm sorry, but I cannot leave my post."

To put my mind at ease, she tried to assure me that the Germans were not likely to bother a working crew. No amount of pleading on my part could dissuade her. That very day, the entire staff of the kitchen was loaded into one of the wagons for deportation. My sister went with them.

Leaving the Ghetto

Vladka Meed

A member of the Polish underground during the war, Vladka Meed is the author of *On Both Sides of the Wall: Memoirs from the Warsaw Ghetto*, which was originally published in Yiddish in 1948 and from which the following excerpt is taken. For additional biographical information on Meed, see page 145.

This excerpt from Meed's memoir tells of her own escape from the ghetto so that she could help those who could not escape.

One evening several weeks later, I heard a knock on my door. In the dim light of the corridor, I did not recognize the tall man asking for me, but I invited him in. It was Michal Klepfisz, an engineer active for many years in the Bund and in *Morgenstern,* a Jewish sports organization.

"Michal, what a pleasant surprise!" I exclaimed. "What brings you here? You've been away from the ghetto for quite a while. How are your wife and child?"

"I've come to take you away, Feigel," he answered. "Get ready; you'll be leaving the ghetto within two days. Meanwhile I'll prepare forged documents for you and try to notify some people in the Polish sector."

My heart seemed to leap into my mouth.

"Get ready," he repeated. "I'll wait for you by the ghetto gate at eight in the morning. You'll have to walk out with a labor battalion on the way to an outside work assignment; that's the best way."

"In case we should miss each other, leave me an addrress where I can find you," I suggested.

He hesitated. "I have no such address yet. I'm still living in someone's cellar. But I'll give you a temporary address, Gornoszlonska 3. Just memorize it; no written notes of any sort."

He could stay no longer, but hurried off to confer with Abrasha. I saw him out into the street, where he joined the last returning labor battalion and disappeared into the night.

I'd be leaving the ghetto in two days! I was aflame with excitement. My coworkers also had an air of secrecy; the first group of resistance fighters had been organized at Toebbens' shop. My head was spinning. Now and then, beyond the ghetto wall running along Zelazna Street, I could make out the movement of adults and children, women carrying baskets, the rushing tempo of life. But here in the ghetto the streets were dead, life was at a standstill. Except for an occasional German patrol, there was seldom a soul in sight.

The thought of escaping from the ghetto kindled new hope among the workers. It seemed the only way to survive. But escape was easier said than done. For one thing, in order to slip across the wall one had to pay an exorbitant sum to the Gentile smugglers. Moreover, while one might bribe the German sentinel, one could never be certain that he might not decide to shoot his victim after all. To walk out with a Jewish labor brigade on the way to an outside work assignment was the only available alternative—but a most dangerous one.

A number of Jews with Aryan features—and well-lined purses—had already attempted to leave the ghetto. Some had been apprehended and either killed on the spot or deported. This did not deter others, and some succeeded in escaping.

Outside the ghetto lay an alien world where one had to seek refuge and contact Gentile friends who might help one obtain forged documents, prepare living quarters, and find a job. Above all, there had to be money—a great deal of money—to pay for every little service. Desperate Jews endeavored to contact Gentile acquaintances on the "other side of the wall," but most of the appeals fell on deaf ears.

Some of those who had succeeded in crossing into the "Aryan sector" returned to the ghetto a few weeks later. They had not been able to cope with the blackmail rampant there.

My way out would be by posing as a member of a labor brigade. No other means of escape was possible. The foremen of the labor gangs employed outside the ghetto were occasionally able to make substitutions for absentees. Such opportunities were rare and expensive. I paid.

I was to take with me the latest issue of the underground bulletin, which carried a detailed description and map of the Treblinka extermination camp. My roommates, aware of my preparations, advised me to hide the bulletin in my shoes. Our leavetaking was tearful. With sad smiles meant to be reassuring, we promised not to forget one another. We parted with handclasps. Would I ever see them again?

December, 5, 1942. At 7:00 a.m. the street was astir with people streaming to work. Brisk bartering went on as Jews traded their last pitiful belongings—a coat, a skirt, an old pair of shoes—to those working on the "Aryan side" for chunks of black bread. Later, the commodities would be smuggled out of the ghetto and sold to Gentile vendors.

After some searching, I found a Jewish leader of a forty-man labor battalion who for 500 zlotys allowed me to join his group. I was the only female in the unit. We marched in column formation to the ghetto gate, where we joined thousands of other laborers, men and women.

The morning guard, heavily reinforced, was busy inspecting the throng. People pushed and jostled wherever they could, hoping to elude the Gestapo scrutiny—to escape to the "Aryan side," to smuggle a few belongings out of the ghetto. The inspection had just started. We waited apprehensively, shivering in the morning frost. One never knew what the Germans might do next.

Some who had just been inspected were retreating, clutching bruised faces. They had been beaten up for carrying items the Germans considered contraband. One was hopping barefoot in the snow; the German had taken a liking to his shoes. Several others, half-undressed, stood trembling in the biting cold, as a warmly-clad German took his time searching them. An old man pleaded with a German trooper that he did not want to be separated from his thirteen-year-old daughter. "She's a regular worker, just like me! Here is her factory card!" he argued heatedly. The soldier rebuffed him brutally. In his despair, the old man looked about with pleading eyes, but no one dared to help him. His daughter was directed aside to a wooden shack from which she gazed forlornly at her father.

My detachment was the next to be inspected. Everything was going smoothly.

"How did you get this woman in here?" the German barked.

"She's employed in the factory kitchen," the group leader explained.

The trooper eyed me with disdain. "I don't like your face," he snapped. "Get in there!" He pointed in the direction of the wooden shack.

"I don't envy her," someone remarked. My blood ran cold at the thought that the underground bulletin might be found on me. In that event the entire labor battalion—not just I—would be detained. Consternation suffused the faces of those around me. A Jewish policeman appeared. The place was swarming with troopers and police; there was no chance of escape.

"Please let me slip out while the German is away." I whispered to the policeman.

"Do you expect me to risk my life for you?" the policeman snapped. "The German will be right back!" At the entrance to the wooden shack lay a man, bruised and bleeding. Off to one side was the young girl. I stood a moment, stunned. The policeman shoved me inside.

I found myself in a dimly lit room, its blood-spattered walls papered with maps, charts, and photographs of half-naked women. Tattered clothing and shoes were strewn about the floor. The only furnishings were a small table and a chair, in the midst of the tangle of discarded apparel—except for the knout that dangled beneath the little window. I stood by the wall and waited. A guard entered and began the interrogation. I fought for control over the terror that seemed about to engulf me.

"Full name."

I answered.

"Place of work."

I named the place for which the battalion was headed.

"I see! Now show me what you are carrying on your person." He pulled off my coat and dress and examined them closely under a light, searching the hems and pockets. My shoes! If he asked about them, I was lost.

"All right, now the shoes!" he demanded.

A chill passed through me. My mind was racing. I started unlacing my shoes slowly, stalling for time. Staring angrily, my interrogator ordered: "Hurry up—stop fiddling around! Let's have those shoes! Do you see this whip?"

As I continued to fumble with the laces, the Nazi seized the whip and started to advance on me.

At that moment, as if miraculously, the door flew open, and someone shouted, "*Herr Leutnant*, please come at once! A Jew has just escaped!"

The officer dashed out, slamming the door behind him. Left alone, I dressed hurriedly and walked through the door.

"Where are you going?" a guard stopped me.

"To the labor battalion," I replied, trying to sound casual. "I have already passed inspection."

The guard eyed me suspiciously for a moment, then waved me on. I was soon swallowed up by the throng on the "Aryan side," about to march out.

Michal Klepfisz was to have been waiting for me at the ghetto gate, but he was nowhere to be seen and I could not linger here, lest my German catch up with me. At last I located the group of laborers with whom I had marched out. They were delighted to see me.

"You're lucky," the group leader told me. "Hardly anyone ever gets out of there unhurt."

Soon we were in a wagon, rolling through the Polish streets. Our white armbands identified us as being Jews. The streets were familiar to me; very little had changed during the past few years. Several Poles chased our wagon, anxious to buy something; but none of us had anything to sell. We were nearing the work project. I racked my brains for a way to break away quickly.

The others, aware that I was on some sort of mission, urged me to discard my armband and jump off the vehicle. Acting on that counsel, I chose a moment when no passersby were in sight and leaped from the slow-moving wagon. I walked away briskly, then turned off into another street and slackened my pace.

Far from the ghetto now, I was free—but my sense of freedom was marred by a strange feeling of restlessness. I was in my own city, but seeing not a single familiar face. Here it was as if nothing had happened in the last two years. Trolleys, automobiles, bicycles raced along; businesses were open; children headed for school; women carried fresh bread and other provisions. The contrast with the ghetto was startling. It was another world, a world teeming with life.

Could the life that I had left behind have been only an illusion? I wondered as I walked the Warsaw streets. How strange and new everything around me was!

At last I arrived at Gornoszlonska 3—the address Michal had given me. I made my way to the cellar, and banged on the door. A blonde woman let me in. Michal was there, to welcome me, relief and joy evident in the warmth of his greeting.

"You're here at last! I was waiting at the gate for hours!"

Michal, along with his landlord, Stephan Machai, had waited at the gate for me since early that morning, and had just gotten back.

"I didn't expect you to venture out today; the guards were very strict," Michal said, after we had regained some composure and were sharing a cup a tea.

I took note of our surroundings: two small, low-ceilinged rooms inhabited by a family of four. Stephan Machai, a Gentile, seemed to like Michal. Before the war they had worked together, he as an unskilled laborer, Michal as an engineer. Now a *ricksha* pusher, the stocky Gentile considered it an honor to have the former engineer as his guest. An old, narrow bunk that Michal used took up half of the kitchen space.

Michal seemed depressed. I asked him what was wrong.

"My sister Gina died in the hospital," he told me quietly. "We're burying her today. If you wish, you can come with me to the cemetery."

I refrained from telling him of the ordeal I had undergone while leaving the ghetto. My experience paled in the presence of death. I had known Gina Klepfisz before the war, having worked with her in the *Zukunft* in a suburb of Praga, where she had organized a children's group. She had been both serious and kindhearted; children adored her. More recently, she had worked as a nurse in the ghetto. Her warm, sympathetic approach to her fellow men and the unique calm with which she met difficult situations had fitted her admirably for such tasks.

Now I had hardly stepped into the Aryan sector, only to hear that she was dead. Michal and I walked silently to the hospital, where he was to meet his wife, Ruszka Perczykow.

Ruszka was all in black, head bowed as she fought back her tears. A nurse led us wordlessly into the morgue. Gina's body was clothed all in white. My eyes were riveted upon this lifeless body—all that remained of the woman whom I remembered as vivacious and energetic, and who, as a hospital employee, had been instrumental in smuggling Jews out of the *Umschlagplatz*. She would steer doomed men and women across the barbed wire, under cover of darkness, at the risk of her own life. On one occasion she had been caught by a Jewish policeman. Her courageous stand had dampened his ire somewhat, but she was dismissed from her job. Thereupon, together with her brother, sister-in-law, and year-old child, she had crossed over to the "Aryan side."

The nurse signaled to us that someone was approaching. We made the sign of the cross, lest anyone suspect that Gina had been Jewish. As a patient, Gina had been registered as a Gentile, under the name Kazimiera Juzwiak; the record had to remain intact. She was to be buried as a Christian.

A small funeral party awaited us at the cemetery. Among them were Yankel Celemenski and Hanka Alexandrowicz. Celemenski had been passing as a Gentile in Cracow—on the Aryan side. He had rescued the thirteen-year-old Hanka from the Cracow ghetto only a few days before. Zygmunt (Zalman Friedrich) was also present. A strange funeral indeed: of the ten mourners following the hearse, only Anna Wonchalska and her sister Marysia Sawicka, were Christians. The funeral was carried out in accordance with Roman Catholic rites. The grave was marked with a cross.

We took our leave of Gina Klepfisz, one of the few Warsaw Jews to be buried in a cemetery at a time when thousands of Jews were being gassed and cremated.

A Cup of Tears

Abraham Lewin

Abraham Lewin was born in Warsaw, Poland, in
1893. Although he and his family had considered
emigrating from Poland to Palestine in 1934, his ill
health precluded their making the move. By 1939,
the invasion of the Nazis made it impossible for them
to leave Warsaw. When Polish Jews were trapped
in the ghettos, Lewin began his meticulously
detailed account of life and death in the Warsaw
ghetto, which was published as *A Cup of Tears: A
Diary of the Warsaw Ghetto*. His diary captures the
daily reality of a community under attack. Lewin was
a member of an underground group established by
the respected historian, Dr. Emmanuel Ringelblum,
to chronicle ghetto life for future generations. The
final entry of Lewin's diary was dated January 16,
1943. After this, it is thought that he and his daughter
were sent to their deaths in the camps.

The following entries from Lewin's diary date
from August 1942, when mass deportations to the
death camps were occurring.

TUESDAY, 11 AUGUST 1942

Things are deteriorating fast. Appalling, horrendous. The brutal expulsion from
the small ghetto. Whole buildings have been emptied of their occupants and all
their possessions left behind. Christians are already beginning to loot. 24 Sienna
Street, 28 Śliska Street. Except for Jakub's family, there is not even a single tenant
remaining in the building; the house-porter is also gone. Aunt Chawa and Dora

Fejga have been seized and deported. The destruction of families. Early this morning the Germans and the rioters spread through the ghetto. By the evening they were distributed throughout the ghetto and were seizing people. In the course of five minutes they drove out all the occupants on Gęsia Street between Zamenhof and Lubiecka Streets. They pay no attention to papers.

The Jewish community offices have moved to 19 Zamenhof Street, the post office building. They have reduced their personnel by half. The number of victims has already risen above 150,000. Today they will complete three weeks since the beginning of the terrible massacre. In the night a large number of women who worked at Többens' were removed. It looks like there is a policy to liquidate women and children. Yesterday at Többens' three Jews died at their work. Blockades and murders in the streets that still belong to the ghetto. The heavy blockade on the entrance to the buildings of the Warschauer Union, with two killed and a vast number seized, nearly 100 women, children and men. The mortal terror that gripped us as we sat in the office.

Smolar rang Sokołów. He was told that those that are deported, or if they are to be deported to Tr., are going to their 'death'. The news that K. brought. In Warsaw there is a Jew by the name of Slawa who has brought reports of Treblinka. Fifteen kilometres before the station at Treblinka the Germans take over the train. When people get out of the train they are beaten viciously. Then they are driven into huge barracks. For five minutes heart-rending screams are heard, then silence. The bodies that are taken out are swollen horribly. One person cannot get their arms round one of these bodies, so distended are they. Young men from among the prisoners are the gravediggers, the next day they too are killed. What horror!

WEDNESDAY, 12 AUGUST 1942

Eclipse of the sun, universal blackness. My Luba was taken away during a blockade on 30 Gęsia Street. There is still a glimmer of hope in front of me. Perhaps she will be saved. And if, God forbid, she is not? My journey to the *Umschlagplatz*—the appearance of the streets—fills me with dread. To my anguish there is no prospect of rescuing her. It looks like she was taken directly into the train. Her fate is to be a victim of the Nazi bestiality, along with hundreds of thousands of Jews. I have no words to describe my desolation. I ought to go after her, to die. But I have no strength to take such a step. Ora—her calamity. A child who was so tied to her mother, and how she loved her.

The 'action' goes on in the town at full throttle. All the streets are being emptied of their occupants. Total chaos. Each German factory will be closed off in its block and the people will be locked in their building. Terror and blackness. And over all this disaster hangs my own private anguish.

THURSDAY, 13 AUGUST 1942

The 23rd day of the slaughter of the Jews of Warsaw. Today about 3,600 people were removed from Többens' buildings, mainly women and children. Today is Ora's fifteenth birthday. What a black day in her life and in my life. I have never experienced such a day as this. Since yesterday I have not shed a single tear. In my pain I lay in the attic and could not sleep. Ora was talking in her sleep: 'mamo, mamusiu, nie odchódź beze mnie!' ['Mother, Mama, don't leave me']. Today I cried a lot, when Gucia came to visit me. I am being thrown out of the flat at 2 Mylna Street: they have already taken most of my things. Those who have survived are thieving and looting insatiably. Our lives have been turned upside down, a total and utter destruction in every sense of the word.

I will never be consoled as long as I live. If she had died a natural death, I would not have been so stricken, so broken. But to fall into the hands of such butchers! Have they already murdered her? She went out in a light dress, without stockings, with my leather briefcase. How tragic it is! A life together of over 21 years (I became close to her beginning in 1920) has met with such a tragic end.

FRIDAY, 14 AUGUST 1942

The last night that I will spend in my war-time flat at 2 Mylna Street. The sight of the streets: the pavements are fenced off, you walk in the middle of the road. Certain streets, such as Nowolipie (on both sides of Karmelicka), Mylna and others are completely closed off with fences and gates and you can't get in there. The impression is of cages. The whole of Jewish Warsaw has been thrown out of the buildings. There is a full-scale relocation of all Jews who have not yet been rounded up and are still in the town. Whole streets that have been given over to the German firms: Müller, Többens, Schultz, Zimmerman, Brauer and others. We have been sold as slaves to a load of German manufacturers. The living-conditions of those in the workshops: hunger and hard labour. Their ration: a quarter kilo of bread a day and a bowl of soup.

The 'action' continues—today is the 23rd day. Yesterday they took away from Többens' workshops about 3,000–4,000 men and women, mostly women and children. This morning the Jewish community-council posted a new announcement: all Jews who live in Biała, Elektoralna, Zielna, Orla, Solna, Leszno, odd numbers in Ogrodowa, Chłodna Streets have to leave their flats by tomorrow, 15 August. Yesterday and today, a huge number of people killed—victims of the blockades. I am moving my things over to Nacia's at 14 Pawia Street.

Setting up of blockades on Nowolipie and Karmelicka Streets. Further victims—there are more deaths today, and very many driven out. There is talk of 15,000. I have heard that measures decreed in the expulsion orders are directed mainly against women and children. The police commandant of the second district is trying to save his wife and children. A new raid on the Jewish Self-help Organization at 25 Nowolipki Street. Dr Bornsztajn and his wife taken away, Elhonen Cajtlin with his son and others. This was carried out by Jewish policemen without the Germans, that is, on their own initiative. Renja Sztajnwajs. I have heard that Yitshak Katznelson's wife and one of his children have been seized. The second day that I am without Luba. I am now also without a place to live. I have nowhere to lay my head. The number rounded up has reached 190,000, just counting those expelled, excluding those who have been killed and those who have been sent to the *Dulag* at 109 Leszno Street.

Every crime in history, like the burning of Rome by Nero, pales into insignificance in comparison with this. Kirzhner has been taken away from work and deported. Together with him they took away a further 28 people. All were aged 35 and over. The same thing has happened, I have learnt, in another *placówka*: 29 people were taken away and deported.

SATURDAY, 15 AUGUST 1942

Today is the 25th day of the bloody 'action' carried out by the butchers. I spent the night at 17 Dzielna Street. The rain of shooting started at half past nine in the evening. Deaths in the street. The whole night incessant movement in and out of the Pawiak. Gutkowski sends his only son, three and a half years old, to the cemetery to have him taken to Czerniaków.

I have nowhere to rest my head at night. Gucia is being thrown out of her flat. Nacia and Frume are not allowed to enter. All the orphanages have been emptied. Korczak went at the head of his children. The pain because of the loss of L. is becoming more intense. My soul can find no peace, for not having gone after her when she was in danger, even though I could also have disappeared and Ora would have been left an orphan. The most terrible thing is that Landau and Sonszajn misled me by saying that Luba wasn't in the queue. Be that as it may, the anguish is terrible and it will never be dimmed.

Rumours about reports arriving from women who were deported from Biała-Podlaska and Białystok.

Today by eight o'clock there was a blockade on Miła, Gęsia, Zamenhof and other streets. 'Our spirit is weary of the killing.' How much longer? Yesterday a huge number of bodies were brought to the cemetery, victims of the blockade of Többens' workshops. Today they were also taking people from the 'shops'. It will soon be seven o'clock and the blockade on Gęsia is still continuing, around our factory. The Jewish police have been looting, breaking open flats, emptying cupboards, smashing crockery and destroying property, just for the fun of it. More people were killed today in the course of blockades. People killed during the blockade. Mirka Priwes, her mother and brother have been deported. Yitshak Katznelson's wife and two of his children have been seized and deported.

The desolation and chaos is greatest on the streets from Chłodna to Leszno Streets, all the Jewish possessions have been abandoned and Polish thugs with the Germans will loot everything. The whole of Jewish Warsaw has been laid waste. That which remains is a shadow of what was, a shadow that tells of death and ruin.

SUNDAY, 16 AUGUST 1942

Today is the 26th day of the 'action', which is continuing with all its atrocities and animal savagery, a slaughter the like of which human history has not seen. Even in the legend of Pharaoh and his decree: every newborn boy will be thrown into the river.

People who have returned from the *Umschlagplatz* have told of women who were seized yesterday who were freed if they sacrificed their children. To our pain and sorrow many women saved themselves in this way—they were separated from their children, aged 3 to 12 to 14, and if they had identity papers, they were freed. Any woman carrying a child or with a child next to her was not freed. The Germans' lust for Jewish blood knows no bounds, it is a bottomless pit. Future generations will not believe it. But this is the unembellished truth, plain and simple. A bitter, horrifying truth.

The Jewish police have received an order that each one of them must bring five people to be transported. Since there are 2,000 police, they will have to find 10,000 victims. If they do not fulfil their quotas they are liable to the death-penalty. Some of them have already received confirmation that they have presented the required number. Since every Jew has some kind of documentation—in the main valid ones—they tear up every document they are shown and round up the passers-by. It is now dangerous for every Jew to go out on to the street. No one goes out.

Rumours have reached me again that letters have allegedly arrived from the deportees saying that they are working in the area of Siedlce and conditions are not bad. Lifschitz's son (my friend from elementary school) told me that his daughter herself had read one of these letters from an elderly couple.

As things are developing, a handful of Jews will be left, those of a designated age. Apart from this there will be no way for a Jew to survive: there will be nowhere to live and no bread. The position of the old is especially tragic: they have no way out. They can either give themselves up into the hands of the butchers, or take their lives themselves, or hide out and live in dark corners and cellars, which is also very difficult because of the general expulsions from the buildings and the upheaval of the residents. In those buildings that have been taken over by new occupants, no strangers are let in. It is easier for an animal to find a hiding place and a refuge in the forest than for a Jew to hide in the ghetto.

Now (four in the afternoon) I have heard that there are no Germans at all in the *Umschlagplatz*. There are only Jews there and they are carrying out the bloody and terrible operation. Today rumours are going round that an order has been issued that all wives and children of officials have to report at the *Umschlagplatz*. Josef Erlich and his family have been killed, so I have heard. According to certain reports, Czerniaków's place here with us—à la Rumkowski—will be inherited by Gancwajch, the man they had been hunting and trying to kill. He is outside the ghetto at the moment.

MONDAY, 17 AUGUST 1942

The 27th day of the annihilation. Yesterday I came to 14 Pawia Street very late at night by a round-about route (via Zamenhof) and was anguished to hear the terrible news about Jakub, Frume and Uri. A very great blow. There is still a faint hope that they can be saved, since there were no train-wagons yesterday and they weren't taken straight to the train. This morning I saw in the streets an announcement about a new reduction in size of the ghetto. Very many streets and sides of streets (the odd or the even numbers) must be vacated by the Jews by 20 August, at four in the afternoon. The ghetto will be a third or a quarter of its original size, if there are no further decrees of this kind. They are emptying those streets that had already been handed over to the German firms, and been fenced off, for example Mylna, Nowolipie, Dzielna Streets and many others. The enemy's claw is reaching out for us and it is still not sated.

Yesterday hundreds of officials of the community and of the Jewish Self-help Organization were taken away. The Gestapo commandant Brandt stood there and struck the detainees with his own hands. Jakub, Uri and Frume were hit. The 'action' is continuing today. There was a blockade on the cemetery. Ora, who works with the group from Hashomer Hatsair, was in great danger. The group was saved today thanks to the intervention of Commissar Hensel. Jewish police-men round up people all day. It is said that they have received an order that each policeman must find six Jews. They abuse those who are rounded up, and smash and loot the empty flats. I have heard that a thousand policemen have received an order to report at the *Umschlagplatz*. This report turns out to be false—for the time being.

Harsh conditions at the factory. Before 80 people were employed there and now almost a thousand are registered there. Hundreds of people wander around bored with nothing to do. They sit around in dread of German blockades and many hide themselves in all kinds of dark corners.

The pain over the loss of L. is getting more and more intense. During the day I am often choked with tears. The fact there is no news about her suffering and torment, whether she is alive or dead, how she died—gives me no peace. If I knew that she was alive and that she was not suffering too much, I would be calm. And if I knew that she had died but did not suffer much at her death—then I would also be calm.

I have been told that Yitshak Katznelson shows great inner strength and endurance, keeping hold of himself after the terrible disaster that has befallen him.

The Ejdus's have been seized. Every day there are killings. When Jakub, Frume and Uri were taken away, someone tried to escape. He was killed on the spot. For a week now we have had no news of the progress of the war. The last report was a few days ago of the heavy bombardment of Mainz. The story about the Jew Chunkis (one of the directors of Adriatika).

Frume and Uri have returned. What they have told me about what is going on at the *Umschlagplatz*. Hell, pure hell. The rich save themselves, if they are not shut into the wagons straight away. The tragic fate of the Taubers. He was killed on the spot, his wife and beautiful and charming son (with statuesque features)—Rapusz—were deported.

TUESDAY, 18 AUGUST 1942

Today marks 4 weeks or 28 days of this blood operation, which has no parallel in history. The Germans and the Jewish police have been carrying out further blockades. Disaster has struck our family once again. Gucia and Hela have been taken away by the Germans, who entered their building. This is a very heavy blow for me. She had been so concerned for us and helped us in the war-years. I have heard talk again about the new rise of Gancwajch. He will take over Lichtenbaum's place and become commissar of the Jewish community.

Today I went with three friends to collect up the books that are in the flats that our firm has been allocated on Miła Street. We set eyes on an appalling vision, all the doors broken open, all the goods and property smashed and scattered through the courtyards. Russian pogromists would have been unable to make a more thorough and shattering pogrom than that carried out by the Jewish police. This sight, which is everywhere to be seen, stunned us. The destruction and the annihilation of the greatest Jewish community in Europe.

New proclamations from the *Judenrat* have been hung up which have caused panic among the Jews. Jews who are not employed are not permitted south of Leszno Street. Those who are caught there will be shot. The families of those working are no longer protected. In fact all those who are not working, even the families of those who are employed, have to report voluntarily at the *Umschlagplatz*. Otherwise their food-cards will be taken away and they will be driven out by force. We can see that the Germans are playing a game of cat and mouse with us. Those employed have protected their families, now the families are being deported (killed) and they want to leave behind the working slaves for the time being. *What horror!* They are preparing to destroy us utterly.

* * *

MONDAY, 4 JANUARY 1943

Once again a few dark, melancholy and very, very gloomy days have gone by. The few who have survived continue to live their lives, which are filled with baseness and bitterness. On the surface everything is quiet and it seems that they do not want to disturb the peace of those who have been left alive. But deep in our hearts is gnawing away the perpetual dread that never lets up for one moment and eats away at us like a moth.

In the past few days we have been seized with anxiety and with a terrible dread. The cause of our disquiet is the arrival of Ukrainians in Warsaw. I have heard that a group of 600 men—Ukrainians—has arrived here. All kinds of theories have been put forward to explain their presence. The Jews have been walking around in gloom and despair. We were afraid that they had come for us, that we were on the brink of a new liquidation, this time a complete one. There were those who reassured themselves and others. They say that their arrival is connected with the 'action' against the Poles that is due to begin shortly. In fact there are reports of unrest and turmoil among the Poles over the mass-expulsions of Poles in the Zamość area. There are also those who say that the Ukrainians have only been sent here for a short period. They are just passing through Warsaw. Whatever the truth may be, the Jews entered the new year—1943—in a depressed and agitated state of mind.

I heard today that the murderers have already left town. As to the reason for their short visit: the same source told me the following: they brought a transport of Poles from Słonim and the surrounding area here. The transport was escorted by the Ukrainians. The town of Słonim, which was once a great Jewish centre, is now 'completely *judenfrei*'. All the Jews have also been expelled. What became of them, whether they were taken to a second location and kept alive, or if they were brought to Treblinka—is not known. One must accept and tell oneself the bitter truth that if the town of Słonim has been emptied of Jews, then these Jews have been wiped off the face of the earth.

The campaign of incitement against Jews in the German press is still continuing and has become even more intense. Much is written about such countries as Romania, Slovakia and Hungary, and about the 'solution' of the Jewish question in these countries. According to what they write, three-quarters of the Jews of Romania and Slovakia have already been exterminated, nearly one million. Hungary is oppressing its Jews economically, but has not yet followed in the footsteps of the Nazis, that is they have not exterminated Jews on a mass scale. All the remaining Jewish communities in Europe face complete annihilation. This is the fate of those countries that find themselves under the rule of these Teutonic butchers: France, Belgium, Holland, Norway, Germany, Denmark, Poland, Czechoslovakia (Bohemia and Moravia), the Baltic countries—Lithuania, Latvia, and Estonia—and the occupied territories of Soviet Russia, as well as Romania, Yugoslavia, Slovakia and Greece. It is to be assumed that about 90 percent of the whole of European Jewry has been destroyed in the ovens of hell that these twentieth-century Huns have erected.

I was told by a certain Jew that a group of Swiss and Swedish journalists have approached German journalists with the question: is there any truth in the stories about the mass-destruction of Jews in German-occupied countries? The Nazi journalists are supposed to have replied that they would give an answer after investigating the matter and researching their sources. A few days later they gave the reply that there had been no mass-murders, but that for economic and supply reasons it has been necessary to shift a percentage of the population to the Eastern territories and resettle them. A certain proportion, especially children, women and old people, had been unable to survive the arduous journey to the new locations and had died. The number of dead is put at only 110,000.

It may be that there is a kernel of truth in this report.

In the proclamations that Hitler has been issuing for the new year he repeats the slanderous lie that Jews were responsible for the outbreak of the war, and that it was only through the Jews that an alliance between the capitalist countries and the Soviet Union became possible. His prophecy of the extermination of European Jewry has already been realized. From his words and from the whole campaign of incitement against Jews in the German press we can see that the active war against us has not eased up in the least.

THURSDAY, 7 JANUARY 1943

Conditions have not changed here either for the better or for the worse. Nothing. We are continually consumed by fear and anxiety. We do not know if today will be our last day, if they will come, surround the ghetto and take us out to our death. Contact with other towns has been almost completely broken. We have no precise idea where there are any other Jewish communities and where they have been completely wiped out. Today I heard a rumour that the whole Jewish community of Lwów has been liquidated and the town has become *judenfrei*. However, it is hard to know how much truth there is in this rumour. We do not even know what is happening on the next street. Just yesterday a rumour went around that the Poles were being driven out of Praga and that they are being brought into the streets that have been left empty by the Jews. Similarly there was also a rumour that at the Eastern Station in Warsaw there are trains standing full of Polish children and that many of them (200) died on the way.

It is hard to determine how much truth there is in either of these reports. We are locked in a cramped and tiny prison and we have no idea what is happening outside the walls of our prison, except in the form of sickening and confused rumours. Indeed there is under present conditions no crime of which the Germans would not be capable. They are turning the whole of Europe outside the

Reich into a wilderness. I am talking about the populations of these areas. They have almost completely wiped out the Jews, now it looks as if it is the turn of the Poles. The Russians are being exterminated, the Czechs are being murdered. The Teutonic sword is destroying the peoples of Europe.

When will this nightmare through which we are living come to an end?

Whole wooden buildings are disappearing from our ghetto. In the course of one or two days they are dismantled and the wood used to heat the homes. Those who have returned from the work-camps (*obozowicze*) are particularly busy at this. The wood-trade is flourishing at the moment in the ghetto. Prices are low, half of what they were a year ago. And it is only thanks to this that we manage not to freeze, and a certain number of unfortunate Jews can support themselves.

SATURDAY, 9 JANUARY 1943

Since yesterday renewed tensions can be felt in the ghetto. The day before yesterday proclamations were posted on the walls forbidding entry or exit from the old ghetto into the new ghetto, or from the new ghetto into the old ghetto without special permission from the *Sonderkommando* at 103 Żelazna Street. This decree, which is signed by the *Judenrat*, is causing great alarm. Once again there is a dread of increased persecutions. In addition, the order issued by the local *Führer* Brandt concerning the buildings at the *Umschlagplatz* that in the course of the summer swallowed around 300,000 Jewish souls has awakened a deep and agitated disquiet. According to Brandt's announcement they plan to make these buildings into a prison or some kind of camp for the Jews who are arrested each day on the Aryan side or in the streets of the old ghetto. These Jews are brought to 103 Żelazna Street. Their quarters are very cramped there and they want to prepare more spacious facilities. This whole business makes every Jew's heart beat with fear. Who can believe the words of a German (after the bitter experiences that we have been through)? All kinds of anxieties have been voiced in this connection. Some believe that this is all a trick on their part and that their real goal is to prepare that place of terror for another slaughter. Others argue that they plan to lock up at the *Umschlagplatz* all those who are registered with the *Werterfassung* and who do not report for work. There are many apprehensions and great is the fear and great is the burden that weighs on our hearts and minds.

Isolated refugees who arrive here literally by miracle from Treblinka bring reports that freeze the blood in the veins. The killing-machine there never rests. In the past few days Jews from Radomsko were brought there and murdered. News of this kind causes us hellish torments. Has anyone ever described the suffering of someone who has been condemned to death and who is to go to the gallows? Even the Russian artists, of whom the greatest is Dostoyevsky, have not succeeded in giving a true description of what transpires in the depths of the soul of an innocent person who has been sentenced to death. When I hear these accounts of Treblinka, something begins to twist and turn in my heart. The fear of 'that' which must come is, perhaps, stronger than the torment a person feels when he gives up his soul. Will these terrible agonies of the spirit call up a literary response? Will there emerge a new Bialik able to write a new Book of Lamentations, a new 'In the Town of Slaughter'?

In recent days there were killings once again in the streets of the ghetto. Yesterday there was talk of a number of victims. One report of a murder on Muranowska Street was confirmed. A relative of the baker at 64 Mylna Street, Goldberg (the name of the baker), was walking at one in the afternoon to take his shoes to the shoemaker for repair. A car drove by. The driver stopped the Jew and asked him why he wasn't working. The Jew replied that he was ill. The German struck him murderous blows. The Jew fell to the ground and the driver was about to go back to his car. At the last moment he changed his mind, took out his revolver and killed the Jew.

I heard confirmation from various sources of the report about the Polish children who were brought to Warsaw from the districts of Lublin and Zamość. They are being distributed among various families. Their parents were taken away to work and the children were brought here.

MONDAY, 11 JANUARY 1943

On Friday in the afternoon there was uproar in several streets of the ghetto. The Jewish police were frightening people into not wandering around in the streets. At that time—half past four—I happened to be on Koża Street (formerly Kupiecka Street, and later named after Rabbi Meisels). The police were shouting: 'Don't bring disaster on yourselves and on us!' People have been saying that Himmler is in Warsaw. The Jews began to run and to hide in the entrance-ways. After a few minutes I continued on my way along Muranowska Street (to my sister and daughter) and three elegant cars [limousines] drove past me. It may be that the head-butcher actually drove by, in order to see with his own eyes the fruits of his 'work', the destruction of the greatest Jewish community in Europe. He was no doubt happy with the results.

Someone who knows many people, including those at present at the head of the *Judenrat*, told me that there really was a very grave danger hanging over our heads these past days. There was a proposal, or a plan, for a new expulsion of the Jews of the ghetto or of the survivors. It was to have been carried out at night, when everyone is asleep in bed and it is impossible for them to take refuge anywhere. This time we escaped disaster because of the opposition of the military authorities, of the *Wehrmacht*. One of the generals opposed the planned expulsion on the grounds that the Jews were working and that their output was necessary at the moment. The opponents of a new slaughter came from the supply authorities, from the *Rüstungskommando* and not from the *Wehrmacht*, as I wrote above. But it is necessary that we recognize the bitter and terrible truth: *over our heads hangs the perpetual threat of total annihilation.* It seems they have decided to exterminate the whole of European Jewry.

Appalling reports are arriving from the provinces: towns that were designated as locations for Jewish ghettos have become *judenrein.* Among them: Siedlce and Sobolew. This means that as far as the Jews are concerned, no promise is binding, no order. There are in fact no human standards in the treatment of us, every trick, every lie, every falsification is legitimate, if it can serve in the destruction of further numbers of Jews.

There are rumours that in Brudno, near Warsaw, barracks are being built which are intended for us . . . if only it was just barracks that they were preparing for us.

A report taken from the Italian newspaper *Corriere della Sera* of 22 December made a strong impression on me. The newspaper carries the contents of the declaration (note) of the German government to the statements of Russia, England and America on the Jewish question, that is, on the extermination of the Jews by Hitler. The German note states that the Jews were well aware of the Nazis' programme with regard to them ten years before they came to power. The Jews knew full well that according to this programme there was no place for them on German soil. The Jews had enough time to leave the Reich and also . . . the other European countries. If they didn't do this—they have only harmed themselves (in Polish: *to tym gorzej dla nich*). Even after the war had broken out they could have left certain countries and even today they can leave several countries. At the end the note mentions the *Führer's* proclamation at the outbreak of the war to the effect that if the Jews cause a new world war they will be the first to suffer the consequences.

It is hardly worth discussing the insanity of this reply: nine million people, men, women and children, were supposed to leave Europe entirely (where, for instance, were they supposed to go?), that is, even those countries where no Germans have ever trod, such as Yugoslavia, Greece, the Russian interior, etc. And if they failed to do this, then they all must die a nameless death, together with their women, children and old people. Words that cut like sharp sword-blades, and we can see from them that the murderers have no intention of halting their terrible crimes. This is their answer to the protests of the nations.

Our mood is one of deep despair and depression. The reports that reach us from various locations show that this time they are intent on the total destruction of the Jews. They are not leaving even a single Jew behind. This is the fate of Radomsko and other towns. These reports plunge us into black despair. We are terrified of a new 'action' here, which will mean the end for us all, that is, for everyone who is left in the ghetto. A few individuals will be saved who have hidden on the other side among the Poles. But the fate of these Jews is also not at all sure, apart from the fact that they live in continual fear, and are liable at any moment to fall into the net of the Germans and of Polish agents. There is also the fear of a special 'action' directed against them.

I heard yesterday that Germans were looking through material in the records of the General Government. It is not known what kind of plan they have in mind: are they going to inspect the new registration of the inhabitants, that is, the Jews, in order to catch them, or do they want to get to know the Polish situation, in order to plan something evil against them—the Poles?

In the town, outside the ghetto, proclamations have been posted about 200 hostages who have been taken from the Poles because of various acts of sabotage and attacks on German soldiers. Great tension and agitation can be felt in the air. The feeling one gets is that the Germans want to drown the disaster that must come to them in a sea of innocent blood. They began with us and will finish with other peoples: Poles, Czechs, Serbs and many others.

My daughter, who is working for the *Werterfassung*, told me the following story: a few days ago three Polish boys and two Polish girls stole into the former ghetto on Leszno and Ogrodowa Streets in order to fill their pockets with Jewish property that is left there that the Germans are collecting. A German soldier, 19 years old, who was guarding the Jewish workers, shot at the Polish children and wounded them all mortally. They all died that day. This soldier is a terrible sadist. One day—perhaps the same day—he beat the Jews savagely, including the women and the young girls. This soldier was removed from his post at the *Werterfassung* in connection with the shooting of the Polish children. But it is interesting to see the reason for his dismissal: not because he shot and killed five human beings, but because he didn't shoot properly, that is, he didn't kill them on the spot, since the five children lived for almost a whole day afterwards and died in the evening. This is the reality in which we live and this is the new order that the Nazis want to erect in the world.

A Girl of Six from the Ghetto

Jerzy Ficowski

Jerzy Ficowski, a Polish
poet and literary critic,
was born in 1924. A
soldier in the Polish
army during World War
II, Ficowski was alarmed
at the Nazi presence in
Poland and at the torture
inflicted upon Jews and
other "undesirables." A
collection of his poetry
entitled *A Reading of
Ashes* was first published
in the United States in
1981.

    In this short poem,
Ficowski captures the
hopelessness of existence
in the ghetto.

she had nothing
but eyes to grow up to
in them quite by chance
two stars of David
perhaps a teardrop would put them out

so she cried

Her speech
was not silver
worth at least
a spit a turning away of the head
her tearful speech
full of hunchbacked words

so she fell silent

Her silence
was not golden
worth at most
3 ha'pence perhaps a carrot or whatever
a very well behaved silence
with a Jewish accent
of hunger

so she died

The Unknown Brother and Sister of the Lodz Ghetto

Laurel Holliday

The identity of the young people who wrote these diary entries is unknown. The entries were written in the margins of a French novel and left in the Lodz ghetto by a young brother and sister who undoubtedly perished. The excerpts appear in *Children in the Holocaust and World War II: Their Secret Diaries*, edited by Laurel Holliday.

Survival in the ghetto was a dehumanizing existence. These diary entries are all that remain to document the suffering that an orphaned Jewish boy and his young sister endured in the Lodz ghetto.

Unknown Girl (as copied into her brother's diary)

JULY 11, 1944

Many a time in the past I began to write my memoirs, but by unforeseen circumstances, I was prevented from putting this mind-easing and soul comforting practice into reality, to begin [to write] of those days when cares and sufferings were unknown to me. I must look back to those bygone days, for my today is quite dissimilar to those which went away.

> Childhood, dear days,
> Alas, so few they were!
> That dimly only I remember them.
> It is only in my dreams that I'm
> Allowed to imagine days bygone.
> Short indeed is human happiness
> In this world of ours!

Unknown Boy

MAY 5, 1944

I committed this week an act which is best able to illustrate to what degree of dehumanization we have been reduced. Namely, I finished up my loaf of bread at a space of three days, that is to say on Sunday, so I had to wait till the next Saturday for a new one. [The ration was about 33 ounces of bread a week.] I was terribly hungry. I had a prospect of living only from the ressort soups [the soup ladled out to forced laborers] which consist of three little potato pieces and two decagrams [three-quarters of an ounce] of flower [sic]. I was lying on Monday morning quite dejectedly in my bed and there was the half loaf of bread of my darling sister. . . . I could not resist the temptation and ate it up totally. . . . I was overcome by a terrible remorse of conscience and by a still greater care for what my little one would eat for the next five days. I felt a miserably helpless criminal. . . . I have told people that it was stolen by a supposed reckless and pitiless thief and, for keeping up appearance, I have to utter curses and condemnations on the imaginary thief: "I would hang him with my own hands had I come across him."

[SEVERAL DAYS LATER]

After my fantasy of writing in various languages, I return to my own tongue, to Yiddish, to *mammelushen*, because only in Yiddish am I able to give clear expression, directly and without artificiality, to my innermost thoughts. I am ashamed that I have for so long not valued Yiddish properly. . . . Yet even if I could rob Homer, Shakespeare, Goethe and Dante of their muses, would I be capable of describing what we suffer, what we sense, what we experience, what we are living through? Is it humanly possible? . . . It is as possible to describe our suffering as to drink up the ocean or to embrace the earth. I don't know if we will ever be believed . . .

[END OF MAY]

Despair increases steadily as does the terrible hunger, the like of which mankind has never yet suffered. With complete assurance we may say that they have not left us even a jot of that which is called body or soul.

   In truth, the world deserves only that we spit in its face and do as Arthur Zygelboim did. [He committed suicide.] . . . Sudden death, hunger, deportation, interrogations, labor, queues, etc., etc. wreak havoc in the ruined vineyard of Israel, among the poor remnant. Will you, O God, keep silent? How can you, having seen it? Send your wrath against these savages, against this scum of humanity, and wipe them out from under your heavens. Let their mothers be bereaved as they have caused Jewish mothers to be bereaved for no cause at all, guiltless Jewish mothers. Let the verse come to pass: "Blessed is he that seizes and smashes on the rock those that have tortured you."

Eli, God, why do you allow it?
Why let them say
You were neutral?
In the heat of your anger
The same that makes
A harvest of us,
Are we the sinners
And they the righteous?
Can it be?
Is that the truth?
After all, you have enough
Intelligence to understand
That it is not thus:
That we are the sinned against
And they are the guilty.

[UNDATED]

We are suffering so much. The old man was savagely beaten up by Biebow. [Hans Biebow, German commander of the ghetto, hanged for his crimes in April 1947.] He had to be taken to the hospital. Five hundred people are to be deported. Again a kind of uncertainty overwhelmed everyone. Have we all gone through all this suffering in order to be liquidated now in their infamous way? Why didn't we die in the first days of the war? My little sister complains of losing the will to live. How tragic. She is only twelve years old! Will there be an end to our suffering? When and how, great heavens! Humanity, where are you?

[UNDATED]

We are so tired of "life." I was talking with my little sister of twelve and she told me: "I am very tired of this life. A quick death would be a relief for us." O world! World! What have those innocent children done that they are treated in such a manner? Truly, humanity has not progressed very far from the cave of the wild beast.

Thank heavens that I'm no realist for to be a realist is to realize and realizing the whole horror of our situation would have been more than any human being could endure. I go on dreaming, dreaming about survival and about getting free in order to be able to " 'tell" the world, to yell and "rebuke," to tell and to protest.

JULY 31, 1944

My after all human heart is cut to pieces when I perceive how terrible my little sister is tormented. She lost literally everything—no stockings, no clothes . . . no tenderness. O you poor orphan, and what you have to suffer by my unjust treatment, because of my destroyed nerves. You, poor being, must help yourself with substitutes: instead of stockings some rags, instead of boots some wooden contrivance. . . . God seems to have abandoned us totally and left us entirely to the mercy of the heartless fiends. Almighty God, how can you do this?

AUGUST 3, 1944

When I look on my little sister my heart is melting. Hasn't the child suffered its part? She has fought so heroically the last five years. When I look on our cosy little room tidied up by the young intelligent poor being I am getting saddened by the thought that soon she and I will have to leave our last particle of home.

Oh God in heaven, why didst thou create Germans to destroy humanity? I don't even know if I shall be allowed to be together with my sister. I cannot write more. I am resigned terribly and black spirited.

[LAST ENTRY. UNDATED.]

Although I write a broken and hesitant Hebrew, I cannot but write Hebrew, for Hebrew is the language of the future, because I shall use Hebrew as a Jew standing proudly upright in the Land of Israel!

Warsaw in April 1943

Stanislaw Marczak-Oborski

Stanislaw Marczak-Oborski was born in Poland in 1921. As a young man, he experienced the anguish of having his country occupied by the Nazis. He was the editor of an underground literary journal. His poem "Warsaw in April 1943" is reprinted from *Poems from the Ghetto: A Testament of Lost Men*, edited by Adam Gillon.

This poem is written in memory of Susan Ginczanka and recounts the Warsaw ghetto uprising. It reflects the futility, shame, and helplessness of not being able to stop the destruction in the Warsaw ghetto.

To the memory of Susan Ginczanka

There are gluey blood and sonorous strings,
A late evening in spring.

Amid explosions in the ghetto
the day is done.
The redness thickens
in the gutters.
And death behind the wall looms dark—
    a threshold of bricks,
and steps towards the execution square are
                                    not mine.

O what striking notes
shall I draw from my fragile lute,
what pain evoke and tone
to make my words resound with fury?

The account is clear—decease,
a payment in stars of gold.
Here a man is dying
To whom I have been no brother.

O what thunderous strain
should pierce the live city
to silence the shame
of the tolling bells?

Did God Create the Nazis?

Lawrence Bush

Lawrence Bush was born in 1951 in New York City. He has been a professional puppeteer, a teacher, a typesetter, and an author and lecturer. He is the author of *Rooftop Secrets and Other Stories of Anti-Semitism*, from which the following story is taken, and a children's book, *Emma Ansky-Levine and Her Mitzvah Machine*. He also wrote the novel *Bessie*, which is based on his grandmother's escape from Siberian prison camps and emigration to the United States.

In this short story, written in diary format, the narrator tells of the daily struggle for survival in the ghetto. He also struggles to reconcile his need for action with his father's religious perspective.

Warsaw, Poland: 1943

FEBRUARY 10

I do believe that Momma's soul has entered heaven because today, for the first time since she died, I can remember her as she used to look, strong, healthy, happy, and big. Just yesterday I could only imagine her as she looked in the end, so shriveled and yellow and old that I could hardly stand to think of her. It felt as if her soul were flying around and around this dark little room like a bat, afraid to leave me, afraid to leave Poppa, unable to rest. But now I do believe her rest has begun, and my memory of her has become beautiful again. This morning I woke up thinking of the sounds her pots and pans used to make. I could almost smell bread baking, and I could imagine her kneading the dough with her fat, jiggling arms.

I have dreams about food all the time, now, and yet I don't feel hungry anymore. I think my stomach has shrunk like a prune. But I must find some food, for Poppa and for me. Dr. Gluckman, who every Friday has visited with a bag of food, has not been here for two weeks. I'm afraid that he, too, must be dead, for he would never forget Poppa, who was his teacher in yeshivah.

I said this just now to Poppa, that I thought Dr. Gluckman is dead. Poppa didn't even hear me. That happens more and more every day—he doesn't hear, though he's sitting right there and never leaves this room. So much of him died with Momma! Every day his head gets heavier, his heart sinks deeper, and he sits at Dr. Gluckman's old desk, buried in his books. Maybe that's why I'm writing in this diary—to have someone who listens, to know that I'm still here.

FEBRUARY 18

This morning I remembered a feeling I once had as a very little boy when Momma took me on the trolley to go shopping. I looked at the passengers and suddenly I realized that each one of them had a whole world of ideas and thoughts, just like me. And each of them could see me only as I saw them, on the surface. Even Momma—even she was separate from me and could never really, really know me.

It was a terrible, scary feeling of being all alone.

That's when the feeling for G-d, the mitzvah of *bitachon*—trust in Hashem—truly entered my heart. G-d would be my friend. G-d would be the one who does come inside of me, who *is* me. Otherwise I would die of loneliness.

But we are dying and, in a certain way, it *is* from loneliness, for, if anyone in the world cared about us, the Nazis could not be doing what they're doing. So where is Hashem now? Are we not His chosen people anymore? Maybe the faith that I thought I had when I was little was just a way of consoling myself, like sucking my thumb?

I wish I could talk about this to Poppa, but he's . . . I don't know what he is or where he is. He's not here. He's not even eating the few remaining bits of food that we have. He just prays, eats words. How can I ever say to him, "Poppa, I think that G-d is just make-believe"?

But I must find out for myself. Let Poppa read in peace, but I cannot believe that Hashem lives inside the Torah anymore. If Hashem is real, then He must be walking the streets of our ghetto. There are such times when G-d comes nearer to us—terrible times, like in the Torah when He at last hears the groaning of the people of Israel in Egypt. And then G-d comes to have a look, to select Moses, to save His chosen people. I do believe that we are living in that kind of time.

I have to go out. I haven't been outside of this room for almost a month, since Dr. Gluckman brought us here and warned us to stay off the streets because the Germans were again going to do a roundup. They're trying to empty out the ghetto by Passover, he said. And now I'm sure that Dr. Gluckman himself is dead, or gone. The Nazis aren't letting anybody escape, I guess, not even members of the Jewish Council.

Still, I must go out. Early tomorrow, before morning prayers, I'll unlock that window in the back and sneak outside for a while. Nobody will see me, I'll make sure. And Poppa probably won't even notice. If he does, good! At least I'll know he's alive!

Oh, why, why, why do I keep having this feeling that Poppa is dying?

O Most High, we are down to our last crust of bread, and my soul is even hungrier than my stomach.

FEBRUARY 19

It has changed out there, a lot. The streets of the ghetto are empty. Everyone who's left is in hiding, like us. There aren't even as many dead bodies as there used to be. And there's nothing to buy on the street. I couldn't find any food, not a thing, until I met the old lady and all that craziness began to happen.

But wait, my diary, wait. Before food, I must tell you about the sky! Big and blue and wide and so magnificent! I tried to take it all in with my eyes, the color, the space, so I could carry it back to our little prison. Oh, blessed art Thou, Lord our G-d, Ruler of the universe who provides us with moments to remind us of Creation!

So I walked and walked, just to feel the air against my face. It's so different outside in the cold, when you're moving, than inside, where you sit and shiver. I even visited our old street, Wolynska, and stopped in front of the building where we used to live. All the glass has been knocked out of the windows so you can't tell who's living where or if anybody's living there at all. I watched my own bedroom window for a while—but what can you see through cardboard? Well, if someone is there, may Hashem place a guardrail around them so they can live a long life.

Then came the old woman out of the doorway of the building. O diary, from the way she looked at me, she must have thought I was crazy. There I was, strolling through hell with a smile on my face! I guess it was crazy, even stupid. Do I really believe that Hashem is going to show me a sign of some kind the way He did for Moses in the wilderness, just because I go around making blessings over everything I see? And yet the ghetto *is* a wilderness—and the thing that happened, wasn't it a kind of sign?

The woman called to me. "There aren't so many youngsters left in Warsaw, sonny," she said. "Don't go showing yourself off in broad daylight. It's just about this time that the Nazis like to get to work, too."

I answered her by saying that there aren't many old people left in the ghetto either.

"Well, then," the old lady said—she had a very nice voice—"we ought to stick together, the young and the old." And then she reached into her apron and brought out a piece of bread for me.

So that's when it happened, just as I went to her for the bread. I was saying the blessing for this bit of nourishment, and suddenly a man came running down the street. The old woman pulled me into her doorway with a yank. I peeked out and saw that the man, a Jew, was breathing like a tired horse and sweating even though there's snow on the ground and it's freezing cold. And then I saw why he was sweating: I heard a gunshot, and the man spun around and almost fell against the wall. Two men were chasing him, two Nazis with guns. I began to pray with all my might that they wouldn't find us in the doorway because they would shoot us, I was sure. But the wounded man kept coming in our direction, and the old lady told me to please shut up. I didn't know what to do.

There were more shots. Then all of a sudden a big explosion tore up the street and blew those Nazis to bits. It must have been a bomb or a grenade of some kind. I could feel the explosion like a hot wind against my face. I don't know where it came from—maybe even from a window in my old building, it was that close! It seemed to drop right out of the heavens.

Then the old lady pulled the wounded man into the doorway and cursed him for coming there, for leading the Nazis to Wolynska Street. They knew each other, I could tell that from the way they talked. Maybe the man was her son— it could be. But I realized from what they were saying that they belonged to the underground, the Jewish Fighting Organization.

I have never before seen people who belong to the underground. I've heard about them, I've seen their newspapers once or twice, but never before did I stand next to them and talk with them. Such ordinary-looking people! From the way Poppa talks about the Jewish Fighting Organization, I expected them to look like horrible madmen. Poppa says that *they* are the sinners for whom G-d is now punishing all of us. Could this be true?

The old lady told me, "You'd better go now, sonny. There will be more of those Nazi swine here at any minute." I wondered where *she* would go, especially with her wounded son or friend, whatever he is. I even thought of inviting them to Dr. Gluckman's office. But I knew that Poppa would throw them out— or else they might shoot him and take whatever we have left. Who can you trust? So I ran as quickly as I could. I suddenly felt terribly afraid. Was I afraid of them, or was I afraid because I was leaving them?

I recited the blessing for deliverance from danger, and then I looked back just before I turned the corner onto Zamenhofa Street. The old woman was standing next to the bloody pieces of the Germans' bodies. Uch! She was taking their guns, their bullets, whatever she could find, like a cat picking clean the bones of a bird. It was a horrible sight, but I must confess, only to you, my diary, that it thrilled me to see an old Jewish woman standing, alive, next to the bodies of our tormentors. Am I bad to have such feelings? It was the first time since Momma died that I felt some hope for the future, some hope that this sight—the Nazis dead, the Jews alive—was a vision of the future. Yet we are not supposed to rejoice at the death of sinners. As it is written in the Talmud: When the angels wanted to sing at the sight of the Egyptians drowning in the Red Sea, Hashem silenced them, saying, "The work of My hands is drowning in the sea, and you desire to sing songs!" But can it be true that the Germans, too, are the creation of Hashem?

FEBRUARY 26

Wonderful news! Dr. Gluckman is alive! He came to see us yesterday. He had two cans of fish stuffed into his pockets, which Poppa opened with a key. A feast! We even drank the oil in the cans. And then Dr. Gluckman told us what had happened to him. The Nazis had arrested him in a sweep on Mila Street, and, even though he's a member of the Jewish Council, they were going to transport him to Treblinka. Then a high Nazi official was wounded badly—either by accident or by the underground, Dr. Gluckman is not sure which—and the Nazis decided that they needed the doctor's services again.

"I saved his life in Gestapo headquarters," Dr. Gluckman told us. "It was a difficult operation. There were five pieces of shrapnel in his back. Both the Gestapo doctor and I worked all through the night."

By saving the Nazi bigshot's life, Dr. Gluckman saved his own. "But," I heard him say in a low voice to Poppa, "I feel unclean."

Poppa tried to make him feel better by quoting from Mishnah Sanhedrin: "If one saves a single life, it is as if one has saved the world." But Dr. Gluckman wondered if the Mishnaic teachings apply to the Nazis. He sounded sick and worried—like a little boy. "Are the lives of the very worst of the *goyim* sacred, Rabbi?"

Again Poppa recited from the Talmud, from Rabbi Hillel: "Whatever is hateful to you, do not do it to others. That is the whole Law." And Poppa also quoted the Rambam, about how true strength is found by being patient, by living with unhappiness, the way Job did. And then he asked Dr. Gluckman: Who was wiser, Bar Kochba, who fought with weapons against the Romans in a war that led to Israel's destruction, or Ben Zakkai, who saved Judaism by leaving Jerusalem before the Romans destroyed the city?

But Dr. Gluckman asked Poppa exactly the question that I was thinking: If Ben Zakkai was wiser, then why are we still in Warsaw? Why haven't we left, the way Ben Zakkai left Jerusalem?

That made Poppa laugh. "And where should we go?" he said. "All of Poland is now Jerusalem! The Nazis have control everywhere! There is nothing, nothing between here and Treblinka but death!"

Can you imagine how I felt when I heard this? O my diary, dear diary! I have gotten used to hearing grownups speak in hopeless words, but still it scares me. If they don't understand what is happening to us, if they have no hope, then what are we young people to think?

Is this really the end of days? If yes, then I have nothing to fear, for I will just die like everyone else. It doesn't matter if Dr. Gluckman saves a Nazi or saves himself—we will all die soon enough. I wonder if that's how the people in the Jewish Fighting Organization feel. That man in the street, and the old woman, do they believe that their guns will bring them life? Or do they know that they're going to die anyway, no matter what they do? And what about Poppa? Does he pray and study and fast in hope of redemption or only to welcome in the Angel of Death?

I got up my courage and asked Poppa this question. It has never been easy to ask him questions; he always turns them around on you, and it becomes a test of your knowledge. "Poppa," I said, "do you believe as Ben Zakkai believed that we and our faith will outlive the Nazis? Or are you just saying Kaddish all the time for Momma, for my sisters, for everybody? Is there any hope, Poppa?"

I can't describe the look that came into my father's eyes. He looked angry at me and frightened of me at the same time. All he said was, "G-d moves in mysterious ways."

Then I said, "But . . ."

And he yelled, "There are no buts! It is the young Jews who say 'But, but' all the time—the Jews without faith, without beards, the Jewish Communists and Bundists and Zionists—*these* are the ones for whom Hashem is punishing all of Israel!" And he kept screaming and screaming at me until I ran and hid my face.

MARCH 7

This morning I began to wonder how many Jews have died since the Nazis appeared? Thousands, maybe hundreds of thousands? Millions? If we've been dying all over as quickly as we are dying in Warsaw, then yes, it is millions. But these are just numbers, thousands, millions. So I began thinking of all the Jewish names I know. Shmul, Mordecai, Leib, Yeshua, Yitzhak, Avrom Asser, Beryl . . . Tsil, Leah, Feige, Hanna, Dvera, Buzie. Ruchel . . . I counted two hundred and forty-five, including every name I could think of from the Torah, and then finally I stopped. Two hundred and forty-five! It takes four times that to make a thousand. It takes four thousand times that to make a million! Four thousand Shmuls, four thousand Moishes, four thousand Chaikas . . .

MARCH 18

Dr. Gluckman says we have to move. He says the Germans are telling him to give over any remaining children in the ghetto. If they ever find out that I'm living here in his own office, we'll all be shot.

How sorry I feel for this man when he comes to us! He has such a guilty look on his face, all because he is on the Jewish Council and must obey the Nazis' orders. He makes lists of people who are able to do labor, which means to live. If you're not on the list that Dr. Gluckman gives to the Germans, either you'd better hide or you're as good as dead. Dr. Gluckman always says to Poppa, "If I don't obey, it will be worse for everybody. This way at least I can protect *some* of our people." But then he also weeps and says things like, "I should strangle myself with my own hands! There is so much Jewish blood on these hands!"

Anyway, we must move. Dr. Gluckman is bringing us tomorrow evening to a place on Smocza Street. It is a bunker, a hiding place, he says. There are Jews there with food, with a radio, with enough things to keep us alive for months. Dr. Gluckman says we should not give up hope. The Nazis have taken a beating from the Russians, he says. Maybe Hitler will at last get what he deserves.

The thought of living through all of this seems awful to me. To have to live and grow up knowing that my mother was murdered, my sisters were murdered, all my friends were murdered, and I'm still alive—I think I'd rather die.

Oh, but if *I* feel this way, my diary, can you imagine how Poppa feels? I've been trying to figure out why he acts so angry with me, why he hardly ever talks unless Dr. Gluckman is here for a visit. Poppa used to be so proud of me. He used to call me his "little scholar," and he would tell me that I would grow up to be a miracle-working rabbi, a great, wise teacher. And yet I am the same person now that I was before the Nazis came and ruined our lives. I'm still a good Jew, and I try to be a good son.

They say that all wisdom is in the Torah. So today I studied the Akedah, the part where Abraham is told to sacrifice his son, Isaac. I thought about how Abraham must have felt when G-d gave him that order. He must have gotten very mad at Isaac even though Isaac hadn't done anything wrong. Because if Abraham didn't get mad at Isaac, he'd have to get mad at Hashem, and that would be a sin. Or else he'd have to get so mad at himself that he would die. He would explode from the anger inside and die. So instead he turned it against his son. I know I'm right, too, because of how Hashem had to call Abraham's name twice before he put down his knife and saw the ram caught in the bushes. Abraham was so angry at Isaac that he didn't hear G-d calling him.

And that's how Poppa feels about me. I've figured it out. He looks at me each day and feels how hopeless our future is. He feels how all his prayers and all his study are unable to save us. He knows that I will probably not even live to be bar mitzvah next year. So the only way that Poppa can keep himself from losing his love for G-d is by taking away his love for me.

So then I was thinking about the old woman from the underground and the way she looked at me—with love in her eyes, with excitement, just because I'm young and alive. I guess she doesn't believe in G-d. Or she believes you can hate the Nazis without hating Hashem because Hashem did not send the Nazis. And because she is able to curse the Nazis and throw grenades at them, she can smile at me.

So maybe Poppa is all wrong about the Nazis. He says that they are doing the work of Hashem, punishing our people for their sins. We should hate the sinful Jews, he says, not the Nazis. But maybe Hashem wants us to fight back. Maybe the fighters of the Jewish Fighting Organization are the righteous ones because they know that G-d is not to blame for our trouble. Maybe it is Poppa who does not understand the will of Hashem! "If I am not for myself," Rabbi Hillel taught us, "who will be for me?" Doesn't the underground obey these words better than Poppa?

I am glad to be leaving this place. It'll be good to live among other Jews, Jews who have hope. Sometimes with Poppa I feel like we're already dead.

But don't worry, diary, I won't abandon you. You are my heart, wherever I go.

MARCH 19

A horrible thing has happened. Dr. Gluckman has killed himself.

It happened just a few hours ago, at about eight o'clock, which was when he was supposed to take us to Smocza Street. An envelope fell onto the floor of our room through the slot that the doctor uses to contact us. Poppa began to read it, and then suddenly we heard a shot in the main part of the house. We would have run there, but the door to this room is locked from the outside. Only Dr. Gluckman has the key. Our only way out of the room has been the window.

The note in the envelope came from the doctor. It said he could not bear to live any more. It said that the place where he was going to bring us is actually a hideout for the Jewish Fighting Organization, and Dr. Gluckman knew that Poppa would feel betrayed when we got there. But there is nowhere else to go in the ghetto. Either you go to Treblinka or you go to the underground. That's what the note says. And maybe by taking his own life, he would be protecting Poppa and me by letting us stay in the office. Yes, the Nazis will come looking for him, but when they find his body, they probably won't search further, G-d willing. Then all we have to do is feed ourselves.

I have been reading and rereading the note for hours. Poppa won't touch it. He acts like it's an unclean thing. This is how it ends:

Goodbye, dear teacher. You were all I had left in this world to make me feel like a human being, but it is not enough to keep me here. Please, do not feel responsible for this. It's just a matter of today or tomorrow or the next week—the Nazis have robbed my soul piece by piece, and I cannot bear to live longer. I know that you and the boy will think, "But just last night, he told us to have hope." Yet I realized afterwards that I do not want to survive this holocaust—there is too much blood on my hands, too much horror in my eyes. Perhaps by dying now, instead of waiting, I can help to preserve this sanctuary for you and help preserve your learnedness for Judaism. If that is so, I will be redeemed. Your loyal servant, Hyman Gluckman.

And now, dear diary, there is lots of noise on the street—gunshots, people yelling. It is much later in the night now, and I guess the Jewish Fighting Organization is doing its work. And that means that more Nazis will visit our neighborhood tonight. They will probably search all the houses and shoot anyone they find. Dr. Gluckman's death will not protect us, not in the slightest.

Poppa stands with his head against the door, crying and praying for the doctor. Somewhere beyond that door Dr. Gluckman's body is lying, and next to it must be the gun that he used. That's all I'm thinking of—his gun! How I wish I could get it and give it to the Jews who are battling for life on the streets of Warsaw!

O Most High! Why should we turn our guns on ourselves? If Dr. Gluckman wanted to die, why didn't he first shoot the biggest and worst Nazi he could find? Isn't it bad enough that we must be slaves to them, that we do whatever they say, work ourselves to death, get on board the trains, give whatever they ask for? Must we also do their dirty work and murder ourselves?

No! As it is written in the Torah: "Choose life!" Let the Nazis be the ones who deliver death to us. Our guns must not kill Jews!

I remember this midrash: When the people of Israel found themselves trapped between the waters of the Red Sea and the spears of the Egyptian army, and the Lord said to Moses, "Why do you cry out to me? Tell the Israelites to go forward," then one man, an ordinary Jew named Nachshon, took the first step into the water—and then the Red Sea split open!

Dear diary, I am leaving as soon as Poppa falls asleep. I am going out the window to the street, into the Red Sea, the Sea of Blood that is our ghetto. Watch over my father, O my heart, and try to preserve him. Preserve yourself, too, my diary, for future generations of Jews to read—if any of our people live to create such a future. But I, I am going out. I am going out to be among Jews who are still alive.

The Lemon

Arnost Lustig

A Holocaust survivor, Arnost Lustig is the author of
several books, including *Night and Hope, Diamonds of
the Night*, from which the following short story is
taken, *A Prayer for Katerina Horovitzova*, and *Street of
Lost Brothers*. For additional biographical
information on Lustig, see page 88.

In this short story, the main character must try to
provide for his mother and sister after his father dies.
On the streets of the ghetto, he must dicker and trade
for even scraps of bread, so how can he get a lemon
for his sick sister? This powerful story illustrates that
it is impossible to know how we will react until we
are actually confronted with the circumstances.

Ervin was scowling. His feline eyes, set in a
narrow skull, shifted nervously and his lips were pressed angrily into a thin blue
arch. He hardly answered Chicky's greeting. Under his arm he was clutching a
pair of pants rolled into a bundle.

"What'll you give me for these?" he demanded, unrolling the trousers, which
were made of a thin nut-brown cloth. The seat and knees were shiny.

Chicky grinned. "Ye gods, where did you pick those up?" He inspected the
cuffs and seams. "Jesus Christ himself wouldn't be caught dead in such a low-
class shroud."

Ervin ignored the sneer. "I'm only interested in one thing, Chicky, and that's
what I can get for them." He spoke fast.

"Listen, not even a resurrected Jesus Christ on the crummiest street in Lodz
would wear a pair of pants like that," Chicky went on with the air of an expert.

He noticed the twitching in Ervin's jaw. "Well, the knees still look pretty good, though," he reconsidered. "Where did you get them?"

It was cloudy and the sun was like a big translucent ball. The barn swallows were flying low. Ervin looked up at the sky and at the swallows swooping toward unseen nests. He'd been expecting Chicky to ask that and he'd prepared himself on the way.

He displayed his rather unimpressive wares again. He knew he had to go through with it now, even if the pants were full of holes. The skin on Chicky's face was thin, almost transparent; he had a small chin and rheumy eyes.

A member of the local security force came around the corner.

"Hey, you little brats," he snapped, casting a quick glance at their skinny bodies, "go on, get out of here!"

They turned around. Fortunately, a battered yellow Jewish streetcar came along just then and diverted the security guard's attention.

"Don't tell me it's a big secret," Chicky said. "Anybody can easily see those pants belonged to some grown-up. What're you so scared of?"

"What should I be scared of?" Ervin retorted, clutching the trousers close. "I've got to cash in on them, that's all."

"They're rags."

"They're English material, they're no rags."

"Well, I might see what I can do for you," Chicky relented. "But on a fifty-fifty basis."

Ervin handed over the bundle, and Chicky took a piece of twine from his pocket and tied up the trousers to suit himself, making a fancy knot. He looked up and down the street.

The security guard was at the other end of the street with his back to the boys. They were on the corner of an alley which hadn't had a name for a long time. It was intermittently paved with cobblestones. People hurried on; Ervin and Chicky moved closer to the wall. The streetcar now took a different route. The next stop was out of sight.

Chicky, the smaller of the two, the one with the shaved head, was clutching the brown checkered pants under his arm as Ervin had done.

"But don't you go having second thoughts, Ervin. Don't let me go ahead and work my ass off and then. . . ."

"My dad died," Ervin said.

"Hm . . . well," Chicky remarked. "It's taken a lot of people these last few weeks," he observed.

"Now there's only one important thing, and that's how you're going to cash in on those pants."

It occurred to Chicky that Ervin might want a bigger share of the take because the pants had been his father's.

"Who's your customer, Chicky?"

"Old Moses," Chicky lied.

"Do I know him?"

"Little short guy."

"First time I've heard of him."

"He just comes up as high as my waist. He's absolutely the biggest bastard in town. But he kind of likes me. Maybe it's because I remind him of somebody."

"He's interested in pants?"

"He's interested in absolutely everything, Ervin."

"Funny I never heard of him."

"Well, I guess I'd better be going," Chicky said.

"What do you suppose your friend would give me for these pants?" Ervin asked.

"Give *us*, you mean," Chicky corrected.

"Anyway, go on and see what you can do," said Ervin, dodging a direct answer.

"He might cough up some bread in exchange for these pants. Or a couple ounces of flour." He unrolled the trousers again. "Like I told you, the knees are still pretty good and the lining's passable. The fly isn't stained yellow like it is in old men's pants. In that respect, these trousers are in good shape and that tells you something about the person who wore them. I'll try to get as much as I can for them, Ervin." He bared his teeth in a tiger grin.

"I need a lemon, Chicky."

"What about a big hunk of nothing?"

"I'm not joking," Ervin said curtly. "All right, then half a lemon, if you can't get a whole one." The expression on Chicky's face changed.

"You know what *I* need, Ervin?" he began. "I need an uncle in Florida where the sun shines all year long and trained fish dance in the water. I need an uncle who would send me an affidavit and money for my boat ticket so I could go over there and see those fish and talk to them." He paused. "A *lemon!* Listen, Ervin, where do you get those ideas, huh, tell me, will you?"

Chicky gazed up into the sky and imagined a blue and white ocean liner and elegant fish poking their noses up out of the silver water, smiling at him, wishing him bon voyage.

Swallows, white-breasted and sharp-winged, darted across the sullen sky. Chicky whistled at them, noticing that Ervin didn't smile.

"That lemon's not for me," said Ervin.

"Where do you think you are? Where do you think Old Moses'd get a lemon? It's harder to find a lemon in this place than . . . ."

But he couldn't think of a comparison.

Chicky's expression changed to one of mute refusal. He thought to himself, Ervin is something better than I am. His father died, Ervin took his trousers, so now he can talk big about lemons. Chicky's mouth dropped sourly.

"It's for Miriam," Ervin said flatly. "If she doesn't get a lemon, she's finished."

"What's wrong with her?"

"I'm not sure. . . ."

"Just in general. I know you're no doctor."

"Some kind of vitamin deficiency, but it's real bad."

"Are her teeth falling out?"

"The doctor examined her this morning when he came to see my mother. The old man was already out in the hall. There's no point talking about it."

"It's better to be healthy, I grant you that," Chicky agreed. He rolled up the pants again. "At best, I may be able to get you a piece of bread." He tied the twine into a bow again. "If there were four of us getting a share of this rag, Ervin—your mom, your sister, and you and me, nobody would get anything out of it in the end."

"If I didn't need it, I'd keep my mouth shut," Ervin repeated.

"I can tell we won't see eye to eye, even on Judgment Day."

A Polish streetcar rattled and wheezed along behind them. The town was divided into Polish and Jewish sectors. The streetcar line always reminded Ervin that there were still people who could move around and take a streetcar ride through the ghetto, even if it was just along a corridor of barbed wire with sentries in German uniforms so nobody would get any ideas about jumping off—or on.

"It's got to be something more than that. Everybody's got a vitamin deficiency here. What if it's something contagious, Ervin, and here I am fussing around with these pants of yours?" He gulped back his words. "And I've already caught whatever it is?"

"Nobody knows *what* it is," said Ervin.

"Well, I'm going, Ervin. . . ."

"When are you coming back?"

"What if we both went to see what we could do?"

"No," said Ervin quietly.

"Why not?"

Ervin knew what it was he had been carrying around inside him on his way to meet Chicky. *It was everything that had happened when he'd stripped off those trousers. His father's body had begun to stiffen and it felt strange. He kept telling himself it was all right, that it didn't matter.* Instead, he kept reciting the alphabet and jingles.

This was your father, a living person. And now he's dead. Chicky was the only one he could have talked to.

"I haven't got a dad or a mother even," Chicky said suddenly. A grin flickered. "That's my tough luck. They went up the chimney long ago."

The sky above the low rooftops was like a shallow, stagnant sea.

Chicky lingered, uncertain.

It was just his body, Ervin told himself. *Maybe memory is like the earth and sky and ocean, like all the seashores and the mountains, like a fish swimming up out of the water to some island, poking out its big glassy eyes just to see how things look. Like that fish Chicky had been talking about. Nobody knows, not even the smartest rabbi in the world. And not the bad rabbis either. But while he was taking his father's trousers off, he knew what he was doing. He wasn't thinking about his father, but about an old Italian tune he used to sing and which Miriam loved. Father sang off key, but it sounded pretty. Prettier than a lot of other things. It was about love and flowers and his father had learned it during the war when he fought in the Piave campaign.*

He already had the trousers halfway off. And he knew the reasons he loved his father would never go away.

The swallows flew quietly in low, skidding arches. Ervin looked around to see how the weather was, and finally his gaze dropped. The rounded cobblestones melted away.

"All right then, I'll bring it around to your place later," Chicky said.

"By when do you think you can do it?"

"In two or three hours."

"But, Chicky. . . ."

Chicky turned and disappeared around the corner as another streetcar came clanging along.

Now Ervin could think ahead, instead of going back to what had been on his mind before. He set off down the alley in the opposite direction, toward the house where he and his family had been living for two years.

The tiny shops upstairs and in the basement had been hardly more than market stalls which had been converted into apartments for several families.

He remembered how be discovered that his father no longer wore underpants. The stringy thighs. The darkened penis, the reddish pubic hair. Rigid legs. Scars on the shin bone. His father had gotten those scars when he was wounded fighting in Italy.

Then that old tune came back to him, sung off key again, the song from somewhere around Trieste that he and Miriam had liked so much.

Hell, who needed those pants more than they did? Father had probably traded in his underpants long ago. Who knows for what?

So Father died, he is no more, Ervin thought to himself.

He reached home, one of the dwarfish shops where he and his mother and sister lived.

The corrugated iron shutter over the entry had broken a spring, so it wouldn't go all the way up or down. He could see a mouse.

He squeezed through a crack in the wall. Mother was scared of mice, so he'd repaired the wall boards through which the mice came in and out. Pressing against the wall, Ervin was suddenly aware of his body, and that reminded him of his father again.

"It's me," he called out.

It had occurred to him that there was nothing to be proud of, being unable to cash in on the trousers *himself.* (Even so, his mother must have known what he had done.) He had to take a deep breath and adjust to the musty smell in the room. It was easier to get used to the difference between the light outside and the darkness inside.

Mother greeted him with a snore. She had long since lost any resemblance to the woman who had come here with him. He peered around him. He had been almost proud of having such a pretty mother. On top of everything else, her legs had swollen. She hadn't been able to get out of bed for the past eight weeks. She'd waited on everything for Father, and now for him.

"Where've you been?" his mother asked.

"Out," he answered.

He crawled into his corner where he could turn his back on everything, including his father who lay out in the hall wrapped in a blanket. Miriam, too, was curled up next to the wall, so he couldn't see her face. He heard her coughing.

He bundled his legs into the tattered rug that used to be his father's. *He'd always had the worst covers. He didn't want to admit he was a loser, and as long as he was able to give up something for them, maybe it wasn't so obvious. The dim light made its way through the thin fabric of dust and dampness and the breath of all three of them. When he lost, he put on the smile of a beautiful woman. He was making a point of being a graceful loser. As if it made any difference to anybody except himself.*

"Did you find anything?" his mother asked.

"No. . . ."

"What are we going to do?"

"Maybe this afternoon," he said, his face to the wall.

"Miriam," his mother called out to his sister. "Don't cough. It wears you out."

"Mirrie," Ervin said. "Miriam." She didn't answer.

"Can't she speak?" he asked his mother.

"It wears her out," she repeated. "You really ought to look around and see if you can't scrape up something."

"There's no point so early in the afternoon."

"You ought to try at least," his mother insisted.

That's how it used to be with Father, Ervin recalled. She always kept sending him somewhere. But Father had gone out just as he'd done now, and, like him, he almost felt better outside; he also may have believed that just by going out he was getting back in shape, that he'd be able to do what he used to do in the beginning. Then Mother started saying things couldn't get any worse. She never went wrong about that. That's because there is no limit to what's "worse." The limit was in his father. And now Ervin had to find it, just like his father.

"I already told you, I can't find anything just now." he said.

"You ought to go out and try, dear," his mother went on. *This was what Father had had to put up with.* "You see how Miriam looks, don't you?" his mother persisted.

"I can see her," he answered. "But I can't find anything now."

"This can't help but finish badly."

"Oh, cut it out. I'm not going anywhere," Ervin declared flatly. "I've already tried. There's nothing to be had."

"For God's sake, listen to me," his mother cried sharply. "Go on out and *try.* Miriam hasn't had a thing to eat today."

The stains on the plaster were close to his eyes. The room was damp, and it almost swallowed up the sound of his mother's voice and his own. The dampness didn't bother him, though. He could hear faint scratching noises in the walls.

The boards he'd put up didn't help much. He almost envied mice. Just as he'd felt envy for trees when he was outside. Ervin suddenly wished he could catch one of those little animals. Pet it, then kill it. Father had told them about the time they were besieged during the First World War and the soldiers ate mice.

To kill and caress. Or simply kill, so you're not always bothered by something or somebody. So it is—to be killed or to kill.

But if Chicky was right, a trained mouse should get along great.

"I wonder if I shouldn't air out the room a bit," he said into the silence.

"Have they been here already?" he asked after a while.

"No."

"They're taking their time about it."

Now, in her turn, his mother was silent. "Who knows how many calls they have to make today?"

"Why don't you want to go out, child?"

"I will. In a while," he answered. "It doesn't make any sense now, though."

"Ervin, child. . . ."

The room was quiet, the silence broken only by Miriam's coughing.

Ervin put his head between his knees, trying to guess where the mouse was and what it was doing. He stuck his fingers in his ears. The scratching continued. *So Father's still lying out there in the hall. He doesn't have any pants and Mother doesn't even know it. He's naked, but that doesn't bother his old Piave scars. Mother could use that extra blanket now,* he thought to himself. *But he left it around his father for some reason which he didn't know himself. So I don't have the feeling that I've stolen everything from him, including our second tattered blanket,* he thought to himself. *It was lucky she couldn't get out of bed now, even if she wanted to. Her legs wouldn't support her. She'd see that Father had no pants. They'll probably take him along with the blanket. What the hell? They were certainly taking their time. They should have been here an hour ago. It was a regulation of the commanding officer and the self-government committee that corpses must be removed promptly. Everybody was scared of infection. The corpse collectors were kept busy. They probably didn't miss a chance to take anything they could get. Everybody knew they stole like bluejays.*

Miriam would probably have been afraid to sleep with a dead person in the same room, even if it was Father, Ervin decided.

"There's some rabbi here who works miracles, I heard," his mother said. "Why don't you go and see him?"

"What would I say to him?"

"Tell him that I'm your mother."

"I don't have any idea where he lives. And even if he could perform a miracle, he certainly won't put himself out to come over here. He waits for people to come to him."

"I feel so weak," his mother told him.

Suddenly it occurred to him that maybe his mother would have been better off lying out in the hall beside his father. It would be better for Miriam too. Mother's gestures and the things she told him were getting more and more indecisive.

"Why don't you want to go anywhere?" Mother said.

"Because there's no point," he replied. "I'd be wearing myself out in vain. I'll find something, but not until this afternoon."

"Miriam won't last long. She can hardly talk anymore."

"Miriam?" Ervin called out.

Miriam was silent and his mother added: "You know how it was with Daddy."

"He'd been sick for a long time."

And when her son said nothing, she tried again. "Ervin. . . ."

"It doesn't make any sense," he growled. "I'm not going anywhere now. Not till later."

He sat quite still for a while, staring at the blotches and shadows moving on the wall. Rabbis say your soul is in your blood, but some kids and old people say it's in your shadow. There are a lot of lies around. Who cares where your soul is? Maybe under your dirty fingernails? Maybe when you have diarrhea? He could hear mice scampering across the floor toward the mattress where Mother and Miriam were lying. Mother screeched, then Miriam.

Ervin was bored.

It might be more comfortable and pleasant to wait outside. But there was something in here that made him stay. He remembered how he and Chicky used to play poker. They always pretended there was some stake. That made it more interesting. You could bluff and pretend to have a full house when you didn't even have a pair. But there was always the chance—which they'd invented—that you might win something.

He remembered how he and Miriam used to go ice-skating. She was little and her knees were wobbly. He'd drag her around the rink for a while, then take her into the restaurant where you could have a cup of tea for ten hellers. Miriam's nose would be running, and she'd stay there for an hour with her tea so he could have a good time out on the ice. Once his mother had given them money to buy two ham sandwiches. His arches always ached when he'd been skating. So did Miriam's.

If they'd come for Father—and he wished it were over with—he wouldn't have to worry that the body would start to decay or that his mother would find out he didn't have any pants on.

"Why don't you go out and see that miracle rabbi?"

"Because it doesn't make any sense."

At first, Mother only had trouble with her legs. And Miriam hadn't coughed *quite* as much.

The sentries along the streetcar line always looked comfortably well-fed, with nice round bellies, as though they had everything they needed. When these sentries passed through the ghetto, they acted as though victory was already theirs, even if they might lose this little skirmish with the Jews. *Daddy once said that this was their world, whether they won or lost.*

Ervin's stomach growled. It was like the noise the mice made. He stretched and waited for his mother to start nagging him again. But she didn't, and it was almost as though something were missing. *He didn't want to think about his father's body wrapped in that blanket out in the hall. Daddy had been sick long enough. He was certainly better off this way.*

After a while, he wasn't sure whether his stomach was making the noise or the mice. His mother groaned. He thought about a nap. Just then he heard someone banging on the iron shutter. He got up.

"Well, I'll be on my way," he said.

"Come back soon," his mother replied. "Come back safe and sound."

"Sure," he answered. As he approached the shutter, he asked, "Is that you, Chicky?"

"No," a voice replied. "It's the miracle-working rabbi with a pitcher of milk."

Ervin pushed the broken shutter and slipped through. It was easy. His body was nothing but skin and bones now. He had a long narrow skull, with bulging greenish blue eyes. He could feel his mother's eyes on him as he squeezed out. Outside in the courtyard he pulled down his shirt and his bones cracked. Chicky was waiting on the sidewalk.

"So?" asked Ervin.

"Even with those stains on the seat," Chicky started.

"What're you trying to tell me?"

"He gave me more than I expected." He smiled slyly and happily.

Chicky produced a piece of bread, carefully wrapped in a dirty scarf. He handed it to Ervin. "This is for you. I already ate my share on the way, like we agreed."

"Just this measly piece?"

"Maybe you forgot those stains on the seat of those pants."

"Such a little hunk?"

"What else did you expect, hm? Or maybe you think I ought to come back with a whole moving van full of stuff for one pair of pants?"

Chicky wiped his nose, offended.

"You just better not forget about those stains on the seat. Besides, almost everybody's selling off clothes now."

Ervin took the bread. Neither one mentioned the lemon. Ervin hesitated before crawling back into the room, half-hoping Chicky was going to surprise him. Chicky liked to show off.

"Wait here for me," he blurted. "I'll be right back."

Ervin squinted through the dimness to where his mother lay on the mattress.

"Here, catch," he said maliciously. He threw the bread at her. It struck her face, bounced, and slid away. He could hear her groping anxiously over the blanket and across the floor. As soon as she had grabbed it, she began to wheeze loudly.

She broke the bread into three pieces in the dark.

"Here, this is for you," she said.

"I don't want it."

"Why not?" she asked. He heard something else in her voice. "Ervin?"

He stared at the cracks in the wall where the mice crawled through. He was afraid his mother was going to ask him again.

"My God, Ervin, don't you hear me?"

"I've already had mine," he said.

"How much did you take?"

"Don't worry, just my share." He felt mice paws pattering across the tops of his shoes. Again, he had the urge to catch one and throw it on the bed.

"Miriam," his mother called.

Ervin left before he could hear his sister's reply. He knew what his mother was thinking.

Chicky was waiting, his hands in his pockets, leaning against the wall. He was picking his teeth. He was looking up at the sky trying to guess which way the clouds were going. There must be wind currents that kept changing.

For a while the two boys strolled along in silence. Then just for something to say, Chicky remarked: "You know what that little crook told me? He says you can't take everything away from everybody."

Everything melted together: father, bread, mother, sister, the moment he was imagining what Chicky might bring back for them. Mice.

"He says we can *hope* without *believing*." Chicky laughed, remembering something else.

"Do you feel like bragging all day?"

"If you could see into me the way I can see into you, you could afford to talk. When my dad went up the chimney, I told myself I was still lucky to have my mother. And when I lost Mother, I told myself that at least I was lucky to have a brother left. He was weaker than a fly. And I said to myself, it's great to have your health at least."

Ervin was silent, so Chicky continued: "Still, we're pretty lucky, Ervin. Even if that's what my little businessman says too. Don't get the idea the world's going to stop turning just because one person in it is feeling miserable at this particular moment. You'd be exaggerating."

They didn't talk about it anymore. They could walk along like this together, so close their elbows or shoulders almost touched, and sometimes as they took a step together, their hips. The mice and the chameleon were gone; Chicky was really more like a barn swallow. Chicky was just slightly crooked. The thought suddenly put him in a better mood. Like when the sun came out or when he looked at a tree or the blue sky.

"He's full of wise sayings," Chicky resumed. "According to him, we have to pay for everything. And money and *things* aren't the worst way to pay."

"Aw, forget it. You're sticking as close to me as a fag."

"What about you?" Chicky's little face stretched.

"They haven't come to get him yet, the bastards."

"I can probably tell you why," Chicky declared. "Would you believe it, my dad's beard grew for two days after he was already dead?"

"Do you ever think you might have been a swallow?"

"Say, you're really outdoing yourself today," Chicky remarked. "But if you want to know something, I *have* thought about it."

Ervin looked up into the sky again. He might have known Chicky would have ideas like that. Ervin himself sometimes had the feeling that he was up there being blown around among the raindrops when there was a thunderstorm. The sky looked like an iron shutter. Sometimes he could also imagine himself jumping through the sky, using his arms and legs to steer with.

"Ervin. . . ." Chicky interrupted.

"What?"

"That old guy gave me a tremendous piece of advice."

"So be glad."

"No, Ervin, I mean it."

"Who's arguing?"

"Aren't you interested? He asked me if your old man had anything else."

"What else could he have?"

"He was just hinting."

"These have been hungry days for us. That crooked second-hand man of yours, his brains are going soft. I hope he can tell the difference between dogs and cats."

"Considering we're not their people, Ervin, what he told me wasn't just talk."

"My dad was the cleanest person in this whole dump," said Ervin.

"He didn't mean that and neither did I, Ervin."

"What's with all this suspense?"

"Just say you're not interested and we'll drop it," Chicky said.

"Come on, spill it, will you? What *did* he mean then?"

"Maybe there was a ring or something?"

"Do you really think he'd have let Mother and Miriam die right in front of his eyes if he'd had anything like a *ring?*"

"He wasn't talking only about a ring. He meant gold."

"Dad had to turn over everything he had that was even gilded."

"He hinted at it only after I tried to explain to him about the lemon."

"You know how it was. Mother doesn't have anything either."

"He only hinted at it when I told him how important it was for you to have that lemon, Ervin."

"Well, what was it he hinted, then?" Ervin noticed the expectant look on Chicky's face.

"He hinted that it wasn't impossible, but only in exchange for something made of pure gold. And that he didn't care what it was."

"Don't be a bastard," said Ervin slowly. "Forget it. My dad didn't have anything like that. Go on, get lost."

"He even indicated exactly *what* and *how.*"

"Look, come on—kindly spill it," Ervin said with irritation. *Once again, he saw his father lying there wrapped in the blanket. It flooded through him in a dark tide, like when his mother didn't believe that he hadn't taken more than his share of the bread. He'd known right from the start what Chicky was talking about.*

Ervin didn't say anything.

"Gold teeth, for instance. It's simply something in the mouth he doesn't need anymore, something nobody needs except maybe you and me."

Ervin remained silent.

"Well, I wasn't the one who said anything about a lemon," he concluded.

Ervin stopped and so did Chicky. Then Ervin turned and looked him up and down, eyes bulging.

"Aw, cut it out," Chicky said wearily. "Don't look at me as though I killed your dad."

Suddenly Ervin slapped him. Chicky's face was small and triangular, tapering off crookedly at the top. It was very obvious because his head was shaved. Then Ervin slapped him again and began to punch his face and chest. When his fist struck Chicky's Adam's apple, Ervin could feel how fragile everything about him was.

Again he saw himself stripping those brown checkered trousers off his father's body. The undertakers would be coming along any minute. (They should have been here long ago.) He thought of how he'd managed to do that before they came and how he'd probably manage to do even this if he wanted to. And he knew that he couldn't have swallowed that piece of bread even if his mother had given it to him without those second thoughts of hers. He kept pounding his fists into Chicky, and it was as if he were striking at himself and his mother. *He kept telling himself that his father was dead anyway and that it didn't matter much and that it didn't have any bearing on the future either.*

Then he felt everything slowing down. Chicky began to fight back. Ervin got in two fast punches, one on the chin, the other in the belly. Chicky hit Ervin twice before people gathered and tried to break it up, threatening to call the security guards.

Ervin picked himself up off the sidewalk as fast as he could. He shook himself like a dog and went home through the courtyard.

"Ervin?" his mother called out. "Is that you?"

"Yeah," he answered.

"Did you find anything else?"

He was shivering as he sometimes did when he was cold because he'd loaned his blanket to his mother or Miriam.

"Mirrie. . . ." he tried.

He bundled himself up into the rug. He was glad Chicky had hit him back. It was hard to explain why. It was different from wanting to catch a mouse and kill it. He touched his cheek and chin, fingering the swollen places. Again he waited for his mother to say something. But she didn't. Mother only knows as much as I tell her, he said to himself. Mother's quite innocent, Ervin decided. Despite everything she's still innocent. Would she have been able to do what she had criticized him for? He wished she'd say something, give at least an echo. He thought of Miriam. For a moment he could see her, tall and slender, her breasts and blond hair.

The twilight began to melt into the dampness of the cellar. The spider webs disappeared in the darkness. He wished they'd muffle the edge of his mother's voice. He waited for Miriam's cough. The silence was like a muddy path where nobody wants to walk. *And his father was still lying out there in the hall.*

When someone dies, Ervin thought to himself, *it means not expecting, not worrying about anything, not hoping for something that turns out to be futile. It means not forcing yourself into something you don't really want, while you go on behaving as though you did. It means not being dependent on anybody or anything. It means being rid of what's bothering you. It's like when you close your eyes and see things and people in your own way.*

That idea of a path leading from the dead to the living and back again is just a lot of foolishness I thought up by myself. To be dead means to expect nothing, not to expect somebody to say something, not to wait for someone's voice. Not to stare enviously after a streetcar going somewhere from somewhere else.

He looked around. Miriam had begun to cough again. She's coughing almost gently, he thought to himself. She probably doesn't have enough strength left to cough anymore.

My God, that lying, thieving, sly old man, that bastard who's fed for six thousand years on Jewish wisdom and maybe would for another half an hour—but maybe not even that long. That dirty louse, full of phony maxims and dreams as complicated as clockwork, lofty as a rose, rank as an onion, who perhaps wasn't quite as imaginary as I wanted to think he was, judging from Chicky's descriptions which made him sound as though he'd swallowed all the holy books. That slimy crook with his miserable messages, that you have to pay for everything and that money and things aren't the most precious currency. But he also said you can't take everything away from everybody, as though he wanted to confuse you by contradicting himself in the same breath. Where did he get those ideas?

"No, I don't have anything," he said suddenly, as if he knew his mother was still waiting for an answer.

He heard her sigh. From his sister's bed he heard a stifled cough. (She's probably ashamed of coughing by now.)

Nothing's plaguing Father anymore either. Not even the craving for a bowl of soup. He wasn't looking forward anymore to seeing Ervin dash out onto the field in a freshly laundered uniform and shiny football boots, which he took care of, in front of crowds of people waiting for entertainment and thrills and a chance to yell their lungs out. If they come for Father now, they'll do just what Chicky said they would. Anyway, the undertakers themselves do it to the old people. He remembered his father's smile which got on his mother's nerves.

He stared into the darkness. His mother was bandaging her swollen legs. Her eyes were very bright. She's probably feverish, he thought. She made a few inexplicable gestures. *What if the rabbis are right and there is some afterwards? Then his father must be able to see him. Where do you suppose he really is, Ervin wondered, and where am I? Does anybody know? Inwardly he tried to smile at his father. It would be nice if I could really smile at him.* To be on the safe side, Ervin tried smiling at his father again.

"I'm going out and take another look around," he said.

Mother ceased her strange movements. "Where do you want to go in the dark?"

"I want to have a look at something."

"Be careful, child."

He went out into the hall and the place he had avoided before, so he wouldn't have to look at the wall beside which his father's body was still lying. He was squeezing through the crack in the wall. For a short while an insurance agent had lived in the corner shop. *But this isn't your father anymore,* he told himself; *he was only until yesterday. Now there is nothing but a weight and the task of carrying it away,* he reminded himself immediately. *But I'll think of him only in good ways. And Mother and Miriam will think about him as if nothing's happened.*

He threw off the old blanket. He closed his eyes for a second. I won't be able to eat very much, he realized, as though he wanted to convince himself that this was the only difference it would make. Everything moved stiffly. He had to turn the head and open its mouth. He grabbed it by the chin and hair and that was how he managed. He couldn't remember exactly which tooth it was. He tried one after another. He was hurrying. He didn't want Chicky and the men with the coffins to catch him at it. Instead, he tried to imagine that lemon. It was like a yellow sphere at the end of the hall. Suddenly he couldn't remember where lemons came from, except that it was somewhere in the south, and whether they grew on trees or bushes. He'd never really known anyway.

He picked up a sharp stone. He had a sticky feeling as though he were robbing somebody. He tried to decide which was the best way to knock it out. He tried several times without success. Then he stopped trying to get at just that one tooth. There is no other way, he kept repeating to himself. Do it. Do it fast. The faster the better.

Finally something in the jaw loosened. Ervin could smell his own breath. He tossed the stone away. He was glad nobody had seen him. Into the palm of his hand he scooped what he'd been seeking. (He was squatting and the head dropped back to the floor.)

Ervin stood up slowly. He felt as though his body and thoughts were flowing into a dark river, and he didn't know where it came from and where it was going. He wiped his hands on his pants. The cellar was dark, like the last place a person can retreat to. For a moment he closed his eyes. He had to take it out into the light. He headed for the other end of the corridor.

He'd hardly stepped out into the street when he saw Chicky's face in the twilight. There, you see, Ervin said to himself. He was keeping watch after all. Chicky would have done what he'd just done if he'd had the chance.

"Hello, kid," Chicky began. "Hello, you Jew bastard." Then Chicky exploded: "You lousy hyena. You son of a bitch. I suppose you've come to apologize. At least I hope so."

Ervin was clutching the thing tightly in his fist. He stared at Chicky for a long time.

"But I got in two good punches, didn't I? Like Max Schmeling." Chicky sounded pleased with himself. His eyes shone.

But then he noticed that the skin under Ervin's eyes was bluer than any bruise could have made it. He noticed, too, the pale blotches on Ervin's face. And how he kept his hand in his pocket.

"No hard feelings," Chicky said.

"I have it."

"I was sure you'd manage. . . ."

Ervin pulled his hand out of his pocket and Chicky's glance shifted swiftly.

"Bring me that lemon, Chicky, but the whole thing." He unclenched his fist. It lay there cupped in his palm, a rather unattractive shell of gold the color of old copper, and very dirty.

"You won't take the tiniest slice for yourself."

"If it's pure, Ervin, you're in luck," Chicky said.

When Ervin did not respond he continued: "Sometimes it's just iron or some ersatz. Then it's worn through on top. The old man warned me about that in advance. But if it isn't, then you're damned lucky, Ervin, honest."

"When will you bring me that lemon?" Ervin asked, getting to the point.

"First hand it over and let me take a look."

Impatiently, Chicky inspected the crown, acting as though he hadn't heard Ervin. He scraped away the blood that had dried around the root and removed bits of cement. He blew on it and rubbed the dull gold between his fingers, then let it rest in his palm again.

"For this, the old runt will jump like a toad."

"I hope so."

"But first, Ervin, it's fifty-fifty."

"The hell it is," he answered firmly.

"I'll only do it for half."

"If Miriam doesn't get that lemon, she won't even last out till evening."

"Why shouldn't she last out? I'm keeping half."

"You're not keeping anything," repeated Ervin. "Now get going before it's too late."

Ervin glared at him, but there was a question in his eyes. Chicky acted calm. None of his self-satisfaction had filtered through to Ervin. His throat tightened. He began to shiver. He could feel the goose pimples on his neck and arms. It wasn't the way he wanted to think it was, *that his father had died and otherwise everything was just the same as before.* And when Chicky looked at him, Ervin could read in his eyes that instead of bringing a lemon or some kind of pills that have the same effect as lemons, Chicky would probably bring another piece of bread.

Ervin heard the quiet gurgle rising in his throat. He tried thinking about that runty second-hand dealer.

"I'd be crazy to do it for nothing," said Chicky slowly. He squinted warily and his nostrils flared. He bared his teeth. There were big gaps between them.

"Either we go halves or I tell your mom how you're treating me."

"You're not such a bastard, Chicky, are you?"

"Well, I'd have to be," replied Chicky.

"Get going," Ervin said.

"That sounds more like it."

"I'll wait at home."

"All right."

"And hurry up. Honestly, it's very important."

"Fast as a dog can do you know what," grinned Chicky.

Small and nimble, he dodged among the pedestrians. In the meantime, two men with tubs had appeared. Chicky must have passed them. The tubs were covered with tattered sheets and something bulged underneath. Everybody stepped aside as the porters passed. They knew what they were carrying.

Ervin didn't feel like going back home. He crawled into the opening of a cement culvert pipe. His long skinny head stuck out as he sat there watching the sun set behind the clouds. It dropped slowly. The barn swallows were flying lower now than they had been earlier that afternoon, flying in flocks, suddenly soaring up, then back toward earth.

He kept looking up and down the alley so he wouldn't miss Chicky when he came back.

It all began to melt together before his eyes: the silhouettes of the buildings and the cobblestones that had been pounded into the earth and then washed loose by long-gone rains. He watched the sky which was full of barn swallows and the sun disappeared. Rain was gathering in the clouds as their colors changed.

I ought to be like a rock, he told himself. Even harder than a rock. He forced his eyes up to the sky where the swallows were wheeling. Maybe swallows are happy, free, without guilt. He tried to swallow the distance, the wet air and the disappearing light, the flowing wind.

And he wept, quietly and without tears, in some little crevice which was inside.

chapter 5

Imprisoned in the Camps

The Nazis imprisoned millions of Jews and others in camps. Some were incarcerated in camps like Auschwitz, where they were told they would be saved by working; others, deemed unfit for work, were sent directly to death camps such as Birkenau, the death camp connected with Auschwitz. Assignment to a work camp, however, did not ensure survival. Often the guards were cruel and capricious in their treatment of the prisoners, food and medicine were in short supply, and the working and living conditions were atrocious. As difficult as life had been in the ghettos, life in the camps was even more difficult.

Heinrich Himmler, Hitler's hand-picked head of the SS, had appointed Reinhard Heydrich to be in charge of dealing with "the Jewish issue." His protégé was Adolf Eichmann, who headed the Jewish desk in Berlin. Heydrich and Eichmann planned the ghettos, ordered the roundup of Jews, and determined their deportation. While there is some uncertainty about the exact date, it is thought that some time during the summer or fall of 1941, Heydrich and Eichmann were charged with developing a plan for the ultimate determination of the fate of European Jews. This plan was revealed on January 20, 1942, in the Berlin suburb of Wannsee, to a group of high-ranking Nazi officials. The plan presented at the Wannsee Conference called for the eastward transportation of all Jews to work camps. Heydrich and Eichmann freely acknowledged that their concern was for the "able-bodied" who could be of service to the war effort. The weak would die off, saving the Nazis from having to kill them. The plan also called for killing the survivors after the Nazi victory, because the "final solution" meant that all Jews must be killed because they represented potential threats to Aryan purity.

The establishment of the camps was an ongoing part of Hitler's plan to quell his enemies. Some of the more famous camps were constructed before the beginning of World War II: Buchenwald in 1938; Mauthausen and Flossenburg in 1938; and Ravensbruck women's prison in 1939. By the beginning of World War II, when Germany invaded Poland, the network of camps was established. They would play a vital part in Germany's war efforts, either as work camps, where slave labor fueled the Nazi war machine, or as death camps.

Frequently, a death camp was built in proximity to a work camp. Such was the case with the largest of all the concentration camps, Auschwitz. Just across the electrified fence was the death camp of Birkenau. Upon arrival at camps like

Auschwitz, prisoners were often separated into two groups. Those fit for work were sent in one direction, while the others were sent to the "showers," the Nazis' gas chambers. Once the prisoners had been gassed, they were then shoveled into furnaces and burned to ashes. The odor of burning flesh could be smelled for miles around the camps.

As long as they were able to contribute to the war effort, prisoners were spared. Yet they were starved, beaten, and made vulnerable to disease. The incarcerations continued, and conditions in the camps deteriorated even as the Allied forces approached. In many cases, the Nazis attempted to destroy as much of the evidence of their atrocities as they could by escalating their program of murder of inmates or by forced marches of prisoners to other camps farther away from the front before the Allied troops arrived.

For many of us, the primary images we have of the Holocaust are of emaciated survivors of the camps at the time of liberation. While these images provide us with an enduring awareness of the magnitude of the horror, the images in films and photographs simply show us the end result of the Nazi attempt to make the world *Judenfrei* (free of Jews). Chapter 5 presents the experiences of some of those imprisoned in the camps.

A Prelude to Hell

Elio Romano

Elio Romano was born in Auschwitz, Poland, in
1923, seventeen years before he was rounded up
by the Nazis as a slave laborer to help with the
construction of the concentration camp there.
During the war, he was moved from camp to camp,
being incarcerated in eleven different camps. In 1945,
he was liberated from Dachau by the United States
Army. He graduated from the University of Munich
before he immigrated to the United States, where he
earned degrees in political science, journalism, and
contemporary history from the University of
California. He has worked as a foreign
correspondent at the United Nations and as a
screenwriter. He is the author of *A Generation of
Wrath: A Story of Embattlement, Survival, and
Deliverance during the Holocaust of World War II*, from
which the following selection is excerpted.

Romano's selection describes the transformation
of the quiet Polish town of Oswiecim, with its two-
cell jail that occasionally housed disruptive drunks,
into Auschwitz, the infamous Nazi camp.

A jail is a place where criminals and other tem-
porary outcasts of society are locked up, I always thought. Being imprisoned
was, of course, harsh punishment. In the town of Auschwitz, formerly the
orderly and peaceful Oswiecim, the only people ever to land in the two jail cells

located in the yard of the town hall, next to the police guardroom, were drunks who made a nuisance of themselves and insulted the town's imperious police constable. Occasionally, socialist and communist agitators during first-of-May demonstrations had been temporarily "re-educated" there, before being sent away to bigger and more frightful installations in the capital. However, since the Germans had arrived, Auschwitz had neither drunks nor radicals. And so the jail block remained empty, until some twenty-five Jews filled its cells.

I was among those locked up and so was my mother. So were the others, either participants of the illegal escapade, parents or organisers. Yossel M was also among us. We never found out who put the finger on us, but betrayed we had been. That much we knew.

The minute the two German border guards took us back to their village post they boasted that they had known we were going to cross the border at a given point. All they had to do, they said, was trap us at the right time.

"You were sold out, you poor saps," the head of the border post, a middle-aged sergeant, told us after we were brought in by the patrol. Knowing the German invaders, we expected to be roughed up, beaten and interrogated, but nothing of the sort occurred. Instead, we were given food and hot tea with rum, as if we were guests instead of prisoners.

Were these soldiers really Germans, I wondered? They were indeed, but not Wehrmacht conscripts, only old border policemen, transferred from the Reich to do noncombatant duty along the new frontier. Old foxes they would be called by some, professionals who had wives and children back home and who apparently were glad to serve in an isolated post, away from the political Nazi Party goons who would see that the ideology of the "New Order" was scrupulously adhered to.

"You should be glad you were caught by us and not by the Gestapo," the sergeant said. We knew what he meant and appreciated his frankness. We hadn't eaten all day and the long march in the mountains froze our bones.

"What will happen to us?" I asked, after we had all been through a preliminary interrogation.

The sergeant shrugged. "Nothing, I suppose," he answered. "You'll go back home tomorrow. After all, you're still under age."

We were glad to hear that, but we knew that our adventure would cause repercussions, once we got back to Auschwitz. The German authorities there wouldn't be as lenient as these old timers, veterans of Kaiser Wilhelm's reign.

"Why couldn't you have let us cross the border?" I asked. "We only wanted to go to Palestine and we were told the Reich was glad to see us go."

"If it were up to me, I would have let you pass," the man answered, "but we received a tip about your intended crossing. You had no valid emigration permits, so we had to stop it. We do have martial law, you know."

It was incredible. These Germans were of a different breed from those we had encountered until now. Had they, however, not been so duty conscious we would already have been in Slovakia. The next morning all eleven of us were given travel orders and train tickets to take us back to Auschwitz. We went all by ourselves.

Our adventure was rather short-lived. At home we had to put the armbands back on and keep a low profile. The meetings with Yossel M had been suspended, but we reported our experiences at a Jewish Council meeting, with our former mentor also present. Nobody could figure out who had given the scheme away. It didn't matter anyway. Youth emigration was dead and buried! But the belated after effects of our journey were soon to be felt.

Only three days after our return home we were called to the German police station and individually interrogated. This time we had to deal with professionals, but still they were only members of the *Schutzpolizei*, regular police constables and officers who went by the book. They, too, bore no grudges against Jews in particular, but had to prosecute a clear offence against their laws. In January 1940, the long arm of the Gestapo and the SS, about whom we had heard from previous Jewish refugees from Germany, had not yet reached Auschwitz.

I actually wondered why they had to grill us so much. They knew everything about our abortive escapade and the part Yossel M played in it. Anyway, I claimed ignorance. I just heard about the planned journey and simply joined in, I maintained. Of the organisers I knew nothing, I insisted. After all, I was only a youngster and still under age.

Again we were released and sent back home, but only temporarily. Within the next few days the German police and the Polish guard of the jail rounded up all the youngsters who had participated in the escape attempt, as well as all the parents they could find. I was thrown into a cell with the males and my mother joined the few females. Since we received no rations, our relatives were obliged to feed us. They were allowed to come once a day, during our fifteen minute walks in the yard, and give us our provisions. My mother and I were visited in the jail by my girl cousin, Hessa, who was about my age and our comforting angel then.

Since we never appeared before a court, we also didn't know how long we would be imprisoned. Yossel M reflected on past events in Europe.

"We have been fools all along," he told us. "In 1938, before the war started, Jabotinsky warned us about our fate, in the wake of Nazi expansionism, and urged us to leave Europe, but we didn't believe him. We were too complacent, too deeply rooted in our age-old habits to risk a change. Now, in 1940, our activities and movements are drastically curtailed and our resources limited. I am afraid that after our latest fiasco the Jewish Council will be unwilling to underwrite any further organised emigration or escapes. From now on every one of you is on his own. That is if we ever get out of this jail and the Germans don't ship us to one of their concentration camps."

Ever since the Nazi rise to power in Germany, in 1933, and from subsequent refugees, we all knew about the existence of such camps in Dachau, in Buchenwald . . . The people who were incarcerated there had been in jails first.

After seventeen days in the cell block we were released and allowed to go back home. That February the Germans weren't yet too preoccupied with Jews. To judge by their newspapers they still hoped Great Britain and France would opt for peace and approve the Reich's territorial gains. After all it was almost six months since the war began and yet all was quiet on the Western front. The game seemed to have been a wait-and-see proposition. It applied to us just as much as to the rest of the world.

Our economic situation however, had worsened. I went to work every day to supplement the family's income. The Maccabean group had been disbanded, but I had been meeting my friends individually and often consulted with Julian and my cousin Jacob. The times weren't conducive to much cultural activity or social life. All we could do was talk about politics and survival.

In March the first SS man arrived in town. He was just a *Scharführer*, a corporal, but an arrogant thug whose sole purpose seemed to be to intimidate us. He arrived one morning in front of the office of the Jewish Council demanding one hundred workers for his command. Since the Council had other requirements to fill for the German Wehrmacht and police, the SS man got only fifty men that day. I was among them.

We were marched off to the former Polish barracks, across the river. The place had seen Jewish slave labour before, when we had had to remove all traces left by the previous occupants, the Polish artillery. This time, the SS man said, he would be in charge and we would be doing some "real work." We were going to be his work team, or *Kommando*, as he called it. Even then this martial term evoked in me a feeling of ominous menace.

As soon as we reached the compound the SS man lined us up in columns of three abreast and had us stand at attention. It looked like some kind of army drill and we didn't know what to make of it. We didn't have to wait long for an explanation. With a horse whip in his hand to make him feel masterly, the *Scharführer* posted himself in front of us and started to give us a lecture.

"Listen carefully, you pigheaded scum! I came here to teach you obedience and subservience. We Germans will make you pay dearly for slandering the Reich and our Fuehrer."

While he looked us over carefully, this conglomerate of shabbily dressed youngsters and middle-aged men, he continued to spill his venom. We were terror-stricken.

"You miserable gang of poor-Johns may not be the real culprits, but the American plutocrats and their Jews are. They forced the war upon us. And so you *Schweinehunde* will suffer for their crimes. All of you are warmongers!"

I stood there petrified. What the man said was hideous and the most terrible slander the Nazis could use against us. Yet we didn't dare to contradict him.

"You see," the SS goon continued in triumph, "your silence proves that I am right. I have seen your crooked kind before, back home, in the concentration camp of Sachsenhausen. Mark that in your cowardly brains!"

So, that was it. The black plague had finally come to Auschwitz. If one SS man came, others were bound to follow. What sinister plans were they hatching?

I had no time to speculate further because the *Scharführer* made us do punishing exercises and push-ups.

"This will circulate your rotten blood," he laughed viciously. "After that you'll be fit for honest work."

Following the drill period we were assigned to work. All the buildings had to be emptied of furniture and all the rubble burned on an empty plot. We started with the first of some 20 one- and two-storey brick buildings spread over the entire compound.

From that first day, the Jewish Council allocated higher pay for all the workers who went out on the barracks detail. It was a case of hardship, but many of our people needed the income, myself included. In about a month all the buildings had been cleared. In the meantime Polish masons and carpenters had been hired by the Germans and a few of the better-kept buildings were renovated. Also, strings of barbed-wire fences had been laid all around the compound and watchtowers built. There was no doubt in our minds that the former barracks would become some sort of prison camp. As time went on our work detail swelled to between two to three hundred men. At first, the SS man had us do the push-up ritual daily, but he soon got tired of it himself and relented. The workday became routine.

Some time in April a troop of about fifteen more SS men, headed by an officer named Höss, arrived in Auschwitz and took up quarters in one of the refurbished buildings. With them German "Aryan" concentration-camp prisoners in striped uniforms, some thirty men in all, also came. We found out that they were from Sachsenhausen, near Berlin. They, too, occupied one of the blocks, but behind barbed wire. Clean-up and restructuring work had then been going on in full swing. We realised with horror that the SS were building another one of their sordid camps, but this time on our own soil! Most ominous, however, was the disinfection process the Germans devised.

As a self-proclaimed superior race, the Germans always held the opinion that other peoples were not hygienic enough, according to their own standards, and therefore their dwellings must surely be infested by vermin. To make the old Polish buildings "habitable" they had to be disinfected. This was done by hermetically sealing a building first, sticking mud into all roof crevices and plastering adhesive tape around door and window frames, and then fumigating the interior. The disinfecting agent was a crystalline chemical in tin cans which, when evaporating, had that cleansing effect. The used-up containers were discarded and, like all other rubbish, landed on a big dump which was periodically set on fire. I once looked at one of the empty cans. It was a sinister, death-bearing vessel and its chemical contents was called Zyklon-B. Had the can not been so bulky, I would have taken it home with me, as I had been pocketing labels which came with various shipments we had to unpack and handle before the items were delivered to their designated places. In all instances the slips said, *Konzentrationslager Auschwitz*, making them valid souvenirs for the collector I was. The tin can was more than that. As I held it in my hands, an awesome, inexplicable premonition struck me that this poisonous chemical could also be used to "disinfect" people. The thought was so morbid that I became distressed and threw the macabre item on to the burning fire.

That day the camp's loudspeakers blared martial music. It was Saturday, the 20th of April 1940. Hitler's birthday.

Little by little the new concentration camp took shape. The compound was a beehive of activity. Several hundred Jews and Poles worked there daily under the supervision of German civilians, while the German prisoners from Sachsenhausen were preparing quarters for more inmates and the SS guards walked around the new installation like peacocks, drinking mineral water at all conceivable hours. At the time, I thought this was some sort of ritual which I could never comprehend. Only later, a friendly German supervisor offered a plausible explanation. Mineral water purified body and mind, according to Himmler, and his SS men were ordered to drink it.

In May, a transport of some forty Polish prisoners arrived from Dachau. They were to become the so-called *Stammhäftlinge*, the basic inmates of the Auschwitz Concentration Camp. Although they were quartered in a compound behind barbed wire, I had a chance to talk to them. Some of them were Jews from Warsaw. They had been taken to Dachau not as Jews, but as part of a raid on Polish intelligentsia. One of them told me that they were to become the camp's administrators, cooks and book-keepers, with the German prisoners from Sachsenhausen, a mixed conglomerate of men, the camp's future "Capos."

"Capos?!" I asked.

"The sons-of-bitches are our supervisors," the gentle-looking Jewish prisoner answered. "The Germans plan to imprison thousands of people here. I hope you won't be one of them."

I was frightened out of my wits. "What can I do for you?" I asked the prisoner. "Do you have relatives?"

"We are allowed to write home, once a month," he answered, "but the food here is poor."

While nobody was looking, I slipped the sandwich I had brought for lunch through the barbed wire. He took it furtively and left. In the days to follow, I could see some of my comrades from the Jewish work detail do the same. We supported the prisoners as much as we could. Bread was the one commodity we could still spare. After all it was heartbreaking to see fellow human beings caged in behind barbed wire. Life in such a spine-chilling camp was anything but recreation, we knew. It was indeed a hell on earth.

Our work detail in the camp lasted till some time in June, after which no Jew from the town of Auschwitz was allowed anywhere near the perimeter of the concentration camp. Occasionally, columns of prisoners marched through town, on the way to their places of work. I saw hundreds of them, flanked by SS guards, while those with armbands designating them as Capos headed the various details.

It was truly a dispiriting sight.

★ ★ ★

That summer the Germans expelled Jews from some of the small towns along their Reich's border. The places were the first to become *Judenrein*, or clear of Jews. At the same time they also brought "back home" thousands of their own nationals who centuries earlier had settled the rich soils of Hungary and Romania. They were called *Volksdeutsche*. To accommodate them, Polish farmers had to give up their homesteads in the sensitive areas and move east. The displaced Jews, however, had not been given new lands to settle. Instead they were thrust upon us as new refugees. We took one such family into our house. They had a daughter of about fifteen. A gentle, beautiful girl with an alabaster face, but a victim of some children's disease which deformed her legs and made her a cripple.

She loved to play with my younger brother and my little sister. When I had to face her, I blushed, but didn't know if it was admiration or pity. To talk to her was a revelation. She wasn't only lovely, she was also incredibly wise.

"How do you feel with us?" I asked her a few days after she and her parents came. I was already in love with her.

"I'll have to get used to it," she answered. "We will manage. But I have been a burden on my parents ever since the war broke out. Without me they would have escaped to safety a long time ago."

"You are safe here," I told her emphatically. "All we have to do is work for the Germans. Otherwise they don't really bother us too much." Even if my statement wasn't wholly true, I still tried to calm her. But she shook her head.

"No," she said sadly. "You don't believe in what you say, do you?"

I bit into my lips instead of answering.

"Things look very bad for us Jews," she continued. "The Nazis want to destroy us and nobody is going to stop them. They'll move us from place to place, until there will be no place left for us to go."

"You actually know that?" I asked her. What the girl said was frightening. I refused to believe it.

"I don't know anything and yet I do," she whispered gently. "A cripple can see more, feel more and tell more than others are willing to admit."

"The bastards have certainly given us samples of their behaviour," I admitted. "We've got the SS in town . . . and a new concentration camp."

"I know," the girl nodded.

"Do you hate them as much as I do?"

She shook her head.

"You don't?" I asked with disbelief.

"No."

"Why?" I just wanted to know what went on in her little, unusual head. I wished I could take her into my arms.

"I pity them," she answered simply.

I couldn't accept that. "Do they seem handicapped to you in any way?" I tried sardonically.

"Yes," she nodded. "They, too, are cripples. They're sick." The girl certainly was generous with kindness.

If Jew-baiting, brutality, mercilessness and all the other insane traits the SS men had so far displayed were signs of sickness then these Germans were certainly maimed for life. I wondered if the devil and the Angel of Death were also cripples. If so, I would have to be careful. I would have to outwit them both.

The little, handicapped Jewish girl, a sheltered refugee in our midst, bore no malice against our tormenters. Why was she, of all people, so magnanimous? Perhaps because she had always been isolated from real cruelty, or maybe she was simply a saintly person. I wasn't. Charity had to be extended to man—not to beast—and piety, I would render only to God!

Judith, that was the girl's name, had to walk with two crutches, but she would let no one help her. Despite her fatalistic outlook she nevertheless loved life and thought of man as a basically good and civilised creature, except that she believed cripples had a right to be eccentric.

"So you believe the Germans are just sick eccentrics?" I asked her. "What, then, are we?"

"Their victims," she replied. "Just like many people are victimised in different parts of the world. Nazism is like bacteria which cause sickness in other healthy beings. But even bacteria are God's creatures."

She proceeded to tell me about the fate of Indians in America, Negroes in Africa and the wars and miseries which plagued Spaniards, Ethiopians, Manchurians, Hindus and Maoris. She had read it all in books, she explained. But the human race was basically good, she added.

"And why do the Germans want to destroy us?" I argued. "Are we worse than the others you mentioned?"

"Not at all," she said. "But our environment today is less favourable." She gave me an angelic smile.

"I don't think we should remain idle and do nothing about it. Pity alone is not going to save us," I told her. "And I am going to care about my own people first."

"The whole human race has to be freed from injustice," she proclaimed loftily. "We are only incidental."

Well, I thought, it was about time we Jews stopped preaching about freedom and started to fight for it. Auschwitz alone was reality. If anyone mattered it was that cripple, Judith.

Indeed, this excessive high-mindedness has always been the malady of our intelligentsia. They were either too parochial or too engrossed in the problems of the world to be able to cope effectively with their own situation. In 1940, some of our rabbinic leaders were no different. Instead of guiding their flocks they turned to mysticism, while the Germans kept reducing us to outcasts. The early and desperate efforts of the Jewish Councils to rationalise our existence failed as well. Inadvertently they, too, slowly became tools of the Germans.

While Jewish labour details weren't sent to the camp area any longer, I had often worked in that part of town, in Zasole, and around the railway station which was close to the compound. By then "K L Auschwitz," as the site was called by the Germans, was full of prisoners from Poland, Czechoslovakia, Austria, Belgium, Holland and France. These were, for the most part, political detainees. Polish civilians from our town and from the villages of Birkenau and Rajsko still worked on the expansion of the camp. It was from them that detailed reports reached us. The rest, I could see quite well with my own eyes. Once our Jewish unit was assigned to help Polish workers who were repairing the railway siding which led to the former Polish Tobacco Monopoly buildings, now part of the camp. I could just about touch the barbed-wire fence; I could see the inside of the camp teeming with prisoners and SS guards and I also got a first-hand impression of what an operating concentration camp looked like. At that time, I was told, Auschwitz already had some ten thousand inmates, with the camp's absorption facilities constantly increasing.

Every so often delegations of Nazi and SS bigwigs came to Auschwitz to inspect the camp. They usually arrived in convoys, some from as far away as Berlin. We never knew who these visitors were, but rumours spoke of many leading SS generals. Police and SS patrols were always strengthened during these tours and, at the same time, we were warned to keep off the streets.

The SS reign of terror in the camp affected us in the town as well. Especially when a Polish prisoner managed to escape from one of the work detachments, which at the time wasn't too difficult since the local peasants always harboured the runaways and turned them over to the underground for safe passage to the east. In those days the escapees were never found. Instead, and in addition to tightened security, squads of SS men rampaged through the streets of the town menacing and manhandling every person whose looks they disliked.

On one such occasion, the commandant of the camp came into town drunk, posted himself in the small square near where we lived and started a long tirade against Poles who hid outlawed criminals, and Jews who, in his words, poisoned the water wells of Auschwitz to such an extent that he no longer dared to take a bath. I could hear every word he said and it sounded so utterly ridiculous that I had to cringe, while hiding behind the doors of our house. Nobody, not even the German police, could stop the maniac. After he ran out of words some of his underlings hustled him away.

There was, of course, nothing wrong with the town's water. It came from springs that were neither poisoned nor in any way polluted. If the commandant's tub seemed contaminated the abomination certainly originated in his own camp, on the other side of the river. The Sola, usually a clear, rushing tributary of the Vistula, had indeed become a stream of murky waters ever since Höss had built his first provisional cremation unit and made the Sola a depository of human ashes.

That evening, in beautiful, late-summer weather, when we all sat in our garden, under my blossoming jasmin tree and talked about the events of the day, my little eight-year-old sister, oblivious of the ghastly times she lived in, and robbed of playmates and schooling, asked the most simple and innocent question I ever heard: "What is a concentration camp?"

Survival in Auschwitz

Primo Levi

Primo Levi was born in Turin, Italy, on July 31, 1919,
and later graduated from the University of Turin
with a degree in chemistry. After graduation, he
tried to join the Italian resistance but was captured
and sent to Auschwitz. His educational background
helped him to survive his experiences in the camp.
After the war, he returned to Italy and had a
successful career in a chemical factory in Turin.
He was named general manager of the factory in
1961. As an author, he is best known for his autobiographical accounts of the years he spent at
Auschwitz. He is a prolific author of fiction, poetry,
and autobiography. His books include *If Not Now,
When?*, *Survival in Auschwitz*, from which the
following excerpt is taken, *Moments of Reprieve*, *The
Drowned and the Saved*, and *The Reawakening*. Levi
died in Turin on April 11, 1987. His death was
apparently a suicide.

In this personal narrative of Levi's Holocaust
experience, Levi clearly demonstrates that the trip
from Italy to Auschwitz was both actual and
metaphorical. The journey was one from reason to
insanity, from a normal life to a tenuous existence,
for those who survived.

The Journey

I was captured by the Fascist Militia on 13 December 1943. I was twenty-four, with little wisdom, no experience and a decided tendency—encouraged by the life of segregation forced on me for the previous four years by the racial laws—to live in an unrealistic world of my own, a world inhabited by civilized Cartesian phantoms, by sincere male and bloodless female friendships. I cultivated a moderate and abstract sense of rebellion.

It had been by no means easy to flee into the mountains and to help set up what, both in my opinion and in that of friends little more experienced than myself, should have become a partisan band affiliated with the Resistance movement *Justice and Liberty*. Contacts, arms, money and the experience needed to acquire them were all missing. We lacked capable men, and instead we were swamped by a deluge of outcasts, in good or bad faith, who came from the plain in search of a non-existent military or political organization, of arms, or merely of protection, a hiding place, a fire, a pair of shoes.

At that time I had not yet been taught the doctrine I was later to learn so hurriedly in the Lager: that man is bound to pursue his own ends by all possible means, while he who errs but once pays dearly. So that I can only consider the following sequence of events justified. Three Fascist Militia companies, which had set out in the night to surprise a much more powerful and dangerous band than ours, broke into our refuge one spectral snowy dawn and took me down to the valley as a suspect person.

During the interrogations that followed, I preferred to admit my status of "Italian citizen of Jewish race." I felt that otherwise I would be unable to justify my presence in places too secluded even for an evacuee; while I believed (wrongly as was subsequently seen) that the admission of my political activity would have meant torture and certain death. As a Jew, I was sent to Fossoli, near Modena, where a vast detention camp, originally meant for English and American prisoners-of-war, collected all the numerous categories of people not approved of by the new-born Fascist Republic.

At the moment of my arrival, that is, at the end of January 1944, there were about one hundred and fifty Italian Jews in the camp, but within a few weeks their number rose to over six hundred. For the most part they consisted of entire families captured by the Fascists or Nazis through their imprudence or following secret accusations. A few had given themselves up spontaneously, reduced to desperation by the vagabond life, or because they lacked the means to survive, or to avoid separation from a captured relation, or even—absurdly—"to be in conformity with the law." There were also about a hundred Jugoslavian military internees and a few other foreigners who were politically suspect.

The arrival of a squad of German SS men should have made even the optimists doubtful; but we still managed to interpret the novelty in various ways without drawing the most obvious conclusions. Thus, despite everything, the announcement of the deportation caught us all unawares.

On 20 February, the Germans had inspected the camp with care and had publicly and loudly upbraided the Italian commissar for the defective organization of the kitchen service and for the scarce amount of wood distribution for heating; they even said that an infirmary would soon be opened. But on the morning of the 21st we learned that on the following day the Jews would be leaving. All the Jews, without exception. Even the children, even the old, even the ill. Our destination? Nobody knew. We should be prepared for a fortnight of travel. For every person missing at the roll-call, ten would be shot.

Only a minority of ingenuous and deluded souls continued to hope; we others had often spoken with the Polish and Croat refugees and we knew what departure meant.

For people condemned to death, tradition prescribes an austere ceremony, calculated to emphasize that all passions and anger have died down, and that the act of justice represents only a sad duty towards society which moves even the executioner to pity for the victim. Thus the condemned man is shielded from all external cares, he is granted solitude and, should he want it, spiritual comfort; in short, care is taken that he should feel around him neither hatred nor arbitrariness, only necessity and justice, and by means of punishment, pardon.

But to us this was not granted, for we were many and time was short. And in any case, what had we to repent, for what crime did we need pardon? The Italian commissar accordingly decreed that all services should continue to function until the final notice: the kitchens remained open, the corvées for cleaning worked as usual, and even the teachers of the little school gave lessons until the evening, as on other days. But that evening the children were given no homework.

And night came, and it was such a night that one knew that human eyes would not witness it and survive. Everyone felt this: not one of the guards, neither Italian nor German, had the courage to come and see what men do when they know they have to die.

All took leave from life in the manner which most suited them. Some praying, some deliberately drunk, others lustfully intoxicated for the last time. But the mothers stayed up to prepare the food for the journey with tender care, and washed their children and packed the luggage; and at dawn the barbed wire was full of children's washing hung out in the wind to dry. Nor did they forget the diapers, the toys, the cushions and the hundred other small things which mothers remember and which children always need. Would you not do the same? If you and your child were going to be killed tomorrow, would you not give him to eat today?

In hut 6A old Gattegno lived with his wife and numerous children and grandchildren and his sons- and daughters-in-law. All the men were carpenters; they had come from Tripoli after many long journeys, and had always carried with them the tools of their trade, their kitchen utensils and their accordions and violins to play and dance to after the day's work. They were happy and pious folk. Their women were the first to silently and rapidly finish the preparations for the journey in order to have time for mourning. When all was ready, the food cooked, the bundles tied together, they unloosened their hair, took off their shoes, placed the Yahrzeit candles on the ground and lit them according to the customs of their fathers, and sat on the bare soil in a circle for the lamentations, praying and weeping all the night. We collected in a group in front of their door, and we experienced within ourselves a grief that was new for us, the ancient grief of the people that has no land, the grief without hope of the exodus which is renewed every century.

Dawn came on us like a betrayer; it seemed as though the new sun rose as an ally of our enemies to assist in our destruction. The different emotions that overcame us, of resignation, of futile rebellion, of religious abandon, of fear, of despair, now joined together after a sleepless night in a collective, uncontrolled panic. The time for meditation, the time for decision was over, and all reason dissolved into a tumult, across which flashed the happy memories of our homes, still so near in time and space, as painful as the thrusts of a sword.

Many things were then said and done among us; but of these it is better that there remain no memory.

With the absurd precision to which we later had to accustom ourselves, the Germans held the roll-call. At the end the officer asked *"Wieviel Stück?"* The corporal saluted smartly and replied that there were six hundred and fifty "pieces" and that all was in order. They then loaded us on to the buses and took us to the station of Carpi. Here the train was waiting for us, with our escort for the journey. Here we received the first blows: and it was so new and senseless that we felt no pain, neither in body nor in spirit. Only a profound amazement: how can one hit a man without anger?

There were twelve goods wagons for six hundred and fifty men; in mine we were only forty-five, but it was a small wagon. Here then, before our very eyes, under our very feet, was one of those notorious transport trains, those which never return, and of which, shuddering and always a little incredulous, we had so often heard speak. Exactly like this, detail for detail: goods wagons closed from the outside, with men, women and children pressed together without pity, like cheap merchandise, for a journey towards nothingness, a journey down there, towards the bottom. This time it is us who are inside.

Sooner or later in life everyone discovers that perfect happiness is unrealizable, but there are few who pause to consider the antithesis: that perfect unhappiness is equally unattainable. The obstacles preventing the realization of both these extreme states are of the same nature: they derive from our human condition which is opposed to everything infinite. Our ever-insufficient knowledge of the future opposes it: and this is called, in the one instance, hope, and in the other, uncertainty of the following day. The certainty of death opposes it: for it places a limit on every joy, but also on every grief. The inevitable material cares oppose it: for as they poison every lasting happiness, they equally assiduously distract us from our misfortunes and make our consciousness of them intermittent and hence supportable.

It was the very discomfort, the blows, the cold, the thirst that kept us aloft in the void of bottomless despair, both during the journey and after. It was not the will to live, nor a conscious resignation; for few are the men capable of such resolution, and we were but a common sample of humanity.

The doors had been closed at once, but the train did not move until evening. We had learnt of our destination with relief. Auschwitz: a name without significance for us at that time, but it at least implied some place on this earth.

The train travelled slowly, with long, unnerving halts. Through the slit we saw the tall pale cliffs of the Adige Valley and the names of the last Italian cities disappear behind us. We passed the Brenner at midday of the second day and everyone stood up, but no one said a word. The thought of the return journey stuck in my heart, and I cruelly pictured to myself the inhuman joy of that other journey, with doors open, no one wanting to flee, and the first Italian names . . . and I looked around and wondered how many, among that poor human dust, would be struck by fate. Among the forty-five people in my wagon only four saw their homes again; and it was by far the most fortunate wagon.

We suffered from thirst and cold; at every stop we clamoured for water, or even a handful of snow, but we were rarely heard; the soldiers of the escort drove off anybody who tried to approach the convoy. Two young mothers, nursing their children, groaned night and day, begging for water. Our state of nervous tension made the hunger, exhaustion and lack of sleep seem less of a torment. But the hours of darkness were nightmares without end.

There are few men who know how to go to their deaths with dignity, and often they are not those whom one would expect. Few know how to remain silent and respect the silence of others. Our restless sleep was often interrupted by noisy and futile disputes, by curses, by kicks and blows blindly delivered to ward off some encroaching and inevitable contact. Then someone would light a candle, and its mournful flicker would reveal an obscure agitation, a human mass, extended across the floor, confused and continuous, sluggish and aching, rising here and there in sudden convulsions and immediately collapsing again in exhaustion.

Through the slit, known and unknown names of Austrian cities, Salzburg, Vienna, then Czech, finally Polish names. On the evening of the fourth day the cold became intense: the train ran through interminable black pine forests, climbing perceptibly. The snow was high. It must have been a branch line as the stations were small and almost deserted. During the halts, no one tried any more to communicate with the outside world: we felt ourselves by now "on the other side." There was a long halt in open country. The train started up with extreme slowness, and the convoy stopped for the last time, in the dead of night, in the middle of a dark silent plain.

On both sides of the track rows of red and white lights appeared as far as the eye could see; but there was none of that confusion of sounds which betrays inhabited places even from a distance. By the wretched light of the last candle, with the rhythm of the wheels, with every human sound now silenced, we awaited what was to happen.

Next to me, crushed against me for the whole journey, there had been a woman. We had known each other for many years, and the misfortune had struck us together, but we knew little of each other. Now, in the hour of decision, we said to each other things that are never said among the living. We said farewell and it was short; everybody said farewell to life through his neighbour. We had no more fear.

The climax came suddenly. The door opened with a crash, and the dark echoed with outlandish orders in that curt, barbaric barking of Germans in command which seems to give vent to a millennial anger. A vast platform appeared before us, lit up by reflectors. A little beyond it, a row of lorries. Then everything was silent again. Someone translated: we had to climb down with our luggage and deposit it alongside the train. In a moment the platform was swarming with shadows. But we were afraid to break that silence: everyone busied himself with his luggage, searched for someone else, called to somebody, but timidly, in a whisper.

A dozen SS men stood around, legs akimbo, with an indifferent air. At a certain moment they moved among us, and in a subdued tone of voice, with faces of stone, began to interrogate us rapidly, one by one, in bad Italian. They did not interrogate everybody, only a few: "How old? Healthy or ill?" And on the basis of the reply they pointed in two different directions.

Everything was as silent as an aquarium, or as in certain dream sequences. We had expected something more apocalyptic: they seemed simple police agents. It was disconcerting and disarming. Someone dared to ask for his luggage: they replied, "luggage afterwards." Someone else did not want to leave his wife: they said, "together again afterwards." Many mothers did not want to be separated from their children: they said "good, good, stay with child." They behaved with the calm assurance of people doing their normal duty of every day. But Renzo stayed an instant too long to say good-bye to Francesca, his fiancée, and with a single blow they knocked him to the ground. It was their everyday duty.

In less than ten minutes all the fit men had been collected together in a group. What happened to the others, to the women, to the children, to the old men, we could establish neither then nor later: the night swallowed them up, purely and simply. Today, however, we know that in that rapid and summary choice each one of us had been judged capable or not of working usefully for the Reich; we know that of our convoy no more than ninety-six men and twenty-nine women entered the respective camps of Monowitz-Buna and Birkenau, and that of all the others, more than five hundred in number, not one was living two days later. We also know that not even this tenuous principle of discrimination between fit and unfit was always followed, and that later the simpler method was often adopted of merely opening both the doors of the wagon without warning or instructions to the new arrivals. Those who by chance climbed down on one side of the convoy entered the camp; the others went to the gas chamber.

This is the reason why three-year-old Emilia died: the historical necessity of killing the children of Jews was self-demonstrative to the Germans. Emilia, daughter of Aldo Levi of Milan, was a curious, ambitious, cheerful, intelligent child; her parents had succeeded in washing her during the journey in the packed car in a tub with tepid water which the degenerate German engineer had allowed them to draw from the engine that was dragging us all to death.

Thus, in an instant, our women, our parents, our children disappeared. We saw them for a short while as an obscure mass at the other end of the platform; then we saw nothing more.

Instead, two groups of strange individuals emerged into the light of the lamps. They walked in squads, in rows of three, with an odd, embarrassed step, head dangling in front, arms rigid. On their heads they wore comic berets and were all dressed in long striped overcoats, which even by night and from a distance looked filthy and in rags. They walked in a large circle around us, never drawing near, and in silence began to busy themselves with our luggage and to climb in and out of the empty wagons.

We looked at each other without a word. It was all incomprehensible and mad, but one thing we had understood. This was the metamorphosis that awaited us. Tomorrow we would be like them.

Without knowing how I found myself loaded on to a lorry with thirty others; the lorry sped into the night at full speed. It was covered and we could not see outside, but by the shaking we could tell that the road had many curves and bumps. Are we unguarded? Throw ourselves down? It is too late, too late, we are all "down." In any case we are soon aware that we are not without guard. He is a strange guard, a German soldier bristling with arms. We do not see him because of the thick darkness, but we feel the hard contact every time that a lurch of the lorry throws us all in a heap. At a certain point he switches on a pocket torch and instead of shouting threats of damnation at us, he asks us courteously, one by one, in German and in pidgin language, if we have any money or watches to give him, seeing that they will not be useful to us any more. This is no order, no regulation: it is obvious that it is a small private initiative of our Charon. The matter stirs us to anger and laughter and brings relief.

On the Bottom

The journey did not last more than twenty minutes. Then the lorry stopped, and we saw a large door, and above it a sign, brightly illuminated (its memory still strikes me in my dreams): *Arbeit Macht Frei*, work gives freedom.

We climb down, they make us enter an enormous empty room that is poorly heated. We have a terrible thirst. The weak gurgle of the water in the radiators makes us ferocious; we have had nothing to drink for four days. But there is also a tap—and above it a card which says that it is forbidden to drink as the water is dirty. Nonsense. It seems obvious that the card is a joke, "they" know that we are dying of thirst and they put us in a room, and there is a tap, and *Wassertrinken Verboten*. I drink and I incite my companions to do likewise, but I have to spit it out, the water is tepid and sweetish, with the smell of a swamp.

This is hell. Today, in our times, hell must be like this. A huge, empty room: we are tired, standing on our feet, with a tap which drips while we cannot drink the water, and we wait for something which will certainly be terrible, and nothing happens and nothing continues to happen. What can one think about? One cannot think any more, it is like being already dead. Someone sits down on the ground. The time passes drop by drop.

We are not dead. The door is opened and an SS man enters, smoking. He looks at us slowly and asks, *"Wer kann Deutsch?"* One of us whom I have never seen, named Flesch, moves forward; he will be our interpreter. The SS man makes a long calm speech; the interpreter translates. We have to form rows of five, with intervals of two yards between man and man; then we have to undress and make a bundle of the clothes in a special manner, the woollen garments on one side, all the rest on the other; we must take off our shoes but pay great attention that they are not stolen.

Stolen by whom? Why should our shoes be stolen? And what about our documents, the few things we have in our pockets, our watches? We all look at the interpreter, and the interpreter asks the German, and the German smokes and looks him through and through as if he were transparent, as if no one had spoken.

I had never seen old men naked. Mr Bergmann wore a truss and asked the interpreter if he should take it off, and the interpreter hesitated. But the German understood and spoke seriously to the interpreter pointing to someone. We saw the interpreter swallow and then he said: "The officer says, take off the truss, and you will be given that of Mr. Coen." One could see the words coming bitterly out of Flesch's mouth; this was the German manner of laughing.

Now another German comes and tells us to put the shoes in a certain corner, and we put them there, because now it is all over and we feel outside this world and the only thing is to obey. Someone comes with a broom and sweeps away all the shoes, outside the door in a heap. He is crazy, he is mixing them all together, ninety-six pairs, they will be all unmatched. The outside door opens, a freezing wind enters and we are naked and cover ourselves up with our arms. The wind blows and slams the door; the German reopens it and stands watching with interest how we writhe to hide from the wind, one behind the other. Then he leaves and closes it.

Now the second act begins. Four men with razors, soap-brushes and clippers burst in; they have trousers and jackets with stripes, with a number sewn on the front; perhaps they are the same sort as those others of this evening (this evening or yesterday evening?); but these are robust and flourishing. We ask many questions but they catch hold of us and in a moment we find ourselves shaved and sheared. What comic faces we have without hair! The four speak a language which does not seem of this world. It is certainly not German, for I understand a little German.

Finally another door is opened: here we are, locked in, naked, sheared and standing, with our feet in water—it is a shower-room. We are alone. Slowly the astonishment dissolves, and we speak, and everyone asks questions and no one answers. If we are naked in a shower-room, it means that we will have a shower. If we have a shower it is because they are not going to kill us yet. But why then do they keep us standing, and give us nothing to drink, while nobody explains anything, and we have no shoes or clothes, but we are all naked with our feet in the water, and we have been travelling five days and cannot even sit down.

And our women?

Mr Levi asks me if I think that our women are like us at this moment, and where they are, and if we will be able to see them again. I say yes, because he is married and has a daughter; certainly we will see them again. But by now my belief is that all this is a game to mock and sneer at us. Clearly they will kill us, whoever thinks he is going to live is mad, it means that he has swallowed the bait, but I have not; I have understood that it will soon all be over, perhaps in this same room, when they get bored of seeing us naked, dancing from foot to foot and trying every now and again to sit down on the floor. But there are two inches of cold water and we cannot sit down.

We walk up and down without sense, and we talk, everybody talks to everybody else, we make a great noise. The door opens, and a German enters; it is the officer of before. He speaks briefly, the interpreter translates. "The officer says you must be quiet, because this is not a rabbinical school." One sees the words which are not his, the bad words, twist his mouth as they come out, as if he was spitting out a foul taste. We beg him to ask what we are waiting for, how long we will stay here, about our women, everything; but he says no, that he does not want to ask. This Flesch, who is most unwilling to translate into Italian the hard cold German phrases and refuses to turn into German our questions because he knows that it is useless, is a German Jew of about fifty, who has a large scar on his face from a wound received fighting the Italians on the Piave. He is a closed, taciturn man, for whom I feel an instinctive respect as I feel that he has begun to suffer before us.

The German goes and we remain silent, although we are a little ashamed of our silence. It is still night and we wonder if the day will ever come. The door opens again, and someone else dressed in stripes comes in. He is different from the others, older, with glasses, a more civilized face, and much less robust. He speaks to us in Italian.

By now we are tired of being amazed. We seem to be watching some mad play, one of those plays in which the witches, the Holy Spirit and the devil appear. He speaks Italian badly, with a strong foreign accent. He makes a long speech, is very polite, and tries to reply to all our questions.

We are at Monowitz, near Auschwitz, in Upper Silesia, a region inhabited by both Poles and Germans. This camp is a work-camp, in German one says *Arbeitslager:* all the prisoners (there are about ten thousand) work in a factory which produces a type of rubber called Buna, so that the camp itself is called Buna.

We will be given shoes and clothes—no, not our own—other shoes, other clothes, like his. We are naked now because we are waiting for the shower and the disinfection, which will take place immediately after the reveille, because one cannot enter the camp without being disinfected.

Certainly there will be work to do, everyone must work here. But there is work and work: he, for example, acts as doctor. He is a Hungarian doctor who studied in Italy and he is the dentist of the Lager. He has been in the Lager for four and a half years (not in this one: Buna has only been open for a year and a half), but we can see that he is still quite well, not very thin. Why is he in the Lager? Is he Jewish like us? "No," he says simply, "I am a criminal."

We ask him many questions. He laughs, replies to some and not to others, and it is clear that he avoids certain subjects. He does not speak of the women:

he says they are well, that we will see them again soon, but he does not say how or where. Instead he tells us other things, strange and crazy things, perhaps he too is playing with us. Perhaps he is mad—one goes mad in the Lager. He says that every Sunday there are concerts and football matches. He says that whoever boxes well can become cook. He says that whoever works well receives prize-coupons with which to buy tobacco and soap. He says that the water is really not drinkable, and that instead a coffee substitute is distributed every day, but generally nobody drinks it as the soup itself is sufficiently watery to quench thirst. We beg him to find us something to drink, but he says he cannot, that he has come to see us secretly, against SS orders, as we still have to be disinfected, and that he must leave at once; he has come because he has a liking for Italians, and because, he says, he "has a little heart." We ask him if there are other Italians in the camp and he says t..ere are some, a few, he does not know how many; and he at once changes the subject. Meanwhile a bell rang and he immediately hurried off and left us stunned and disconcerted. Some feel refreshed but I do not. I still think that even this dentist, this incomprehensible person, wanted to amuse himself at our expense, and I do not want to believe a word of what he said.

At the sound of the bell, we can hear the still dark camp waking up. Unexpectedly the water gushes out boiling from the showers—five minutes of bliss; but immediately after, four men (perhaps they are the barbers) burst in yelling and shoving and drive us out, wet and steaming, into the adjoining room which is freezing; here other shouting people throw at us unrecognizable rags and thrust into our hands a pair of broken-down boots with wooden soles; we have no time to understand and we already find ourselves in the open, in the blue and icy snow of dawn, barefoot and naked, with all our clothing in our hands, with a hundred yards to run to the next hut. There we are finally allowed to get dressed.

When we finish, everyone remains in his own corner and we do not dare lift our eyes to look at one another. There is nowhere to look in a mirror, but our appearance stands in front of us, reflected in a hundred livid faces, in a hundred miserable and sordid puppets. We are transformed into the phantoms glimpsed yesterday evening.

Then for the first time we became aware that our language lacks words to express this offence, the demolition of a man. In a moment, with almost prophetic intuition, the reality was revealed to us: we had reached the bottom. It is not possible to sink lower than this; no human condition is more miserable than this, nor could it conceivably be so. Nothing belongs to us any more; they have taken away our clothes, our shoes, even our hair; if we speak, they will not listen to us, and if they listen, they will not understand. They will even take away our name: and if we want to keep it, we will have to find ourselves the strength to do so, to manage somehow so that behind the name something of us, of us as we were, still remains.

We know that we will have difficulty in being understood, and this is as it should be. But consider what value, what meaning is enclosed even in the smallest of our daily habits, in the hundred possessions which even the poorest beggar owns: a handkerchief, an old letter, the photo of a cherished person. These things are part of us, almost like limbs of our body; nor is it conceivable that we can be deprived of them in our world, for we immediately find others to substitute the old ones, other objects which are ours in their personification and evocation of our memories.

Imagine now a man who is deprived of everyone he loves, and at the same time of his house, his habits, his clothes, in short, of everything he possesses: he will be a hollow man, reduced to suffering and needs, forgetful of dignity and restraint, for he who loses all often easily loses himself. He will be a man whose life or death can be lightly decided with no sense of human affinity, in the most fortunate of cases, on the basis of a pure judgement of utility. It is in this way that one can understand the double sense of the term "extermination camp," and it is now clear what we seek to express with the phrase: "to lie on the bottom."

Street for Arrivals, Street for Departures

Charlotte Delbo

Charlotte Delbo was born near Paris in 1913. When
France was invaded by the Germans, she was
touring in South America with a company for which
she worked as a theatrical assistant. She decided to
return from safety abroad to join her husband,
Georges Dudach, in occupied Paris. Dudach was
involved in the resistance movement. Delbo and
Dudach were arrested, and he was subsequently
executed by the Nazis. Delbo, a political prisoner,
was incarcerated in Paris before she was sent to
Auschwitz in January 1943. She was incarcerated
there and in Raisko for the next year. She was
transferred to Birkenau and then to Ravensbruck,
where she remained until her release shortly before
the end of the war. The Red Cross sent her to
Sweden to recover from her experiences in the
camps. These experiences provided Delbo with the
subject matter for her books, including *None of Us
Will Return*, from which the following excerpt is
taken, *Days and Memory*, and *Auschwitz and After*. She
died in 1985.

This powerful selection creates a haunting
metaphor of the concentration camp as a railway
station.

T here are people arriving. They scan the crowd of those who wait seeking those who wait for them. They kiss them and they say that they are tired from the journey.

There are people leaving. They say good-by to those who are not leaving and they kiss the children.

There is a street for people arriving and a street for people leaving.

There is a café called "Arrivals" and a café called "Departures."

There are people arriving and there are people leaving.

But there is a station where those arriving are the same as those leaving
a station at which those arriving have never arrived, to which those leaving have never returned
it is the biggest station in the world.

This is the station at which they arrive, wherever they come from.

They arrive here after days and nights
after crossing whole countries
they arrive here with children, even babies, who were not supposed to have been taken

They have brought their children because you do not part with children for this journey.

Those who had gold brought it along because they thought that gold might be useful.

Everyone brought his dearest possession because you must not leave what is dear to you when you go far away.

Everyone has brought his life along, above all it was his life that he had to bring along.

And when they arrive
they think they have arrived
in Hell
possibly. Still they did not believe it.

They did not know that you could take a train to Hell but since they are here, they steel themselves and feel ready to face it
with women, children, aged parents
with family keepsakes and family documents.

They do not know that you do not arrive at that station.

They expect the worst—they do not expect the unthinkable.

And when the soldiers shout to them to line up by fives, men on one side, women and children on the other, in a language they do not understand, they understand the blows of the truncheons and line up by fives since they are ready for anything.

226

Mothers clutch their children—they shudder at the thought that the children might be taken away from them—because the children are hungry and thirsty and crumpled from not having slept across so many lands. At long last they are arriving, they will be able to take care of them.

And when the soldiers shout to them to leave bundles and blankets and keepsakes on the platform they leave them because they ought to be ready for anything and do not wish to be surprised at anything. They say "We'll see"; they have already seen so much and they are tired from the journey.

The station is not a station. It is the end of a line. They look and they are stricken by the desolation about them.

In the morning, fog hides the marshes.

In the evening, spotlights illuminate the white barbed-wire fences with the sharpness of stellar photography. They believe that this is where they are being taken, and they are terrified.

At night, they wait for daylight with the children weighing down their mothers' arms. Wait and wonder.

In the daytime they do not wait. The lines start moving right away. Women and children first, they are the most weary. The men next. They are also weary but relieved that wives and children are being taken care of first.

For the women and children always go first.

In the winter they are gripped by the cold. Especially those who come from Crete. Snow is new to them.

In the summer the sun blinds them as they step down from the dark boxcars that were sealed shut at the start of the journey.

At the start of the journey from France from the Ukraine from Albania from Belgium from Slovakia from Italy from Hungary from the Peloponnesus from Holland from Macedonia from Austria from Herzegovina from the shores of the Black Sea from the shores of the Baltic from the shores of the Mediterranean and from the banks of the Vistula.

They would like to know where they are. They do not know that this is the center of Europe. They look for the name of the station. It is a station without a name.

A station which for them will never have a name.

There are some who are traveling for the first time in their lives.

There are some who have traveled to every part of the globe, businessmen. All landscapes were familiar to them but they do not recognize this one.

They look. Later on they will be able to tell how it was.

Everyone wants to recall what his impression was and how he had the feeling that he would never return.

It is a feeling one might have had already in one's life. They know feelings should not be trusted.

There are those who come from Warsaw with big shawls and knotted bundles
those who come from Zagreb, women with kerchiefs on their heads
those who come from Danube with garments knitted by the hearth in multi-colored yarns
those who come from Greece, bringing black olives and Turkish Delight
those who come from Monte Carlo
they were in the casino
they are in white tie with shirt fronts that the journey has completely ruined
pot-bellied and bald
they are bankers who played at banking
newlyweds who were leaving the synagogue with the bride dressed in white, wearing a veil, all wrinkled from lying on the floor of the boxcar
the bridegroom dressed in black and top hat with soiled gloves
the relatives and guests, women with beaded bags
who all regret that they were not able to stop off at their homes and change into something less fragile.
The rabbi holds his head up high and walks first. He has always set an example for the others.
There are little girls from boarding school with their identical pleated skirts and their hats with blue streamers. They pull up their stockings carefully as they alight. They walk demurely five by five as though on a Thursday outing, holding one another by the hand and not knowing. What can they do to little girls from boarding school who are with their teacher. The teacher tells them: "Be good, children." They have no wish not to be good.
There are old people who have had news from their children in America. Their knowledge of foreign lands came from postcards. Nothing looked like what they see here. Their children will never believe it.
There are intellectuals. Doctors or architects, composers or poets, recognizable by their walk, by their glasses. They too have seen a great deal in their lifetimes. They have studied a lot. Some have even imagined a great deal in order to write books and nothing they have ever imagined resembles what they see here.
There are all the furriers of the big cities and all the gentlemen's and ladies' tailors all the clothiers who had emigrated to the West and who do not recognize in this place the land of their forebears.
There are the inexhaustible multitudes of the cities where each man occupies his own pigeonhole and now in this place they form endless lines and you wonder how all that could fit into the stacked pigeonholes of the cities.

There is a mother who slaps her five-year-old because he does not want to give her his hand and because she wants him to keep still at her side. You run the risk of getting lost you must not become separated in a strange place in such a crowd. She slaps her child and we who know do not forgive her for it. Besides it would make no difference if she were to smother him with kisses.

There are those who journeyed eighteen days who went mad and killed one another in the boxcars and

those who had been suffocated during the journey because they had been packed in so tightly

of course they do not get off.

There is a little girl who hugs her doll to her heart, you can smother dolls too.

There are two sisters in white coats who went out for a walk and did not return for dinner. Their parents are still worrying.

In ranks of five they move along the street for arrivals. They do not know it is the street for departures. You only pass this way once.

They move in strict order—so that you cannot fault them for anything.

They come to a building and they sigh. At last they have arrived.

And when the soldiers shout to the women to strip they undress the children first taking care not to wake them up completely. After days and nights of travel they are fretful and cross

and they begin to get undressed in front of their children, it can't be helped

and when the soldiers hand each one of them a towel they worry if the water in the shower will be warm because the children might catch cold

and when the men come in to the shower room through another door naked too the women hide their children against their bodies.

And then perhaps they understand.

And it is useless for them to understand now since they cannot tell those who are waiting on the platform

cannot tell those who are riding in the dark boxcars across all the countries on the way here

cannot tell those who are in detention camps and are apprehensive about their departure because they fear the climate or the work and because they are afraid of leaving their belongings

cannot tell those who are in hiding in the mountains and in the woods and who no longer have the patience to stay in hiding. Come what may they will return to their homes. Why would they be taken away from their homes they have never done any harm to anyone

cannot tell those who did not want to go into hiding because you cannot go and leave everything cannot tell those who thought they had put their children in a safe place in a Catholic boarding school where the sisters are so kind.

A band will be dressed in the little girls' pleated skirts. The commandant wants Viennese waltzes on Sunday mornings.

A blockhova, to give her window a homey touch, will make curtains out of the holy cloth the rabbi wore so that he would be ready to perform services no matter what happened wherever he might be.

A kapo will dress up in the morning coat and top hat and her girlfriend in the veil and they will play bride and groom at night when the others have collapsed in their bunks from exhaustion. The kapos can have a good time they are not tired in the evening.

Black olives and Turkish Delight will be distributed to the German women prisoners who are sick but they do not like Calamata olives nor olives in general.

And all day and all night

every day and every night the chimneys smoke with this fuel from all the countries of Europe

men assigned to the chimneys spend their days sifting the ashes to recover melted gold from gold teeth. They all have gold in their mouths these Jews and they are so many that it makes tons.

And in the spring men and women spread the ashes on the marshes drained and plowed for the first time and fertilize the soil with human phosphate.

They have bags tied to their bellies and they stick their hands into the human bone meal which they scatter by the handful over the furrows with the wind blowing the dust back into their faces and in the evening they are all white with lines traced by the sweat that has trickled down over the dust.

And no fear of running short train after train arrives they arrive every day every night every hour of every day and every hour of every night.

It is the biggest railway station in the world for arrivals and departures.

It is only those who go into the camp who find out what has happened to the others and who weep at having left them at the station because that day the officer ordered the younger people to form a separate line

there has to be someone to drain the marshes and to scatter the ashes of the others

and they say to themselves that it would have been better never to have entered and never to have found out.

You who have wept for two thousand years
for one who suffered three days and three nights

230

what tears will you have
for those who suffered
many more than three hundred nights and many more than three hundred
   days
how much
will you weep
for those who suffered so many agonies
and they were countless

They did not believe in resurrection to eternal life
And they knew that you would not weep.

Treblinka

Frank Stiffel

A survivor of the camps, Frank Stiffel wrote his
memoir, *The Tale of the Ring: A Kaddish*, based on
diaries he kept while he was in the camps. After the
war, he immigrated to the United States. In the early
1980s, he retired from the New York Department of
Labor.

In this selection, Stiffel relates his experience of
arriving at Treblinka. He details his experiences
moving from the transports to the division of the
men into two lines—to work or to die—and he
captures the acts of dehumanization and humiliation
that the camp inmates were forced to endure.

Before now, it had always been I who watched
the others being dragged out of their homes and deported from the Ghetto. I
had looked at them as though a member of the audience observing the actors
in a play, seldom even trying to imagine what they could be feeling at such a
moment.

But now, it was different. It was really happening to me. I looked around
as we were driven by a horde of yelling Germans and Lithuanians, forced into
a column, four abreast, and made to march to the sound of the whips and rifle
butts falling upon us. A formation of Jewish workers passed by, marching smartly.
They must have been going home from work, as we had, until yesterday. Some
of them looked away from us. Some looked at us with curiosity, and I knew so
well what they were feeling: "Another day has passed; another transport has left;
maybe tomorrow, no more deportation." As for me, the whole thing was so far

beyond my capacity to feel that I was unable to grasp its meaning. We marched crisply, I at the left flank, Father next to me, then Mother and Dr. Saks. Behind me, marched Martin with Pola, and the young engineer Zmigród with his pretty wife. I looked at Father and smiled. I knew that my smile in these circumstances must have seemed very stupid. He was serious. From time to time, he tried to take Mother under the arm, to help her in this excruciating march, but the German guard who walked near me yelled, "Was ist los?" ("What's the matter?") and waved his rifle threateningly.

It was not far to go. We were now approaching the Umschlagplatz. I was thinking how different the same place can be if it is seen on different occasions. It didn't even resemble the Stawki Hospital in which I had worked for three months and which I had known so well. Now it was a set of gloomy buildings surrounded by barbed wire and inhabited by a huge crowd of Jews who had been brought there before us. After our Astrawerke detachment of about one hundred and twenty people had been driven into this enclosure, feeling like cattle being readied for the butcher, we were left alone. Our little group, with the Zmigróds and Dr. Saks, entered the hospital building. People were everywhere: sitting people, standing people, lying people. The corridors, the wards, the stairways, all smelled of people and their excrements. People were sitting in their own feces, jealously clutching their bundles and their bread.

"How long have you been here?" I asked somebody.

He looked at me with distrust and didn't answer.

Someone else said, "Four days, five days—what's the difference?"

I wanted to know whether there were any transports leaving *now*; I felt nauseated; I wanted to leave this place.

There was a sudden uproar downstairs. Several men swiftly climbed the stairs past me. One whispered to the others, "Quick! Let's find a place to hide!"

The guards were chasing everybody out. A German in SS uniform stepped into human excrement, cursed, and didn't go any further in his search for Jews who might be hiding in some of those ill-smelling corners. I realized that the men who had gone upstairs would avoid this transport.

We were driven into a formation as before, four abreast, only this time it was all mixed. I could see in our immediate group maybe twenty or thirty people from the Astrawerke. An SS man with a huge belly and a leather whip in his hand gave the order. We were marched away, toward the railroad platforms. As we were passing by the big-bellied SS man, he noticed a blonde girl marching in my group. He stopped the group and motioned her out. They exchanged a few words, and she handed a document over to him. He glanced at it briefly, then motioned her back to the group. He might have taken her for an Aryan, I thought.

Now, we were led toward a long freight train. Our group was stopped in front of one of the boxcars. On its side was still written the old military sign going back to World War I: "Eight Horses, or Forty Men." We were whipped into the car within minutes. I counted one hundred and twenty people. Just enough for most of us to have standing room, with only a few women, old or sick, able to sit. The door hinges jarred. The guards locked us in. The transport was ready for dispatch.

Mother sat on the floor, old and defeated. She wouldn't talk. Besides, what was there to talk about? When she had said, during our travel from Lvov, that she would never see Lvov again, that she would never see her son Max again, her words were prophetic. She had also said that she wouldn't leave the Ghetto alive. But was she now leaving the Ghetto, or simply traveling toward its annex?

Poor Mother. Tenderness for her flooded me. She and Father had always been so far away from me, so far in age, so far in understanding my hopes and my drives, that all my life I had been building a wall of silence between me and them, hurting them unwillingly by my aloofness. I would have liked now to pour this huge volume of tenderness, suddenly overflowing me, right into them, to soothe the aching effect of all the years that were gone without our having been able to express our emotions. All I could do was to caress her hair slightly with my fingers.

Father stood up against the back wall of the boxcar. His eyes were fixed on Mother. Never in my life had I heard him say to her, "I love you." Indeed never in my life had I heard them addressing each other by their first names. They had always called each other "Old Man" and "Old Lady," although they weren't old when I was a child. All these years, it had never occurred to me to ask myself this simple question, "Do they love each other?" As I remembered the scene in Astrawerke, when he wanted to join her for the Umsiedlung, I knew he loved her. And now, they traveled together.

Pola sat next to Mother. Unconsciously she kept pulling her hair, the person-ification of Tragedy, and I could hear her saying, "Now we are lost."

Martin stood against the locked gates of the boxcar, as if in a vain hope that it was all a mistake, that the car would open and a cheerful voice from the outside would call, "Come out, my good friends! You've just had a nightmare. Wake up to love, to life, and to laughter." He kept twisting a lock of his hair with a finger, his eyes fixed on the darkness of the car.

The car was hot, the air was foul. I could see a woman defecating directly under herself. A man urinated over another man, and an argument broke out between them. Mother said, "I'm thirsty," and I would have given my life for some water for her. But it had been an exceptionally beautiful September, and there was no rain in sight. Strange how much importance we had learned to give to rain in September. When the Germans had invaded Poland three years before, it was also in September, September 1. And everybody said, "Oh, just watch and see! Come the second week of September, the rains will fall, the roads will become muddy, and the German armor will drown—and that is when we'll hit them." The rains never fell, and we never hit them. And it was September again, and again there was no rain, and Mother needed water.

Suddenly there was lightning outside and thunder. "Must be from a clear sky," I thought. I didn't remember seeing the clouds. Rain fell on the train. I believed it was a miracle. I stuck an arm through the small rectangular airhole at the top of the boxcar wall. I squeezed my arm through the barbed wire that covered the outside of the slit and cupped my palm, trying to catch the heavy drops of rain. Not one drop fell into my hand. The eave of the car's roof was keeping the rain away. A heavy wind blew along the train, enveloping it in a nightmarish howling and giggling. I was not sure whether it was the wind that giggled, or the Lithuanian guards seated in the sentry booth behind the car. I prayed to God for a miracle.

"God," I said in my mind, "stop the train. Derailments, collisions, wreckages do occur. Let this train wreck. Let it collide. Let it jump off the rails."

But the train continued on its pitiless voyage forward.

The people in the boxcar had been affected by the heat, the lack of water, the imminence of danger, and the deep differences in their own individual backgrounds. Everybody hated everybody, and cursed everybody, and would have liked to survive at everybody else's expense. It wasn't a car full of Jews; it was Noah's ark all over again. Suddenly, these were not people but animals. Sick animals, dying animals, raging animals. The air of the slaughterhouse was all over us.

The train stopped in the middle of the night, the gate opened up, and two guards entered, a Lithuanian and a Latvian. They hit Martin, who was standing next to the gate, and asked him for his money. He handed over the little he had, and they proceeded to hit people, one by one, and to rob them. Father whispered, "What are we going to do?" I took his little cotton bag and hung it from the barbed wire that covered the airhole. The guards hit me for not having money for them and continued robbing other people. As they were getting ready to leave the car, I pulled Father's little bag in. A minute later, they searched the outside of the car, using strong flashlights. Probably my trick wasn't unknown to them.

As the train moved again, Father wanted me to keep his bag. "You saved it," he said. "We might still need it one day." I knew he was proud of me.

Dawn peered in through the air hole. The train came to a stop in the middle of the countryside. I could see, far away in front of me, the dark line of a thick forest. Closer, against the background of the forest, there was a peasant cottage, whitewashed, small, and simple. A peasant woman was bending over her plants, minding the garden. Outside, all was quiet, all was peace. I felt something like a spasm in my heart. I wanted to be a part of this universal peace that had always been denied me because I was a Jew. I was still allowed one last dream. I said to myself, "If I come out alive, I want to have such a cottage one day, with flowers in the front, and vegetables in the back, and peace in it and around it."

Two uniformed railroad workers were walking slowly along the train. They spoke Polish to each other. I recognized the Mazur accent. Then we weren't far from Warsaw, in spite of our long travel. Maybe it meant hope. Somebody yelled from one of the cars, "We are dying of thirst! Will you give us a drop of water?" The workers made believe they didn't hear him. Somebody else yelled a question, "How long are we going to stay here, before we move on?" The two workers stopped. One of them raised his blue Mazur eyes and said in his sing-song accent: "People, poor people! If you only knew where you are going, you would like to stay here forever, and without water." The railroad workers wandered off, leaving the train in bewilderment.

It was already nine in the morning when the first twenty cars in the back were uncoupled from the rest of the train, and a locomotive pulled them away on a track parallel to ours. At nine-thirty, a second row of twenty cars was pulled away. As they were passing by, I recognized the Zmigróds in the vent of one of the boxcars. At ten o'clock, the irons jarred and jerked, and our portion of the train moved forward.

It didn't take long now. Within twenty minutes the locomotive moaned, and the train came to a full stop. Someone outside shoved the heavy doors of the box cars. From this point on, everything happened so suddenly, and so rapidly, and in such a shocking way, that even today, after over thirty-five years, I am still overcome by a mixture of emotions: blind anger and hatred, hope and misery, prayer and blasphemy were all drowning in a sea of hoarse commands, of whipping, hitting, kicking, and shooting.

It had taken on the shape of a square dance. I was again a student in Naples. Giacomino Biondi, a lieutenant of the Black Shirts, led the quadrille: gentlemen to the right—ladies to the left—vite! vite! vite!—Giacomino threw his orders energetically, and the row of ladies bowed graciously, and ran, and ran, and ran— vite! vite!—schnell! schnell!—run, you dog—you verfluchter hund—you sow.

All I could see was a moving body of martyred humanity. I didn't see Mother and Pola. When I finally started accepting the reality, the last women from the transport were disappearing into a long wooden barrack to the left of the square sandy yard where only the men were now kept in formation. Martin and Father stood next to me.

A man in front of me said in a colorless voice: "God! We are in Treblinka!"
I asked him, "What is Treblinka?"

He looked at me as if he had seen a tropical bird in the Arctic. "You don't know of Treblinka! It's even worse than Auschwitz!"

But then, I didn't know what Auschwitz was either.

We were standing along the barrack where the women had gone in. We must have been some six hundred men, all the men left from the last twenty boxcars of our train. It was already ten-thirty, and the September sun was burning unceasingly. A pile of loaves of bread was lying in front of us, some of the loaves bearing signs of having been bitten into. It must have been the bread belonging to the people on our train. I hadn't eaten anything in twenty-four hours, but I wasn't hungry. I asked Father whether he wanted some, but he wasn't hungry either. He said he would like a little water to drink.

There was a round wooden well, with a little decorative roof above it, in front of us and to the right, not far from the wide opening in the barbed-wire fence through which we had been chased into the yard upon our arrival. Two Ukrainian guards were standing at the well. I left the formation and approached it. A few others followed me. One of the guards twirled his rifle and hit one of the men with its butt. The other aimed his rifle, ready for firing. We all returned, running to our posts. I felt depressed. I wanted that water for Father. And I suddenly felt terribly thirsty myself. Father said, "Don't worry."

In the middle of the yard, fixed to two tall poles, was a huge placard, a welcome to Treblinka. It said in large, neat letters: "THIS IS A LABOR CAMP. YOU ARE REQUESTED TO SURRENDER YOUR CIVILIAN CLOTHES AND DEPOSIT YOUR MONEY AND YOUR VALUABLES WITH THE CASHIER. YOU WILL TAKE SHOWERS IN GROUPS. AFTER THE SHOWER, WORKING CLOTHES WILL BE DISTRIBUTED AND ROOM IN THE BARRACKS ASSIGNED. FAMILIES OF THE WORKERS WILL BE EMPLOYED IN AGRICULTURAL JOBS."

And now, two Jews, obviously workers in this labor camp, walked slowly in front of us, calling in sad voices: "Surrender your diamonds. Surrender your valuables. Surrender your money. You won't need it here any longer. This is the end of the road. This is Treblinka."

They carried small wooden boxes in their hands, shaking them occasionally, encouraging us to throw our valuables in. Various people did.

Father whispered, "Oh, God! What are we going to do?"

I answered in a whisper, "Nothing. I'm going to keep your things."

The placard said one thing; the wretches asking us for our money were saying something else. And then, in front of us, in the hot white sand, I saw American dollars torn in half, and ripped Polish five-hundred-zloty banknotes, and pieces of jewelry, like orphans crying out for their departed owners.

A tall, blond, handsome German in an SS uniform, with a leather whip in his left hand, stopped in front of us, and his steel-blue eyes embraced the group in a swift glance. A little girl, a child of three or four, wandered in front of the group. She cried desperately, calling, "Mommy! Mommy!" With her long blond curls and her beautiful face shiny with tears, she looked like one of Titian's cherubs. The handsome SS man took the child in his arms, caressed her head, and gave her a candy he got out of his pocket.

He asked, "Do you see your mommy here? Look around. Do you see her?"
The child shook her head.

He put her down, turned to an elderly man in the first row, and said, "I make you personally responsible for this child. When you go to the bath, you'll take her with you. We'll find her mother later on."

A second SS man arrived, and they had a quick conference. Then the handsome one ordered, "Present yourselves to me, one by one, for work assignment!"

One by one, we stood in front of him at attention, each stating his age and occupation. In an elegant gesture, he motioned us to the left or to the right, one by one, one by one. Soon, there were two groups of us: a large group composed of people who looked old or tired or sick; and a small group of some two hundred younger men, or men who looked young. Father was in the former group; Martin, Zmigród, and I in the latter.

The command fell now: "Undress for the shower!" It was directed at Father's group.

I said, "I'd like to take a shower, too. I'm so hot."

A man next to me, who looked like a Ghetto smuggler, said, "Shut up, you shmok!"

The Ukrainians went into action. They yelled and used the rifle butts. The handsome SS man walked among the undressing men, letting his leather whip fall on them with an elegant motion. Father was not undressing quickly enough. I didn't want him to be whipped. I wished he could undress faster. By now, they had almost all disappeared into the barrack. Father was the last one to go. He walked slowly, naked but dignified, and they didn't hit him. I lifted a hand, and it clenched into a fist. Father waved to me. It was a goodbye. I felt an urge to ask him this last important question: "Father, is this the end of the world?" And, as if he had heard me, he shrugged his shoulders. And now I could almost hear him saying, "This is the end of my road. But it is not the end of the world."

Later that day, a feeling of guilt overcame me that I was to carry for many years thereafter. Long after that day, I told myself that had I known my Father was going to his death, I would have joined him. Today, I am no longer ashamed to admit the obvious truth: I knew where he was going. I must have known by intuition that we were drowning in a sea of death, and I wanted to steer away from it, toward some shore of salvation.

Our group was called to order by a big husky Jew with an armband saying, "Kapo," and with the raucous, gravelly voice of somebody suffering chronic laryngitis. He told us that we were lucky, that the Lagerkommandant needed two hundred able-bodied Jews to take the place of those workers whose productivity had fallen off, and that he had decided to give us a chance. Then he said that he needed immediately fifty unskilled laborers to take care of various odd jobs, and he asked for volunteers. Martin and I stepped out, followed by many others. Our intuition had become our guide. The ones who didn't volunteer, hoping for better work, were immediately rounded up, stood in front of a thicket of fir growth along one of the fences, and machine-gunned. We were led off to work.

Our assignment that first afternoon was in the *Lumpenkommando*—the "Rag Detail"—where we had to work at sorting clothing into uniform groups: dresses with dresses, jackets with jackets, shoes with shoes. Our group was divided into several teams of twenty people, each team having a Jewish foreman who, a stick in his hand, made sure that the work proceeded quickly and expertly.

Martin was marched away to another location, while I worked in a barrack positioned directly behind the barrack of doom, and parallel to it. The barrack was bursting with Jewish clothing.

While sorting, we were supposed to look for valuables and to report each find to the foreman. As we were working, the foreman kept yelling in both German and Yiddish, "Schneller! Schneller! Gicher! Gicher!" ("Faster! Faster! Quicker! Quicker!"), and whenever an SS man approached, the foreman ran into the barrack, hitting us with his stick. Sometimes, this was sufficient for the SS man, but sometimes, dissatisfied with our performance, he dropped in himself and hit us with his leather whip. All of this lasted until late in the afternoon, at which time all the teams were marched off into the camp, surrounded by the Ukrainian guards.

As we were marching, the chief guard ordered us to sing. It seemed unbelievable to me, but the old timers in the group—people who had already been there for two or three days—knew better, and they intoned a joyous song of the Ukrainian peasant festivals, "Szczoby nie Marusia." It was a dance tune, and it was incongruous with either a march or this sort of camp, but the guards laughed contentedly. It must have been just what they wanted.

It was still hot when the entire work force of Treblinka was gathered for the evening report. We were all waiting in formation along three sides of the yard, while the Ukrainian guards were getting together in the middle of it. I was dizzied by that awful thirst. I could hardly understand Martin when he whispered, looking directly in front of him, "Sonny, our folks are gone."

Martin always called me "Sonny," because he was fourteen years my elder. But I was now twenty-six. Going to be twenty-six in November. On November

23. If I lived that long. "Sonny, our folks are gone." I nodded my head, looking into the hot, white sand.

And there, watching me intensely, as if she were trying to call me back to my senses, was the Girl. I bent down and picked up a ring. It was a heavy piece of gold, set around a chunk of fluorescent tiger's eye stone with a soft cameo of a girl's face carved into it. Perhaps I had become an easy prey to superstition by now, but as I clutched the Ring, I had a vivid sensation of holding the Spirit of Life, and I could hear the voice I knew so well from my dreams: "This is me."

"Sonny, our folks are gone."

I clasped the Ring in my hot, sweating hand. And the Girl repeated, "It is really me."

The time had arrived for the evening report.

We were gathered in a U-shaped formation, four to a line, facing the center of the yard. My group was standing along the barrack where this morning's arrivals had been taken to death. Across the yard was another barrack, similar in shape and size, with a group of workers standing along it. Between these two groups, to my left, a third was standing, at the bottom of the U. Behind them was a long barbed-wire fence with a thicket of tall fir trees just behind it. This was the place where, earlier this afternoon, people who hadn't volunteered for unskilled labor had been shot.

While waiting for the report I noticed a few details. The fir trees along the fence weren't alive. They were dead trees that had been cut away at the roots to become the woof for the warp of the barbed wire. The trees were just another fence with a make-believe life in it, holding forth a false promise in much the same way as the placard about the showers. Now I noticed another fence of fir trees, out at the other side of the entrance, across the railroad tracks. I could also see now, next to the entrance but in its own separate barbed-wire enclosure, a third, smaller barrack. In front of it, a small formation of perhaps fifty people was standing. They wore civilian clothing, like all of us, but on their pants, over the right knee, each of them had a large yellow triangular patch. I learned that they were the Jews who had helped to build Treblinka. They were all craftsmen, and all had been brought in from the little surrounding towns. Now they were considered permanent workers, had special privileges, like being able to move around unattended by the ubiquitous Ukrainians, and were known by the Jewish proletariat of the camp as the *Geyle Lattes*—the "Yellow Patches." Behind the barrack of the Yellow Patches, I saw a wooden sentry tower, from which two Ukrainians with a machine gun controlled this side of the camp. I noticed three more such towers in the remaining corners of the camp.

So, this was all? I knew better than this. This yard, with the three barracks and the four towers, was just a molecule. The real Treblinka must be lying behind the jealous fence of mummified firs. A continuous grinding sound was coming from there, something like a dentist's drill magnified to the millionth power. This sound was the real Treblinka. And the smell. The nauseating sweetish smell, similar to the one emitted by burning pork sausages. This smell, too, was the real Treblinka. And the shots. And the little explosions that sounded like grenades. They erupted sporadically there, at the other side of the firs. They, also, were the real Treblinka.

The administration of the camp was almost ready for the evening report. In the center of the yard, a group of Ukrainians stood in a single line. They wore SS uniforms, and each had a rifle. Next to them and to their right stood four strange figures. They wore impeccable white uniforms, but their husky bodies, huge hands, and oafish faces seemed awkward in all that unblemished white. Nobody knew who they were, but we were to see them, during the days to come, at each morning and evening report. Further away, stood the big Jew with the Kapo's armband and a dozen other Jewish foremen. The handsome, tall blond SS officer who had sorted us this morning was standing in front of the group. By now, I knew that he was known by the Treblinka Jews as the "Golem" and that his name inspired awe among the people here. But I did not know what a "Golem" actually was until it was later explained to me that a "Golem" was a figure from Jewish folklore, a mechanical being without a soul who if uncontrolled would easily fall into a murderous rage. The other SS officer who was helping the Golem this morning now counted us. He walked along my group, a leather whip in his left hand, and he was counting, "Ein-und-zwanzig, zwei-und-zwanzig," he punctuated his bookkeeping by slightly knocking the handle of the whip on the chests of the people in the first row.

Finally, the stage was set. An officer in a crisp white uniform, a slight figure with a pince-nez, marched in accompanied by two SS officers. The man who had counted us, and whom the Jews knew as "Franz," stepped forward, stopped at attention, saluted dutifully, and reported to the officer in white, "Eight-hundred men, Herr Kapitan! All present and accounted for."

We slept in the barrack through which the doomed ones had passed—this day and for many days and weeks before. The barrack was empty, except for us, lying on the earthen floor, body to body, exhausted yet unable to fall asleep, confusing our own sobbing with imagined sighs and whispers of the dead, having daydreams of bloody revenge, and nightmares of inevitability. There, at the narrow far end of the barrack was a locked door. This must be the exit from life, into a death without dignity.

There was a gas chamber beyond that door, people were saying. And there was another door, leading from the gas chamber into the ditches. But between the gas chamber and the ditches, there was a barber detail, where the hair was cut off of the bodies, to be shipped to Germany to stuff mattresses; and there was the dentist detail, where gold crowns were extracted; and there was even, they were saying, a chemical detail where it was attempted, on a laboratory scale, to salvage human fat to make soap out of it.

I couldn't sleep. My tongue was dry as parchment. It seemed to have reached the dimension of a calf's tongue. I had to get water.

There were some stray objects spread here and there in the barrack, among them an aluminum canteen. I took it and crawled out of the barrack. Out there, it was all darkness, except for a little field kitchen near the wooden well, where a small group of people were doing some work. On all fours, making sure that no guard could see me, I approached the group.

As they noticed me, one hissed, "Idiot! What are you doing here? They'll shoot you!" I could see the yellow triangle over his knee.

"Water!" I whispered back hoarsely.

A finger on his lips, he motioned me toward a pail filled with water. Still on all fours, I dipped my entire head into the pail, drinking the cool liquid like a horse. It had a strong smell of burnt skin, but so did all of Treblinka. I filled up the canteen.

A guard yelled out of the darkness, "Hey! What's going on there?"

A Yellow Patch yelled back, "Nothing! We are preparing the breakfast!"

"Then shut up!" screamed the voice.

By then, I was back in the barrack, giving Martin the water. As he drank avidly, he looked like a helpless baby, and I felt like calling him, "Sonny."

At four o'clock, we were up and ready for the morning report. The field kitchen was giving out something, and a number of people were waiting in line, some holding a plate, some holding a pot. We still weren't hungry. We still needed a lot of readjusting. What we did feel very strongly was a continuous, gnawing thirst. I drank again, and again filled up the canteen, which I then fastened to my belt.

After the report, my detail was marched back to the same barrack where we had sorted clothes the day before. Martin's group went to the adjacent barrack, also filled with clothes. Other, smaller groups went in various different directions. There was a group called the "Lime Detail" which went to work behind the firs mixing lime to be spread over the ditches of death. Another group was called the "Tower Detail," and I imagined that they must be employed in constructing additional sentry towers. There was also a "Ditch Detail" and a "Garden Detail," and a few others, but obviously the largest group was the "Rag Detail," the Lumpenkommando in which Martin and I worked.

As I was going toward my work site, I could see several neat, colorful wooden cottages, in front of which young Jewish women were washing and hanging linens. Probably the SS lived in the cottages.

Later that morning, we were ordered to interrupt the sorting and were taken back to the yard, where one last group of a new transport was waiting in front of our barrack, and the yard was littered with clothing. We were whipped into quickly collecting the clothing and carrying it in large bundles to the sorting barracks. Each of us worked at a trot, to avoid a beating. I was told that any signs of beating on your face were a step closer to death. I ran across Martin. He had a huge bump on his forehead. I kept running in my direction, he in his. As I was trotting past two German SS men, one remarked, laughing, to the other, "Look at these Jews, how they work! They think they're going to stay alive!"

I now had a three-day-old beard. A thought occurred to me: Could I ask them to lend me their razor, so that I might die looking neat?

The group that waited in front of the barrack wasn't there any longer. We were led inside the barrack, to collect women's garments. Women didn't undress in the yard. Hidden under some clothes was a live infant. A Ukrainian caught him by the tiny arms and carried him out and beyond the firs. A worker was caught in the middle of the yard. It was a woman dressed like a man. A German SS man was whipping her while she was stripping naked as ordered. She cried that she could be as good a worker as a man, but she was soon whipped behind the fir fence. I thought about the little girl who had been looking for her mommy yesterday. When the Golem asked her whether she saw her mommy in the group of men, he had expected the child to betray her mother. Possibly other women before had tried to stay alive by passing for men.

Still later that day, an SS man led me to a huge hole in the middle of a forest within the camp. There a detail of Jews was making bricks. A guard indicated a wooden rack to me and ordered me to start carrying bricks to the opposite side of the camp, beyond the railroad platform.

I loaded the rack half full, and it still was very heavy. The day was hot, and I worked in my pants only, with naked torso and bare feet. I tried to trot in the hot sand, even with this heavy burden on my shoulders, so as not to be marked for death by the whip of a guard. I reached the platform onto which we had been discharged only yesterday. It seemed like a year ago.

I walked along a low concrete structure built on one of the sides of the platform. Some Jews were inside, working at sorting food. A foreman was yelling at them, "Schneller! Schneller! Gicher! Gicher!" marking his order rhythmically with a stick he held in his hand. Further down, a group of three foremen were having breakfast, helping themselves to some jars found in the bundles of deportees. I left the bricks at the spot indicated by a guard who was posted there and ran back for more bricks. As the time passed, the sun became hotter, and I dragged my feet at a slower pace in the burning sand of Treblinka. I felt dizzy from dehydration, and as I walked doggedly with my burden, both shoulders already two open wounds, I kept repeating automatically in my mind, *Avadim*

Hainu L'Paroh b'Mizraim—"We were Pharoah's slaves in the Land of Egypt"—
the sentence with which Father had started each Passover recounting of Jewish
suffering and miraculous salvation three thousand years ago.

A Ukrainian guard stopped me. He was big and awkward and smelled of
vodka. He told me in a kind voice that what I was doing was incorrect. That I
was killing myself. He picked up some rags from the sand and slipped them
under the arms of the rack, between the rack and my wounds. He said that this
was the right way to carry bricks. Then he hit me with the butt of his rifle, right
on the head. For a moment, I lost consciousness. When I came to, I heard the
guard's voice: "Get up, you! Get up!" The words reached me as through a fog
and through a distance, and I well remember my deep sense of regret that I was
back there, to continue paying my dues.

That evening, we helped Mr. Zmigród to die. Martin and I, and a couple of
more people from Astrawerke sat around him, while he swallowed a bottle
of barbiturate pills, taking them, one by one, like a gourmet enjoying an hors
d'oeuvre. He had decided today that he didn't want to live without his wife.
Now, he was having his last cigarette. Later, he asked Martin to take it out of his
mouth, as his hands were already asleep. And then he was lying in his last happy
doze, which tomorrow no amount of kicking and hitting would be able to
interrupt.

Terezin

Hanuš Hachenburg

Hanuš Hachenburg was one of fifteen thousand young people under the age of fifteen who were sent to the "model" camp at Terezin that the Nazis established to mislead the world about their treatment of the Jews. Only one hundred of these children survived.

Born on July 12, 1929, in Prague, Hachenburg was deported to Terezin on October 24, 1942. He died at Auschwitz on December 18, 1943. His poem is reprinted from *I Never Saw Another Butterfly: Children's Drawings and Poems from Terezin Concentration Camp, 1942–1944*.

At Terezin, there was an organized effort to use the arts to help the children deal with the bitter circumstances of their daily lives. Hachenburg's poem expresses the reactions of young people to their world in the camp.

That bit of filth in dirty walls,
And all around barbed wire,
And 30,000 souls who sleep
Who once will wake
And once will see
Their own blood spilled.

I was once a little child,
Three years ago,
That child who longed for other worlds.
But now I am no more a child
For I have learned to hate.
I am a grown-up person now,
I have known fear.

Bloody words and a dead day then,
That's something different than bogeymen!

But anyway, I still believe I only sleep today,
That I'll wake up, a child again, and start to
  laugh and play.
I'll go back to childhood sweet like a briar rose,
Like a bell that wakes us from a dream,
Like a mother with an ailing child
Loves him with aching woman's love.
How tragic, then, is youth that lives
With enemies, with gallows ropes,
How tragic, then, for children on your lap
To say: this for the good, that for the bad.

Somewhere, far away out there, childhood
  sweetly sleeps,
Along that path among the trees,
There o'er that house
That was once my pride and joy.
There my mother gave me birth into this world
So I could weep . . .

In the flame of candles by my bed, I sleep
And once perhaps I'll understand
That I was such a little thing,
As little as this song.

These 30,000 souls who sleep
Among the trees will wake,
Open an eye
And because they see
A lot

They'll fall asleep again . . .

Stars

Yaffa Eliach

A Holocaust survivor, Yaffa Eliach was born in
Vilna, Poland, in 1935. Although she, her parents,
and one brother survived the war by hiding in caves,
in the woods, and among the partisans, her mother
and brother were later killed by Poles after they
returned home, and her father was imprisoned by
the Russians and sent to Siberia. Eliach was taken to
Israel by her uncle; she remained there until 1954,
when she immigrated to the United States. After
earning a doctorate in Russian intellectual history,
she became a professor at Brooklyn College of the
City University of New York, where she also
founded the Center for Holocaust Studies. She is the
editor of *Hasidic Tales of the Holocaust*, from which
the following selection is taken.

The following selection dramatically retells the
experience of Michael Schwartz as he "beat the
Nazis' system" and saved his cousin from the gas
chamber.

Michael Schwartz arrived in Auschwitz-
Birkenau in August of 1944 with one of the last transports from the Lodz ghetto.
Though a veteran of this first and last ghetto of Nazi Europe, Michael was in
a state of shock when he was shoved out of the cattle car into the Auschwitz
kingdom. The railway platform with its barking dogs, screaming S.S. men, kicking Ukrainians, and the sorrowful eyes of quick-moving prisoners in striped
uniforms inspired terror, hopelessness, and a strange wish to get it over and

done with as quickly as possible. Before he realized what was happening, he was separated from his family and was led away in the opposite direction with a group of young men. The men marched beneath a barrage of leather truncheons, near the edges of flaming pits where people were tossed alive. The air was filled with sulfur and the stench of burning flesh.

A few hours later, his hair shaven, his body stinging from disinfectants, wearing a striped, oversized uniform and a pair of skimpy, broken clogs, Michael along with hundreds of young men was led off to a barracks. There in the barracks, he found a cousin from whom he had been separated earlier at the platform. Only after looking at his cousin did Michael realize the transformation that he himself had undergone since his arrival on that accursed platform. That night in the barracks the cousins promised each other never to part again. It was the first decision Michael had made since his arrival in Auschwitz.

Michael quickly learned the realities of Auschwitz. Survival depended on one's ability to "organize" anything and everything, from an additional sip of coffee to a better sleeping place on the three-tiered wooden planks, and of course one had to present a healthy and useful appearance if one hoped to pass selections.

One day rumors spread in Michael's barracks that the impending selection was of particular importance, for those selected would be transferred out of Auschwitz to work at another camp. Michael was especially anxious to pass that selection. In the few months he had been in Auschwitz he had learned that Auschwitz would eventually devour everybody, even those who deciphered its survival code.

Dr. Joseph Mengele himself was supervising the selection. It was apparent to Michael that Mengele was using what was known among the Auschwitz old-timers as the "washboard" criterion. Each inmate was ordered to lift his hands high above his head as he approached Mengele. If his rib cage protruded and each vertebra was clearly visible, Mengele would smile and motion with his snow-white glove to the left.

The moment came. Michael and his cousin stood in front of Mengele, whose clean, shaven face glittered in the sun and whose eyes shown. The angel of death was in his moment of bliss. Michael's turn came and Mengele's finger pointed: "Right!" Then Michael heard Mengele's death sentence on his cousin: "Left!"

A moment later Michael stood before a table where three people sat dressed in white coats. One was holding a stamp pad, one a huge rubber stamp, and the third a pen and a white sheet of paper. Michael felt the cold rubber stamp press against his forehead and saw a pen mark a line on the white sheet of paper.

Michael moved on to a group of young men, all naked like himself, wearing only a huge ink star on their foreheads. Michael realized that this star was the passport that would take him out of the camp, and that his cousin in the other group just a few meters away would be taken to the chimneys.

In the commotion of the selection Michael decided to act. He walked briskly over to his cousin, spat on his cousin's forehead, pressed his own forehead against his cousin's, took his cousin by the hand, and led him to the group marked with stars. Only then did he dare look at his cousin. There in the middle of his forehead was the imprint of the lucky star, the passport that would lead them out of the Auschwitz hell.

From Birkenau, Michael and his cousin were transported to Neuengamme, Braunschweig, Watenstadt, Beendorf, Ravensbrück, and Ludwigslust, where they slaved in the Hermann Goering works in private German companies engaged in the war industry.

On a May day in 1945 a tank entered a camp near Ludwigslust. On it was painted a huge white star and inside the tank sat a black-faced soldier wearing a steel helmet. After six years in the Nazi slave kingdom, Michael and his cousin were once again free men.

September 1944

Charles Fishman

Charles Fishman was born in Freeport, New York, in 1942. He earned a doctorate in creative writing with a concentration in contemporary American poetry and Holocaust poetry. An award-winning poet, Fishman is also a highly regarded scholar. He is Distinguished Service Professor of English and Humanities at the State University of New York, Farmingdale. Fishman is the editor of *Blood to Remember: American Poets on the Holocaust*, from which the following poem is taken.

This short but poignant poem provides vivid images of the camps. Fishman wrote the poem as a variation on a theme by the highly regarded Czech poet Arnost Lustig.

variations on a theme
by Arnost Lustig

I stood in the gypsy camp
by the high-voltage wires,
around us the bare Polish
plains and forests.
A thin transparent fog
enveloped the ground, the people.
It penetrated the soul.
A purple fire flashed
from the chimneys,
glowing a deeper purple
before turning into black
smoke. Everything stank.
The smoke became a cloud,
and slowly a black rain—
ashes—dropped down.
Like everyone else, I wished
the wind would shift
or the earth reverse its
direction. The ashes had
a bitter taste. The were
not from coal or burnt wood,
rags or paper.
They fell on us—mute, deaf,
relentless ashes, in which
human breath, shrieks and tears
could be felt.
I stood at a concrete fence post
with white porcelain insulators,
taking it all in like
an hallucination.
A tune from Strauss's *Die Fledermaus*
ran through my mind.

Gypsies

CHARLOTTE DELBO

> ## Charlotte Delbo
>
> Charlotte Delbo's experiences as a Holocaust
> survivor provided her with the subject matter for
> her books, including *None of Us Will Return, Days and
> Memory*, from which the following excerpt is taken,
> and *Auschwitz and After*. For additional biographical
> information on Delbo, see page 225.
>
> In this selection, Delbo reflects on the fate of the
> Gypsies by relating the experience of one woman
> trying to save her infant child.

The projectors light the barbed wire strung
between high white poles. Encircled by light, the camp lies in darkness and in
this black abyss nothing can be distinguished
   nothing except darker shapes swaying
   ghostlike upon the ice.

The roll-call siren has emptied the barracks. By swaying clusters, the women
have all stumbled out, clinging to each other so as not to fall

And when one does fall, the whole cluster reels and falls and gets back up,
falls again and rises, and in spite of it all moves on.

Without a word.

There is only the screaming of the furies who want the barracks to empty
faster, want the reeling shades to move faster from the barracks to the space
where the roll is called.

In the darkness, for the beams of the projectors do not reach the spaces
between the barracks. They light only the gate and the barbed wire enclosure
so that the sentinels up in the watchtowers may spot those trying to escape
and shoot

✗ format structure

as if one could escape

as if one could cut through the fence of high-tension live barbed wire

as if . . .

In the dark you cannot see where you step, you fall into holes, stumble into drifts of snow.

Clutching one another, guided by shouts and blows of clubs, the shades of the night take the places where they must be to await the break of day.

Panic sometimes. Where are you? I'm right here.

Hold on to me, or a voice full of despair: My galoshes. I've lost my galoshes. It's from a woman who slipped, got up, but without her galoshes, flown off who knows in what direction, and the whole group stops, stoops over the snow, gropes unseeingly. The galoshes must be found.

Barefoot at roll-call is certain death. Barefoot in the snow for hours—death.

They're all hunting for the galoshes and others behind them grow impatient and shove because the fury, the barracks leader, in her boots and steady on her feet, comes down on them with her club, screaming as she swings at everyone within reach. In the dark she can't see where she's hitting, the club always strikes someone, lands on those shapes that are squatting and groping and straightening up and, beneath the blows, there fall again those who had succeeded in rising to their feet.

Here, I've got one of them. I've got the other. The galoshes pass from hand to hand until they reach the one they belong to, who murmurs her thanks but is not heard, so exhausted is she by fear, by falls, clubbing, and the hallucinations of the night.

The group sets off again, a chaotic procession. Tortuous wending of its way between obstacles: piles of brick covered with frozen snow, piles of snow, holes full of water turned into ice

a ditch to step over

and the frozen earth, bristling and jagged, like a plowed field petrified into clods of ice.

At last they're all in place, lined up for the roll-call, on each side of the road running down the middle of the camp.

They shall have to wait hours and hours before daybreak, before the counting. The SS do not arrive until it is light.

First you stamp your feet. The cold pierces to the marrow. You no longer feel your body, you no longer feel anything of your self. First you stamp your feet. But it's tiring to stamp your feet. Then you huddle over, arms crossed over your chest, shoulders hunched, and all squeeze close to one another

but keeping in rank because the club-wielding furies are there and watching.

Even the strength to raise one's eyes, to look to see if there are stars in the sky
there's a chilling effect to stars
to cast a glance about
even the strength that takes must be saved and no one looks up.
And to see what in that darkness?
The women from the other barracks, also reeling and falling, trying to form
their ranks?
all these ranks stretching from one end of the camp to the other, on each side
of the road,
that makes how many women, how many thousands of women, all these
ranks?
these ranks bobbing up and down because the women are stamping their
feet and then they halt because to stamp one's feet is exhausting
You see nothing, each one is enclosed in the shroud of her own skin,
you feel nothing, neither the person next to you, huddling against you, nor
that other who has fallen and is being helped up.
You don't speak because the cold would freeze your saliva.
Each feels she is dying, crumbling into confused images, dead to herself
already, without a past, any reality, without anything,
the sky must have grown light without anyone noticing.
And now, in the pallid light of the night drawing to a close,
the ranks across the way suddenly emerge, the ranks of the Gypsy women
like ourselves all blue from cold.
How would you know a Gypsy if not by her tattered dress? The Jewish
women do not have striped uniforms either, they have grotesque clothing,
coats too long or too tight, mud-spattered, torn, with a huge red cross painted
on the back.
The Gypsy women have tatters, what's left of their full skirts and their
scarves.
And suddenly there she is, you can make her out, the one in the front row,
holding, clutched to her breast, a bundle of rags.
In her gaunt face, eyes gleaming so bright that you must look away not to be
pierced by them
her eyes gleaming with fever, with hatred, a burning, unbearable hatred.
And what else but hatred is holding together these rags this spectre of a
woman is made of, with her bundle pressed against her chest by hands purple
from cold?
She holds the bundle of rags to her, in the crook of her arm, the way a baby
is held, the baby's head against its mother's breast.
Daylight.

The Gypsy stands straight, so tense that it is visible through her tatters, her left hand placed upon the baby's face. It is an infant, that bundle of rags she is clutching. It became obvious when she shifted the upper part of the bundle, turning it outward a little, to help it breathe perhaps, now that daylight has come.

Quickly she shelters the baby's face again and hugs it tighter

then she shifts the bundle of rags to her other arm, and we see the infant's head lolling, bluish, almost black.

With a gentle movement she raises the baby's head, props it in the hollow between her arm and her breast,

and again she lifts her eyes, and again the impression she gives is of tension and fierceness, with her unbearable stare.

The SS arrive. All the women stiffen as they move down the ranks, counting. That lasts a long time. A long time. Finally, one side is done. You can put your hands back in the sleeves of your jacket, you can hunch up your shoulders, as if it were possible to make yourself a smaller target for the cold.

I look at the Gypsy holding her baby pressed against her. It's dead, isn't it?

Yes, it's dead. Its purplish head, almost black, falls back when not supported by the Gypsy's hand.

For how long has it been dead, cradled in its mother's arms, this rag-swaddled infant? For hours, perhaps for days.

The SS move past, counting the ranks of the Gypsies. They do not see the woman with the dead baby and the frightening eyes.

A whistle blows. The roll-call is over. We break formation. Again we slide and fall on the sheet of ice, now spotted here and there with diarrhea.

The Gypsies' formation breaks up too. The woman with the baby runs off. Where is she heading for shelter?

The Gypsies are not marched out of the camp for work. Men, women, children are mixed together in a separate enclosed area. The camp for families. And why are there Gypsy women over here, in our camp? Nobody knows.

When the roll was called that evening she was there, with her dead baby in her arms. Standing in the front row. Standing straight.

The following morning at roll-call she was there, hugging her bundle of rags, her eyes still brighter, still wilder.

Then she stopped coming to roll-call.

Someone saw the bundle of rags, the dead baby, on the garbage heap by the kitchen.

The Gypsy had been clubbed to death by a policewoman who'd tried to pull the dead baby away from her.

This woman, hugging her baby to her, had fought, butting her head, kicking, protecting herself and then striking with her free hand . . . a struggle in which she had been crushed despite the hate that gave her the strength of a lioness defending her brood.

The Gypsy had fallen dead in the snow. The corpse collection squad had picked up her body and carried it to where the corpses are stacked before being loaded on the truck which dumps them at the crematorium.

The mother killed, the policewoman had torn the baby from her arms and tossed it on the garbage heap in front of which the struggle had taken place. The Gypsy woman had raced to the edge of the camp, tightly cradling the baby in her crossed arms, had run till she was out of breath and it was when she was blocked by the garbage pile that she turned to face the fury and her club.

The corpse collection squad picked up the mother. The baby, in its rags, remained on the garbage heap, mixed with the refuse.

All the Gypsies disappeared very fast. All gassed. Thousands of them. The family camp was emptied out, that made room for the next arrivals. Not Gypsies. We saw nothing more of Gypsies at Birkenau. Gypsies are less numerous than Jews, it didn't take much time to dispose of them.

The Shawl

Cynthia Ozick

Cynthia Ozick was born in New York City on April 19, 1928. Her short stories and novels are highly regarded for their reflection of Jewish life and faith in the twentieth century. She has explored the psychological implications of the Holocaust in a number of works, including *Levitation: Five Fictions* and *The Cannibal Galaxy*. Among her other works are *The Messiah of Stockholm* (a novel) and *Metaphor and Memory* (a collection of essays).

In this powerful short story, Ozick examines the horror of a mother desperately trying to help her infant survive.

Stella, cold, cold, the coldness of hell. How they walked on the roads together, Rosa with Magda curled up between sore breasts, Magda wound up in the shawl. Sometimes Stella carried Magda. But she was jealous of Magda. A thin girl of fourteen, too small, with thin breasts of her own, Stella wanted to be wrapped in a shawl, hidden away, asleep, rocked by the march, a baby, a round infant in arms. Magda took Rosa's nipple, and Rosa never stopped walking, a walking cradle. There was not enough milk; sometimes Magda sucked air; then she screamed. Stella was ravenous. Her knees were tumors on sticks, her elbows chicken bones.

Rosa did not feel hunger; she felt light, not like someone walking but like someone in a faint, in trance, arrested in a fit, someone who is already a floating angel, alert and seeing everything, but in the air, not there, not touching the road. As if teetering on the tips of her fingernails. She looked into Magda's face through a gap in the shawl: a squirrel in a nest, safe, no one could reach her inside the little house of the shawl's windings. The face, very round, a pocket mirror of a face: but it was not Rosa's bleak complexion, dark like cholera, it was another kind of face altogether, eyes blue as air, smooth feathers of hair nearly as yellow as the Star sewn into Rosa's coat. You could think she was one of *their* babies.

Rosa, floating, dreamed of giving Magda away in one of the villages. She could leave the line for a minute and push Magda into the hands of any woman on the side of the road. But if she moved out of line they might shoot. And even if she fled the line for half a second and pushed the shawl-bundle at a stranger, would the woman take it? She might be surprised, or afraid; she might drop the shawl, and Magda would fall out and strike her head and die. The little round head. Such a good child, she gave up screaming, and sucked now only for the taste of the drying nipple itself. The neat grip of the tiny gums. One mite of a tooth tip sticking up in the bottom gum, how shining, an elfin tombstone of white marble gleaming there. Without complaining, Magda relinquished Rosa's teats, first the left, then the right; both were cracked, not a sniff of milk. The duct-crevice extinct, a dead volcano, blind eye, chill hole, so Magda took the corner of the shawl and milked it instead. She sucked and sucked, flooding the threads with wetness. The shawl's good flavor, milk of linen.

It was a magic shawl, it could nourish an infant for three days and three nights. Magda did not die, she stayed alive, although very quiet. A peculiar smell, of cinnamon and almonds, lifted out of her mouth. She held her eyes open every moment, forgetting how to blink or nap, and Rosa and sometimes Stella studied their blueness. On the road they raised one burden of a leg after another and studied Magda's face. "Aryan," Stella said, in a voice grown as thin as a string; and Rosa thought how Stella gazed at Magda like a young cannibal. And the time that Stella said "Aryan," it sounded to Rosa as if Stella had really said "Let us devour her."

But Magda lived to walk. She lived that long, but she did not walk very well, partly because she was only fifteen months old, and partly because the spindles of her legs could not hold up her fat belly. It was fat with air, full and round. Rosa gave almost all her food to Magda, Stella gave nothing; Stella was ravenous, a growing child herself, but not growing much. Stella did not menstruate. Rosa did not menstruate. Rosa was ravenous, but also not; she learned from Magda how to drink the taste of a finger in one's mouth. They were in a place without pity, all pity was annihilated in Rosa, she looked at Stella's bones without pity. She was sure that Stella was waiting for Magda to die so she could put her teeth into the little thighs.

Rosa knew Magda was going to die very soon; she should have been dead already, but she had been buried away deep inside the magic shawl, mistaken there for the shivering mound of Rosa's breasts; Rosa clung to the shawl as if it covered only herself. No one took it away from her. Magda was mute. She never cried. Rosa hid her in the barracks, under the shawl, but she knew that one day someone would inform; or one day someone, not even Stella, would steal Magda to eat her. When Magda began to walk Rosa knew that Magda was going to die very soon, something would happen. She was afraid to fall asleep; she slept with the weight of her thigh on Magda's body; she was afraid she would smother Magda under her thigh. The weight of Rosa was becoming less and less; Rosa and Stella were slowly turning into air.

Magda was quiet, but her eyes were horribly alive, like blue tigers. She watched. Sometimes she laughed—it seemed a laugh, but how could it be? Magda had never seen anyone laugh. Still, Magda laughed at her shawl when the wind blew its corners, the bad wind with pieces of black in it, that made Stella's and Rosa's eyes tear. Magda's eyes were always clear and tearless. She watched like a tiger. She guarded her shawl. No one could touch it; only Rosa could touch it. Stella was not allowed. The shawl was Magda's own baby, her pet, her little sister. She tangled herself up in it and sucked on one of the corners when she wanted to be very still.

Then Stella took the shawl away and made Magda die.

Afterward Stella said: "I was cold."

And afterward she was always cold, always. The cold went into her heart: Rosa saw that Stella's heart was cold. Magda flopped onward with her little pencil legs scribbling this way and that, in search of the shawl; the pencils faltered at the barracks opening, where the light began. Rosa saw and pursued. But already Magda was in the square outside the barracks, in the jolly light. It was the roll-call arena. Every morning Rosa had to conceal Magda under the shawl against a wall of the barracks and go out and stand in the arena with Stella and hundreds of others, sometimes for hours, and Magda, deserted, was quiet under the shawl, sucking on her corner. Every day Magda was silent, and so she did not die. Rosa saw that today Magda was going to die, and at the same time a fearful joy ran in Rosa's two palms, her fingers were on fire, she was astonished, febrile: Magda, in the sunlight, swaying on her pencil legs, was howling. Ever since the drying up of Rosa's nipples, ever since Magda's last scream on the road, Magda had been devoid of any syllable; Magda was a mute. Rosa believed that something had gone wrong with her vocal cords, with her windpipe, with the cave of her larynx; Magda was defective, without a voice; perhaps she was deaf; there might be something amiss with her intelligence; Magda was dumb. Even the laugh that came when the ash-stippled wind made a clown out of Magda's shawl was only the air-blown showing of her teeth. Even when the lice, head lice and body lice, crazed her so that she became as wild as one of the big rats that plundered the barracks at daybreak looking for carrion, she rubbed and scratched and kicked and bit and rolled without a whimper. But now Magda's mouth was spilling a long viscous rope of clamor.

"Maaaa—"

It was the first noise Magda had ever sent out from her throat since the drying up of Rosa's nipples.

"Maaaa . . . aaa!"

Again! Magda was wavering in the perilous sunlight of the arena, scribbling on such pitiful little bent shins. Rosa saw. She saw that Magda was grieving for the loss of her shawl, she saw that Magda was going to die. A tide of commands hammered in Rosa's nipples: Fetch, get, bring! But she did not know which to go after first, Magda or the shawl. If she jumped out into the arena to snatch Magda up, the howling would not stop, because Magda would still not have the shawl; but if she ran back into the barracks to find the shawl, and if she found it, and if she came after Magda holding it and shaking it, then she would get Magda back, Magda would put the shawl in her mouth and turn dumb again.

Rosa entered the dark. It was easy to discover the shawl. Stella was heaped under it, asleep in her thin bones. Rosa tore the shawl free and flew—she could fly, she was only air—into the arena. The sunheat murmured of another life, of butterflies in summer. The light was placid, mellow. On the other side of the steel fence, far away, there were green meadows speckled with dandelions and deep-colored violets; beyond them, even farther, innocent tiger lilies, tall, lifting their orange bonnets. In the barracks they spoke of "flowers," of "rain": excrement, thick turd-braids, and the slow stinking maroon waterfall that slunk down from the upper bunks, the stink mixed with a bitter fatty floating smoke that greased Rosa's skin. She stood for an instant at the margin of the arena. Sometimes the electricity inside the fence would seem to hum; even Stella said it was only an imagining, but Rosa heard real sounds in the wire: grainy sad voices. The farther she was from the fence, the more clearly the voices crowded at her. The lamenting voices strummed so convincingly, so passionately, it was impossible to suspect them of being phantoms. The voices told her to hold up the shawl, high; the voices told her to shake it, to whip with it, to unfurl it like a flag. Rosa lifted, shook, whipped, unfurled. Far off, very far, Magda leaned across her air-fed belly, reaching out with the rods of her arms. She was high up, elevated, riding someone's shoulder. But the shoulder that carried Magda was not coming toward Rosa and the shawl, it was drifting away, the speck of Magda was moving more and more into the smoky distance. Above the shoulder a helmet glinted. The light tapped the helmet and sparkled it into a goblet. Below the helmet a black body like a domino and a pair of black boots hurled themselves in the direction of the electrified fence. The electric voices began to chatter wildly. "Maamaa, maaa-maaa," they all hummed together. How far Magda was from Rosa now, across the whole square, past a dozen barracks, all the way on the other side! She was no bigger than a moth.

All at once Magda was swimming through the air. The whole of Magda traveled through loftiness. She looked like a butterfly touching a silver vine. And the moment Magda's feathered round head and her pencil legs and balloonish belly and zigzag arms splashed against the fence, the steel voices went mad in their growling, urging Rosa to run and run to the spot where Magda had fallen from her flight against the electrified fence; but of course Rosa did not obey them. She only stood, because if she ran they would shoot, and if she tried to pick up the sticks of Magda's body they would shoot, and if she let the wolf's screech ascending now through the ladder of her skeleton break out, they would shoot; so she took Magda's shawl and filled her own mouth with it, stuffed it in and stuffed it in, until she was swallowing up the wolf's screech and tasting the cinnamon and almond depth of Magda's saliva; and Rosa drank Magda's shawl until it dried.

Taut as a String

Sara Nomberg-Przytyk

Born into a prominent Hasidic family in Lublin,
Poland, in 1915, Sara Nomberg-Przytyk fled Lublin
when the Germans invaded Poland in 1939. She
settled in Bialystok, Poland, where she was later
confined in the ghetto. In 1943, she was deported
from the ghetto to the concentration camp in
Stutthof; later, she was sent to Auschwitz, where she
worked as an attendant in Dr. Josef Mengele's
hospital. After she was liberated, she went back to
Lublin and worked as a journalist. She married
during this time. She fled from the communists in
1968 and immigrated to Israel. In 1975, she left Israel
to live closer to one of her sons in Canada. She is the
author of *Auschwitz: True Tales from a Grotesque Land*,
from which the following selection is taken. Her
narratives explore the moral conflict between
fighting to survive and acting ethically.

Karola was a registered nurse. Before the war
she had worked in a hospital in Krakow. If it is true that the practice of a profession influences a person's outward appearance as well as a person's psyche,
then Karola was an excellent example of the rule. All you had to do was to take
one look at her and you would instantly know what her profession was. The
tranquil expression on her face, the calmness of her movements, her quick, light
step, and the nobility of her figure all indicated that Karola must have been a

wonderful nurse. When I first met her in Auschwitz she was about thirty-five years old.

She was not eager to reveal her intimate secrets. Always she seemed to be lost in thought. I knew very little about her. Her coolness was intimidating. I saw her often, since Karola worked on the hospital block. Her manner was unchanging: calm and quiet.

It was rumored in the camp that Karola had left two children with her sister—a thirteen-year-old daughter and five-year-old son. She very rarely spoke about them. Apparently she feared that the mere mention of them might have the power to bring them here to her. Rumor had it that Karola's sister had found a place outside the ghetto, among good gentile friends, and that there she took care of Karola's children.

I remember that hot summer day when Karola was informed that her sister, along with the children, was on the ramp in Auschwitz, waiting with the others for the arrival of the German doctor.

It was twelve o'clock. Dr. Koenig was in the clinic, looking over the sick. He was tall and skinny and gloomy. Even so, we preferred him to Dr. Mengele, who often talked to the sick like a benefactor. Suddenly the door of the infirmary opened and Karola burst in like a hurricane. She kneeled in the middle of the infirmary and stretched out her hands to Dr. Koenig in a beseeching way. She begged for the lives of her children. Orli, who had come into the infirmary with Karola, was standing next to her. Karola was lucky. Mengele was not in the infirmary that day. If he had been there he would have sent her to the gas chamber along with the children, because the children could not live in the camp and they could not be sent to the gas chamber by themselves. It would not be humanitarian.

Koenig was taken aback for a moment, and Orli added hurriedly that Karola was a professional nurse and a very good worker.

Koenig said, "Come with me, then, and take your children!"

Orli went with Karola in order to help her get the children through the gate.

In the evening I went to the neighboring block where Karola lived. She was sitting with her children on the highest bed. Since the girl was tall and, like her mother, well-built, Karola had no trouble in adding three years to her recorded age. She was put down as sixteen on her registration card, and a number was tattooed on her arm. The age of little Zbyszek was difficult to cover up. He was five years old and small-framed. Slim, though tall, he had dark brown hair, bangs combed onto his forehead, and a dark complexion, all of which were brightened by beautiful blue-gray sparkling eyes. He sat cuddled up to his mother with fear in his eyes. He looked at that terrible world, at those sick lying in the beds around him, and he listened. His head was held at a tilt as though he was constantly listening and was ready to escape.

Karola's daughter Krysia had to start work as a *läufer* the next day. She started her adult life, if that is what you can call it, in Auschwitz. What was to be done with Zbyszek? With Orli's help she had smuggled him into the camp. Since he did not have a number he did not actually exist. Koenig knew about the boy, and the question was how would he behave? Would he appear one day and take Zbyszek to the gas chambers with the other children? The mercy of the German gods rode a fitful horse—that we knew very well.

Karola withered and aged. Zbyszek lay hidden on the top bunk when she was at work. You can imagine what Karola went through on every visit from Mengele or the other SS men on the block. She could never be certain that the boy would not become frightened and do something to draw attention to himself. Koenig never asked her about her children. He acted as if he knew nothing about the matter. There was no danger from that quarter.

A few months went by in this way. In the evening, after roll call, Zbyszek would crawl out of his hiding place, and Karola would go out to the front of the block with him. The boy had to walk and run a little.

Once I met them as they were going about their nightly exercise. It was the end of the summer and the chimneys were smoking without stop. Karola stood at an angle, looking around with the watchfulness of a hawk. Zbyszek ran around the block, taut as a string.

"You know, he is very frightened," Karola told me. "I had to tell him what would happen to him if the Germans see him. It is very important that he doesn't leave his bed during the day. He brought a book of poems with him. I taught him to read, and now he reads all day. He knows everything by heart. If I could get him some Polish books what a joy it would be for him."

Zbyszek came running toward us, fatigued, like any boy his age.

"You didn't see any Germans?" he asked with an air of sadness and tragedy, a vigilant look on his face.

The Germans did not visit us on Sundays. We felt freer than we usually did, and we would meet in the infirmary. That Sunday Karola came with her children. With her *läufer's* armband Krysia felt completely safe. Zbyszek recited some poems. He stood in the middle of the infirmary, quite handsome, and talked about a train sweating grease and oil. I looked at him and simply could not believe that there were people who desired his death. It was quiet in the infirmary, and Zbyszek's every word rang like the most beautiful music.

Suddenly the *sztubowa* ran into the infirmary from the next block.

"Mengele," she shouted.

I looked at Zbyszek. Till this day I see his pale face. He stood there as if turned to stone. We all jumped up. We hid Zbyszek under a mattress and made the bed over him. He did not protest. He did not say that he was uncomfortable or that he could not breathe. Karola ran to her block.

Half an hour later we pulled a barely breathing child from under the mattress. "Has he gone for sure?" he asked. "Because I can lie here till evening."

Zbyszek lived through Auschwitz. Although all the prisoners knew about him, no one betrayed him to the Germans.

A Living Torch

Sara Nomberg-Przytyk

An Auschwitz survivor, Sara Nomberg-Przytyk is
the author of *Auschwitz: True Tales from a Grotesque
Land*, from which the following selection is taken.
For additional biographical information on
Nomberg-Przytyk, see page 261.

This selection presents a horrifying account of
the murder of the innocent.

Every day of that macabre last summer of
Hitler's reign twenty thousand people were killed in Auschwitz. The crematoria
were unable to burn all of the dead who were being gassed in Auschwitz. Large
ravines were excavated next to the crematoria. The dead bodies were thrown
into them, and then they were doused with benzine and set aflame. The flames
leaped upwards, and the sky was turned red by the gigantic fire. At night the
entire scene looked grotesque. We would go out to the front of the block and
stare at the reddened sky. We were not so much mesmerized by the flames as by
the sea of human blood. Burning human flesh gives off a sweet, choking odor
that makes you feel faint. That summer we were saturated with that indescribable choking odor. All summer we groped our way around in the smoke that
belched from the chimneys of the crematoria above and from the burning bodies
in the ravines below. That July and August the weather was very hot and stuffy.
It was a terrible summer. Looking back, now, it is difficult for me to say how we
were able to live through those times, conscious of human life oozing out of
existence everywhere. How is it that we did not all go crazy? How is it that we
were able to vegetate, keeping our composure in this unbearable world? The
time arrived when a scream tore itself involuntarily out of one's throat.

We were standing, as was our wont, in front of the block, watching the sky turn to a deeper red. All around us was quiet that night, because there was no transport. Apparently there was a large backlog of corpses that had to be burned before the new raw material essential to the functioning of the death factory could be brought in. Suddenly, the stillness was broken by the screaming of children, as if a single scream had been torn out of hundreds of mouths, a single scream of fear and unusual pain, a scream repeated a thousand times in the single word, "Mama," a scream that increased in intensity every second, enveloping the whole camp and every inmate.

Our lips parted without our being conscious of what we were doing, and a scream of despair tore out of our throats, growing louder all the time. The *blokowa* and the *sztubowa* chased us into the block and threw blankets over us to smother our screams. They were afraid that our despair would communicate itself to the rest of the women, those who lay sick and dying in this oppressive hospital block.

Finally, our screaming stopped. On the block we could still hear the screams of the children who were being murdered, then only sighs, and at the end everything was enveloped in death and silence. The next day the men told us that the SS men loaded the children into wheelbarrows and dumped them into the fiery ravines. Living children burned like torches. What did these children do to suffer such a fate? Is there any punishment adequate to repay the criminals who perpetrated these crimes?

Man's Search for Meaning

Viktor E. Frankl

Viktor E. Frankl was born in Vienna in 1905. He and
his wife were imprisoned at Auschwitz, where his
wife perished. Frankl was a physician prior to the
war and served as the director of the department of
neurology at the Rothchild Hospital in Vienna. After
the war, he earned a doctorate in psychology.

Frankl has been a lecturer and visiting professor
at many universities in the United States. He is
probably best known as the psychiatrist who
developed a school of psychotherapy known as
logotherapy, which was designed to humanize the
field of psychiatry. He is the author of several books,
including *Man's Search for Meaning: An Introduction to
Logotherapy*, from which the following excerpt is
taken, and *Will to Meaning*.

Frankl's search for meaning in the midst of the
horror, degradation, and inhumanity of the camps
has had a profound impact on the fields of
psychology and psychiatry. In this selection, Frankl
describes how his rich inner life and his belief in the
power of love helped him to survive.

In spite of all the enforced physical and mental
primitiveness of the life in a concentration camp, it was possible for spiritual life
to deepen. Sensitive people who were used to a rich intellectual life may have

suffered much pain (they were often of a delicate constitution), but the damage to their inner selves was less. They were able to retreat from their terrible surroundings to a life of inner riches and spiritual freedom. Only in this way can one explain the apparent paradox that some prisoners of a less hardy make-up often seemed to survive camp life better than did those of a robust nature. In order to make myself clear, I am forced to fall back on personal experience. Let me tell what happened on those early mornings when we had to march to our work site.

There were shouted commands: "Detachment, forward march! Left-2-3-4! Left-2-3-4! Left-2-3-4! Left-2-3-4! First man about, left and left and left and left! Caps off!" These words sound in my ears even now. At the order "Caps off!" we passed the gate of the camp, and searchlights were trained upon us. Whoever did not march smartly got a kick. And worse off was the man who, because of the cold, had pulled his cap back over his ears before permission was given.

We stumbled on in the darkness, over big stones and through large puddles, along the one road leading from the camp. The accompanying guards kept shouting at us and driving us with the butts of their rifles. Anyone with very sore feet supported himself on his neighbor's arm. Hardly a word was spoken; the icy wind did not encourage talk. Hiding his mouth behind his upturned collar, the man marching next to me whispered suddenly: "If our wives could see us now! I do hope they are better off in their camps and don't know what is happening to us."

That brought thoughts of my own wife to mind. And as we stumbled on for miles, slipping on icy spots, supporting each other time and again, dragging one another up and onward, nothing was said, but we both knew: each of us was thinking of his wife. Occasionally I looked at the sky, where the stars were fading and the pink light of the morning was beginning to spread behind a dark bank of clouds. But my mind clung to my wife's image, imagining it with an uncanny acuteness. I heard her answering me, saw her smile, her frank and encouraging look. Real or not, her look was then more luminous than the sun which was beginning to rise.

A thought transfixed me: for the first time in my life I saw the truth as it is set into song by so many poets, proclaimed as the final wisdom by so many thinkers. The truth—that love is the ultimate and the highest goal to which man can aspire. Then I grasped the meaning of the greatest secret that human poetry and human thought and belief have to impart: *The salvation of man is through love and in love.* I understood how a man who has nothing left in this world still may know bliss, be it only for a brief moment, in the contemplation of his beloved. In a position of utter desolation, when man cannot express himself in positive action, when his only achievement may consist in enduring his sufferings in the right way—an honorable way—in such a position man can, through loving contemplation of the image he carries of his beloved, achieve fulfillment. For the first time in my life I was able to understand the meaning of the words, "The angels are lost in perpetual contemplation of an infinite glory."

In front of me a man stumbled and those following him fell on top of him. The guard rushed over and used his whip on them all. Thus my thoughts were interrupted for a few minutes. But soon my soul found its way back from the prisoner's existence to another world, and I resumed talk with my loved one: I asked her questions, and she answered; she questioned me in return, and I answered.

"Stop!" We had arrived at our work site. Everybody rushed into the dark hut in the hope of getting a fairly decent tool. Each prisoner got a spade or a pickaxe.

"Can't you hurry up, you pigs?" Soon we had resumed the previous day's positions in the ditch. The frozen ground cracked under the point of the pickaxes, and sparks flew. The men were silent, their brains numb.

My mind still clung to the image of my wife. A thought crossed my mind: I didn't even know if she were still alive. I knew only one thing—which I have learned well by now: Love goes very far beyond the physical person of the beloved. It finds its deepest meaning in his spiritual being, his inner self. Whether or not he is actually present, whether or not he is still alive at all, ceases somehow to be of importance.

I did not know whether my wife was alive, and I had no means of finding out (during all my prison life there was no outgoing or incoming mail); but at that moment it ceased to matter. There was no need for me to know; nothing could touch the strength of my love, my thoughts, and the image of my beloved. Had I known then that my wife was dead, I think that I would still have given myself, undisturbed by that knowledge, to the contemplation of her image, and that my mental conversation with her would have been just as vivid and just as satisfying. "Set me like a seal upon thy heart, love is as strong as death."

This intensification of inner life helped the prisoner find a refuge from the emptiness, desolation and spiritual poverty of his existence, by letting him escape into the past. When given free rein, his imagination played with past events, often not important ones, but minor happenings and trifling things. His nostalgic memory glorified them and they assumed a strange character. Their world and their existence seemed very distant and the spirit reached out for them longingly: In my mind I took bus rides, unlocked the front door of my apartment, answered my telephone, switched on the electric lights. Our thoughts often centered on such details, and these memories could move one to tears.

As the inner life of the prisoner tended to become more intense, he also experienced the beauty of art and nature as never before. Under their influence he sometimes even forgot his own frightful circumstances. If someone had seen our faces on the journey from Auschwitz to a Bavarian camp as we beheld the mountains of Salzburg with their summits glowing in the sunset, through the little barred windows of the prison carriage, he would never have believed that those were the faces of men who had given up all hope of life and liberty. Despite that factor—or maybe because of it—we were carried away by nature's beauty, which we had missed for so long.

In camp, too, a man might draw the attention of a comrade working next to him to a nice view of the setting sun shining through the tall trees of the Bavarian woods (as in the famous water color by Dürer), the same woods in which we had built an enormous, hidden munitions plant. One evening, when we were already resting on the floor of our hut, dead tired, soup bowls in hand, a fellow prisoner rushed in and asked us to run out to the assembly grounds and see the wonderful sunset. Standing outside we saw sinister clouds glowing in the west and the whole sky alive with clouds of ever-changing shapes and colors, from steel blue to blood red. The desolate grey mud huts provided a sharp contrast, while the puddles on the muddy ground reflected the glowing sky. Then, after minutes of moving silence, one prisoner said to another, "How beautiful the world *could* be!"

Another time we were at work in a trench. The dawn was grey around us; grey was the sky above; grey the snow in the pale light of dawn; grey the rags in which my fellow prisoners were clad, and grey their faces. I was again conversing silently with my wife, or perhaps I was struggling to find the *reason* for my sufferings, my slow dying. In a last violent protest against the hopelessness of imminent death, I sensed my spirit piercing through the enveloping gloom. I felt it transcend that hopeless, meaningless world, and from somewhere I heard a victorious "Yes" in answer to my question of the existence of an ultimate purpose. At that moment a light was lit in a distant farmhouse, which stood on the horizon as if painted there, in the midst of the miserable grey of a dawning morning in Bavaria. *"Et lux in tenebris lucet"*—and the light shineth in the darkness. For hours I stood hacking at the icy ground. The guard passed by, insulting me, and once again I communed with my beloved. More and more I felt that she was present, that she was with me; I had the feeling that I was able to touch her, able to stretch out my hand and grasp hers. The feeling was very strong: she was *there*. Then, at that very moment, a bird flew down silently and perched just in front of me, on the heap of soil which I had dug up from the ditch, and looked steadily at me.

Letters from Westerbork

Etty Hillesum

Etty Hillesum was born in the Netherlands in 1914.
She served as a member of the Jewish Council in the
Netherlands, a position that permitted her to remain
free in Amsterdam when many Dutch Jews were
sent to the camp at Westerbork before being sent
to Auschwitz. Although she was exempt from
incarceration, she elected to go to Westerbork as a
social worker. She recorded the realities of Nazi
occupation in her letters and diary, which were
published in *Letters from Westerbork*. Although she
had been able to avoid incarceration for several years
during the war, in September 1943 she was sent with
her parents to Auschwitz, where she died two
months later.

Hillesum's letters to friends reveal both the
misery of the camp at Westerbork and her own
indomitable spirit. This letter provides a vivid
description of people waiting for the dreaded
selection that meant they would be transported to
another camp and thus, one step closer to death.

[Probably to Father Han and friends]

24 August 1943

There was a moment when I felt in all seriousness that after this night, it would
be a sin ever to laugh again. But then I reminded myself that some of those who
had gone away had been laughing, even if only a handful of them this time . . .
There will be some who will laugh now and then in Poland too, though not
many from this transport, I think.

When I think of the faces of that squad of armed, green-uniformed guards—my God, those faces! I looked at them, each in turn, from behind the safety of a window, and I have never been so frightened of anything in my life. I sank to my knees with the words that preside over human life: And God made man after His likeness. That passage spent a difficult morning with me.

I have told you often enough that no words and images are adequate to describe nights like these. But still I must try to convey something of it to you. One always has the feeling here of being the ears and eyes of a piece of Jewish history, but there is also the need sometimes to be a still, small voice. We must keep one another in touch with everything that happens in the various outposts of this world, each one contributing his own little piece of stone to the great mosaic that will take shape once the war is over.

After a night in the hospital barracks, I took an early-morning walk past the punishment barracks. And prisoners were being moved out. The deportees, mainly men, stood with their packs behind the barbed wire. So many of them looked tough and ready for anything. An old acquaintance—I didn't recognize him straightaway; a shaven head often changes people completely—called out to me with a smile, "If they don't manage to do me in, I'll be back."

But the babies, those tiny piercing screams of the babies, dragged from their cots in the middle of the night . . . I have to put it all down quickly, in a muddle, because if I leave it until later I probably won't be able to go on believing that it really happened. It is like a vision, and drifts further and further away. The babies were easily the worst.

And then there was that paralyzed young girl, who didn't want to take her dinner plate along and found it so hard to die. Or the terrified young boy: he had thought he was safe, that was his mistake, and when he realized he was going to have to go anyway, he panicked and ran off. His fellow Jews had to hunt him down. If they didn't find him, scores of others would be put on the transport in his place. He was caught soon enough, hiding in a tent, but "notwithstanding" . . . "notwithstanding," all those others had to go on transport anyway, as a deterrent, they said. And so, many good friends were dragged away by that boy. Fifty victims for one moment of insanity. Or rather: he didn't drag them away—our commandant did, someone of whom it is sometimes said that he is a gentleman. Even so, will the boy be able to live with himself, once it dawns on him exactly what he's been the cause of? And how will all the other Jews on board the train react to him? That boy is going to have a very hard time. The episode might have been overlooked, perhaps, if there hadn't been so much unnerving activity over our heads that night. The commandant must have been affected by that too. *"Donnerwetter,* some flying tonight!" I heard a guard say as he looked up at the stars.

People still harbor such childish hopes that the transport won't get through. Many of us were able from here to watch the bombardment of a nearby town, probably Emden. So why shouldn't it be possible for the railway line to be hit too, and for the train to be stopped from leaving? It's never been known to happen yet. But people keep hoping it will, with each new transport and with never-flagging hope . . .

In the afternoon I did a round of the hospital barracks one more time, going from bed to bed. Which beds would be empty the next day? The transport lists are never published until the very last moment, but some of us know well in advance that our names will be down. A young girl called me. She was sitting bolt upright in her bed, eyes wide open. This girl has thin wrists and a peaky little face. She is partly paralyzed, and has just been learning to walk again, between two nurses, one step at a time. "Have you heard? I have to go." We look at each other for a long moment. It is as if her face has disappeared; she is all eyes. Then she says in a level, gray little voice, "Such a pity, isn't it? That everything you have learned in life goes for nothing." And, "How hard it is to die." Suddenly the unnatural rigidity of her expression gives way and she sobs, "Oh, and the worst of it all is having to leave Holland!" And, "Oh, why wasn't I allowed to die before . . ." Later, during the night, I saw her again, for the last time.

There was a little woman in the washhouse, a basket of dripping clothes on her arm. She grabbed hold of me; she looked deranged. A flood of words poured over me: "That isn't right, how can that be right? I've got to go and I won't even be able to get my washing dry by tomorrow. And my child is sick, he's feverish, can't you fix things so that I don't have to go? And I don't have enough things for the child; the rompers they sent me are too small, I need the bigger size, oh, it's enough to drive you mad. And you're not even allowed to take a blanket along, we're going to freeze to death, you didn't think of that, did you? There's a cousin of mine here, he came here the same time I did, but he doesn't have to go, he's got the right papers. Couldn't you help me to get some too? Just say I don't have to go, do you think they'll leave the children with their mothers, that's right, you come back again tonight, you'll help me then, won't you, what do you think, would my cousin's papers . . . ?"

If I were to say that I was in hell that night, what would I really be telling you? I caught myself saying it aloud in the night, aloud to myself and quite soberly, "So that's what hell is like." You really can't tell who is going and who isn't this time. Almost everyone is up, the sick help each other to get dressed. There are some who have no clothes at all, whose luggage has been lost or hasn't arrived yet. Ladies from the "Welfare" walk about doling out clothes, which may fit or not, it doesn't matter so long as you've covered yourself with something. Some old women look a ridiculous sight. Small bottles of milk are being prepared to take along with the babies, whose pitiful screams punctuate all the frantic activity in the barracks. A young mother says to me almost apologetically, "My baby doesn't usually cry; it's almost as if he can tell what's happening." She picks up the child, a lovely baby about eight months old, from a makeshift crib and smiles at it. "If you don't behave yourself, Mummy won't take you along with her!" She tells me about some friends. "When those men in green came to fetch them in Amsterdam, their children cried terribly. Then their father said, 'If you don't behave yourselves, you won't be allowed to go in that green car, this green gentleman won't take you.' And that helped—the children calmed down." She winks at me bravely, a trim, dark little woman with a lively, olive-skinned face. She is dressed in long gray trousers and a green woollen sweater. "I may be smiling," she says, "but I feel pretty awful!" The little woman with the wet washing is on the point of hysterics. "Can't you hide my child for me? Go on, please, won't you hide him, he's got a high fever, how can I possibly take him along?" She points to a little bundle of misery with blond curls and a burning, bright-red little face. The child tosses about in his rough wooden cot. The nurse wants the mother to put on an extra woollen sweater, tries to pull it over her dress. She refuses. "I'm not going to take anything along, what use would it be? . . . my child." And she sobs, "They take the sick children away and you never get them back."

Then a woman comes up to her, a stout working-class woman with a kindly snub-nosed face, draws the desperate mother down with her on the edge of one of the iron bunks, and talks to her almost crooningly. "There now, you're just an ordinary Jew, aren't you? So you'll just have to go, won't you . . . ?"

A few beds further along I suddenly catch sight of the ash-gray, freckled face of a colleague. She is squatting beside the bed of a dying woman who has swallowed some poison and who happens to be her mother . . .

"God Almighty, what are You doing to us?" The words just escape me. Over there is that affectionate little woman from Rotterdam. She is in her ninth month. Two nurses try to get her dressed. She just stands there, her swollen body leaning against her child's cot. Drops of sweat run down her face. She stares into the distance, a distance into which I cannot follow her, and says in a toneless, worn-out voice, "Two months ago I volunteered to go with my husband to Poland. And then I wasn't allowed to, because I always have such difficult pregnancies. And now I do have to go . . . just because someone tried to run away tonight." The wailing of the babies grows louder still, filling every nook and cranny of the barracks, now bathed in ghostly light. It is almost too much to bear. A name occurs to me: Herod.

On the stretcher on the way to the train, her labor pains begin, and we are allowed to carry the woman to the hospital instead of to the freight train—which, this night, seems a rare act of humanity . . .

I pass the bed of the paralyzed girl. The others have helped to dress her. I never saw such great big eyes in such a little face. "I can't take it all in," she whispers to me. A few steps away stands my little hunchbacked Russian woman;

I told you about her before. She stands there as if spun in a web of sorrow. The paralyzed girl is a friend of hers. Later she said sadly to me, "She doesn't even have a plate, I wanted to give her mine, but she wouldn't take it. She said, 'I'll be dead in ten days anyway, and then those horrible Germans will get it.' "

She stands there in front of me, a green silk kimono wrapped around her small, misshapen figure. She has the very wise, bright eyes of a child. She looks at me for a long time in silence, searchingly, and then says, "I would like, oh, I really would like, to be able to swim away in my tears." And "I long so desperately for my dear mother." (Her mother died a few months ago from cancer, in the washroom near the WC. At least she was left alone there for a moment, left to die in peace.) She asks me with her strange accent in the voice of a child that begs for forgiveness, "Surely God will be able to understand my doubts in a world like this, won't He?" Then she turns away from me, in an almost loving gesture of infinite sadness, and throughout the night I see the misshapen, green, silk-clad figure moving between the beds, doing small services for those about to depart. She herself doesn't have to go, not this time, anyway . . .

I'm sitting here squeezing tomato juice for the babies. A young woman sits beside me. She appears ready and eager to leave, and is beautifully turned out. It is something like a cry of liberation when she exclaims, arms flung wide, "I'm embarking on a wonderful journey; I might find my husband." A woman opposite cuts her short bitterly. "I'm going as well, but I certainly don't think it's wonderful." I remembered admitting the young woman beside me. She has been here only a few days and she came from the punishment block. She seems so level-headed and independent, with a touch of defiance about her mouth. She has been ready to leave since the afternoon, dressed in a long pair of trousers and a woollen sweater and cardigan. Next to her on the floor stands a heavy rucksack and a blanket roll. She is trying to force down a few sandwiches. They are moldy. "I'll probably get quite a lot of moldy bread to eat," she laughs. "In prison I didn't eat anything at all for days." A bit of her history in her own words: "My time wasn't far off when they threw me into prison. And the taunts and the insults! I made the mistake of saying that I couldn't stand, so they made me stand for hours, but I managed it without making a sound." She looks defiant. "My husband was in the prison as well. I won't tell you what they did to him! But my God, he was tough! They sent him through last month. I was in my third day of labor and couldn't go with him. But how brave he was!" She is almost radiant.

"Perhaps I shall find him again." She laughs defiantly. "They may drag us through the dirt, but we'll come through all right in the end!" She looks at the crying babies all around and says, "I'll have good work to do on the train, I still have lots of milk."

"What, you here as well?" I suddenly call out in dismay. A woman turns and comes up between the tumbled beds of the poor wailing babies, her hands groping around her for support. She is dressed in a long, black, old-fashioned dress. She has a noble brow and white, wavy hair piled up high. Her husband died here a few weeks ago. She is well over eighty, but looks less than sixty. I always admired her for the aristocratic way in which she reclined on her shabby bunk. She answers in a hoarse voice, "Yes, I'm here as well. They wouldn't let me share my husband's grave."

"Ah, there she goes again!" It is the tough little ghetto woman, who is racked with hunger the whole time because she never gets any parcels. She has seven children here. She trips pluckily and busily about on her little short legs. "All I know is, I've got seven children and they need a proper mother, you can be sure of that!"

With nimble gestures she is busy stuffing a jute bag full of her belongings.

"I'm not leaving anything behind; my husband was sent through here a year ago, and my two oldest boys have been through as well." She beams. "My children are real treasures!" She bustles about, she packs, she's busy, she has a kind word for everyone who goes by. A plain, dumpy ghetto woman with greasy black hair and little short legs. She has a shabby, short-sleeved dress on, which I can imagine her wearing when she used to stand behind the washtub, back in Jodenbreestraat. And now she is off to Poland in the same old dress, a three days' journey with seven children. "That's right, seven children, and they need a proper mother, believe me!"

You can tell that the young woman over there is used to luxury and that she must have been very beautiful. She is a recent arrival. She had gone into hiding to save her baby. Now she is here, through treachery, like so many others. Her husband is in the punishment barracks. She looks quite pitiful now. Her bleached hair has black roots with a greenish tinge. She has put on many different sets of underwear and other clothing all on top of one another—you can't carry everything by hand, after all, particularly if you have a little child to carry as well. Now she looks lumpy and ridiculous. Her face is blotchy. She stares at everyone with a veiled, tentative gaze, like some defenseless and abandoned young animal.

What will this young woman, already in a state of collapse, look like after three days in an overcrowded freight car with men, women, children, and babies all thrown together, bags and baggage, a bucket in the middle their only convenience?

Presumably they will be sent on to another transit camp, and then on again from there.

We are being hunted to death all through Europe . . .

This Way for the Gas, Ladies and Gentlemen

Tadeusz Borowski

Tadeusz Borowski, a highly regarded author of
poetry and fiction, was born on November 12, 1922,
in Zhitomir, Ukraine, in the Soviet Union. In 1942,
he defied the occupying German army by publishing
an illegal collection of poems entitled *Wherever the
Land.* The following year he was incarcerated at
Auschwitz, where he remained until the end of the
war. In 1945, he published another collection of
poems before turning his talents to writing
collections of stories. His writing often reflected
themes of despair, depravity, and the humiliation of
life in the Nazi concentration camps. One of his
best-known works is *This Way for the Gas, Ladies and
Gentlemen*, from which the following selection is
taken. He died on July 3, 1951, in Warsaw.

Borowski's work is noted for its controversial
portrayal of how atrocities became an ordinary part
of life and how the line between normal and
abnormal, sane and insane disappeared.

All of us walk around naked. The delousing is
finally over, and our striped suits are back from the tanks of Cyclone B solution,
an efficient killer of lice in clothing and of men in gas chambers. Only the inmates in the blocks cut off from ours by the "Spanish goats"[1] still have nothing

---

[1] Crossed wooden beams wrapped in barbed wire.

to wear. But all the same, all of us walk around naked: the heat is unbearable. The camp has been sealed off tight. Not a single prisoner, not one solitary louse, can sneak through the gate. The labour Kommandos have stopped working. All day, thousands of naked men shuffle up and down the roads, cluster around the squares, or lie against the walls and on top of the roofs. We have been sleeping on plain boards, since our mattresses and blankets are still being disinfected. From the rear blockhouses we have a view of the F.K.L.—*Frauen Konzentration Lager*; there too the delousing is in full swing. Twenty-eight thousand women have been stripped naked and driven out of the barracks. Now they swarm around the large yard between the blockhouses.

The heat rises, the hours are endless. We are without even our usual diversion: the wide roads leading to the crematoria are empty. For several days now, no new transports have come in. Part of "Canada"[2] has been liquidated and detailed to a labour Kommando—one of the very toughest—at Harmenz. For there exists in the camp a special brand of justice based on envy: when the rich and mighty fall, their friends see to it that they fall to the very bottom. And Canada, our Canada, which smells not of maple forests but of French perfume, has amassed great fortunes in diamonds and currency from all over Europe.

Several of us sit on the top bunk, our legs dangling over the edge. We slice the neat loaves of crisp, crunchy bread. It is a bit coarse to the taste, the kind that stays fresh for days. Sent all the way from Warsaw—only a week ago my mother held this white loaf in her hands . . . dear Lord, dear Lord . . .

We unwrap the bacon, the onion, we open a can of evaporated milk. Henri, the fat Frenchman, dreams aloud of the French wine brought by the transports from Strasbourg, Paris, Marseille . . . Sweat streams down his body.

"Listen, *mon ami*, next time we go up on the loading ramp, I'll bring you real champagne. You haven't tried it before, eh?"

"No. But you'll never be able to smuggle it through the gate, so stop teasing. Why not try and 'organize' some shoes for me instead—you know, the perforated kind, with a double sole, and what about that shirt you promised me long ago?"

"*Patience, patience.* When the new transports come, I'll bring all you want. We'll be going on the ramp again!"

"And what if there aren't any more 'cremo' transports?" I say spitefully. "Can't you see how much easier life is becoming around here: no limit on packages, no more beatings? You even write letters home . . . One hears all kind of talk, and, dammit, they'll run out of people!"

---

[2] "Canada" designated wealth and well-being in the camp. More specifically, it referred to the members of the labour gang, or Kommando, who helped to unload the incoming transports of people destined for the gas chambers.

"Stop talking nonsense." Henri's serious fat face moves rhythmically, his mouth is full of sardines. We have been friends for a long time, but I do not even know his last name. "Stop talking nonsense," he repeats, swallowing with effort. "They can't run out of people, or we'll starve to death in this blasted camp. All of us live on what they bring."

"All? We have our packages . . ."

"Sure, you and your friend, and ten other friends of yours. Some of you Poles get packages. But what about us, and the Jews, and the Russkis? And what if we had no food, no 'organization' from the transports, do you think you'd be eating those packages of yours in peace? We wouldn't let you!"

"You would, you'd starve to death like the Greeks. Around here, whoever has grub, has power."

"Anyway, you have enough, we have enough, so why argue?"

Right, why argue? They have enough, I have enough, we eat together and we sleep on the same bunks. Henri slices the bread, he makes a tomato salad. It tastes good with the commissary mustard.

Below us, naked, sweat-drenched men crowd the narrow barracks aisles or lie packed in eights and tens in the lower bunks. Their nude, withered bodies stink of sweat and excrement; their cheeks are hollow. Directly beneath me, in the bottom bunk, lies a rabbi. He has covered his head with a piece of rag torn off a blanket and reads from a Hebrew prayer book (there is no shortage of this type of literature at the camp), wailing loudly, monotonously.

"Can't somebody shut him up? He's been raving as if he'd caught God himself by the feet."

"I don't feel like moving. Let him rave. They'll take him to the oven that much sooner."

"Religion is the opium of the people," Henri, who is a Communist and a *rentier*, says sententiously. "If they didn't believe in God and eternal life, they'd have smashed the crematoria long ago."

"Why haven't you done it then?"

The question is rhetorical; the Frenchman ignores it.

"Idiot," he says simply, and stuffs a tomato in his mouth.

Just as we finish our snack, there is a sudden commotion at the door. The Muslims[3] scurry in fright to the safety of their bunks, a messenger runs into the Block Elder's shack. The Elder, his face solemn, steps out at once.

"Canada! *Antreten!* But fast! There's a transport coming!"

---

[3] "Muslim" was the camp name for a prisoner who had been destroyed physically and spiritually, and who had neither the strength nor the will to go on living—a man ripe for the gas chamber.

"Great God!" yells Henri, jumping off the bunk. He swallows the rest of his tomato, snatches his coat, screams *"Raus"* at the men below, and in a flash is at the door. We can hear a scramble in the other bunks. Canada is leaving for the ramp.

"Henri, the shoes!" I call after him.

"Keine Angst!" he shouts back, already outside.

I proceed to put away the food. I tie a piece of rope around the suitcase where the onions and the tomatoes from my father's garden in Warsaw mingle with Portuguese sardines, bacon from Lublin (that's from my brother), and authentic sweetmeats from Salonica. I tie it all up, pull on my trousers, and slide off the bunk.

"Platz!" I yell, pushing my way through the Greeks. They step aside. At the door I bump into Henri.

"Was ist los?"

"Want to come with us on the ramp?"

"Sure, why not?"

"Come along then, grab your coat! We're short of a few men. I've already told the Kapo," and he shoves me out of the barracks door.

We line up. Someone has marked down our numbers, someone up ahead yells, "March, march," and now we are running towards the gate, accompanied by the shouts of a multilingual throng that is already being pushed back to the barracks. Not everybody is lucky enough to be going on the ramp . . . We have almost reached the gate. *Links, zwei, drei, vier! Mützen ab!* Erect, arms stretched stiffly along our hips, we march past the gate briskly, smartly, almost gracefully. A sleepy S.S. man with a large pad in his hand checks us off, waving us ahead in groups of five.

"Hundert!" he calls after we have all passed.

"Stimmt!" comes a hoarse answer from out front.

We march fast, almost at a run. There are guards all around, young men with automatics. We pass camp II B, then some deserted barracks and a clump of unfamiliar green—apple and pear trees. We cross the circle of watch-towers and, running, burst on to the highway. We have arrived. Just a few more yards. There, surrounded by trees, is the ramp.

A cheerful little station, very much like any other provincial railway stop: a small square framed by tall chestnuts and paved with yellow gravel. Not far off, beside the road, squats a tiny wooden shed, uglier and more flimsy than the ugliest and flimsiest railway shack; farther along lie stacks of old rails, heaps of wooden beams, barracks parts, bricks, paving stones. This is where they load freight for Birkenau: supplies for the construction of the camp, and people for the gas chambers. Trucks drive around, load up lumber, cement, people—a regular daily routine.

And now the guards are being posted along the rails, across the beams, in the green shade of the Silesian chestnuts, to form a tight circle around the ramp. They wipe the sweat from their faces and sip out of their canteens. It is unbearably hot; the sun stands motionless at its zenith.

"Fall out!"

We sit down in the narrow streaks of shade along the stacked rails. The hungry Greeks (several of them managed to come along, God only knows how) rummage underneath the rails. One of them finds some pieces of mildewed bread, another a few half-rotten sardines. They eat.

"*Schweinedreck,*" spits a young, tall guard with corn-coloured hair and dreamy blue eyes. "For God's sake, any minute you'll have so much food to stuff down your guts, you'll bust!" He adjusts his gun, wipes his face with a handkerchief.

"Hey you, fatso!" His boot lightly touches Henri's shoulder. "*Pass mal auf,* want a drink?"

"Sure, but I haven't got any marks," replies the Frenchman with a professional air.

"*Schade,* too bad."

"Come, come, Herr Posten, isn't my word good enough any more? Haven't we done business before? How much?"

"One hundred. *Gemacht?*"

"*Gemacht!*"

We drink the water, lukewarm and tasteless. It will be paid for by the people who have not yet arrived.

"Now you be careful," says Henri, turning to me. He tosses away the empty bottle. It strikes the rails and bursts into tiny fragments. "Don't take any money, they might be checking. Anyway, who the hell needs money? You've got enough to eat. Don't take suits, either, or they'll think you're planning to escape. Just get a shirt, silk only, with a collar. And a vest. And if you find something to drink, don't bother calling me. I know how to shift for myself, but you watch your step or they'll let you have it."

"Do they beat you up here?"

"Naturally. You've got to have eyes in your ass. *Arschaugen.*"

Around us sit the Greeks, their jaws working greedily, like huge human insects. They munch on stale lumps of bread. They are restless, wondering what will happen next. The sight of the large beams and the stacks of rails has them worried. They dislike carrying heavy loads.

"*Was wir arbeiten?*" they ask.

"*Niks. Transport kommen, alles Krematorium, compris?*"

"*Alles verstehen,*" they answer in crematorium Esperanto. All is well—they will not have to move the heavy rails or carry the beams.

In the meantime, the ramp has become increasingly alive with activity, increasingly noisy. The crews are being divided into those who will open and unload the arriving cattle cars and those who will be posted by the wooden steps. They receive instructions on how to proceed most efficiently. Motor cycles drive up, delivering S.S. officers, bemedalled, glittering with brass, beefy men with highly polished boots and shiny, brutal faces. Some have brought their briefcases, others hold thin, flexible whips. This gives them an air of military readiness and agility. They walk in and out of the commissary—for the miserable little shack by the road serves as their commissary, where in the summertime they drink mineral water, *Studentenquelle,* and where in winter they can warm up with a glass of hot wine. They greet each other in the state-approved way, raising an arm Roman fashion, then shake hands cordially, exchange warm smiles, discuss mail from home, their children, their families. Some stroll majestically on the ramp. The silver squares on their collars glitter, the gravel crunches under their boots, their bamboo whips snap impatiently.

We lie against the rails in the narrow streaks of shade, breathe unevenly, occasionally exchange a few words in our various tongues, and gaze listlessly at the majestic men in green uniforms, at the green trees, and at the church steeple of a distant village.

"The transport is coming," somebody says. We spring to our feet, all eyes turn in one direction. Around the bend, one after another, the cattle cars begin rolling in. The train backs into the station, a conductor leans out, waves his hand, blows a whistle. The locomotive whistles back with a shrieking noise, puffs, the train rolls slowly alongside the ramp. In the tiny barred windows appear pale, wilted, exhausted human faces, terror-stricken women with tangled hair, unshaven men. They gaze at the station in silence. And then, suddenly, there is a stir inside the cars and a pounding against the wooden boards.

"Water! Air!"—weary, desperate cries.

Heads push through the windows, mouths gasp frantically for air. They draw a few breaths, then disappear; others come in their place, then also disappear. The cries and moans grow louder.

A man in a green uniform covered with more glitter than any of the others jerks his head impatiently, his lips twist in annoyance. He inhales deeply, then with a rapid gesture throws his cigarette away and signals to the guard. The guard removes the automatic from his shoulder, aims, sends a series of shots along the train. All is quiet now. Meanwhile, the trucks have arrived, steps are being drawn up, and the Canada men stand ready at their posts by the train doors. The S.S. officer with the briefcase raises his hand.

'Whoever takes gold, or anything at all besides food, will be shot for stealing Reich property. Understand? *Verstanden?*'

"*Jawohl!*" we answer eagerly.

"*Also los!* Begin!"

The bolts crack, the doors fall open. A wave of fresh air rushes inside the train. People . . . inhumanly crammed, buried under incredible heaps of luggage, suitcases, trunks, packages, crates, bundles of every description (everything that had been their past and was to start their future). Monstrously squeezed together, they have fainted from heat, suffocated, crushed one another. Now they push towards the opened doors, breathing like fish cast out on the sand.

"Attention! Out, and take your luggage with you! Take out everything. Pile all your stuff near the exits. Yes, your coats too. It is summer. March to the left. Understand?"

"Sir, what's going to happen to us?" They jump from the train on to the gravel, anxious, worn-out.

"Where are you people from?"

"Sosnowiec-Bedzin. Sir, what's going to happen to us?" They repeat the question stubbornly, gazing into our tired eyes.

"I don't know, I don't understand Polish."

It is the camp law: people going to their death must be deceived to the very end. This is the only permissible form of charity. The heat is tremendous. The sun hangs directly over our heads, the white, hot sky quivers, the air vibrates, an occasional breeze feels like a sizzling blast from a furnace. Our lips are parched, the mouth fills with the salty taste of blood, the body is weak and heavy from lying in the sun. Water!

A huge, multicoloured wave of people loaded down with luggage pours from the train like a blind, mad river trying to find a new bed. But before they have a chance to recover, before they can draw a breath of fresh air and look at the sky, bundles are snatched from their hands, coats ripped off their backs, their purses and umbrellas taken away.

"But please, sir, it's for the sun, I cannot . . ."

"*Verboten!*" one of us barks through clenched teeth. There is an S.S. man standing behind your back, calm, efficient, watchful.

"*Meine Herrschaften*, this way, ladies and gentlemen, try not to throw your things around, please. Show some goodwill," he says courteously, his restless hands playing with the slender whip.

"Of course, of course," they answer as they pass, and now they walk alongside the train somewhat more cheerfully. A woman reaches down quickly to pick up her handbag. The whip flies, the woman screams, stumbles, and falls under the feet of the surging crowd. Behind her, a child cries in a thin little voice "Mamele!"—a very small girl with tangled black curls.

The heaps grow. Suitcases, bundles, blankets, coats, handbags that open as they fall, spilling coins, gold, watches; mountains of bread pile up at the exits, heaps of marmalade, jams, masses of meat, sausages; sugar spills on the gravel.

Trucks, loaded with people, start up with a deafening roar and drive off amidst the wailing and screaming of the women separated from their children, and the stupefied silence of the men left behind. They are the ones who had been ordered to step to the right—the healthy and the young who will go to the camp. In the end, they too will not escape death, but first they must work.

Trucks leave and return, without interruption, as on a monstrous conveyor belt. A Red Cross van drives back and forth, back and forth, incessantly: it transports the gas that will kill these people. The enormous cross on the hood, red as blood, seems to dissolve in the sun.

The Canada men at the trucks cannot stop for a single moment, even to catch their breath. They shove the people up the steps, pack them in tightly, sixty per truck, more or less. Near by stands a young, cleanshaven "gentleman," an S.S. officer with a notebook in his hand. For each departing truck he enters a mark; sixteen gone means one thousand people, more or less. The gentleman is calm, precise. No truck can leave without a signal from him, or a mark in his notebook: *Ordnung muss sein.* The marks swell into thousands, the thousands into whole transports, which afterwards we shall simply call 'from Salonica', "from Strasbourg," 'from Rotterdam'. This one will be called "Sosnowiec-Będzin." The new prisoners from Sosnowiec-Będzin will receive serial numbers 131–2— thousand, of course, though afterwards we shall simply say 131–2, for short.

The transports swell into weeks, months, years. When the war is over, they will count up the marks in their notebooks—all four and a half million of them. The bloodiest battle of the war, the greatest victory of the strong, united Germany. *Ein Reich, ein Volk, ein Führer*—and four crematoria.

The train has been emptied. A thin, pock-marked S.S. man peers inside, shakes his head in disgust and motions to our group, pointing his finger at the door.

"*Rein.* Clean it up!"

We climb inside. In the corners amid human excrement and abandoned wristwatches lie squashed, trampled infants, naked little monsters with enormous heads and bloated bellies. We carry them out like chickens, holding several in each hand.

"Don't take them to the trucks, pass them on to the women," says the S.S. man, lighting a cigarette. His cigarette lighter is not working properly; he examines it carefully.

"Take them, for God's sake!" I explode as the women run from me in horror, covering their eyes.

The name of God sounds strangely pointless, since the women and the infants will go on the trucks, every one of them, without exception. We all know what this means, and we look at each other with hate and horror.

"What, you don't want to take them?" asks the pockmarked S.S. man with a note of surprise and reproach in his voice, and reaches for his revolver.

"You mustn't shoot, I'll carry them." A tall, grey-haired woman takes the little corpses out of my hands and for an instant gazes straight into my eyes.

"My poor boy," she whispers and smiles at me. Then she walks away, staggering along the path. I lean against the side of the train. I am terribly tired. Someone pulls at my sleeve.

"*En avant*, to the rails, come on!"

I look up, but the face swims before my eyes, dissolves, huge and transparent, melts into the motionless trees and the sea of people . . . I blink rapidly: Henri.

"Listen, Henri, are we good people?"

"That's stupid. Why do you ask?"

"You see, my friend, you see, I don't know why, but I am furious, simply furious with these people—furious because I must be here because of them. I feel no pity. I am not sorry they're going to the gas chamber. Damn them all! I could throw myself at them, beat them with my fists. It must be pathological, I just can't understand . . ."

"Ah, on the contrary, it is natural, predictable, calculated. The ramp exhausts you, you rebel—and the easiest way to relieve your hate is to turn against someone weaker. Why, I'd even call it healthy. It's simple logic, *compris?*" He props himself up comfortably against the heap of rails. "Look at the Greeks, they know how to make the best of it! They stuff their bellies with anything they find. One of them has just devoured a full jar of marmalade."

"Pigs! Tomorrow half of them will die of the shits."

"Pigs? You've been hungry."

"Pigs!" I repeat furiously. I close my eyes. The air is filled with ghastly cries, the earth trembles beneath me, I can feel sticky moisture on my eyelids. My throat is completely dry.

The morbid procession streams on and on—trucks growl like mad dogs. I shut my eyes tight, but I can still see corpses dragged from the train, trampled infants, cripples piled on top of the dead, wave after wave . . . freight cars roll in, the heaps of clothing, suitcases and bundles grow, people climb out, look at the sun, take a few breaths, beg for water, get into the trucks, drive away. And again freight cars roll in, again people . . . The scenes become confused in my mind— I am not sure if all of this is actually happening, or if I am dreaming. There is a humming inside my head; I feel that I must vomit.

Henri tugs at my arm.

"Don't sleep, we're off to load up the loot."

All the people are gone. In the distance, the last few trucks roll along the road in clouds of dust, the train has left, several S.S. officers promenade up and down the ramp. The silver glitters on their collars. Their boots shine, their red, beefy faces shine. Among them there is a woman—only now I realize she has been here all along—withered, flat-chested, bony, her thin, colourless hair pulled back and tied in a "Nordic" knot; her hands are in the pockets of her wide skirt. With a rat-like, resolute smile glued on her thin lips she sniffs around the corners of the ramp. She detests feminine beauty with the hatred of a woman who is herself repulsive, and knows it. Yes, I have seen her many times before and I know her well: she is the commandant of the F.K.L. She has come to look over the new crop of women, for some of them, instead of going on the trucks, will go on foot—to the concentration camp. There our boys, the barbers from Zauna, will shave their heads and will have a good laugh at their "outside world" modesty.

We proceed to load the loot. We lift huge trunks, heave them on to the trucks. There they are arranged in stacks, packed tightly. Occasionally somebody slashes one open with a knife, for pleasure or in search of vodka and perfume. One of the crates falls open; suits, shirts, books drop out on the ground . . . I pick up a small, heavy package. I unwrap it—gold, about two handfuls, bracelets, rings, brooches, diamonds . . .

"*Gib hier,*" an S.S. man says calmly, holding up his briefcase already full of gold and colourful foreign currency. He locks the case, hands it to an officer, takes another, an empty one, and stands by the next truck, waiting. The gold will go to the Reich.

It is hot, terribly hot. Our throats are dry, each word hurts. Anything for a sip of water! Faster, faster, so that it is over, so that we may rest. At last we are done, all the trucks have gone. Now we swiftly clean up the remaining dirt: there must be "no trace left of the *Schweinerei.*" But just as the last truck disappears behind the trees and we walk, finally, to rest in the shade, a shrill whistle sounds around the bend. Slowly, terribly slowly, a train rolls in, the engine whistles back with a deafening shriek. Again weary, pale faces at the windows, flat as though cut out of paper, with huge, feverishly burning eyes. Already trucks are pulling up, already the composed gentleman with the notebook is at his post, and the S.S. men emerge from the commissary carrying briefcases for the gold and money. We unseal the train doors.

It is impossible to control oneself any longer. Brutally we tear suitcases from their hands, impatiently pull off their coats. Go on, go on, vanish! They go, they vanish. Men, women, children. Some of them know.

Here is a woman—she walks quickly, but tries to appear calm. A small child with a pink cherub's face runs after her and, unable to keep up, stretches out his little arms and cries: "Mama! Mama!"

"Pick up your child, woman!"

"It's not mine, sir, not mine!" she shouts hysterically and runs on, covering her face with her hands. She wants to hide, she wants to reach those who will not ride the trucks, those who will go on foot, those who will stay alive. She is young, healthy, good-looking, she wants to live.

But the child runs after her, wailing loudly: "Mama, mama, don't leave me!"

"It's not mine, not mine, no!"

Andrei, a sailor from Sevastopol, grabs hold of her. His eyes are glassy from vodka and the heat. With one powerful blow he knocks her off her feet, then, as she falls, takes her by the hair and pulls her up again. His face twitches with rage.

"Ah, you bloody Jewess! So you're running from your own child! I'll show you, you whore!" His huge hand chokes her, he lifts her in the air and heaves her on to the truck like a heavy sack of grain.

"Here! And take this with you, bitch!" and he throws the child at her feet.

"*Gut gemacht,* good work. That's the way to deal with degenerate mothers," says the S.S. man standing at the foot of the trunk. "*Gut, gut, Russki.*"

"Shut your mouth," growls Andrei through clenched teeth, and walks away. From under a pile of rags he pulls out a canteen, unscrews the cork, takes a few deep swallows, passes it to me. The strong vodka burns the throat. My head swims, my legs are shaky, again I feel like throwing up.

And suddenly, above the teeming crowd pushing forward like a river driven by an unseen power, a girl appears. She descends lightly from the train, hops on to the gravel, looks around inquiringly, as if somewhat surprised. Her soft, blonde hair has fallen on her shoulders in a torrent, she throws it back impatiently. With a natural gesture she runs her hands down her blouse, casually straightens her skirt. She stands like this for an instant, gazing at the crowd, then turns and with a gliding look examines our faces, as though searching for someone. Unknowingly, I continue to stare at her, until our eyes meet.

"Listen, tell me, where are they taking us?"

I look at her without saying a word. Here, standing before me, is a girl, a girl with enchanting blonde hair, with beautiful breasts, wearing a little cotton blouse, a girl with a wise, mature look in her eyes. Here she stands, gazing straight into my face, waiting. And over there is the gas chamber: communal death, disgusting and ugly. And over in the other direction is the concentration camp: the shaved head, the heavy Soviet trousers in sweltering heat, the sickening, stale odour of dirty, damp female bodies, the animal hunger, the inhuman labour, and later the same gas chamber, only an even more hideous, more terrible death . . .

Why did she bring it? I think to myself, noticing a lovely gold watch on her delicate wrist. They'll take it away from her anyway.

"Listen, tell me," she repeats.

I remain silent. Her lips tighten.

"I know," she says with a shade of proud contempt in her voice, tossing her head. She walks off resolutely in the direction of the trucks. Someone tries to stop her; she boldly pushes him aside and runs up the steps. In the distance I can only catch a glimpse of her blonde hair flying in the breeze.

I go back inside the train; I carry out dead infants; I unload luggage. I touch corpses, but I cannot overcome the mounting, uncontrollable terror. I try to escape from the corpses, but they are everywhere: lined up on the gravel, on the cement edge of the ramp, inside the cattle cars. Babies, hideous naked women, men twisted by convulsions. I run off as far as I can go, but immediately a whip slashes across my back. Out of the corner of my eye I see an S.S. man, swearing profusely. I stagger forward and run, lose myself in the Canada group. Now, at last, I can once more rest against the stack of rails. The sun has leaned low over the horizon and illuminates the ramp with a reddish glow; the shadows of the trees have become elongated, ghostlike. In the silence that settles over nature at this time of day, the human cries seem to rise all the way to the sky.

Only from this distance does one have a full view of the inferno on the teeming ramp. I see a pair of human beings who have fallen to the ground locked in a last desperate embrace. The man has dug his fingers into the woman's flesh and has caught her clothing with his teeth. She screams hysterically, swears, cries, until at last a large boot comes down over her throat and she is silent. They are pulled apart and dragged like cattle to the truck. I see four Canada men lugging a corpse: a huge, swollen female corpse. Cursing, dripping wet from the strain, they kick out of their way some stray children who have been running all over the ramp, howling like dogs. The men pick them up by the collars, heads, arms, and toss them inside the trucks, on top of the heaps. The four men have trouble lifting the fat corpse on to the car, they call others for help, and all together they hoist up the mound of meat. Big, swollen, puffed-up corpses are being collected from all over the ramp; on top of them are piled the invalids, the smothered, the sick, the unconscious. The heap seethes, howls, groans. The driver starts the motor, the truck begins rolling.

"Halt! Halt!" an S.S. man yells after them. "Stop, damn you!"

They are dragging to the truck an old man wearing tails and a band around his arm. His head knocks against the gravel and pavement; he moans and wails in an uninterrupted monotone: "*Ich will mit dem Herrn Kommandanten sprechen—* I wish to speak with the commandant . . ." With senile stubbornness he keeps repeating these words all the way. Thrown on the truck, trampled by others, choked, he still wails: "*Ich will mit dem . . .*"

"Look here, old man!" a young S.S. man calls, laughing jovially. "In half an hour you'll be talking with the top commandant! Only don't forget to greet him with a *Heil Hitler!*"

Several other men are carrying a small girl with only one leg. They hold her by the arms and the one leg. Tears are running down her face and she whispers faintly: "Sir, it hurts, it hurts . . ." They throw her on the truck on top of the corpses. She will burn alive along with them.

The evening has come, cool and clear. The stars are out. We lie against the rails. It is incredibly quiet. Anaemic bulbs hang from the top of the high lamp-posts; beyond the circle of light stretches an impenetrable darkness. Just one step, and a man could vanish for ever. But the guards are watching, their automatics ready.

"Did you get the shoes?" asks Henri.

"No."

"Why?"

"My God, man, I am finished, absolutely finished!"

"So soon? After only two transports? Just look at me, I . . . since Christmas, at least a million people have passed through my hands. The worst of all are the transports from around Paris—one is always bumping into friends."

"And what do you say to them?"

"That first they will have a bath, and later we'll meet at the camp. What would you say?"

I do not answer. We drink coffee with vodka; somebody opens a tin of cocoa and mixes it with sugar. We scoop it up by the handful, the cocoa sticks to the lips. Again coffee, again vodka.

"Henri, what are we waiting for?"

"There'll be another transport."

"I'm not going to unload it! I can't take any more."

"So, it's got you down? Canada is nice, eh?" Henri grins indulgently and disappears into the darkness. In a moment he is back again.

"All right. Just sit here quietly and don't let an S.S. man see you. I'll try to find you your shoes."

"Just leave me alone. Never mind the shoes." I want to sleep. It is very late.

Another whistle, another transport. Freight cars emerge out of the darkness, pass under the lamp-posts, and again vanish in the night. The ramp is small, but the circle of lights is smaller. The unloading will have to be done gradually. Somewhere the trucks are growling. They back up against the steps, black, ghostlike, their searchlights flash across the trees. *Wasser! Luft!* The same all over again, like a late showing of the same film: a volley of shots, the train falls silent. Only this time a little girl pushes herself halfway through the small window and, losing her balance, falls out on to the gravel. Stunned, she lies still for a moment, then stands up and begins walking around in a circle, faster and faster, waving her rigid arms in the air, breathing loudly and spasmodically, whining in a faint voice. Her mind has given way in the inferno inside the train.

The whining is hard on the nerves: an S.S. man approaches calmly, his heavy boot strikes between her shoulders. She falls. Holding her down with his foot, he draws his revolver, fires once, then again. She remains face down, kicking the gravel with her feet, until she stiffens. They proceed to unseal the train.

I am back on the ramp, standing by the doors. A warm, sickening smell gushes from inside. The mountain of people filling the car almost halfway up to the ceiling is motionless, horribly tangled, but still steaming.

"*Ausladen!*" comes the command. An S.S. man steps out from the darkness. Across his chest hangs a portable searchlight. He throws a stream of light inside.

"Why are you standing about like sheep? Start unloading!" His whip flies and falls across our backs. I seize a corpse by the hand; the fingers close tightly around mine. I pull back with a shriek and stagger away. My heart pounds, jumps up to my throat. I can no longer control the nausea. Hunched under the train I begin to vomit. Then, like a drunk, I weave over to the stack of rails.

I lie against the cool, kind metal and dream about returning to the camp, about my bunk, on which there is no mattress, about sleep among comrades who are not going to the gas tonight. Suddenly I see the camp as a haven of peace. It is true, others may be dying, but one is somehow still alive, one has enough food, enough strength to work . . .

The lights on the ramp flicker with a spectral glow, the wave of people—feverish, agitated, stupefied people—flows on and on, endlessly. They think that now they will have to face a new life in the camp, and they prepare themselves emotionally for the hard struggle ahead. They do not know that in just a few moments they will die, that the gold, money, and diamonds which they have so prudently hidden in their clothing and on their bodies are now useless to them. Experienced professionals will probe into every recess of their flesh, will pull the gold from under the tongue and the diamonds from the uterus and the colon. They will rip out gold teeth. In tightly sealed crates they will ship them to Berlin.

The S.S. men's black figures move about, dignified, businesslike. The gentleman with the notebook puts down his final marks, rounds out the figures: fifteen thousand.

Many, very many, trucks have been driven to the crematoria today.

It is almost over. The dead are being cleared off the ramp and piled into the last truck. The Canada men, weighed down under a load of bread, marmalade and sugar, and smelling of perfume and fresh linen, line up to go. For several days the entire camp will live off this transport. For several days the entire camp will talk about "Sosnowiec-Będzin." "Sosnowiec-Będzin" was a good, rich transport.

The stars are already beginning to pale as we walk back to the camp. The sky grows translucent and opens high above our heads—it is getting light.

Great columns of smoke rise from the crematoria and merge up above into a huge black river which very slowly floats across the sky over Birkenau and disappears beyond the forests in the direction of Trzebinia. The "Sosnowiec-Będzin" transport is already burning.

We pass a heavily armed S.S. detachment on its way to change guard. The men march briskly, in step, shoulder to shoulder, one mass, one will.

"*Und morgen die ganze Welt* . . ." they sing at the top of their lungs.

"*Rechts ran!* To the right march!" snaps a command from up front. We move out of their way.

Resisting Evil

The power and threat of the Nazis were overwhelming. They were highly organized, well-armed, and dedicated to conquering Europe and destroying the Jews and other enemies. Against their might and numbers, there were acts of resistance by individuals and groups. Many of the Jews who escaped from ghettos, trains, camps, or even from sites of mass executions went into the forests and joined groups of predominately young people who had established underground resistance movements. There were groups of freedom fighters or partisans in every German-occupied country. The partisans, who were ill-equipped, provided more of an annoyance to the Nazis than a genuine threat; however, they fought with pride and dedication. Some activities of the resistance were less public. Many members of the underground were dedicated to helping Jews escape to nonoccupied countries where they would be safe. For example, the small French village of Le Chambon defied the Nazis and the Vichy government as it conspired to hide Jews and to help them to freedom.

Between the fall of 1942 and the summer of 1943, Jews in twenty ghettos in Eastern Europe revolted against their Nazi oppressors. In some cases, they were armed only with bricks, rocks, and sticks, while in others they had weapons that had been smuggled in to them, such as a few handguns and even fewer rifles, gasoline bombs, and grenades. In the Warsaw ghetto, nearly 1,000 Jewish rebels continued their violent resistance for several weeks before the Nazis destroyed the whole ghetto. Yet, as the word spread, outbreaks occurred in other ghettos and in five of the death camps. The Nazis crushed these rebellions and emptied the ghettos as they sought to carry out the "final solution"—the destruction of all European Jews.

Chapter 6 provides the stories of some of those who resisted the evil of the Nazis. Also included are the stories of rescuers—people who risked their own safety to help others in danger.

There Were Those

Susan Dambroff

Susan Dambroff is a San Francisco poet and performer. Her collection of poems, *Memory in Bone*, includes poetry about the Holocaust. She teaches special education.

Dambroff's poem explores some of the many ways in which individuals resisted the Nazis.

There were those
who escaped to the forests
who crawled through sewers
who jumped from the backs of trains

There were those
who smuggled messages
who smuggled dynamite
inside breadloaves
inside matchboxes
inside corpses

There were those
who were shoemakers
who put nails
into the boots
of German soldiers

There were those
who wrote poetry
who put on plays
who taught the children

There were those
who fed each other

I Did What *Everyone* Should Have Done

Arie van Mansum
(as told to Gay Block and Malka Drucker)

A Dutch Christian, Arie van Mansum quit his job to
work full-time for the resistance during World War II.
Even after he was captured, imprisoned, and
eventually released, he continued to help Jews. Arie
van Mansum, as do many other rescuers, believes
that what he did was nothing special. His story is
reprinted from *Rescuers: Portraits of Moral Courage in
the Holocaust*, which was edited by Gay Block and
Malka Drucker.

Arie van Mansum's narrative describes how he
repeatedly risked his life to resist evil.

Well, the Holocaust didn't start with the
Germans picking up Jews and sending them to concentration camps and putting
them in gas chambers. The Holocaust started in the hearts of the people. As
soon as you go and say, "That Jew!" or whatever, that's where it starts, you know.
That was the beginning. As soon as you put one race higher than another one,
you get that.

I was born in 1920 in Utrecht, but we moved to Maastricht in the south of
Holland when I was six years old. I was the second child, one sister was older
and one brother and sister were younger. We were simple people with not
much education. My father was a laborer with the Dutch railroad, and I was
very close to my mother, who stayed home with the children.

We were members of the Reform Church of the Netherlands, which is more strict than the Dutch Reformed. When we moved to Maastricht we were in the minority because the city was 90 percent Catholic. There were about seventy or eighty Jewish families but we didn't know them. We had no contact because we were a laborer's family and the Jews were businesspeople; we went to the Protestant school and they went to public school. In 1939, I was active in the young people's group of our church, and we went to a meeting at City Hall to discuss what to do about refugees coming in from Germany. I was the representative from the church, to try to decide how to help them. You couldn't tell the difference between Jews in Holland and others, anyway. But we had no chance to make any decisions before the war broke out.

In 1940, I was working as a traveling salesman for a wholesale wallpaper company. A man from my church who was an accountant for some Jewish people asked me to become the representative for distributing the underground newspaper, *Free Netherlands*. I agreed, and every month I took 500 to 1,000 newspapers and distributed them on my trips. I came in contact with a man in the Socialist movement, Van Assen, who told me a Jewish family needed help, and asked if I would accompany them to the hiding place he had found for them. I did it. Then, after I had done more of this, he approached me to find a hiding place for a Jewish family. I contacted Mrs. Fralich and found a place for her and her daughter in Haarlem. But her son, Fritz, looked too Jewish, so I took him home myself. He was my age and my parents liked him. He had to stay in the house all the time, since he looked so Jewish, but it was through him that I came into contact with more families who needed help. Then I needed to get food stamps for all these people. I figured out a way to forge the food-stamp cards, and every week I went from one food-stamp office to another to get them because I needed so many. Soon I was getting 150 ration cards, and I finally met a man in the food-stamp office who was willing to get them all for me. When I needed 250 cards to deal with he got scared, so then a man who was the head of the police department in Haarlem did it for me.

One day some students in Amsterdam contacted me. The Germans were putting all the Jewish children together in the nursery, and the overflow in a converted theater across the street. Each day when the Germans took them out for a walk, the students would kidnap some of them and take them to hiding places in other parts of Holland. I began finding places for them, mostly in the south of Holland because there people had come from Poland and were darker skinned, so it was easier for a Jewish child to live among them. One day I was told of a Jewish boy in the hospital who would be shipped to Westerbork if we didn't get him out. I had a friend who was a nurse and she rescued him. I placed him with a Catholic family where he stayed till the end of the war.

Another time I needed to find a place for a baby fast because the family had already been summoned to Westerbork. My mother said she would take this eleven-day-old baby, and my girl friend and I went to pick her up. People thought we were a married couple with a newborn child. My mother really loved that baby. Later I placed another baby someplace else. I could go on telling these stories. Every day a new problem came up that I had to figure out a way to solve.

I quit my job and did this resistance work full-time. Every month I visited the people I had placed to take them food stamps and mail with news from their families. Many were very depressed, and I had the opportunity to lift them up a little and they appreciated that.

I was still living at home with my parents, and my sister, Margarete, helped me as well. When I was arrested in October 1943, she took over all the work I had been doing. I ended up in Haarlem in prison, for six months of solitary confinement. Then I was sent to Amersfoort concentration camp until September 1944. I was mistreated during interrogation, and was scared to death like anyone else. According to me, the Germans were stupid. When they arrested me, I had some addresses on me of families in hiding, but they never checked them out. I was taking care of about a hundred people, but they never found them. Only one family I had placed, the Vesleys, was found and arrested, and the son was killed. A three-year-old boy. But this wasn't because of the list.

I was released from prison in Utrecht, which was in an area already liberated by the Allies. I couldn't go home because Maastricht was still occupied, so I stayed in Utrecht with an aunt and began underground work again. I was delivering *Free Netherlands* when I was again arrested in February 1945, and sent back to the concentration camp. I stayed there until the end of the war. All this time my sister did the work with the food stamps and the families in hiding that I had been doing. She died last year of a stroke at sixty-five, in Holland.

The baby stayed with my mother until June 1945, when the parents picked her up. It was hard on my mother; she was very attached. But the parents said, "We don't have family anymore. Can we adopt you as grandparents?" So we all remained like family until they emigrated to Israel.

I'll tell you, the best years of my life were when I could help Jews in the wartime. That was one of the best time periods of my life because it gave such satisfaction. I mean, the moment that I came back from prison in May 1945, I walked through the streets of Maastricht, and I saw Jews walking there, Jews I helped in the wartime, I started to cry. That was the satisfaction, you know. You saw those people walking through the street! And then it was a double satisfaction when I saw them in Israel, in their own country. It was fabulous!

Fritz lives in Belgium now. He is the secretary of the Jewish community. I moved to Canada because I was very disappointed in Holland. Many people who did no resistance work took the most prominent positions after the war. I'll give you an example. I had a friend I worked with, he was a Socialist, a teacher in the public high school. And one day he approached me. He said, "There's a Jewish family, the Spitz family, and the chances are that they're gonna pick them up, either today or tomorrow. We need a place for them quick! Please help."

So I found a temporary place for the family, a family with four children. They were a poor family, he had a used furniture store. So that night we went over to get the people from their house and when we were sitting and they were packing, all of a sudden two Dutch policemen came in and told them that a Gestapo van would come in an hour or so to pick them up. And they asked us what we were doing there. We said, "Well, we were just buying some furniture." And he said, "You'll have to discuss that with the trustees because you'll have to leave now." So we walked outside and waited, walked up and down in front of the house for over an hour. One policeman came out to call the Germans because it was taking so long for the van to come to pick up these people. I asked that policeman, "Please, stay away for half an hour—give us a chance." He said, "I'm sorry, sir, I'm just doing my duty." This family was picked up and never returned. But this same man, after the war, got a promotion in the regular police force. That made me so furious. And besides, this policeman was assigned to the police force responsible for punishing NSBers. We registered a complaint when we saw him but nothing was done. They said he was just doing his duty. And those people were all picked up, the six people, and none of them came back. That makes you furious!

But I still say there was nothing special about what I did. I did what *everyone should have done.* Those people who did nothing on either side were scared and only looked after themselves. But I had feelings during wartime, and after the wartime even more, that I could have done more. I remember one day when I was walking through a rail station and a train came in loaded with Jewish people in those, you know, those livestock wagons. I, I stood there, you know, and I could do nothing, you know.

All of my Jewish friends are in Israel now, and we're like one big family. They called a few days ago to ask when I will come again. I went to Israel for the first time in 1981, with a tourist group, and when they met me at the hotel, they were mad. They said, "You shouldn't go with a tour; you should have stayed with us." I had received my medal from Yad Vashem in 1970; my sister was one of the first to be honored. When I went to Yad Vashem to look for my tree, it wasn't there. They said, "No, we have been waiting for you to come to plant it yourself." So I said, "Okay, give me a shovel." But they said, "No, it's a celebration and a ceremony." So my friends said, "You come next year and we'll pay for the trip, and you'll stay with us." But I said, "I'll pay for it." So we went back the next year. I think people don't understand what goes on in Israel. Maybe the Palestinians have a better PR department than the Israelis.

My children never knew what I did until recently. They asked, "Dad, why didn't you tell us?" But first, I'm afraid people will think I'm bragging, and I'd hate that. It's nothing to brag about. My sister went to Israel four times, and I keep in close contact, but otherwise I don't want to brag. Now, lately, some people in the Jewish community convinced me to share my story for the next generation. So I talked to kids, to churches, to memorial gatherings of Jews. And my children think it's enormous. My six-year-old grandson called and said, "Hey, Grandpa, I heard you were in jail!" So my daughter has started to tell them.

I guess I have helping in my blood. After the war a large group of people came from Indonesia, and my sister and I helped them. And here in Canada I work for a rescue mission. But, you know, not everyone had the opportunity to help during the war. I wouldn't say I had courage. If you'd have asked me before if I could have done it, I'd have said, "Oh, no, not me!" But if the moment's there and there's somebody in need, you go help, that's all.

Lest Innocent Blood Be Shed

Philip P. Hallie

Philip P. Hallie is the author of *Lest Innocent Blood Be Shed: The Story of the Village of Le Chambon and How Goodness Happened There*, which tells of Le Chambon, a small Protestant village in southern France. The villagers, led by their clergy, put their beliefs about nonviolence into practice during the Holocaust. Undaunted by the Nazi SS and the collaborationist Vichy government, they quietly and peacefully organized to save thousands of Jewish children and adults.

The following excerpt illustrates the courage and fear that coexisted in Le Chambon during the winter of 1940–1941.

T he winter following the conquest of France—the winter of 1940–1941—was one of the most ferocious in the history of modern France. In Le Chambon the snow was piled high against the gray walls and buildings, and *la burle* seemed never to stop its whirling. In the granite presbytery Magda Trocmé was putting small pieces of wood and dried genets into the kitchen stove to keep the heat as high as possible without wasting fuel. The big black stove stood against the wall facing the Rue de la Grande Fontaine, the crooked street along which her husband would later walk on his way to an internment camp.

Concentrating—as she always did—upon the details of what she was doing, the calculation of just the right number of bits of fuel to put in the stove, she was slightly startled to hear a knock at the outer door of the presbytery. Someone had come through the "poetic gate" that opened onto the Rue de la Grande

Fontaine, and was standing in the shallow doorway of the presbytery itself, standing in the wind and snow blowing off the Lignon River. She closed the stove, went through the dark little hallway, and opened the outer door.

There before her, only the front of her body protected from the cold, stood a woman shawled in pure snow. Under her shawl her clothes, though once thick, had been whipped thin by the wind and the snow of that terrible winter. But her face had been whipped even thinner by events; she was visibly frightened, and was half-ready to step back, trembling with fright and cold. The first thing that Magda Trocmé recalls seeing was the hunger in that face and in those dark eyes.

Here was the first refugee from the Nazis to come to the presbytery door. This is the way Magda Trocmé started her description of the incident in a conversation with me thirty-six years later:

"A German woman knocked at my door. It was in the evening, and she said she was a German Jew, coming from northern France, that she was in danger, and that she had heard that in Le Chambon somebody could help her. Could she come into my house? I said, 'Naturally, come in, and come in.' Lots of snow. She had a little pair of shoes, nothing. . . ."

There was a big wooden table in the middle of the kitchen, and, after asking her to take off her shawl and coat, Magda had the woman sit at the side of the table facing the stove, where she gave her something to eat. They started to talk. The pastor's wife spoke German, and she soon learned a story that was to become familiar. The woman had run away from Hitler's Germany because of the increasingly vicious racial laws, and had found herself in the Occupied Zone, where the lives of foreign Jews were in constant danger; and so she had kept running until she crossed the demarcation line and entered the Free Zone, where there were fewer German troops and less danger.

Magda Trocmé is not given to long, ruminative chats. When she talks, she does so swiftly, with a breathless, heavy voice whose pace and tone seem to be saying, "Come, now, let's get this talking over with and *do* what we're supposed to be doing." She has powerful arms that are frequently being used to move things and to push herself away from tables and up from chairs so that she can cope with human physical needs instead of the "nonsense" she often finds in conversations between idle people. Accordingly, her first reaction, after seeing that the woman was fed and comfortable, was to get up and go for help. Idle compassion was as alien to Magda Trocmé as idle talk.

Standing, she calmed the woman with a few words, urged her to warm herself at length near the stove, and to put her soaking-wet shoes, for a little while, in the oven attached to the stove. Then she put on her own shawl, pushed open the kitchen door, went through the little hallway, out into the bitterly cold courtyard, through the "poetic gate," and into the streets of Le Chambon. She walked west toward the square and the town hall.

The snow and wind were incidental to her; mainly she was thinking that the woman had to have *papers*, especially identification papers. There were frequent surprise checks for papers and frequent roundups, even this early in the Occupation. Without papers, the woman was in danger of deportation back to Germany and Hitler.

She walked up the few steps of the village hall and into the mayor's office. She remembers that she was confident that the papers would be forthcoming; after all, there were Frenchmen in this village, not Nazi racists. Almost as a matter of course, she told the mayor about her German refugee, expecting him to sit down with her and help her make plans for the welfare of the refugee.

And so the mayor's response surprised her. "What?" he said. "Do you dare to endanger this whole village for the sake of one foreigner? Will you save one woman and destroy us all? How dare you suggest such a thing to me? I am responsible for the welfare of this French village. Get her out of Le Chambon tomorrow morning, no later."

She did not argue; she simply arose and went back into the snow. As she went down the hill toward the presbytery, she analyzed the situation. She had gone to the authorities and revealed to them the presence of an illegal, unregistered refugee in her home. The fact that the refugee was in the home of the Protestant minister of a Protestant village not only exposed the refugee to action by those authorities; it seemed to invite such action, since the presbytery was the single most conspicuous home in the village, and the duties of the authorities were clear. The mayor, Frenchman though he was, was still under the command, ultimately, of Hitler. The mayor could justify his action not only by pointing to the photograph of the handsome, eighty-four-year-old Marshal Pétain, who had ordered the "surrender on demand" of foreign refugees, but also he could and did justify it by pointing to his own role as leader and protector of the village of Le Chambon-sur-Lignon. For him, moral obligations held only in the realm of "one of us": native Frenchmen; they did not apply to "one of them": foreigners, German Jews. For him, it was "our people, our lives"; it was the trust laid upon us by our leaders that determined what was good and what was evil.

All of this had something to do with the mental fog in southern France, the incapacity to resist a French leader above whom the French saw only vaguely, in a cloud of doubts, the Nazi Führer. But the mayor had emphasized the other source of paralysis in France: fear of reprisals, fear that a whole village might become an object of suspicion, and, because of the Nazi conquerors in great numbers above the demarcation line, even a target for destruction.

But Magda Trocmé did not dwell upon these matters during that walk down from the town hall. Her main thought was that the refugee was now in great danger because she was known to the mayor. For her to stay in Le Chambon against the orders of the official leader of the village, *and with his full knowledge of her presence and location,* was absurd. If Magda allowed her to stay in the presbytery, she would, in effect, be dooming her to capture.

And so Magda Trocmé had to get her out of Le Chambon. Like others in the Unoccupied Zone, she had a "line" to other people who opposed Pétain's measures. Even in those early days of the Occupation, many resisters knew of others who could be trusted in an emergency; and Magda Trocmé knew of a certain Catholic family who were enemies of the National Revolution and who were courageous and compassionate persons. She would send the refugee to them.

Probably because of the separation of Catholics from Protestants in France (I have met some French Catholic families who have never knowingly met a French Protestant), she did not know that there was growing near Lyons, not more than a hundred miles from Le Chambon, a powerful Catholic network whose main task was to save Jewish refugees: the *Témoignage Chrétien* (Christian Witness), the organization of the courageous Father Chaîllet. In any case, at this early stage in the Resistance, people had only the names of scattered individuals on their "lines."

When she came back into the kitchen, she saw the woman still sitting before the stove, shoeless. Swiftly Magda ran to the oven beside the stove and opened the oven door. The shoes were still in the oven, burned black. The two women gasped.

For the refugee to leave by the next morning, she had to have shoes. But Le Chambon was a poor village, especially in the winter months when there were no tourists. And Le Chambon was poorer than ever now, what with this extremely severe weather and the difficulty of finding supplies after the supply lines to the cities had been smashed in the sudden, overwhelming defeat of France. It was especially difficult to find shoes, since the adults in the village could not buy shoes legally and could not afford to buy them on the black market; only children could buy them, one pair a year, on their birthdays and with a coupon. This was one of the reasons why the awkward wooden shoes of old were being used more and more of late; there was wood enough in the forests in and around Le Chambon, and there were still some woodworkers. But shoes for long walks were almost an impossibility to find for adults of modest means. André Trocmé—who had agreed completely with every move she had made on behalf of the refugee—once got a pair of leather shoes for his big feet only because somebody about his size had died in the not-too-distant city of Saint-Étienne, and a friend had arranged for him to receive them.

Magda Trocmé is not one to work hard before a crowd of idle onlookers; she is like *la burle*—busy, but also making everything around her busy as well. That night there was a network of shoe-seekers in the village, and she was pushing through the snow in the middle of the network. Even in that harsh winter she brought back the shoes before the night was far gone.

The next morning, the woman left. Later Magda was to reflect, "She was a Jew. What did she think of a Christian community, walking in the snow without knowing where she was going?"

It is true that Magda Trocmé had sent her to another family, but who was to help the woman get there? And exactly what would she find there? For the rest of the Occupation, Magda Trocmé and all the other people of Le Chambon would know that from the point of view of the refugee, turning somebody away from one's door is not simply a refusal to help; it is an *act of harmdoing*. Whatever one's excuses for not taking a refugee in, from the point of view of that refugee, your closed door is an instrument of harmdoing, and your closing it does harm.

A while later—while her husband was away—another Jewish refugee appeared at the presbytery door. Magda Trocmé had a fresh idea. Vichy is Vichy. Understood. But what about Jews helping their fellow Jews? At this time, the French wife of an influential French rabbi was staying in Le Chambon to escape the rigors of the Occupied Zone where she and her family were permanent residents. Magda went to visit her and asked her to help with this German Jew. The answer she received struck the iron of egotistic human reality even more deeply into her soul than had the answer of the mayor: "A German Jew? But it is because of the foreign Jews that our French Jews are persecuted. They are responsible for our worries and difficulties." Again that hard line between "one of us" and "others"; again the idea that moral obligation has to do only with "one of us," not "one of them."

These two events were important in the history of the presbytery and of the refugees in Le Chambon. They were important not only because these two refugees were the first of hundreds who would come to the presbytery door, and not only because these two events showed how narrow the domain of love was to some people, but also because they helped the Trocmés realize the concrete meaning of the "city of refuge" passage in Deuteronomy 19:10: "lest innocent blood be shed in your land . . . and so the guilt of bloodshed be upon you."

And there was another lesson, a very practical one, that the Trocmés and Le Chambon learned from these events: they must *conceal* from the authorities and from unsympathetic citizens any help they were giving refugees. To reveal that help would be to betray the refugees, to put them in harm's way. Either conceal them or harm them—those were the alternatives.

But in Le Chambon in the beginning of the 1940s, concealment meant lying— lying both by omission and by commission. It meant not conveying to the authorities any of the legally required information about new foreigners in Le Chambon, and it meant making false identity and ration cards for the refugees so that they could survive in Vichy France. It meant, for example, changing the name Kohn to the good old French name Colin so that the refugee could have the life-giving identity and ration cards to protect against roundups, when identity cards were usually checked, and to protect against hunger, since the basic foods were rationed. Such cards made it unnecessary to report a new foreign refugee to the mayor—only a Frenchman with, perhaps, an accent had come to town.

But for Magda and the other Chambonnais, the making of counterfeit cards was not simply a matter of practicality. It raised profound moral problems. To this day, Magda remembers her reaction to hearing about the making of the first counterfeit card. During that first winter of the Occupation, Theis came into the presbytery and said to her, "I have just made a false card for Monsieur Lévy. It is the only way to save his life." She remembers the horror she felt at that moment: duplicity, for any purpose, was simply wrong. She and the other leaders knew that ration cards were as important as identity cards—the Chambonnais were so poor that they could not share their food with refugees and hope to survive themselves. Nonetheless, none of those leaders became reconciled to making counterfeit cards, though they made many of them in the course of the Occupation. Even now, Magda finds her integrity diminished when she thinks of those cards. She is still sad over what she calls "our lost candor."

How, then, could they lie and violate one of the commandments given to Moses? Theis and Trocmé saw that deep in Christianity is the belief that man is never ethically pure—in this world he finds himself sinning no matter what his intentions are. The best he can do is acknowledge and lessen his sins. Such a view is part of Judaism, too. In 1972, Magda Trocmé went to Israel to participate in the ceremony awarding her husband—posthumously—the Medal of Righteousness. Part of the ceremony involved planting a tree in memory of André Trocmé (there is a tree in Israel for every person who has received the Medal of Righteousness). During the ceremony, one of the speakers said, "The righteous are not exempt from evil." Magda remembers the sentence word for word. The righteous must often pay a price for their righteousness: their own ethical purity.

She is aware of these depths, but they do not comfort her. She still feels anguish for the children of Le Chambon who had to unlearn lying after the war, and who could, perhaps, never again be able to understand the importance of simply telling the truth. But usually when she says this, she suddenly straightens up her body, with typical abruptness and vigor, and adds, "Ah! Never mind! Jews were running all over the place after a while, and we had to help them quickly. We had no time to engage in deep debates. We had to help them—or let them die, perhaps—and in order to help them, unfortunately we had to lie."

But her daughter, Nelly, points out that the children, as far as Nelly could see, never had the problem of unlearning lying. She remembers the children, among them herself, seeing the situation with the clear eyes of youth. She remembers their seeing that people were being helped in a desperate situation by these lies. And the children were convinced that what was happening in the homes of Le Chambon was right, simply right.

What the children saw was what the rest of the Chambonnais saw: the *necessity* to help that shivering Jew standing there in your door, and the necessity not to betray him or her to harmdoers. In this way of life the children were raised, and—at least according to Nelly—they did not feel their parents to be guilty of any wrongdoing.

There were many women in Le Chambon whose homes were the scenes of events like those in Magda Trocmé's kitchen. There was, for instance, round-faced, sparkling-eyed Madame Eyraud, whose husband was *très chic* in the violent Maquis, despite her own nonviolence. When I asked her why she found it necessary to let those refugees into her house, dragging after them all those dangers and problems, including the necessity of lying to the authorities, she could never fully understand what I was getting at. Her big, round eyes stopped sparkling in that happy face, and she said, "Look. Look. Who else would have taken care of them if we didn't? They needed our help, and they needed it *then*." For her, and for me under the joyous spell she casts over anybody she smiles upon, the spade was turned by hitting against a deep rock: there are no deeper issues than the issue of *people needing help then*.

The fact is that the Chambonnais were as candid, as truthful with the authorities as they could have been without betraying the refugees. Trocmé was perfectly willing, as were the other Chambonnais, to tell the authorities that there were refugees in Le Chambon. As a matter of fact, they felt that it was their duty to do so, and the letter to Lamirand says this outright: "We feel obliged to tell you that there are among us a certain number of Jews." The spirit of Le Chambon in those years was a strange combination of candor and concealment, of a yearning for truth and of a commitment to secrecy. They were as open as love permits in a terrible time.

Jew, Go Back to the Grave!

Yaffa Eliach

A native of Vilna, Poland, Yaffa Eliach is the editor of
Hasidic Tales of the Holocaust, from which the
following selection is taken. For additional
biographical information on Eliach, see page 247.

Based on interviews with a Holocaust survivor,
Zvi Michalowski, and several other people from the
town of Eisysky, Lithuania, Eliach paints a chilling
portrait of the events leading to the birth of the
Jewish resistance in this area.

On Rosh Hashana, 1941, when all the Jews of
Eisysky and nearby towns awaited their fate in the shtetls' synagogues, watched
over by lunatics whom their Lithuanian captors had appointed as their supervisors, it was clear to the Rabbi of Eisysky, Rabbi Shimon Rozowsky, that his
beloved shtetl was doomed. A few days earlier he had called the town's notables
together and told them, "Jews, our end is near. God does not wish our redemption; our fate is sealed and we must accept it. But let us die with honor, let us not
walk as sheep to the slaughter. Let us purchase ammunition and fight until our
last breath. Let us die like judges in Israel: 'Let me die with the Philistines.' "

Some had supported him, but the opposition, led by Yossel Wildenburg,
prevailed. Now it was too late. From the synagogues, they were led to the horse
market. At the head of the strange procession, more than 4,000 Jews, walked
Rabbi Shimon Rozowsky, dressed in his Sabbath finery and his tall silk yarmulke.
Next to him walked the handsome hazan of Eisysky, Mr. Tabolsky. The hazan,
wrapped in his talit, was holding the holy Torah scrolls. The rabbi and the hazan
together were leading the congregation in reciting the Vidduy, the confession of
the dying.

In groups of 250, first the men and then the women, the people were taken to the old Jewish cemetery in front of the open ditches. They were ordered to undress and stand at the edge of the open graves. They were shot in the back of the head by Lithuanian guards with the encouragement and help of the local people. The chief executioner was the Lithuanian Ostrovakas. Dressed in a uniform, a white apron, and gloves, he personally supervised the killing. He reserved for himself the privilege of shooting the town's notables, among them Rabbi Shimon Rozowsky, and he practiced sharpshooting at the children, aiming as they were thrown into the graves.

Among the Jews that September 25, 1941, in the old Jewish cemetery of Eisysky was one of the shtetl's melamdim (teachers), Reb Michalowsky, and his youngest son, Zvi, age sixteen. Father and son were holding hands as they stood naked at the edge of the open pit, trying to comfort each other during their last moments. Young Zvi was counting the bullets and the intervals between one volley of fire and the next. As Ostrovakas and his people were aiming their guns, Zvi fell into the grave a split second before the volley of fire hit him.

He felt the bodies piling up on top of him and covering him. He felt the streams of blood around him and the trembling pile of dying bodies moving beneath him.

It became cold and dark. The shooting died down above him. Zvi made his way from under the bodies, out of the mass grave into the cold, dead night. In the distance, Zvi could hear Ostrovakas and his people singing and drinking, celebrating their great accomplishment. After 800 years, on September 26, 1941, Eisysky was Judenfrei.

At the far end of the cemetery, in the direction of the huge church, were a few Christian homes. Zvi knew them all. Naked, covered with blood, he knocked on the first door. The door opened. A peasant was holding a lamp which he had looted earlier in the day from a Jewish home. "Please let me in," Zvi pleaded. The peasant lifted the lamp and examined the boy closely. "Jew, go back to the grave where you belong!" he shouted at Zvi and slammed the door in his face. Zvi knocked on other doors, but the response was the same.

Near the forest lived a widow whom Zvi knew too. He decided to knock on her door. The old widow opened the door. She was holding in her hand a small, burning piece of wood. " Let me in!" begged Zvi. "Jew, go back to the grave at the old cemetery!" She chased Zvi away with the burning piece of wood as if exorcising an evil spirit, a dybbuk.

"I am your Lord, Jesus Christ. I came down from the cross. Look at me—the blood, the pain, the suffering of the innocent. Let me in," said Zvi Michalowsky. The widow crossed herself and fell at his blood-stained feet. "*Boże moj, Boże moj* (my God, my God)," she kept crossing herself and praying. The door was opened.

Zvi walked in. He promised her that he would bless her children, her farm, and her, but only if she would keep his visit a secret for three days and three nights and not reveal it to a living soul, not even the priest. She gave Zvi food and clothing and warm water to wash himself. Before leaving the house, he once more reminded her that the Lord's visit must remain a secret, because of His special mission on earth.

Dressed in a farmer's clothing, with a supply of food for a few days, Zvi made his way to the nearby forest. Thus, the Jewish partisan movement was born in the vicinity of Eisysky.

August–November 1943

Primo Levi

Primo Levi is considered one of the great
memoirists of the Holocaust. His books include *If
Not Now, When?*, *Survival in Auschwitz*, *Moments of
Reprieve*, *The Drowned and the Saved*, and *The
Reawakening*. For additional biographical
information on Levi, see page 213.

The following excerpt from Levi's novel *If Not
Now, When?* is based on the experiences of Jewish
partisans who, under desperate circumstances,
actively resisted and fought the Nazis.

It wasn't exactly a village: it was a "republic of the
marshes," the man explained to Mendel, not without pride. It was rather an
encampment, a haven, a fortress; and the two of them would be welcome, because hands capable of working were scarce, and men able to handle weapons
were even scarcer. His name was Adam. As night was about to fall, he collected
the children, who were hunting grasses at the edge of the clearing; and he invited Mendel and Leonid to follow him. The children, boys and girls, numbered
about a dozen, between the ages of five and twelve; and each had gathered a
little bundle of grasses, separated into several bunches. "Here everybody has
to make himself useful, even the children. There are herbs for curing diseases,
others are good to eat, cooked or raw. Grasses, berries, roots: we've taught the
children to identify them. Eh, we don't teach them much else here."

They started on their way. The children looked at the two soldiers with
distrustful curiosity. They didn't ask the men any questions, and they didn't talk
among themselves, either. They were shy, wild little animals, with restless eyes;

without Adam's giving them any order, they spontaneously formed a line, two by two, and set off towards the rise, following a trail that they seemed to know well. They, too, were wearing sandals cut from tires; their clothes were old army uniforms, tattered and ill-fitting. The little girl who had recovered her doll held it tight against her chest as if to protect it, but she didn't speak to it or even look at it: she looked to either side, with the uneasy, darting glances of a bird.

Adam, on the contrary, had a great desire to talk and to listen. He was fifty-five years old, he was the oldest of the camp, and therefore he was charged with minding the children: yes, there were women, but not many, and they were suited for heavier tasks; one of them was his daughter. Before answering their other questions, he wanted to know the story of the two newcomers: Mendel was glad to satisfy him, and in detail, but Leonid managed it in a few words. He, Adam, came from far away: he had been a textile worker in Minsk, active in the Bund, the Jewish labor organization, since he was sixteen. He had been in time to get a taste of the czar's prisons, which still hadn't saved him from going to the front in the First World War. But a Bundist is a Menshevik, and as a Menshevik he had been tried and again imprisoned in 1930: it hadn't been nice, they had put him in freezing cells and in others that were torrid and airless, they wanted him to confess that he had been bribed by foreigners. He held out through two interrogations, then slashed his wrists. They sewed him up again so he could confess: for two weeks they didn't allow him an hour's sleep, and then he confessed everything the judges wanted. He spent another couple of years in prison and three more in a camp, at Vologda, halfway between Moscow and Arkhangelsk: that was better than a prison, he worked in a kolkhoz, which was where he had learned what grasses are good to eat. There are a lot more than city people know, and so even from confinement some good can come. In the summer, grasses are important, they contain some nourishment, even if you eat them without seasoning. Of course, winter is another matter: it was best not to think about winter.

After his confinement was over, they had sent him home, but the war came and the Germans reached Minsk in a few days. Well, Adam felt a weight on his conscience, because he, and other old men like him, had known the Germans in the other war, and had tried to reassure everybody: the Germans were good soldiers, but civilized people, why hide or run away? At most, they would give the land back to the peasants. Instead, in Minsk, *those* Germans had done a thing that he couldn't tell about. He couldn't and wouldn't and shouldn't. "It's the first rule of our republic. If we kept on telling one another what we've seen, we'd go crazy, and instead we all have to be sane, children included. Besides the different grasses, we teach them to tell lies, because we have enemies on all sides, not only the Germans."

While he was talking like this, they had arrived at the camp. Actually, it would have been difficult to define it with a single word, because it was something Mendel had never seen and couldn't have imagined possible. In any case, it was much more a refuge than a fortress. On the hillock they had glimpsed from the distance, and which didn't rise more than twenty meters or so above the plain, there was an old monastery, hidden among the thick trees. It consisted of a brick construction forming three sides of an open quadrangle, two stories above-ground. At the two corners, two squat towers rose, one supporting what remained of a bell chamber. The other, half-destroyed then reconstructed in wood, must have been used as a lookout post. Not far away, opposite the open side of the quadrangle, there was the monastery barn, a building of roughly stripped logs, with a wide wagon entrance and some tiny windows.

The monastery was not so much hidden by the trees as besieged by them. Of its three wings, only one was intact; the other two bore signs of destruction, ancient and recent. The roof, originally of tiles, had collapsed in several places, and had been haphazardly patched up with straw and reeds; the outside walls also displayed big gaps through which you could see the rooms inside, filled with rubble. Everything must have been abandoned dozens of years before, perhaps even at the time of the civil war, because alders, oaks and willows had grown against the walls, and some even inside, sending roots down into the piles of detritus and seeking the light through gaps in the roof.

It was almost dark by now. Adam had the two men wait outside in the court-yard invaded by trampled weeds; he returned a little later and led them into a big room, its floor covered with straw and sunflower stalks, where many people were already waiting, some seated, some lying down. The children also arrived, and in the semidarkness a grass soup was distributed to all. There were no lights; two women prepared the children for sleep; Adam came back and cautioned the newcomers not to strike any matches. Mendel and Leonid felt guarded and protected. They were tired: only for a few minutes were they aware of the murmuring of their neighbors, then they fell into the unawareness of sleep.

Mendel woke in the morning with the happy-uneasy impression of being in another world and another period: perhaps in the midst of the desert, on the march for forty years towards the promised land, perhaps inside the walls of Jerusalem besieged by the Romans, or perhaps in Noah's ark. In the big room, besides the two of them, only two men and a woman had remained, all three middle-aged, and apparently ill: they spoke neither Russian nor Yiddish, but some Polish dialect. Children, perhaps the same as the previous evening, peered in at the door, curious but silent. A girl entered, small and thin, with a sub-machine gun slung over her shoulder; she saw the two strangers and went out at once, asking no questions. A subdued bustle could be heard all around, as of mice in an attic: brief calls, a hammering, the creak of a well chain, the hoarse cry of a rooster. The air that came through the open windows, bringing the damp breath of the marsh and the wood, dragged other, sharper and unfamiliar smells, of spices, singed fur, of cramped rooms, poverty.

A little later Adam came and asked them to follow him: Dov, the chief, was waiting for them. He was awaiting them at headquarters, Adam specified proudly, which meant a little room with paneled walls of fir planks, half-occupied by a built-in stove, at the heart of a big shed that had been the outbuilding of the monastery. On the stove and beside it were three pallets, and near the door there was a table of rough planks nailed together: there was nothing else. Even the chair on which Dov sat looked solid but crude, the work of expert hands with little help from tools. Dov was middle-aged, short, but with strong bones and broad shoulders: without actually being hump-backed, he was bent and carried his head down, as if he were wearing a burden; so he looked up at his interlocutors from below, as if above the rims of nonexistent eye-glasses. His hair, which must once have been blond, was almost white, but still thick: he wore it carefully combed, parted straight down the middle. His hands were big and strong; when he spoke, he kept them motionless, hanging from his forearms, and he looked at them from time to time as if they weren't his. He had a square face, steady eyes, honest features, worn and vigorous; he was slow of speech. He had the two men sit down on the pallet nearest the stove, and spoke these words:

"I would have received you in any case, but it's good luck that you're soldiers: we already have too many people who've come here looking for protection. They come even from far away, seeking safety. They aren't mistaken, this is the safest place a Jew can find within a radius of a thousand kilometers, but that doesn't mean the place is safe. It isn't, not at all: we are weak, poorly armed, we are in no condition to defend ourselves against a serious attack. There are also too many of us: actually, we don't even know how many of us there are at any given moment. Every day there are people who come and people who leave. Today there must be about fifty of us, not all Jews: there are also two or three families of Polish peasants. The Ukrainian nationalists stole their provisions and livestock and burned their houses, they were terrified, and so they came here. The Jews come from the ghettos, or have escaped from the German labor camps. Each of them has a terrible story behind him: there are old people, women, children, sick. Only about a dozen young people know how to handle weapons."

"What weapons do you have?" Mendel asked.

"Very few. A dozen hand grenades, a few pistols and submachine guns. A heavy machine gun with ammunition for five minutes' fire. Luckily for us, the Germans have rarely been seen around here so far; their best troops have been recalled to the front, which is hundreds of kilometers away. In these parts there are only a few garrisons scattered here and there, for requisitioning provisions and labor and guarding the roads and railway. The Ukrainians are the most dangerous; the Germans have organized and armed them, and they indoctrinate them: as if there were any need for that! The Ukrainians have always considered Poles and Jews their natural enemies.

"The best protection the camp has is the marshes. They go on and on for dozens of kilometers in every direction, and to cross them, you have to know them well: in some the water comes up to your knees, but in others it's over a man's head, and there are few fords and they're hard to find. The Germans don't like them because you can't have a blitzkrieg in marshes: even tanks get stuck, and the heavier they are the worse it is."

"But the water must freeze during the winter."

"Winter is a time of terror. In winter the woods and the marshes become our enemies, the worst enemies of people in hiding. The trees shed their leaves, and it's like being naked: reconnaissance planes can see everything that happens. The marshes freeze, and they're not a barrier any longer. You can read footprints on the snow. And your only protection against the cold is a fire, but any fire makes smoke, and smoke can be seen far off.

"And I still haven't mentioned food. For food, too, we have no certitude. Some we get from the peasants, obtained politely—or otherwise—but the villages are poor and far away, and the Germans and the bandits are already quick to strip them. We get some things from the partisans, but in the winter they have the same problems we have; still they sometimes receive supplies by parachute drops, and then we get something too. And, finally, some food comes from the woods: grasses and herbs, frogs, carp, mushrooms, berries, but only in summer. In winter, nothing. In winter only terror and hunger."

"Isn't there some way to establish better contacts with the partisans?"

"So far our contacts have been irregular. For that matter, what is more irregular than the *partizanka*? I was with them, until winter before last: then they declared me unfit, because for them I was an old man, and besides I was wounded and couldn't run any more. The local bands are like drops of mercury: they come together, they break apart, they join up again: they are destroyed and new ones are formed. The biggest and most stable have radios and keep in contact with the Great Land . . ."

"What's the Great Land?"

"We call it that, too: it's the Soviet territory beyond the front, the part not occupied by the Nazis. The radio is like blood: thanks to the radio they receive orders, reinforcements, instructors, arms, provisions. Not only by parachute: when it's possible, planes from the Great Land come down in the partisan zone, unload men and goods, take away the sick and the wounded. For this, on the contrary, things go better in winter, because for planes you need an airfield, or at least a stretch of flat, open land; but land like that can be seen clearly from the air, and the Germans, as soon as they see it, they promptly drop bombs to make it unusable. But in the winter any lake or marsh or river will do, provided the ice is thick enough.

"But you mustn't imagine a regular service. Not all the drops and the landings end happily, and not all the bands are prepared to share their things with us. Many partisan leaders consider us useless mouths because we don't fight. For that very reason we have to prove ourselves useful, and we can do this in various ways. First of all, anyone able to walk and shoot must consider himself a partisan, contribute to the defense; and if the partisans ask for him, he has to go with them. Practically speaking, between the bands and the monastery there is a constant exchange, and the monastery itself, until the Germans discover it, is not a bad refuge for tired or wounded partisans, too. But there are other things that can be done, and we do them. We mend their clothes, do their laundry, tan hides with oak bark and make boots from the hides: yes, the smell you smell comes from the tanning vats. And with birch bark we make pitch so the boot leather will remain soft and waterproof. Do you have a trade?" he asked, addressing Mendel.

"I'm a watchmender by trade, but I also worked as a mechanic in a kolkhoz."

"Good. We'll find work for you right away. What about you, Muscovite?"

"I studied to be a bookkeeper."

"That's a bit less useful, for us." Dov laughed. "I'd like to keep accounts, but it's impossible. We can't even count the people who come and go. Here we get Jews who have miraculously escaped the SS massacres; peasants come seeking protection; and dubious people we have to watch out for. They could even be spies, but what can we do? There's nothing to do but trust their faces, the way I trust yours now: we don't have a secret service. Many arrive, others leave, or die. The young leave, with my permission or without: they prefer to join up with the partisans properly, rather than vegetate in this republic in hunger and fear. The old and the sick die, but young and healthy people also die, of despair. Despair is worse than disease: it attacks you during the days of waiting, when no news comes and no contacts, or when they announce German troop movements or movements of Ukrainian and Hungarian mercenaries: waiting is as fatal as dysentery. There are only two defenses against despair: working and fighting; but they're not always enough. There's also a third, which is telling one another lies: we all fall into that. Well, that's the end of my speech; it's good you've come here armed, but if you'd brought a radio transmitter it would have been better still. So it goes, you can't have everything, not even in Novoselki."

Silence, and a Starry Night

Hirsh Glik

Hirsh Glik was born in 1920 in Vilna, Poland. Although he was a well-known poet and songwriter, most of his work did not survive the war. His poetry was written in either Hebrew or Yiddish. He was incarcerated in the Vilna ghetto before being deported to the Estonia concentration camp in 1943. He escaped the following year and died while fighting for the underground in 1944. The poem reprinted here was originally published in *A Treasury of Jewish Folksongs* by Ruth Rubin.

In this poem, Glik pays tribute to the Jewish partisans of Vilna who, in the summer of 1942, fought the German army. Two women, Itzik Matzkevitch and Vitke Kempner, were credited with launching the first attack, blowing up an ammunition column.

Silence, and a starry night
Frost crackling, fine as sand.
Remember how I taught you
To hold a gun in your hand?

In fur jacket and beret,
Clutching a hand grenade,
A girl whose skin is velvet
Ambushes a cavalcade.

Aim, fire, shoot—and hit!
She, with her pistol small,
Halts an autoful,
Arms and all!

Morning, emerging from the wood,
In her hair a snow carnation.
Proud of her small victory
For the new, free generation!

Underground Networks for Child-Rescue

Anny Latour

As a historian, Anny Latour is recognized for her
meticulous research. Her account of the resistance
in France is based on conducting numerous
interviews and compiling eyewitness accounts and
documents. She then framed the information within
the context of her own experiences. During World
War II, she was a member of the French
underground. Her resistance activities included
helping to smuggle children out of Nazi-occupied
territories, transporting arms to the partisans, and
forging identity cards and documents. The following
excerpt is from *The Jewish Resistance in France
(1940–1944)*.

Jewish rescue networks in France had their
origin in Jewish social services and other groups
already in existence. After the Nazi occupation,
these organizations went underground and were
responsible for saving tens of thousands of lives.

Providence occasionally picks certain people
who must leave their accustomed paths, to take up entirely new duties. George
Garel was one of these men. And even if he had long since returned to his original profession, his name will remain forever tied to the work he—undaunted
and courageous—accomplished underground, to make possible the saving of
thousands of Jewish children.

I, personally, do not believe in chance. Even if George Garel says it was purely
by accident that he became involved in the affair of the "children of Vénissieux,"

it was, in reality, no chance occurrence that he was totally committed, or that this particular business became the starting point for activity evolving onto a much grander scale; really, it was here that began what we now refer to as "the Garel circuit."

Lyon, the end of August, 1942. George Garel, an engineer in charge of a large electrical engineering department, has his meals in a boarding house; at his table sit Nina Gourfinkel, Raymond Winter (later to be shot by the Germans), all three already involved in clandestine activities.

It was here that Garel first learned of the 1,200 foreign-born Jews arrested on the night of August 26, and imprisoned in the fort of Vénissieux, transformed into a camp; the Jews' only crime was having come to France after 1936; by an agreement between Laval and the Germans, they would all be deported.

A screening commission—of which Abbé Glasberg, "king-pin of the *Amitiés Chrétiennes*" is a member—has headquarters in the camp. Charles Ledermann, an attorney, as representative of the O.S.E., has the job of overseeing the fate of children who may, for the moment, remain free, being under sixteen years of age. He and Garel know each other, Ledermann having belonged to a resistance network in which Garel also worked.

Under these dual auspices, then, Garel is authorized to enter the camps. He is assigned the almost impossible task of determining, during one night, who may leave, and who must remain.

Straining to control his emotion, Garel speaks of this frightful night:

A power failure had plunged the camp into total darkness, to last for several hours. During the night, we went from group to group, among people insane with fear. Imagine the scene when we had to tell parents: "You must trust your children with us." But some understood, and gave their children willingly; we attached small tags around necks and wrists, so the children could retain at least a portion of their identities, their names and birth dates.

I was of course aware that the fates of many of the adults would soon be sealed. But we could not say outright: "You, you are condemned to death; at least allow your children to survive." We thought saying as little as possible of what was in store for those who would be leaving, would do the most to persuade the parents. With the electrical blackout, however, there were still certain shacks with children in them, which we could not find . . . Our task was made the more difficult by constant interruptions: people would tug at our arms, saying: "Come here, I must talk with you—" And all this amidst shouting and weeping. I recall one man who, on the verge of hysteria, threw himself on me bodily: "Now you must listen to me! I fought in the International Brigade—if the Germans find out, I'm lost! You must get me out!"

Seeing that time was growing short, we became more authoritarian, telling parents: "We have come for your children—give them to us!" Many complied, but the new attitude didn't work all the time, and, almost coming to blows, we took many despite parents' physical resistance. When mothers held tight to their children, we had to try prying them loose in as civilized a way as possible. . . .

By daybreak the group consisted of eight hundred children.

Among their number were two sisters, one of whom was 16 years, 2 months old—just over the age limit—and the other, 18 years old. They were the same height, and for the first time the idea came to me of falsifying papers. I made twins of them. But they had a brother, 22 or 23, and I remember one of the girls kept following me, everywhere, and in a voice soft, but tireless, repeated: "I beg of you, save my brother . . ." This went on, twenty, thirty times—the same words. At first I gently replied I could not—that it might compromise the whole rescue operation. But after her constant pleading, in the darkness, amidst cries and shouts, I grew brusquer, saying that no, it was impossible. By morning the two young girls were veritable statues of despair; they simply had refused to admit I was unable to save their brother.

The entire camp echoed with cries and groans. The police administrator of Lyon, who was present, asked Abbé Glasberg: "Why are they shouting like that?" The Abbé replied: "If someone were taking your children, wouldn't you cry out?" After a pause, the policeman responded, "Yes, I guess so."

"In the morning," Garel continues, "the eight hundred children were put aboard buses. By a dreadful coincidence we passed close by other buses holding the parents about to be deported. Though after that long night many of the children were dozing, the parents were awake; that poignant scene, of the parents pressing against the windows for one last look at their children, I'll never forget."

The children, then, were temporarily out of danger. But how might we thwart attempts by Lyon's police prefect Angeli, who, acting under order of Vichy, could wish to "recapture" them?

Abbé Glasberg alerts Mgr. Gerlier, who declares himself the children's protector.

Father Braun, who was present at that unforgettable meeting, says:

If I remember correctly, it was the 2nd of September. Mgr. Gerlier was at his desk, Abbé Glasberg, Father Chaillet, Abbé Lagarde, Jean-Marie Soutou and myself there, too. Mgr. Gerlier told us: "All of you will have to disappear; the prefect can't do anything to me, but he could try to pressure you, to learn the children's whereabouts." Suddenly the telephone rang. It was Angeli himself, calling to tell Mgr. Gerlier: "At 6:00 tonight a train is arriving from the camp at Milles, with Jews to be handed to the Germans. We're adding a car for all the children you took out of Vénissieux—I want them brought to the station." Mgr. Gerlier replied: "Monsieur le préfet, the families of those children made me their guardian; you would not force a father to hand over his children to the police . . ." The telephone conversation was long, and I must say we all became rather agitated. What especially upset me was Mgr. Gerlier's always covering the mouthpiece to make jokes—it seemed not quite the right time. We finally heard Mgr. Gerlier say: "Well, monsieur le préfet, come up to the archdiocese if you like! But you won't get the children." And he hung up. He turned to us, saying: "You all must leave, and I don't want to see you again: the prefect is on his way to ask me for the children—I certainly don't want to know where they are! Do your best! Good bye!"

Mgr. Gerlier's vacillating politics led George Garel to remark: "In this instance, he comes off very well. Perhaps he realized that if he let himself be manipulated this time, it would be an eternal stain on his reputation."

In any case, the "children of Vénissieux" were dispersed into different Christian homes and, fortunately, saved. Some were taken in by the *Amitiés Chrétiennes*, many others remaining for a while under the aegis of the O.S.E.

Yes, the children were saved; but they were never again to see their parents. Dr. Weill comments:

> We knew Laval had ordered the deportation of children, and, as we had "stolen" them, prefect Angeli became furious. He had his secretary telephone and threaten me personally with arrest if the children were not found within 24 hours.

As for Reverend Father Chaillet—another of those responsible for the refusal to hand over the children—he was placed under house arrest in Privas. Dr. Weill paid him a visit, and recalls: "I barely escaped arrest myself; while I was away, the Gestapo had come to my house."

For Garel—shaken by the events at Vénissieux—to undertake secret rescue work, his moral spirit and determination required the support of Dr. Weill's diplomatic efforts. He was convinced the Germans intended exterminating the Jews, and thus assigned the child rescue effort top priority. The first step in the rescue operation became separating children from the Jewish milieu and integrating them fully into non-Jewish surroundings.

Dr. Weill explains that none of the official leaders of Jewish relief organizations could undertake such clandestine activity, because they would be spotted too quickly; the work would have to be assumed by unknown newcomers, such as Garel. Having seen Garel in action in the camp of Vénissieux, Dr. Weill had faith in his abilities.

Garel accepted the responsibilities entrusted him, and was to continue his work through the entire war. But he does mention an "appealing" position offered him by the regular Resistance: being in charge of arms for the entire southern zone. As he could not work at both clandestine activities, though, he declined this offer, to devote himself to the Jewish children—work that might seem less glamorous but equally fraught with risk.

Garel's organizing the O.S.E.'s secret work consisted of several steps. First, an effective "cover" had to be found. Mgr. Salièges, the first prelate to make official protest against the deportations, seemed the right man to second Garel's efforts.

Garel uses Charles Ledermann's acquaintance with Mgr. Salièges as a starting point.—It had been Ledermann, in fact, who kept the archbishop informed about the deportations; thus had been initiated the famous letter of protest.

Garel, then, with an introduction from Ledermann, goes to the archdiocese to meet Mgr. Salièges for the first time. "I cannot," remarks Garel, "say we became close friends, because that would be an inadequate definition of the relationship we developed; but certainly there was an element of friendship—though, for my part, there was much respect, and for his, I think the feelings were more paternal. From our first meeting, I had the feeling of being in the presence of a unique man. I can and must say it: he had the makings of a saint. It was all the more striking, because, except for his eyes—which were radiant and from which intelligence seemed to shine—he was physically very broken down, and expressed himself, both orally and in writing, with only the utmost difficulty."

Garel outlined his project. To save the greatest number of children, there could be no thought of establishing a new philanthropic organization—which would only draw attention—but, instead, work would have to be carried out under cover of existing charities; it was here that Garel thought Mgr. Salièges could help.

The archbishop listens to Garel without interrupting, and replies that the plan is consistent with Christian concepts, and that he will cooperate.

"Thus," Garel points out, "his willingness was immediate—he didn't ask for even two or three days to think about it. Subsequently, when I went to visit him—often with no opportunity of announcing myself ahead of time—he always received me, always found some time. From all this contact with the man, I gleaned something indefinable, but very precious and exhilarating. He asked me to keep him informed about my work, and added that his blessing would be with me always."

Garel stresses: "On this subject, let me tell you that, unbeliever that I am, all the same, this blessing carried importance."

At their very first meeting, Mgr. Salièges introduced Garel to his coadjutor, Mgr. de Courrèges. Garel says: "If the archbishop had first struck me as a saint, the bishop seemed one of those Medieval or Renaissance princes of the Militant

Church where cassocks were donned over coats of mail. Energetic face, precise speech—he was the apotheosis of the leader who knows how to take command."

Contact was direct, understanding—immediate.

Such were the beginnings of the "Garel circuit." Mgr. de Courrèges introduced Garel to a philanthropic organization of the diocese called *Sainte-Germaine*. Headed by Mlle. Thèbes, the charity attended to needy children, family placements, youth clubs, and after-school activities for Catholic children. It was agreed Garel would place the Jewish children here, with "Aryan" identities. Some of the Vénissieux group were included.

That was the first victory. The rescue operation had finally gotten off the ground.

Such Things Are Not Going to Happen to Us

Chaim Asa
(as edited by Carol Rittner and Sandra Myer)

Chaim Asa was a young boy when the Nazis occupied his native Bulgaria. His father, who was the president of the Burgas Jewish community, inadvertently received secret information that the Nazis planned to deport the Jews. His position enabled him to make contact with members of the local non-Jewish community who mobilized support to save the Jews. Asa now lives in California, where he is a rabbi. His story appeared originally in *The Courage to Care: Rescuers of Jews during the Holocaust*, which was edited by Carol Rittner and Sandra Myer.

In 1943, the Nazis planned to begin the mass deportation of the Jews of Bulgaria. But their plans were thwarted by the efforts of the Jewish federation of organizations and the non-Jews of Bulgaria.

My father was the president of the Burgas Jewish community on the Black Sea, which meant that he received all the official mail directed to the Jewish community. In January 1943, he received, in error, a telegram addressed to the commissar of Jewish affairs in Burgas from the commissar of Jewish affairs in Sofia, the person in charge of the commissariat created by the secretary of the interior. The mailman, who was not smart enough to know that there was a commissar of Jewish affairs as well as a president of the Jewish community, gave the telegram to my father because he associated him with Jewish affairs, not anyone else.

My father accepted the telegram, opened, and read it. The message informed all the local commissars for Jewish affairs that they had six weeks to prepare the Jewish community for deportation, or as the telegram put it, "resettlement." The commissars were instructed to prepare lists and send them back to Sofia immediately. Information also was given about train schedules—dates, times, locations—and about how the Bulgarian Jewish community was to be divided into two parts—A and B—so that they could be more efficiently loaded into the trains and transported to the camps.

Of course, he memorized it, then immediately put the telegram back in the envelope and went to the postmaster, who was a personal friend of the family, living on the third floor in our house. (We used to go to his quarters every night so we could listen to the "Voice of London in Bulgaria" at nine o'clock.) The postmaster said, "Ah, those peasants, they don't know how to read. Don't worry, I shall rechannel it." Then he opened the telegram and read it himself. He nearly fainted, then he said to my father, "Asa, did you read this?" My father replied, "Of course not!" But they both knew he was lying.

The postmaster sealed the envelope, re-routed it, sending it on to its proper destination. You might wonder why they didn't just destroy the telegram but they didn't, probably because they viewed it as an official communication and for whatever reason simply felt that one did not do such things. Who knows?

My father immediately made arrangements to take the night train to Sofia and rushed to the *consistoria*, which was the Sephardic equivalent to what we might call today the Jewish federation of each country or the organization of presidents of major Jewish organizations. An emergency meeting of the *consistoria* was called the next morning, and he told them about what he had read in the telegram. The majority reacted by saying, "Oh come on, Asa, that's impossible. This is not Germany. This is not Poland. Such things are not going to happen to us. Don't worry about it." And my father said to them, "I'd like to believe what you are saying, but I have read it with my own eyes."

Fortunately, there was another person at the meeting who said, "Look, I've known about this telegram, but I didn't have any proof, so I didn't know how to bring it up, what to say. But now that somebody has seen it—believe me, this is the reality."

The *consistoria* decided to mobilize itself. They organized lobby groups. For six weeks and more, there was intense lobbying of members of parliament (which was still in session), the labor unions, and the Agricultural Union. They decided to go to King Boris III, to contact the metropolitan of the Orthodox Church in Sofia, as well as to canvass ordinary Bulgarian citizens in order to force the Germans to abandon their plans to deport the Jews of Bulgaria.

I would say that the complete answer to who saved and what saved the Jews of Bulgaria is not within our reach. There is no one clear factor to which one can point and say, "This is exactly what happened and why." But let us remember that Bulgaria was the only country where the native, non-Jewish people—the proletariat, the simple people—marched in the streets, as they did in Sofia, protesting. This did not happen so much in March 1943 because the deportation of Bulgarian Jews was averted, but it did occur later on that spring, in May. In fact, some non-Jewish people were killed by the police at night during the protests.

The Bulgarians were simple, good-hearted people who refused, up to a point, to go ahead with the edict either from the fascist government of Bulgaria or from the Nazis. And what is remarkable is that they succeeded in preventing the Jews of "Old Bulgaria" from being deported.

While I was not saved individually but as a member of a group, there was a wonderful Christian woman by the name of Marika Karolova who was prepared to hide me if it became necessary. Fortunately, this never came to pass, but several years ago I asked her why she was ready to help me, and she said, in her simple way of speaking: "How could I, as a good Christian, let little Enrico [that was my nickname] go with those people? Who knows where they were going to take him? I was going to keep him; I was going to protect him."

The Warsaw Ghetto Uprising

Vladka Meed

Vladka Meed is the author of *On Both Sides of the Wall: Memoirs from the Warsaw Ghetto*, from which the following excerpt is taken. For additional biographical information on Meed, see page 145.

The Warsaw ghetto uprising is the most well-known of the ghetto revolts. Badly outnumbered and with limited resources, the Jewish resistance fighters valiantly and fiercely fought from April until June 1943, when the ghetto was burned and destroyed. Meed was a young member of the underground who, because of her Aryan appearance, was able to live and work for the resistance movement outside of the ghetto. In this selection, she describes the early days of the uprising. Following this selection is the last letter the commander of the Jewish fighters, Mordecai Anielewicz, sent to a comrade on the Aryan side of the wall that further demonstrates the spirit of those resisting evil.

On the morning of April 19, 1943, the eve of Passover, sporadic gunfire erupted in the ghetto. It was not the usual gunfire one heard from the ghetto; this time the bursts were deafening. Powerful detonations made the earth tremble. The ghetto was surrounded by soldiers. Special S.S. detachments, in full battle array, stood opposite the ghetto wall. Machine-gun muzzles protruded from balconies, windows and roofs of the adjacent Aryan homes. German scouts reconnoitered through holes drilled through the bricks of the ghetto wall. The streets alongside were blocked off, patrolled by German police on motorcycles.

The battle had begun.

Although all of us had anticipated the uprising, the actual outbreak caught us by surprise. Spontaneously, a number of activists on the "Aryan side" gathered in the apartment of Samsonowicz, a member of the Central Committee. The group consisted of Bolek (Chaim Ellenbogen), Czeslaw (Benjamin Miedzyrecki), Stephen (S. Mermelstein), Celek (Yankel Celemenski) and myself. Our assignment was to obtain arms, to break through the German lines, and to cooperate with the Fighting Organization in the ghetto. Mikolai was to reach an accord with the Polish underground in the hope that they would help us implement our plans.

We waited for an answer from the Polish partisan leadership. Things in the ghetto were relatively quiet that morning, but by noon sporadic fire had resumed on both sides of the wall. The Germans had wheeled in artillery along Krasinski, Bonifraterska, and Muranowska Streets and it was keeping up a steady barrage. German planes, gleaming in the sun, swooped low and circled above the ghetto. Muranowska Street was ablaze, thick black smoke billowing from its north side. Every few minutes, the ground shook from an explosion; with every artillery volley, windowpanes shattered and buildings crumbled into rubble.

I looked at Swientojerska Street. Machine guns had been trained at the remains of the brush factory. Evidently, the Germans were encountering strong resistance there; the air was filled with gunfire. I could see familiar buildings, now in ruins, floors collapsed, huge gaping holes, pillars of rising dust.

Suddenly, there was a deafening explosion, louder than anything yet heard.

Tanks rolled along Nalewki Road toward the ghetto wall. Thousands of Poles had gathered in the streets near the wall to watch the struggle. They came from all over Warsaw; never before had the city witnessed so bitter a struggle in its very heart. The Poles found it almost impossible to believe that the Jews were confronting the Germans without outside support.

"They must have some of our officers over there," they insisted. "Our men must have organized the resistance." They were stirred, thrilled, exhilarated. They had never expected the miserable Jews to put up a fight. The steady stream of ambulances carrying dead and injured Germans to their field hospitals gave them satisfaction. "Look at all those casualties," they cried with delight as the ambulances rushed by, sirens screaming.

A broadside of fire from the ghetto sprayed the "Aryan" streets beyond the ghetto wall. The bystanders scattered and the Germans threw themselves flat on the ground. During a lull in the shooting, everyone dashed for cover. Afraid to get too close to the wall, the Germans posted Ukrainian guards there to counter the Jewish guns.

That evening Mikolai briefly summarized the situation for us. On the night of April 19th, he said, he had been awakened by a telephone call from Abrasha Blum in the ghetto.

"Active resistance has begun," Abrasha told him. "All the groups of the Fighting Organization are participating in the struggle. It's all very well organized and disciplined. We are now engaged in a battle near the brush factory. For the time being there have been only a few casualties among our fighters. There are more casualties among the Germans."

That was all: no appeals for help, no wail of despair. Just a simple, terse communique from the battle-front.

A second telephone call came on the night of April 22. "Michal Klepfisz is dead. He fell in the fighting. We are short of ammunition. We need arms." The conversation had been interrupted by the telephone central office. It was the last phone call from Abrasha Blum.

What was there to add? Our dear Michal was no longer among us. I could not even bring myself to think about it.

On April 17, his own birthday, as well as the birthday of his two-year-old daughter, Michal had succeeded in obtaining a revolver. Celek and I had visited him in the morning and examined the weapon. Michal was ecstatic; he caressed the weapon and played with it like a child with a new toy.

"If only I could keep it!" he sighed.

Because it was his birthday, we suggested that Michal give us the revolver, and we would try to smuggle it into the ghetto. Michal insisted that since he had bought the gun himself, he had the right to smuggle it in himself. "Who knows," he said, "perhaps I will teach them a little lesson with this little instrument." We pleaded with him, but to no avail. That very day he took the gun into the ghetto, and he remained there to fight, once the uprising had erupted, rather than return to the "Aryan side." We learned later that Michal had fought in the neighborhood of the brush factory, where he had set up the "munition plants." On the third day of the revolt, Zalman, Marek and Michal had gone out to scout the enemy positions. While crossing from one house to another, they were met by a fusillade of machine-gun fire. Zalman and Marek managed to escape. After the shooting stopped, they recovered Michal's bullet-riddled body.

Our thoughts were constantly with the fighters in the ghetto. All our plans seemed to have come to naught. The Polish underground kept dragging its feet, urging us to be patient, to hold on a little longer, another day. Restless and depressed, we idled about the Polish streets, trying to establish contact with the ghetto.

Cut off from the ghetto, we were aliens on the "Aryan side," all alone. Aryan Warsaw watched the Jewish resistance with amazement and observed its toll of hated Germans with grim pleasure; but it scarcely lifted a finger to help.

The ghetto was isolated; we on the "Aryan side" were helpless. Extra guards had been posted around the ghetto, making it all but impenetrable.

On the sixth day, the gunfire subsided; the Germans withdrew their heavy artillery and mounted machine guns instead. Stuka dive bombers continued their deadly rain of incendiary bombs. The muffled detonations of bombs and grenades in the ghetto never stopped. Dense clouds of smoke streaked with red flames rose from all over the ghetto, spiralling upward, obscuring the buildings. The ghetto was on fire.

That day I succeeded in getting past a German outpost on the corner of Nalewki and Dluga after I had persuaded the sentry that I was on my way to see my mother at Swientojerska 21, the house of the Dubiels. Perhaps, from the vantage point of their dwelling just outside the ghetto wall, they might have seen something or heard some news. The streets were filled with soldiers. The entire quarter from Nalewki to Swientojerska had been barred to civilians. Numerous German and Ukrainian guards patrolled the ghetto gates, through which a brisk traffic of military vehicles and ambulances passed. The cars of high-ranking S.S. officers stood parked alongside the wall.

I was stopped and interrogated several times by German sentries. Reaching the house of the Dubiels at last, I found it virtually in ruins, littered with debris and dust, windows shattered, walls riddled with bullets. The elderly Mrs. Dubiel was confused and frightened. Every once in a while her husband let some Germans into what remained of the building to search for Jews. Nellie and Vlodka moved about listlessly with silent, frightened faces, occasionally peeping out of a window at the burning ghetto.

During the German raids, old Dubiel had barely managed to conceal the children. The girls had to be rescued—but how? I tried to get near the window, but Mrs. Dubiel held me back; it was too risky. Her husband had almost been killed the day before. No Pole could show himself at a window. I peered through the window from behind a closet. Swientojerska and Wolowa Streets were deserted, glowing dim red from the fires raging in the distance, outlined by the billowing black clouds of smoke that hung over the ghetto. Two groups of German machine-gunners hunched behind a fence at the intersection of the two streets. Germans and Ukrainians in full battle array were stationed every fifteen feet along the wall. At intervals, Germans armed with machine guns darted past on motorcycles, amid occasional bursts of gunfire.

"The shooting comes from our roof," Dubiel told me. "The Germans mounted a machine gun up there. This has been going on all night. Today it's been a little quieter than usual."

"Could I make contact with the ghetto through this house?" I asked.

"No, the area is crawling with Germans," he told me. "You could never slip past them. Stay here for the night, and you'll see for yourself."

Several squads of Germans were now moving among the houses on Wolowa Street, sprinkling some sort of liquid from cans onto the houses and then retreating.

"They're trying to set the houses on fire," old Dubiel said. "Yesterday they tried the same thing, but it didn't work." As he spoke, I could see Germans throw burning rags on the houses and then hastily withdraw. The building caught fire amid a rain of heavy gunfire. Grenades exploded nearby. The earth shook. The flames spread.

"Look over there," Dubiel pointed. On the balcony of the second floor of the burning house stood a woman, wringing her hands. She disappeared into the building and a moment later returned carrying a child and dragging a feather-bed, which she flung to the sidewalk. Obviously, she meant to jump, or perhaps to drop the child, hoping that the featherbed would break the fall. Clutching the child, she started to climb over the railing. Amid a spray of bullets she slumped. The child dropped to the street. The woman's lifeless body remained draped over the railing.

The flames had enveloped the upper floor by now and explosions were occurring with increasing frequency and intensity. Figures appeared in windows, jumped, only to die by gunshot in mid-air or on the ground.

From the third floor, two men fired a few rounds, then retreated.

I turned from the window in horror, unable to watch any more. The room was now filled with the acrid smoke and stench of the burning ghetto. No one spoke.

The gunfire continued sporadically throughout the night. There were no more screams now. The crackling of dry woodwork, the occasional collapse of a weakened floor were the only sounds heard in the eerie stillness that had settled over Swientojerska and Wolowa while the blazing buildings turned night into day.

All night long I stood at the window in a state of near-shock, the heat scorching my face, the smoke burning my eyes, and watched the flames consume the ghetto. Dawn came quiet and ghastly, revealing the burned-out shells of buildings, the charred, bloodstained bodies of the victims. Suddenly one of these bodies began to move, slowly, painfully, crawling on its belly until it disappeared into the smoking ruins. Others, too, began to show signs of life. But the enemy was also on the alert. There was a spatter of machine-gun fire—and all was lifeless again.

The sun rose higher over the ghetto. There was a knock on the door. Quickly I moved away from the window; Dubiel moved to the door. Two German officers entered.

"Anyone except your family living here?"

"No, I do not harbor any Jews."

The Germans did not even bother to search the place; they went straight to the window and unslung cameras.

"It's a good site for pictures," one remarked, "if it weren't for those damned fires."

For a half hour they continued their picture-taking, laughing and joking about those "Jewish clowns" and their comical contortions.

When they had gone, the old woman begged me to go, too. She was terrified, crossing herself and mumbling prayers. The little girls bade me a silent farewell. Dubiel escorted me through the courtyard, the steps, and the street, all swarming with Germans. Afraid even to look in the direction of the ghetto, I walked quickly away, without a backward glance. Somehow, the ghetto fought on. On the fifth day of the uprising the Coordinating Committee on the "Aryan side" issued an appeal in the name of the ghetto. The message was drafted and written at Zurawia 24. From there I brought the manuscript to a store which served as our "drop," and later brought back a package of printed appeals. Written in Polish and signed by the Fighting Organization, the appeal stressed the heroism of the fighters and the ferocity of the struggle. Every home was a fortress against the Germans. The insurgents sent their fervent salutations to all those fighting the Nazis.

"We will avenge the crimes of Dachau, Treblinka and Auschwitz," the appeal proclaimed. "The struggle for your freedom and ours continues."

On my way back from Zoliborz with the package of printed pamphlets, I found Bonifraterska Street impassable because of the acrid smoke. Waves of intense heat rolled in from the ghetto; tongues of fire flicked hungrily across the wall at the Aryan homes. Polish firemen had mounted the roofs of the houses in an attempt to stave off the flames advancing from the ghetto. A German sentry stood by, halting pedestrians and searching them thoroughly.

I turned quickly onto Konwiktorska Street where I came upon some 60 Jews—men, women and children—facing the wall, surrounded by guards with fixed bayonets. The unfortunates, including some very small children, looked gaunt and wild-eyed. Yet none of them cried. Their fate was sealed.

Three days later I happened to pass the same way. A crowd of Poles was impassively staring at a roof nearby.

"Some Jews broke out of the ghetto and hid in the loft of a Polish house," one of the spectators was telling a newcomer as I came within earshot. "But the Germans found them and attacked the place. The Jews returned fire and tried to escape over neighboring roofs. Soon afterwards a tank drove through, firing broadsides. Now you can see dead Jews lying along the roof."

The burning had now gone on for two nightmarish weeks. Some areas had been reduced to smoldering ruins. The gunfire had diminished, but it had not stopped. The Germans marched into the ghetto every morning and each evening at dusk they withdrew. They worked only in broad daylight. The Stukas still circled and swooped overhead, raining incendiaries on the ghetto without letup; the explosions could be heard throughout the city.

At night, however, things were quiet. Poison gas was released into the water mains and sewers to kill any Jews who might be hiding there. Gentile homes facing the ghetto along Leszno, Przejazd and Swientojerska were burned to the ground by the Germans. Among the houses that fell victim to the flames was the house of the Dubiels.

Nevertheless, the revolt continued unabated. Jewish resistance continued. The Germans had succeeded in penetrating only a few outer sections of the ghetto, and had contented themselves with setting the Jewish homes afire.

Before long the admiration and excitement of the Poles over the Jewish uprising was replaced by a gnawing apprehension. "What's next now?" the Poles wondered. "Will the Germans turn on us also?"

With their pitiful assortment of arms and explosive-filled bottles our comrades in the ghetto had dared to challenge the modern, sophisticated weapons of the enemy. We on the "Aryan side" were bursting with admiration for them, but we were consumed also by a sense of guilt at being outside the ghetto, in relative safety, while they were fighting and dying. We should have been there with them, amid the roaring fires and the crashing walls.

We stared into the fiery sky over Warsaw. Why was there no response from the rest of the city? Where was the help our neighbors had promised? And the rest of the world—why was it so silent?

*   *   *

It is impossible to put into words what we have been through. One thing is clear, what happened exceeded our boldest dreams. The Germans ran twice from the ghetto. One of our companies held out for 40 minutes and another—for more than 6 hours. The mine set in the "brushmakers" area exploded. Several of our companies attacked the dispersing Germans. Our losses in manpower are minimal. That is also an achievement. Y [Yechiel] fell. He fell a hero, at the machine-gun. *I feel that great things are happening and what we dared do is of great, enormous importance.* . . .

Beginning today we shall shift over to the partisan tactic. Three battle companies will move out tonight, with two tasks: reconnaissance and obtaining arms. Do remember, short-range weapons are of no use to us. We use such weapons only rarely. What we need urgently: grenades, rifles, machine-guns and explosives.

It is impossible to describe the conditions under which the Jews of the ghetto are now living. Only a few will be able to hold out. The remainder will die sooner or later. Their fate is decided. In almost all the hiding places in which thousands are concealing themselves it is not possible to light a candle for lack of air.

With the aid of our transmitter we heard a marvelous report on our fighting by the "Shavit" radio station. The fact that we are remembered beyond the ghetto walls encourages us in our struggle. Peace go with you, my friend! Perhaps we may still meet again! *The dream of my life has risen to become fact. Self-defense in the ghetto will have been a reality. Jewish armed resistance and revenge are facts. I have been a witness to the magnificent, heroic fighting of Jewish men of battle.*

M. Anielewicz

chapter 7

Liberation

Liberation was not a single act or event; it was a series of events that happened throughout the winter and spring of 1945 as the Allied troops freed countries, cities, towns, and camps that had been under Nazi domination. By the time of liberation, millions of victims had already been killed; many others would die in the following days and weeks. For the survivors, liberation elicited a range of emotions and reactions. Initially, some survivors felt joy and relief, while many others experienced guilt and depression; still others, who had lived with numbness for too long, felt nothing.

While images of liberation frequently focus on the haggard, emaciated inmates of the camps, liberation freed all of the victims of the Holocaust. Liberation brought with it an outpouring of emotions from some of the survivors and a sense of emptiness for others. Regardless of their initial response, the survivors faced a difficult transition.

Of primary importance was their continued survival. The survivors needed food, clothing, and often medicine. Many survivors died immediately or in the days or weeks following liberation because their systems had been malnourished for so long that they could not deal with the richness of the rations they received.

The selections in Chapter 7 relate a range of experiences and emotions that survivors endured. Clearly, for the survivors, while liberation represented an ending, it also represented a beginning, and that beginning was filled with new challenges and continued hardships.

I, the Survivor

Bertolt Brecht

Born February 10, 1898,
in Augsburg, Germany,
Bertolt Brecht became
one of the leading
authors of the twentieth
century. Fearing
persecution because of
his Marxist views, he left
Germany in 1933,
spending the next
fourteen years in exile,
first in Scandinavia and
then in the United States.
His German citizenship
was revoked by the
Nazis, and his works
were burned in Germany
during the Third Reich.
Brecht left the United
States for Europe in 1947.
In 1949, he returned to
Germany. He remained
in Berlin until his death
on August 14, 1956.

Brecht's brief poem
mirrors the guilt that
survivors often
mention—that they
survived while others
perished.

I know of course; it's simply luck
That I've survived so many friends. But last
    night in a dream
I heard those friends say of me: "Survival of
    the fittest"
And I hated myself.

Death against Life

Elie Wiesel

Elie Wiesel, born in Sighet, Transylvania, on
September 30, 1928, is considered by many to be the
foremost spokesperson for the survivors of the
Holocaust. He grew up in a devoutly religious
community that was untouched by the war until
1944, when the whole community was sent to
Auschwitz. Wiesel's avowed goal was that he and his
father survive the camp, but after they were sent to
Buchenwald as slave laborers, his father died. After
the war, Wiesel studied in France and became a
journalist. In 1958, he wrote his first book, a
semiautobiographical novel about his experiences,
Night, from which the following excerpt is taken.
Wiesel received the Nobel Peace Prize in 1986 and
remains one of the most eloquent voices speaking
about the horrors of the times. He is currently a
professor at Boston University.

In this excerpt, Wiesel poignantly recounts his
liberation, which occurred only a few months after
his father died.

I had to stay at Buchenwald until April eleventh. I
have nothing to say of my life during this period. It no longer mattered. After
my father's death, nothing could touch me any more.

I was transferred to the children's block, where there were six hundred of us.
The front was drawing nearer.

I spent my days in a state of total idleness. And I had but one desire—to eat. I no longer thought of my father or of my mother.

From time to time I would dream of a drop of soup, of an extra ration of soup.

On April fifth, the wheel of history turned.

It was late in the afternoon. We were standing in the block, waiting for an SS man to come and count us. He was late in coming. Such a delay was unknown till then in the history of Buchenwald. Something must have happened.

Two hours later the loudspeakers sent out an order from the head of the camp: all Jews must come to the assembly place.

This was the end! Hitler was going to keep his promise.

The children in our block went toward the place. There was nothing else we could do. Gustav, the head of the block, made this clear to us with his truncheon. But on the way we met some prisoners who whispered to us:

"Go back to your block. The Germans are going to shoot you. Go back to your block, and don't move."

We went back to our block. We learned on the way that the camp resistance organization had decided not to abandon the Jews and was going to prevent their being liquidated.

As it was late and there was great upheaval—innumerable Jews had passed themselves off as non-Jews—the head of the camp decided that a general roll call would take place the following day. Everybody would have to be present.

The roll call took place. The head of the camp announced that Buchenwald was to be liquidated. Ten blocks of deportees would be evacuated each day. From this moment, there would be no further distribution of bread and soup. And the evacuation began. Every day, several thousand prisoners went through the camp gate and never came back.

On April tenth, there were still about twenty thousand of us in the camp, including several hundred children. They decided to evacuate us all at once, right on until the evening. Afterward, they were going to blow up the camp.

So we were massed in the huge assembly square, in rows of five, waiting to see the gate open. Suddenly, the sirens began to wail. An alert! We went back to the blocks. It was too late to evacuate us that evening. The evacuation was postponed again to the following day.

We were tormented with hunger. We had eaten nothing for six days, except a bit of grass or some potato peelings found near the kitchens.

At ten o'clock in the morning the SS scattered through the camp, moving the last victims toward the assembly place.

Then the resistance movement decided to act. Armed men suddenly rose up everywhere. Bursts of firing. Grenades exploding. We children stayed flat on the ground in the block.

The battle did not last long. Toward noon everything was quiet again. The SS had fled and the resistance had taken charge of the running of the camp.

At about six o'clock in the evening, the first American tank stood at the gates of Buchenwald.

Our first act as free men was to throw ourselves onto the provisions. We thought only of that. Not of revenge, not of our families. Nothing but bread.

And even when we were no longer hungry, there was still no one who thought of revenge. On the following day, some of the young men went to Weimar to get some potatoes and clothes—and to sleep with girls. But of revenge, not a sign.

Three days after the liberation of Buchenwald I became very ill with food poisoning. I was transferred to the hospital and spent two weeks between life and death.

One day I was able to get up, after gathering all my strength. I wanted to see myself in the mirror hanging on the opposite wall. I had not seen myself since the ghetto.

From the depths of the mirror, a corpse gazed back at me.

The look in his eyes, as they stared into mine, has never left me.

Liberation

Lucille Eichengreen

Lucille Eichengreen was born in 1925 and grew up
in Nazi Germany, where she experienced persecution. She survived incarceration at Auschwitz,
Neuengamme, and Bergen-Belsen. Her parents and
sister did not survive the Holocaust. Following the
war, she immigrated to the United States. She is
the author of *From Ashes to Life: My Memories of the
Holocaust*, from which the following material is
taken.

The reality of liberation was not always what
survivors, desperately clinging to life, imagined it
would be. In this excerpt, Eichengreen describes her
liberation from Bergen-Belsen by the British army
and the revival of feelings that had for so long been
numbed.

It was an unusually quiet morning. The sky was
overcast. The guard towers were manned, and as usual, the SS kept their
machine guns aimed at us. But something was different . . . odd. Although the
SS wore their usual uniforms, they had added white armbands. We wondered
what it might mean.

At noon Elli[1] and I stood outside the barracks, the sun straight overhead.
Suddenly, the ground trembled beneath our feet, and a rumbling noise filled the
air. Cautiously, we ventured toward the middle of the compound, then closer
to the barbed wire that separated us from the main camp road. There, we saw
tanks—huge, crawling monsters beginning to line the street from end to end.

---

[1] Her friend.

The men on top of the tanks wore khaki uniforms. We watched, stunned and bewildered. A woman's shrill, hysterical cry pierced the air as she pointed to the soldiers, "Look, they're British . . . They've come, the war must be over! We are free!"

We watched with both fear and disbelief. Could it be true? We stood motionless until the soldiers jumped off the tanks and walked toward the camp gate. Some of us began to cry, others cheered and laughed as several uniformed British officers entered the camp. The Germans seemed suddenly to have disappeared. The women pressed against the fence and the gate, now guarded by the soldiers in khaki. We followed their every gesture, still not sure that these were our liberators.

Finally, one of them spoke to us in English. "We have liberated this camp. But we are not prepared for what we have found and seen with our own eyes. We'll try to rush in food, water, and medical supplies."

So it was true. We were liberated— finally! Tears, laughter, hugging, and uncontrollable senseless screams burst out of us. The British watched in silence, staring at us, their eyes reflecting horror and disbelief. When we calmed down, the same soldier asked if anyone understood English.

Along with several others, I raised my hand.

"Good, we can use you. We need you to translate for us." They watched us carefully. They looked at our torn, filthy clothing and our thin faces, stained with tears. We saw the troubled bewilderment in their eyes.

I was immediately assigned to three officers. The tall one introduced himself. "I'm Major Brinton. I'm from Scotland. You'll get used to my accent," he laughed. "I'd like to see the inside of several barracks, talk to people, and ask some questions. You'll translate for me."

With more energy than I thought I could muster, I led the way. We walked into the nearest barracks building. Most of the women there had been too weak to come out; some were on the verge of death. The major asked for names, nationalities, and how long they had been in the camps. Most inmates cried; some tried to kiss the hands of the officers. All of them begged for food. I looked at the British. There was horror in their faces. They were unable to comprehend what they saw. They stared at human beings who were barely human, reduced to skeletons with burning eyes and halting voices, bearing little resemblance to women. These still-breathing collections of bones all hoped to live. Their hollow eyes followed us.

The compound housing the men was even worse. I had never been there before. These men had been in Bergen-Belsen a long time; they no longer talked or smiled. On a corner bunk, we saw a skeleton of a man, so emaciated that his skull showed every bone. He stared at us through sunken, feverishly blank, burning eyes. He held a knife in one hand, and as we watched, he slashed away

341

at the thigh of a nearby corpse and then hungrily devoured the flesh. Two of the three officers turned and ran; the third vomited where he stood.

One of the officers screamed, "For Christ's sake, let's get some help!"

I was paralyzed. I had seen and experienced much, but this man left me shaken. What had we become? The Germans had succeeded in reducing us to subhumans. Would we ever be normal again? It seemed impossible. Despite our liberation, I was totally without hope.

The British were quiet. They had seen more than they had bargained for. "Enough for today. Come to the camp gate tomorrow morning at 8:00," they said to me, "and we'll see where we can use you."

The major pressed a small packet of biscuits and several cigarettes into my hand.

"Thank you," I murmured.

"Don't mention it," he sadly replied.

It was late when I returned to our barracks. Elli and I sat on the floor and shared the biscuits and cigarettes. We were silent, still too numb to comprehend all that had happened. Sleep was impossible. My mind raced with plans for the future. I'd have to write to my family in Palestine, in England, and in the United States. They had not heard from any of us in more than four years. They did not know that Mother and Father had been murdered. And Karin—where was she now? I could only wonder and hope. Maybe I would hear from her . . . maybe she would come to Hamburg . . . maybe . . . I thought about our separation during the selection in the Lodz ghetto. Where had they taken her? Had she been liberated, too?

Even though liberation seemed to promise a return to a normal life, it did not bring happiness. Instead, it revived feelings that had long been numbed by the daily struggle for both mental and physical survival—feelings of guilt, loneliness, and utter devastation. The reality of liberation was so different from what I had imagined. I had dreamed of a great party, with fanfare, music, dancing, and fireworks. There was, however, only renewed sorrow for the dead and little hope for the living. Liberation had come quietly, and it had brought with it the realization that thousands of us had not lived to see this moment. Many of us would not live even until the end of the week.

It was almost midnight when the British troops managed to bring drinking water into the camp. This was followed by a huge supply of two-pound tins filled with pieces of pork and lard. Most of the former inmates gulped down the contents of the entire can in minutes. I still chewed on my biscuits, afraid to touch the pork. Within less than an hour, those who had eaten the pork were vomiting and writhing with stomach cramps. Elli and I walked outside; the smell inside the barracks had become more unbearable than ever. I decided to beg the British for more biscuits or bread until our stomachs could get used to food again.

As dawn broke the next morning, the five of us chosen to translate already stood at the gate. Finally, as the sun appeared on the horizon, the major and several officers arrived. The major wanted to know how long we had been waiting. When we told him, "Since daybreak," he looked perplexed. We explained that we had no watches, that they had been taken by the Germans in Auschwitz.

"Come with me," said the major.

For the first time since my arrival at Bergen-Belsen, the camp gate was opened for us, and we walked through it. We had never before left the confines of the camp, and walking into the former SS area without a single German confronting us seemed unbelievable.

We followed the major to the German barracks and stopped in front of a green building marked "Supplies." Inside, on tables, benches, and the floor were hundreds of boxes, neatly sorted and filled with ladies' watches, men's watches, rings, bracelets, brooches, and strings of pearls. Along the far wall were huge boxes filled to the brim with gold coins and foreign currency. We stared in stunned silence, reluctantly remembering Auschwitz and how these heirlooms had been torn from our arms, fingers, and necks. Piles of gold teeth, removed from the mouths of the dead, were hoarded here, destined for distribution or sale to Germans.

"I want each of you to choose a watch so you can be on time for work. Just make sure it still runs," the major said, rather matter-of-factly.

I stretched out my hand, only to pull it back. I wondered about the owners. I could still see the faces of my fellow prisoners as they stood huddled, fearing the worst. Where were they now? Major Brinton's voice ended my ruminations: "Come on, make up your mind!"

I picked up a small, oblong silver watch, wound it, and saw the second hand move. Unbelievable! The back of the watch was slightly rusty, the leather strap black and worn. I put the watch around my wrist with a silent prayer that its owner was alive and that someday she would recognize the watch and claim it. She never did.

Several days after liberation, life at Bergen-Belsen started to take on a certain routine. My work as an interpreter kept me busy, and I momentarily forgot everything else. Food improved; there was hot stew now, dark bread, hot tea. No one went hungry. Still, hundreds died daily. For them, food and freedom had come too late.

Two weeks after I began working, I summoned enough courage to ask the major if I could shower or bathe. He looked at me, embarrassed. How could he understand? It had been almost four years.

"Of course. I'll make arrangements for you and the others," he said.

A young woman officer of the British Red Cross took the five of us to the showers in the former SS barracks. We were handed a small piece of soap and a towel. The showers worked! Hot water streamed over our cropped hair and thin bodies. It was heaven. I soaped and rinsed again and then again, hoping that perhaps the clean, hot water would put distance between the dark, bloody past and the present. But it didn't work. The past could not be forgotten, not then—perhaps not ever. I finally stepped outside, dried myself, and put on my ragged, dirty clothing. In time perhaps we would have new, clean clothes.

During the days that followed, huge bulldozers were brought into the camp. They dug deep craters. Then they shoveled the thousands of dead bodies that lay in a heap into the gaping pit. Those who could attended the services. I stood at the rim of the pit, listening to the army chaplain recite prayers in English and the Kaddish in Hebrew. Suddenly the earth heaved, my head spun, my arms flailed, and the world around me turned black.

Later, when I opened my eyes, I found myself in a light, airy room. A kind voice told me that I had fainted. Gentle hands were applying cool compresses to my head, and I burst into uncontrollable sobs. I could neither talk nor explain; no words could sound the depths of my pain and sorrow or articulate the agony of total loss.

The Thaw

Primo Levi

Primo Levi was a prolific author of fiction, poetry,
and autobiography. His books include *If Not Now,
When?*, *Survival in Auschwitz*, *Moments of Reprieve*,
The Drowned and the Saved, and *The Reawakening*,
from which the following excerpt is taken. For
additional biographical information on Levi, see
page 213.

In this memoir, Levi describes the liberation of
Auschwitz by the Russian army and the strange
mixture of feelings that it evoked in the prisoners.

In the first days of January 1945, hard pressed by
the Red Army, the Germans hastily evacuated the Silesian mining region. But
whereas elsewhere, in analogous conditions, they had not hesitated to destroy
the Lagers and their inhabitants by fire or arms, they acted differently in the
district of Auschwitz: superior orders had been received (given personally, it
would seem, by Hitler) to recover at all costs every man fit for work. Thus all
healthy prisoners were evacuated, in frightful conditions, in the direction of
Buchenwald and Mauthausen, while the sick were abandoned to their fate. One
can legitimately deduce from the evidence that originally the Germans did not
intend to leave one man alive in the concentration camps; but a fierce night air
raid and the rapidity of the Russian advance induced them to change their
minds and flee, leaving their task unfinished.

In the sick bay of the Lager at Buna-Monowitz eight hundred of us remained.
Of these about five hundred died from illness, cold and hunger before the
Russians arrived, and another two hundred succumbed in the following days,
despite the Russians' aid.

The first Russian patrol came in sight of the camp about midday on 27 January 1945. Charles and I were the first to see them: we were carrying Sómogyi's body to the common grave, the first of our room mates to die. We tipped the stretcher on to the defiled snow, as the pit was now full, and no other grave was at hand: Charles took off his beret as a salute to both the living and the dead.

They were four young soldiers on horseback, who advanced along the road that marked the limits of the camp, cautiously holding their sten-guns. When they reached the barbed wire, they stopped to look, exchanging a few timid words, and throwing strangely embarrassed glances at the sprawling bodies, at the battered huts and at us few still alive.

To us they seemed wonderfully concrete and real, perched on their enormous horses, between the grey of the snow and the grey of the sky, immobile beneath the gusts of damp wind which threatened a thaw.

It seemed to us, and so it was, that the nothing full of death in which we had wandered like spent stars for ten days had found its own solid centre, a nucleus of condensation; four men, armed, but not against us: four messengers of peace, with rough and boyish faces beneath their heavy fur hats.

They did not greet us, nor did they smile; they seemed oppressed not only by compassion but by a confused restraint, which sealed their lips and bound their eyes to the funereal scene. It was that shame we knew so well, the shame that drowned us after the selections, and every time we had to watch, or submit to, some outrage: the shame the Germans did not know, that the just man experiences at another man's crime; the feeling of guilt that such a crime should exist, that it should have been introduced irrevocably into the world of things that exist, and that his will for good should have proved too weak or null, and should not have availed in defence.

So for us even the hour of liberty rang out grave and muffled, and filled our souls with joy and yet with a painful sense of pudency, so that we should have liked to wash our consciences and our memories clean from the foulness that lay upon them; and also with anguish, because we felt that this should never happen, that now nothing could ever happen good and pure enough to rub out our past, and that the scars of the outrage would remain within us for ever, and in the memories of those who saw it, and in the places where it occurred and in the stories that we should tell of it. Because, and this is the awful privilege of our generation and of my people, no one better than us has ever been able to grasp the incurable nature of the offence, that spreads like a contagion. It is foolish to think that human justice can eradicate it. It is an inexhaustible fount of evil; it breaks the body and the spirit of the submerged, it stifles them and renders them abject; it returns as ignominy upon the oppressors, it perpetuates itself as hatred among the survivors, and swarms around in a thousand ways, against the very will of all, as a thirst for revenge, as a moral capitulation, as denial, as weariness, as renunciation.

These things, at that time blurred, and felt by most as no more than an unexpected attack of mortal fatigue, accompanied the joy of liberation for us. This is why few among us ran to greet our saviours, few fell in prayer. Charles and I remained standing beside the pit overflowing with discoloured limbs, while others knocked down the barbed wire; then we returned with the empty stretcher to break the news to our companions.

For the rest of the day nothing happened; this did not surprise us, and we had long been accustomed to it. In our room the dead Sómogyi's bunk was immediately occupied by old Thylle, to the visible disgust of my two French companions.

Thylle, so far as I then knew, was a "red triangle," a German political prisoner, and one of the old inhabitants of the Lager; as such, he had belonged by right to the aristocracy of the camp, he had not worked manually (at least in the last years), and he had received food and clothes from home. For these reasons the German 'politicals' were rarely inmates of the sick bay, where however they enjoyed various privileges: the first of them that of escaping from the selections. As Thylle was the only political prisoner at the moment of liberation, the SS in flight had appointed him head of Block 20, where, besides our room of highly infectious patients, there were also the TB and dysentery wards.

Being a German, he had taken this precarious appointment very seriously. In the ten days between the departure of the SS and the arrival of the Russians, while everyone was fighting his last battle against hunger, cold and disease, Thylle had carried out diligent inspections of his new fief, checking the state of the floors and the bowls and the number of blankets (one for each inmate, alive or dead). On one of his visits to our room he had even praised Arthur for the order and cleanliness he kept; Arthur, who did not understand German, and even less the Saxon dialect of Thylle, had replied *"vieux dégoutant"* and *"putain de boche,"* nevertheless, Thylle, from that day on, in open abuse of his authority, had acquired the habit of coming into our room every evening to use the comfortable latrine-bucket installed there, the only one regularly cleaned in the whole camp, and the only one near a stove.

Thus, up to that day old Thylle had been a foreigner to me, and therefore an enemy—a powerful person, moreover, and therefore a dangerous enemy. For people like myself, that is to say for the majority of the Lager, there were no other distinctions: during the whole interminable year spent in the Lager, I had never had either the curiosity or the occasion to investigate the complex structure of the hierarchy of the camp. The gloomy edifice of vicious powers lay wholly above us, and our looks were turned to the ground. Yet this Thylle, an old combatant hardened by a hundred struggles both for and within his party, and petrified by ten years of ferocious and ambiguous life within the Lager, was the companion and confidant of my first night of liberty.

For the whole day we had been too busy to remark upon the event, which we still felt marked the crucial point of our entire existence; and perhaps, unconsciously, we had sought something to do precisely to avoid spare time, because face to face with liberty we felt ourselves lost, emptied, atrophied, unfit for our part.

But night came, and our sick companions fell asleep. Charles and Arthur also dropped into the sleep of innocence, because they had been in the Lager for one month only, and had not yet absorbed its poison. I alone, although exhausted, could not fall asleep because of my very tiredness and illness. All my limbs ached, my blood throbbed violently in my head and I felt myself overwhelmed by fever. But it was not this alone; in the very hour in which every threat seemed to vanish, in which a hope of a return to life ceased to be crazy, I was overcome—as if a dyke had crumbled—by a new and greater pain, previously buried and relegated to the margins of my consciousness by other more immediate pains: the pain of exile, of my distant home, of loneliness, of friends lost, of youth lost and of the host of corpses all around.

In my year at Buna I had seen four-fifths of my companions disappear, but I had never faced the concrete presence, the blockade, of death, its sordid breath a step away, outside the window, in the bunk next to me, in my own veins. Thus I lay in a sickly state of semi-consciousness, full of gloomy thoughts.

But very soon I realized that someone else was awake. The heavy breathing of the sleepers was drowned at intervals by a hoarse and irregular panting, interrupted by coughs and groans and stifled sighs. Thylle was weeping, with the difficult and shameless tears of an old man, as intolerable as senile nudity. Perhaps he saw me move in the dark; and the solitude, which up to that day we had both sought for different reasons, must have weighed upon him as much as upon me, because in the middle of the night he asked me "are you awake?" and, not waiting for a reply, toiled up to my bunk, and, without asking permission, sat beside me.

It was not easy to understand each other; not only because of linguistic difficulties, but also because the thoughts that weighed upon us in that long night were immense, marvellous and terrible, but above all confused. I told him that I was suffering from nostalgia; and he exclaimed, after he had stopped crying, "ten years, ten years"; and after ten years of silence, in a low stridulous voice, grotesque and solemn at the same time, he began to sing the *Internationale*, leaving me perturbed, diffident and moved.

The morning brought us the first signs of liberty. Some twenty Polish men and women, clearly summoned by the Russians, arrived and with little enthusiasm began to fumble around, attempting to bring some order and cleanliness into the huts and to clear away the bodies. About midday a frightened child appeared, dragging a cow by the halter; he made us understand that it was for us, that the Russians had sent it, then he abandoned the beast and fled like a bolt. I don't know how, but within minutes the poor animal was slaughtered, gutted and quartered and its remains distributed to all the corners of the camp where survivors nestled.

During the following days, we saw more Polish girls wander around the camp, pale with disgust and pity: they cleaned the patients and tended to their sores as best they could. They also lit an enormous fire in the middle of the camp, which they fed with planks from broken-down huts, and on which they cooked soup in whatever pots came to hand. Finally, on the third day, we saw a cart enter the camp led joyfully by Yankel, a Häftling: he was a young Russian Jew, perhaps the only Russian among the survivors, and as such he naturally found himself acting as interpreter and liaison officer with the Soviet HQ. Between resounding cracks of his whip, he announced that he had the task of carrying all the survivors, in small groups of thirty or forty a day, beginning with the most seriously ill, to the central Lager of Auschwitz, now transformed into a gigantic lazaret.

In the meantime, the thaw we had been fearing for so many days had started, and as the snow slowly disappeared, the camp began to change into a squalid bog. The bodies and the filth made the misty, muggy air impossible to breath. Nor had death ceased to take its toll: the sick died in their cold bunks by the dozen, and here and there along the muddy roads, as if suddenly struck down, died the greediest of the survivors, those who had followed blindly the imperious command of our age-old hunger and had stuffed themselves with the rations of meat that the Russians, still engaged in fighting, sent irregularly to the camp: sometimes little, sometimes nothing, sometimes in crazy abundance.

But I was aware of what was going on around me in only a disconnected and hazy manner. It seemed as if the weariness and the illness, like ferocious and cowardly beasts, had waited in ambush for the moment when I dismantled my defences, in order to attack me from behind. I lay in a feverish torpor, semiconscious, tended fraternally by Charles, and tormented by thirst and acute pains in my joints. There were no doctors or drugs. I also had a sore throat, and half my face had swollen; my skin had become red and rough and hurt me like a burn; perhaps I was suffering from more than one illness at the same time. When it was my turn to climb on to Yankel's cart, I was no longer able to stand on my feet.

I was hoisted on to the cart by Charles and Arthur, together with a load of dying men, from whom I did not feel very different. It was drizzling, and the sky was low and gloomy. While the slow steps of Yankel's horses drew me towards remote liberty, for the last time there filed before my eyes the huts where I had suffered and matured, the roll-call square where the gallows and the gigantic Christmas tree still towered side by side, and the gate to slavery, on which one could still read the three, now hollow, words of derision: *"Arbeit Macht Frei,"* "Work Gives Freedom."

Night of Surrender

Ida Fink

Ida Fink was born in Poland in 1922. After the Nazis invaded Poland, she was forced into a ghetto until she escaped in 1942 and went into hiding for the remainder of the war. In 1957, she and her family immigrated to Israel. Her stories often provide readers with a human perspective about hiding. She was the first recipient of the Anne Frank Prize for Literature for her collection of original stories entitled *A Scrap of Time and Other Stories*.

Survival during the Holocaust often meant lying and hiding one's identity. In this short story, Anna wonders if she can really be herself again after the war.

I met Mike in a park, in a pretty little town on the Alsatian border. I had been imprisoned there briefly in 1943, which was complicated, considering that I was a Jew using Aryan papers. Now the war was ending, the front was falling apart around Stuttgart, and the surrender was expected any day.

Mike was a very nice fellow, and in those first days of freedom I was feeling very lonely and sad. I used to go to the park every day. It was immaculately kept and the rhododendrons were in full bloom, covered with pale violet flowers. I would walk to the park, sit on a bench, and tell myself that I should be happy to have survived, but I wasn't happy, and I was upset to be so sad. I went there every day and the girls from the camp figured that I had met a boy; they were envious and curious. Their suspicions were confirmed on the day Mike walked me back to the camp; and from then on he would come to get me every day at four and we would go for a stroll.

Michael was very tall, he had funny long legs, his uniform trousers fit tightly, his waist was as slender as a girl's. He wore large eyeglasses with rectangular frames. He smiled like a child, and if he wasn't so big, you could have mistaken him for a teenager; but he was a serious grown man, a professor of mathematics, already twenty-seven, ten years older than I.

He would take my hand—my head came up to his elbow—and we would go strolling in the park or along the Rhine, and he would always whistle the same tune. Much later, I found out that it was Smetana's *Moldau*, but at that time I didn't know its name or who had composed it. My knowledge of the world and of life was one-sided: I knew death, terror, cunning, how to lie and trick, but nothing about music or poetry or love.

This is how I met him: One day I was sitting on the bench beside the pale violet rhododendrons. It was evening and I should have gotten up and returned to the camp for supper, but I kept on sitting there, I didn't feel like getting up even though I was hungry, and I didn't notice the lanky boy with the glasses and the American uniform who had sat down on the edge of the bench. When he asked, "What are you thinking about?" I was terrified, and he burst out laughing.

I answered in my broken English, "I was in a German prison here,"—though I hadn't been thinking of that at all, only about supper, because I was hungry.

"Did they beat you?"

"No."

He looked closely at me, then said, "That's funny."

I didn't know what was funny—the fact that I had been in prison or that they hadn't beaten me. Some kind of moron, I thought, but he kept on asking me questions.

"And why did the Germans lock you up in prison?"

I looked at him as if he were a creature from another world.

"Don't worry. I just wanted to know what it was like for you."

He looked at me seriously, and his eyes shone with a warm, golden light. Maybe he's not such a fool, I thought. But watch out, I told myself, wait a bit. You held out for so many years, you can hold out for another week or two. The war is still going on.

But already I anticipated the enormous relief it would be to say those three words—their weight was growing more unbearable each day. I smiled faintly, and in that teary voice befitting the revelation of one's life story, said: "Ah, my history is very sad, why return to those matters? I don't want to."

"Poor child!" He stroked my hair and took some chocolate out of his pocket. "But you will tell me some day, won't you?"

It was milk chocolate. I love milk chocolate; it's light and melts in your mouth. The last time I ate chocolate was before the war, but I didn't say anything, I just got up to go to supper—the potatoes and canned meat in gravy we got every day.

The next afternoon Mike brought me some enormous, dark violets, and I rewarded him with the life story I had patched together over the last three years; it moved him as it was meant to. I was sorry that I was still lying, but consoled myself with the fact that the true story would have been a hundred times more horrifying.

The girls from the camp were jealous, and in the evening they would ask in detail about everything. After a week, they asked, "Has he kissed you?" and when I answered, "No," they were very disappointed. And that was the truth. Mike brought me more chocolate (because I had told him, after all, that not since before the war . . .). He bought me ice cream, he held my hand, and sometimes, when we lay near the Rhine, he stroked my hair and said it was silken and shiny. He also told me about his home and the school where he taught, and about the garden he worked himself. It all sounded like a fairy tale from a storybook for well-brought-up children, and sometimes I smiled to myself, especially when he talked about flowers and mowed grass. I never asked him if he had a girlfriend in America. It was obvious that he did, but he never mentioned her.

Sometimes we didn't say anything. The water in the Rhine glittered like fish scales, the weeds flowered in the ruins, airplanes circled overhead and they too were silvery and long, like fish. But there was no reason to fear them, and now, without getting that tightness in your throat, you could watch them dive, grow huge, and mark the earth with the shadow of a cold black cross.

"Ann," Mike would say, giving my name, Anna, its English form, "isn't this nice?"

"Very nice," I would answer, and he would say, "Very, very nice, my dear," but it wasn't very nice at all and it couldn't be very nice as long as I was lying to him.

That day, when we were returned from the park, the rhododendrons were already yellow and withered. Mike asked, "Why won't you tell me everything about yourself? It would make you feel better."

I was well trained. I replied instantly, "But I told you."

"Not everything, Ann. I'm sure that was only a part, maybe not even the most important part. Why don't you trust me?"

Again he had that warm, golden glow in his eyes, and I thought: I am mean and nasty.

"The war taught all of you not to trust anyone. I'm not surprised. But listen, the war is over. You have to learn to believe in people, in happiness and goodness."

"You're talking like a professor, and a stupid one. You think everything can change just like that? Believe in people? It makes me laugh"—I wanted to say throw up—"when I hear such idiotic stuff."

"Ann, I want to ask you something."

My heart began to pound, because that was what everyone said before they asked, "Are you a Jew?"

"Well, ask," I said, but he didn't say anything; he just looked at me and I couldn't help seeing the tenderness and concern in his glance. I felt like touching his face, pressing close to him, asking him not to go away, telling him that I didn't want to be alone anymore, that I was tired of standing outside myself and watching every move.

"Well, ask. I'm waiting," I said.

We were standing at the gate to the camp. It was supper-time. A crowd of DPs with aluminum mess kits for their potatoes and canned meat with gravy were crossing the large square where, every morning, roll call and edifying prayers were held.

I looked at Mike and noticed that a muscle in his right cheek was quivering.

"Would you go away with me?"

"With you? Well . . . where?" I asked only to gain time and calm down. I knew very well what he meant.

"Where? Where? To the moon!" All at once, he grew serious. "You know what I'm asking and you know that I mean it. I've thought about it for a long time and I've come to the conclusion that it's very nice for us both when we're together. Right?"

"You're saying this out of pity, aren't you?" I laughed. "A poor victim of the war, she lost her parents in the uprising, she's all alone in the world."

"Stop it, that's horrible. You know that isn't true. It's not pity, I just want things to be nice for us. I know that together . . . Don't answer now. Think about it. I'll come tomorrow. You can tell me then. We've known each other for almost a month, and I want you to stay with me. But Ann," he didn't let go of my hand, "get rid of all those defenses. Trust me. I want to bring you up all over again, teach you to live again."

For the first time he looked like a serious, grown-up man.

"All right, Professor," I said, and then ran away. The next day the surrender came and everyone was going wild. I waited for Mike for a whole hour on the low wall in front of the camp. By the time he arrived that evening, I had lost hope. Lying on my bunk in the empty room—all the girls had gone to a party— I thought, with the army you never can tell, they might have transferred him suddenly, and goodbye! I lay there dazed, trying to recall the melody he always whistled, and which I still didn't know the name of. But I couldn't, so I tried to summon up his smile and his long funny legs. When he walked into the room,

I was very happy—but only for the second it took me to remember that today I had to tell him everything. Though I very much wanted to be rid of the burden of those three words, I was frightened. Mike seemed like a total stranger. But that feeling, too, lasted only a moment, because he said, "My God, you look like a schoolgirl, like a child, and I'm an old man." He began singing to that *Moldau* melody, "Such an old man, but so very much in love," and we laughed till tears came to our eyes. Only on the way to the Rhine did I remember the gnawing fear inside me and though the night was quite warm, I felt cold.

The river no longer looked like a silver scale; it was dark and the water babbled against the shore. From the direction of town came songs, shouts, the noise of fireworks.

I thought, what a shame to ruin this night. We should be drinking and celebrating like normal people.

"Ann," Mike said softly, "today is doubly important. Right? The war has ended and we are beginning a new life. The two of us. I know your answer; I can read it in your eyes. I know—you'll stay with me."

He kissed me tenderly on the mouth; his lips were soft and gentle.

"Michael," I said, "before I tell you I'll stay with you, you have to know the truth about me. You have to know who I am."

"Do you think I don't know? You're a small, lost child of the war. You're seventeen years old, but you're just a little girl who needs protection and tenderness."

I looked at the sky. A rain of man-made stars showered down, falling like fiery fountains. The water in the river was sparkling with color, the ruins of the town were colored, the whole night was colored.

"Michael." I looked into his eyes. Now I couldn't afford to miss even the tremor of an eyelid. "I am Jewish."

Perhaps it was because I was hearing those words for the first time in three years, those words I had carried inside myself constantly, or because none of the things I had feared registered on Mike's face, but I felt tears well up, and I opened my eyes wide so as not to burst out crying.

"And that's what you were hiding from me so carefully? Whatever for?"

I spoke quickly, feeling lighter with every word.

"You don't know, and you can't know. You don't know what it means to say, 'I am Jewish.' For three years I heard those words day and night but never, not even when I was alone, did I dare to say them aloud. Three years ago I swore that until the war ended no one would hear them from me. Do you know what it means to live in fear, lying, never speaking your own language, or thinking with your own brain, or looking with your own eyes? Michael, it's not true that my parents died in the uprising. They were killed right in front of me. I was hiding in the wardrobe that the Germans forgot—just think, they forgot!—to open. You don't know what an action means. You don't know anything, and I won't tell you. When I came out of the wardrobe, I found my parents' bodies on the floor. I ran out of the house. I left them there just as they were, it was night, deathly still. I ran to the village where friends of my father lived and they gave me their daughter Anna's birth certificate. I got on the train and got off in a big city, but there was a round-up in the station—you don't even know what a round-up is!—and they shipped me directly to Germany to do forced labor. I was lucky, very few people had such good luck, because others saw their parents' bodies and then were tortured and killed. But I milked cows, mowed grass, knew how to lie, to invent stories at the drop of a hat. I was lucky, no one found me out, and except for the few days spent in prison, I lived in peace until the end of the war. But at night I dreamed all the time that I was hiding in a wardrobe and was afraid to come out. But I don't want to tell you about it, why did I tell you? Tonight is such a joyous night, and I've ruined it completely."

His kind eyes were so sad. He didn't stop stroking my hand and I didn't want him to stop. I longed to go to sleep, I felt as if I had been in labor, with its healthy pain and healthy exhaustion.

"What's your real name?" he asked.

"Klara."

"Klara," he repeated. "Clear one . . . but you'll always be Ann to me."

The sky above us was golden and red. We could hear the noise of the rockets, and red stars were falling into the river. I bowed my head and heard that wondrous music: the beating of a human heart.

"I will do everything to make you forget that nightmare. And you will forget," Mike said after a moment. "You're very young. You'll see, time will cover over all this the way grass grows over the earth. But promise me one thing: that you will remain Ann—and not just in name. It will be better that way, believe me."

I felt a chill down to my fingertips.

"For whom?" I asked clearly, because suddenly it seemed to me that the river was making a lot of noise and that my words were drowning in that noise.

"For you, for us. The world is so strange, Ann, it will be better if no one other than me knows about Klara."

"Michael, *you too?*"

"Oh, you child, it's not a question of anti-Semitism. I have no prejudices, it'll simply be easier that way. You'll avoid a lot of problems, it'll be simpler for you to cast off the burden of your experiences. You've suffered so much already! I'm not saying this out of prejudice, but for your own good. And since you've already left it behind . . ."

The river was still roaring, the river that was flowing inside me.

"If you don't want to I won't insist. You can decide for yourself, but believe me, I have experience, it'll be easier for you this way."

He touched his lips to my hair; in the glare of the rocket exploding into light above us I saw the anxiety in his eyes. I felt cold and once again I didn't know how to cry.

"Let's not talk about this now, it's not important," he pleaded. "Not tonight, the night of the surrender . . ."

He didn't finish. He wasn't stupid.

I silently shook my head. Maybe he didn't notice, maybe he didn't understand.

The water in the river was burning with the fire of victory and in the pure air of the May night we could clearly hear the singing that welcomed the end of the war.

1728 Hours: A Time to Remember

Michael Selzer

A writer and lecturer, Michael Selzer was born in
1940 in Lahore, India, where both of his parents were
physicians. He earned a bachelor's and master's
degree from Balliol College, Oxford, and his
doctorate from the City University of New York.
Selzer has been a professor of political science at
Brooklyn College of the City University of New
York, specializing in Jewish studies. He has also
worked as a stockbroker with Lehman Brothers in
New York City. In 1979, he received the National
Jewish Book Award for *Deliverance Day: The Last
Hours at Dachau*, from which this selection is taken.

Liberation of the camps was often a tumultuous,
confusing experience, bordering on the chaotic. In
this selection, Selzer describes the liberation of
Dachau by the U.S. Army.

They poured out of their huts. Frenzied, starving,
sick. Screaming like banshees. Bumping blindly into each other, tripping, picking themselves up, and rushing forward again. Impelled by unknown reservoirs
of energy that had been filled, drop by drop, for just this occasion. Frantic
to reach the fence. Conscious of no other purpose and not recognizing any
meaning in this purpose. The heavy machine-gun fire from the towers and the
answering staccato of American carbines did not drown out their insane shrieks
but seemed to assist them. The chorus of thousands was unlike any heard before
or since, a cacophony of anguish, rage, despair, joy, and hope that combined the
wail of a funeral and the triumph of a football game and virtually every other
sound known to man.

Hopman, in better physical condition than many of the other men, pushed through the throng at the same time that he ran along with it. But he was also big enough to delay, for just a split second, a sudden surge that tumbled hundreds of men to the ground of the *Appellplatz*. And as he fell, he saw what they were trying to duck—the spectacularly rapid advance of a line of angry eruptions on the ground as an SS soldier, in a last desperate affirmation of his faith, turned his heavy machine gun away from the advancing Americans and onto the hordes of prisoners rushing to meet them. The line of bullets sped directly toward him. Desperately, shocked not only by the sight but by the drastic return of reality, he pushed his falling body to one side. But it was too late.

It was as if a white-hot poker had been drawn across the top of his skull. "Oh, God!" he shrieked. "Not now. Not now!" He fell over a body, which cushioned his fall. Incredulous despite the pain, he realized that he was not dead, and that the bullet had only grazed him. The others were on their feet again, resuming their rush across the *Appellplatz*. Hopman looked around. Fantastically, no one else seemed to have been hit—let alone killed—by that savage burst of machine-gun fire. Far from deterring the prisoners, the shots from the guard tower, after the one brief lull, renewed their bestial outpouring of sound and emotion, raising it to even greater intensity.

The Americans, too, had seen the machine gun on the tower open up on the prisoners. That unleashed the last restraints on their inhibitions. Light machine guns were brought up and within seconds had saturated the platforms on top of the guard towers with a deadly assault of lead. Now GIs stormed across the moat separating them from the towers. But even before they reached them their doors swung open and SS men came stumbling out. Their hands weren't exactly raised in surrender. Or perhaps they were. But everything happened too quickly to be sure, and, surrender or no, the Nazis were pulverized by fire from a score of rifles as they stepped out. Climbing over their corpses, the GIs rushed into the towers. More shots were heard. More Nazi corpses were thrown onto the piles outside.

The prisoners had reached the *Jourhaus* gate, and others were crowding up near the electrified fence. As each Nazi was shot, the mob let out a roar of jubilation that defied the impossible by making the incredible tumult out of which it arose seem like silence itself. Hopman, who had pushed his way against the wave of prisoners rushing toward the Americans, now stood up against a windowsill of the *Revier Block* while a Polish doctor divided his attention between the events unfolding close by and the more practical matter of stitching the wound in Hopman's head.

To their horror, the two men saw a sudden rush near the electrified fence and the brief—and to them, all too familiar—scream of a prisoner dying as the voltage surged through his body. Firing continued in several locations and did not, in fact, die down for about half an hour. But already, groups of soldiers, freed from combat in their immediate zones, were staring across the fence at the prisoners and digging in their pockets and packs for cigarettes, candy bars, and rations to throw over to them. But the savage fights that erupted as the prisoners tore at each other for these unheard-of luxuries dissuaded the GIs from continuing the handouts.

"Where's the powerhouse?" one of the Americans at the *Jourhaus* gate asked. A hundred prisoners volunteered to show the way. Cautiously, the Americans opened the gate and allowed two prisoners to step forward. They disappeared for about ten minutes. When they returned, the electricity in the wire had been disconnected.

The men milling behind the fence were the stronger and healthier prisoners. Nonetheless, from time to time their hysterical outpouring of emotion abated somewhat, from sheer exhaustion, and was transmuted into coherent expressions of joy and relief. Strangers and friends alike embraced each other. "We've made it! We've made it!" they exulted to each other in the scores of languages spoken in the camp. "Now everything will be OK." And they noticed for the first time the individual men who were their liberators. The general consensus was that the Americans were overfed, and that their helmets and asses were both far too large. Maas, hobbling up on his crutches, was distressed. He found the shooting of the SS men unnecessary, a violation of the laws of decency and war. But no less than any other man, he was overwhelmed with the desire to shake hands with an American soldier, to touch an American arm or shoulder, and to say anything, no matter how inconsequential, to an American. For this, however, he would have to wait several hours. But long afterward, the sheer magic of Americanness would remain with him.

Wiley was troubled by many cares. His men were fighting with deadly effectiveness, but they were once again close to the point where he could no longer control them. And how was he going to secure a perimeter of this size with the 150 unnerved men at his disposal? Soon another problem presented itself, one for which his military training and experience left him entirely unequipped.

While the shooting was still continuing in several zones, he was startled to see an American Jeep drive right up to the *Jourhaus* gate. A major general, whom he at once recognized as the commander of the division in the adjoining zone of combat, sat in the front seat next to the driver. In the rear seats were a lieutenant colonel and a woman—a very attractive blonde—in the uniform of a war correspondent.

Wiley set off at a trot and arrived at the *Jourhaus* gate a moment after the Jeep. He saw the woman correspondent get to her feet and jump out of the vehicle even before it had braked to a stop. She stumbled, caught herself, and then pushed past the two GIs standing by the gate. They watched passively as she fumbled with its bolt and swung the gate open.

"Shut that gate at once, for Christ's sake!" Wiley roared. All he needed now were thousands of half-crazed prisoners running all over the place. It was already too late. The woman, standing in the opened gateway, was brushed aside by a throng of prisoners who swept past her to freedom. Ludicrously, she tried to stop them. She wanted her interview.

The threat of being overwhelmed by a flood of prisoners mobilized a group of GIs nearby. Without a direct command from Wiley, they linked arms and formed a barrier across the narrow roadway leading to the gate. Slowly, and with great effort, they forced the prisoners back. Swearing and grunting, pushing as though they were dealing with a horde of animals, they nevertheless kept their cool. The problem now was to extricate the woman from this crowd. In forcing the prisoners back behind the gate, the GIs had shoved her into the compound with them.

"Get me outta here!" she shrieked, close to tears. The prisoners ignored her, their eyes focused crazily on the spectacle of American soldiers. They didn't prevent her from getting out, but they didn't open a way for her, either. Now she began to feel desperate and pushed her arms forward, as if doing a breaststroke through this ocean of bodies in an effort to reach the gate. She was taller than most of the men, and stronger, and before long had reached the metal grilles.

Wiley stared down at her. His voice trembling with fury, he said, "I should shoot you for this!" Maliciously, he let her be flattened against the gate for a few seconds. Then he opened it the few inches necessary for her to pass. Leaning with all his weight to prevent the prisoners from sweeping the gate open, and with his arm stretched across the gap to prevent anyone from escaping, he banged the grille shut again the moment she was through. He half hoped that it would graze her heel in closing, but her alacrity, and her desperation to get out, had her almost all the way back to the Jeep before Wiley had secured the heavy metal bar across the gate.

He stormed back toward her, determined to throw her out of his zone. By the time he was near her, however, she had recovered her composure and was staring up at him in a sexy, provocative fashion. "Thanks, Colonel!" She smiled, as though he had done nothing more than hold open a door for her.

"You get out of here, lady, and that's an order!" Wiley growled, turning on his heel and setting out down the road to check the situation at the guard towers.

"Colonel!" It was the general speaking. Wiley had actually forgotten about him in the absurd little drama that had just taken place. He turned back and saluted. Slowly, arrogantly, the general got out of his Jeep. He returned Wiley's salute. "Colonel, this lady here's a correspondent, and I've okayed it for her to be here to interview the VIPs in this camp she wants to do a story about."

"What VIPS, sir?"

The general seemed uncertain, but the woman answered for him. "There's Schuschnigg and Léon Blum and some of the people involved in the bomb plot against Hitler last year, and all sorts of other people who the world thought died years ago. It's a great story, Colonel, and I'm sitting on top of it. So I've gotta go inside and get my story!"

"Sorry, lady. This is all the story you're getting for now," Wiley answered brusquely. "My orders are to let no one in and no one out of this compound. You can see how crazed the men in there are, and no one's going in until things settle down here and we get medics to check them out for contagious diseases and—"

"That's OK, Colonel," the general interrupted, winking at the woman. "I'm taking over command here, and you let me worry about those things."

For a moment, Wiley was speechless. "I'm sorry, sir, but with all respect I have my orders from General Collins, who is my commanding officer, and only he can change them. Until I hear from him, I'm running the show here." He couldn't resist taking a swipe at the headline-hunting general. "Lieutenant Colonel Robert Wiley, ma'am!" He smiled at the correspondent. "Now, if you'll kindly get back into your Jeep—"

"I'm taking over here, Wiley," the general roared, "and that's a direct order."

"I'm afraid that's impossible, sir," Wiley answered. He was suddenly very conscious of the scores of men pressing up against the gate only a few feet away from him. They were getting a fine impression of the United States Army in action, he thought bitterly, hoping that they could not hear or understand the exchange that was taking place.

"You can't talk to my general that way!" the colonel who had been sitting in the back of the Jeep warned Wiley.

"Oh, yeah?" Wiley answered. "And what are you going to do about it?"

"If there wasn't a lady here, I'd show you soon enough!" the gallant colonel responded.

Wiley ignored him. "Soldier!" He beckoned a GI over to the group. The man came up and saluted. "See this lady gets safely into the Jeep, will you?" The soldier gave him the slightest hint of a grin.

"This way, lady," he said, taking the woman's elbow and guiding her the two steps back to the Jeep.

The general's face flushed. "Take your hands off her," he ordered. And then, in the next second, he whipped him across the arm with the riding crop he carried in his hand, a hard, painful blow.

The group froze. The general flushed. The woman blushed. The soldier winced but did his utmost to hide the pain. Wiley's mind momentarily went blank. He became conscious again of the prisoners at the gate and realized that in their continuing frenzy they evidently hadn't so much as noticed what had just happened. But he was also conscious of the other soldiers standing around who *had* witnessed this extraordinary scene. Wiley sensed that unless he did something drastic, his own men would do it for him.

He broke the silence. Hardly bothering to disguise the gesture, he put his hand on his hip, just above the holster in which he carried his .45. "General," he said in a flat tone, but looking his superior officer directly in the eye, "I'm ordering you out of this camp. I want you out of this camp altogether, not just the prison area here but the whole camp. Either you get out now or I'll have you thrown out. And take that lady with you!"

The general forced an expression of outrage onto his face. "I'm gonna get your hide for this," he snarled at Wiley.

Like hell you think you are, Wiley thought to himself, noticing how the general was unable to bring himself to confront him eye to eye. You're going to be hoping and praying that I don't get yours. Even in Patton's army you're not going to get away with horsewhipping a GI!

The general and his party left. Wiley took out a pack of chewing gum, helped himself to a stick, and passed the rest around. Secure the perimeter! he told himself. You've got to secure the perimeter. Keep the Krauts from getting in and the prisoners from getting out! Through the gateway he could see that the prisoners were still as excited and out of control as before. He would have to pacify them, get them organized. But later. Right now, it would be impossible to do that. And he would need Stock around to translate for him. He sent a soldier to find Stock.

"The towers are all out, Colonel," Jackson said as he came up to join him. "One of our boys got grazed in the arm, but that's the only casualty. The men are fanning out to search for Krauts hidden in the buildings. Some have already surrendered. But we understand there's more. Those sure weren't no *Volksturm* guys, Colonel. Real fanatics."

He's right, Wiley thought to himself, remembering the false intelligence report that the SS had vacated the camp. "So much for G-2," he said aloud.

Jackson smiled. "Yeah. And if that woman correspondent knew there are VIPs in the camp, how come G-2 didn't?" he added.

"I want the area behind that wall there set up for Kraut prisoners," Wiley said, pointing to a concrete wall about ten feet high that stretched across an area about fifty yards away. "Take a squad with you to guard them, and a machine gun. Leave a platoon here with me to secure the perimeter, and send the rest of the boys off to look for more Krauts."

Already a group of about twenty Germans, guarded only by three GIs, was coming down the road toward them. Surrendering Germans had become a familiar enough sight to Wiley in recent weeks. But he felt different about these men. He remembered the corpses piled outside the guard towers. Too bad they didn't get it, too, he thought to himself. The road down which the Germans, a shabby, dispirited-looking group, were walking paralleled the moat behind which the howling, shrieking mob of prisoners was still engulfed in frenzied exultation. For a brief but identifiable and distinct moment the sight of the captured Germans being paraded past them robbed the mob of its voice. An awesome, and awed, hush gripped the crowd. Dead Germans, shot out of this life in front of their eyes, was one thing for the prisoners, yet another variant of the pervasive encounter with death that they had been having for years. But this: live German soldiers, Nazi SS men, in abject, helpless surrender! This was a far more astonishing and persuasive spectacle.

But the prisoners' astonishment lasted only a moment. Their silence gave way almost at once to a vast paroxysm of jeering, hooting, derisive hatred. Even some GIs joined in, adding their catcalls to the hubbub and shaking their fists at the Nazis. Altogether a terrible sound. The Germans looked as though they would gladly have escaped from it into the jaws of hell itself. They shuffled their feet more rapidly in a desperate endeavor to block their ears to the tumult. But it was at least five minutes before they came to the end of the road and were led off behind the wall to await their captors' pleasure.

Images danced in Jackson's mind. Emaciated bodies spread out in the contortions of painful death pirouetting frantically around invisible axes. Stick figures tumbling endlessly out of their cattle cars, skulls plowed open by rifle butts. Scenes made all the madder by the silence in which they were performed. Made all the more inevitable by the movielike slow motion of their fatal gymnastics. Dead, they came to life again as jumping, screaming skeletons in striped uniforms stampeding behind a barbed-wire fence. Those little, little, helpless bodies. So little. Poor, little, helpless bodies. His anguish for them was authentic, but it also merged with deep racial memories. This, he felt sure, though without articulating the thought to himself, is what it must have been like for his Indian ancestors. This is what they must have looked like. Driven off their hunting grounds, mercilessly tracked down and exterminated by the white man. Starved and battered to death.

Wiley had taken away his command. Left him with a squad to do guard duty. He looked at the Kraut prisoners. They were being brought in in small groups, ten or fifteen at a time. Small enough groups to make out the individual faces and to sense the fear and humiliation that each man felt. He had them line up against the high concrete wall facing the machine gun on its tripod. He stood next to the gun. His men fanned out to either side of him, their rifles pointing menacingly at the Nazi prisoners.

A fresh group of Nazis was brought in. Only five men this time, but one of them was a tall, blond-haired officer in an immaculate black uniform, peaked cap, shiny boots, and all. "This here guy says he's the commander, sir," Hardwick called out. "He wants to speak to you." Jackson walked over and looked the man up and down.

Skodzensky gave a military salute, which Jackson ignored. "I am the commanding officer of the guard in the camp," he said in fluent, British-accented English. "And I herewith surrender the camp to your forces." He looked down at Jackson, perfectly at ease, it seemed, as if waiting for Jackson to thank him for his courtesy.

"Line this piece of shit up with the rest of 'em over there," Jackson said to Hardwick in a quivering voice. "And I want to see his hands higher than anyone else's." He turned and strolled back to the machine gun.

Skodzensky's arrival had an extraordinary effect on the GIs. The previous batches of Nazis had been men of all ages, but uniformly shabby and despondent-looking. Skodzensky, on the other hand, looked—and behaved—as though he were on a parade ground. There was nothing dejected or servile about his appearance, and his manner was just a little too cocky. Lined up against the wall with his men, he conveyed some of his arrogant assurance to them. Almost imperceptibly, their bearing changed, and this change did not go unnoticed by either Jackson or his men.

Up to now, the GIs had stood guard in tense silence, each man lost in his own thoughts, coping in his own way with the shock of the past couple of hours. Now, however, as though responding to the Nazis' provocative self-assurance, the men began swearing threats at their prisoners. At first they only muttered them, scarcely audibly, under their breaths. Rapidly their curses escalated—in volume as well as in intensity, fusing into a chorus whose backdrop was the distinctly audible howls and screams from the prison compound not far away.

Jackson understood that his men were going berserk with murderous rage and that there was nothing he could do about it. Not only because he had lost control of them, but because he was feeling everything they were and was losing control over himself, too.

"They're vermin, sir," Smitty, looking up from the machine gun, said to him. Tears were rolling down his cheeks. "They don't deserve to live another minute. But there's no death that's bad enough for them."

"I'd like to kill 'em with my bare hands," Jackson agreed.

"Kill 'em!" someone echoed. "Kill 'em! Kill 'em!" Others took up the cry until it seemed that the whole squad was chanting the same refrain: "Kill 'em!"

Screaming the words now, his body convulsed with sobs, Smitty let off a burst of fire from his machine gun. Noiselessly, ten or twelve Nazis slipped to the ground, dead. The spectacle did not propitiate any of the men. Without even pausing, they continued to scream. "More, more! Kill 'em all!" they yelled. Again Smitty pulled the trigger, and again Nazis fell to the ground—this time about thirty of them. Skodzensky was in this batch. But his death did not appease the GIs, either. Smitty took his time. The seconds ticked by until the suspense became unbearable. Again he opened fire, in a long, raking action that felled thirty, forty, fifty, and finally nearly eighty Nazis. Now only three remained standing, miraculously unscathed by the spray of lead. Two had their hands dutifully in the air, as they had been ordered, while a third, whether out of defiance or despair, crossed his arms in front of him and awaited his fate. Smitty, however, noticing that some of the men on the ground were wounded rather than dead, temporarily ignored the three still on their feet and directed the gun at the pile of bodies on the ground. They soon stopped twitching. Now he turned his attention to the three survivors.

"Stop that crazy bastard!" The shout rang out loud and clear despite the murderous chanting of the GIs. Seemingly out of nowhere, Wiley came charging into the scene, his holster and canteen flapping crazily at his waist. He was no more than ten or fifteen feet away when Smitty loosed off the final burst. In frustration, or because the momentum of his charge could not be broken in time, Wiley continued his dash forward and, leaping in the air, kicked Smitty with enormous force in his head. His helmet prevented the kick from shattering the soldier's skull. But the blow sent him sprawling onto the muddy ground in a daze. Even then he continued muttering, "Kill 'em, kill 'em."

But there were no more to kill. One hundred and twenty-two Nazis lay dead in a neat row along the base of the wall.

Wiley established his command post in an office on the ground floor of the *Jourhaus*, a sparse, orderly room messed up only by the shattered fragments of two large framed portraits of Hitler and Himmler which had hung on the wall behind a desk.

He felt drained. This day was unlike any in his life, and now there was passing through him a feeling unlike any he had ever felt. Or perhaps he had felt it once or twice in his life, long ago, when he was a small kid. Still, a very unfamiliar feeling, but one that he had no trouble identifying. Self-pity. Why the hell did *he* have to be subjected to all this in one day? He sighed deeply. With a vast effort of the will, he pulled himself together. The prisoners' howling continued unabated, reaching through the thick walls of the *Jourhaus* to haunt his soul. He searched for a way of calming himself. If he could get the prisoners to settle down, his own men might ease up, too, and discipline could be restored. But how to do that? He toyed with the idea of ordering the prisoners back into their barracks. But he recognized that there was nothing he could do to force them if, as seemed probable, they disobeyed the order. And in that case he would only complicate matters still further in terms of restoring discipline. Besides, the thought of ordering the prisoners into their huts was distasteful. He didn't want them to think of him as a Nazi.

And as for his own men . . . he would have to do something about Jackson and that GI at the machine gun. A court-martial, probably. Not probably, he corrected himself, but certainly. They had massacred 122 Nazis in cold blood, and that was not the kind of thing that could be tolerated in the United States Army. Cold blood? Well, hardly. He shivered, recognizing how easily he could have done the same thing. But that was no excuse. And talking of court-martials, what was he going to do about that dumb-ass general? There were probably about five separate charges that could be filed against him.

"Geez!" he muttered out loud, glad that he was alone in the room and that his men couldn't see his face right now. It's going to take a miracle to get things here straightened out, he thought to himself.

Stock came excitedly into the room, a smile breaking out on his haggard face as he said, "I was just thinking that what we need most to settle ourselves down is a real good prayer, and no sooner did I think that than this chaplain appeared out of the blue, said he'd heard we'd liberated Dachau, and wanted to come over right away to see if there was anything he could do to help. I don't know what unit he's with, sir, but he'd like to see you."

Even without seeing the chaplain, Wiley felt a great weight removed from his mind. He broke into a smile. "Show him in!" he ordered Stock.

Wiley never learned the chaplain's name. Or his denomination. "Padre," he said, when the young man was ushered in, "what we need now is just what Stock says. A real good prayer. For us. For the prisoners. For the dead."

The chaplain nodded. Without a further word, Wiley took him by the elbow to a staircase that led up to a large, turretlike structure on top of the *Jourhaus*. The landing on which they stood faced the crowded *Appellplatz* but commanded a view of the entire compound. Stock followed them a couple of seconds later, bringing with him a bullhorn that he had managed to find somewhere. He gave it to the chaplain.

For some moments, the chaplain stood facing the *Appellplatz*, his arms spread out as though he were crucified. Wiley, standing behind him, could not see his face, but he sensed the tension that held the chaplain's body rigid. Slowly, the men below saw the clergyman and began to fall silent. It was as if little pockets of calm surfaced at different points in the crowd and then rippled through it until every person on the *Appellplatz* was standing peacefully, his eyes lifted up to the crucifix on top of the *Jourhaus*. Christian eyes. Jewish eyes. Communist eyes. Agnostic eyes. It did not seem to matter to any of the prisoners who the clergyman was, what his denomination was. For each man this was a moment of mournful thanksgiving, a moment of sublime recognition.

He spoke first in English. It was, Wiley suddenly realized, the first time he'd heard the chaplain's voice. It was clear and healthy, and gave just the right quality of reassurance to his words. "Comfort ye, comfort ye my people, saith the Lord your God." His voice faltered, and he paused to regain his composure. "Comfort ye my people," he repeated. "We thank you, O God, for preserving us to this moment of deliverance. We pray that you return us speedily to our homes and to the embrace of our loved ones."

He lowered the bullhorn and gave it to Stock, who now stepped forward and translated the prayer into German, first, and then into French. When he was finished, the chaplain turned toward Wiley. Tears were rolling down both men's faces. Wordlessly, they shook hands, and the chaplain disappeared down the steps. Wiley never saw him again.

Wiley stepped forward for a clearer view of the *Appellplatz*, taking care not to intrude on the privacy of Stock's thoughts and feelings. A profound calm had settled on the crowd. Hardly a man stirred, though some turned to their neighbors and embraced each other. Some men were shaking in what appeared to Wiley to be deep, if silent, sobs. The calm settled on Wiley's mind, too. But he had never known such sadness as he now felt. "Comfort ye my people." The words echoed in his ears. For him they were associated with *The Messiah*, and thus with Christmas, and thus with warm and innocent happiness. Comfort! Where would these people find that? he wondered bitterly.

He and Stock stayed up there for many minutes after the chaplain had left, each man lost in his own thoughts and watching the crowd below slowly disperse to different parts of the compound. A soldier came up to find Wiley. He handed him a message that had just come in from division headquarters.

For Wiley it was the second miracle of the afternoon. Units of the neighboring division were coming to take over control of the prison compound, the message informed him, and would be arriving within the hour. Wiley's men were to remain at Dachau overnight, but would be responsible for security only in the part of the camp that contained the SS quarters and the workshops. Tomorrow morning, Wiley's job at Dachau would be done and he would rejoin the attack on Munich.

"Well, bless that dumb-ass general!" Wiley said to himself with a smile.

Already the first frenzied outpouring of emotions had passed, sealed off by the soothing balm of the chaplain's prayer from the *Jourhaus* tower. Now was the time to try to collect one's thoughts, to catch up with the fantastic sequence of events that had occurred during the past forty-five minutes. Deeply ingrained instincts prompted Piet Maas to leave the *Appellplatz*, that field of danger, but he was too drained to gather up the energy to hobble off back to his *Block*. A shed stood on a nearby corner of the *Appellplatz*, just in front of the *Wirtschaftsgebäude*, and he made his way slowly to it. He sat down, his back leaning heavily against the wall.

To catch his thoughts. To put some recognizable framework on what had transpired, and on his feelings. A single phrase repeated itself in his mind, either because he would not allow anything else into his consciousness or because there was nothing else, in these moments, that was possible for it. *Himmelhoch jauchzend, zum Tode betrübt.* "Divinely happy, depressed to death." It seemed inappropriate to have a German phrase in his mind at this time. Was it Goethe? he wondered, but he couldn't identify the line for sure. What does that matter? he asked himself impatiently, recognizing the appropriateness, to him, of these words—German or no. He forced himself to reach for his diary and to record the momentous happenings that had just taken place. But even with the pencil in his hand he could not begin to write. Almost idly, he turned the pages of the little book to the end. He looked down at the list of names, neatly inscribed in double columns on each page. Nearly five pages were filled with these names. Over 230 Dutchmen he had known who had not lived to see this day. Softly, he read them out as his private memorial service to his dead comrades.

His pencil was a two-colored one, black lead at one end, and red at the other. This entry, he decided, definitely called for red. He began writing:

1728. First American comes through the
entrance. Dachau free!!! Indescribable
happiness. Insane howling.

He paused, uncertain of how to continue. Howling didn't seem to go with happiness; but then, as he recognized, *Himmelhoch jauchzend* didn't go with *zum Tode betrübt*, either, but that was how things were.

He tried to continue the entry; there seemed so much to record—the things he had seen, his feelings. But words would not come. He began recalling incidents and found that doing so at last enabled him to put some words down on paper. Briefly, he jotted them down. How the first men to reach the *Jourhaus* broke through the door reserved for SS personnel and, climbing to the second floor, threw portraits of Hitler and Himmler out of the window to the crowd gathering below. He recorded that, and the surrender of the first German soldiers. "Indescribable" was the only word he could find for the sight of them marching forward with their hands in the air. Although he had not been able to get close to the fence, he had succeeded, somehow, in catching one of the cigarettes that the GIs threw over the wire to them. It was, he noticed, a Camel. He smoked it then and there, delighting in the luxurious indifference he felt to the great value it had in the prison's barter economy. He recorded the Camel in his diary too.

He paused again. It all seemed so trivial. Trivial? It suddenly occurred to him that to find such things trivial you had to be alive and free—and he was alive and free! He had made it through, and he was alive! "It's happened," he told himself. "I've survived. It's over, and I'm alive!" He began crying.

Minutes later, he realized that the faithful Plaga had found him and was sitting on the ground next to him. "Up we get again, Piet," Plaga said presently. He laughed. "I seem to have said that ten times to you today. But look—the Americans are entering the compound!"

Maas looked up and dried his eyes. By the *Jourhaus* gate a mob of two or three hundred men was once again milling around excitedly. A big cheer went up from the crowd, and a moment later a GI was lifted up into the air and balanced precariously on the thin shoulders of some of the prisoners. Arms reached up to touch him. Even from this distance Maas could detect the man's discomfort and embarrassment. He saw the soldier self-consciously wave his arms to acknowledge the prisoners' greetings. The gesture displaced his weight in a way that almost caused him to topple over backward, but he was caught by other prisoners and let gently down onto his feet. Rather brusquely, now, he pushed some of the men aside and shook himself free. Prisoners struggled to reach him, hungering to shake his hand, even just to touch his uniform. The GI looked bewildered and a bit frightened. Soon, however, other Americans came in to join him, and there were enough American hands for the crowd to shake. Shortly after, Maas and Plaga saw Connally step out of the crowd, flanked by two Americans and followed by three more. Since neither of the two in front carried rifles or submachine guns, Maas guessed that they were officers. They headed down the *Appellplatz* toward the *Lagerstrasse*.

Wiley wondered who this man Connally was. What a story *he* must have to tell, he thought to himself. He was quite certain, though, that he did not want to hear it now. He looked across at Frazer. He seemed like a good man, he decided, and he'd kept his unit together pretty well. Better than I did, he thought bitterly.

"I warned my men at the front gate that they'd never seen anything like they were about to see," Frazer said to Wiley. "But when they saw that train back there, I thought they'd go berserk. I'm glad you had to shoot it out with the Krauts, Wiley, because I'm telling you, I don't think my boys would have taken one of them alive!" His voice trembled with emotion.

My boys didn't take one of them alive, Wiley was about to say, but checked himself. Instead, he said, "I know what you mean."

"There have been lots of trains like that in the last few months," Connally broke in. "They've come from all over, sometimes weeks on the way. I don't think there's been one in which as many as half of the people arrived alive."

"Are there likely to be more Krauts around?" Frazer asked.

"I'd guess there are dozens of them here. Some are hiding inside the *Lager* as prisoners. Others, we think, are still in the administrative buildings. And there are also a number of prisoners who collaborated with the SS. Many of them are as guilty as the SS."

"Well, you just tell us who they are and we'll round 'em up," Frazer said with enthusiasm.

There was a long pause. Halfway across the *Appellplatz* Connally turned to face Frazer. "I'm not sure, Colonel," he said ironically, "how many of them will be alive until we are able to point them out to you."

Just then a hideous shriek rang out, almost instantly to be engulfed in an angry roar from the direction of the *Lagerstrasse*.

"This way, if you please, gentlemen," Connally said quietly.

Silence

Tadeusz Borowski

A survivor of Auschwitz, Tadeusz Borowski is the author of *This Way for the Gas, Ladies and Gentlemen*, from which the following selection is taken. For additional biographical information on Borowski, see page 277.

Survivors responded to liberation in many different ways. Here, Borowski tells a horrifying tale of revenge against a particularly brutal guard by former camp prisoners.

At last they seized him inside the German barracks, just as he was about to climb over the window ledge. In absolute silence they pulled him down to the floor and panting with hate dragged him into a dark alley. Here, closely surrounded by a silent mob, they began tearing at him with greedy hands.

Suddenly from the camp gate a whispered warning was passed from one mouth to another. A company of soldiers, their bodies leaning forward, their rifles on the ready, came running down the camp's main road, weaving between the clusters of men in stripes standing in the way. The crowd scattered and vanished inside the blocks. In the packed, noisy barracks the prisoners were cooking food pilfered during the night from neighbouring farmers. In the bunks and in the passageways between them, they were grinding grain in small flour-mills, slicing meat on heavy slabs of wood, peeling potatoes and throwing the peels on to the floor. They were playing cards for stolen cigars, stirring batter for pancakes, gulping down hot soup, and lazily killing fleas. A stifling odour of sweat hung in the air, mingled with the smell of food, with smoke and with steam that liquified along the ceiling beams and fell on the men, the bunks and the food in large, heavy drops, like autumn rain.

There was a stir at the door. A young American officer with a tin helmet on his head entered the block and looked with curiosity at the bunks and the tables.

He wore a freshly pressed uniform; his revolver was hanging down, strapped in an open holster that dangled against his thigh. He was assisted by the translator who wore a yellow band reading "interpreter" on the sleeve of his civilian coat, and by the chairman of the Prisoners' Committee, dressed in a white summer coat, a pair of tuxedo trousers and tennis shoes. The men in the barracks fell silent. Leaning out of their bunks and lifting their eyes from the kettles, bowls and cups, they gazed attentively into the officer's face.

"Gentlemen," said the officer with a friendly smile, taking off his helmet—and the interpreter proceeded at once to translate sentence after sentence—"I know, of course, that after what you have gone through and after what you have seen, you must feel a deep hate for your tormentors. But we, the soldiers of America, and you, the people of Europe, have fought so that law should prevail over lawlessness. We must show our respect for the law. I assure you that the guilty will be punished, in this camp as well as in all the others. You have already seen, for example, that the S.S. men were made to bury the dead."

". . . right, we could use the lot at the back of the hospital. A few of them are still around," whispered one of the men in a bottom bunk.

". . . or one of the pits," whispered another. He sat straddling the bunk, his fingers firmly clutching the blanket.

"Shut up! Can't you wait a little longer? Now listen to what the American has to say," a third man, stretched across the foot of the same bunk, spoke in an angry whisper. The American officer was now hidden from their view behind the thick crowd gathered at the other end of the block.

"Comrades, our new Kommandant gives you his word of honour that all the criminals of the S.S. as well as among the prisoners will be punished," said the translator. The men in the bunks broke into applause and shouts. In smiles and gestures they tried to convey their friendly approval of the young man from across the ocean.

"And so the Kommandant requests," went on the translator, his voice turning somewhat hoarse, "that you try to be patient and do not commit lawless deeds, which may only lead to trouble, and please pass the sons of bitches over to the camp guards. How about it, men?"

The block answered with a prolonged shout. The American thanked the translator and wished the prisoners a good rest and an early reunion with their dear ones. Accompanied by a friendly hum of voices, he left the block and proceeded to the next.

Not until after he had visited all the blocks and returned with the soldiers to his headquarters did we pull our man off the bunk—where covered with blankets and half-smothered with the weight of our bodies he lay gagged, his face buried in the straw mattress—and dragged him on to the cement floor under the stove, where the entire block, grunting and growling with hatred, trampled him to death.

Chorus of the Rescued

Nelly Sachs

Nelly Sachs, a German
poet and playwright,
was born in Berlin on
December 10, 1891. With
the help of the Swedish
Nobel Laureate Selma
Lagerlof, she and her
mother escaped from
Germany in 1940. Sachs
became a powerful and
poignant voice for
alerting the world to the
conditions in Germany.
In 1966, her work was
honored when she
shared the Nobel Prize
for Literature with S. Y.
Agnon. She died on May
12, 1970, in Stockholm.
She is the author of *O the
Chimneys!* from which
the following poem is
reprinted.

   As Sachs relates in
this poem, many sur-
vivors, though rescued,
would never be the same.

We, the rescued,
From whose hollow bones death had begun
   to whittle his flutes,
And on whose sinews he had already stroked
   his bow—
Our bodies continue to lament
With their mutilated music.
We, the rescued,
The nooses wound for our necks still dangle
before us in the blue air—
Hourglasses still fill with our dripping blood.
We, the rescued,
The worms of fear still feed on us.
Our constellation is buried in dust.
We, the rescued,
Beg you:
Show us your sun, but gradually.
Lead us from star to star, step by step.
Be gentle when you teach us to live again.
Lest the song of a bird,
Or a pail being filled at the well,
Let our badly sealed pain burst forth again
and carry us away—
We beg you:
Do not show us an angry dog, not yet—
It could be, it could be
That we will dissolve into dust—
Dissolve into dust before your eyes.
For what binds our fabric together?
We whose breath vacated us,
Whose soul fled to Him out of that midnight
Long before our bodies were rescued
Into the ark of the moment.
We, the rescued,
We press your hand
We look into your eye—
But all that binds us together now is leave-
   taking,
The leave-taking in the dust
Binds us together with you.

chapter 8

The Days After

Liberation of the camps brought freedom to the imprisoned, release to the hidden, and return to the exiles, yet most of the survivors had no place to return to: their homes, businesses, and possessions were gone or now belonged to others. While the victims of the Holocaust knew that they had been spared from almost certain death, they did not know what they had been liberated to, what the future would be. Certainly, for the older survivors, the world that they had known prior to 1933 was altered forever. But for some of the younger survivors, liberation was often even more unsettling, because they had never known life without danger, hardships, and persecution. For all survivors, the future was disconcerting and even frightening. In addition, many survivors suffered from guilt that they had survived while so many others had perished. This was especially true for the sole survivors of families.

Many survivors had nothing to return to; their homes were destroyed and their possessions stolen. In some cases, wealthy Jews had asked Christian friends to protect and keep their possessions; unfortunately, when many of these Jews returned to reclaim their possessions, they were disappointed. Some keepers had themselves fled or died, while others had sold the possessions to stave off wartime hardships. In some cases, the keepers refused to return the possessions to their rightful owners.

Complicating matters even further for the survivors was that they were returning either to a defeated nation or to countries that had been occupied and, in many cases, continued to be occupied. Much of Western Europe had been a battlefield; food and supplies were not readily available; transportation and fuel were scarce but in high demand. The liberation and its aftermath signaled the end of one type of hardship but did not bring with it a return to a normal way of life.

Many of the people released from concentration camps ended up in displaced person camps; others wandered from village to village, city to city, or country to country, searching for surviving relatives. Many survivors waited for the papers that would enable them to immigrate to new countries or found other ways of making new lives for themselves. Even as they prepared for a new life, many survivors continued to hope for reunions that seldom happened. The hope that they would find a relative or a friend who also had survived sustained a number of the survivors.

A tragic footnote to the Holocaust was that, in the six months following the war, over five hundred Jews were killed in Poland as the anti-Semitic feelings that the Nazis had fueled continued to rage in Eastern Europe.

The selections in Chapter 8 explore varied experiences that survivors endured at the end of World War II. These stories provide valuable insights into a chapter of the Holocaust experience that is often overlooked.

Steps beyond the Grave

Simon Wiesenthal

A Holocaust survivor, Simon Wiesenthal is the
author of numerous books, including *Krystyna: The
Tragedy of the Polish Resistance* and *The Sunflower*, a
collection of personal narratives about the
Holocaust. The following selection is reprinted from
Hunter and Hunted: Human History of the Holocaust,
edited by Gerd Korman. For additional biographical
information on Wiesenthal, see page 136.

Former concentration camp prisoners were often
ill and depressed during the days immediately
following their liberation. The desire to find their
families became paramount. In this memoir,
Wiesenthal describes the experiences he and his wife
encountered as they tried to find each other.

It was ten o'clock on the morning of May 5, 1945, when I saw a big gray tank with a white star on its side and the American flag waving from the turret. I stood on the windswept square that had been, until an hour earlier, the courtyard of the Mauthausen concentration camp. The day was sunny, with a scent of spring in the air. Gone was the sweetish smell of burned flesh that had always hovered over the yard.

The night before, the last SS men had run away. The machinery of death had come to a stop. In my room a few dead people were lying on their bunks. They hadn't been taken away this morning. The crematorium no longer operated.

I do not remember how I'd got from my room into the courtyard. I was hardly able to walk. I was wearing my faded striped uniform with a yellow *J* in a yellow-red double triangle. Around me I saw other men in striped dungarees.

Some were holding small flags, waving at the Americans. Where had they gotten the flags from? Did the Americans bring them? I shall never know.

The tank with the white star was about a hundred yards in front of me. I wanted to touch the star, but I was too weak. I had survived to see this day, but I couldn't make the last hundred yards. I remember taking a few steps, and then my knees gave way and I fell on my face.

Somebody lifted me up. I felt the rough texture of an olive-drab American uniform brush against my bare arms. I couldn't speak; I couldn't even open my mouth. I pointed toward the white star, I touched the cold, dusty armor with my hands, and then I fainted.

When I opened my eyes after what seemed a long time, I was back on my bunk. The room seemed changed. There was only one man on each bunk, no longer three or four, and the dead had been taken away. There was an unfamiliar smell in the air. It was DDT. They brought in big kettles with soup. This was *real* soup, and it tasted delicious. I took too much of it—my stomach wasn't used to such nourishing fare—and I got violently sick.

The next days went by in a pleasant apathy. Most of the time I dozed on my bunk. American doctors in white coats came to look at us. We were given pills and more food—soup, vegetables, meat. I still was so weak that a friend had to help me when I wanted to go out. I had survived, I didn't have to force myself to be strong any longer; I had seen the day I'd prayed for all these years, but now I was weaker than ever. "A natural reaction," said the doctors.

I made an effort to get up and walk out alone. As I shuffled through a dark corridor, a man jumped at me and knocked me down. I collapsed and lost consciousness. I came to on my bunk, and an American doctor gave me something. Two friends sat next to me. They had picked me up in the corridor and carried me to my bunk. They said that a Polish trusty had beaten me. Perhaps he was angry because I was still alive.

People in room A said I must report the trusty to the American authorities. We were free men now, no longer *Untermenschen*. The next day my friends accompanied me to an office in the building that had formerly been the camp headquarters. A handwritten sign WAR CRIMES was on the door. We were told to wait in a small anteroom. Somebody brought me a chair, and I sat down.

Through the open doors, I saw American officers behind desks who interrogated SS men who stood at attention in front of them. Several former prisoners worked as typists. An SS man was brought into the room. Instinctively I turned my head sideward so he wouldn't see me. He had been a brutal guard; when he walked through the corridor and a prisoner did not step aside quickly and snap to attention, the SS man would whip the prisoner's face with the riding crop he always carried. The sight of this man had always brought cold sweat to the back of my neck.

Now I stared; I couldn't believe it. The SS man was trembling, just as we had trembled before him. His shoulders were hunched, and I noticed that he wiped the palms of his hands. He was no longer a superman; he made me think of a trapped animal. He was escorted by a Jewish prisoner—a *former* prisoner.

I kept staring, fascinated. I didn't hear what was said as the SS man stood before the American interrogator. He could hardly stand at attention, and there was sweat on his forehead. The American officer motioned with his hand and an American soldier took the SS man away. My friends said that all SS men were being taken to a big concrete pillbox, where they were to be kept under guard until they were tried. I made my report on the Polish trusty. My friends testified that they had found me lying unconscious in the corridor. One of the American doctors also testified. Then we went back to our room. That night the trusty apologized to me in front of our comrades, and extended his hand. I accepted his apology but did not give him my hand.

The trusty wasn't important. He was already part of the past. I kept thinking of the scene at the office. Lying on my bunk with my eyes closed, I saw the trembling SS man—a contemptible, frightened coward in his black uniform. For years that uniform had been the symbol of terror. I had seen apprehensive German soldiers during the war (the soldiers, too, were afraid of the SS men), but never a frightened SS man. I had always thought of them as the strong men, the elite, of a perverted regime. It took me a long time to understand what I had seen: the supermen became cowards the moment they were no longer protected by their guns. They were through.

I got up from my bunk and walked out of the room. Behind the crematorium, SS men were digging graves for our 3000 comrades who had died of starvation and exhaustion after the arrival of the Americans. I sat down, looking at the SS men. Two weeks ago they would have beaten me half-dead if I had dared look at them. Now they seemed to be afraid to walk past me. An SS man begged an American soldier for a cigarette. The soldier thew away the cigarette that he'd been smoking. The SS man bent down, but another SS man was faster and got hold of the butt, and the two SS men began to scuffle until the soldier told them to get away.

Only two weeks had gone by, and the elite of the Thousand Year Reich were fighting for a cigarette butt. How many years had it been since we had been given a cigarette? I walked back to my room and looked around. Most of my comrades were lying apathetically on their bunks. After the moment of exhilaration many of them suffered attacks of depression. Now that they knew they were going to live, they were aware of the senselessness of their lives. They had been spared—but they had no one to live for, no place they could go back to, no pieces they could pick up. . . .

[Days later]. They would ask each other: "Who else is alive?" One couldn't understand that one had survived, and it was beyond comprehension that others should still be alive. They would sit on the steps to the office [of the Jewish Central Committee in Linz] and talk to one another. "Can it be that my wife, my mother, my child is alive? Some of my friends, some of the people in the town where we lived?"

There was no mail service. The few available telephone lines were restricted to military use. The only way to find out whether someone was alive was to go and look. Across Europe a wild tide of frantic survivors was flowing. People were hitchhiking, getting short jeep rides, or hanging onto dilapidated railway coaches without windows or doors. They sat in huddled groups on haycarts, and some just walked. They would use any means to get a few miles closer to their destination. To get from Linz to Munich, normally a three-hour railroad trip, might take five days. Many of them didn't really know where to go. To the place where one had been with his family before the war? To the concentration camp where the family had last been heard of? Families had been torn apart too suddenly to make arrangements for the day when it would be all over.

. . . And yet the survivors continued their pilgrimage of despair, sleeping on highways or in railroad stations, waiting for another train, another horse-drawn cart to come along, always driven by hope. "Perhaps someone is still alive. . . ." Someone might tell where to find a wife, a mother, children, a brother—or whether they were dead. Better to know the truth than to know nothing. The desire to find one's people was stronger than hunger, thirst, fatigue. Stronger even than the fear of border patrols, of the CIC and NKVD, of men saying "Let's see your papers."

The first thing we did at the Committee in Linz was to make up lists of known survivors. People who came in to ask for someone were asked where *they* were from. They were nomads, vagabonds, beggars. But once upon a time they had had a home, a job, savings. Their names were put on the list of some town or village. Slowly the lists grew. People from Poland, Czechoslovakia, or Germany brought us lists. We gave them copies of our lists. We worked long into the night to copy these lists. Early in the morning, the first people would arrive to look up names. Some waited all night to get in. Behind a man another waited for a glance that might mean hope or despair. Some people were impatient and there were brawls. Once two men began to scuffle because each wanted the same list. In the end they tore up the precious piece of paper. Another time two men started to argue, their eyes glued to the list in the hands of a third man. Each wanted it next. Suddenly they looked at each other and gasped, and the next moment they were in each others' arms. They were brothers and each had been trying to find the other for weeks.

And there were moments of silent despair when someone discovered that the person he was looking for had been there only a few days before, looking for him. They had missed each other. Where should one look now? Other people scanned the lists of survivors, hoping against hope to find the names of people they had seen killed before their very eyes. Everybody had heard of some miracle.

I hardly ever looked at the lists. I didn't believe in miracles. I knew that all my people were dead. After the Pole from Warsaw had told me what happened in Topiel Street, I had no hope that my wife was alive. When I thought of her, I thought of her body lying under a heap of rubble, and I wondered whether they had found the bodies and buried her. In a moment of illogical hope I wrote to the International Committee of the Red Cross in Geneva. They promptly answered that my wife was dead. I knew that my mother did not have a grave; she had died in the death camp of Belzec. I hoped that at least my wife might have a grave.

One night, when I had nothing else to do, I looked at a list of survivors from the Polish city of Cracow and found the name of an old friend from Buczacz, Dr. Biener. I wrote him a letter. I told him that my wife's body might still be lying under the ruins of the house in Topiel Street. I asked him to go to Warsaw and look at what was left of the house. There was no mail service to Poland, so I gave the letter to a man who specialized in getting things through Czechoslovakia to Poland.

I didn't know that a miracle had indeed happened. My wife told me all about it later. When the German flame-thrower squads had closed in on Topiel Street, in the darkness and confusion my wife and a few other people had managed to get away. For a while they hid. After the battle of Warsaw, the few survivors were driven together by the Germans and assigned to forced-labor transports for Germany. My wife was sent to a factory in Heiligenhaus, near Gelsenkirchen in the Rhineland, where they made machine guns for the Wehrmacht. The Polish laborers were decently housed and fed, and the Gestapo left them alone. The Germans knew that the war was lost.

My wife was liberated by the British, who marched into Gelsenkirchen on April 11, 1945. (That day I was lying on my bunk in the death block of Mauthausen.) My wife went to the British authorities and reported that she was Cyla Wiesenthal, a Jewish woman from Poland. Six women in her group turned out to be Jewish, but they had not known of each other. One of them told my wife that she was going home.

"Home?" asked my wife. "Where is home?"

"To Poland, of course. Why don't you come with me?"

"What for? My husband was killed by the Gestapo in Lwow last year. Poland has become a large cemetery to me."

"Have you proof that he's dead?"

"No," said my wife, "but . . ."

"Don't believe it. Now, suppose he were alive: where is he likely to be?"

Cyla thought it over. "In Lwow, I would think. We spent the years before the war there."

"Lwow is now in the Soviet Union," said her friend. "Let's go there."

The two women left Gelsenkirchen in June 1945. (At one point on her journey, we later discovered, my wife had been less than thirty miles from Linz.) After an arduous trip, they reached the Czechoslovak-Polish border at Bohumin. They were told that a train left that night for Lwow. They got on the overcrowded cars and arrived in Cracow, Poland, in the morning. It was announced that there would be a four-hour stop.

At the Cracow railroad station somebody stole my wife's suitcase with everything she owned. That was her homecoming. To cheer her up, her friend suggested that they walk into town. Perhaps they would meet someone they had once known. The beautiful old city of the Polish kings looked deserted and ghostlike that morning. Suddenly my wife heard her name called out, and recognized a man named Landek, who had been a dentist in Lwow. (Landek now lives in America.) For a while they exchanged hectic questions and unfinished sentences, as always happened when survivors met. Landek had heard that Simon Wiesenthal was dead. He told my wife to talk to Dr. Biener. He might know more.

"Dr. Biener from Buczacz?" asked my wife. "Is he in Cracow?"

"He lives five minutes from here." Landek gave her the address and hurried away.

When they came to Dr. Biener's house, my wife asked her friend to wait downstairs. She walked up the stairway with a heavy heart. On the third floor she saw a sign reading Biener and rang the bell. The door was opened. For a moment she saw Dr. Biener's face and heard a muffled cry. Then the door was quickly shut again.

"Dr. Biener!" my wife shouted, banging her fists against the door. "Open up! It's Cyla. Cyla Wiesenthal from Buczacz!"

The door was opened. Dr. Biener was pale, as if he were seeing a ghost.

"But—you are dead," he said, "I just got a letter. . . ."

"I'm very much alive," my wife said angrily. "Of course I *look* half-dead, after spending the night on the train."

"Come in," Dr. Biener said hastily, and closed the door. "You don't understand. Yesterday I had a letter from your husband. Simon writes that you died under the ruins of a house in Warsaw."

Now my wife got pale. "Simon? But he's dead. He's been dead for over a year."

Dr. Biener shook his head. "No, no, Cyla. Simon is alive, in Linz, Austria. Here, read the letter."

They called my wife's friend from downstairs. She was not at all surprised. Hadn't she told Cyla that her husband might be alive? They sat down and talked, and when they remembered the train it was much too late. If my letter hadn't reached Dr. Biener the day before, if my wife hadn't met Landek, if Dr. Biener hadn't been at home, the two women would have gone back to the station and continued their journey to the Soviet Union. My wife might have been sent into the interior of the USSR, and it would have taken years to find her again.

My wife stayed in Cracow, and tried to get in touch with me. Dr. Biener knew several illegal couriers who would carry letters for a fee, with no guarantee of delivery. She wrote three letters and gave them to three men working different routes. I received one of them, from a man who had come to Linz by way of Budapest—which is quite a detour.

I'll never forget the moment when I saw Cyla's handwriting on the envelope. I read the letter so many times that I knew it by heart. I went to see the OSS captain for whom I was then working and asked him to give me travel orders to Cracow. He didn't like the idea of my going to Poland. He said I might never be able to come back. He suggested we think it over until next morning.

I didn't go to the Jewish Committee that afternoon. I was happy and perhaps feeling a little guilty at being a happy man among so many unhappy people. I wanted to be alone. I knew a peasant not far from where I lived who had a few horses. I thought of my summer vacations in Dolina, where I loved to ride horses. I asked the peasant to let me have a horse for an hour. I forgot that I was a little older and not yet in good physical condition. I mounted the horse. Something went wrong. I suppose the horse sensed at once that I was still weak. I was thrown and landed in a potato field with a broken ankle.

I had to stay in bed. That settled the matter of my projected journey to Poland. I asked a Jewish friend, Dr. Felix Weisberg, to go to Cracow and gave him a letter for my wife. He promised to bring her back to Linz. My OSS friends made out the necessary travel documents for her, so she would have no difficulty in getting into the U.S. Zone of Austria.

They were fine travel documents, but unfortunately my wife never received them. Crossing Czechoslovakia on his way to Poland, Dr. Weisberg was warned that there was an NKVD roadblock ahead, with "very strict controls." He got nervous; if the Soviet secret police found any American *dokumenty* on him, they might arrest him as a spy. He destroyed the documents. Too late he realized that he had also destroyed my wife's address in Cracow. As it turned out, NKVD didn't even search him. In Cracow, he went to the local Jewish Committee and put a notice on the bulletin board. Mrs. Cyla Wiesenthal, the wife of Simon Wiesenthal, was asked to get in touch with Dr. Felix Weisberg, who would take her to her husband in Linz.

My wife saw the notice the next morning and went to see Dr. Weisberg. She was not the first visitor. Two other women were already there, each claiming to be the one and only Cyla Wiesenthal. A lot of people in Poland were trying to get to Austria, hoping they might later try to get to America. Poor Felix Weisberg had a trickier problem than the mythological Paris. Weisberg didn't know my wife. In all the excitement preceding his sudden departure, I had foolishly forgotten to give him her exact description. He faced the unpleasant possibility of bringing back the wrong Mrs. Wiesenthal. Weisberg told me later that he'd asked each of the three women to describe how I looked. Two seemed rather vague, but one knew a lot of details, naturally. Also, Weisberg admitted to me, he'd liked her best. He decided to take a chance and bought false travel papers for her in the black market.

One evening, late in 1945, I was early in bed as usual. My broken ankle still gave me a lot of trouble. There was a knock at the door. Felix Weisberg came in, confused and embarrassed. It took him quite a while to explain how he'd foolishly thrown away the American documents, and his dilemma over three women each claiming to be Mrs. Cyla Wiesenthal.

"I brought one of them with me. She's waiting downstairs. Now, don't get excited, Simon. If she isn't your wife, I'm going to marry her myself."

"You?"

"Yes, my word of honor. You're under no obligation whatsoever. To tell the truth, I thought it safest to bring the one I liked best. That way, I knew even if she was not your wife I would —"

But then she came into the room, and Felix Weisberg, God bless him, knew that he could not marry her.

Searching

Dov Beril Edelstein

Dov Beril Edelstein grew up in a religious family in the Carpathian Mountain region of Hungary. He was ordained as a rabbi the day before the Germans invaded Hungary. He and his family were sent to the ghetto and later were deported to Auschwitz. He is a member of the Rabbinical Assembly and has served a number of congregations in the United States and Canada. He is the author of *Worlds Torn Asunder*, from which the following personal narrative is taken. Edelstein and his wife live in Israel.

Liberation did not automatically bring stability and safety. Political alliances in Europe continued to shift for some time. In this selection, Edelstein describes his encounters with various people as he recovered from concentration camp imprisonment and began the search for his family.

A most consuming urge immediately following liberation was the need to search for food. An insatiable passion to eat loomed high above all other desires. This need of ours for food, however, was less than matched by the ability of our British liberators to feed us. They may not have been provided with what was needed for such a gigantic task. The fact remains that for several days following the liberation, there was no noticeable change in our situation. David and I were fortunate, though, to have established contact with the Hungarian soldier. From our first visit to the village we brought back, among other things, a skinned and cleaned rabbit, ready for cooking, an atonement offering from one of the villagers. Nor did we forget to ask for some eggs and sugar, a goodwill offering for our new friend and benefactor, so that our secret path would be kept open for future trips. One of our biggest problems upon returning to the camp was how to conceal our provisions so that we wouldn't be attacked and robbed by the starving inmates who were roaming the streets in search of food.

Our first encounter with German civilians in their home was dramatic. It was about eight o'clock in the morning. Only the lady, in her mid-thirties, her two young children, and an elderly woman were at home. David's and my sudden appearance threw them into panic and shock. We must have been the first *Musulmen* they had encountered face-to-face. They looked at us dumbfounded and speechless, examining us nervously from top to bottom, not knowing what to say or what to expect. They seemed tremendously relieved when I asked whether we could have something to eat. David and I then were served our first normal breakfast in almost a year. To us it looked more like a royal banquet. Both women showed great eagerness to serve us well and to please us, while the two children looked at us in amazement. No questions were asked and no meaningful conversation developed, as both parties, hosts and guests alike, sensed the uniqueness of the encounter.

It must have been that somehow the lady managed to summon her husband home from wherever he was. Only then did I notice that while David and I were glutting ourselves with our royal banquet, the older of the two children had disappeared. He now returned with his father, a robust farmer of about forty, quite tall, and heavily mustached. Not overly successful in trying to conceal his surprise, Herr Gerhard went out of his way to make us welcome and extend his hospitality. When David and I had finished breakfast, our host went into another room and soon returned with a small, fancy box in his hand. With a gesture of special importance he opened the box and took out of it two enormous cigars, handing one to me and one to David. Never before had I smoked either cigars or cigarettes. As I took the first inhalation of the aromatic smoke, I almost suffocated. For a long time I continued coughing and choking intermittently. Herr Gerhard hit me on my back and pressed with his hands against my chest, while the two ladies and the children looked on in terror. When I eventually relaxed and threw the cigar away with disdain, a loud laugh of relief burst forth from everyone present, and the atmosphere became less tense.

The spontaneous group relaxation surely had an easing impact on Herr Gerhard, who now produced from somewhere a pitcher full of beer and three schooners. Placing these at the center of the table, he seated himself directly across from the place where David and I were sitting. Filling up the schooners with gold-brilliant, foaming beer, our host imbibed a long sip of the liquid, leaving his schooner half-empty, then wiped his mouth with his sleeve. Looking alternately at David and at me, Herr Gerhard made it obvious that he was about to say something, but he took his time and carefully chose his words. Then, putting his right hand on his chest, he started.

"What the German people have done to the Jews is atrocious and cannot be excused. I know we shall have to pay a heavy price for it. Yet I would like you to believe me, that we, the populace, the simple people, were not aware of what was happening. We simply did not know. Please, believe me."

On that morning when I had for the first time breathed anew free air and eaten my first normal breakfast, I was not, either physically nor emotionally, up to entering into a historical debate on the guilt or the lack of it of the German people. Nor did I possess at that time adequate and comprehensive information on what really had happened. I had not read a newspaper nor listened to a radio since my deportation from Szatmár about a year earlier. Yet I could not refrain from asking my friendly host how it was possible for him and the simple people of his village not to know what was going on within seeing distance of their homes. How could they not have been aware of the transports of thousands of prisoners arriving by train day and night? How could they be oblivious to the hundreds of dead corpses strewn all over their fields? Yet Herr Gerhard kept on insisting they knew nothing. So we left it at that. Before we departed, our host showed us a rabbit he had shot early that morning and asked us to come back later for the animal, after he had time to skin and clean it.

Some three weeks following the liberation, the first signs of life from other camps began reaching us through the lists of survivors' names that were posted at our camp office. The first published list impressed on me the frightful realities I was now to face. I knew that the search for surviving parents, brothers, and relatives would be much more traumatic and exhausting than the search for food. I also knew by then that not all the names I was searching for would ever appear on the lists. With trepidation and anxiety I stood in a long line of people with somber looks, who, like me, had come to search for the names of survivors on a list that carried a message of life, yet also implied death. From time to time, shouts of joy burst forth from the mouth of one who had just read the familiar name of one of his relatives. Many, however, left sullen and dejected.

When my turn came, I read the names over once, and then again, but found none of the names for which I was searching. In three days, a new list arrived in the camp and was posted for public view. Again, I found none of the names of my family. When the third list was posted and I read it, my blood rose to my head, and my heart pounded heavily. I saw the name Frida Herskovitz.

Frida was my first cousin; our mothers had been sisters. She too had been taken to Auschwitz from the Szatmár ghetto. According to the list, she was now at a place called Salzwedel. Without further delay, I decided to go and find her.

The best transportation system operating in Germany at that time was hitchhiking. A German truck driver took me halfway and dropped me off in some city near the office of the British military commandant. When I told the officers that I had just found the first, and perhaps the only, survivor of my family, they seemed moved and eager to help. Before anything else, however, the commandant ordered the attendant sergeant to serve me a meal. While I ate, the officers discussed various options of transportation to Salzwedel. When I finished, the sergeant gave me two packs of English cigarettes and five bars of chocolate, all of which I promptly put into my pockets for future bartering.

While I was eating, I noticed in the room a man wearing a uniform unlike the British military uniforms, which I had already learned to recognize by that time. I identified this person by the shiny metal letters attached to his lapel that read U.S. Army. It was the first time I had seen an American. Since we were in the British Zone, I assumed that the American was there on some official business. When the U.S. captain learned about my case, he came over to me, introduced himself, and told me that he was on his way to Salzwedel but had stopped at this place for some routine business, and that he would be glad to take me along in a short while. The fine meal I had been served, the chocolate and the cigarettes, and now the good news I heard from the American captain made my day.

Hardly was I seated in the U.S. Army jeep when I thought I was flying in a helicopter. In order not to be thrown out of the jeep, I had to hold fast to my seat with both of my hands. Following a ride of approximately two hours, I saw a sign that read "Salzwedel."

While I was hitchhiking, and while I was riding in the American jeep, a gnawing doubt disturbed my peace of mind. The list that contained the name Frida Herskovitz did not give any additional information about her, except the fact that she was at Salzwedel. It could be that she was not my cousin but another person with the same name. The captain, to whom I revealed my doubts, tried to assure me that it was, indeed, my cousin. He also promised not to just drop me off at camp, but to stay with me until I found Frida.

We arrived at a place that had long rows of nice-looking brick buildings, many trees, green lawns, and many flower beds. Well-dressed girls in their upper teens and young ladies were strolling among the blooming trees or resting on the well-tended lawns. Pleasant sounds of music coming from various directions permeated the afternoon air, creating a sensation of nostalgia and peacefulness. Later I learned that the place had previously served as a vacation resort for the German military and their families, but had been converted by the British into a temporary home for some two thousand former female prisoners, mostly Jewish, who had been liberated by the British in various concentration camps in the area. By the time I came to Salzwedel, there were also some fifty men at the camp. Like me, they had come there to search for surviving family members.

The U.S. captain kept his promise. He took me to the camp office and did not leave until I had, indeed, found my cousin. Both he and his driver watched the emotional reunion of two survivors, and both he and his driver turned aside for a moment to wipe away a tear, so as not to betray a momentary sentimental weakness unbecoming two hardened military men.

Ever since, the suspicion has not escaped me that the U.S. Army captain really had no business to attend to at Salzwedel. His only reason for driving all the way there, I suspect, was to bring about a reunion between two survivors, "charred sticks plucked from the fire."

It is difficult to describe the regal treatment I was accorded by Frida and her seven roommates. Each of the eight girls tried to outdo the other in showering attention and affection on me. It was the first time since my deportation that I was sitting with my own people in a relaxed atmosphere with no fear or anxiety.

Life in Salzwedel was a veritable vacation. We, the campers, had to do nothing at all, but were given everything necessary to satisfy our needs. German civilians from the vicinity worked in the kitchens, in the dining halls, and even cleaned our rooms. Everyone was certainly free to leave the compound and go wherever he wished, yet very few left. The future was so uncertain that no one really knew what to anticipate or what course to take. The British were generous in giving us the best of everything—clothing, food, even entertainment. Many girls willingly accepted offers by British soldiers to teach them English, and they learned the new language most eagerly. During the evenings there were parties, music, and dances. The survivors enjoyed themselves. Still, maybe it was a final desperate attempt to avoid the inevitable blow of coming face-to-face with the brutal realities. No one, as yet, knew the full depth of the tragedy, and no one was eager to hasten the day when the naked truth would slap him or her in the face. The good life at Salzwedel might have continued for a long time, but it was drastically interrupted by changing circumstances.

One day, British soldiers drove through camp and announced from loudspeakers that as a consequence of territorial adjustments between the British and the Russians, Salzwedel would be evacuated by the former and handed over to the latter. The announcer added that all who wished to go along with the British should register at the camp office. The British promised to maintain at the new location the same services they had been providing us with at Salzwedel.

A heated campaign engulfed our camp as pro-British and pro-Soviet agitators roamed the streets trying to convince the inhabitants to leave with the former or to stay and wait for the arrival of the latter. Psychologically, the majority of the survivors were already conditioned to favor the Russians. While still in Hungary, we had hoped and prayed for the Russian forces to arrive and liberate us from the Nazi death grip. In their desperation, the Hungarian Jews had conceived of the Russians as redeemers and saviors who were late in coming. Now that they were at last coming to us here in Salzwedel, the excitement was great. To be sure, the British were nice guys, polite, and compassionate. One could hardly encounter a British soldier without being offered chewing gum, a cigarette, or a piece of chocolate. Yet there was nothing exciting about them. The Russians, on the other hand, had a mysterious aura surrounding them; they were still the great unknown.

By the time the deadline for registration was over, only fifty people had registered. Yet the British would not accept that as the final verdict. When evacuation hour arrived, fifty lorries pulled into the camp, their loudspeakers announcing that it was still possible to join the evacuating forces even if one had not signed up. This last-ditch attempt of the British to convince the stubborn Jewish girls to go with them ended in humiliating failure. No one took seriously the British admonition that as soon as they left, even crying would not help those who stayed behind. Typical British gentlemanliness and the comradeship forged on the battlefield prevented the British from openly saying anything nasty about their Russian comrades at arms. Yet it did not prevent them from uttering veiled hints about the type of behavior to be expected of Russian soldiers. Nothing, however, prevailed on those who had their minds already firmly made up. The lorries returned empty. It took us only one hour to find out how prophetic the British had been when they spoke of crying.

As we watched the British contingent depart in one direction, we saw in the distance, in the opposite direction, a huge moving mass—the Russians were coming. Loud applause rose from our midst. Yet something puzzled us; the Russians were moving very slowly. Why did it take them such a long time to reach us when we could already see them? Gradually the picture became clear. The Russian units assigned to take over Salzwedel were not mechanized. They rode neither tanks nor troop carriers, not even jeeps. They arrived in horse-drawn carts. The soldiers were unkempt, unshaven, and smoked vile-smelling cigarettes they themselves had made out of newsprint and cheap tobacco they called *machorka*. There was a crying contrast between the polished and refined British soldiers who had just left and their Russian replacements, who looked to us as though they had come out of the pages of a medieval-history book. Our bewilderment and disappointment were great. We looked in the opposite direction, but our British friends had already disappeared from sight. Still worse things were in store for us.

In the eyes of our new masters we were enemies, collaborators with the Germans. How otherwise could we explain the enviable living conditions we were enjoying? Besides, what were we doing in Germany in the first place if we had not come there to help the Germans in their war effort? All our explanations and pleas that we had been concentration camp inmates, and that our dear ones had been gassed, fell on deaf ears. They simply refused to believe us. Already, the girls were having a tough time warding off the insulting advances of the Russian soldiers. There was, indeed, much bitter crying, perhaps more than the British had foreseen. Still, the worst was yet to come.

A few days following their arrival, the Russian authorities told us that they needed the Salzwedel compound for their own personnel and we would have to evacuate it. They did not tell us, however, where they would take us. As we later learned, they themselves did not know what to do with us.

A day or two later, we were placed under military surveillance. Again we had become prisoners. This time we were prisoners of the Russians. We remained confined to the compound, our freedom of movement suspended. Soon after, a long convoy of military trucks moved into the camp and we all were ordered into the trucks. Unlike the British, the Russians did not ask anyone whether he wished to stay or to go; they simply gave orders. We rode off in search of a new place. Our convoy stopped at several refugee camps, but all refused to take us in, as they were already overcrowded. Once, in the middle of the night, we stopped at a camp that housed Ukrainians who had collaborated with the Germans, and who were now awaiting their forced shipment back to Russia. Horror overtook us as we contemplated the possibility of being placed together with those Nazi criminals and then being shipped to Russia as collaborators. To our delight, there too we were refused for reasons of overcrowdedness. The ride in search of a place resumed. The next day, our Russian masters simply dumped us at a huge field where the only building was a large stable. They left us in the charge of a unit of Tito's partisans who had their camp nearby. The Russians ordered the partisans to guard us and supply us with food.

There were heartrending scenes: girls wept in hysteria, bemoaning the terrible mistake we had committed by ignoring the British pleas to go with them. Yet, as the British had told us, crying made no difference in our desperate situation. Fortunately, the partisans were sympathetic and friendly, trying to alleviate our plight as much as was possible.

One afternoon, as we were cooking supper in the open field, a high-ranking Russian officer and his aide entered our compound. Of short stature and dark skin, the officer engaged in a friendly conversation with us. He inquired who we were and how we had ended up in that place. When he heard our story, he tried to remain calm, but I remember that he turned all tense and his voice became slightly tremulous. Following several minutes of tense silence, the short, dark skinned officer pointed in a certain direction and said resolutely, "Do you see those nice little brick houses over there, uphill? Well, tonight you all will be sleeping in those houses."

We stood in silent awe, not knowing what to say, nor how to take his words. Was it a cruel joke he was playing on us, or did he have some evil design on us? Before long, however, we realized he meant every word he had said, and that he intended to live up to his words. The Germans who had been living in the houses the officer had pointed at were given two hours to evacuate them. Then, we moved in. The homes were nicely furnished, and their pantries were well stocked with a variety of foodstuffs. The partisans still looked after our needs, except that they did not guard us any more. We were free people again.

Later we walked to the nearest town and in the street were identified as survivors by some local Jews. When we told them our story and of our encounter with the mysterious, high-ranking, dark-skinned Russian officer, they told us that they knew him well and suspected he was Jewish, although he had never told them so.

In a few more days, a representative of the newly established Czechoslovak government came to see us. He told us that everyone who wanted to return to Czechoslovakia should register with him. Most of the girls had been deported by the Hungarians from areas ceded to them by Hitler's edict. Those territories had by now been returned to Czechoslovakia and to Romania. Since it was unlikely that a Romanian representative would ever come to that place, I too registered with the Czech official. In a few days we were in Prague. . . .

In a day or two I learned that although the original Jewish community of Prague had been almost entirely annihilated during the war, there was a new nucleus of a Jewish community in the capital city comprised of survivors who came to Prague from various parts of the country. Most of them had served in the notorious forced-labor brigades and had been liberated by the Russians. Several meetings with those survivors and some follow-up investigation resulted in the joyous news that two of my brothers, Hershil and Yosil, had survived, and that Hershil was in a hospital in Budapest. Without wasting any more time, I headed for Budapest.

After I arrived there, I began searching for the hospital in which my brother was confined. When I located it, I readied myself for my first meeting with a survivor of my immediate family. Not having been told anything about his condition, nor the reason for his being hospitalized, I had serious misgivings and prepared myself for the worst.

The hospital was crowded, even its corridors filled with beds. The sharp odors of medications present everywhere impressed on me my own hospital experience at Buna. Before I was led to my brother's room, a nurse was dispatched to prepare him for the visit. For some reason, whether a shortage of electricity or overcrowding, the visitors' elevators were not operating, and I had to climb to one of the upper floors on foot. All along the way on the various floors I saw maimed people, one missing a hand or a leg, one missing an eye or

otherwise severely injured. These sights in no way bolstered my already flag-
ging spirit.

As I entered Hershil's room, I saw him lying on a tall bed, slightly slanted
toward his feet. His left leg was elevated and attached to a system of rails and
chains from which a set of weights was suspended. A faint smile appeared on his
face as he saw me entering. The stark realities of the hospital coupled with the
impact of reunion under the given circumstances caused me sudden dizziness. I
saw a chair nearby and sat down quickly. As I looked at Hershil, I felt somewhat
reassured. His situation, after all, seemed not to be too bad, I reasoned with
myself, since his head, eyes, and both hands were intact and functioning well.

It was Hershil who broke the silence, asking me whether I knew anything of
Shiele or of Antshil. When I replied in the negative, his pale face trembled, and
a fleeting spasm appeared at the left corner of his mouth. He did not ask about
our parents. Instead, he told me that Yosil was home, and that he came quite
frequently to Budapest. After a somewhat lengthy pause, and without waiting
for me to ask about his leg, Hershil began telling his story.

From the day the Germans invaded Hungary, hiding in Budapest under an
assumed identity had become ever more difficult. In the course of less than six
months, Hershil was forced to change his identity three times. In addition, he
succeeded in obtaining a Swedish *schutzpass*, which bestowed a certain degree
of protection on its bearer. Yet, despite all of his papers, he was always fearful
that he might be arrested as a suspect and interrogated. There was in Budapest a
Jewish woman and her four children who had escaped from Poland. They posed
in Hungary as Catholics, scrupulously observing the church's tenets, including
regular church attendance. Originally, the children had an Orthodox Jewish up-
bringing. While in flight from their persecutors, they too had to change their
identity several times. One Sunday in the church, when the eight-year-old boy's
turn came to be given the holy wafer by the priest, the youngster asked the
latter for a yarmulke. The poor, confused soul could not conceive of eating the
holy bread without his head being covered.

Not only was it difficult at the critical moment for one to remember his
identity, it was no less frustrating trying to follow the tilting political realities in
Hungary.

On October 15, 1944, the remnant of Hungary's Jewry in Budapest rejoiced,
hailing Miklós Horthy as their redeemer, for on that day the Hungarian regent
proclaimed the extrication of Hungary from the Axis alliance. Since Horthy had
already stopped the deportation of Jews from the country, the Jews of Budapest
believed that he had also extricated them from the death grip of the Nazis. Their
jubilation, however, was short-lived. It did not last for even one full day.

On the same day, the most rabid of Hungary's Jew-haters and the most
avowed of Hungary's Nazis staged a coup, and, with the help of the Germans,

took power in Budapest. Ferenc Szálasi, head of the infamous Arrow Cross Party, became the country's new prime minister. If up to now life in Budapest had been hell, it now became a real inferno. Sensing the dramatic changes, Eichmann returned to Budapest and feverishly threw himself into the business of liquidating the final remnants of Hungarian Jewry, now concentrated mainly in Budapest.

By that time, any semblance of law and order in the capital had completely broken down, and anarchy and terror reigned supreme. The new government almost daily issued new and often contradictory decrees concerning the Jews. Although Hungary was faced with one of the grimmest moments in her history, and the nation's most existential interests were at stake, the government was consumed with one overriding issue—the Jewish question. The Russian armies were already making deep inroads into the country, and German resistance was collapsing all along the front, yet the Hungarian leaders were able to conceive of only one menace—the Jews. The ferocious hatred manifested toward the Jews of Budapest during those final days of the war can only be categorized in terms of insanity and madness.

Rampaging bandits of the Arrow Cross took the law into their own hands, looting, shooting, and murdering any Jew whose ill fortune brought him into their reach. They also broke their way into Jewish homes, harassing and killing young and old. At two hospitals they murdered all the Jewish patients, and the Jewish doctors and nurses. A favorite pastime of the gangs was to drag their victims to the banks of the Danube River before shooting them, so that the victims' bodies would automatically fall into the water. In the city proper, thousands of Jewish bodies were piling up in hospitals and synagogues awaiting burial.

All that time, Hershil was living with a Jewish family at Teleki Tér. One night he was awakened by shouts, "They are coming, they are at the gates!" All knew who "they" were. It was enough to send anyone running for his life. Hershil, who always had a proclivity for original thought, considered it unwise to run into the street, directly into the hands of the Arrow Cross death squads. Instead, he tied a rope to a window facing a shaft, and lowered himself down from the second floor. To his misfortune, the rope broke before he even reached halfway, sending him to his destination much faster than he had planned. Immediately following his fall, Hershil felt a sharp pain in his left thigh, which he attributed to the blow he had just sustained. In order not to be discovered by his pursuers should they search the shaft, and also because the barren cement floor was quite cold, he decided to hide in an old laundry basket someone had thrown long ago into the shaft. Only then did he realize that he could not stand up on his feet. Through a strenuous effort, however, he crawled into the basket and waited for further developments.

Soon the noises quieted down and everything seemed to have returned to normal—everything, that is, except my brother's thigh, which hurt more and more. He shouted for help, and neighbors came and pulled him out of the basket and then out of the shaft. As it turned out, no Arrow Cross gangs had been active in the vicinity that night. The entire confusion was the result of someone's strained nerves, which brought about everybody's running, which in turn caused Hershil to tie a rope to his window, which broke while he was lowering himself, which resulted for my brother in a broken left thighbone.

The bandits, however, did come the next day.

In the streets of Budapest there was utter chaos, and death loomed everywhere. One never knew whether he was going to be hit by a bullet fired by a member of an Arrow Cross gang, a German tank, or a low-flying Russian airplane. While the Russian bullets were nondiscriminatory, the former two aimed their weapons mainly at Jews.

Hershil was lying in bed with a high fever and in acute pain when he heard shouts, "All Jews immediately to present themselves in the courtyard. Anyone found inside the building will be shot." All the Jewish residents began running in panic down the stairway and toward the courtyard, some of them carrying my brother with them. When, however, he shouted terribly on account of his pain, they put him down in the corridor and left him there, running for their lives. Hershil heard shots being fired all around, and fearful for his life if found by the gangs inside the building, he started crawling down the stairs on his hands and knees. An Arrow Cross gangster, however, seized him and dragged him to the sidewalk. In the street, bullets were flying in all directions, everyone shooting at everyone. Seeing him wounded and lying on the sidewalk, one of the Nazis pulled his pistol. Aiming it at Hershil he shouted wildly, "You perfidious Jew, you were wounded while shooting at our forces." "No," Hershil replied, "please, don't shoot. I was wounded in the Hungarian Labor Service, where a heavy load fell on my left leg. Besides," Hershil continued, "I am a bearer of a Swedish *schutzpass*, and the head of the Swedish legation in Budapest is personally concerned with my well-being."

The gangster put his pistol away, called over a coachman, and ordered him to "drive this Jew to the designated place." The two of them tied my brother's hands and fixed a rag over his eyes. Following an arduous ride that even more aggravated my brother's pain, he was driven into a large enclosure that had been used for cattle auctions and was dumped on the wet ground. There he joined thousands of other Jews who had been brought there during the past several days. All of them spent that night in the open, in a drizzling rain that soaked them to their bones.

The next day, the Szálasi government issued yet another of its contradictory orders, now calling for the return of all arrested Jews to their homes. Hershil and the other wounded and sick were taken to a hospital. They remained there until the liberation of Budapest by the Russian army. During that period, a Swedish diplomat, Raoul Wallenberg, paid several visits to the hospital, which was enjoying the protection of the Swedish flag.

It goes without saying that in those chaotic times and unusual circumstances my brother's leg was never given a thorough checkup. It was enough that the hospital provided him with a haven from the ravages of the streets and a certain measure of safety. Several months after the liberation, still limping on his left side, he returned to the hospital, where he underwent complicated surgery during which his left thighbone had to be broken again and properly reset. The weights I saw suspended from his left leg when I entered his room were arranged so as to pull apart the two sections of the bone that had grown together the wrong way.

The story left my brother exhausted. He was now much more pale than when I had entered his room some hours earlier. I tried to encourage him to take a nap, promising I would be back next morning. Still, he asked me to stay a little longer. I sat at his bedside until he fell asleep, then left quietly.

Jewish relief organizations, like the American Joint Distribution Committee, were already active in Budapest in extending help to survivors. I was given a small amount of cash and allocated a place where I could have room and board. My future course, however, was entirely blurred. I had a great desire to go to Szatmár, my hometown, yet I was also apprehensive about the idea of returning there. My brother's confinement in the hospital temporarily aided my decision to stay in Budapest and extend him moral support. Yet, following some two weeks of aimlessness and heightened anxiety, I made the decision to continue to Szatmár and see for myself.

Displaced Person's Camp

Lucille Eichengreen

A Holocaust survivor, Eichengreen is the author of
From Ashes to Life: My Memories of the Holocaust, from
which the following material is taken. For additional
biographical information on Eichengreen, see page
340.

For some survivors, liberation from the
concentration camp was but the beginning of life in
yet another kind of camp, the displaced person's
camp. Here Eichengreen describes her attempts to
find a way to leave Germany with no passport, birth
certificate, or official papers and with limited
financial resources.

The war, for me, had ended on April 15, 1945, at
Bergen-Belsen when I was liberated by the British Army. Liberation was still
almost unbelievable. I had survived. No more beatings, hunger, or killings—yet
the realities of liberation were not what I had expected. There was no euphoria
or joy. But perhaps I was no longer capable of experiencing joy. I had day-
dreamed about life after the war. My dream was of a return to life the way it had
been before the war: our sunny apartment, our close family, my friends, a navy
silk dress with a full, sweeping skirt. Five years ago, I had been thinking of
parties, dances, boys, going to art school. Instead of parties—mass murders.
Instead of dances—Mengele's selections. Instead of my full sweeping skirt—a
striped rag with a yellow star. Instead of art school—the art of death, dehumanization, and despair.

Until now I had not been conscious of the fact that the one short happy
period of my life was gone, never to return. I was physically and emotionally
scarred. My family and friends no longer existed. Everything and everyone

important to my life were gone forever. Slowly I realized that I could not turn back to what had been but only toward something different, unknown, and uncertain. Even the future was blocked; I was still not free.

Like so many others, I became ill. We all suffered the aftereffects of malnutrition. Typhus and tuberculosis were the main problems. I vaguely recall drifting in and out of consciousness with a high fever but refusing to go to the hospital. My friend Sabina was dabbing my face, applying cool compresses to my hot forehead, and making me drink water. My kidneys were not functioning well, and I was in constant, almost unbearable pain. Large boils began to appear on my neck and shoulders; they opened, drained, and healed, but new ones took their place. The British doctors had neither explanations nor medication; they thought the combination of dirt, unsanitary conditions, and a "deprived system" might be the cause.

"They'll disappear in six months. All you need is a regular diet," they told me. But when or where could one get it? The food that was cooked for us in army kitchens consisted of a piece of dark bread and a stew made with shredded, dried vegetables. There was no meat, fruit, or fresh vegetables, and no one had heard of vitamins.

Elli was so gravely ill that she was hospitalized. When I visited her, she looked pale and thin between the white sheets.

"Will I make it?" she whispered. "They tell me that I have diseased lungs and might need surgery. The war is over now, but I'm sicker than I ever was."

I held her hands and silently demanded, "Dear God, don't let her die now."

My visit a few days later threw me into a panic. Elli's bed was empty. "Where have you taken her? What have you done with her?" I screamed at the nurses.

They tried to calm me down, explaining that they had sent her to a sanitorium in Switzerland where she would have surgery and the special care she needed. In a daze, I left the hospital feeling tired and sad, wondering if Elli and I would ever see each other again.

We were warehoused in large, red-brick barracks, the former German "Kasernen," which had been used as military housing for the German army. Six or seven women occupied one large room, slept in gray metal bunk beds, and shared a dormitory-type bathroom at the end of the hall. I longed for some privacy. Although we were allowed free run of the entire camp, the British did not permit us to leave it. Sometimes these rules were ignored, and now and then someone would come back from a "trip" into occupied Germany with stories of the country's total defeat. They would often bring back little trinkets of china or jewelry, some of which had been bartered for, others stolen. "Why pay?" was the attitude. "Didn't the Germans take all our possessions, even the gold teeth from both the living and the dead?" Occasionally, there were incidents, altercations between displaced persons and German civilians, but the British tried to ignore them.

People were constantly inquiring about missing family members and friends. One woman, Hela, was looking for her father. "He was always tough, indestructible, a hard worker—I'm sure he must have survived."

But not a trace was to be found. He had been seen at Auschwitz. There the trail ended.

Sabina was luckier. She located her younger sister, Dzuta, through the Red Cross. She had been sent with a children's transport to Sweden. Sabina now concentrated on getting permission to enter Sweden.

Lola was looking for her mother. We heard that she had worked under horrible conditions in Mauthausen and had died there of hunger and exhaustion. Two women in her group had managed to survive, and the news of her death, passed from person to person, finally reached Lola.

I kept searching for any scrap of information about my sister and about Julie and Julius, the elderly couple who had befriended me in the ghetto. My inquiries always met with the same response: all of the children and old people deported from the ghetto in 1942 had been murdered by the Germans. Memories of Karin[1] and of my unfulfilled promise to Mother haunted my nights and days. Karin's frightened, tearstained face kept reappearing. Coming to terms with the loss of Karin, of Mother and Father, was impossible. My desolation and despair over their deaths made me question my own right to survive. And I was alone with my guilt.

Almost daily, visitors from other camps arrived, straggling men and women who were traveling from camp to camp in search of their families. Some stayed, others made their way west, and some even returned to Poland. One morning an old friend, Chawa Levi, whom I had not seen for more than a year, stopped me on my way to work. We had worked together in the same office in the Lodz ghetto. She told me that she had walked and hitched rides from a camp in southern Germany in search of her younger sister, Dorka. She asked me if I had any information, but I could not help.

"I have talked to many of our former friends," she said, "and I heard that Szaja[2] is alive. He is supposed to be traveling back to Poland." Chawa's information took me by surprise. The mention of Szaja's name dredged up a mixture of feelings. I remembered our closeness, our walks through the ghetto streets, the love, the abandonment, his saving my life. It all seemed so very long ago, yet the feelings were alive, and the images remained vivid.

---

[1] Her sister.

[2] Her former boyfriend.

"Did he ask about me?" I queried.

"I have no idea," Chawa replied.

I still wanted him to care. I wondered if he would pass through Bergen-Belsen and look for me. I wished he would, but a little voice inside my head told me that he would not. As the months passed, I often thought about Szaja, but I never heard from him. I reasoned that he had probably returned to Lodz—a place I never wanted to see again. I resigned myself to memories.

Fortunately, my work forced me to confront each day and to live in the present. I hoped that this would keep me sane. I knew English and German, could manage Polish and French. I was working for Major Brinton, a burly man, dark-haired, dark-eyed, about six feet tall, with a bellowing voice. I worked as an interpreter and translator from 8:00 to 6:00, six days a week. Whenever he needed conversations and letters translated, he would call on me. He demanded fast, spontaneous translations and asked that they be only more or less accurate. Speaking English was a challenge, and my work and contact with the British helped me, at least for a few hours, to forget the past.

Displaced persons (DPs) were paid little, and the money we received, "Occupation marks," had been issued by the army for interim use until a stable currency could be established. The marks were worthless; one could buy very little with them. The real currency in occupied Germany was food, coffee, and cigarettes.

Most of my friends spent their days visiting, gossiping, and waiting for charitable organizations, such as the Hebrew Immigration Aid Society (HIAS) or the Joint Distribution Committee, to come and send them to a new home—that is, to any country willing to accept DPs. Few were willing. Furthermore, because we lived in a displaced persons' camp, it was almost impossible to obtain entry visas.

I had hoped to emigrate to Palestine or the United States where I had family and friends, but the war had left me without any documents—no passport, no birth certificate, no proof at all that I existed or that I was the person I said I was. Paris and London, the two cities with embassies from which one could obtain visas, were far away, and I lacked both the financial means and the proper documents to get there. I felt trapped in a bureaucratic nightmare. Nevertheless, my hopes for pursuing a normal life depended on getting out of Germany—Europe, if necessary—as quickly as possible. I had no intention of waiting.

I began to devise various schemes for leaving Germany. Since I had only limited power over my own destiny, my plots always involved contacting friends or family abroad, although this approach had its own obstacles. Postal service out of the country was not available to anyone except military personnel. I asked one of my British coworkers if I could use his name and APO number to write to family and friends in Palestine and the United States. He agreed. I immediately dashed off several letters, one to my uncle Herman, my father's brother in Palestine, others to friends in the U.S. and Great Britain. I wanted them to know that I was alive and, more importantly, that my parents and my sister had been killed.

Finally, after a month's wait, my uncle's first letter reached me. I was overjoyed. As I mulled over his letter, I hit upon an idea. If I married a Palestinian citizen, I would be able to leave. In my reply, I asked my uncle if he would please, please, help get me out of Germany and into Palestine by marrying me.

A month passed before I received an answer. Uncle Herman wrote that he was old and ailing, no longer able to travel. However, he had contacted my cousin Fred, a cousin on my mother's side, who was stationed in Holland and serving in the Palestine brigade of the British army. He said that Fred had consented to marry me and that I could expect to hear from him soon. I would have preferred my uncle, but in desperation I was willing to marry anyone to get out. A divorce later would take care of such a marriage.

Returning from work one evening in July, I found Fred waiting for me. I recognized him by his striking resemblance to my mother and knew who he was before he even got up to embrace me. He was good-looking—my friends even thought handsome—in his late twenties, pleasant and well mannered. We took a long walk that evening; there was much I wanted to know about the family in Palestine, but mostly I wanted to know if he would indeed marry me.

"Of course I will," he answered immediately. "My parents think this is a very good idea." I was delighted with the news—but only for a moment. Casually, he continued, "Even though we are cousins, we can still have a wonderful life together."

I was stunned. Did he and his parents actually think that our marriage was to be permanent? For some reason, I had assumed that Fred knew that this arranged marriage was merely a device to get me out of Germany. Although his attitude promised to be yet another obstacle, I said nothing and decided to go ahead with my plan for a temporary marriage. Everything else could be worked out later; first, I simply had to get out. As we continued walking, I asked about his work as a civilian, what he did in his spare time, if he was interested in music or the theater, and whether he had any hobbies.

He said he worked as a carpenter, did not care for books, museums, or the theater. He spent his free time helping his parents around the house and garden and in their small food store. He did not have a car but rode a bike. He closed by telling me that I would enjoy their quiet little place in Palestine and that we would, of course, live with his parents.

He stayed only three days, but at the end of that time, I knew that if I did go through with the plan, I definitely would not stay married to him. He was kind but uninteresting. We had nothing in common other than the fact that his father and my mother were brother and sister. To think that the family had already decided on our marriage and had determined our future made me angry. I began to panic, but I tried to put all these feelings aside and concentrate on my main goal: getting out of Germany.

"I'll make the necessary arrangements with my commanding officer so we can marry as soon as possible. I'm sure the request will be granted." He looked happy, and I could tell that he fully intended to make this marriage a real and permanent arrangement. I was relieved when he left—and apprehensive about the future.

For the next six weeks, Fred's letters arrived regularly from Holland. The more he wrote, the more I knew that I could not possibly live with him. Still, he represented my best hope for getting out of Germany.

One morning, several weeks after Fred's visit, two British officers appeared in the office.

"Are you Cecilia Landau? We would like to talk to you."

"Of course," I replied quickly, pulling up some chairs. I knew that everyone who worked for the British was being investigated for security reasons, and I wanted to keep my job.

"Where were you born?" one of them continued.

"Hamburg, Germany," I replied.

"Your nationality?"

"Polish," I replied.

"How is that possible when you were born in Germany?"

"My parents were Polish nationals living in Germany, and I also held a Polish passport since birth," I responded.

"That does not seem likely; can you prove it?"

"I was born in Hamburg, Germany, but held a Polish passport, like my parents, since birth. I spent the war years in Poland, but after Auschwitz I was left without documents of any kind."

"You were born in Germany, and that, in our eyes, makes you a German national."

"Maybe in your eyes, but I'm not a German. I always had Polish papers." Being Polish was not such a bargain, I thought to myself, but it was infinitely better than being German.

The two officers thanked me politely, got up, and left the office. I was worried about losing my job. Had I given the right answers?

Several weeks later, Fred called from Holland. He sounded upset and disappointed. "My application to marry you has been rejected. No reason was given. I am angry and so very, very sorry."

I was crushed. My plan had failed. But in the back of my mind, there was also a tiny speck of relief—I wouldn't have to marry Fred.

Reunions

Bernard Gotfryd

Born in Radom, Poland, in 1924, Bernard Gotfryd was involved in the Polish resistance movement during World War II. He was captured by the Nazis, who sent him to a series of concentration camps. He, his brother, and his sister survived the war, but their parents were killed. Gotfryd was a slave laborer in the stone quarry at the Mauthausen concentration camp. After the war, he immigrated to the United States. He had a successful career as a staff photographer for *Newsweek* magazine. The following story is from *Anton the Dove Fancier and Other Tales of the Holocaust*, a collection of stories and vignettes, which is Gotfryd's first book.

Even after the war was over, Jews in some European countries were not entirely safe. In this short story, Gotfryd describes the dangers a young man faced as he searched for his sister.

I t was May, 1945, and the war was over. For two days I had been in Linz, Austria, alone, living in constant anxiety over the fate of my family. I was afraid to think about who was still alive. Every day I crisscrossed the city of Linz, hoping to find a trace of something familiar, a clue, a contact of some kind. I wasn't even sure if I still remembered the faces of my brother and sister or my parents; I wasn't sure that they would recognize me if we were to meet.

Nightmarish images were always before my eyes, keeping me awake at night. I had nothing left, not even a picture, to prove that I had once belonged to a family. I didn't know who I was; I had doubts about my own name. I remembered only my prisoner number, as if it were engraved on my brain.

Who am I, I kept asking myself, and what am I doing here? I looked and searched but kept running away from myself.

Soon I moved on to Salzburg, about seventy-five miles from Linz, to get away from an imaginary SS man I thought was out to kill me. In my mind he looked like Horst Gartner, whose parents had invited me to stay at their house. Salzburg was no better, only somewhat larger than Linz; registrations and inquiries, survivors looking for relatives, lists of survivors on walls, and notices in different languages were everywhere. Everybody was looking for somebody else, but no one, it seemed, was looking for me. I found no familiar names, not even that of a neighbor. Slowly I was coming to terms with the fact that, at the age of twenty, I was alone in the world.

One early morning, while walking near the railway station in search of a photo shop, I heard someone calling from the other side of the street. The call came again; it was my name. At first I couldn't identify with it; when I finally turned I saw a stocky young man of medium height with a full, round face and closely cropped hair. Who was he? He had the face of a stranger, and his voice was unfamiliar. He was wearing a pair of baggy pants and a striped shirt with rolled-up sleeves; he carried a small suitcase with reinforced metal corners.

When I stopped he started running toward me, yelling my name at the top of his lungs. When he realized I wasn't responding he dropped the suitcase, grabbed me by my shoulders, and shook me hard, as if trying to wake me from a sleep.

"I'm your brother, don't you recognize me?" he yelled. He had heard that I was in Austria and had traveled for two days from Stuttgart, sitting on top of a coal car, to look for me. "Are you all right?" he asked. "Or is there something wrong with you?" We hugged, and he nearly squashed me; he was strong.

"I just couldn't recognize you," I said, fighting back my tears. "I didn't think I would ever see you again. It's almost unreal how different you look; you've gained a lot of weight, your hair is short. God, you look like a different person. How could I have recognized you?"

"I had a bad case of typhoid," he said, "and since I got well I haven't been able to stop eating. I've been liberated since April and have been living on a farm with some friends. Recently we slaughtered a pig; you can imagine how well we eat.

"You probably don't know that Father was shot," my brother went on to say. He had witnessed Father's execution. Matter-of-factly he described the whole scene to me. "I begged the SS man to let Father go," he told me, "but he threatened to shoot me, too, and I think he would have if I hadn't stepped back into the ranks. I remember him very well. I even know his name and where he came from. It was terrible and frightening. I can't forget it."

For a split second I remembered my father throwing the egg to me at the Szkolna camp. I remembered his tears when the SS guard hit him with a stick for doing so; every time I thought of my father there were tears; still, I couldn't cry. It seemed impossible that I was talking to my brother.

An Austrian woman with big, sad eyes and a knapsack strapped to her back stopped to watch us; she stood a few feet away shaking her head. I didn't think she knew what was happening or who we were, but when we started walking away she looked back over her shoulder, still shaking her head. I heard her say "*Wie traurig*"—how sad—before we disappeared around the corner.

My brother had heard rumors from survivors who traveled across Europe looking for their families that our sister Hanka was alive and looking for us in Poland.

We stayed together for a while, but toward the end of the summer we parted again. My brother remained in Germany; I went to Poland via Prague to search for our sister.

It was a difficult and lonely journey that took me back to a country I dreaded, a journey full of strange and unpredictable encounters. I traveled in the backs of trucks or in unheated trains, standing up for hours on steps or in open freight cars, often enough in the rain. The Nazis had robbed the country of everything; there were few scheduled trains or buses. The same hateful faces greeted me wherever I went. The same resentment came through all of their eyes; I could see they were wondering why I had come back.

Cold winds and rain blew incessantly across the Polish landscape, turning it into one huge mud pie. I traveled from one city to another searching for my sister, only to find that she had eluded me each time by leaving a day or two before I arrived. I kept moving from place to place, hoping to catch up with her; in Lodz a Polish friend of the family, Mr. S., gave me some money my parents had left with him for safekeeping and told me that my sister had left for Stettin on her way to the west.

The following day I hitched a ride on a truck going toward the German frontier. As soon as I climbed in the back of the truck it started raining, so I slipped under the tarpaulin and stretched out on a pile of potato sacks behind some wooden crates. It was late in the evening when the truck approached the first intersection; it slowed down. I heard part of a conversation with the driver, and soon I saw two armed men in uniforms climb in the back. They settled themselves directly across from where I was lying; even in the dark something told me that they weren't friendly.

I was correct in my assessment; when the truck started moving again I heard the two men talking. They complained about what a wasted day it had been; they hadn't found a single Jew. I broke out in a cold sweat. What if they discovered me? Suppose they decided to lift the tarpaulin. That would be the end of me. What could I possibly tell them? About my time in the camps, and how much I longed to get back to my home town and find my people? How could they understand me if they were out to kill me? Only several days before I had heard someone talk about armed bands of Polish nationalists who were organizing pogroms against Jewish survivors. These people were no better than the Nazis; I hated the thought that I might have survived the camps to meet my fate at the hands of Polish hooligans.

My stomach felt as if it were tied into a knot. I tried not to move or even breathe. If only I could shrink to the size of an insect or change into an earthworm! Kafka's *Metamorphosis* came to my mind, and I prayed for a miracle.

Suddenly I felt like sneezing. I was terrified; instinctively I pressed my nose against the edge of a crate and stopped breathing. It worked. I hoped I wouldn't have to repeat the trick; next time I might not be as lucky. I could still hear my traveling companions making threats against the Jews.

It must have been well past midnight. There was no moon, and the rain was coming down incessantly. One side of my face kept getting wet, and drops of water were rolling down my neck behind my shirt collar. It was getting cold; I began to shiver. From time to time the truck would zigzag to avoid a pothole, and the smaller load at the tail of the truck would slide and bounce against the crates, pushing them against my legs.

The two men continued to discuss their exploits and their frustrations. The one with the hoarser voice was recounting how he and some of his friends had recently executed a whole Jewish family who had survived the war in an underground shelter in the woods. He described the episode in vivid detail. It was a bloodcurdling story. The two men sat at the edge of the truck with their feet hanging down and with their backs to me. With one eye I was able to make out their silhouetted torsos against the misty night.

Some hours passed, and finally I heard a knocking above my head, at the driver's cab window. At the next intersection the truck came to a stop, and the two men got off. I watched them jump across the ditch and disappear into the woods. I felt as though I had been liberated for the second time.

I didn't know how far it was to Stettin, but I didn't care. I crawled from under the tarpaulin and looked out. It had stopped raining, and the haze was lifting. There was a strong aroma of rotting leaves mixed with cow manure. At the side of the road I could see faint outlines of bare trees with twisted branches, as if multitudes of crisscrossing arms were reaching for the sky. Some distance away I could make out farm huts with thatched roofs; the flickering lights of kerosene lamps reflected against their tiny windows, making them look like squatting monsters with burning eyes.

It was a sad and desolate landscape. Here and there were clusters of birch and pine trees. The white birch trunks seemed to be moving across the fields like ghosts, as though they were racing with the truck. From time to time I could hear the driver curse in Polish or sing old Jewish tunes. I was astounded. How did he know Jewish tunes? He had a husky voice and a rich vocabulary of four-letter words with which he seemed to amuse himself.

It was dawn when the truck reached the gates of the city. When it came to a full stop the driver clambered out of the cab, yawning and stretching, to announce our arrival in the city of Stettin. This was as far as he was going.

"This is it," he said. "Last stop." I jumped off the truck holding on to my knapsack. Every muscle in my body ached. I walked over to the driver. He was a husky blond man, perhaps in his thirties. "How do you happen to know Jewish tunes?" I asked him carefully.

"Oh, well," he answered, "it's a long story, but since you ask I'll tell you. I happen to be Jewish. Simple as that. So are you, right? I didn't even have a good look at you, but my antennae tell me you must be one, too," he said, winking at me.

"How could I deny it?" I asked him, and the two of us laughed. It felt so much safer now that the trip was over.

"By the way," I said, "do you happen to know who those two armed men were you had on your truck?"

"I don't know them personally, but I imagine they were members of some political faction; fanatics. There are quite a few of them around, and they always hitch rides; it could be dangerous for me to refuse them. Don't forget, they're armed, and I'm not."

"I was frightened when they got on the truck," I admitted. "They were really dangerous."

"Frankly, I had no idea you were Jewish," he said. "I never had a good look at you before you got on the truck. But don't be afraid, it's over. God protected you."

"You look so Polish, so Christian," I said. "I would have never taken you for a Jew."

"That is exactly what saved me," he said. "My looks. But who are you, and where are you going?" he asked. I told him briefly where I came from and for whom I was looking. "My God," he exclaimed, "it must have been real tough for you. You should be happy to be alive and have a sister. Look at me; I'm the only one from my family left alive. I know what it is like to be left alone."

When I tried to reward him for his trouble he wouldn't accept any money. I offered him my last pack of Chesterfields, but he would only take a few cigarettes. He drove me closer to the center of the city and let me off in front of a teahouse surrounded by ruins. "This is the only place in Stettin where you can get some food. Good luck. I hope you find her," he said, smiling and shaking my hand.

I was in a strange city in which only a few buildings remained standing. It was still early. The teahouse was open, however; I could smell freshly baked bread, and the aroma reminded me of my hunger. I hadn't eaten since I got on the truck in Lodz almost twelve hours before. In the teahouse marble tables stood on massive wrought-iron stands; a long marble counter adorned with brass fixtures, a reminder of better times, ran the length of the room. On the wall hung a small Polish flag.

A young woman was filling orders behind the counter, and a teenager with a blond ponytail was waiting on tables. They didn't have much to offer; only hot tea and buttered rolls or bread. For me that fare was a treat. I sat there warming my hands on a tall glass full of steaming tea, feeling the warmth travel all the way down to my frozen toes. The place began to fill up. People were drifting in, settling in at the tables, dragging metal chairs noisily over the marble floor. I noticed a young man enter the teahouse. He wore a creased raincoat tied with a wide leather belt and carried a knapsack. He looked around as if searching for someone, then proceeded directly toward my table, where there was an empty chair. "Is it all right if I join you?" he asked.

"Please do; I haven't talked to a soul in days," I answered.

"My name is Moshe, Moshe Feingold. I'm a survivor," he introduced himself, shaking my hand rather vigorously. He pulled out the chair across from me and quickly sat down, dropping his knapsack under the table next to mine. I told him my name, and he leaned forward, coming closer to me, as if he had difficulty hearing.

"I think you must be a survivor," Moshe said in a low voice, looking at me suspiciously. "Yes, I am," I answered. "Now that our hair is still short, our clothing fits badly, and we look hungry, lost, and frightened, it must be easy to tell," I said.

"You're quite right," Moshe said, biting into his buttered roll. He was thin, and his eyes were dark and intense. When he talked his head kept turning like a radar dish, left to right, right to left. His short, curly hair was growing in in a very odd shape; the curls were connecting and pressing on each other, as if fighting for space. We sat there exchanging stories, ordering more and more tea. As far as he knew, his entire family had disappeared.

"I crisscrossed Poland, I went to see every camp that ever existed, and all I found were piles of ashes. Poland is one huge cemetery. What else is left?" he asked. "I come from Otwock, not far from Warsaw. There is not a single Jew left in the town. I got married one week before the war started. I had a wife and a little son. My son would have been four years old by now. My parents, my wife's parents, and the rest of the family were shipped to Treblinka. This much I found out."

I felt bad for him and didn't think it was appropriate for me to talk about my losses. Moshe was on his way to the west, he told me, to join some friends who were getting ready to emigrate to Palestine. We wished each other luck; a few hours into the morning he left.

I got up and went over to the counter to buy some more rolls, but before I had a chance to place my order the young woman behind the counter asked me excitedly, "Do you happen to have a relative named Hanka? I don't know her last name. You look just like her, the same mouth and eyes, the same face. She's my neighbor. She lives right around the corner, on the second floor to the right. I know her. She usually comes here for her rolls. I'm surprised she didn't show up yet this morning. I noticed the strong resemblance as soon as you came in, but then I got busy, and I lost track of you."

"I'm her brother," I answered, my knees shaking. "I've been looking for her everywhere for weeks."

"Please sit down and have some more tea," she suggested. "You must be starved. All this traveling in such bad weather." I thanked her and told her I had already eaten well, paid my check, and ran outside.

It was still early when I knocked at my sister's apartment. A young woman dressed in a long robe opened the door and instantly threw her arms around me.

"How did you find me? This is a miracle. I've been looking for you all over Poland," I heard her say into my shoulder. I couldn't speak. There were no tears, only sadness, and when we hugged a strange feeling came over me. It was as if something inside me was asking me why I was alive while so many others weren't. It pressed and nagged at me, bringing back images of those who were gone. Should I tell my sister immediately what had happened to our father? Or should I wait? I had a feeling that she already knew, that she, too, must have been wondering if I knew about Father.

I wanted to tell my sister how happy I was to find her, but I couldn't find the words. It all seemed abstract, hardly believable. What was one supposed to talk about at such moments? There was no point in recalling the tragic events; it was simply good to be alive, and to be together. Over the next few days we talked at length about many different things but never mentioned the war, nor the camps, as if it had never taken place, as if the six years had just dropped out of the calendar and disappeared. I was getting used to the idea that I was free, no longer alone, and that there were others like myself, roaming, searching, and wandering.

About ten days after my arrival my sister left Stettin, heading for the west to join our brother, and I set out in search of Alexandra, my wartime underground contact. I planned to rejoin my family as soon as I found her.

Saving the Fragments

Isabella Leitner

Isabella Leitner is an Auschwitz survivor. As a young
woman, she and her family were sent to the camp
from their home in Hungary. She spent the last year
of the war at Auschwitz, an experience that she later
described in her first book, *Fragments of Isabella*. In
1945, she immigrated to the United States, where she
married Irving A. Leitner, with whom she has
written her memoirs, including *Saving the Fragments:
From Auschwitz to New York*, from which the
following excerpt is taken, and *Isabella: From
Auschwitz to Freedom*.

In this lyrical and haunting selection, Leitner
describes her experiences after liberation from
Auschwitz as she and her sisters continued their
struggle for survival. The emotional intensity of her
writing underscores their transition from a living
death to life with its many possibilities.

From time to time it dawns on us that we have
been detached from the rest of humankind. We will have to relearn how to live,
how to hold a fork, how to live with the family of man. Too great a task. The
resources within us will have to stand up to a nearly impossible struggle.

We have reverence for life, or no reverence at all. We have flare-ups of hope,
or are dead within. We know almost everything about life or death. Still, we
have to relearn how to walk, step by painfully fragile step. What will, what can,
prop us up through these delicate inner negotiations?

A warring land is not without its share of decomposing bodies. They are strewn all around us. We step over them, devoid of any emotion. Where have we become so hardened? In Auschwitz. All that burning of our mothers, our children, our kin of every shape, gender, and age—all that was only one aspect of the Auschwitz aberration. There were many other sides.

One: the daily removal of the night's dead from the *Blocks* (barracks). Corpses piled high in front of each *Block* every morning, waiting for the *Totekommando* (death squad) to slap them onto their wagons to convey them to the almighty crematorium. There were so many of these emaciated skeletons greeting the morning dew, sun, or rain daily that we no longer had a tear left to shed from our ducts, not even a flutter, just a tiny flutter, to beat in our hearts. Everything inside us had been used up over and over again. We could no longer locate the mourning niche for the dead in our shriveled souls.

We would perk up only if some rags on the dead could be stolen, if something on the bodies was better than what we, the "living," were wearing. It hardened us so, these bodies that were more touchable, more immediate than the burning stench of thousands floating in the sky.

There, but for the grace of each deadly night, was I. It was good to see that my body was missing each morning from the pile of corpses in front of *Block* 2, *Block* 13, *Block* 9.

Our training ground was Auschwitz. It is easy to step over the bodies on the roads of murder country. It is even easier when the bodies are clad in Nazi uniforms. Yet, whatever a body wears, parts of us are dead, and for moments we hurt from our inability to retrieve the heart or hurt of yesteryear. We want to cry not for the dead but for what is dead in us.

Will what we were return? A silent prayer is etched into our footsteps as we heartlessly step over a decomposing arm, a hip, or a head. Hitler's imprint is on the roads, in the sky, everywhere. He tore our insides into unbearable memories. He also set us up for hopes we should not have.

We try not to remember. We try not to think. Hitler, Hitler, why didn't you let us have normal deaths? Funerals? Tears? Why did you set us apart? Just graves, Hitler—we have survived into an age where a grave is a mark of humanity.

When we were growing up, our mothers and teachers taught us other values. The inspirations we were nurtured on were examples of humaneness. We read and wrote poetry of heroism, learned of a common goal for common man, of justice, of being in the service of common good, of becoming healers—doctors, nurses.

Our songs were love songs. We knew and felt tenderness. Were we misled by all who had a share in shaping us into young women and men? Is this the age of mockery, or were the years that sculpted us the mockery?

411

Hitler, we will forgive nothing you wrought. Even before you murdered us you tried to cripple our minds. We, the people of the Book, had to endure your book burnings. Knowledge in flames.

Some of us will forever weep for the books and schooling you denied us. The broken wings of our minds will always curse you for that. I curse you. So do Sally, Philip, Berta, Sam, Morris, Helen, Edith, Harry, Jacob, Nathan. . . .

There is no peace on the roads, no peace in our hearts. Marchers, where are you marching? Step out of this age. Step off this planet. Life is tainted too much. Auschwitz is even bigger and more than whatever transpired before.

How will the world heal itself of Auschwitz? Is there a large pill for a large virus called hate? Is the world terminal? Can it get well? Can shattered lives ever be mended? Will saving the fragments be an impossible task?

All these unanswerable ponderings are floating about within our exhausted minds. They are not questions properly formed. They just take up chaotic residence within our souls.

We will have to learn how to cry. . . .

But if we let the tears flow, how long would we weep? For all eternity? For six million years?

The cows are gone. Now there is no basic food supply from anywhere. The available food in the area keeps diminishing. Only the people absolutely necessary for managing things will be permitted to remain. The others will have to move on. They will have to try to make their way to their various homelands.

We hope that the war will soon be won and trains will become available. We have consumed everything edible. Food that is scarce cannot be fairly divided. It is clear that we will have to leave.

The Russians provide us with some kind of discharge papers, attesting to our work record, or whatever. They seem regretful and honorable, but it doesn't satisfy us. We want to remain. Our minds understand that we must leave, but our emotions react in a deeply wounded way. In our hearts, we feel that the curse of the wandering Jew is upon us again. . . .

We are desperate. We do not want to give up the relative security of what we have here. For six weeks we have had some kind of home. Diabolical, ironic that we should consider as something good an abandoned house in this vile land.

It is still cold and wintry. We know that no one is waiting for us at home in Hungary. If Cipi and Philip are alive, they know that, too. If ever we can go anywhere, we will go to America, to New York, to our father, our only living parent.

We love being liberated. We think of the Russian soldiers as life-givers. They kept the Germans from annihilating us. They are responsible for our reentering life. They let no dogs loose on us. They let no Dr. Mengele loose on us. Their smoke emits the smell of food, not the scent of burning flesh.

Now they are imploring us to leave. When we procrastinate, they order us to go.

"We need more healing."

"Food is scarce. Can't you see that?"

"Yes, but we are afraid. Let us stay a little longer."

Our pleas are to no avail. We must leave, like all the others. We will join the road people until we find a train that will deliver us to a land of peace.

Where is that land of peace? How long are we to wander before we can cry ourselves to sleep on our own pillows?

We organize and organize until we accumulate a heap of clothes. What to sort out, what to take on this, our new unknown journey? What will be warm enough to fend off the cold, light enough to carry, strong enough to protect us?

The last time we made such decisions, we found ourselves at journey's end in the cannibal kingdom of Auschwitz. Where will this journey lead?

We are glum, contemplative. Our last march, the death march, is still burned into the soles of our feet. We look for an image of solace and come to rest on the hope that while on the road, we might bump into the missing members of our family.

We find a small wagon on which to load our belongings. We load items, remove them, put them back again. It is so difficult to part with any of our new-found riches. Our wagon, we know, must not be overburdened. We will have to pull it wherever we go, and our trip may be long and wearisome. We choose, discard, reacquire. We have a special fondness for a large robe. It is dark red with white checks. It is too heavy, but we pile it on the wagon.

Slowly we make peace with the prospect of living a road life. There will be, we pray, compensating factors. We say good-bye to those who remain, knowing well that we will never share good or bad again, and join the multinational, multilingual remnants of the bloodbath.

Almost immediately we begin to make friends and share the tales of common horrors.

"Which camp were you in? How many were in your family? How many survived? Who are you looking for? Do you have any hope?"

We talk and walk. We walk and remember. We walk and hurt. We wipe away tears that haven't surfaced yet. Sometimes we hum tunes.

Each day, as dusk approaches, we look for deserted homes to sleep in, homes that lodged yesterday's travelers. This kind of life calls for intuition and ingenuity. We have to share, be compassionate, crowd together, grab, run before others get there. Some villages yield an abundance of empty homes, others only a scant few.

We are helpful and kind to one another. The food we have brought along keeps us well. We keep walking during daylight, settle before dark.

On the third night we find shelter in a room with two large mattresses on the floor. A middle-aged woman joins us to share our "beds." She keeps talking about her twin daughters who were separated from her by Dr. Mengele upon their arrival at Auschwitz. She insists that her daughters are alive. Her faith in their survival is like a religious fervor.

We are skeptical, but we haven't the heart to tell her otherwise. We know that Mengele's particular passion was to perform medical experiments on twins.

We prepare for bed. Rachel and I take one mattress, Chicha and the woman the other. Suddenly, a drunken soldier enters the room. He sizes up the situation and chooses a bedmate. *"Chornaya,"* he mutters, selecting Chicha, my dark-haired sister. He quickly undresses and turns out the light.

In the dark the middle-aged woman switches places with Chicha.

In the morning the soldier realizes the deception. He smiles, dresses, and departs. On his way out he tosses a gold watch to his most recent conquest. The woman becomes part of our wandering family.

Finally, we lose her on the road, and much later we learn that she has actually, miraculously, found her twins alive in Budapest.

On our journey the woman never stopped talking about her children. She was certain the gods had decreed that somewhere another mother would give her body to a drunken soldier, as she had done, to save her daughters' virginity. We shall always remember her faith. We do not remember her name. . . .

We begin to climb aboard the train, we and the others, the dear others from around the globe: Jews who weren't murdered, and liberated soldier prisoners, soldiers who killed in order to stop Hitler from murdering us. Tall Englishman, short Hindu, blond Scot, smiling American, Palestinian Jew, Sino-European, Czech Jewess, French fighter, people from tiny hamlets and great nations—and three Jewish girls from Kisvarda, Hungary. All these, plus the Russian soldiers responsible for our journey and our liberation.

Our commonality is overwhelming. We are all survivors of the same disease, hate. In this moving venture we nourish each other with care and concern. There is no common language between us, yet we speak the same tongue. With the touch of a hand, a comforting gesture, a look, we understand each other's recent past.

Those who are returning to their homes and families seem fully to comprehend that we three—Rachel, Chicha, and I—and the other liberated Jewish survivors are a breed separate and apart. No one will be brewing coffee, serving drinks, baking bread and cookies for us at the end of our journey, wherever that end will be. Families will not be waiting for us; no one will be sitting around listening to our war stories. Our mothers and fathers did not accumulate letters from us while we were gone. There will be no parties to celebrate our kind of heroism. There will be no music and no neighbors weeping with joy for us, no salty tears for our dead.

Wherever we go, we will be alien orphans. Home is nowhere for us—not in our native land, not in any new land that will have us. We will have to learn a new language, a new culture, a new mode of dress and behavior. We will have to learn to control the rage inside us or make peace with it. We will have to learn how to communicate the unbelievable or keep silent and make believe that we just happened upon this side of the ocean or the other.

In this train we have an identity: we are little girls from a big war. On the other side of the ocean, should we ever reach that haven, we will be the strangest of strangers, from a continent of killing that contained within it yet other continents called Auschwitz and Bergen-Belsen and other strange names.

The Hindu sits in the lotus position and never talks. Does he ever sleep? It doesn't seem so. The Czech Jewess falls in love with the tall Englishman. The Palestinian promises the blessings of the kibbutz, the whole kibbutz, to Rachel. The New Zealander promises New Zealand to Chicha. And Les, the dearest, gentlest American soldier, mothers me with the most exquisite sensitivity.

Les is about twenty-two, a little older than I, but he adopts me as though I were an infant in need of ceaseless care. He must have seen Auschwitz or some other death camp, for he looks at me in total awe. In his every move he seems determined to somehow make up for the ferocious crime committed against me.

For two weeks, as the train rolls toward Odessa, Les seems to suspend his own person so that all he has, all he is, can be put in the service of healing. I don't think he is in love with me—he *is* love, total love. He provides something warm for my shoulders, something cool to quench my thirst, something nourishing to make me gain weight. Where does he get it all?

Each time the train stops, Les disappears and comes back with the sweetest balms. His delicacy is so unique that everyone is touched by it. Never have I seen such gentleness, as if some mysterious force willed the antithesis of Auschwitz upon me. Les asks for nothing in exchange.

I wonder now, so many years later, how much that young American was able to glean from my awe of him, from the depth of my loving appreciation, from my loving gratitude.

For two weeks the train keeps stopping in all kinds of places for all kinds of intervals. We visit with the other riders; by now, we all feel like kin. We do not understand the logistics of travel in a war-torn land. Are the frequent stops necessary for the movement of more urgent cargo in the other direction? Ammunition? Guns? The war is still in progress. It is March 1945. When will the war end? Are there concentration camps still to be liberated? Is Cipi in one of them? Is Philip?

War is noisy as hell, but it is silent concerning its secrets. It is so hard to find out anything. Gossip of great victories abounds. We love the stories. Are they true? Will the war be over soon?

The train is very long. Masses of people are riding on it, but we have all been on board for so long that to us it is a traveling community. Food is available or not. The motherly Russian cook concocts a magic all-in-one meal whenever she gets a delivery of ingredients from who-knows-where. In her huge cauldron she stirs vegetables and meat with a giant wooden spoon. We watch her prepare the "family meal" with delicious excitement. If only food were cooking around the clock . . . but it is not.

On some days we are terribly hungry. We talk about nothing but food. We are frustrated by the British. They alone seem to be different. They do not complain. They talk about the weather, the dog that runs past the train, the countryside—anything but food. Were they not to eat for a year, it seems, they would not complain. They are stony-faced at the mention of food. What makes them the way they are? Why can't they say they are hungry?

In certain villages the train stops long enough for us to go to the open farmers' markets, which are filled with the aroma of the morning's harvest. The peasants are kindly, but we have no money. We hardly remember what money looks like.

The peasants have food but lack clothing. We barter our stockings and other items from the "wardrobe" we dragged along from the blacksmith's house. Some peasants want our stockings more than anything else. We do not understand why. We barter with them for eggs and return to our train home.

In a battered pan, Rachel collects scalding water droplets from the steam plumes of the locomotive. We keep the eggs in the hot water long enough to half cook them, then enjoy a sumptuous feast; we are happy again.

We roll along and stop again. We barter for potatoes and cook them in an instant fireplace of burning twigs. They are tastier, it seems, than any dish that any gourmet chef could prepare. Our battered pan is lovable and lickable whenever sticky food graces its contours.

We are happy with our lot, with our train, with our companions. The Russian cook is cooking again. We love her food. We love her.

At each stop, romance is refueled. We roll cigarettes and stroll flirtatiously in the sun. Our hair has grown a bit. We can actually begin to use a comb. We have not had any use for one in nearly a year. It is an uncanny sensation.

We stroll beside the train displaying our short crowns of an inch of hair. With our newly found womanhood, we attract the attention of the men of our world.

We are our very attractive selves again, and the soldiers on our train admire us, are ready to whisk us away to cities and hamlets we have never heard of.

But our plans are different. We have yet to search, to find parts of our old family before we try to create a new one. Our yearnings are fixed on what was: Cipi, Philip, my father.

Innocent, global flirtations en route to Odessa are such fun, but we are on our way to America, not Australia, New Zealand, or India. We are looking for Kisvarda. We will go all the way to America to try to find it. We are not in love yet, only intrigued by the very real possibility that someday we will be.

As I sit on the train, Les sensitively bandages my inner wounds. Chicha and Rachel report on new conquests. "I was proposed to," says Chicha. "So was I," says Rachel.

All a beautiful thing has to do is get off the train for a walk and she gets a marriage proposal. However playful and unserious these promises of heaven are, they nurture the long-dead womanhood in us, and we are grateful to these Don Juans of a devastating war. May you never war again, handsome soldiers. May this train, with its gathering of exiles, travel into an age of peace. We are all so tired.

We Didn't Know That You Were Alive

Helen Epstein

Born in 1947, Helen Epstein is the daughter of
Holocaust survivors, who had been incarcerated at
Auschwitz and Terezin. Like many children of
survivors, Epstein felt the need to understand the
Holocaust. She is a freelance writer and a professor
of journalism at New York University. After
interviewing hundreds of children of survivors, she
gathered their stories in *Children of the Holocaust:
Conversations with Sons and Daughters of Survivors*,
from which the following narrative is taken.

In this section, Epstein describes her mother's
return to Prague after the war. While the city was
virtually the same, everything was different for
Franci.

It was nearly four months after liberation. One
could not go on pretending that home was in a British administrative center. In
the first week of August, 1945, the two cousins set out by bus and truck, with
eleven pieces of luggage, for Prague. They traveled slowly, from the British into
the American war zone, and then into the Russian zone, across the country in
ruins that was Germany.

They arrived in Prague one week later at four in the morning. Their driver
honked the truck horn in the dark, empty street in front of the house where a

former classmate of Kitty's lived. The apartments both my mother and Kitty had lived in before the war were now occupied by strangers and Kitty's friend had kindly invited them to stay with him. He came down to greet them now, followed by a group of neighbors who helped the two cousins unload their baggage and plied them with pastries and coffee until my mother felt paralyzed by solicitousness.

"I don't know what I was expecting," she told me when I was older. "But whatever I had expected, whatever I had dreamed it would be like, it was different. I kept thinking that I had come home to strangers. That I was in Prague, the place I had lived all my life, and I was staying with strangers."

Later that morning, my mother and Kitty went downtown. They walked to the back of the streetcars and remained standing there although they saw seats vacant. They had not had time to accustom themselves to the fact that the Nazi transportation regulations concerning Jews had been rescinded. As the red streetcar clattered through the morning streets, my mother grew gloomy. It seemed to her that the war had bypassed the people around her. She compared the cloth of their suits and dresses to the flimsy cotton sundress she wore, the one that had seemed a miracle just four months before. The conversations she overheard around her seemed peppered with new Czech expressions which had not been fashionable three years before. There were small changes in the shop windows and street signs of the city. Life had gone on here, she saw, while for her it had stopped for three years.

Kitty, standing beside her in the tram, seemed oblivious to any of these things. She was busy taking in old sights, chattering on about the changes in a bright, happy voice. When they reached the center of town, the two women went their separate ways. My mother had an appointment with Max, who had been her parents' friend. It was at his home that her family had planned a re-union when the war was over. She walked to the café where they had agreed to meet, her dark eyes following the faces in the street, searching for one that was familiar. She imagined her mother's figure, small, elegant and soft, each time she turned a corner. She was twenty-five now, a woman who had survived Hitler and even typhus, she told herself. But her feet dragged on the pavement and she felt like a lost child.

"Franci?" a man asked as she walked into the café.

She sat down with Max and neither knew what to say. Then he told her that her husband, Pepik Solar, was dead. He returned to my mother a letter she had written her husband in the belief he had survived. She held the unopened envelope between her fingers and felt nothing. Numbness was becoming part of her nature. She had first noticed the loss of feeling in Auschwitz, after they had given her the blue number. She had been sitting in a bunk watching a Jewish *kapo* deride some fellow prisoners. *A striped S.S.*, she had thought to herself.

How strange to see. She had stared at her forearm then and the forearm became two arms, one that belonged to her, Franci Solar, and one that belonged to that other woman, the one that looked exactly like her but had a number on her arm. From that moment on, she had become two people: one who acted and one who watched. She watched herself now, holding the unopened envelope between her fingers. And she watched Max.

"Vera told me to ask you to dinner tonight," he said. "That is, if you have no other plans."

"I have no other plans," she replied, staring into his face and finding it terribly stupid. What other plans could she possibly have? She wanted to hear that Max was happy to see her back, that he was glad she had survived. But Max seemed tongue-tied. Why did he not understand that she did not need this silence, this embarrassment, this awkwardness? She had wanted warmth.

Max thrust his hand toward her. It was filled with bills. "Just to tide you over," he said, blushing so that his summer tan showed even more prominently. "It's not really as much as it looks. The currency's been devalued so many times. I'll see you tonight."

My mother sat with the devalued bills in her hand for several minutes after he left. Then she walked in the direction of the Jewish Community Center, where Jews returning to Prague were issued documents to replace those confiscated by the Gestapo three years before. At that moment, had she been stopped by a policeman or accused of a crime, my mother could not have proved who she was. She did not possess a single document. Her birth certificate, her passport, working papers, and health records had been taken from her in 1942. She watched herself waiting her turn, answering questions in a monotone, filling out forms.

"Where can I find a room?" she asked a clerk.

"Are you married?"

"My husband is dead."

"Children?"

"None."

"There's a terrible housing shortage," the clerk told her patiently. "It's a difficult situation. We give preference to families. Then, married couples."

That made sense, my mother told herself. It was only fair. But a terrible anger burned inside her as she walked the streets to kill time before dinner at Max's house. By what right were strangers living in her parents' house? Was this what they called repatriation, to be sent home only to find no roof to live under? Why hadn't she stayed in Celle? Or married one of the Englishmen like some of the girls had? She wandered past the bookstores that she had spent hours in before the war, seeing nothing, aimless and blank. When she stopped, she found herself standing before the door of what had been her mother's dress salon.

Without thinking, she rang the bell and Marie, the Czechoslovak woman who had been her mother's assistant, came to the door.

"Franci. You're back."

The tone of her voice was not happy or welcoming, just surprised, my mother thought. She imagined her former employee was thinking: *What does she want? How did she get back? What did she do to survive?*

"Come in. Please come in." Marie recovered quickly. She took my mother into the workroom where Franci had, as a teen-ager, learned to cut and baste and finish the dresses and coats that her mother designed.

"Almost nothing that was yours is here any longer," Marie said. "I put everything in storage. I didn't want the authorities to make trouble for us. I mean, we had to protect ourselves against the charge of enriching ourselves with Jewish property. Do you see what I mean?"

My mother nodded and understood nothing. Marie seemed to be talking gibberish. Nothing was in its proper place in the workroom. Her favorite sewing machine was gone. There were fewer tables. The room was poorly swept. There was grime on the windows.

"Business is off," Marie continued. "The old customers, the ones who came to your mother? They don't come here anymore. Some of them emigrated, I've heard. At any rate, I don't see them. We refurnished the place, you see. And the lease came up for renewal last year. Of course we had no idea where you were. We took it out in our own name."

"Yes," my mother said.

Something in her face seemed to frighten Marie.

"There was nothing else to do," she said loudly. "We didn't know that you would be coming back. We didn't know that you were alive."

My mother's mouth had swelled and her jaw thrust out as it had when she had been a child affecting indifference.

"Your mother . . ."

"She's dead."

"I'm so sorry," Marie said and that part of my mother that was observing the scene observed that Marie seemed sincerely distressed.

"Thank you," my mother said mechanically, and then wondered what she was thanking Marie for.

"You should have the address of the warehouse where your mother's things are stored. There should be no problem requisitioning them. Not now. It's been very hard these past few years but it's easier now." She gave my mother a slip of paper with the name of the warehouse written on it. "I'm sure we will be seeing one another now that you're back. We're in the same business after all, no?"

The door closed and my mother wandered through the streets again. A hazy August light had settled over the city, warming the gray stone buildings and sending glints of gold off the tips of church spires. People hurried home with packages of bread or potatoes. Prague had been bombed less than other major European cities during the war. Most of it was intact, just as my mother remembered it. Only she was different.

At seven, she presented herself at Max and Vera Bocek's house. Her mother had very much liked the couple. They were people to be trusted. They had two teen-age boys whom she had watched grow from babies into adolescents. The Boceks were old family friends. It would be all right.

When Vera Bocek opened the front door, her face showed a prepared smile. She served dinner almost immediately after my mother arrived and then busied herself so effectively with the ladling of soup and the cutting of bread that she was able to disregard the dearth of conversation.

As soon as she sat down at the table my mother had seen the "R" on the tablecloth. It stood for Rabinek and it came from the linen closet in her parents' home. The heavy silver knife and fork at the sides of her plate were part of the set of silverware my mother had, as a small child, helped her polish. The crystal wine glass which she held between her fingers was from the dark wood cupboard that had stood in the dining room. She had helped her mother pack the glasses carefully and brought them over to the Boceks for safekeeping until the war was over. Vera Bocek said nothing about the pale-blue tablecloth, the silverware, the glasses, or anything else. At first my mother thought these things had been brought out of storage in her honor. But as the meal drew to a close without mention of them, she understood that Vera Bocek had forgotten, or had made herself forget, that they were not her own.

My mother caught herself staring at the "R" in the table-cloth so fixedly that she became embarrassed. She wanted to change the subject that claimed her mind, so she asked about the Bocek children. How old were they? What were they doing?

At the time my mother and her parents were deported to Terezin in 1942, Pavel and Edvard Bocek were twelve and thirteen.

"You won't recognize either of them, they've grown so," said Vera Bocek, and as she spoke Pavel walked in, taller and skinnier than my mother had remembered him. He was wearing one of Pepik Solar's suits, one of the many items of clothing my mother had carried over to the Boceks' house for safekeeping.

But for reasons that my mother did not understand, it was she—not Vera Bocek—who was embarrassed by the sight of her dead husband's suit on Pavel. Her embarrassment grew as they finished dinner and sat down in the living room for coffee. Max had said little. Conversation was stilted and my mother saw no smooth way to pose the question she had to ask. Finally, she took a breath and asked it.

"You know the jewelry my mother left with you," she asked Vera Bocek. "I thought maybe I'd sell one of the rings. I don't have a place to live. Or a job. All I own is a couple of suitcases."

Vera exchanged glances with her husband. "I'm terribly sorry," she said, "but we were very hard up the last year of the war. We had the same idea. We sold your mother's jewelry. It's gone."

My mother felt the way she had in the Jewish Community Center that afternoon looking for a place to live. There was nothing to say, nothing to do. She could hardly haul Vera Bocek to court for stealing her family's possessions. She didn't even have an address of her own or a piece of paper proving she was a Czech citizen. Besides, they had been close friends of her parents. The war had been hard for them too. They had not expected she would come back.

The encounter with the Boceks was typical of several reunions my mother was to have in the following weeks and months. The gist of the conversations and the embarrassment of things left unsaid were repeated so many times that my mother came to expect them. Soon she only wanted to see people she had known in prison. Or entirely new people, people she had never seen before the war, people who could not compare her to the person she had been before. During the day, she walked through Prague, turning the corners with the impossible hope of seeing her parents walking toward her arm in arm, the way they had walked away from her in Terezin, on their way to the transport which took them to Poland. At night she saw Kitty or sat in small rooms rented by other survivors who drank ersatz coffee and argued politics. Only Communism could prevent another Fascist regime in Czechoslovakia, some said. Others argued that only a strong Socialist party could prevent the Communists from becoming new Fascists. She sat listlessly, uninterested in politics, and then went home with one of the debaters. Neither she nor Kitty had been able to find a room of their own. They moved from one place into another, always on the understanding that it was temporary. There were no apartments to be had.

Autumn came to Prague, bringing bad weather and another currency devaluation. My mother had retrieved small amounts of cash she had left with friends but the devaluation reduced them to one-tenth their value. The rain put an end to her walks, and she needed money so badly that she accepted a job as assistant to a former competitor of her mother.

"Franci Solar!" old clients would exclaim when they saw her buying in the fabric shops. "You're back! Have you opened the business?"

My mother shook her head. "I need a license," she would say. "There's too much red tape. I need documents I don't have. I need a place to work. I have no equipment. I'd have to buy everything from scratch."

What she did not say was that the long lines at the Community Center, the questions the clerks asked her and the forms she had to fill out terrified her. She was frightened by any form of authority. How could she run a business? She would have to give orders to her employees and she was incapable of giving orders to anyone. She could barely take care of herself.

Autumn became winter. There were fewer people on the streets. Many of the ex-prisoners who had returned to Prague along with my mother married and emigrated to England or America, propelled by the fear that the Russians would take over Eastern Europe bit by bit, just as Hitler had done not even a decade before. My mother spent long evenings alone. For a time, she had a puppy, a terrier who reminded her of the puppy she had before the war. During the last few months before she was deported, when it was too dangerous for her to continue appearing in the workroom, she had spent hours sewing fancy covers for his collar. Once she had made him a yellow Star of David. "Take that off him!" her mother had warned as they set out for a walk far from the center of the city. In a meadow filled with wildflowers and rabbits, the puppy had disappeared. That evening someone had found him. He had been shot dead. My mother became certain that if she kept the second puppy, he would die too, and one day she gave him away.

On New Year's Eve of 1946, my mother lay in a luke-warm bath, listening to the shouts and songs coming in through the window from the street. She had been invited to several parties but did not feel like going. She was too lonely. Her documents were still not in order. She still did not have her own place to live. She had lost all interest in men. She had decided never to marry again. Every day she imagined that she heard her mother's voice correcting her as she pinned dresses to headless dummies. She wanted all the noise in her head, all the images that passed through it day and night, to stop.

My mother got out of the tub, got dressed and walked to the Vltava River, which runs through Prague. She passed partygoers bundled up against the cold and a few drunks who wished her a Happy New Year. But apart from them, the streets were deserted. Once, as a child walking home from school with her governess, my mother had seen a dead man dredged up out of the Vltava. His body was tinged with green and reeked of dead fish. For several nights after that, she had dreamed about the mythical Water Man of Czech folklore who was said to lure young girls into the water. The servants had always told her that the Water Man would take her away if she misbehaved. My mother remembered those stories now. She kept looking at the river in the darkness, thinking how peaceful it would be to sink down into the water and forget everything.

She walked along the river until a policeman stopped her. It was one o'clock, he said. Not the best time to be walking alone by the side of a half-frozen river. He smiled at her, then offered to walk her home. It was the first day of the new year, 1946, eight and a half months after the British tanks had rumbled into Bergen-Belsen.

My War Began in 1945

Debórah Dwork

Debórah Dwork teaches in the Department of
Religious Studies and has an appointment at the
Child Study Center at Yale University. She is the
author of *Children with a Star: Jewish Youth in Nazi
Europe*, which is based on hundreds of oral histories
of survivors who were children during the Holocaust
and from which the following selection is taken.

In this excerpt, Dwork describes the plight of
Jewish children after liberation when they learned
that their families had been destroyed, that their
possessions had been taken, and that few people or
organizations were concerned about their welfare.

For those Jewish children who were old enough
to remember, the memory alone of family life was a source of strength and
solace. Children who were separated from their parents when they went into
hiding or through the hazards of deportation, daughters who lost contact with
their fathers and brothers through the separation of sexes in the camps or
because the latter had been picked up in the streets for a forced labor detail, sons
who no longer saw their mothers and sisters, and siblings who were not able
to remain together remembered each other as they were at the time of parting.
Throughout the war they preserved the hope or dream that some day the
family would be reunited. In a vague, inchoate way, they presumed that when
the war was over they would resume their former life, and the old structures
and certainties would be restored. Even those who had seen family members
killed, or who had been told that such a fate had befallen them, held out hope

for the rest. This was not a clearly formulated or articulated principle, but a fundamental assumption, an interior conviction that carried a certain stability.

Maurits Cohen was eight years old when he went into hiding; his older brothers who also hid were ten and eleven. Neither of the latter survived. One was picked up by the Germans when he and a grandson of the farmer Boogaard (who, it may be remembered, with his family saved over 300 Jews and others hunted by the regime) had bicycled into the nearby village. The other was hiding with a family and attended the local school; he had been told to say that he was an evacuee from Rotterdam. One day, German soldiers entered his classroom and asked which children came from Rotterdam. The little boy said he was, and he was caught. Maurits Cohen was not told of these tragedies at the time. "I learned of everything after the war," he explained.

> During the war, I was a child and I was engaged with everyday living. The very impact of the consequences of the war I experienced after the war ended. My war began in 1945, and not in 1940. When I learned that my father and mother would not come back, and my brothers, then the war started. It took me years to get used to the idea, to find my own place, an only child, of course. We had had a very big family, so as a child I had to carry the whole weight of survival.

The children discovered after the war that their dreams had been fantasies, their hopes, illusions. Very few nuclear families were reunited after the war in their entirety, and no extended family escaped without losses. The survivors returned to their homes to find that their loved ones would never join them and that the Jewish community itself had been destroyed. Pre-war society had changed and the life they had known, the habits, manners, tenets, and beliefs had vanished. Indeed, the very shards of their lives had disappeared. Nothing that had been left in their homes was to be found and little that had been entrusted to friends and neighbors was recovered. The plunder of their possessions was permanent. The Germans had done their work thoroughly and, in spiritual collusion with them, the victims' neighbors looted whatever was left. The survivors returned to naught.

When the war ended, María Ezner was convinced that her father, who had been arrested before the rest of the family was deported, would survive. Her mother and sister shared her belief, and together they walked and jumped trains from Strasshof to Budapest. The roads and rail lines overflowed with people as the Soviet Army moved west and those who were liberated streamed east. The Ezners were debilitated and exhausted but they continued, driven by the urgent expectation of their reunion with their father and husband. As they trudged on, they saw "Cossacks on their horses. And we saw Tartars [Mongolians], like the great, great Plague of Europe, the Tartars in 1241, the same people. We saw elite troops coming, and Russian soldiers—women—who with two flags organized the traffic at the bridges, and so on." They slept in abandoned homes and ate the food they found in the larders. And then Ezner's mother fell horribly ill with dysentery. "One day she fell, and she thought she couldn't get up. We stood and cried that she should stand up, and then she got the strength and she stood up and we went on and on. If she had known that our father wouldn't come back, maybe she wouldn't have managed. But she said she had the feeling that she had to lead her two children home." Finally they arrived in Budapest, where they stayed with friends of relatives who had not yet returned. They checked the lists of survivors posted by the Joint Distribution Committee, but "the name of my father never showed up on the list." A few days later, "somebody said he had met a peasant from our community and this peasant had said, 'Oh, the lawyer Ezner is at home!' And then my mother said, 'We'll go home.'" They organized transport with a peasant who brought a laden cart to the market-place in Pest and returned with it empty. Leaving in the early morning, they arrived in Abádszalók the following morning.

> The house was empty. Not only was Father not there, the whole house was totally empty. No bed, no table, not a chair, nothing. Only one thing remained: my mother's piano was brought into the garden. Maybe it was too heavy. The people who had robbed everything had just left it. That one thing was in the garden. My mother still had her blanket with the SS stamp with her and we laid down on the floor and went to sleep. That was our homecoming.
>
> If I had known that my father would not come back, maybe I would have told my mother that we should go to Vienna and not return. I adored my father more than anybody. I have never met a man such as he. So there was no question as to whether we would return to Hungary, because we hoped that Father was working under similar conditions to ours. . . . We didn't know that Auschwitz existed. . . .
>
> We came back because we didn't know that our father wouldn't come back. And we were there; Mother on the ruins of her life. We imagined that when we returned we would come back to our old lives. The old life never came back. . . . And we had nothing.

A couple of their former friends returned bits of their furniture. "Some of our neighbors came and denounced other people who had our things. We went to them, and there were people who said, 'Surely, surely we'll bring it back.' But there were others who said, 'We?' and we knew that it was hidden in the attic or cellar." Ezner, her mother, and her sister were devastated, depressed, and impoverished. "We had no money. We had nothing."

The Ezners' homecoming was a common occurrence throughout Europe. Older and younger children, from the cities and the villages, of all social classes, degrees of religious observance, and nationalities experienced the same return to a void. Mária Ezner had recently turned fourteen when she, the child of a lawyer, went back to the small village where she had lived an assimilated, Jewishly unobservant life before the war. Gerry Mok, by contrast, was just eight years old when the Netherlands was liberated. His father had owned a small fruit shop in the Jewish neighborhood in east Amsterdam where they lived, and they had had a very Jewish life. Yet, essentially they confronted the same reality. "My personal Auschwitz came after 1945, not before," Mok explained. "I didn't really lose anyone during the war. People left, and I knew that was a disaster, supposedly a disaster, that anything might happen to them. But more or less, I expected them to come back, reasonable or not, and even notwithstanding the fact that people told me that probably my parents were dead. Do you think I believed them? . . . I thought I knew better. I was wrong." He waited and waited. "I expected my parents to come back. I expected everyone to come back. And no one came." It was a loss from which, in a certain sense, he never recovered. Since that time, "I have been missing my parents, I have been missing my grandparents and I have been missing my neighborhood. And I still do."

No one from his enormous extended family returned, and few of his family possessions were given back to him. The day Mok left his parents in February 1942, his father confided their valuables to a gentile man with whom he did business from time to time; "they bought fruits together, things like that." This business associate "came before I left and was asked to take care of all the things that belonged to my parents and my grandparents. He got a big iron box with all the jewels and things of my grandmother, who had a lot of such pieces. He took the box and put it on the back of his car." Mok remembered it well, because it was a sure sign that his parents intended to join him in his hiding home, as they told him they would. "I knew that they would follow me because they gave those valuable things to this man. I knew if my parents did that, they really were planning also to come." When the war was over, and Mok came to the painful realization that his parents would not return and he would not go back to his home, he recalled that some of his parents' things would have been saved, and he would have something that had belonged to them and to his grandparents. "I remembered who had taken the box, and I remembered the man's address because I had been there a thousand times. [My step-parents and I] went there, and oh yes, the man lived at that address and, oh yes, he knew I had lived there, and how fine that little Gerry survived. And I got fruit from him, and he was very nice, but 'the child must be completely mistaken because I never got anything.'" It was frustrating and infuriating, and especially so for Mok whose claim had no authority precisely because he was a child. "I remembered his name, I remembered his address, I remembered his car, I remembered the place he put it on his car, I remembered that he came, I remembered the fuss that was made about it. And then I went there, he recognized me, yes he knew my father, yes he knew my grandfather's wagon driver, he knew everybody.

And everything was true except, coincidentally, strangely enough, what I told about valuables. So: 'The child must be wrong; how nice that a child can imagine a thing like that.' "

The extent of the neighborly theft and the degree to which these ordinary people had justified their gains to themselves ranged from the astounding to the bizarre. Many children who survived and returned to their home towns after the war have related that, when they went to visit neighbors, friends of their parents, they were nicely treated and amiably received. They even were invited to come in, to sit down, and to eat. But the same people denied having received jewelry, china, linen, or silverware from the deported family. And there the child sat, eating off her mother's own dishes. In rural areas, where land and livestock were the valuables a family owned, children returned to villagers who denied that they or their families had ever existed. In some cases their reception was benign: the children simply never had lived there. In other instances, people who had the temerity to return were murdered. Wealth so easily obtained was not so easily renounced. In many places, Jews who survived were an unwanted encumbrance, an intolerable presence. Moishe Koblansky and his family were hidden by several people in and around their village of Gruszwica in the Ukraine, some of them Ukrainian and some Czech. The last family to take them in were Czech farmers who lived very near to the Koblanskys' own home. From late 1943 until the beginning of February 1944 the Koblansky family hid in a six by six by four foot pit which had been dug out under the pigsty. The wooden floor of the pigsty was their roof. "When the Russians came in, February 2nd of 1944, we were about two blocks away from our house. The Russians came one day, and early the next morning, before dawn we got out of the hole. We didn't wait to have breakfast with these people. We didn't want to compromise them. We left the hiding place in the pigsty and we went to our house. That way, no one knew where we came from, no one would know where we had been. The people who hid us would be safe and no one would know that they had hidden Jews, because some people might take retribution against them." The Koblanskys returned to their home only briefly. They did not stay. They were no longer members of that community. "There was no question. We left the house. Everything was very casual. There was no sense of belonging and no sense of things belonging to us. The term 'my house' had no meaning. I think that's how I felt at that time. The house was just another encumbrance. We couldn't carry it with us, we couldn't sell it. So the hell with it." To wait until they could sell it was out of the question. It was too dangerous. Once again, they left their home for safety elsewhere.

Returning children received little sympathy from their neighbors, and they encountered indifference from their national governments. In the immediate post-war period (from 1945 to 1950) politicians were preoccupied with the business of rebuilding their countries, and the plight of Jewish children did not figure prominently in that agenda. The cities had been bombed, the infrastructure shattered, and the financial system was in ruins. The population, which had been united under a national flag before the war, had been riven apart by Nazism, Fascism, and the occupation. Resisters and collaborators had fought against each other for years while the great majority of people simply had endured the hardships of war. There was no solidarity between these three factions; they had not experienced the war in the same way and there was no sympathy between them. It was the politicians' job to stitch their citizenry together. This was the predominant national project, and the issue of the Jews, the iniquities that had been perpetrated against them during the war, their current plight, and their uncertain future, was a low-priority problem.

The Awakening

Primo Levi

As an author, Primo Levi is best known for his autobiographical accounts of the years he spent at Auschwitz. His books of fiction, poetry, and autobiography include *If Not Now, When?, Survival in Auschwitz, Moments of Reprieve, The Drowned and the Saved*, and *The Reawakening*, from which the following excerpt is taken. For additional biographical information on Levi, see page 213.

In this selection, Levi reveals his complex emotions during the long journey back to his home in Italy after his release from Auschwitz in January 1945.

Austria borders on Italy, and St Valentin is only 180 miles from Tarvisio; but on 15 October, the thirty-first day of our journey, we crossed a new frontier and entered Munich, prey to a disconsolate railway tiredness, a permanent loathing for trains, for snatches of sleep on wooden floors, for jolting and for stations; so that familiar smells, common to all the railways of the world, the sharp smell of impregnated sleepers, hot brakes, burning fuel, inspired in us a deep disgust. We were tired of everything, tired in particular of perforating useless frontiers.

But from another point of view, the fact of feeling a piece of Germany under our feet for the first time, not a piece of Upper Silesia or of Austria, but of Germany itself, overlaid our tiredness with a complex attitude composed of intolerance, frustration and tension. We felt we had something to say, enormous things to say, to every single German, and we felt that every German should have something to say to us; we felt an urgent need to settle our accounts, to ask, explain and comment, like chess players at the end of a game. Did "they" know about Auschwitz, about the silent daily massacre, a step away from their doors? If they did, how could they walk about, return home and look at their children, cross the threshold of a church? If they did not, they ought, as a sacred duty, to listen, to learn everything, immediately, from us, from me; I felt the tattooed number on my arm burning like a sore.

As I wandered around the streets of Munich, full of ruins, near the station where our train lay stranded once more, I felt I was moving among throngs of insolvent debtors, as if everybody owed me something, and refused to pay. I was among them, in the enemy camp, among the *Herrenvolk*; but the men were few, many were mutilated, many dressed in rags like us. I felt that everybody should interrogate us, read in our faces who we were, and listen to our tale in humility. But no one looked us in the eyes, no one accepted the challenge; they were deaf, blind and dumb, imprisoned in their ruins, as in a fortress of wilful ignorance, still strong, still capable of hatred and contempt, still prisoners of their old tangle of pride and guilt.

I found myself searching among them, among that anonymous crowd of sealed faces, for other faces, clearly stamped in my memory, many bearing a name: the name of someone who could not but know, remember, reply; who had commanded and obeyed, killed, humiliated, corrupted. A vain and foolish search; because not they, but others, the few just ones, would reply for them.

If we had taken one guest on board at Szób, after Munich we realized that we had taken on board an entire contingent: our train consisted no longer of sixty, but of sixty-one trucks. A new truck was travelling with us towards Italy at the end of our train, crammed with young Jews, boys and girls, coming from all the countries of Eastern Europe. None of them seemed more than twenty years old, but they were extremely self-confident and resolute people; they were young Zionists on their way to Israel, travelling where they were able to, and finding a path where they could. A ship was waiting for them at Bari; they had purchased their truck, and it had proved the simplest thing in the world to attach it to our train: they had not asked anybody's permission, but had hooked it on, and that was that. I was amazed, but they laughed at my amazement: "Hitler's dead, isn't he?" replied their leader, with his intense hawk-like glance. They felt immensely free and strong, lords of the world and of their destinies.

We passed through Garmisch-Partenkirchen and in the evening reached the fantastically disordered transit camp of Mittenwald, in the mountains, on the Austrian border. We spent the night there, and it was our last night of cold. The following day the train ran down to Innsbruck, where it filled up with Italian smugglers, who brought us the greetings of our homeland, in the absence of official authorities, and generously distributed chocolate, grappa and tobacco.

As the train, more tired than us, climbed towards the Italian frontier it snapped in two like an overtaut cable; there were several injuries, but this was the last adventure. Late at night we crossed the Brenner, which we had passed in our exile twenty months before; our less tired companions celebrated with a cheerful uproar; Leonardo and I remained lost in a silence crowded with memories. Of 650, our number when we had left, three of us were returning. And how much had we lost, in those twenty months? What should we find at home? How much of ourselves had been eroded, extinguished? Were we returning richer or poorer, stronger or emptier? We did not know; but we knew that on the thresholds of our homes, for good or ill, a trial awaited us, and we anticipated it with fear. We felt in our veins the poison of Auschwitz, flowing together with our thin blood; where should we find the strength to begin our lives again, to break down the barriers, the brushwood which grows up spontaneously in all absences, around every deserted house, every empty refuge? Soon, tomorrow, we should have to give battle, against enemies still unknown, outside ourselves and inside; with what weapons, what energies, what willpower? We felt the weight of centuries on our shoulders, we felt oppressed by a year of ferocious memories; we felt emptied and defenceless. The months just past, although hard, of wandering on the margins of civilization now seemed to us like a truce, a parenthesis of unlimited availability, a providential but unrepeatable gift of fate.

With these thoughts, which kept us from sleep, we passed our first night in Italy, as the train slowly descended the deserted, dark Adige Valley. On 17 October, we reached the camp of Pescantina, near Verona, and here we split up, everyone following his own destiny; but no train left in the direction of Turin until the evening of the following day. In the confused vortex of thousands of refugees and displaced persons, we glimpsed Pista, who had already found his path; he wore the white and yellow armband of the Pontifical Organization of Assistance, and collaborated briskly and cheerfully in the life of the camp. And then we saw advance towards us a figure, a well-known face, a full head higher than the crowd, the Moor of Verona. He had come to say good-bye to us, to Leonardo and me; he had reached his home, the first of all of us, for Avesa, his village, was only a few miles away. And he blessed us, the old blasphemer: he raised two enormous knobbly fingers, and blessed us with the solemn gesture of a Pontiff, wishing us a good return and a happy future.

I reached Turin on 19 October, after thirty-five days of travel; my house was still standing, all my family was alive, no one was expecting me. I was swollen, bearded and in rags, and had difficulty in making myself recognized. I found my friends full of life, the warmth of secure meals, the solidity of daily work, the liberating joy of recounting my story. I found a large clean bed, which in the evening (a moment of terror) yielded softly under my weight. But only after many months did I lose the habit of walking with my glance fixed to the ground, as if searching for something to eat or to pocket hastily or to sell for bread; and a dream full of horror has still not ceased to visit me, at sometimes frequent, sometimes longer, intervals.

It is a dream within a dream, varied in detail, one in substance. I am sitting at a table with my family, or with friends, or at work, or in the green country-side; in short, in a peaceful relaxed environment, apparently without tension or affliction; yet I feel a deep and subtle anguish, the definite sensation of an impending threat. And in fact, as the dream proceeds, slowly or brutally, each time in a different way, everything collapses and disintegrates around me, the scenery, the walls, the people, while the anguish becomes more intense and more precise. Now everything has changed to chaos; I am alone in the centre of a grey and turbid nothing, and now, I *know* what this thing means, and I also know that I have always known it; I am in the Lager once more, and nothing is true outside the Lager. All the rest was a brief pause, a deception of the senses, a dream; my family, nature in flower, my home. Now this inner dream, this dream of peace, is over, and in the outer dream, which continues, gelid, a well-known voice resounds: a single word, not imperious, but brief and subdued. It is the dawn command of Auschwitz, a foreign word, feared and expected: get up, *"Wstawàch."*

1945

Bernard S. Mikofsky

Bernard S. Mikofsky
served as an intelligence
officer in the U.S. Army
Signal Corps from 1943 to
1946. He has taught
Russian and other Slavic
languages at several
universities, including
Indiana University and
Kent State. His articles
on Slavic linguistics and
opinion pieces have
appeared in a number of
newspapers.

In this poem,
Mikofsky explores how
the Holocaust continues
to trouble our memories.

And that year
When the fires ceased
And the ovens were finally cool
A strange wind moved out
In slow, grief-laden eddies
And sooty swirls
Across Europe—
And even beyond.

And those with conscience
(And even those without)
Heard faint sounds from afar,
Echoes from an age-old abyss,
And sometimes these seemed to come
From inside one's ear—
So tiny and yet so persistent,
Echoes of the anonymous cries
Of numbered millions.

And far from the ovens,
Far from the funeral fires,
This wind still carried
Wraiths of soot
Too fine to water the eye
Yet searing the heart.

That year the strange wind
Moved slowly across Europe—
And even beyond,
Now and then pausing
To eddy into the deepest corners
Of our minds
To remind us,
To stir us for an instant
From our dream of well-being.

1945, The Silence

Burton D. Wasserman

Burton D. Wasserman lives in Mount Vernon, New York. His work has been published in a number of poetry magazines.

After liberation, some Holocaust survivors found it difficult to track down family members. As Wasserman's poem suggests, bad news was common and often had a devastating impact.

It was a letter
From Poland,
Delivered simply
With the junk mail
And the butcher's bill,
Yet breathing the bristle
Of military commands
And commanding the sight
Of dragging, bleeding feet.

The letter seized my mother
Read itself aloud in her quivering
Voice, on and on
And on
Until she fell;
Father, speaking in his father's voice,
Emptied its final silence
Into our mouths.

My little sister asked
"Why did the Nazis kill mama's family?" Father
Would not or could not answer, instead
Kissed his child's eyes full of tears.

I, almost thirteen,
Suddenly saw my parents
As smaller than life.

We all carried mother to bed;
For months after, we tried to reason,
To love her, to beg—but she
Would not listen
Or become part of us again:
She had become
The Silence.

The Accident

Elie Wiesel

Elie Wiesel remains one of the most eloquent voices
speaking about the horrors of the Holocaust. For
additional biographical information on Wiesel, see
page 337.

This poignant Wiesel piece illustrates the guilt
and sorrow that survivors often experience.

Every morning Dr. Russel came to chat. He had
made it a habit to end his daily rounds with me. Often he would remain an hour
or more. He would walk in without knocking, sit on the window sill, his hands
in the pockets of his white coat, his legs crossed, his eyes reflecting the changing
colors of the river.

He spoke a lot about himself, his life in the army—he had been in the Korean
War—his work, the pleasures and disappointments that came with it. Each prey
torn away from death made him as happy as if he had won a universal victory. A
defeat left dark rings under his eyes. I only had to look at him carefully to know
whether the night before he had won or lost the battle. He considered death his
personal enemy.

"What makes me despair," he often told me bitterly, "is that our weapons
aren't equal. My victories can only be temporary. My defeats are final. Always."

One morning he seemed happier than usual. He gave up his favorite spot
near the window and started walking up and down the room like a drunkard,
talking to himself.

"You have been drinking, Doctor!" I teased him.

"Drinking!" he exclaimed. "Of course I haven't been drinking. I don't drink.
Today I'm simply happy. Awfully happy. I won! Yes, this time I won. . . ."

His victory tasted like wine. He couldn't stand still. To split up his happiness he would have liked to be simultaneously himself and someone else: witness and hero. He wanted to sing and to hear himself singing, to dance and to see himself dancing, to climb to the top of the highest mountain and to shout, to scream with all his strength, "I won! I conquered Death!"

The operation had been difficult, dangerous: a little twelve-year-old boy who had a very slim chance of surviving. Three doctors had given up hope. But he, Paul Russel, had decided to try the impossible.

"The kid will make it!" he thundered, his face glowing as if lit up by a sun inside him. "Do you understand? He's going to live! And yet all seemed lost! The infection had reached his leg and was poisoning his blood. I amputated the leg. The others were saying that it wouldn't do any good. That it was too late. That the game was lost. But I didn't hesitate. I started to act. For each breath, I had to fight with every weapon I had. But you see: I won! This time I really won!"

The joy of saving a human life, I thought. I have never experienced it. I didn't even know that it existed. To hold in your hands a boy's life is to take God's place. I had never dreamt of rising above the level of man. Man is not defined by what denies him, but by that which affirms him. This is found within, not across from him or next to him.

"You see," Paul Russel said in a different tone of voice, "the difference between you and me is this. Your relation with what surrounds you and with what marks the limits of your horizon develops in an indirect way. You only know the words, the skin, the appearances, the ideas, of life. There'll always be a curtain between you and your neighbor's life. You're not content to know man is alive; you also want to know what he is doing with his life. For me this is different. I am less severe with my fellow men. We have the same enemy and it has only one name: Death. Before it we are all equal. In its eyes no life has more weight than another. From that point of view, I am just like Death. What fascinates me in man is his capacity for living. Acts are just repetitions. If you had ever held a man's life in the palm of your hand, you too would come to prefer the immediate to the future, the concrete to the ideal, and life to the problems which it brings with it."

He stood at the window for a moment and stopped talking, just long enough to smile, before continuing an octave lower.

"Your life, my friend, I had it right there. In the palm of my hand."

He turned slowly, his hand held out. Little by little his face became as it usually was and his gestures became less abrupt.

"Do you believe in God, Doctor?"

My question took him by surprise. He stopped suddenly, wrinkling his forehead.

"Yes," he answered. "But not in the operating room. There I only count on myself."

His eyes looked deeper. He added, "On myself and on the patient. Or, if you prefer, on the life in the diseased flesh. Life wants to live. Life wants to go on. It is opposed to death. It fights. The patient is my ally. He fights on my side. Together we are stronger than the enemy. Take the boy last night. He didn't accept death. He helped me to win the battle. He was holding on, clinging. He was asleep, anesthetized, and yet he was taking part in the fight. . . ."

Still motionless, he again stared at me intensely. There was an awkward silence. Once more I had the impression he knew, that he was speaking only to penetrate my secret. Now, I decided. Now or never. I had to put an end to any uncertainty.

"Doctor, I would like to ask you a question."

He nodded.

"What did I say during the operation?"

He thought a moment. "Nothing. You didn't say anything."

"Are you sure? Not even a word?"

"Not even a word."

I was relieved and couldn't help smiling.

"My turn now," the doctor said seriously. "I also have a question."

My smile froze. "Go ahead," I said.

I had to fight an urge to close my eyes. All of a sudden the room seemed too light. Anxiety took hold of my voice, my breath, my eyes.

The doctor lowered his head slightly, almost imperceptibly.

"Why don't you care about living?" he asked very softly.

For a moment everything shook. Even the light flickered and changed color. It was white, red, black. The blood was beating in my temples. My head was no longer my own.

"Don't deny it," the doctor went on, speaking still more softly. "Don't deny it. I know."

He knows. He knows. He knows. My throat was in an invisible vise. I was going to choke any moment.

Weakly I asked him who had told him: Kathleen?

"No. Not Kathleen. Nobody. Nobody told me. But I know it anyway. I guessed. During the operation. You never helped me. Not once. You abandoned me. I had to wage the fight alone, all alone. Worse. You were on the other side, against me, on the side of the enemy."

His voice became hard, painfully hard. "Answer me! Why don't you want to live? Why?"

I was calm again. He doesn't know, I thought. The little he is guessing is nothing. An impression. That's all. Nothing definite. Nothing worked out. And yet he is moving in the right direction. Only he's not going all the way.

"Answer me," he repeated. "Why? Why?"

He was becoming more and more insistent. His lower lip was shaking nervously. Was he aware of it? I thought: he's angry at me because I left him alone, because even now I escape him and have neither gratitude nor admiration for him. That's why he's angry. He guessed that I don't care about living, that deep inside me there is no desire left to go on. And that undermines the foundation of his philosophy and his system of values. Man, according to his book, must live and must fight for his life. He must help doctors and not fight them. I had fought him. He brought me back to life against my will. I had nearly joined my grandmother. I was actually on the threshold. Paul Russel stood behind me and prevented me from crossing. He was pulling me toward him. Alone against Grandmother and the others. And he had won. Another victory for him. A human life. I should shout with happiness and make the walls of the universe tremble. But instead I disturb him. That's what is distressing him.

Dr. Russel was making an obvious effort to restrain himself. He was still looking at me with anger, his cheeks purple, his lips trembling.

"I order you to answer me!"

A pitiless inquisitor, he had raised his voice. A cold anger made his hands rigid.

I thought: he is going to shout, to hit me. Who knows? He might be capable of strangling me, of sending me back to the battlefield. Dr. Russel is a human being, therefore capable of hatred, capable of losing control. He could easily put his hands around my neck and squeeze. That would be normal, logical on his part. I represent a danger to him. Anyone who rejects life is a threat to him and to everything he stands for in this world where life already counts for so little. In his eyes I am a cancer to be eliminated. What would become of humanity and of the laws of equilibrium if all men began to desire death?

I felt very calm, completely controlled. If I had searched further I might have discovered that my calm also hid the satisfaction, the strange joy—or was it simply humor?—that comes from the knowledge of one's own strength, of one's own solitude. I was telling myself: he doesn't know. And I alone can decide to tell him, to transform his future. At this very moment, I am his fate.

"Did I tell you the dream I had during the first operation I ever had?" I asked him smilingly in an amused tone of voice. "No? Shall I tell you? I was twelve. My mother had taken me to a clinic that belonged to my cousin, the surgeon Oscar Sreter, to have my tonsils removed. He had put me to sleep with ether. When I woke up, Oscar Sreter asked me, 'Are you crying because it hurts?' 'No,' I answered. 'I'm crying because I just saw God.' Strange dream. I had gone to heaven. God, sitting on his throne, was presiding over an assembly of angels. The distance which separated Him from me was infinite but I could see Him as clearly as if He had been right next to me. God motioned to me and I started to walk forward. I walked several lifetimes but the distance grew no shorter. Then two angels picked me up, and suddenly I found myself face to face with God. At last! I thought. Now I can ask Him the question that haunts all the wise men of Israel: What is the meaning of suffering? But, awed, I couldn't utter a sound. In the meantime other questions kept moving through my head: When will the hour of deliverance come? When will Good conquer Evil, thus allowing chaos to be forever dispelled? But my lips could only tremble and the words stuck in my throat. Then God talked to me. The silence had become so total, so pure, that my heart was ashamed of its beating. The silence was still as absolute, when I heard the words of God. With Him the word and the silence were not contradictory. God answered all my questions and many others. Then two angels took me by the arm again and brought me back. One of them told the other, 'He has become heavier,' and the other replied, 'He is carrying an important answer.' That is when I woke up. Dr. Sreter was leaning over me with a smile. I wanted to tell him that I had just heard the words of God, when I realized to my horror that I had forgotten them. I no longer knew what God had told me. My tears began to flow. 'Are you crying because it hurts?' the good Dr. Sreter asked me. 'It doesn't hurt,' I answered. 'I'm crying because I just saw God. He talked to me and I forgot what He said.' The doctor burst into a friendly laugh: 'If you want I can put you back to sleep; and you can ask Him to repeat. . . .' I was crying and my cousin was laughing heartily. . . . And you see, Doctor, this time, stretched out on your operating table, fast asleep, I didn't see God in my dream. He was no longer there."

Paul Russel had been listening attentively. Leaning forward he seemed to be looking for a hidden meaning in every word. His face had changed.

"You haven't answered my question!" he remarked, still tense.

So he hadn't understood. An answer to his question? But this was an answer! Couldn't he see how the second operation was different from the first? It wasn't his fault. He couldn't understand. We were so different, so far from each other. His fingers touched life. Mine death. Without an intermediary, without partitions. Life, death, each as bare, as true as the other. The problem went beyond us. It was in an invisible sphere, on a faraway screen, between two powers for whom we were only ambassadors.

Standing in front of my bed, he filled the room with his presence. He was waiting. He suspected a secret that made him angry. That's what was throwing him off. We were both young, and above all we were alive. He looked at me steadily, stubbornly, to catch in me that which eluded him. In the same way primitive man must have watched the day disappear behind the mountain.

I felt like telling him: go. Paul Russel, you are a straightforward and courageous man. Your duty is to leave me. Don't ask me to talk. Don't try to know. Neither who I am, nor who you are. I am a storyteller. My legends can only be told at dusk. Whoever listens questions his life. Go, Paul Russel. Go. The heroes of my legends are cruel and without pity. They are capable of strangling you. You want to know who I am, truly? I don't know myself. Sometimes I am Shmuel, the slaughterer. Look at me carefully. No, not at my face. At my hands.

They were about ten in the bunker. Night after night they could hear the German police dogs looking through the ruins for Jews hiding out in their underground shelters. Shmuel and the others were living on practically no water or bread, on hardly any air. They were holding out. They knew that there, down below in their narrow jail, they were free; above, death was waiting for them. One night a disaster nearly occurred. It was Golda's fault. She had taken her child with her. A baby, a few months old. He began to cry, thus endangering the lives of all. Golda was trying to quiet him, to make him sleep. To no avail. That's when the others, including Golda herself, turned to Shmuel and told him: "Make him shut up. Take care of him, you whose job it is to slaughter chickens. You will be able to do it without making him suffer too much." And Shmuel gave in to reason: the baby's life in exchange for the lives of all. He had taken the child. In the dark his groping fingers felt for the neck. And there had been silence on earth and in heaven. There was only the sound of dogs barking in the distance.

A slight smile came to my lips. Shmuel too had been a doctor, I thought. Motionless, Paul Russel was still waiting.

Moishe is a smuggler. He too comes from Sighet. We were friends. Every morning at six, ever since we were eight years old, we met in the street and, lantern in hand, we walked to the *cheder* where we found books bigger than we. Moishe wanted to become a rabbi. Today he is a smuggler and he is wanted by every police force in Europe. In the concentration camp he had seen a pious man exchange his whole week's bread rations for a prayer book. The pious man passed away less than a month later. Before dying he had kissed his precious book and murmured, "Book, how many human beings have you destroyed?" That day Moishe had decided to change the course of his existence. And that's how the human race gained a smuggler and lost a rabbi. And it isn't any the worse off for it.

You want to know who I am, Doctor? I am also Moishe the smuggler. But above all I am the one who saw his grandmother go to heaven. Like a flame, she chased away the sun and took its place. And this new sun which blinds instead of giving light forces me to walk with my head down. It weighs upon the future of man. It casts a gloom over the hearts and vision of generations to come.

If I had spoken to him out loud, he would have understood the tragic fate of those who came back, left over, living-dead. You must look at them carefully. Their appearance is deceptive. They are smugglers. They look like the others. They eat, they laugh, they love. They seek money, fame, love. Like the others. But it isn't true: they are playing, sometimes without even knowing it. Anyone who has seen what they have seen cannot be like the others, cannot laugh, love, pray, bargain, suffer, have fun, or forget. Like the others. You have to watch them carefully when they pass by an innocent looking smokestack, or when they lift a piece of bread to their mouths. Something in them shudders and makes you turn your eyes away. These people have been amputated; they haven't lost their legs or eyes but their will and their taste for life. The things they have seen will come to the surface again sooner or later. And then the world will be frightened and won't dare look these spiritual cripples in the eye.

If I had spoken out loud, Paul Russel would have understood why one shouldn't ask those who came back too many questions: they aren't normal human beings. A spring snapped inside them from the shock. Sooner or later the results must appear. But I didn't want him to understand. I didn't want him to lose his equilibrium; I didn't want him to see a truth which threatened to reveal itself at any moment.

I began to persuade him he was wrong so he would go away, so he would leave me alone. Of course I wanted to live. Obviously I wanted to live, create, do lasting things, help man make a step forward, contribute to the progress of humanity, its happiness, its fulfillment! I talked a long time, passionately, using complicated, grandiloquent words and abstract expressions on purpose. And since he still wasn't completely convinced, I threw in the argument to which he couldn't remain deaf: love. I love Kathleen. I love her with all my heart. And how can one love if at the same time one doesn't care about life, if one doesn't believe in life or in love?

The young doctor's face gradually assumed its usual expression. He had heard the words he wanted to hear. His philosophy wasn't threatened. Everything was in order again. Nothing like friendship between patients and doctors! Nothing is more sacred than life, or healthier, or greater, or more noble. To refuse life is a sin; it's stupid and mad. You have to accept life, cherish it, love it, fight for it as if it were a treasure, a woman, a secret happiness.

Now he was becoming friendly again. He offered me a cigarette, encouraging me to accept it. He was no longer tense. His lips had their normal color again. There was no more anger in his eyes.

"I'm glad," he said finally. "At the beginning I was afraid. . . . I admit my mistake. I'm glad. Really."

A Mosaic of Courage

This chapter explores the experiences of some of the many people who defied the Nazis in some way. At a time when the Nazis succeeded in dehumanizing or destroying millions of European Jews, individual acts of courage took on a new dimension. During the reign of the Third Reich, numerous people, known and unknown, sought to make a difference, one person at a time, whether by giving food to a Jewish child by the ghetto gate, providing a hiding place, working with the resistance, or in some other way.

In Chapter 9, we see the faces of some of those individuals who demonstrated profound personal courage. This chapter pays tribute to a number of people who are largely unknown except to those who are alive because of them. Still others, perhaps better known, found ways to help more publicly, flouting Nazi authority to save lives. Some perished because of their courageous actions, while others are still alive to tell their stories.

For Jews in the camps, it took courage just to face daily existence. They had little reason to expect that they would be able to survive. If they were not immediately gassed or beaten to death, they were likely to perish from hunger or disease. The seeming inevitability of death inspired a range of reactions among prisoners: some fought to survive or somehow to undermine their captors; others gave up.

For those outside the camps, courage often meant hiding Jews or helping them to escape, even though such acts were punishable by death. Yet for all those who defied the Nazis, there were also those who stood by and watched as their neighbors were rounded up and taken away.

Some of the faces of courage are well-known, such as Raoul Wallenberg, Hannah Senesh, Oskar Schindler, and Janusz Korczak. The actions of all of these people, both well-known and nameless, comprise a mosaic of courage.

Nobody Has a Right to Kill and Murder Because of Religion or Race

Irene Opdyke
(as edited by Carol Rittner and Sandra Myer)

Irene Opdyke was born in Poland in 1920. Raised as a Catholic, she hid twelve Jews during the German occupation of Poland. She now lives in southern California and is an interior decorator. Her story appeared originally in *The Courage to Care: Rescuers of Jews during the Holocaust*, which was edited by Carol Rittner and Sandra Myer. She was honored by Yad Vashem for her humanitarian work and appeared in the film *The Courage to Care*, based on the book of the same name, in which she tells of her wartime experiences. Opdyke also has co-authored a book entitled *Into the Flames: The Life Story of a Righteous Gentile*.

In this selection, Opdyke, who was a young Polish Catholic during the war, describes why she could not stand idly by while the Nazis hunted and killed Jews.

In my house a Polish girl, a woman, wasn't expected to be involved with politics. We were prepared to be married, to be good wives and good mothers, so I really wasn't affected by political issues or anti-Semitism. Besides, I did not have that in my home.

My mother was just the most wonderful woman, a saint. She was a woman with very little education. When she was only a little girl, her father was killed and she was left to raise her brother and sister. She probably taught me more than anything else to keep my heart, my hands, my ears open for anybody needy. These were her ABCs and she taught them to us. We always had people coming—they were poor, sick—and my mother always knew how to help and what to do to help.

I have often tried to discover in myself what gave me the courage to help Jews during the war. I am sure that it was due to my parents, who always played and prayed together with us children. Although we had a sheltered life, my parents raised me to respect the Ten Commandments and to be at peace with God and people.

I was a 19-year-old student when the war started in 1939. I was happy and proud to have been born in Poland, a free country after 143 years. Maybe that also was the reason I did what I did later: I was Polish, I was proud, I wanted the best. I wanted my parents and my country to be proud of me. That's why I wanted to be a nurse. I was trying to be another Florence Nightingale. I had big ideas: I wanted to go to other countries, I wanted to help. But my dream never got finished because the Germans, without declaring war, invaded Poland. Immediately, I was cut off, separated from my family.

The hospital where I was working and studying started to fill up with wounded and dying people. We tried to help, to save lives, but the Germans were pushing like lightning. In a couple of days, they were almost at the door. The Polish military had to evacuate. Since I could not go home—the Germans were already there—I joined the Polish Army. For days we were on the run. The Germans were pursuing us with unbelievable speed, creating destruction and death everywhere. And in three weeks, with us almost at the Russian border, the war was over. The Polish Army was defeated. I was far from home, and I did not know what to do and where to go. With the remnants of the Polish Army some other nurses and I escaped to a big Ukrainian forest, close to the Russian border. That was the beginning of the Polish underground.

Just before Christmas, a small group of soldiers, a nurse, and I went to the villages and tried to exchange coffee, tobacco, and sugar for something to eat. They left me on guard. I saw them spread around to go to the houses. I heard noise. Before I had a chance to know where it was coming from or what it was, I saw a truck and Russian soldiers jumping off. I ran like a scared little rabbit for the forest. That was the only thing I knew to do, but it was too late. They knocked me down. I was beaten and raped. They left me lying there. When I was found by other Russian soldiers, I was taken to a hospital. And when I came to, I felt two warm arms around my shoulders, and a hand was petting my hair. I thought for a minute that it was a dream, that my mother was there. I looked up and saw a woman doctor speaking a language that I did not understand, but her emotion, her embrace, maybe saved my sanity. She was a Russian doctor who was the head of that hospital.

When I started to feel better, she assigned me to work in the hospital. In 1940 the Russians were fighting the Germans, and she was sent to the front. For me, it was awful because I was assigned to work in a hospital that had infectious diseases—typhus, meningitis—but little medicine, only a little sulphur. But the Lord had other plans for me, so I survived.

In 1941 there was an exchange of Polish population between the Russians and the Germans. I wanted to go back to Poland, which was occupied by the Germans, because I was hoping to find my family. On the way home to Kozlowa Gora, which is three kilometers from the Russian border, I stopped in Radom. I went to church one Sunday. After the mass and other services, the church was surrounded by the Germans, who picked up all the young men and women to send them to Germany to work. Young German men were needed to fight, so the Nazis needed slaves to do their work. But before I was sent with the others, a group of officers came in, and one man, in the uniform of a major, started pointing at random and saying, "this one, this one, this one." I was picked also and by God's miracle, I was not sent to Germany. Instead, I was sent to work in an ammunition factory.

I wanted to work because I was hungry, and I didn't have my parents and family there to care for me. One day, maybe because I had developed anemia, I fainted right in front of the whole plant. When I came to, a German, an older man in his late sixties, was standing before me. He asked me what had happened, and I answered him in German. He was very impressed. I told him, "Please forgive me. I want to work, but I am not well." So he said, "OK, you report to another part of the plant and I will give you another job." I was inexperienced and not well educated, but I knew then that the Lord had put me in the right place at the right moment to make that German major notice me. My new job was serving breakfast, lunch, and dinner to the German officers and secretaries, and to the head of the local Gestapo. I started to feel better because the food was good and it was clean. But it was while I was working there that for the first time I realized what was happening to the Jewish people, because behind the hotel there was a ghetto, and I could see for myself.

It was unbelievable to me that any human being could be so mean to others. I saw the people in the ghetto: families, older parents, little children, pregnant women, the crippled, the sick. The Nazis put them all in the ghetto for later disposal. One day, I saw a death march. They pushed the people like cattle through the middle of the town. And the Gestapo was kicking and pushing those who walked too slowly or that were not in line. I saw an old man who looked to me like a rabbi, with a white beard, white hair. He was carrying a Torah. Next to him I saw a beautiful woman in her last months of pregnancy. And next to her I saw another young woman with a little girl holding her skirt with all her might. There were old women, men hobbling on crutches—a long,

long procession. Most of all, I remember the children—all sizes, all ages. The little ones screaming, crying, "Mama, Mama," and the bigger ones—they were even too scared to cry. One thing I remember: the eyes—big, scary; looking, searching, as if asking, "What did I do? What did I do?"

We were standing, watching that inhuman march, but what could we do? We were a few women and men standing. There were dozens of Gestapo with guns. Later, I went with someone whose husband was a Jew and saw a nightmare that I will never forget: bodies plowed into a shallow grave. The earth was heaving with the breath of those who were buried alive. It was then that I prayed and promised that I would do whatever I could.

The whole plant was moved to Tarnopol and I was moved with them. I was transferred from factory work and was assigned to serve breakfast, lunch, and dinner for the German officers and secretaries, and also sometimes for the local head of the Gestapo, because I knew German.

I also took care of 12 Jewish people who washed clothes for the Germans. Once they had been people of means. They had been nurses, businessmen, businesswomen, a medical student, a lawyer. Now they had to do that dirty work or die. We became good friends. I didn't have a family. They were persecuted. It was a human bond. That's how I felt. I did not think of them as different because they were Jews. To me, we were all in trouble and we had a common enemy.

We created a grapevine information center. I became the eyes and the ears for the Jewish people. And these 12 would use their footwork to spread the news to other Jews—when there would be unexpected raids on ghettos and so on. We saved many lives because people were warned. Some of them could escape, if they had a place to hide, and some escaped to the forest. There was a place, Janowka, about eight kilometers from Tarnopol.

In Janowka, about three hundred Jewish people escaped. Some of them were from our plant, and some were from other German plants. And all because those 12 Jews were carrying information to the ghetto. (It spread around, you know, to the people.)

There was a priest in Janowka. He knew about the Jews' escape—many of the Polish people knew about it. Can you imagine living underground as the Jews were forced to do when the winter came? Many people brought food and other things—not right to the forest, but to the edge—from the village. The priest could not say directly "help the Jews," but he would say in church, "Not one of you should take the blood of your brother."

When the time came for the total liquidation of the ghetto, those 12 people in my factory did not have a place to go. They asked me for help. What could I do? I, at that time, lived in a tiny little room by the diner. I didn't have a home to take them to. There was only one thing left for me to do. I did not have any resources; I didn't have my parents. I prayed. And as I prayed that night, I threw a tantrum at my Maker: "I do not believe in you! You are a figment of my imagination! How can you allow such a thing to happen?" The next day I was on my knees, saying, "Forgive me. I don't know what I'm talking about. Your will be done."

The next morning, like a miracle, the major asked me to be his housekeeper. He said, "I have a villa. I need a housekeeper. Would you do it?" The decision was made for me. Like a young child, without thinking or preparing anything, I told the 12 Jewish people I knew that I would leave open the window in the villa where the coal chute led to the cellar. One by one, they went there.

The major was an old man. He was sick. I cooked his special dinners for him. He liked me. I was with him for about three years. He wanted to take a man to be there with me also, but I told him I didn't want it. So I pleaded with him. "Please," I said, "I was held by the Russians, I was beaten and raped by Russian soldiers before I was even kissed by a boy." He said, "OK. Fine. We will try it with you alone for a while. Let's wait and see how it goes."

During the next couple of weeks there were posters on every street corner saying, "This is a Jew-free town, and if any one should help an escaped Jew, the sentence is death." About three months after that, in September, I was in town, and all of a sudden the Gestapo were pushing the people from the town to the marketplace, where there were Polish families being hung with Jewish families that they had helped. We were forced to watch them die, as a warning of what would happen if we befriended a Jew.

When I came home, I locked the door as I always did, but I usually left the key turned in the lock so that if the major would come unexpectedly, he could not open the door. But I was so shaken up that I locked the door, and I pulled out the key. I came in to the kitchen, and there were Ida, Franka, Clara, Miriam—the women came out because that's what they usually did, to help me. I was white like snow, so they asked me what had happened. I said "I don't feel good." I could not tell them. What could they do? We were talking when the door suddenly opened and the major was standing in front of us. I still can see his chin shaking, his eyes glaring with unbelief. We were all frozen like statues. He turned around in silence and walked to his office.

I had to go face him; there was not any other way. He yelled at me. He said, "Irene, how could you do it? I trusted you. I give you such a nice home, protection—why?" I said, "I know only one thing. They're my friends. I had to do it. I did not have a home to take them to, I don't have a family. Forgive me, but I would do it again. Nobody has a right to kill and murder because of religion or race."

He said, "You know what can happen to you?" I said, "Yes, I know, I just witnessed what can happen." By that time I was crying; I could hardly talk.

450

Finally he said to me, "Look, I cannot do that to you. I cannot just let you die." And when he said that, believe me, I knelt down, and kissed his hand; not for me, but for those people, not only for the ones in the villa, but for the people in the forest who depended on me. They remained, and they had hope that they could survive.

Then the major had to leave the villa, as the Germans were retreating, but I could not leave the people in the villa because in time of war you never know what's going to happen. It could last another day, a month, two months. One of the women was pregnant. A little Jewish boy was born two months after freedom came.

Just before the war was over we decided that I would take those Jewish people to the forest. I also was helping the partisans in the forest the whole time, in whatever way I could. Three days after I took the Jews to the forest, the Red Army freed us. My Jewish friends were free to make a new life, even though they were broken in spirit and body. I have often wondered how anyone could continue to live without a family, with their children killed, having lost everything.

When the Russian army rescued us I went with the partisans, and I remained with them until Russia took all of Poland. I was on my way to see my family when I was arrested by the Russians because of my association with the partisans. This time, my Jewish friends helped me, and wrote my story to the historical committee in Krakow. Then I was sent to a displaced persons camp in Germany. Finally, in 1949, just before Christmas, I came to the United States, and now I live in California.

People sometimes ask me what the lesson is from all this. I think it is that we have to teach that we belong all together. That no matter what a person's color, race, religion, or language, we are created by one God, no matter what you call Him. And I think that if there would be less hate, if people would try to understand each other more, there would not be the wars.

I myself realize that when I came to the United States, I put a "Do Not Disturb" sign on my mind. I did not want to talk about the war. I wanted to have a normal life. I wanted to marry. I wanted to have a child. I wanted to create a new family to replace the one that I had lost.

I had tried to forget, to put this experience out of my mind. But in 1975, there was a neo-Nazi organization that started spreading a lie that the Holocaust never happened. That it was only propaganda. Well, that put me on fire. Why? Because I was there. I lived through it, and I realized that it is my duty to tell the truth about what the Nazis and their collaborators did to the Jews, to tell so that those people that died will not have died in vain; to tell so that a new generation will learn the truth. I know I don't speak correctly, that I have an accent. But believe me, I want the new generation to know so that we will not go through another Holocaust.

What Happened
That Day

*Luba Krugman
Gurdus*

Luba Krugman Gurdus
survived the German
occupation of her native
Poland. She is an artist
and an author, exploring
the Holocaust in both her
drawings and her writ-
ings. Her drawings are
part of the permanent
collection at Yad Vashem.
The State University of
New York at Albany
honored her in 1986 with
the Louis Yavner First
Citizen Award for her
"contributions to educa-
tion about the Holocaust
and other violations of
human rights." She is the
author of *Painful Echoes:
Poems of the Holocaust*,
from which the following
poem is taken, and *The
Death Train*.

In this poem, Gurdus
pays tribute to her
parents, who helped their
children escape while
they awaited their own
deaths.

For years I wondered
What happened that day
When Mother and Father
Pushed us on our way

I still remember
Their bent gray heads
And emaciated arms
In tender embrace

I see their drawn faces
And eyes with teary blur
And hear their pleading voices:
"Look after yourselves, take care!"

Days later, we heard from the local Poles
That resisting the Nazis, they were
            killed on the spot
Their battered bodies remained on the road
And Polish peasants commented in wonder
That a Jew and Jewess defied the order
And refused to part even in death . . .

A Poem for Anton Schmidt

William Pillin

William Pillin was born
in 1910 in Russia.
Although he attended
the Lewis Institute of
Chicago, Northwestern
University, and The
University of Chicago, he
believed that his poetry
was related more to
European influences
than to American. He
was well known as a
potter in the Los Angeles
area, where he and his
wife created and exhib-
ited their pottery. Pillin
died in 1985. He is the
author of *Another Dawn*.

This poem pays
tribute to a German
army sergeant who was
executed for providing
the Jewish underground
with forged credentials
and military vehicles.

*A German army sergeant, executed in March 1942 for
supplying the Jewish underground with forged
credentials and military vehicles.*

I have properly spoken
hymns for the dead, have planted
white roses in the high air.

And because my pen is a leech
to suck out blood's poison
I had a need to write

of death's clerks and doctors;
but my pen dissolved
in an inkwell of acid

and my paper, litmus of shame,
crumbled to ashes.
Anton Schmidt, I thank you

for breaking the spell that numbed
the singing mouth. I need not write
of the mad and the murderous.

That a vile camaraderie
caused streets and meadows to weep
no longer surprises us;

but a lone soldier's
shining treason
is a cause for holy attention.

Anton Schmidt, whose valor
lessened the vats of human fat
and looms of human hair

I thank you that no poison
is burning my veins
but a wine of praise

for a living man
among clockwork robots
and malevolent puppets.

453

The Mosaic Artist's Apprentice

Yaffa Eliach

Yaffa Eliach is the editor of *Hasidic Tales of the Holocaust*, from which the following selection is taken. For additional biographical information on Eliach, see page 247.

Acts of courage and bravery occurred in many quiet ways. In this selection, based on a story told by Jacob Garfein, a lie saves a boy's life.

Jacob (Jack) Garfein was only thirteen years old when he was deported to Auschwitz with a transport of Hungarian Jews. As the men were separated from the women and children upon arrival on the platform, Jacob was clinging to his mother's skirt. Suddenly he felt his mother's hand tearing him away from her and pushing him in the direction of the men's column. Jacob ran back to his mother, pleading with her to let him stay with her. "Mommy, I love you, please let me stay with you, please, Mommy, don't send me away."

His mother had a strange look in her eyes that he had never seen before. She did not look at him; her glance was fixed far away on the distant glow of the chimneys. Her teeth were clenched and she looked as if she was holding back her tears, but Jacob was not sure. Jacob tried again to plead with her. Once more her firm hand pushed him away.

Feeling betrayed and abandoned by his beloved mother, Jacob, with tears in his eyes, was pushed into a stream of men amidst dogs and S.S. men that carried him in an unknown direction.

"Boy," he heard from behind him a voice in a distinct Polish-Yiddish accent, "when you reach the man on the podium, stretch yourself out as tall as you can."

"How old are you?" Jacob now heard the voice of the man on the podium.

"Sixteen," said the voice from behind him.

"What is your occupation, young lad?" Mengele continued to question him. Before he had a chance to reply "student," the Polish Jew behind him hastily replied, "Your honor, he is my apprentice. The two of us are among the world's greatest mosaic artists." Jacob turned his head, and only then, for the first time in his life, did he see the face of the Polish Jew; his big, deep-set eyes, his white, stubby beard, and his long, delicate, almost transparent fingers. "His fingers must have turned thousands of Germara pages," thought Jacob when he saw those exquisite hands. Mengele lifted his own glove-clad hand and motioned to the right.

Jacob's face was burning with insult and shame. First he had been rejected by his beloved mother and now he was guilty of being an accomplice to a lie. He was not an apprentice to a mosaic artist, he did not even know what the word *mosaic* meant. He was a student, a yeshiva bocher. And he had never seen that man before in his life. He turned back to complain to the Polish Jew, but the man was gone, lost in the crowd. Jacob tried to go back to the nice, elegant man on the podium to tell him that he had been party to a lie and to ask for his forgiveness. But as he was trying to push his way against the streaming mob of men, a Kapo kicked Jacob in the stomach and ordered him to turn back.

All that night Jacob searched for the old Polish Jew with the white beard. All the men had been shaven, all were bald, all were wearing striped camp uniforms, but Jacob was sure that he would recognize the man's voice and his long delicate fingers.

For months, during his stay at Auschwitz, Jacob searched in vain for the old man, wishing to thank him for saving his life on the selection line. He never saw him again.

One day, at dusk, as the chimneys were spitting out thousands of lives in strange red clouds, Jacob was searching for his old savior. Suddenly it occurred to him that he would never find him, for the old man must have been Elijah the Prophet who was sent by his mother's prayers to save him, a mother's last prayers to save her only beloved son.

Natasha's Triumph

Sara Nomberg-Przytyk

A Holocaust survivor, Sara Nomberg-Przytyk is the author of *Auschwitz: True Tales from a Grotesque Land*, from which the following selection is taken. For additional biographical information on Nomberg-Przytyk, see page 261.

In this selection, a Russian concentration camp prisoner feigns madness as she intimidates the infamous Dr. Mengele with her courageous expression of the truth about the Nazis.

Every day deathly undernourished women and hundreds of mortally sick people came through the doors of the infirmary to which was attached a little cottage that housed the personnel who worked in the infirmary. Actually, it was not really a cottage but a little shack without windows. The total area of the shack was about two by six meters. Inside there were two three-decker beds and a small table. We thought that it was the most wonderful habitation in the world. It was our corner, different from the terrible barracks.

One sunny day we received a notice that hit us like a clap of thunder. It was a summer evening in 1944 when Orli brought us the news that we would have to move out of our little shack because Mengele had decided to create a ward for mentally disturbed women. At night we removed our meager possessions. The next morning we waited for the patients. The whole affair looked very suspicious to me. It was difficult to understand why Mengele would create a ward for the mentally sick in the infirmary. Until now there had been no such ward. We had a feeling that Mengele must have a new trick up his sleeve.

First thing in the morning they brought the first patient. Her name was Natasha. The *blokowa* brought her in.

"She has to stay here with you in the infirmary," the *blokowa* said and left.

Before me stood a young girl, straight as a tree, with a gloomy, rebellious face. She was nineteen years old and from Leningrad. She would not tell us anything else. Our Jewish doctors were not invited to examine her, since their findings were set at no value. Natasha immediately took an upper bunk. She lay there quietly, saying nothing, but when we brought her some soup she came to life, and a big smile brightened up her face. She ate while she continued to lie there without saying a word.

The same afternoon, five new patients were brought in, including two German, one Dutch, and two French women. They were all very young and very sad. At first we were afraid of them. We imagined that they would cause trouble, maybe have fits. Perhaps we would have to use physical force to subdue them. We had no experience in handling such cases. But the new patients lay quietly in their beds, or else they sat bent over on the edge of the bed.

I remember that I made several attempts to talk to them, but my words did not reach them. That same day, just before roll call, a few more women were brought in. By this time a few of the beds were being shared by two women. A couple of mornings later we prepared the infirmary to receive a visit from Dr. Mengele. We knew that he would come to examine the new "ward." That morning, as we were admitting the sick to the hospital, we did not accept the very sick ones. We sent them back to the blocks. We knew that if he started looking at them he would certainly send them to the ovens. It was with heavy hearts that we sent those women away to do heavy labor, women who were barely alive, with swollen legs and terrible sores all over their bodies. But we well knew the monster in the white coat who had the face of a Romeo. He would assign them to the gas and then would say to us, "You see yourselves that these women are not strong enough to live. Why should they suffer? I am sending them to the gas for their own good."

Mengele arrived about twelve o'clock.

"Achtung," shouted Marusia.

The selection of the sick and the signing of the cards started. Everything was going smoothly, without a hitch. All of a sudden, from the next room, we heard a loud, happy voice calling,

"Hey, you! Doctor! Maybe you can come in and see us."

It was Natasha calling to Mengele; she was speaking to him in beautiful German, her voice radiant with happiness.

"What are you afraid of, coward, you who can murder women and children? Come here. We will discuss your Hitler's crimes. Maybe you want to discuss Stalingrad, where you are dying like mad dogs."

We turned to stone. Every one of us pretended to be very busy. We were afraid to look in his direction. We knew that in a minute something terrible would happen. Natasha's ringing, violent voice floated in from the other room.

"You will all die in Russia, the way Napoleon did. You are afraid to come to me. You don't want to listen to the truth, you specialist of the gas chambers."

Suddenly we saw Mengele get up and go into the other room. I waited for a shot and automatically covered my ears with my fists.

"Come, sit next to us. We will have a chat."

Mengele did not say a thing. Only the voice of Natasha could be heard.

"Hitler, that human garbage, destroyed Germany. All the nations will hate you through the ages. You will see. Even if you live through the war, you will have to hide from human revenge like a worm."

We stood there completely motionless, as though hypnotized. Natasha started to sing. What a wonderful voice she had.

She finished the interview with an abrupt, "Get out of here. I can't stand to look at your shiny mug any more."

Mengele got up and left without a word. Only after he had crossed the threshold of the infirmary and had looked at our pale faces did he shout out the order to dress all the sick, because the orderly would come to pick them up after lunch.

"The Russian is to stay here," he added in closing.

We knew what that meant. The orderly would give them an injection of phenol, and in the evening the *leichenauto* would take them to the gas chambers. Natasha had to remain here. Why? Maybe he was preparing a more agonizing death for her.

The next day they brought a new batch of women. They, too, were sad and silent. About lunch time Mengele came in again.

"Come here, hero of the gas chambers," Natasha called again. "We will discuss your death. If you wish, I will tell you how you're going to die."

With wonder we watched him approach Natasha. For an hour she carried on a tirade against Hitler. She sang Russia's praises. Mengele sat on the chair with his head hung low on his chest.

I remember looking at him and not believing my own eyes. What was going on here? What was drawing that predator to his prey? To this very day I cannot understand what secret was lurking behind his behavior. Maybe it was just one more aberration. Perhaps the flagellation he received from Natasha's tongue gave him some sort of satisfaction.

Every day the sanitation worker took the sick for the *szpryce* (injection). That was their term for murder by phenol in Auschwitz. Every day Mengele came to listen to Natasha's speeches. One evening I decided to have a talk with Natasha.

I told her everything about myself, waiting for her to get up enough confidence so that she would be willing to tell me about her life. I was not mistaken.

Natasha had been a student. Her parents had been professors of German. It was from them that she had learned such elegant German. After that conversation I was certain that Natasha was not mentally ill and that she was feigning mental illness in order to be able to get away with telling the Germans exactly how she felt about them.

"But dear Natasha," I screamed with anguish, "do you know what they do to mentally ill people? They don't heal but kill."

"I know," said Natasha. "But I don't want to live in this rotten world."

The next day Dr. Koenig came for the inspection instead of Mengele. We closed the door to the little room. Maybe we could hide the sick from him.

"Hey, you, Doctor of death," Natasha shouted in a loud voice. "Come here, we will discuss your Hitler."

Koenig shuddered. He pushed open the door and went into the little room. The room was almost completely dark. On the beds sat the huddled figures.

"What, you're afraid to come in, you Hitler's coward?"

Then there was a shot. All the sick screamed at the same time, with a terrible, hollow voice.

When we reached Natasha she was already dead.

Schindler's Legacy

Elinor J. Brecher

Elinor J. Brecher has been a journalist with the
Miami Herald. She is the author of *Schindler's Legacy:*
True Stories of the List Survivors, from which the
following excerpt is taken.

Oskar Schindler was a businessman and Nazi
Party member who helped to save his Jewish
workers from the SS. In this excerpt, Brecher
provides a sketch of Schindler as a complex man
whose motives in helping Jews to survive are even to
this day not clearly understood.

Adolf Hitler came to power on January 30, 1933.
He soon began restricting the rights of Germany's Jews. From the first official
government act of persecution on April 1 of that year—the boycott of Jewish
businesses—through the 1935 "race shame" laws prohibiting sex and/or marriage between Jews and Gentiles, the Nazis relentlessly regulated every facet
of Jewish life. By 1935, 75,000 Jews had fled. After Kristallnacht—the "Night of
Broken Glass"—on November 9, 1938, any Jew who didn't leave Germany was
confined to a concentration camp. Thousands more crossed over to Poland,
which would boast Europe's largest Jewish population on the eve of World War II:
3,300,000. By war's end, only 10 percent remained alive.

The Nazis invaded Poland on September 1, 1939. They took Kraków on the
sixth, then home to 60,000 Jews, 26 percent of the city's population. By year's
end, Jews lost the right to attend school, keep bank accounts, own businesses,
or walk on the sidewalks. They were tagged by a yellow Star of David. By the
following April, evacuation orders would pare Kraków's Jewish community to
35,000.

All this transformed Poland into the land of economic opportunity for German entrepreneurs. They swarmed the cities, snapping up forfeited Jewish firms as their Treuhanders, or trustees. One of them was a young salesman named Oskar Schindler, born April 28, 1908, in the Sudetenland. He applied for Nazi Party membership on February 10, 1939. By then, he was an agent of the German Abwehr, the intelligence. In fact, he had been jailed in 1938 as a spy by the Czechs (he was released when Germany annexed the Sudetenland). Oskar Schindler provided Polish Army uniforms to the German provocateurs who attacked a German border radio station the night before the invasion.

Schindler took over an idled enamelware plant at 4 Lipowa Street in Kraków, capital of the occupation government. A Jew named Abraham Bankier had owned the plant. Schindler renamed it Deutsche Emailwaren Fabrik, and began turning out pots, pans, and mess kits for the German military. He had come to seek his fortune, and with Jewish slave labor, he made one.

By the end of 1942, Schindler employed 370 Jewish workers, all from the Kraków ghetto. He paid their wages directly to the Nazi general government. Word quickly spread that his factory, outside the ghetto, in the Zablocie district, was a safe haven. With copious bribes, Schindler kept the SS at bay, so nobody was beaten on the job. He winked at the flurry of illegal "business" between the factory's Jewish and Polish workers. He lied for people so they could bring in friends and relatives. Most of his "skilled" workers had no skills at all. Eventually one thousand Jews would gain sanctuary at the DEF (called Emalia by its workers).

Hans Frank, the Nazi governor of the Kraków district, established the Kraków ghetto in March 1941; there were 320 residential buildings for 15,000 Jews (the rest had been driven off into the suburbs). Transports and massacres decimated the ghetto population over the next two years. Between June and October 1942, 11,000 ghetto dwellers were sent to the Belźec death camp. Then, on March 13, 1943, *Untersturmführer* Amon Goeth liquidated the ghetto. Those who lived through it became inmates at the Kraków-Płaszów labor camp— later a concentration camp—on the outskirts of the city, under Goeth's bloodthirsty command.

For a few months, Schindler's workers lived in the camp barracks and marched every day to the factory at 4 Lipowa Street. At the end of their shifts, they would return to Amon Goeth's hell, and the very real possibility of ending up dead on Chujowa Górka, the camp's notorious execution hill. . . .

Daily life at Płaszów proved unbearable for some people: They lost the will to live and so they died. Conditions were so bad that only internal fortitude kept people going. "You knew when people stopped washing themselves, stopped pushing themselves in the line, they were giving up," says Cleveland survivor Jack Mintz. "They didn't answer or ask questions. They became like zombies. If they got torn shoes, they didn't try to find something else to put on."

Schindler's Emalia subcamp extracted his workers from that hell, but in August of 1944 he was ordered to reduce his workforce by about seven hundred. In September, the Emalia subcamp shut down and its remaining workers were sent to Płaszów. In October, Schindler moved his operation to a new plant at Brinnlitz, Czechoslovakia, near his hometown. A second list was drawn up, providing the nucleus of the one in circulation today. The October list consisted of three hundred original Emalia workers and seven hundred replacements for those shipped out in August.

Before Schindler's workers got to Brinnlitz, they made intermediate stops: the women at Auschwitz, the men at a transit camp called Gröss-Rosen. Memories vary, but most survivors think the men stayed about a week at Gröss-Rosen. It was nightmarish, even by Płaszów standards. Chaskel Schlesinger of Chicago remembers the humiliating body searches when they arrived: "You had to open your mouth and spread the fingers and bend over and lift up your feet because you could have [something taped] on the bottom."

The men were run through delousing showers, and then, soaking wet and naked, they were made to stand outside in frigid temperatures. Brooklynite Moses Goldberg remembers a German officer on a white horse approaching the group and yelling to the guards, "'Those are *Schindlerjuden!* Put them in a barracks and give them nightshirts, otherwise our hospital will be full of them tomorrow.' "

Schindler's three hundred women left Płaszów two days after his men and spent about three weeks at Auschwitz. It's clear that he knew they would have to stop there, and that a few of the women knew it, too. However, neither he nor they realized they would languish there so long. He had to bribe their way out. In one of the most dramatic scenes in the film *Schindler's List*, the women—stripped and shaved—are shoved into a locked, windowless room. Shower heads stud the ceiling. The Auschwitz gas chambers are no longer a secret. Suddenly, the lights go out, as someone throws a heavy switch. The women are hysterical. Then water blasts from the jets. The women survivors confirm that it actually happened.

"There were old prisoners who were quite rough," remembers Betty Schagrin, a Florida survivor. "They were saying, 'You go in through the big doors and you go out through the chimney.' In the shower, they waited ten minutes to panic people. We started to go crazy."

As awful as they looked, the women were a welcome sight to the worried men at Brinnlitz, where the copy of Schindler's list currently circulating was drawn up on April 18, 1945. In a clunky, manual typeface, it logs the names of 297 women and 800 men, each page headed: "K.L. Gröss-Rosen–A.L. Brunnlitz/ Liste der mannl.Haftling [or weibl.Haftling, for the women] 18.4.45." *Haftling* is German for prisoner. K.L. stands for *Konzentrationslager.*

The only difference between the *Frauen* (women) and the *Manner* (men) is that the women are listed alphabetically. Otherwise, both read from left to right: list number, prisoner number, name, date of birth, job classification.

The April 18 list is a jumble of inaccuracies: phony birth dates—some off by decades—and altered identities. Some mistakes are intentional; others resulted from confusion or disinformation, or simple typos. There are German spellings, Polish spellings, and Hebrew transliterations into both languages.

By April 18, Janka Feigenbaum and a Mrs. Hofstatter had died of natural causes. About ten young boys and their fathers had been taken to Auschwitz soon after arriving at Brinnlitz in the fall, so they weren't listed. Canadian journalist Herbert Steinhouse, who interviewed Schindler at length in 1949, estimates that about eighty names were added from the "frozen transport": men from Goleszów, an Auschwitz subcamp, who had been locked in two side-tracked freight cars without food or water for ten days in subzero temperatures. Abraham Bankier, the enamelware plant's original owner, appears twice, and some people who unquestionably were at Brinnlitz don't appear at all. According to Steinhouse, Schindler also gathered in Jewish fugitives who escaped transports leaving Auschwitz, including Belgians, Dutch, and Hungarians.

All in all, the composition of the list is as much of a puzzle as Oskar Schindler's motives, a topic of endless debate among the *Schindlerjuden*. Was he an angel masquerading as an opportunist? An opportunist masquerading as an angel? Did he intend to save eleven hundred Jews, or was their survival simply one result of his self-serving game plan? Did he build the Emalia subcamp to protect Jews or to keep Amon Goeth from interfering in his lucrative black marketeering?

"I think he was a gambler and loved to outwit the SS," says Rena Finder of Massachusetts. "In the beginning, it was a game. It was fun at first. He joined the [Nazi party] to make money. But he had no stomach for the killing. He enjoyed the wheeling and dealing and doing outrageous things—living on the edge. But then he realized if he didn't save us, nobody would."

Did he have a sudden change of heart, or undergo a gradual metamorphosis? It's hard to say. Henry Rosner of Queens, New York, claims that there was a definitive moment: "Two girls ran away to Kraków. Goeth sent two Jewish policemen and said, 'If you don't find them, ten OD men will be hanged.' They found those girls. All women [were ordered] to *Appell* for hanging. Schindler came and saw Goeth shoot them two seconds before they died hanging. Schindler vomited in front of everybody. He would never be working for the Germans again, he said to me."

In 1964, a decade before Schindler's demise from alcoholic complications, a German television news crew caught up with him on the streets of Frankfurt and asked him the question directly. He replied, "The persecution of the Jews under the General Government of Poland meant that we could see the horror emerging gradually in many ways. In 1939 the Jews were forced to wear the Star of David and people were herded and shut up into ghettos.

"Then in the years 1941 and 1942, there was plenty of public evidence of pure sadism. With people behaving like pigs, I felt the Jews were being destroyed. I had to help them."

The bottom line for most is this: "If I hadn't been with Schindler, I'd be dead." And that's all that matters. (It's thought that nearly four hundred *Schindlerjuden* are still alive; about half live in Israel.)

Clearly, Oskar Schindler was a sybarite, a sexually voracious, thrill-seeking dandy. He wore so much cologne that you could smell him before you saw him. Apparently he considered his sexual magnetism negotiable capital in situations where gemstones or vodka might have had a less dramatic impact. One of the Schindler women told me that a group complained to Herr Direktor about the abuses of a female camp guard at Brinnlitz. He said he would take care of things. Later, he remarked to the women that someone should have warned him about how bad the guard smelled. He seemed to have had an infinite capacity for alcohol. When he came to New York in 1957, he stayed with Manci and Henry Rosner in Queens. Manci remembers how "every single night, we got him a bottle of cognac, and in the morning, I found an empty bottle. But he was never drunk."

One of the survivors told Steinhouse, "It's the personality more than anything else that saved us." Another, who hailed from Schindler's hometown, said, "As a Zwittau citizen, I never would have considered him capable of all these wonderful deeds. Before the war, you know, everybody here called him *Gauner* [swindler]."

He permitted the Jews to observe holidays (secretly) and, at Brinnlitz, to bury their dead traditionally. He got them extra food and rudimentary medical care. He accepted the frozen transport when no one else would, and, with his wife, Emilie, lavished personal attention and resources on the half-dead survivors.

According to Steinhouse, the Schindlers "never spent a single night" in their comfortable "villa" at Brinnlitz, sleeping instead in a small room at the factory, because Oskar understood how deeply the Jews feared late-night visits by the SS.

It's hard to say what was in that sort of thing for him, except the creation of goodwill, which in itself was a valuable commodity. Were his humane actions really planned to ensure that the grateful Jews would protect him after the Germans lost and support him for the rest of his life? Some people think so.

Sol Urbach of New Jersey has one theory: "Oskar Schindler, on April eighteenth, recognized that everything was over, so he told somebody in Brinnlitz, 'Make me a list of all the people who are here.' That's when Oskar Schindler hatched his plan of escape. There is no question in my mind that that was going through his mind. He needed this list of who survived in his camp because he was going to go to Germany and take this list into some agency."

It's commonly believed that Schindler had far less to do with compiling the list than Marcel Goldberg, the greedy Jewish policeman. (In the film, Goldberg takes Oskar's gold watch and cigarette case as a payoff to place Jewish workers at Emalia.) Most people who saw the movie will recall the scene in which Oskar and his faithful accountant, Itzhak Stern (played by Ben Kingsley), laboriously construct the list from their hearts and minds. In reality, it was Marcel Goldberg who controlled the list, not Stern or even Schindler. According to many survivors, Goldberg demanded payment directly from those who wanted to get on the list.

What's definite is that seven hundred Emalia workers were sent to death camps. Some survived; others didn't. There's no small amount of bitterness among the former group and among the surviving relatives of the latter. After the war, some confronted Schindler, demanding to know why they had been left behind. He said he couldn't stand over Goldberg's shoulder keeping track all the time.

When Oskar left Brinnlitz, he was accompanied by Emilie, a mistress, and eight Jewish inmates assigned to safeguard him. The group left the factory on May 8, 1945, in Oskar's Mercedes. A truck pulling two trailers followed. The interior of the Benz—the seats and door panels—had been stuffed with valuables. The Schindlers also carried a letter, signed by some of his workers, explaining his role in saving their lives.

The entourage headed southwest, first getting stuck in a Wehrmacht convoy, then halted by Czech partisans. They stopped over for the night in a town called Havlickuv Brod. They spent the night at the town jail—not as prisoners, but for the accommodations—then awoke to find their vehicles stripped, inside and out. They proceeded by train, then on foot.

In the spring of 1945, Kurt Klein, an intelligence officer in the U.S. Army—a German-born Jew—encountered Oskar's traveling party near the Czech village of Eleanorenhain, on its way from Brinnlitz to the Swiss border. Klein got permits for the group to remain in the American Zone of Occupation until it could find transportation for the rest of the trip.

"Nobody knew who he was at the time," Klein has said. "They were all dressed in prison uniforms and presented themselves as refugees from a German labor camp. They didn't let on that Schindler, their Nazi labor camp director, was in their midst, probably because they were afraid I would arrest him as a POW. They were correct, because my assignment was to interrogate and segregate Germans caught fleeing from Russian and Czech guns." Klein (now retired in Arizona) enlisted the aid of other Jewish American servicemen to ensure the group's safe passage to the Swiss border town of Konstanz.

When Steinhouse met Oskar, he found that the forty-year-old Schindler was "a man of convincing honesty and outstanding charm. Tall and erect, with broad shoulders and a powerful trunk, he usually has a cheerful smile on his strong face. His frank, gray-blue eyes smile too, except when they tighten in distress as he talks of the past. Then his whole jaw juts out belligerently and his great fists are clutched and pounded in slow anger. When he laughs, it is a boyish and hearty laugh, one that all his listeners enjoy to the full."

According to Steinhouse, Schindler helped American investigators gather evidence against Nazi war criminals by "presenting the occupying power with the most detailed documentation on all his old drinking companions, on the vicious owners of the other slave factories . . . on all the rotten group he had wined and flattered while inwardly loathing, in order to save the lives of helpless people."

But in 1949, Oskar Schindler was "a lost soul. Everyday life became more difficult and unsettled. A Sudeten German, he had no future in Czechoslovakia and at the time could no longer stand the Germany he had once loved. For a time, he tried living in Regensburg. Later he moved to Munich depending heavily on Care parcels sent to him from America by some of the *Schindlerjuden*, but too proud to plead for more help.

"Polish Jewish welfare organizations traced him, discovered him in want, and tried to bring some assistance even in the midst of their own bitter postwar troubles."

A New York woman and Płaszów survivor who had relatives on the list recalls that in the summer of 1945, Schindler told her that he'd been warned to stay out of Poland, "because he'd meet the same fate as had Dr. Gross and Kerner, the OD men [Jews killed for their war crimes]. He'd meet it at the hands of those who got knocked off the list."

The Jewish Joint Distribution Committee gave Oskar money and set up the Schindlers in Argentina on a nutria ranch, where they tried raising the minklike animals. He failed. Survivors bought him an apartment in Buenos Aires, but he left Emilie in 1957 and went back to Germany. He tried running a cement plant but failed at that, too. He just couldn't seem to adjust to the banality of life in peacetime.

He visited Israel in 1962. The *Schindlerjuden* there received him like a potentate. From then on, he never lacked for support from his "children." Before he died in 1974, he asked that the *Schindlerjuden* take his remains to Israel and bury him there. He lies in the Catholic cemetery on Mount Zion.

Whatever he was between 1939 and 1945, he has come to represent so much more than a mere flesh-and-blood mortal. He has become, in legend, what most people want to believe they themselves would become in situations of moral extremis. "Each one of us at any time, faced with the particular circumstances, has the power to stand on the side of right," a California survivor named Leon Leyson told me. "Ninety-nine percent of the time, we simply don't. This is an ordinary man, not a special hero with super powers, and yet he did it."

He also has allowed hundreds of men and women to answer at least part of the imponderable question: *Why did I survive and six million perish?* Answer: *Because of Oskar Schindler.*

I Gambled on What Mattered Most

Hannah Senesh

Hannah Senesh was born into a family of privilege in Budapest in 1921. Her father was a well-respected playwright who died when Hannah was a young child. She inherited his talent with words and began writing poetry at an early age. She grew up with few connections to her Jewish heritage until, as a result of the ever-increasing Nazi influence, she experienced discrimination at school. She then developed an interest in Judaism and began to study her heritage. Senesh became a Zionist and immigrated to Palestine after she graduated from high school. She learned Hebrew quickly and worked on a kibbutz. Senesh volunteered to serve with the British military and parachuted into Nazi-occupied Yugoslavia on a secret mission. Crossing into Hungary with the resistance, she was captured and held in jail in Budapest. Senesh was executed at age twenty-three shortly before the liberation. Her story is told in *Hannah Senesh: Her Life and Diary*, from which the following material is taken.

The following material includes some of Senesh's poetry and letters to her beloved brother, George.

Cairo

January, 1944

My Darling George,

We arrived safely after an approximately ten-hour ride by car. The drive was pleasant since I came with a group of good-natured people. We sang, talked, and even slept (of course this last is not a sign of good spirits, but it made the trip pass more quickly). I drove a part of the way, though of course not all the way because there were three drivers besides myself. I had plenty of time to think, and thus naturally thought about you. Again and again I thanked Providence that we could at least meet, even though only for such a very short time.

You can imagine how interested I am in your first impressions of the Land, and of the kibbutz. You don't have to hurry too much in forming opinions; try to know the country first—which will not be an easy achievement. (I'm not thinking of knowing it geographically, but its way of life and its society.)

At the moment it is difficult for me to write because everything is considered a 'military secret' and I'm afraid the censor will delete something. In short, I am well, there are a lot of soldiers (boys and girls) here from Eretz among whom I can find a good many to be friendly with. During the day I'm busy, at night we go to the cinema, or I stay home and read. Fortunately I am not in the barracks but in the city, so I can take advantage of my free time.

George, please write about everything. You know how much it all interests me. Did you send Mother a telegram? I will try to write more in the immediate future, and will send a picture as well.

A million hugs.

Cairo
February 27, 1944

My Darling George,

The only fortunate thing is that there are so many soldiers here from Ma'agan, and that one by one they take trips home so I can send you a letter, and along with this one a little gift. I would like to send you every nice thing I see, to make up for the many years I could send nothing. But I don't know what you need, and of course I am not exactly wealthy so my gifts are not very impressive. I am also sending you my fountain pen as I have been given a new one.

I received your first letter with the greatest possible joy. It took about a week for it to arrive which is not terribly long. But send one back with Yona and that way I'll get it even more quickly.

Not long ago I talked to someone who has just returned from Turkey and asked for news of Mother's arrival. He said everything possible has been done, but that so far there has been no sign that Mother has even thought of Aliyah. Of course one does not know anything to the contrary either. I hope my letter, which Mother probably received, has convinced her of all the advantages of coming as quickly as possible. That it's impossible at the moment to come through Bulgaria is a great obstacle, but there is some hope that there will be a new way soon.

As for me, there is a good chance we will soon be leaving here, and in that case I will be writing shorter letters. But in any event I'll make every attempt to keep you informed of my well-being. I'm preparing several letters for Mother which you'll have to send her later. She must not know, under any circumstances, that I've enlisted.

I hope you're guarding those addresses I gave you in connection with matters to do with you and Mother. You can use them safely at any time should you have need of them.

I hug you. With everlasting love.

Cairo

February, 1944

Dear George,

Today I went on an excursion again. This time to the royal graves of Luxor. They are interesting, monumental creations. But as a matter of fact I don't have the patience for such things now. As far as I can see, we're moving on next week, and I am tensely awaiting the new assignment.

Should Mother arrive during my absence you will have to explain the situation. I know, darling, this is a difficult task for you, and I don't know if Mother will understand what I've done. I can't find words to express my pain at the thought that once again I am going to cause the darling so much worry, and that we can't be together. All my hopes are that you two will soon be united.

Unending love.

The following letter was written to the secretary of the kibbutz, who arranged her mission.

Cairo

March, 1944

Dear Braginsky,

Before my departure, I would like to send you a few words. This is not goodbye; we already said goodbye in Eretz. But I feel the need of saying a few words to you, my close good friend.

I know that uncertain situations can arise. To be exact, difficult situations which can affect our fate. I know in that event you will ask yourself certain questions—and I want to answer them beforehand. Not on behalf of others, only on behalf of myself, even though everyone feels as I do.

I leave happily and of my own free will, with full knowledge of the difficulties ahead. I consider my mission a privilege, and at the same time a duty. Everywhere, and under all conditions, the thought that all of you are behind us will help.

I have something to ask of you which it is perhaps unnecessary to ask, but I must. We have grown used to the fact that a lot of comrades know about our affairs since we all live our successes and difficulties together. But you must be aware that in fulfilling the curiosity of those who are interested in knowing our fate we might well have to pay a very high price. You know how much all information or disclosure of fact can mean. I don't want to multiply these words.

Before my departure I must express my appreciation for your help, for all I've received from you, and for the friendliness you always extended to me.

We will talk about everything else upon my return. Until then, warmest regards from Hagar.[1]

April 2, 1944[2]

Dear George,

As I thought I would, I left my former place. I am well and like my work, which is all I can tell you now. I know this laconic communication doesn't say much, but you, darling, can write to me about everything. How are you fitting into the new life? It should be easier for you to judge things now that you have had time to become acquainted with the good and the bad. I think the people are quite decent there, which helps considerably to create a feeling of being at home.

I don't envy you the approaching summer. One doesn't exactly freeze in the Emek Hayarden. But Kinneret is close by and that's not exactly bad! Any news from Mother?

My darling, a thousand hugs.

May 10, 1944

Dear George,

Though air-mail traffic is not too good I've received three letters from you, and I am so happy I've finally had news of you. It makes me feel well to know everything is in order, and that you're content. I, too, am well, but it hurts that we are so far from each other. I've enjoyed some fine and interesting experiences, but we'll have to wait until I can tell you all about them.

Darling, I am as concerned about Mother as you, and it's terrible that I can do nothing for her. Without knowing any of the details I can envisage the horrible situation. You can imagine how much I think of both of you, and more than ever before of Mother.

Forgive this brief letter, but by now you must be used to these succinct messages. Some day I will make up for all the omissions.

Thousand kisses.

---

[1] Hagar was her code name during the mission.
[2] The following four letters were sent from Yugoslavia. At the time, though, her whereabouts were a military secret, and even her brother did not know where she in fact was.

May 20, 1944

George Darling,

Again a short letter so you'll know everything is all right with me, and that's all. I have a suspicion all my friends and acquaintances are annoyed because I don't write. Perhaps they are even angry with me. Please try to explain the situation, and if you can't perhaps they'll forgive me later.

I don't write to Mother at all, so your letters will have to take the place of mine. In fact I even give you permission to forge my signature with the hope that you won't one day take advantage of this to 'extort large sums'.

It is unnecessary to tell you how much I would like to see you, talk to you, or at least be able to write in more detail. I hope you know all this anyway. Your letters arrive with great delay, but sooner or later they do get here and I am always so happy when I have news from you.

A thousand kisses, and warmest regards to our friends.

The following letter was written the day before she crossed the Hungarian border.

June 6, 1944

Darling George,

Once again I'm taking advantage of an opportunity to write, even though I have nothing to write about.

The most important thing: most heartfelt wishes for your birthday. You see, I was so hopeful that this time we could celebrate it together, but I was mistaken. However, let us hope we can next time.

I would be very pleased, George dear, if you would write a few lines to M. at our kibbutz. It has been a long time since I wrote but think a great deal about all of them. I am well. I have reason not to write to them at this particular time.

Any news of Mother? I beg you, please write about everything. Your letters reach me sooner or later, and I am always so happy to read them.

My darling, I wish you the very best of everything. A thousand kisses.

This letter was written to her comrades in Caesarea an hour before she flew from Italy to Yugoslavia.

March 13, 1944

Dearest Comrades:

On sea, land, in the air, in war and in peace, we are all advancing towards the same goal. Each of us will stand at his post. There is no difference between my task and that of another. I will be thinking of all of you a great deal. That's what gives me strength.

Warmest comradely greetings.

This letter was written the day she parachuted into Yugoslavia and was received by her mother very much later; it was forwarded by an unknown route.

March 13, 1944

Mother Darling,

In a few days I'll be so close to you—and yet so far. Forgive me, and try to understand. With a million hugs.

Blessed Is The Match

Blessed is the match consumed
    in kindling flame.
Blessed is the flame that burns
    in the secret fastness of the heart.
Blessed is the heart with strength to stop
    its beating for honour's sake.
Blessed is the match consumed
    in kindling flame.

One—Two—Three

One—two—three . . .
    eight feet long,
Two strides across, the rest is dark . . .
Life hangs over me like a question mark.

One—two—three . . .
    maybe another week,
Or next month may still find me here,
But death, I feel, is very near.

I could have been
    twenty-three next July;
I gambled on what mattered most,
The dice were cast. I lost.

Yugoslavia, 1944

Adrienne Rich

One of the United States'
most highly regarded
poets, Adrienne Rich was
born in Baltimore in
1929. A noted feminist
scholar and lecturer, her
poetry has received
numerous awards. Active
in the civil rights,
antiwar, and women's
movements, the themes
of social justice, women's
consciousness, and a
sense of authentic
community are reflected
in her work. She is a
professor of English and
feminist studies at
Stanford University.
Among her many
publications is *Time's
Power: Poems 1985–1988*,
from which the
accompanying poem is
taken.

In this poem, Rich
pays tribute to the
heroism of Hannah
Senesh.

Dear Chana,
                    where are you now?
Am sending this pocket-to-pocket
(though we both know pockets we'd hate to lie in).
They showed me that poem you gave Reuven,
about the match:
Chana, you know, I never was
for martyrdom. I thought we'd try our best,
ragtag mission that we were,
then clear out if the signals looked too bad.
Something in you drives things ahead for me
but if I can I mean to stay alive.
We're none of us giants, you know,
just small, frail, inexperienced romantic people.
But there are things we learn.
You know the sudden suck of empty space
between the jump and the ripcord pull?
I hate it. I hate it so,
I've hated you for your dropping
ecstatically in free-fall, in the training,
your look, dragged on the ground, of knowing
precisely why you were there.
                                        My mother's
still in Palestine. And yours
still there in Hungary. Well, there we are.
When this is over—
                            I'm
your earthbound friend to the end, still yours—
                                                    Esther.

Raoul Wallenberg: Angel of Rescue

Harvey Rosenfeld

Harvey Rosenfeld was born in New York in 1939. He
earned a doctorate from St. John's University and
has been a professor of English since 1976. Rosenfeld
has been editor of *Martyrdom and Resistance*, a
journal devoted to the study of the Holocaust. He is
the author of *Raoul Wallenberg: Angel of Rescue*, which
was named one of the ten best books of 1982 by the
National Catholic News Service.

Raoul Wallenberg was a young, American-
educated Swedish diplomat who repeatedly risked
his life to help save the lives of the Jews in Budapest,
Hungary, who were targeted for death by the
German SS and the Arrow Cross, the Hungarian
fascists. Sent to Hungary through a cooperative
Swedish and American effort, he is credited with
saving thousands of lives. Although he was
recognized as a hero for his tireless efforts to protect
Hungarian Jews and to provide them with hope, the
Soviets arrested and imprisoned him when they
liberated Hungary from the Germans. His
disappearance remained a mystery for many years,
but it is now assumed that he died in Soviet captivity.

"There are no great men, only ordinary men
facing a great challenge." Winston Churchill's words certainly describe Raoul
Wallenberg and his rescue mission in Budapest. With only the meager personal protection offered by a diplomatic passport, he confronted SS and Nyilas

gunmen: racists, psychopaths, torturers, murderers, the dregs of a civilized society. Wallenberg literally snatched thousands of Jewish victims from the jaws of death using the only weapons at hand: some money, his wits, his courage, and an overwhelming moral commitment to save lives. His sense of responsibility to humanity allowed him to transcend his personal fears and shortcomings in order to overcome seemingly insurmountable obstacles with the perseverance of a true hero.

On the surface Raoul Wallenberg did not look like a hero, an Angel of Rescue. He certainly lacked the traits of the Scandinavian prototype of courage and strength, the dauntless Beowulf. With Wallenberg's medium height, dark eyes, and dark, thinning hair, he did not even resemble the Swedish stereotype. However, unlike exploits of Beowulf, the superhuman heroics of Raoul Wallenberg are not legend; they are fact. Colleagues, classmates, and family have all reflected on Raoul's phenomenal achievements.

Tibor Baranski had much in common with Wallenberg: they were both young, nonprofessional representatives of neutral legations, highly motivated for idealistic reasons, who succeeded through resourcefulness and indefatigable dedication.

Baranski's first impressions of Wallenberg were of "a thin man, rather shy and virtually fearless. He dressed elegantly and was always clean-shaven. He had a good nose to sniff out danger and immediately respond with the appropriate action. Although we did get to know one another, there was little time for friendship in those hectic times."

The representatives of the neutral legations met regularly, always at a different place so as to escape detection by the SS and the Arrow Cross. After one of these meetings, Baranski approached Wallenberg and asked if he would like to meet the nuncio. Wallenberg, very enthusiastic about the idea, asked Baranski to find out if the hour was not too late for the nuncio. "I called the nuncio, and he was excited." Baranski recalled the nuncio's words. " 'Would he really like to come? Are you sure?' "

Wallenberg visited with the nuncio for about an hour and a half. "They spoke about many things," Baranski said, "mostly about their countries. I tried to ensure their privacy, so most of the time I was at a distance from them." The next morning, Baranski was anxious to get the nuncio's opinion of Wallenberg. The nuncio was "very much impressed by him," Baranski said. "In fact, he said, 'I never met such a nice Protestant.' " Wallenberg's impressions of the papal representative were reciprocal. "It was amazing," Baranski said. "Wallenberg told me, 'I never met such a nice Catholic.' You could say that Wallenberg and the nuncio both saw each other as human beings, both on missions motivated by divine love towards man."

After one meeting of the neutral legations, Baranski and Wallenberg sat together for two hours in a Budapest restaurant.

> We were fantastically near to each other. We were both nondiplomats who acted for the sake of humanity. At one point, he asked me whether I was Jewish. "Why, just because I look Jewish?" I quipped. "No," Wallenberg answered, "I just imagined that you must be Jewish because you were so zealous in trying to save them." I then asked him about his zealousness. He told me that he had a Jewish ancestor, but that had little influence on his motivation. He did say that he spent some time in Palestine and met refugees who fled from German persecution. At that time he made a commitment to help such victims if he ever got the opportunity.

According to Baranski, Wallenberg had much to say about his family, especially about his mother. "Wallenberg was a very loving son, who wanted me to meet his mother. His mother had always told him that he was too shy. 'You should come to Sweden,' Wallenberg told me. 'You have the big mouth that mother would want me to have.' "

No one is better acquainted with Raoul Wallenberg than his family. Mrs. Nina Lagergren, his half sister, expresses no surprise at Raoul's feats. "I always felt my brother would do something very special with his life. My family was not surprised at his acts. We knew what he did was the greatest challenge of his life. It took hold of him."

Mrs. Lagergren recalled that Raoul had said that he was going to Budapest with "all sorts of lists with people to contact." The family never actually thought that his life would be constantly on the line. "Raoul knew that it would be a very difficult undertaking, but no one expected that he would risk his life. One did not think of such things because diplomatic immunity has been accepted worldwide."

Mrs. Lagergren said that Raoul approached the mission with "much energy and eagerness. Because of his business trips, Raoul had developed many pleasant relationships. So in that sense, the mission became something very personal for him. His many business trips abroad had proven that Raoul was a skillful negotiator and that he could deal effectively with people. Undoubtedly, this is one factor which helps explain why my brother was able to accomplish so much in Budapest."

Mrs. Lagergren added that her brother was very skillful at intimidation. "He was a great actor. He could imitate brilliantly. If he wanted to, he could be more German than a Prussian general. Shouting louder, sounding more authoritative than the higher-ups, he could wrest concessions from the Nazis."

On one occasion before a train departed for Auschwitz, Wallenberg appeared on the scene with several lists of his protégés. Per Anger observed, "He demanded in an authoritative tone whether any such persons had by mistake been taken aboard. The Germans were taken by surprise and, right under their noses, Wallenberg pulled out a large number of Jews. Many of them had no passport at all, only any kind of paper whatever in the Hungarian language— driver's licenses, vaccination records or tax receipts—that the Germans did not understand. The bluff succeeded" (84–85).

Anger also tells about Wallenberg's arrival in Budapest with a revolver in his pocket. "He said he was never going to use the revolver because he was too afraid, too much of a coward. But of course he was very courageous."

Lars Berg describes Wallenberg:

> Wallenberg's daring appearance at the scene of rescue was all the more admirable, as Raoul was not at all a brave man by nature. During the air raids he was always the first to seek shelter, and he was sometimes affected when the bombs fell too close. But when it was a question of saving the lives of his protégés, he never hesitated a second. He acted with a challenging boldness and bravery, though his life then mostly hanged by much thinner than a thread during the air raids.

Thomas Veres experienced Wallenberg's bravery firsthand. Mr. Veres, a commercial photographer in New York, rode in Wallenberg's big black Studebaker almost daily, taking pictures of the rescue mission. Thomas Veres's father, Paul Veres, a well-known Hungarian photographer, stopped practicing his trade when the Germans took over Hungary, and Thomas found himself with an abundant supply of film and other photographic supplies. Per Anger introduced the younger Veres, then twenty, to Wallenberg and the right person and a vital assignment coincided.

Veres recalled the dangers involved, both for him and for Wallenberg. But, he said, Wallenberg never backed away from a dangerous situation:

> I came to the Swedish embassy in October, 1944. Raoul Wallenberg said that he would like to take advantage of my profession and take pictures of the life-saving activities. He said that the pictures would serve as historic documentation. At that time, it was dangerous, in a sense forbidden, to take pictures on the streets. When I mentioned this point to Wallenberg, he said that he had already signed a pass for me, and thereby it would be legal for me to take pictures. In spite of this, Wallenberg constantly put his life in danger. Wallenberg dealt constantly with the Nyilas, and he knew their underhanded behavior. Legal or no, Wallenberg certainly knew that it was dangerous to take pictures, and at the beginning I couldn't bring myself to take pictures. However, the bravery of Raoul Wallenberg got to me. It may seem that I am exaggerating or just being trite, but the truth is that Raoul Wallenberg didn't know the meaning of danger.

Wherever Wallenberg's rescue operation went, Thomas Veres followed. He witnessed the death marches to Hegyeshálom and includes in his "collection" a "before and after" picture of a mother and daughter who survived the march, but whose excruciating experience is apparent in their faces. He recorded the freeing of Jews at the rail station and their return to the Swedish safe houses. He photographed hundreds of Wallenberg's protégés for identification on the protected passes.

Because of his many experiences with Raoul Wallenberg, Veres saw not only the bravery of the Swede but also his delightful sense of humor.

> One day our car was in heavy artillery fire and there was our car with one license plate in the front, a different license plate in the back. In fact, we had many plates and signs, depending on who asked: the SS or the Arrow Cross. For example, we had a sign that said "rushing mail," to avoid being stopped. On that particular day, in the midst of gunfire, Wallenberg jokingly remarked, "We should get an automatic gadget so that when one license plate appears the others will disappear."

Despite Wallenberg's bravery and determination, Veres remembers times when even Wallenberg couldn't succeed. At the end of December, 1944, the Arrow Cross attacked a protected house and dragged out some of the protégés. Veres reconstructed the following dialogue between Wallenberg and a member of the Nyilas:

Wallenberg: "Where are the protected ones?"

Nyilas: "In the Danube."

Wallenberg: "Why?"

Nyilas: "They were dirty Jews."

"At that point," Veres said, "even Wallenberg was stunned and couldn't help."

Another Wallenberg aide presently heads a pharmaceutical company in Los Altos, California. He was one of the Swede's personal drivers on the rescue missions. Although he did not want to be identified, he said that "after years of silence, it is important to tell the story of Raoul Wallenberg. Perhaps all the talk, all the print will help locate this heroic person."

The driver presented himself at the Swedish legation when the Nazi invasion forced the closing of the universities. "Wallenberg was a modest, retiring individual with steellike determination," the driver said. "He wasn't the Patton type. He was adept in administrative detail and understood the German mentality. He knew that Germans reacted to formal documents and authority. When it came to rescue work, he was workmanlike, precise, and cold."

Taking Wallenberg to many deportation points, the driver got a firsthand view of the Wallenberg modus operandi: "He always overwhelmed the German

SS with double talk. Wallenberg would threaten to call their superiors if they didn't cooperate. He used every possible deception and trick, including bribing them and telling the SS he would write a favorable report about them after Germany lost the war."

Wallenberg's daring spread among his workers.

> Raoul usually had with him a book with names of passport holders. Sometimes the book had all blank pages. When he arrived at the train, he then made up Jewish names and began calling out. Three or four usually had passports. For those who didn't, I stood behind Raoul with another fifty or more unfilled passports. It only took me ten seconds to write in their names. We handed them out calmly and said, "Oh, I'm terribly sorry you couldn't get to the legation to pick it up. Here it is. We brought it to you." The passport holder showed it to the SS and was free.
>
> I myself carried forged identity papers for various occasions. One set identified me as a doctor for the German SS; another proved I worked for the Swedish legation. If anybody had ever searched and found those phony papers, I would have been shot there and then. All those who worked with Raoul Wallenberg took unbelievable risks. But we were his disciples and followed his courageous example.

The driver never really got to know Wallenberg personally—few did. Raoul Wallenberg had a mission—that was all that mattered. "We never got very close," the driver said. "He never shared chitchat or confidences. It was strictly business. Wallenberg went to fulfill a mission. He never once thought of personal glory."

Another of Wallenberg's workers was his driver, Sandor Ardai. (Actually, Wallenberg had another chauffeur, Wilmos Langfelder, who was abducted along with him by the Russians.) Ardai was summoned to Wallenberg's office in November after Langfelder had been arrested by the Arrow Cross. Wallenberg asked Ardai to become his driver, but pointed out the dangers of the assignment. Ardai reflected on this meeting and on Wallenberg in the weekly journal *Aret Runt* (July 4–11, 1957):

> "It is dangerous and difficult," underlined Wallenberg. "You do not need to if you do not want it."
>
> I did not hesitate a second but accepted. And many times afterwards I have remembered my meeting with this remarkable Swede. He did not at all look like a hero, not as you imagine a courageous, strongwilled and freeborn hero type. He rather seemed dreaming and weak. My first mission was to drive him to the headquarters of the Arrow Cross and wait outside until he got Langfelder back. I thought silently "that this will never go well," when he disappeared with long strides. How could the Hungarian Arrow Cross release a prisoner, just because one man requested it?

But when I saw him again on the stairs he brought Langfelder along. They jumped into the car and I drove them to the legation. Nobody commented on what had happened and I started to understand the extraordinary force which was in Raoul Wallenberg.

I never heard Wallenberg speak an unnecessary word during the month and a half I and Langfelder took turns as a driver—not a single comment, never a complaint, even if he could not sleep more than a few hours for several days.

On one occasion we had come to a station where a train full of Jews was on the point of leaving for Germany and the concentration camps. The officer of the guard did not want to let us enter. Raoul Wallenberg then climbed up on the roof of the train and handed in many protective passports through the windows. The Arrow Cross men fired their guns and cried to him to go away, but he only continued calmly to hand out passports to the hands which reached for them. But I believe that the men with the guns were impressed by his courage and on purpose aimed above him. Afterwards he managed to get all Jews with passports out from the train. His only aim was to save as many as possible. And by his personal courage he managed to save thousands.

Wallenberg's insistence on helping groups rather than individuals became even firmer during his hectic round-the-clock rescue mission after the Arrow Cross took over. However, a dramatic, storybook episode, that of the Vandor family, proved an exception. On November 3, a frantic Tibor Vandor sought out Wallenberg. Vandor's wife was in labor with their first child, but all hospitals refused to help. In the middle of the night Wallenberg took the Vandors to his room, while he slept in the corridor, covered with his coat. At 7 A.M. the Vandors invited Wallenberg into the room to see the new arrival and to name the dark-haired girl. He chose the names Nina Maria Ava. "She looks like my grandmother," Wallenberg laughed. "I am honored to be her godfather." With Wallenberg's permission the name was changed to Yvonne Maria Ava.

After the war the Vandors went to Switzerland, Holland, and then Montreal, where Yvonne was raised as a Christian. "My parents always wanted to forget the past," Yvonne, now Mrs. Ron Singer of Toronto, recalled. "All I knew was that I was born in Hungary during the war. I always felt that I had roots, that I didn't belong. When I married Ron fourteen years ago I converted to Judaism because I wanted to identify with Ron and with a group that had roots."

Years later, when the Singers were living in England, a relative told Yvonne that she was Jewish by birth. "I became driven with a desire to know more about my past, but my parents refused to say more." Then like a bolt from the blue, on October 20, 1979, a story dealing with the heroics and search for Raoul Wallenberg appeared in the *Toronto Star*. This article referred to the Vandors and the birth of Yvonne. In Mrs. Singer's words:

I was reading the story aloud to Ron, when I came to those lines where I read my own name. I burst out crying. Ron and I clung to each other and we were both crying. It became very difficult to go on reading. I finally found myself. The reaction in the community has been incredible since that day. There is a sizable Hungarian Jewish community in Toronto. Many others have also found their roots. They have discovered that they are Jewish. They have come to the realization that they are only alive because of Raoul Wallenberg.

If Raoul Wallenberg could be said to be the Angel of Rescue, one could also say that the forces of Satan were arrayed against him. Chief among these infamous Nazi devils was Adolf Eichmann, Hitler's Bloodhound, the man who made mass murder into an efficient, mechanized process. The conflict between these two men provides a study in contrasts: the Angel of Rescue versus the Bloodhound. Whereas the arrival of the Swede in Budapest was an event of joy, the Nazi's appearance in Hungary prompted gloom and despair. While Wallenberg was a man of culture and learning, Eichmann was an individual of little knowledge but much pretense. Lévai describes Eichmann's entrance into Hungary in the *Black Book on the Martyrdom of Hungarian Jewry*:

There is reason to believe that "Eichmann" used a new name in every country he went in order to prevent creating a panic, so terrible was the record of the atrocities for which he was responsible. Eichmann was fond of pretending that he was born in Palestine and spoke Hebrew fluently; in point of fact, no one ever heard him say anything in that ancient tongue beyond a Biblical quotation regarding the creation of the universe, and that can hardly be taken as conclusive proof of his knowledge of the language. . . . When Eichmann made his first appearance at the headquarters of the Jewish Congregation in Budapest, he opened the conversation with the following pleasantry: "Sie wissen nicht wer ich bin? Ich bein ein Bluthund!" (So you don't know who I am? I am a bloodhound!) (108).

In his relentless efforts to save Jews, Wallenberg worked around the clock, at times without eating and sleeping. He was forced to change apartments to escape the assassination plots of the Nazis and the Nyilas. Eichmann, however, was immersed in a hedonic existence. He was a permanent guest at the estate of László Endre, where they were united, according to Lévai, by three things: "their passion for horses, their love of alcohol, and their insane hatred of everything Jewish" (109). The wild orgies at the Endre estate were common knowledge.

The Angel of Rescue and the Bloodhound both resorted to deception: the Swede used subterfuge to save the targets of the Holocaust; the Nazi employed chicanery to facilitate his plans for genocide. After learning of the atrocities taking place in the provincial ghettos, the Jewish Council of Budapest compiled a memorandum and turned to Eichmann requesting an improvement of the situation. The Bloodhound responded with typical Eichmann dishonesty: "Not a single word of the report is true, for I have just inspected the provincial ghettos. I really ought to know. The accommodation of the Jews is no worse than that of German soldiers during manoeuvres and the fresh air will only do their health the world of good!" When the Jewish leadership continued to press, the Bloodhound replied with another attempt at deception. The treatment of the Jews was no fault of the Nazis, but of Endre, who "will die Juden mit Paprika fressen!" (who wants to devour the Jews with sweetpepper). When the Jewish leadership later received reports of the deportations in Sub-Carpathia and in the northern and trans-Danubian districts, Eichmann lied brazenly once more, telling the leaders: "If the Hungarian Jews behave themselves and do not join the Ruthenian partisans, there will be no deportations."

Wallenberg's family, friends, colleagues in Hungary, and the protégés whom he saved have attested to his graciousness, gentility, and courage. Before his execution in Bratislava after the war, Dieter von Wisliceny, the Bloodhound's collaborator in Budapest, enlarged upon Eichmann's boorishness, crudity, and cowardice:

> In 1944 Eichmann met a woman in Budapest, whose name was Ingrid Schama (?). She was living separated from her husband and I think she had private means. She had absolute power over Eichmann. When the Russians were advancing in Hungary, Eichmann prepared poison for the woman in case she was captured by the Russians.
>
> In Hungary Eichmann had another love affair, too, with a young Viennese woman, called Margrit Konschir. In the last years preceding the debacle, Eichmann, who would get drunk by night, was anyway an easy prey to women.
>
> In spite of his high rank, Eichmann could never get rid of his lower middle-class habits and mentality. He most carefully avoided any encounter with personalities of the elite. He sent his deputy, Günther, to official receptions. Not as though he had been reluctant to receive any honours; it was rather because he did not trust himself; he was afraid of making a fool of himself in a milieu alien to him. He always wished to remain "the mystery man." He was living in constant fear that they were after his life. He only travelled by his own personal motorcar and never dared to fly because he was afraid the plane might crash.
>
> There were always weapons in his car: two revolvers and hand grenades. In one of his pockets he always had a hand grenade and in the other a percussion cap. . . . Actually Eichmann was afraid.
>
> In September, 1944, in Hungary, he feared lest the house he was staying at would be blown up. He had bunkers built in his garden. So cautious was he that he did not let himself be photographed. When he needed a photograph for an identity card, he had his likeness taken at the photographic studio of the Gestapo and ordered only a few prints.

The adversaries first caught sight of each other at the bar of the Arizona nightclub in Budapest. Eichmann appraised Wallenberg as yet another effete diplomat, a playboy as dissolute as himself. His misperception of the Swede's character was quickly corrected as their opposing missions came into conflict.

Wallenberg was probably the first person who had ever dared to frustrate and countermand Eichmann's orders. As he thrust his type of devastation on Europe, Eichmann had met only token resistance to his wishes. Wallenberg's presence, therefore, became a new and unwelcome experience for Eichmann. As a means of becoming "acquainted" with the opposition, Wallenberg invited Eichmann and a top aide to his home for dinner. "Wallenberg was well aware," Berg said, "how much easier it is to bring a difficult transaction to a successful conclusion after an indulgence of good food and fine wines." Unfortunately, the overburdened Wallenberg completely forgot about his "distinguished" dinner guests. When Wallenberg arrived home at his usual late hour, the exasperation of the hungry, thirsty Nazis had peaked: not only had Wallenberg forgotten about the invitation, but it was the cook's day off. Wallenberg, never easily rattled, kept the Nazis at bay with a few drinks and called Lars Berg, who agreed to have all the guests for dinner. With typical poise Wallenberg told the placated guests that there had been a misunderstanding and that the dinner had been set in the home of attaché Berg.

Berg and coworker Göte Carlsson had a most charming residence at Hunfalvi Street and a cook of the highest quality. The house had previously belonged to nobility, and the owner left the new tenants his exquisite tableware. "The count's best porcelain and silver were laid out for the guests," Berg said, "and thanks to our excellent cook, the dinner was a great success. I am sure that Eichmann never even suspected that Wallenberg had forgotten him."

Berg recalls that the dinner was held late in the fall of 1944, and as they dined the Russian guns could be seen on the distant horizon. "Raoul was very relaxed that evening," Berg recalls, "since there were no emergencies or interventions which required his attention at that moment. Our little salon became a battle-field for one of Eichmann's many defeats against Raoul Wallenberg." The latter's opening salvo was a cool discussion of Nazi doctrines and the military outlook for Germany. Berg observed, "With clarity and logical precision, Wallenberg fearlessly tore Nazi doctrines into shreds and predicted that Nazism and its leaders would meet a speedy and complete destruction. I must say that these were rather unusual, caustic words from a Swede who was far away from his country and totally at the mercy of the powerful German antagonist Eichmann and his henchmen."

But Wallenberg's attack on Eichmann had a definite purpose: he actually sought to influence Eichmann. "In his prediction of the imminent doom of Nazism," Berg said, "there was also a sincere exhortation to Eichmann to bring to an end the senseless deportations and the unnecessary killing of Hungarian Jews."

Wallenberg pointedly put the question to Eichmann: "Look, you have to face up to the facts. You have lost the war. Why do you not give up now?"

As the discussion went on, Eichmann could not conceal his surprise that anyone would have the gall to attack not only him, but also Hitler so openly! "He soon discovered," said Berg, "that he was losing the battle to Wallenberg. Eichmann's well-learned propaganda phrases sounded empty and had little strength against Raoul's forceful, intelligent presentation." Stunned, Eichmann replied in a very open, revealing manner:

> I admit that you are right, Mr. Wallenberg. I actually never believed in Nazism as such, but it has given me power and wealth. I know that this pleasant life will soon be over. My planes will no longer bring me women and wines from Paris nor any other delicacies from the Orient. My horses, my dogs, my palace here in Budapest will soon be taken over by the Russians, and I myself, an SS officer, will be shot on the spot. But for me there is no rescue any more. If I obey my orders from Berlin and exercise my power ruthlessly enough here in Budapest, I shall be able to prolong my days of grace.

After making this admission and stating his resolve to continue, Eichmann served notice on Wallenberg: "I warn you, Herr Legationsekretär. I shall do my very utmost to defeat you. And your Swedish diplomatic passport will not help you, if I consider it necessary to do away with you. Even a neutral diplomat might meet with accidents."

According to Berg, the Germans are very "correct" in diplomatic dealings. And, not surprisingly, Eichmann left without anger or bitterness. "With the unfailing politeness of a well-brought-up German officer, Eichmann bid us goodbye and thanked us for a charming evening."

Berg speculated on the purpose behind Wallenberg's lecture and rebuke of Eichmann: "Perhaps Raoul did not achieve much by his frank argumentation, but sometimes it could be quite a relief for a Swede to be able to tell his straightforward opinion to a German SS officer. Without doubt Eichmann left the house very much impressed by Raoul's fearlessness and strong personality."

Wallenberg certainly left an imprint on Eichmann. A few days after their charming evening together, Wallenberg's private car was out on official business, but Wallenberg was not inside. A big, heavy German truck rammed straight into Wallenberg's car, wrecking it completely. Wallenberg lodged a firm protest directly to Eichmann regarding the attempt on his life. Eichmann was "sorry" about the "accident," but quickly told his adversary "I will try again."

However, Eichmann had more important things to attend to, such as the planning and implementation of the death marches and other schemes to complete the final solution, so neither Wallenberg nor his cars were ever attacked again. In fact, Wallenberg is reported to have dealt directly with Eichmann in bargaining for the release of Jews. But Eichmann continually voiced his hatred of the Swede. One of his outbursts sparked an international incident. During a conversation with a staff member of the Swedish Red Cross, Eichmann made known his desire to shoot "Jew-dog" Wallenberg. "It is possible that Eichmann's statement was an empty threat," Anger said, "but we were not prepared to leave it unchallenged." After receiving a telegram from the Swedish legation, the Foreign Office in Stockholm instructed the embassy in Berlin to lodge a protest to the Germans, complaining about the threat against Wallenberg and demanding that the SS command in Budapest respect the legation members and their staffs. Edmund Veesenmayer, Hitler's ambassador in Budapest, "apologized" to Stockholm, assuring Sweden that Eichmann's words were not to be taken literally. However, Veesenmayer explained, Eichmann's reaction had to be understood in light of Wallenberg's illegal activities on behalf of the Jews. Wallenberg acted in a "far too unconventional and unacceptable way." In that sense, Veesenmayer maintained, Eichmann's words should be viewed as a future warning, meant to restrain Wallenberg from persisting in his rescue efforts.

Unwilling to be on hand for the arrival of the Russians, Eichmann hurried out of Budapest on December 23, 1944, but before leaving, he conceded that Wallenberg had been "a brilliant chess player." Their conflicting goals—Wallenberg's, to save as many Jews as possible; Eichmann's, to kill as many Jews as possible—had made them bitter, determined foes, but Wallenberg had outfoxed and outmaneuvered the Bloodhound. With his chief adversary Eichmann gone, the Angel of Rescue next directed his efforts towards outsmarting the Nyilas and contending with a more deadly group of villains.

Wallenberg's rescue activities brought him many potent enemies—aside from Eichmann. Although Wallenberg was able to influence Foreign Minister Kemény through the baroness, he had no success in dealing with Deputy Foreign Minister Zoltan Bagossy, Wallenberg's "particular antagonist," according to Berg.

> Bagossy was a real sadistic Nazi and hated Jews with all his heart, if he had any heart at all. He was absolutely unsusceptible to persuasion whether in form of bribes or reasoning. He remained the master spirit of the deportation of the Jews. Not even the menace of blacklisting him with the Russians seemed to have any effect on him. In distinction to almost all other German and Hungarian Nazi bigshots he was not even interested in Wallenberg's very last means of influence—a Swedish protection passport either for the person in question himself or for his mistress or somebody else near of kin. Bagossy could just not be swayed (29).

Despite Bagossy's animosity towards Wallenberg, the deputy foreign minister never considered having his foe assassinated. The same could not be said for two other satanic forces: Kurt Rettmann and SS Hauptsturmführer Theodore Dannecker. An instigator of the Nyilas' atrocities, Rettmann was quite incensed over Wallenberg's continual thwarting of his plans to "kill all Jews." Rettmann sent a warning to Wallenberg that he would have him murdered if he did not cease his rescue work. Dannecker also wanted to do away with Wallenberg. He planned the near catastrophe of a German truck ramming into Wallenberg's car and publicized it, by bragging that it was his scheme. Wallenberg's worker Charles Wilhelm was also aware of Dannecker's intentions and warned Wallenberg.

Despite these warnings, Wallenberg's response always remained the same: the Angel of Rescue would never give up his mission. In answer to Rettmann's death threats, Wallenberg said, "It is not my intention to worry about myself or about my safety. The more help I can dispense, the more safe passes I can give out, the happier I am."

Mrs. Paula Auer, of Newark, New Jersey, recalled Wallenberg's heroism during the final days of 1944. On February 14, 1947, the Newark *Jewish News* presented her experiences in perhaps the first account of a Wallenberg rescue. Mrs. Auer and her family had found refuge in a Swedish protected house. She said, "When the Russians reached the gates of Budapest, the Nazis broke into this and other Swedish homes and like crazed beasts shot all the Jews they saw. They then threw the bodies into the Danube. Somehow I escaped the Nazis' search and got word to the Swedish legation. Wallenberg and his assistants arrived in time to prevent the massacre of the remaining 160 Jews in the home."

From his home in Stockholm, Georg Libik related Wallenberg's fearless adventure during Christmas week. Now a civil engineer, Libik was a slalom champion in his native Hungary. His father was a commissioner in a Nazi war factory; his father-in-law, Albert Szent-Györgyi, was a Nobel laureate in medicine. During the war, Libik said, his father-in-law was a leader of the Hungarian resistance movement and a "personal enemy of Hitler." After the Arrow Cross came to power, the Nyilas raided a meeting of resistance leaders, at which Libik was present. The Arrow Cross seized his address book with its listings of underground workers. Libik managed to escape from the clutches of the Arrow Cross and warn all those in his address book.

At this time, Per Anger took Libik onto his staff under the pseudonym of Bela Ratkovsky, while sheltering Szent-Györgyi at his residence in Buda. Libik joined his father-in-law at the Anger residence around Christmas time.

Georg Libik reconstructed that memorable evening. "It was one night, some time after 10, when Wallenberg showed up at Per Anger's apartment. He looked like a student with his red scarf and black winter coat. He was bareheaded and looked very pale." Libik first thought that Wallenberg must be some sort of lunatic. "This fellow must be mad, I said to myself. It's suicidal to be out so late at night, with all the Nyilas roaming the streets."

Wallenberg and Anger went to a corner and began conversing in low tones, first in Swedish and then in German. "The situation was obviously very serious," Libik said. "The Arrow Cross had bullied their way into a protected house on Benczur Street, drove the people out into the courtyard, searched them, and treated them brutally. One could expect, Wallenberg said, that 'they would be shot in the Danube.' "

Wallenberg's car and chauffeur were missing, and for that reason he had come to Anger. "Wallenberg was afraid that he could not get to Benczur Street in time to stop the massacre from being carried out. There were many lives to be saved. Despite some misgivings about the recklessness of Wallenberg, Anger was agreeable and asked me to drive Wallenberg to Pest before the bridges over the Danube were blown up."

Libik left with a false identification and a gun at his side. According to Libik, "Wallenberg had a different outlook. 'I do not rely on power,' Wallenberg told me. 'My strength is that I can bribe or threaten the Arrow Cross.' We drove off with no lights on. It was a frightful scene on the streets of Pest. Everywhere there were houses on fire. It was my country, part of my life being destroyed. But with all the human corpses, all the dead horses strewn along the streets, there was no time for meditation."

Wallenberg entered the building on Benczur Street alone, telling Libik to park the car where the Nyilas could not see it. "I thought to myself," Libik said, "why is Wallenberg doing this? Why didn't he stay at home, even if the unfortunate people were to die. How could a foreigner—and a Swede—be more noble and a truer patriot than the Hungarians. If the Hungarians didn't care about their own people, why should a foreigner? My head was filled with such medieval, romantic wanderings while I thought of Wallenberg with admiration."

Libik waited an hour in the car for Wallenberg to return. "He came out and happily announced, 'Everything is okay. Everyone has permission to return to the house.' I never for a moment doubted the truth of Wallenberg's claim, but I admit it was difficult to believe."

An anonymous Hungarian Jew who was saved because of Wallenberg's refusal to be coerced, to give up, gave the following account in the March 6, 1945, *Dagens Nyheter* about a Nyilas armed patrol invading a protected house:

Wallenberg: "This is Swedish territory. You have got nothing to do here."

Chief of Patrol: "I have orders to take the able-bodied men away from here."

Wallenberg: "Nobody will get out. If you try to take anybody away from here you will get into trouble with me. As long as I am alive, nobody will be taken from here. You will have to shoot me first."

Tibor Vayda still vividly recalls the December rescue operation on Üllöi Street.

There were more than three hundred men and women at our office, which was also a Swedish protected house on Üllöi Street. The Nyilas stormed in and shouted, "Wallenberg is not here. Everybody, get out. Swedish protection means nothing. Protective passes mean nothing." People wanted to take their luggage, but the Nyilas sneered. "You don't need luggage because you will be dead soon." About noon we were marched to SS headquarters. We expected to be shot after being thrown into the Danube. Somehow—and I still do not know how—a message was gotten to Wallenberg. At 2:00 in the afternoon his car roared through the courtyard. Not one of the three hundred was lost. He simply put it straight to the SS commando: "You save these men, and I promise your safety after the Russians win the war."

Tibor Vayda never saw Wallenberg again. "He was a quiet hero. Few people got to know him on a personal level, except perhaps his secretary, Mrs. Falk, and our fellow worker, Vilmos Forgacz."

Per Anger describes his last meeting with his colleague on January 10, 1945. "I remember reminding him once again of the extremely dangerous position he was in, and advised him to move over with us on the Buda side from the Pest side. The Hungarian Nazis were especially at this point hunting for him and he endangered himself by continuing his rescue work. But he turned a deaf ear to this. He wanted to be near the Jews who needed his help."

During January, amid the infernolike fires in Budapest, Wallenberg received death threats in the mail. Stones were thrown against his car. Armed gangsters hunted him. Everything was done to make it impossible for him to visit his protégés, but nothing could make Wallenberg give up his work.

Although Wallenberg refused to give up his rescue work, he was neither naive nor foolhardy. He was fully aware of the dangers surrounding him. He continually changed apartments as well as his sleeping place for the evening. One of his last apartments was on the sixth floor of Madách Street. Lévai succinctly captured the historical charm and allure of the lodging: "He [Wallenberg] found a haven at the apartment of writer Magda Gabor. He had been there many times before and had spent much time with Baroness Kemény" (167).

But, while Raoul Wallenberg was a veritable Angel of Rescue, he was still a mortal possessing normal fears. After an encounter with the Nyilas official Vöczköndy, Wallenberg remarked, "I have never been closer to death." On January 10, Anger and Wallenberg were on a mission together. Bombs fell continually. Proceeding with the car was most difficult, as the roads presented obstructions of human bodies, dead horses, fallen trees, and demolished houses. Anger turned to his colleague and asked whether he was frightened.

The response tells the story of Raoul Wallenberg—as the Angel of Rescue, but equally as an ordinary mortal: "Sure, it gets a little scary, sometimes, but for me there's no choice. I have taken on this assignment and I would never be able to go back to Stockholm without knowing inside myself I had done all a man could do to save as many Jews as possible."

In explaining why Raoul Wallenberg could not return home, one of his protégés compared him to an obsessed, overworked violinist. "He was a driven man, unable to let go of what had become an obsession," according to Edith Wohl-Ernster, first violinist of the Stockholm opera. "He was like a violinist playing an extremely difficult concerto. His work sapped all his strength, but he refused to quit."

Wallenberg's nonprofessional counterpart at the nunciature, Tibor Baranski, recalled the Swede as an "extraordinary" person, but with the usual apprehensions of mortals.

> We were normal human beings. Certainly we both were afraid at times of the dangers in our path. What is important is that Wallenberg was able to rise above and defeat these fears and accomplish so many wonderful things. He saved 70,000 Jews when he prevented the central ghetto from being destroyed. More than 25,000 life-saving Swedish protection passes are the result of his initiative and actions. That's almost 100,000 lives saved by one man! What else is there to say?

Remember My Name (Act 1, Scenes 1–3)

Joanna H. Kraus

Joanna H. Kraus was born in 1937 and was raised in
Portland, Maine. She has made significant
contributions to the theater, most notably in the
area of child drama. Educated at the University of
London, Sarah Lawrence College (B.A., 1959), the
University of California, Los Angeles (M.A., 1963),
and Columbia University (Ed.D., 1972), Kraus taught
at the State University of New York, Brockport, until
1995. The New York State Theatre Education
Association gave her their Lifetime Achievement
Award in 1995. Among Kraus's best-known works
are *The Shaggy Dog Murder Trial, Remember My Name,*
from which the following excerpt is taken, *Mean to
Be Free,* and *The Ice Wolf.* Kraus now resides in
Walnut Creek, California.

Remember My Name is the story of ten-year-old
Rachel Simon and the people of St. Laurent de Pins,
France, who sheltered Rachel when her parents sent
her there from Marseilles for safety. Living under the
name Madeleine Petit, the child is aided and
sheltered by a priest, a war widow, a teacher, and a
member of the underground. In this excerpt, Rachel
takes on her new name and begins her journey to
safety.

ACT 1

Scene 1

SCENE: *A city street in Marseilles. The Unoccupied Zone of France. November, 1942. The WHISTLE of a French train. School boys BEATING someone up.*

RACHEL.   (*Voice offstage.*) No! Leave me alone. Let me go. No-o!

(*SOUND: A GUN SHOT. The wailing of a French SIREN.*
RACHEL races on, fleeing a gang of school boys. SHE is resourceful, idealistic, and curious. But at present SHE is beaten up. Her uniform is torn and her face and knees are bleeding. SHE turns and realizes they're not pursuing her. RACHEL stops to collect herself, discovers injuries, wipes the blood from her face and puts a handkerchief around her bleeding knee. Stifling the tears, SHE continues running, halting only in the momentary safety of shadows.
RACHEL exits.
SOUND: The WHISTLE of a French train.
LIGHTING comes up on a basement hotel room in Marseilles.)

AT RISE: PAULINE is setting the table for supper. PAULINE SIMON is married to LÉON and is the mother of Rachel. She is religious, family-centered and cautious. 32.
LÉON peers out through a slit in the hotel curtain. LÉON SIMON is married to Pauline and the father of Rachel. He is a man of action. 37.
SOUND: GUNFIRE, followed by the wailing of a French SIREN.
PAULINE freezes.
Suddenly past the basement window, there are running feet. Then the THUDDING SOUND of heavy boots and the blare of a military BRASS BAND.
LÉON slumps in a chair.

PAULINE.   What's happened?
LÉON.   They're here. In Marseilles.
PAULINE.   This is the Free Zone. That's why we came here. The French and German governments made a pact.
LÉON.   A devil's pact. (*LÉON crosses to the desk, searching for papers.*)

(*PAULINE rushes to the window.*)

LÉON.   Stay away from the window!!! PAULINE!!
PAULINE.   Where's Rachel?

(*RACHEL SIMON stands in the doorway.*)

RACHEL. Maman.
PAULINE. (*Runs to her.*) RACHEL!
RACHEL. I don't have the bread, Maman. I don't have . . . (*Bursts into tears in her mother's arms.*)
PAULINE. Léon, some clean rags and some hot water quickly.

(*LÉON goes.*)

PAULINE. Where were you?
RACHEL. Outside the cinema.
PAULINE. But that's nowhere near the bakery!
RACHEL. (*Between sobs.*) I wanted . . . to find out . . . what was playing. But I saw a big sign, "No Jews Allowed." Maman, it wasn't there yesterday.

(*LÉON returns with rags. PAULINE begins to cleanse wounds.*)

LÉON. Who was it? Who beat you up like this?
RACHEL. Some boys. A gang.
PAULINE. If you'd do what you're told and not be so headstrong! The cinema!
LÉON. Did you recognize any of them?
RACHEL. Some were from my school.
PAULINE. Your new school!
RACHEL. They had the same uniforms. But, Papa, they all had Nazi armbands. Except one. Brand new armbands. And one of them had a flag.
LÉON. The Nazis do a thorough job.
RACHEL. They started hitting me. One of them yelled, "Forget it. She's just a kid." But the one carrying the flag, said, "This'll teach her a lesson she won't forget."
LÉON. Why didn't you run?
RACHEL. I did. They came after me. The one with the flag yelled, "We'll get rid of your kind."
PAULINE. Rachel, are you hurt? Is anything broken?
RACHEL. Oh, Maman, it wasn't the sticks. They were laughing at me!
PAULINE. Léon, she is not going back to that school!
LÉON. (*Thoughtfully.*) No. No, she's not.
RACHEL. But I didn't cry, Papa. No matter how hard they hit me.
PAULINE. You can cry all you want now.
LÉON. How did you get home?

493

RACHEL.   There was a gunshot. They turned to look. The boy without the armband whispered, "Run!" But, Maman, I forgot the bread.

LÉON.   Never mind about the bread. (*Hugs her.*) Tonight we'll eat less.

RACHEL.   Papa, why do they hate us so much? WHY?

LÉON.   Because . . . we are a little different. (*Shrugs.*) Because it's easy.

RACHEL.   Easy?

LÉON.   Easier to blame us than try to solve the problem. (*To Pauline wearily.*) That's our history, isn't it?

RACHEL.   Papa, I was scared. Awful scared. But I didn't let them know. And I bit one of them, too. He yelled!

LÉON.   (*Laughs.*) Next thing you know you'll be a French spy!

PAULINE.   How can you laugh at a time like this?

LÉON.   There are times, Pauline, when you can either laugh or cry. Léon Simon chooses to laugh. My one and only daughter is saved by the gunfire of the Nazi invasion. But just before that happened, she bit the enemy, and he howled like a baby. It's a story for her grandchildren.

RACHEL.   (*Giggles.*) Papa, you make things seem all right. You make me laugh. You always do.

LÉON.   It comes with the job of being papa. And right now that's the only job I have. The only job I have—worth keeping. (*LÉON goes to the drawer and takes out an official identity card and an ink pad.*) Rachel, put your thumb in this, and then press it on the square right here.

(*RACHEL does.*)

LÉON.   Now say, "My name is Madeleine Petit."

RACHEL.   (*Repeats.*) My name is Madeleine Petit. But why, Papa? My name's Rachel Simon. Who's Madeleine Petit?

(*SOUND: CLOCK striking five.*)

LÉON.   As of five o'clock—you are!

RACHEL.   But that's lying. You told me never to lie.

LÉON.   The world's just turned upside down. When it's right side up, we can live again—and stop lying. For now you must forget you were ever Rachel Simon.

PAULINE.   NO!

RACHEL.   Why, Papa? I don't want to forget.

LÉON.   You must forget you are a brave and beautiful Jewish girl.

RACHEL.   PAPA!

LÉON.   Not that Madeleine isn't brave and beautiful. She is. Definitely. But she is not Jewish. And she has never heard of Léon and Pauline Simon.

PAULINE.   Léon, we discussed this, and I said, "No." Only if it were an emergency.

LÉON.   What do you call this? They've invaded Marseilles.

PAULINE.   She's not ready.

LÉON.   Ready? Who is ready? Do you think I want to do this? But alone she has a chance to survive.

RACHEL.   Alone? ALONE! Maman?

PAULINE.   Léon, she's only ten years old.

LÉON.   With a whole life ahead of her! And I won't let those barbarians take it away!

PAULINE.   (*Frantic.*) The family should stay together.

LÉON.   The only way to survive is to separate.

RACHEL.   Why can't we go together?

LÉON.   Because, you're the only one who has the right papers. I am sending you to St. Laurent des Pins.

RACHEL.   Where?

LÉON.   A tiny village in the mountains. Snowed in all winter. A perfect place to hide.

RACHEL.   But where is it?

LÉON.   Auvergne.

RACHEL.   I never heard of it.

LÉON.   With a little luck the Nazis never heard of it either.

RACHEL.   Do we have relatives there?

LÉON.   No.

RACHEL.   Friends?

LÉON.   Madeleine Petit will make some.

RACHEL.   Papa, Auvergne is so far away.

LÉON.   Yes. Far from all this madness. That's why I'm sending you. Now here's your new papers: your identity card with photograph and thumb print, your birth certificate, a food ration card. You'll need these. Don't lose them. You're going to start a whole new life.

RACHEL.   Papa, I can't.

LÉON.   (*His gesture interrupts her.*) You don't know what you can do until you try. Now, this is the most important of all. Don't ever tell anyone that you had another name. Not even someone you think you can trust. NEVER!

RACHEL.   Why not?

LÉON.   (*Stern.*) Promise me!

RACHEL.   All right, I promise, but why not, Papa?

LÉON.   Because one slip of the tongue, and you're dead.

RACHEL.   (*Scared.*) Papa, can't you and Maman come too? Please!

LÉON.   It's safer this way.

RACHEL.   How will I get there?

LÉON.   By train.

PAULINE.   They'll arrest her. Jews can't travel.

LÉON.   No. But Madeleine Petit can. And she will. Three hundred and fifty kilometers. All the way from Marseilles to St. Laurent des Pins. (*To Rachel.*) Don't look so frightened. Above all, don't give them any cause for suspicion.

RACHEL.   But I am frightened.

LÉON.   Of course, you are! It's dangerous. Some people think when you're brave, you have no fear. No. To be brave means you don't *show* your fear.

PAULINE.   Léon, she's just a child.

LÉON.   Not any longer! Go change. Your bag is under the bed. Packed. The train's at eight. Hurry.

(*RACHEL exits.*)

PAULINE.   She won't know what to do.

LÉON.   She'll learn.

PAULINE.   It isn't right.

LÉON.   The whole war isn't right.

PAULINE.   I only have one child.

LÉON.   And I will do anything to save her!

PAULINE.   What if something happens to her?

LÉON.   Did you forget what happened to our neighbors in Paris? The reason we ran?

PAULINE.   Why St. Laurent des Pins?

LÉON.   I told you before. They'll never let a child go hungry.

PAULINE.   (*Desperate.*) Léon, can't we decide this tomorrow?

LÉON.   Tonight there's confusion. Easier for her to escape. And wait for what? They took our business. They took our home. They're not going to take our daughter.

PAULINE.   There must be some other way.

(*SOUND: GUNFIRE and the wail of a French SIREN.*)

LÉON.   Not now! (*Persuading her.*) In St. Laurent des Pins she'll lead an ordinary life.

PAULINE.   Ordinary! Away from her own mother and father?

(*SOUND: Marching JACKBOOTS and ORDERS shouted in German.*)

LÉON.   We are sending her away to live, Pauline. TO LIVE!
PAULINE.   (*Looks at him shocked. Pause. Softly.*) All right. (*Deliberately.*) All right.

(*LÉON kisses Pauline.*)

PAULINE.   Léon, I want her to remember the Sabbath.
LÉON.   I'll get her. (*Exits.*)

(*PAULINE gets out three Sabbath candles on a tray, one for each member of the family, and a wine goblet. As the reality hits her, SHE loses control and cries. But quickly SHE straightens herself up. SHE lights the three candles, covers her head with a white shawl, closes her eyes, and waves her hands toward her three times in the traditional welcoming of the Sabbath blessing.*
RACHEL and LÉON enter.
PAULINE puts her hands before her face, closes her eyes and recites the Sabbath blessing.)

PAULINE.	(Translation)
(*Recites in Hebrew.*)	Blessed art Thou, the Eternal our
Ba-ruch a-ta, ha-shem E-lo-hei-nu,	God, King of the Universe, Who
me-lech ha-o-lam, a-sher kid-sha-nu	has sanctified us with His
b'mitz-vo-tav ve-tsi-va-nu le-had-lik-	commandments and enjoined us
ner shel sha-bat.	to kindle the Sabbath lights.

(*LÉON raises the wine goblet and says the traditional blessing.*)

LÉON.	(Translation)
(*Recites in Hebrew.*)	Blessed is the Lord our God, Ruler
Ba-ruch a-ta, ha-shem E-lo-hei-nu,	of the Universe, Creator of the fruit
me-lech ha-o-lam, bo-rei pe-ri ha-go-	of the vine.
fen.	

(*LÉON sips the wine. PAULINE and RACHEL each take a sip from the same goblet.*)

PAULINE.   We'll have to imagine the Sabbath loaf is in front of us.

LÉON,	(Translation)

PAULINE, and RACHEL.
(*Recite in Hebrew.*)

Ba-ruch a-ta, ha-shem E-lo-hei-nu,	Blessed art Thou, the Eternal our
me-lech ha-o-lam, ha-mo-tzi le-chem	God, King of the Universe, who
min ha-a-retz.	brings forth bread from the earth.

(*PAULINE mimes taking a piece of the Sabbath loaf and hands the tray to LÉON and RACHEL who each mime taking a chunk.*)

PAULINE.   (*Kisses Léon and Rachel.*) Good Shabbas.
LÉON.   Good Shabbas.
RACHEL.   Good Shabbas.
RACHEL.   Maman, where's the lace tablecloth?
PAULINE.   Rented rooms cost money.
RACHEL.   (*Horrified.*) You sold it!

(*PAULINE nods upset.*)

RACHEL.   You said you'd never do that. No matter what happened.

(*PAULINE looks at Léon unable to respond.*)

LÉON.   Things are replaceable. Lives are not! (*Gestures to soup tureen.*) She's got to hurry.

(*THEY sit down to their meager supper. PAULINE ladles out soup.
LIGHTING: The street is now dark.
As they eat. RACHEL looks out the window nervously trying to gather courage. THEY eat a few spoonfuls in silence.*)

RACHEL.   I've never been out alone after dark.
PAULINE.   I never let you!
RACHEL.   When will—
LÉON.   (*Interrupts.*) When the war's over. But stay in St. Laurent des Pins. (*A lighter tone.*) I don't want to have to hunt all over France for you!
RACHEL.   What do I do first?
PAULINE.   You see!
LÉON.   A sensible question! Just what I'd expect from Madeleine Petit. The directions are easy. Finding a home will be harder. As soon as you arrive go to the village priest or the school teacher.
RACHEL.   What do I tell them?

LÉON.   Don't mention Paris. Just say that you've come from Marseilles.
RACHEL.   I have.
LÉON.   Tell them that when the Nazis invaded, you lost your home.
RACHEL.   We did.
LÉON.   And that your parents were deported for forced labor.
PAULINE.   Léon!
LÉON.   (*To Pauline.*) She has to know! Marseilles was safe until today.
    Tomorrow it could be Paris all over again. (*To Rachel.*) Say you need a place
    to stay, and you'll work hard in exchange. A farm can always use extra hands.
RACHEL.   It won't be long, will it, Papa? Will it?

(*SOUND: Roar of MOTORCYCLES, tramp of soldiers' JACKBOOTS. LÉON can't
answer. PAULINE embraces her.*)

PAULINE.   My dearest, as soon as the first star appears, say goodnight; and
    I'll say goodnight too. For as long as we're apart.
RACHEL.   Oh, Maman. Like letters. Our own special letters.
PAULINE.   Be a good girl. Remember all I've taught you. But most of all,
    remember that I love you. (*Covering her emotions.*) You'll need your winter
    coat. I'll get it. (*Exits.*)
LÉON.   You know the way to La Gare Saint Charles. You pass it every day.
RACHEL.   Can't you go with me? Just that far?
LÉON.   No. If they stopped us for an identity check, none of us would get
    through. Maman and I have to . . . arrange . . . for new
    papers . . . Remember how we used to make up stories?

(*RACHEL nods.*)

LÉON.   This one you must always tell the same way. Ready?
RACHEL.   Ready.
LÉON.   Name?
RACHEL.   Madeleine Petit.
LÉON.   Occupation?
RACHEL.   Uh . . . uh . . . student.
LÉON.   Good. Which school?
RACHEL.   Elementary school.
LÉON.   Where are you going?
RACHEL.   St. Laurent des Pins.
LÉON.   Why?
RACHEL.   Uh . . . uh . . . to see . . . uh . . . my relatives.
LÉON.   Good. But don't hesitate. (*With a feigned kindly tone.*) Now what's
    your real name?

(*PAULINE returns with coat and beret.*)

RACHEL. (*Slips.*) Rachel Simon.

LÉON. (*Slaps her face.*) NO!!!

RACHEL. PAPA!

PAULINE. LÉON! How could you?

LÉON. You don't think the Nazis will do worse? This is a game of life and death. One mistake—and it's over. (*To Rachel.*) Let's try again. Your name is?

RACHEL. (*Sniffling.*) Madeleine.

LÉON. (*Shakes her roughly.*) Madeleine what?

RACHEL. MADELEINE PETIT!

LÉON. Good! Say it again.

RACHEL. Madeleine Petit.

LÉON. Say it over and over. Until it's second nature.

RACHEL. (*Muttering.*) Madeleine Petit. Madeleine Petit. Madeleine Petit.

LÉON. Good. Good. Now I'm going to give you some money. I wish it were more. But it'll get you there. Are you ready?

RACHEL. (*Scared.*) So soon? What time is it?

(*Peeks in his vest pocket, an old familiar gesture.*)

RACHEL. Papa, where's your watch?

LÉON. (*Picks up identity papers.*) Here! Genuine forged false identity papers. The best in the black market. And here. The money for your train ticket. It was a good watch. It fetched a good price. (*Hands envelope to her.*)

RACHEL. Oh, Papa, you loved that pocket watch. It was Grand-père's.

LÉON. Yes. (*Hugs Rachel tightly.*) But I love my daughter more!

RACHEL. (*Crosses to Pauline and THEY hug goodbye.*) Maman!

(*PAULINE gives her coat, which RACHEL puts on.*)

LÉON. (*Shows directions on envelope.*) Here's the numbers of the trains. From Marseilles you take one train direct to St. George d'Aurac. You'll have to change trains there for Le Puy. From Le Puy, it's only about twenty kilometers to St. Laurent des Pins. (*Looks out the window.*) Better go out the back way. Wait until the street is empty. Make sure no one follows you. Go straight to the station. When you've bought your ticket get on the train immediately. Don't talk to anyone. I'm counting on you, Madeleine Petit!

RACHEL. (*Crosses to Pauline, scared.*) Adieu, Maman.

PAULINE. (*Quickly.*) No, no, not adieu. Adieu means goodbye forever. Au revoir means till we see you again. And we will see you again. I promise. (*Kisses Rachel tenderly.*) Au revoir, my darling.

(*RACHEL picks up suitcase. LÉON and PAULINE cross with her to hotel door.*)

LÉON.   Au revoir, Madeleine.
RACHEL.   (*Turns for one last look at her parents.*) Au revoir. (*Exits.*)

(*PAULINE turns to Léon crying. HE holds her in his arms. LIGHTING fades.*)

End of ACT 1, Scene 1

ACT 1

Scene 2

SCENE: *A carriage in a French train bound for the Haute-Loire region in Auvergne in South Central France. Two days later.*
RACHEL *sits stiffly in the carriage.*

AT RISE: PÈRE ANTOINE, *a Jesuit priest, a man who follows his conscience, 55, sits reading a book.*
YVETTE REYNAUD, *an opportunist, 45, is dozing.*

SOUND: *The TRAIN stops abruptly.*

YVETTE.   (*Wakes up with a start.*) Where are we?
PÈRE ANTOINE.   (*Peering out the window.*) Just outside the station. Le Puy.
   (*Still peering.*) There's some sort of trouble.
YVETTE.   (*Sighs.*) That's all there is these days.

(*SOUND: VOICES shouting.*)

YVETTE.   I can't make it out. It's all in German. What are all those soldiers doing?
PÈRE ANTOINE.   Chasing someone.
YVETTE.   Oh, I see him! I see him! (*Calls out window.*) Over there! (*Pause.*)
   The horse just knocked down the flower cart!

(*SOUND: A GUNSHOT. RACHEL screams and buries her head. PÈRE ANTOINE immediately tries to calm her.*)

YVETTE.   Must they do such things in public! Scaring women half to death.
PÈRE ANTOINE.   My God! They've just left the man. Beside the tracks!

YVETTE.   Who was it?

PÈRE ANTOINE.   (*Shakes his head.*) A poor Jew trying to escape.

(*PÈRE ANTOINE quietly recites a prayer in Latin from the liturgy of Good Friday under Yvette's next speech.*)

Ego eduxi te de Aeypto	I led you out of the land of Egypt
Demerso Pharone in Mare Rubrum, et tu me tradidisti	Destroyed Pharoah in the Red Sea, and you handed me over
Principibus sacerdotum.	To the authorities of the Church.
Ego ante te aperui mare,	I opened the sea before you,
Et tu apereruisti lancea Latus meum.	And you have opened my side with a lance.
Ego ante te praeivi in columna nubis,	I went before you in a pillar of cloud,
Et tu me duxisti and Praetorium Pilatis.	And you led me to the Tribunal of Pilate.
Ego te pavi manna per desertum, Et tu me cecidisti a lapis et fiagellis.	I fed you with manna in the desert And you have struck me down with slaps and scourging.
Ego dedi tibi sceptrum regale, Et tu dedisti capiti meo spineam coronam.	I gave you a royal sceptre, And you gave my head A crown of thorns.
Ego te exaltavi magna virtute, Et tu me suspendisti, In patibulo Crucis.	I raised you up in great power, And you have suspended me On the gibbet of the cross.

YVETTE.   He must have been a criminal! (*Grabs newspaper, searching.*) Why . . . did you know? There's a five hundred franc reward for turning in a Jew! Right here. Look. On page two. And I saw him. Five hundred francs! I could have fed my whole family for a month! (*SOUND: The TRAIN starts to move again.*) All this stopping and starting. Next time my sister's sick, she can come and visit me.

(*PÈRE ANTOINE finishes prayer.*)

YVETTE.   Père Antoine, you know I never pry; but why on earth did you say a prayer for him? Someone who doesn't even go to our church? And a criminal?

PÈRE ANTOINE.   My dear Madame Reynaud, perhaps the differences down here don't seem as important up there!

GÉRARD.   (*Calling offstage.*) Papers! All identification papers. Please, have
your papers ready!

(*GÉRARD LA SALLE enters. He is a gendarme, who enforces the laws of France, no
matter what they are. Sentimental, 55. GÉRARD checks Yvette's papers.*)

GÉRARD.   Yvette Reynaud. Ah, but you look younger than your
photograph, madame.
YVETTE.   (*Pleased.*) Oh, monsieur. Well, it's a wonder I do. Tending an ill
sister all week.
GÉRARD.   You'll soon be home, now. (*GÉRARD inspects Père Antoine's
photograph closely.*)
PÈRE ANTOINE.   (*Laughs.*) I can see you notice the difference. I'm thinner
now. Before the war I ate better.
GÉRARD.   We all did. These are hard times. Thank you, Père Antoine.

(*PÈRE ANTOINE resumes reading. GÉRARD crosses to Rachel.*)

GÉRARD.   Hello, there, young lady. And what is your name?

(*RACHEL opens her mouth to speak and no sound comes out. Mutely she hands her
papers over.*)

GÉRARD.   Madeleine Petit. (*Looks sharply at her.*) Don't you know your own
name?

(*RACHEL nods.*)

GÉRARD.   (*Shakes his head disapprovingly.*) Such times! I certainly wouldn't
let my young daughter travel alone. Where are you going?
RACHEL.   To . . . to . . . visit . . . relatives.
GÉRARD.   Let's see your train ticket.

(*RACHEL hands it to him.*)

GÉRARD.   St. Laurent. That's the next stop. (*Scrutinizing papers.*) Ah, from
Marseilles. I know it well. The best fish on the Mediterranean. (*Kisses his
fingers.*) Ah, Père Antoine, what I wouldn't give for some bouillabaisse à la
Marseillaise!

(*PÈRE ANTOINE nods in agreement.*)

GÉRARD. (*To Rachel.*) Is someone meeting you in St. Laurent des Pins?

(*RACHEL hesitates.*)

PÈRE ANTOINE. (*Takes him aside.*) Officer, can't you see the child is upset? She saw what happened.

YVETTE. It was practically under this carriage window. Almost like . . . the movies!

GÉRARD. Ah! Ah, Père Antoine, something like that's happened every day this week. After awhile you get used to it. They try to run away. Our job is to stop them.

PÈRE ANTOINE. What kind of job is that for a decent Frenchman?

GÉRARD. We stop them . . . if we see them. Me? I never see them.

PÈRE ANTOINE. Officer, I was so absorbed in my book, I wasn't paying attention. The child is travelling with me.

YVETTE. She is!

GÉRARD. Well, well, why didn't you say so? Sorry, Father. (*Checks papers.*) Regulations. You understand.

PÈRE ANTOINE. Certainly. But she's very tired. It's a long way from Marseilles, officer—and good bouillabaisse!

GÉRARD. Ah, Père Antoine, for a man who loves fish, as I do, to work in Auvergne . . . is purgatory! (*Catches himself.*) I hope I didn't offend you, Father.

PÈRE ANTOINE. (*Laughs.*) Not at all. Not at all. (*To Rachel.*) Rest now, Madeleine. I'll wake you, when we get there.

(*RACHEL pretends to sleep.*)

GÉRARD. Why is she going to St. Laurent des Pins?

PÈRE ANTOINE. If I had my way, officer, I'd take all the children out of the city. War's no place for a child.

GÉRARD. (*Agreeing.*) No. (*Hands papers to Père Antoine.*) Here. Let her sleep. We have to check the papers on all the trains. Just following orders.

PÈRE ANTOINE. So am I.

GÉRARD. (*Exiting.*) Papers. All identification papers.

YVETTE. Such a quiet little thing. I had no idea that she was with you, Père Antoine. Why, she hasn't spoken the whole way to you.

PÈRE ANTOINE. Or to anyone else. She's well brought up. (*Pointedly.*) She knows better than to chatter, when I'm trying to prepare a Sunday sermon.

YVETTE. Oh! (*Pause.*) Then, is she a relative of yours?

PÈRE ANTOINE. In a way.

YVETTE.   Oh, you people from Auvergne! You never ever talk. It's maddening. Where I come from in the south, we practice the art of conversation. But you Auvergnats, you hardly ever open your mouths. It must be the climate. Why my husband's family . . .

(*SOUND: TRAIN lurches to a stop.*)

PÈRE ANTOINE.   Ah, here we are! Permit me to help you with your baggage, Madame Reynaud.
YVETTE.   Why, thank you. Thank you, Père Antoine.

(*PÈRE ANTOINE opens carriage door and puts Yvette's luggage out.*)

YVETTE.   But why didn't you introduce us, when I got on at Nimes? Now, I know all about little girls. I raised six of them. So be sure to . . .
PÈRE ANTOINE.   (*Assisting Yvette out.*) Thank you, Madame Reynaud.

(*YVETTE exits.*)

PÈRE ANTOINE.   Madeleine. Madeleine, we're here.
RACHEL.   I'm awake. Why did you lie?
PÈRE ANTOINE.   Lie? I didn't lie.
RACHEL.   You said I was with you.
PÈRE ANTOINE.   You are. I vowed to look after any child who's in need. But I didn't introduce myself. I'm Père Antoine from St. Laurent des Pins.
RACHEL.   I'm Madeleine Petit.
PÈRE ANTOINE.   Yes. But when the police officer asked you, you forgot.
RACHEL.   No! No, I just lost my voice.
PÈRE ANTOINE.   Madeleine, your name must be comfortable—like an old shoe. Particularly, if the name is new.
RACHEL.   (*Stiffens.*) How do you know?
PÈRE ANTOINE.   I don't! And what I don't know, I can't tell! Remember that.
RACHEL.   You saved my life just now.
PÈRE ANTOINE.   (*Lifts suitcase down and takes her hand. Casually.*) Just following orders.

(*PÈRE ANTOINE and RACHEL exit through carriage door.*)

End of ACT 1, Scene 2

ACT 1

Scene 3

SCENE: *Immediately afterwards. The traditional kitchen-room of Mme. Barbière's
stone farm house. There is a black cast iron stove with iron cooking pots and
utensils hanging above it. There are fresh lace curtains at the windows and framed
ornamental patterns of lace hanging on the wall.*

AT RISE: *MARIE-THÉRÈSE BARBIÈRE is making lace, peering through her glasses
at the netlike fabric of thread. SHE is a war widow, independent, proud, 60. SHE
wears mourning black continually, and her white hair is pulled off her face in a
bun. Over her somber attire is an apron that she rarely removes, as SHE is always
hard at work.*

PÈRE ANTOINE *watches.*

MARIE-THÉRÈSE.   . . . and they'd hung their Nazi flag in front of the Town
Hall. The mayor stood there, tears in his eyes. But he could do nothing.
Nothing. Then the regiment marched on to Le Puy. Ah, Père Antoine,
what will happen to us now? Now, that they're here.

PÈRE ANTOINE.   I don't know. In Paris meat's practically disappeared. The
bread ration would barely keep a sparrow alive. Women are crying in the
streets, because they can't feed their children.

MARIE-THÉRÈSE.   Savages! What they can't kill, they starve! Well, they
won't starve the Auvergnats! We can make a cabbage grow from a stone.
(*Inviting him.*) I have some hot soup on the stove.

PÈRE ANTOINE.   Thank you. Not now. I don't think they'll bother us.
We're a poor mountain village. There's nothing to steal.

MARIE-THÉRÈSE.   Except our five-month winter. And we'll give them
that!

(*THEY laugh. MARIE-THÉRÈSE holds her lace up to the light and deftly corrects a
stitch.*)

PÈRE ANTOINE.   Madame Barbière, your lace is the finest in St. Laurent
des Pins.

MARIE-THÉRÈSE.   Thank you, Père Antoine. My lace is my company,
since Henri died. (*Looks at him sharply.*) But whenever you compliment me

there's a favor not far behind. Have I ever refused? What is it?

PÈRE ANTOINE.   This is different.

MARIE-THÉRÈSE.   What?

PÈRE ANTOINE.   A child.

MARIE-THÉRÈSE.   What kind of child?

PÈRE ANTOINE.   Intelligent. Polite. They lost their home to the Nazis.

MARIE-THÉRÈSE.   Her parents?

PÈRE ANTOINE.   Deported.

MARIE-THÉRÈSE.   Such times! French!

PÈRE ANTOINE.   French!

MARIE-THÉRÈSE.   An orphan?

PÈRE ANTOINE.   (*Carefully.*) Alone.

MARIE-THÉRÈSE.   Ah! Ah, no, Père Antoine. It is too dangerous!

PÈRE ANTOINE.   She has papers. All in order.

MARIE-THÉRÈSE.   Did you see them?

PÈRE ANTOINE.   Yes. She boarded the train at Marseilles. She stared out the window for hours. In utter silence. I've never seen anyone look so forlorn. Then at Le Puy the Nazis killed a man, and she screamed.

MARIE-THÉRÈSE.   Naturally!

PÈRE ANTOINE.   When the gendarme came through, she couldn't speak. She needs a home.

MARIE-THÉRÈSE.   Père Antoine, you can't hide her here. If she's caught, we'll both be shot. The way they killed my husband.

PÈRE ANTOINE.   Henri was a brave soldier, Madame Barbière. Very brave.

MARIE-THÉRÈSE.   I don't want any more trouble.

PÈRE ANTOINE.   I understand. (*Picks up his hat casually.*) I thought she might be company.

MARIE-THÉRÈSE.   My neighbor across the field, Madame Reynaud looks in on me, even when the snow is knee deep. So how could I hide her with that one poking her nose into my cabbage soup every day?

PÈRE ANTOINE.   Madame Reynaud! She was on the same train. I said Madeleine was with me.

MARIE-THÉRÈSE.   Madeleine?

PÈRE ANTOINE.   The child.

MARIE-THÉRÈSE.   Where is she now?

PÈRE ANTOINE.   Outside. (*Crosses to window.*)

MARIE-THÉRÈSE.   Outside! Good Lord! Outside in the cold! Père Antoine, what were you thinking of? (*Crosses beside him.*)

(*PÈRE ANTOINE points out the window.*)

507

MARIE-THÉRÈSE.   She looks half frozen. You didn't say she was so little! Poor child so young to be alone in the world. Bring her in to sit by the stove, Père Antoine. At least she can get warm and have some hot soup. How could you leave a little child like that out in the cold? Bring her in here at once!

PÈRE ANTOINE.   (*Suppressing a smile.*) Certainly, Madame Barbière.

(*PÈRE ANTOINE exits.*)

(*MARIE-THÉRÈSE rustles about the stove and stirs pot.*)

(*PÈRE ANTOINE enters with RACHEL.*)

PÈRE ANTOINE.   Madame Barbière, this is Madeleine Petit. Madeleine, this is Madame Barbière.

RACHEL.   (*Shyly.*) Hello, Madame Barbière.

MARIE-THÉRÈSE.   (*Warmly.*) Come in, Madeleine.

(*MARIE-THÉRÈSE takes Rachel's coat. RACHEL shivers. MARIE-THÉRÈSE looks at Père Antoine disapprovingly.*)

MARIE-THÉRÈSE.   Sit by the stove and get warm. (*Puts coat near stove.*) This is ice cold! Where are you from Madeleine?

RACHEL.   Marseilles.

MARIE-THÉRÈSE.   No wonder you're shivering. It's always summer there, isn't it?

RACHEL.   (*Agreeably.*) Yes, madame. (*Shivers again.*)

MARIE-THÉRÈSE.   Here, have some hot soup.

RACHEL.   Thank you, Madame Barbière.

(*RACHEL eats hungrily. Her manners disappear, and SHE gulps soup. MARIE-THÉRÈSE and PÈRE ANTOINE exchange glances. RACHEL stops embarrassed by her appetite.*)

RACHEL.   This is wonderful soup.

MARIE-THÉRÈSE.   (*Laughs.*) Hunger is the best seasoning, little one. But we are famous in St. Laurent des Pins for our cabbage soup.

PÈRE ANTOINE.   And our lace.

(*RACHEL looks up at framed lace. Puts bowl down and goes to look more closely.*)

RACHEL.   Oh-h-h-. Each one's different! Oh, Madame Barbière . . .

(*RACHEL stops in front of one particular piece.*)

RACHEL.   I like that one!

MARIE-THÉRÈSE.   (*Softly.*) That's my favorite too. It's my own design. Do you think it would make a nice wedding dress?

RACHEL.   Oh, yes!! Is it very difficult to make lace?

MARIE-THÉRÈSE.   Come here. (*Shows Rachel how to do a stitch.*) Lace making requires sharp eyes, careful fingers, and patience. And while you work on each tiny piece you have to see the whole design in your head.

RACHEL.   We had a lace tablecloth . . . once. It was for Sh . . . holidays. Maman said one day, when I got married, it would be mine. But . . . but . . . but now, it's gone.

MARIE-THÉRÈSE.   (*Briskly.*) Well, then you must make your own. Just like the girls do here. They all have lace trousseaus. Madeleine, how old are you now?

RACHEL.   Ten.

MARIE-THÉRÈSE.   Well then, there's plenty of time before you get married! Plenty of time. (*Spontaneously takes Rachel's small hand.*) Oh, your hands are so cold! (*Rubs them.*) There! You need wool mittens when you go out in weather like this. (*Looks down.*) And wool socks. Madeleine, do you know how to knit!

RACHEL.   No, Madame Barbière.

MARIE-THÉRÈSE.   Good heavens! What do they teach at school these days?

RACHEL.   I was learning French, history, geography, arithmetic, science, art and music. Oh, and sewing, too.

MARIE-THÉRÈSE.   Sewing. Now, that's something useful.

RACHEL.   I was at the top of my class, too. I was even learning English.

MARIE-THÉRÈSE.   English? Sometimes at night we can pick up the British broadcast on the radio.   (*To Père Antoine.*) Now, the Nazis arrest you for listening. They don't want us to hear the *real* news! But I say no one is going to tell me what to do in my own house, in front of my own fire. No one.

PÈRE ANTOINE.   It's getting dark, Madame Barbière. We'd better be on our way.

MARIE-THÉRÈSE.   It gets dark so early these days. (*Looks out the window.*) It's starting to snow. (*Goes to get Rachel's coat.*) And her coat's not even warm yet. And she has no mittens.

PÈRE ANTOINE.   But in an hour the roads will be too slippery.

MARIE-THÉRÈSE.   Madeleine, someone must have sent you to St. Laurent des Pins. Who? Why?

PÈRE ANTOINE.   Madame Barbière, the best kept secrets are the ones we don't know.

(*Pause.*)

MARIE-THÉRÈSE.   That's true. Madeleine, I'd like to help you, but I can't. If the Nazis pound on the door, and they find you curled in a closet, that will be the end of both of us.

RACHEL.   (*Rises.*) Thank you for the hot soup, madame. (*Puts her coat on. Crosses to door.*)

MARIE-THÉRÈSE.   Not so fast! Not so fast! Where will she go tonight, Père Antoine?

PÈRE ANTOINE.   I'll think of something. The Lord provides. Come, Madeleine.

MARIE-THÉRÈSE.   The Lord has more sense than to be out in a St. Laurent blizzard. Wait a minute. Let me think. When it snows here, Madeleine, it can be up to your waist in no time. But that can keep the soldiers away as well. (*Thinking of a plan.*) I can't hide her, Père Antoine, . . . but . . . you say she has papers?

PÈRE ANTOINE.   Yes. The gendarme inspected them. A food ration card too.

MARIE-THÉRÈSE.   Hmm. We'd need that if . . .

(*PÈRE ANTOINE and RACHEL look at one another.*)

RACHEL.   Oh, Madame Barbière, I wouldn't be any trouble, I promise! I'd be so quiet, you wouldn't even know I was here.

MARIE-THÉRÈSE.   No, no, no, little one. A child should laugh. A child should sing. We were never blessed with a child. But there's a time in life, for everything. Père Antoine, I can't hide her but . . . but . . . my husband's cousin could come to visit, couldn't she? And she could go to school with the other girls, couldn't she? And in the evening she could learn to make lace.

RACHEL.   Oh, yes, madame, yes! And I could wash the dishes and run to the bakery for you and . . . and . . . (*Hides tears.*)

MARIE-THÉRÈSE.   (*Gently puts an arm around Rachel.*) She can't leave without warm clothes, and that's that. Not with winter on its way. She needs warm wool mittens and socks . . . and a scarf. And she's not leaving till she has them. But, Madeleine, you'll have to knit them yourself!

RACHEL.   (*Crushed.*) But I don't know how to knit!

MARIE-THÉRÈSE.   I will teach you, little one. I will teach you.

PÈRE ANTOINE.   Madame Barbière, just how long do you think it will take to make all those clothes?

MARIE-THÉRÈSE.   Oh, that's hard to say, Père Antoine. Hard to say. It could take . . . awhile. (*Removes Rachel's beret.*) It could take . . . till the end of the war.

End of ACT 1, Scene 3

chapter 10

Echoing Reflections

For some who lived through the Holocaust—the survivors, their protectors, and the Allied troops who liberated Nazi-held territories—images of devastation will never fade. Because of the magnitude of their painful recollections, many survivors remained silent for decades after the Holocaust. However, in recent years, numerous survivors have realized that they must share their experiences to document what happened during those years. Consequently, many have chosen to tell their stories. Whether their accounts have been told to historians, in autobiographies, or in talks with civic or school groups, the survivors relate a fundamental message in their testimonies: The brutalities of the Holocaust must never be forgotten. Remembering also helps to honor those who were lost.

There is a sense in the words of many survivors that they feel obligated to speak not only for themselves but also for those who have been silenced forever. The selections in Chapter 10 explore the ongoing aftermath of the Holocaust. As time passes, the atrocities of the Nazis might become muted, but their actions and intentions should never be forgotten or even minimized. The words and messages of the survivors, their families, and those who have devoted years of study to this period echo in the conscience of humanity.

Why Me?

Ernst Papanek

Dr. Ernst Papanek was born in Vienna in 1900. He
was an eminent teacher and child psychologist who
fled from Austria. In 1938, he was asked to become
the director of homes that were being established in
Southern France as shelters for refugee children.
Many of these children were Jewish, and their
parents had been sent to the camps or killed.
Papanek's foremost goal was to help these children
not only to survive but also to survive whole. From
1943 to 1945, he worked as a social worker at the
Children's Aid Society in New York. Later, he served
as executive director of the Brooklyn Training
School for Girls and the Wiltwyck School for Boys in
the United States. Well known and highly respected
throughout the world for his work with juvenile
delinquents, his lectures, and his publications,
Papanek died in 1973. He is the author of *Out of the
Fire*, from which the following excerpt is taken.

Many of the children who survived the
Holocaust were left with unanswered questions and
conflicting emotions that persisted for many years.
In this selection, Papanek describes their experiences.

The guilt of the survivor. I saw it unfold before
my eyes in classic form soon after the war had ended. By that time, I was the
executive director of American Youth for World Youth, an organization which

eventually involved ten million students in this country. (The program called for young people to make direct contact with their counterparts abroad; i.e., adopt schools, organize their own money-raising events, grow and can food, assemble kits and generally find their own ways to be helpful.)

One of the men working with us was Paul Goldberg, a Polish refugee who had been delegated to us by the World Jewish Congress, one of the many agencies cooperating with us. Like so many refugees, Goldberg had his own tragedy to live with. The war had broken out while he was in Switzerland attending an international congress and he had been forced to go to London, leaving behind a wife, an eleven-year-old daughter named Sue and a seven-year-old daughter with the unforgettable name of Aurora. At his request we made constant inquiries to every agency in the field, private and governmental. What little information we were able to get clearly indicated that they had been wiped out during the uprising in the Warsaw ghetto.

And then, one morning while I was leafing through the mail I flipped over a routine thank-you letter from an orphanage in Russian-occupied Poland— and felt my heart skip a beat. The letter had been signed by five of the children representatives, and one of the signatures leaped right off the paper at me. Aurora Goldberg. Immediately, I called Paul. How many Aurora Goldbergs, after all, could there be in the world?

Any number, as far as the Polish authorities were concerned. The countries of Europe, bled white by the war, were fighting to hold onto every unattached child they could lay their hands on. Since Paul had no papers, the authorities maintained over a period of months that he could offer no real proof that he was the girl's father. At length, with great difficulty, we were able to arrange for Aurora to be sent to a recuperation camp in Sweden, and once she was there it became an easy matter to whisk her onto a ship for England and on to the United States.

By that time, we knew that her mother and sister had indeed been killed during the Warsaw Uprising. Aurora had survived only because she had been among the rather large group of younger children who had been smuggled out of the ghetto and placed with Polish farmers.

After all that waiting, Paul was almost destroyed by the reunion. For by this time Aurora was thirteen years old and not at all reluctant to accuse her father of saving himself and leaving her mother and sister to die. They would come to the office, first one and then the other, to complain about each other. The relationship between them deteriorated so badly that she would insult him in the presence of others.

For five or six months I took those accusations of hers at face value. Until . . . well, I had been invited to their apartment for dinner, and after we had eaten I was out in the kitchen helping Aurora with the dishes. Exactly what was it, I asked her, that she thought her father could have done. "He didn't know where any of you were. How could he? Even you—did you know where your mother and sister were?"

The dish fell from her hand and shattered against the floor. "You don't like me anymore," she cried.

Of course I liked her. Why shouldn't I like her?

"No, you think it should have been them that were saved. Them, not me! You think Sue was better than me, don't you? He told you how good she was."

She was trembling worse than I had ever seen anybody tremble in my life. "It should have been me that was killed," she moaned. "It should have been me." Over and over. "It should have been me."

And there it was. It wasn't anything that had to be interpreted. She had said it all.

I had survived too, I reminded her. So had millions of others. And most of them hadn't suffered the losses or undergone the hardships she had. "What right do we have to hate millions of people because they stayed alive while others died?" I asked her. No more right, as she should have been able to see, than they had to hate us.

Intellectually, she could accept that. Emotionally, she couldn't.

For Aurora, it has been a long walk down an endless road. She came to work with American Youth for World Youth, doing contact work with Polish children, particularly with her former friends at the orphanage. Since she spoke very limited English, she entered a private school where she could get special help. Three years later, she was graduated as valedictorian of her class.

She had also become a leader of a Zionist youth group in high school. Upon graduation she went to Israel to live in a kibbutz, discovered very quickly that it wasn't the life for her and returned to America to enter college. Gradually, her attitude toward her father improved, although their relationship didn't become cordial until she moved into her own apartment and consulted a psychiatrist.

The sense of guilt was never completely eradicated. She found she was able to function best while she was helping other people, and so she went back to college to get her degree in social work. She manages. She copes. She functions. But to this day, she finds it necessary to pay an occasional visit to a psychiatrist.

I am not suggesting that everybody emerged with this sense of guilt or, even, that it so completely overpowered those who did. Most of them understood, emotionally as well as intellectually, that survival was a matter of luck. And had a story they could tell to prove it. I had an aunt who was at Ravensbrueck, the notorious concentration camp for women in which the inmates were used as guinea pigs for medical experiments. One night, shortly after she arrived, there was an alarm. "Everybody out of bed and out into the yard!"

The count came up one short. Unbelievable! While the SS commander was raging and threatening and bullying, out walked my aunt, a handsome, tiny lady of about sixty.

Where had she been? screamed the SS leader. How dare she come out late!

"I do not go out to meet people, no matter how late," said my aunt, regally, "until after I have washed myself and put up my hair."

The SS man's mouth fell open. Nobody had ever dared to speak up like that before. Or, need it be said, to confront him with a logic so far removed from the logic of a concentration camp. In the long, trembling silence that followed, everybody in the yard was aware that her life was on a razor's edge. And then the SS commander scowled ferociously. Not at my aunt. At the other prisoners. "I want you all to follow this little lady's example," he shouted. "*She* knows how to behave properly. I don't want to see any of you people fall in again unless you have washed up and combed your hair and made yourself presentable."

It made absolutely no sense. It was grotesque. Any woman who had dared to *ask* for permission to put up her hair would not have lived to ask another question. How do you explain it? Maybe the SS commander had hesitated too long; maybe she reminded him of somebody in his own family. Maybe he had yelled himself out in those last few seconds before the decision had to be made. Or maybe it had just been a long day for him, too. Who knows?

Having allowed her to get away with it, he had to go all the way. My aunt was made the capo of her barracks charged, presumably, with keeping everybody else in line. Once the SS commander had shown such respect for her, the guards were afraid not to. And so it was that one old Jewish woman survived.

There were also those who set out to survive, refused to consider the possibility of not surviving and therefore accepted survival as no more than their due. A friend of mine named Hugo Price would boast how he had worked like a buffalo in the concentration camps. Hugo, who was very Jewish-looking, would labor until his hands were bloody, and then work even harder while he made jokes about his bloody hands. "This impressed the Nazis very much," he would laugh. "I was their star performer." For people such as Hugo, survival became exactly that, a personal triumph.

Abraham, a Polish Jewish boy I met at a camp for displaced persons, had come home one afternoon to find that the Nazis had taken away his whole family; his father, mother, three brothers and sister. For two months he was hidden by a Christian family who shared their meager provisions with him. At the end of those two months, he came to the decision that he had no right to allow them to risk their lives for him. So he walked out of the house and went to the Karzyso Work Camp, which was run by the Nazis. "I am a Jew," he announced at the gate. "I have come to report for work."

At first, they didn't know what to make of him. "You are volunteering to work here?" And then they began to laugh. "Sure, we have plenty of work for an ambitious young man. Come on in, we can use you."

He became the camp joke, and when the joke began to pall they shipped him around from one camp to another, always billed as The Volunteer. By the time he landed in Mauthausen, a work quarry which was also used as an extermination camp, the war was almost over.

In his own eyes, Abraham—unlike Hugo—was no hero. He had merely calculated the odds for prolonging his own life, he said, without risking the lives of his friends. If he was discovered in hiding, he would be treated as an enemy; if he surrendered, he might be viewed more like a prisoner of war.

In my eyes, this boy had a powerful instinct for survival although I'm aware that others might disagree. A contrary case could be made that his act revealed a distinct ambivalence about survival. That perhaps he had simply decided to get it over with, one way or another, and was able to console himself that if he was indeed rushing to his death he was at least holding his fate in his own hands.

Because our children were in a protected position their fate, by and large, was not in their own hands. And if that wasn't true of all of them it was certainly true of those who were brought to the United States.

The question asked of me again and again as these children married, settled down and began to raise families of their own was: "Why did you bring me over and not someone else?"

Many years after I had come to New York I received a call from a girl who identified herself as Sarah Cohen and wanted to know if I remembered her?

Of course I did. "I'll be over in half an hour," she said. She didn't ask whether I wanted to see her; she didn't even ask whether I was free. She would be over. Period. As it turned out, she was married, had four children and was teaching school in Canada. It also turned out that although she had identified herself by the name by which I knew her, she now called herself Nora. Quite a few of the girls changed their first name, a phenomenon I wouldn't want to overinterpret. In some cases, it was no more than a free-style anglicizing of their German names; in other cases, they preferred the name they had been given on their false passports. With most of them, I suppose, starting a new life in a new country had offered them a chance to drop a name they didn't like and adopt one they did.

The first thing she said after our greeting was: "Why was I chosen to come over, and what happened to those who were not?"

That was easy. She had come over, because she had been among the first to be processed in Marseilles. The only criteria for that, as far as I knew, were "good health" and random chance. Of those who had not been brought over, about a hundred had been killed.

That wasn't good enough for her. "You did not save me because I was such a good student?"

"I did not know whether you were a good student or a bad one."

"Did you save me because my uncle was a professor and told you I was an intelligent girl?"

"I did not know you had an uncle. As far as I know neither did anybody else."

She jumped up and kissed me. "Thank you! Oh, thank you! I was afraid you might have become one of those snobs who only wanted to save the intelligent children who would have the best chance of making good."

The question persists. Twenty-seven years after the children had reached the shores of this country it came up again in a letter from a Cuban girl who had married one of the Cuban boys. "Both Hank and I think of our arrival in the U.S. as coming into the promised land in spite of Congress's earlier refusal. We still feel that way. We also feel an obligation to justify our survival somehow because of the recurring question, 'Why us?' This obligation calls for service to others, but it will never really answer the question."

It is not an obligation, I must hasten to add, which was felt by everybody. There are, for instance, two brothers. The older one went into business for himself, worked very hard and has done very well. The younger one has always sponged off him. "I'm worried about my brother," the successful one told me during a visit. "He simply refuses to apply himself to anything long enough to hold a decent job." It wasn't that he begrudged him the money. "I'm only glad I'm able to give it to him. But I'm afraid for him. I'm afraid that something was destroyed in him over there. He thinks his experiences in the war entitle him to ask the world for anything. I can't even talk to him about it. Everything irritates him, and the hell of it is that he believes he's entitled to be irritated, too."

Tell Them I Was There.
I'm Real. It Happened

David A. Adler

David A. Adler wrote *We Remember the Holocaust*, from which the following excerpt is taken, because he wanted his own children to learn more than just the dates, names, and places of the Holocaust. For additional biographical information on Adler, see page 14.

The Holocaust continues to have an impact on the lives of the survivors and the lives of their children. In this selection, Adler retells the experiences of a number of survivors and concludes with a plea that the world learn the lessons of the Holocaust.

The anti-Jewish policies of the Nazis were widely known as early as the 1920s, when Hitler first began attracting a following. And even before the liberation of the death camps, the camps' true nature was certainly known to leaders of various governments and to the media. But much of what was reported about the camps was hidden in the middle pages of newspapers and magazines. Average citizens in countries not overrun by Germany may have had only a vague knowledge of what was happening. But in April 1945, when photographs of the victims filled newspapers and magazines and were shown on newsreels, the world truly understood the horrors of the Holocaust.

In the months and years since liberation, thousands of Nazis have been brought to trial. The first trials were at Nuremberg, Germany. On November 20, 1945, when twenty-two leading Nazis were accused of "crimes against humanity," the Nazis claimed they were blameless, that they were only following orders. Ten and a half months later the trials ended, and nineteen of the twenty-two were found guilty. Seven were imprisoned. Twelve were executed.

In April 1947 Alfred Lipson was a witness at one of the later trials at Nuremberg. He remembers: "I was more anguished sitting there, waiting to testify, than the prisoners. I imagined them sitting there full of regret. But no, they hoped to escape punishment. They seemed almost smug."

On December 9, 1946, at one of the first trials in Nuremberg, Germany, U.S. Brigadier General Telford Taylor made an opening statement that included an explanation of the importance of the trials. "The mere punishment of the defendants," he said, "or even thousands of others equally guilty, can never redress the terrible injuries which the Nazis visited on these unfortunate peoples. For them it is far more important that these incredible events be established by clear and public proof, so that no one can ever doubt that they were fact and not fable."

The chief British prosecutor, Sir Hartley Shawcross, said of the Holocaust, "History holds no parallel to these horrors." And Hans Frank, the former general governor of Nazi-occupied Poland and one of the defendants at Nuremberg, declared, "A thousand years will pass and this guilt of Germany will still not be erased."

The guilt may not be erased, but as time passes, people forget. The survivors, however, did not and cannot forget. Even today their memories haunt them.

Al Feuerstein remembers when he came to the United States, in 1946: "I was afraid. I was afraid to be a Jew. My friends told me, 'Don't worry. We have a constitution. It can never happen again.' I said, 'Germany was a democracy. It had a constitution too.' "

Shulamit Erlebacher remembers: "My parents were sent to the Warsaw ghetto and were later killed. My aunt died in Auschwitz. She was the one who raised me. My two sisters died working in coal mines. My brother died in Dachau with his wife and child. Sometimes I ask, 'Why was I the only one to survive?' "

More than forty years after Irene Hizme and her brother, Rene Slotkin, were separated from their mother, they found her death certificate. It was in a small museum in Israel. Rene Slotkin remembers: "I felt a terrible sadness for her and for me. And that terrible moment of separation came back to me. I heard my mother crying out. It was difficult, very difficult, to walk away from that paper."

Memories of the Holocaust intrude every day on Irene Hizme. "Every time I take a shower, I think of Auschwitz. There's a great deal of sadness in my life because of the Holocaust."

Esther Himmelfarb Peterseil is not free from the past. I have nightmares. I remind myself of something and it brings tears to my eyes. I'm more touchy. I'm afraid of gentiles. Since Auschwitz, I have never taken a shower, only baths."

And Judy Schonfeld Schabes is not free from the past. "Every time we have a cookout, I say, 'There is that smell.' I'm forever thinking what I would be like today if I hadn't gone through it, if a single parent had survived, or a sibling. I'm very overprotective of my family now."

Ernest Honig's daughter once asked him, "Daddy, did you have a mommy?" All her friends had grandparents. She didn't.

Clara Wachter Feldman is still not free from the past. "I go to a bar mitzvah now and think of all the bar mitzvahs that have never been, the children who will never be. I'm ambivalent about my own survival. The happiest years since 1933 were the years I was raising my children. Then I was making a statement. They didn't defeat us."

Aron Hirt-Manheimer was born in a Displaced Persons camp in Feldafing, Germany. He is the child of survivors. He remembers: "I felt rage. I felt my parents were dishonored, humiliated. I felt I had to fight back, but there was no one to fight. Later I became active in the effort to track down and prosecute escaped Nazi war criminals. I feel privileged to be the child of survivors. I represent the future of many people who perished: my aunts, my uncles, and their children. It is a tremendous responsibility.

"My parents called me their *oytzer*, their treasure. But I was also their helper. I taught them English. I taught them how to drive. I had to contribute to their healing. My sister and I proved that Hitler had not destroyed the Jewish family. We meant continuity."

Florence Bauman Wiener is the daughter of Holocaust survivors. She grew up without grandparents, aunts, uncles, or cousins. "Both my parents came from large families. I don't know how large. They were both married to other people and had children. But only my parents survived. They met and married in Bergen-Belsen in 1945 after liberation. The death camp had become a Displaced Persons camp. That's where my brother Jacob and I were born. When I was eight, someone asked me where I was born, and I said, 'Bergen-Belsen.' To me that was as natural as saying Brooklyn or Staten Island."

Florence Bauman Wiener's parents were very protective. She remembers: "My mother never wanted to let me out of her sight. When I was sixteen, I was going to the beach with friends. My mother said she would follow me. She said she would sit far away on a bench and watch. No one would even know she was there. My mother often said, 'You should never have to know why I feel the way I do.' "

Auschwitz remains as a museum and a monument. Erwin Baum returned there in June 1988. "I hired a taxi and went to the camp. I went to the bunk where I slept. I went to where they put on my number. I went to the bench where they beat us. When I was thirteen and went there for the first time, there was no way out. This time I walked in because I wanted to, and on the other side of the gate there was a taxi waiting for me whenever I was ready to leave. I felt truly liberated for the first time. I had walked in and out with my own free will. To the people who say there was no Holocaust, tell them I was there. I'm real. It happened."

As a result of mistreatment by the Nazis, Aron Hirt-Manheimer's father contracted tuberculosis. After the war he spent several years in a sanatorium but had trouble breathing for the rest of his life. He died in 1984. Aron Hirt-Manheimer remembers his father: "Even if he wanted, my father couldn't hide the scars. His body was a map of the Holocaust. He was shot with a machine gun while trying to escape the train which was taking him to Auschwitz, and his back was bent from the bullets which left their mark on his back and chest. He had a number, a blue tattoo, on his left arm. Because he had been beaten so often, he had a permanent black-and-blue mark on his knuckles. The pain he endured was unbelievable. But my father did not give up on humanity. He continued to care about others and refused to judge people collectively.

"Twenty years ago I escorted my father on his only trip to Israel. Ironically, our itinerary called for a stopover in Frankfurt. As we filed into the airport terminal, we saw uniformed German sentinels all around us. 'Damn murderers,' I whispered. 'We never should have come here.' My father turned to me and said in Yiddish, '*Aron, nish alle Deutschen zenen gevein schlecht*—Aron, not all Germans were bad.' He tried to pass on to us, to me and my sister Rose, all the best values of Judaism, to be a *mensch* [a decent, honorable person]. 'You be what you want others to be.' "

People who have read about and studied the history of the Holocaust wonder how a tragedy of such unparalleled dimensions could have occurred. Historians, philosophers, religious thinkers, have asked, "Where was God? Where was man?"

"Where was God?" is a difficult, perhaps impossible, question to answer. Some feel it is not even a proper question to ask. But "Where was man?" Where were the basically good people of this world, the people who consider themselves free of prejudice and hate, the people who would never willfully harm others?

These people were in many places. They were at home in the 1930s, calmly reading newspaper reports of the weather, of baseball games, and of Jews losing their rights as citizens of Germany. They were standing outside Jewish-owned stores in Germany on April 1, 1933, but they did not go in. These people were watching as Jews were forced from their homes and into ghettoes. They were standing by and watching as Jews were rounded up and taken off in locked cattle cars. They were living near enough to the death camps to smell the burning flesh. They were in positions of leadership with the power to help but not caring enough to stop the massacre. There were good, brave people too, who were protesting the discrimination, helping people to escape, and hiding Jews from the Nazis at great personal risk.

No words, no book, can fully describe the humiliation, the pain, the horror, of that time. The lives lost cannot be reclaimed. And still the lesson the Holocaust has to teach us has not been learned. Prejudice, bigotry, and hatred have not disappeared. On the contrary, in the past few years violent acts motivated by prejudice have increased. And often the people guilty of painting swastikas on Jewish buildings, of attacking Jews, blacks, and others, are young people.

People today must learn not to hate, to teach their children not to hate. They must understand that hatred can lead to discrimination and violence. What happened once must not happen again.

I Must Tell the Story

Emily Borenstein

Emily Borenstein was
born in Elizabeth, New
Jersey, in 1923. She was a
psychiatric social worker
in Middletown, New
York. She is the author of
a book-length collection
of poems on the
Holocaust, *Night of the
Broken Glass*, in which the
following poem
originally appeared. In
1978, she received the
Poetry Award from
Jewish Current for her
poem, "Holocaust."

    As Borenstein attests
in this poem, bearing
witness to the Holocaust
is regarded by many as an
important responsibility.

I press my face to the pane of death to
    witness
the slaughter of Jews in Warsaw.
I must tell the story of this tragic event.
I write for my friend Pesha.
I write for my cousin Perelke who was
    going to be
an actress
for my nephew Wiernicka who wrote
    poetry
for Chaim Kaplan and his *Scroll of Agony*
for half-witted Nathan who was hanged
    from a tree
for Hinda, the bride, who died in her
    husband's arms
for Motl, the tailor
for Bruno Schulz, his stories, his dreams
for Emanuel Ringelblum who preserved for
    posterity
the record of the slaughter.
Names pile up like pebbles on tombstones.
To forget you is to let you die twice.
To forget you is to hear forever blasting in
    my head
the single long note of the Shofar sounding
    in the houses
of the dead.

The Next Generation

Arnold Zable

Arnold Zable was born to a young Jewish couple
who emigrated from Poland to New Zealand and
Australia before the Holocaust. Their families
remained in Poland, however, and many perished.
Zable relates his parents' story in *Jewels and Ashes*,
from which the following material is taken.

In this excerpt, Zable tells of traveling to Krakow,
Poland, in search of family history and surviving
relatives, and encountering a young German man
who was also born after the war.

It is cool and quiet in the walled courtyard, protected from the winds. We sit on benches awaiting the Sabbath. One by one they pass beneath the arched entrance, the minyan gradually assembling in the waning light. "You come from Australia?", an old man sitting beside me asks. "So why didn't you do something? Why didn't you tell the world what was happening?"

"How could I do anything?", I reply. "I was not even alive at the time." But my words do not seem to have registered. "Why didn't you do anything? Eh? Why didn't you scream? Why didn't you let the world know what was happening to us?" Only when we have entered the prayer-hall does he cease, for a while, to pursue his obsession.

There is no longer a rabbi in Krakow, and no cantor to lead the prayers. Members of the kehilla take turns at the pulpit. Of the fifteen assembled, several sit in the back row reading newspapers, others hold whispered conversations, while half a dozen or so concentrate on the prayers. Yet a sense of intimacy pervades the hall, and from time to time we unite in a common chorus of amens.

Some way into the service a young man enters the hall. He is tall, lean, his physique sharp and angular, his face pale and tense. He reaches into a pocket for a black skull cap, and hovers behind the back row of lacquered pews, scanning the congregation. He observes the proceedings from the fringes, like a stranger who wants to come out of the cold and close to the fire.

After the service the narrow foyer inside the entrance of the shul is thick with the din and hubbub of quick introductions, cries of *"Shabbat Shalom,"* and rapid-fire exchanges of the latest communal gossip. The young man remains on the perimeter hesitantly, as if looking for an opening, a polite way of entering the animated circle of well-wishers.

When I approach and introduce myself he is visibly relieved at having made some contact. We converse in English, although it is not his mother tongue. He seems reluctant to reveal where he is from, and constantly deflects the conversation away from the issue. He is in Krakow for a quick visit, he informs me. He has arrived today from nearby Auschwitz. He will return on Monday to continue work as a volunteer in the camp museum. There is a small group who do so every year, for several weeks at a time. They sift through archival material, help assemble exhibits, clean and dust, and do whatever is needed. The facilities are undermanned. Workers are urgently required to maintain the camp for the many thousands who come on pilgrimage from all parts of the globe.

It is obvious where he is from, and it has been from the beginning. Now he confesses, with embarrassment. He was born in Germany, soon after the War. His story tumbles out quickly, in staccato-like whispers, as if he wants to tell it before I can judge him. I have to strain to hear him. His father had been a soldier during the War. "What did you do, father, during the War?" And year after year, the same answer. "I was a soldier. I did my duty. There is no more to be said." But the son had stumbled upon clues, documents, photos. He had made enquiries, talked to family acquaintances, and had pieced it together. Father had been an SS man. He had served in Poland. He had worked in Auschwitz. "What did you do, father?" The questions became more insistent. The answers were always the same. "I did my duty. I was a soldier. I had orders."

"If only he would have admitted it. That would have been at least something. And mother. Always a hausfrau. She had seen nothing, known nothing. Merely maintained a household while her husband was away on duty, for the Fatherland. I grew up in a house of denials and secrets."

The son atones for the father. He goes on a journey to Israel. He lives in Jerusalem for two years and works among the elderly, as a nurse's aide. Since then, for several years now, he has journeyed to Auschwitz with a group he has formed—the sons and daughters of former SS men. Together they make the annual pilgrimage to atone for the crimes of their elders: "I cannot comprehend how an Auschwitz could have existed. It eludes me, constantly. But I will continue to work there. We must maintain it for everyone to see what our elders once did."

We keep talking in the courtyard, long after the others have gone. Feigl Wasserman, the caretaker of the Rema, has turned off the lights and is locking the synagogue doors. "I cannot comprehend how they could have committed such deeds," Werner muses, as if conducting aloud an inner dialogue he has pursued for years. "But in the work, in my travels throughout Poland, I escape my father's cold silence, my mother's pursed lips and, for a while at least, I am free of the shadow that has clung to me since birth."

Survivor

Florence Weinberger

Florence Weinberger is
the wife of a Holocaust
survivor and lives in
California. Her first
collection of poetry, *The
Invisible Telling Its Shape*,
was published in 1989 by
Ambrosia Press. The
poem reprinted below
first appeared in *Poetry/
LA* in 1985.

As Weinberger re-
lates, for many survivors,
it is important that their
children understand the
past.

for Ted

He knows the depths of smokestacks,
from their bleak rims down
their spattered walls, from their ash cones
to the bone-bottom ground.
Once he could see under skin,
inside the body, where deprivation
thins the blood of all desire
except hunger.
For years he wanted to forget
everything. He knows it is possible
to live only at the surface,
it is possible to work,
to marry and have daughters.
But his daughters
look like people he once knew,
and he dreams them.
He dreams them opening doors,
sending letters. When he wakes,
he knows he has been dreaming.
This year, he will show his daughters
where he was born. He will show them
the chimney, the iron gate,
the deep oven where his mother baked bread.

Children of the Holocaust

Helen Epstein

The daughter of Holocaust survivors, Helen Epstein
interviewed hundreds of children of survivors,
gathering their stories in *Children of the Holocaust:*
Conversations with Sons and Daughters of Survivors,
from which the following narrative is taken. For
additional biographical information on Epstein, see
page 418.

During childhood and—for some—throughout
their lives, children of survivors of the Holocaust
often struggle with confusing emotions and issues.
In this selection, Epstein and several other adult
children of survivors discuss their experiences.

On a Sunday morning in the spring of 1977, in
a blizzard that threatened to close down several airports, I flew to Toronto,
Canada on the first leg of a journey that would take me into the homes and lives
of several hundred children of Jewish survivors of the Second World War. I was
twenty-nine years old, a New Yorker, a university professor, and a writer who
had been reporting for newspapers and magazines since I was twenty. For nine
years, I had been writing about other people's lives, learning to extract the
essence of their experience and sensibility. Now, for the first time, I wanted to
apply those skills to myself and to a group that had never before been the subject of journalistic inquiry—the children of the survivors of the Holocaust.

I had talked with other children of survivors before. Three of my closest
childhood friends belonged to that quiet, invisible community, that peer group
without a sign. After school, my friend Evelyn and I would often take our
homework into Central Park and study Latin together, bound by a tacit affinity

that we did not understand. Evelyn's parents, like mine, had insisted that she study Latin. They spoke English with thick accents; they had fled Vienna just as my parents had fled Prague. They read the newspapers as avidly as my own parents. A seemingly innocuous headline could plunge them into an hour-long debate. Like me, Evelyn did not have grandparents or any family besides her mother and father. Like my friend Jimmy, whose family had also fled Vienna, Evelyn never spoke about family, or history, or how her parents came to be living in New York City. But when I visited them, I felt at home. There was an intensity there, a kind of fierceness about living that was absent from the more casual, easygoing atmosphere of other homes. There was mystery of great consequence.

At my friend Mary's house, that mystery was sharpened by sadness. Her parents came from Poland and when they were alone they spoke Yiddish instead of German. They owned the small house in which they lived on West End Avenue and they rarely left it. Once Mary told me that they were afraid it would burn down or be looted if they left. I accepted that without question, as if it were a natural consideration. Neither did I wonder why they had given their only child a Christian name. All of our parents, the ones who had come to America after the war, were eccentric in my eyes. They were not like Americans, and we children were not like other American children. That fact was so obvious it did not require discussion and Mary, like Jimmy and Evelyn, never ventured to speculate on why that should be so. Friends, like family, are quick to shield each other from pain and although we all knew that a great deal of pain pervaded the households in which we were raised, we never addressed it by name.

At twenty-nine, I had decided to address it.

That was why I flew to Toronto. I was going to a strange city to meet a stranger as different from myself as another child of survivors who had grown up in the United States could possibly be. Her name was Deborah Schwartz, and she had grown up in the South. She had been crowned her state's first Jewish beauty queen, and had spent a year behind the wheel of an official beauty pageant Oldsmobile that was turned in for a replacement every three thousand miles. Deborah had played the role of a Southern beauty queen to the hilt. She had visited county fairs, supermarkets and military bases. She had given dozens of gracious interviews to journalists representing city dailies, country weeklies, and even high school papers. She had addressed her state's legislature. She corresponded with hundreds of admirers on special stationery that had the imprint of her face and figure welded to the outline of her state. And she had walked down the runway in the Miss America Pageant in Atlantic City, a participant in one of the most American of rituals.

Her "talent" in the Miss America contest had been playing the piano and she had chosen Chopin's *Revolutionary Etude* because it had been played twenty-four hours a day over Polish radio when Adolf Hitler invaded Poland in 1939. The Second World War had greatly affected her family and, as a result, her own life, Deborah told the judges and newspaper reporters in Atlantic City. Her father, who came from a small town in Hungary, had spent the war in a labor camp and then in the underground. Her mother, who was also from a small town in Hungary, had celebrated her sixteenth birthday in the concentration camp of Auschwitz.

In the South, where the lives of local beauty queens are prime newspaper material, Deborah's story was published in dozens of versions. "Out of Horror—Love and Beauty" ran one headline. "No Negative Attitudes for Deborah" proclaimed another. The newspaper accounts of her reign made much of her family history, largely because Deborah herself stressed its importance to her. "When I think of what my mother was going through at my age—do you realize that her head was shaved completely?" she asked a newsman in Atlantic City. "She had nothing to eat. She was running around in the snow without shoes, and here I am, state queen at the Miss America contest—it's really unbelievable."

I felt utter bewilderment as I looked at the full-page features on Deborah Schwartz that appeared in Southern newspapers. It had never occurred to me that people like my parents could have emigrated to rural backwaters, places thick with tobacco fields, Baptist churches and trailer parks. I tried to imagine Hungarian accents softened by a Southern drawl, and what it was like to grow up rootless in a region which so clearly prized its history. I wondered at Deborah's unequivocal identification of herself as a child of survivors, the assurance of her voice.

I had often heard my own voice, sounding as if it belonged to someone else, explaining to people about the war. When I was small, the questions came from the other children: "Why does your Mommy wear that number on her arm?" I don't remember what I told them but none asked me a second time. It was later, in conversation with adults, that I remember how and what I replied. I no longer answered questions in the quick, unthinking way of a child. Discussion of the war split my being in two. My face remained calm, my voice matter-of-fact, but my feelings froze, keeping the conversation at bay, outside my body.

"You say you weren't born in New York?"

"No. In Prague. Czechoslovakia."

That part was easy. I was proud of being Czech.

"Your parents came here before the war then?"

"No. I was born in 1947."

"Oh, I see. So during the war they . . ."

"They were in concentration camp," I would say helpfully. "Each was the only survivor of the family."

The conversation usually died there. Few people questioned me further and those who did received flat, factual replies. *They were in concentration camp* was a warning. It meant don't step across this line I've drawn; watch the careless things you might otherwise say.

I had, by the time I was old enough to understand, heard what people said about survivors of the war: "Strange people. Crazy, some of them. You know, a human being can only take so much. Those people went through living hell. They went through things we can't imagine. It made them hard."

"I know a survivor," a woman had told me. "That man at the meat market with the blue number on his arm. Sweet man. Never raises his voice. Not like the others I've come across. You'd think they'd have learned something from their experience, wouldn't you? No. Those people seem to have learned nothing. Making money. That's all they're interested in."

I may have said *my parents were in concentration camp* calmly, smoothly, but in my ears the sentence rang like a declaration of loyalty. It put me squarely on the side of "those people," far away from the complacent, untouched Americans—Jews or Gentiles—who seemed to be so quick to make assumptions about things they did not understand. I answered their pity or embarrassment or confusion with pride. My parents were not particularly interested in money, they were not hard and they were not crazy, I told myself. They hadn't gotten divorced, like so many parents did. They never got drunk. They did not do illegal things. They were always home, unlike other parents who left their children behind and went on trips.

Although I thought these things to myself, I never said them out loud. I did not like talking about my parents or the war, because talk meant accepting that the war had happened and, more than anything else in the world, I wished it had not. The idea that my mother and my father had been forced out of their homes and made to live like animals—worse than animals—was too shameful to admit. To tell people that my parents had been in concentration camp in a cool, rational tone of voice was a kind of denial. Concentration camp became a location, not a prison or a death house or a human mill that turned free people into slaves. It became a badge of courage rather than a degradation. It became an untouchable standard of fortitude.

It suddenly occurred to me as I drove into Deborah's neighborhood, an upper-middle class Toronto suburb, that she might never have had any of those thoughts and reactions. It was six years since she had given interviews. In the interval, she had married a Canadian whose parents were also survivors and also came from small towns in Hungary; she had given birth to one child and was expecting another. Their house, a massive, split-level structure, stood at the end of a quiet street, frosted with snow. Its garage door was shut, all the curtains were drawn, and as I walked up the front steps with my tape recorder and suitcase I felt like an interloper, someone bringing unnecessary trouble.

I had had a hint of that feeling a week before in New York, when Deborah had telephoned me to confirm the date of my visit. In the first rush of excitement, we had agreed that I would stay with her in Toronto. Then came a cooler, more distanced telephone call. Perhaps it would be better if I found a hotel or made other arrangements? Her husband was studying for exams. It really wasn't a good time to have guests. There was a guardedness in Deborah's voice that had not been there the first time we spoke and it triggered a reserve of my own. We were strangers, after all, and I would be asking her questions that she was not accustomed to answering or even thinking about. A friend of mine, another child of survivors, who over the years had tried to talk me out of my plan to write about others like us, had told me that I was engaged in "stirring up shit to no good purpose." On that Sunday afternoon, as I knocked on Deborah's door, his words came back to me, and I waited, more than a little anxious, for her to appear.

The young woman who opened the door was eight months pregnant and still moved like a beauty queen. For a moment her face looked blank and then she smiled—a full, unmistakably American smile brimming with self-possession. Deborah was accustomed to greeting strangers. Her poise and physical grace threw me into a confusion that I would spend the next few hours trying to shake.

Deborah prepared two cups of coffee. Her manner was leisurely. It was the only obviously Southern characteristic she had brought with her to Toronto. But reinforcing that unhurriedness was a reluctance to plunge too quickly into the topic that had led to our meeting. I sipped the coffee, thinking that it would not be easy to interview her. She was not an introspective person. She had spent a great deal of time presenting and living up to a Grace Kelly public image. The beauty pageant business had taught her to be careful, even suspicious. I had sent her some articles I had written and I had told her that a psychiatrist had found children of survivors severely traumatized by their parents' experiences. The very idea of psychiatric studies put her off.

"I became infuriated," she told me later. "I never felt abnormal in any way, shape or form. In fact, I always felt very much the opposite. I was living a very typical, normal, average life, playing the role of wife and mother to the best of my ability. I resented being talked about and categorized by anyone, especially by psychiatrists who were making strong negative remarks about my personality."

She was also wary of talking in depth to a stranger about her family even though she had done so many times before. "I was suspicious of your motives," she told me later. "I didn't know you and I wasn't sure how you would handle the whole thing. It seemed to me there were people trying to capitalize on the Holocaust and I object to seeing the memory of my family sensationalized."

But Deborah said nothing of the sort to me at the time. She was gracious. She asked me questions about myself. *Where had I been born? Where had my parents been during the war? Had any of my family survived? What did my parents do for a living? What had they done in Czechoslovakia?* She was checking me out, with the peculiar brand of questions I would hear from many people before they would talk about themselves. Even after I had answered her questions, Deborah was reluctant to talk. "There're plenty of survivors in Toronto," she told me. "It was one of the cities they came to after the war. I called a couple of people I knew, because I thought this afternoon might be a good time to interview some of them. During the week, it will be harder."

Deborah looked at me over her coffee cup, her blue-gray eyes managing a combination of distance and cordiality. She wanted, I thought, to hear what kind of questions I intended to ask before answering them herself. She also wanted to watch me work and to decide whether I could be trusted. Many children of survivors whom I would encounter would do exactly what Deborah did that first day. I had to prove myself, make myself vulnerable before they would do the same.

A short time later, there was a knock on the front door and Deborah brought two young men into the living room. One was Irwin Diamond, a short, robust, extroverted man with a thick mustache under his nose and a small knitted skullcap on his head. Irwin was the first person Deborah had called when she knew I was arriving because he was active in the Jewish community. He was a teacher and vice-principal of one of its religious schools and the kind of guest who could always be relied on to keep a party lively. Irwin had brought along his close friend Eli Rubinstein who was, in perfect complement to Irwin, tall, thin and very shy. He was a doctoral student in philosophy who, I suspected, vastly preferred opening unfamiliar books to meeting strangers. Like Irwin, he was an observant Jew who lived within walking distance of *shul*, refrained from traveling, using electricity or answering the telephone on the Sabbath, and kept a strictly kosher household. As Deborah ushered us all into the den and set about serving more coffee and cakes, I fiddled nervously with my tape recorder, as unconfident as though I were interviewing people for the first time in my life.

Stammering a little bit, I explained why I had come to Toronto, that I was interested in hearing the experiences of other children of survivors in order to clarify some things for myself, that I had no theories to prove. Irwin Diamond took this in with good humor and asked me a few questions about myself. Eli Rubinstein said nothing. His dark eyes seemed to be floating in his pale, fine-boned face and I had no clue as to what he was thinking.

Both men were twenty-nine years old, like me. Irwin had been born in Cheb, Czechoslovakia; Eli, in a Displaced Persons camp in Torino, Italy. Both had arrived in Canada as babies when their parents immigrated in 1948. They had attended religious schools, then university. Both had married daughters of Holocaust survivors and both were now enthusiastic fathers. "It isn't just the normal parental instinct," Eli Rubinstein said. "I really feel that my raising a family has cosmic significance. I feel I have a sacred duty to have children. I feel it's the only way to respond to the evil of the Holocaust and to assure that the death of my family and the Six Million was not in vain."

The import of his words and the clarity with which they were expressed startled me, Deborah, Irwin and even Eli himself. It was as if Eli had been waiting for years for an opportunity to say what he had just said.

"Are you named after someone who died in the war?" I asked him.

"Yes. My full name is Robert Eli Rubinstein," he replied, in the quiet voice that would not rise or fall very much for the next two hours. "But my Hebrew name is Eliahu Mordechai. I was named after both my grandfathers who were murdered by the Germans. Although it's a weak substitute for not having grandparents, I've always felt that having their name enables something to live on in me."

A door slammed, and Joseph, Deborah's younger brother, hurried in. He was twenty-two, red-haired, broad-shouldered and thoughtful, a sociology student. Without a word, he sat down in the circle. There were five of us now. All of us, like Eli, were named after people who had been murdered during the war, and as Eli continued speaking, his story merged with the stories each of us had heard at home, so much that the feelings he described became our own.

Eli's father, Béla Rubinstein, had been one of twelve children in a small town in Hungary before the war. Four survived; his father by working in a labor camp. Eli's mother, Judith, was one of four children. Only she and one brother were left of her family.

"I always had a feeling of something different in our house," Eli said, "but I couldn't ever really pin it down. I sensed there was something mysterious, something peculiar about the past, about the place where I was born but I didn't know what. I wondered about it: How did my parents end up here in Canada? It's obviously so difficult for them."

In 1948, I discovered later, representatives of the Canadian International Fur and Leather Workers Union, together with the Jewish Immigrants Aid Society and the Canadian government formed a commission to visit the Displaced Persons camps in Europe and bring back two hundred furriers and their families. When they arrived in Torino, Béla Rubinstein and his older brother claimed that their father had been a fur trader although, in fact, they knew nothing at all about furs. A few months later they were given the choice of emigrating to

Montreal, Toronto or Winnipeg—all unfamiliar names. The Rubinsteins made inquiries. Winnipeg, people said, was very cold, and Montreal was a bilingual city. So they settled on Toronto where they knew not a soul. For the first three years, the men and their wives all worked as furriers, six days a week, at home as well as in the factory, from early in the morning until late into the night.

"I was aware that we lived in considerable poverty despite all this work," Eli said, "and that I had to do without a lot of things my friends had. Other children had grandparents and I didn't have a single one. When I asked my mother about that, she said that bad people had killed them. I didn't understand who these people were or why they would want to kill my grandparents. I wasn't aware of any connection between their being killed and their being Jewish.

"I knew there was this country, Hungary, far across the ocean, where my parents used to live. Somehow, something had happened, that world came to an end and now we were here in a new world. Their lives consisted of two parts: pre-War and post-War. That's how their calendar worked if they wanted to place an event. The war was such a turning point in their lives that they would constantly be referring to it without talking about it. So I was aware there had been a war with a capital 'W' which was very different from the kind of war I saw on TV with cowboys and Indians. But I didn't pursue the mystery. I just lived with it until one day when I was ten my cousin made the revelation to me."

The two boys were playing together when Eli's cousin began talking about a man named Hitler who had killed all their relatives because they were Jewish. Eli, as he recalled, could not make any sense of it. He had never heard of Hitler before. And what reason would he have had for killing all their relatives? His cousin could not elaborate. The Rubinstein family did not believe in talking to the children about the war, Eli's mother told me later. "Some of the kids still don't know anything about it," she said, "and their parents feel this is a good thing. They say, 'Why should they find out? It has nothing to do with them.' I waited to tell Eli. I waited until he was sixteen."

"My father to this day rarely says anything about the war," Eli said. "He gets jumpy, very edgy, when my mother starts talking about it. He tries to change the subject or shifts around in his chair or finds an excuse to leave the room. Once in a while, he'll blurt something out and then regret it afterwards. What I know of my father's experience I learned mainly from my mother."

Like my mother, and Deborah and Joseph's mother, Eli's mother would often drift into a memory of the war as she stood in the kitchen preparing dinner, or sat at the kitchen table afterwards. "I have a very difficult time recalling the stories she told me exactly. I couldn't tell you one and be sure I had the details right if my life depended on it," Eli said. "It was very painful to listen to. These were things that had happened to my mother and who's closer to me than my mother? Sometimes I cried but I was embarrassed to have her see me doing that. I certainly didn't want to hurt my mother further by upsetting her. I would feel the tears billowing up in my eyes and I would force myself not to cry. I would wipe my eyes so that she wouldn't see. I rarely asked a question, but I felt compelled to listen. I wanted to hear and I didn't want to hear. And I had extraordinary difficulty remembering what she told me. I have a pretty good memory and I usually recall the most basic trivia very well. But about this, my memory is very poor. I can't even remember the number on my mother's arm. I don't know what it is."

Eli glanced up at the four people watching him. His dark brown eyes shone against the pallor of his skin. No one said a word. None of the children of survivors I spoke with could recall the numbers, their order, or even the arm on which their parents bore a tattoo. Those whose parents had not been tattooed were relieved that they had escaped the procedure. It was an indelible brand, a constant reminder of suffering. The thought of it drew us together. I had the peculiar sensation of plasma flowing through the five of us. An intimacy had settled in. Eli was no longer shy or tentative; he spoke fluently.

"By the time I began school, my mother had stopped working, to stay at home with me and my baby sister, Rochelle. My father still did not feel financially secure but the family had set up their own fur business and even employed a man or two. When I refused to speak Hungarian anymore, my parents cooperated. They had every intention of adapting to the new reality and my mother always said she learned along with me when she helped me with my schoolwork. My parents always said that a person can lose everything, but what's inside his head stays there. I had to acquire an education, they said, because our enemies could take everything away from us but that. Little by little, as I became aware of who the enemies were, I began to understand. Education is closely related to the idea of being self-sufficient."

Deborah looked up at him. She had been listening attentively, more than a little surprised. Like the rest of us, she was hearing Eli describe her own family.

"I was a fairly usual, though introverted, little boy. My parents were religious Jews and I was a dutiful child. I was never a rebel. I never violated the Sabbath or ate non-kosher food. But I wondered about things. I wondered about God. The standard question of how a merciful, beneficent God could allow millions of innocent men, women and children to perish. That was the question for me and it never, ever came up in school. It was taboo. In *yeshiva*, the religious high school I attended, the emphasis was on rabbinic texts. If you spend all your waking hours absorbed in them, you don't have any energy left for worrying about troublesome questions. In *yeshiva*, there is no such thing as free time. You go from early morning until night with prayer three times a day and required study sessions in the evening.

"We never touched upon the Holocaust in *yeshiva*. No one was competent; everyone was afraid. It could lead you into dangerous territory. Only once, during the Eichmann trial, did we talk about it. We had a substitute teacher from Israel. He told us that Israeli agents had just apprehended a man called Eichmann in Argentina. I had never heard of Eichmann. The other kids hadn't either. So he told us. It gave me a nice feeling to know they had caught him. When you are twelve or thirteen, you're a bit bloodthirsty and after the teacher had explained what he had done, I identified him as one of the people responsible for killing my family. I had a certain satisfaction knowing that they were no doubt going to kill him.

"But we never got into the really weighty problems of the Holocaust with him or any other teacher. I don't know how many other boys were troubled by these things. Probably not many. But there just wasn't anyone to talk to about them. I admired and respected my teachers in *yeshiva*. I figured they're the experts. If they can't cope with these things, nobody can. So I just let it go at that. But privately, I continued to ask all kinds of questions, questions of good and evil and how it was possible that these things could have happened. I thought it was blasphemous to give the traditional answer that God in His wisdom knows what He's doing and it is not for us finite mortals to question His ways. That's the stock answer that's been given by Jewish thinkers throughout the ages to the various catastrophes that have befallen the Jewish people.

"I found that answer very hard to accept. I don't think that someone who lives in the twentieth century can be satisfied with it. What happened during the Holocaust is not merely quantitatively different from what happened to the Jews earlier but qualitatively different as well. There is something demonic about the goal of the Nazis to exterminate the Jewish people in their entirety, something that was totally lacking in all previous persecutions. For the first time in history, the murder of Jews became the national policy of a 'civilized' government, an end in itself. That idea is virtually impossible to relate to our experience in North America. My parents had come through that ordeal and I had boundless admiration for both of them, for surviving with dignity, for pulling the pieces together and succeeding so beautifully in their new life. I'm very proud of the fact that my father, my uncle, and my cousin, who arrived in this country as penniless refugees, managed to create a highly successful business instead of succumbing to despair. I never thought of my parents going through indignity or humiliation. I don't remember ever being angry at them or ashamed of them because of what they went through. But I always wanted to talk about it with someone. Talking about your experience legitimizes it in a way. It lets you know you are normal."

Eli's questions led him to philosophy. He entered the University of Toronto as a philosophy student, one of the only two graduates of his *yeshiva* ever to do so. His parents, who had always stressed the importance of acquiring skills as well as knowledge, were not pleased with their son's decision, but they put no obstacles in his way.

When he was twenty-one, Eli startled them, his friends and himself by suddenly emerging from reclusiveness and becoming a leader of the Toronto Student Committee for Soviet Jewry. "I still don't understand exactly how it happened," Eli said, "but I found myself making speeches at rallies, shouting into a megaphone outside the Soviet Embassy in Ottawa and even applying for a visa to go to Russia. That was in 1971, when there were no Soviet Jews in Canada and when there was not much public awareness of the problem. It was very much out of character for me. I had never done anything like that before, and my parents worried that something would happen to me."

They became even more alarmed the following year when Eli decided to go to Hungary to visit the town in which his family had lived. "It was a pilgrimage," Eli told us. "I just wanted to establish some sort of contact with my past. I wanted to stand in the place where all the lost people I never knew had lived. By standing there, by being among the people they had lived with, I thought I could come as close as possible. Otherwise, they would be just phantoms, names my parents mentioned.

"When my parents left Hungary they both vowed never to set foot in the country again. They couldn't understand what would drive their son, who had been born outside, to go back. They had nightmares about what might happen to me. I had to find a way of reporting back to them in Toronto every other day, to let them know I was okay.

"I didn't make it back to my mother's hometown but I did make it to where my father grew up. It is a little hamlet. Everyone came out to look me over. All the peasant women were chattering, gossiping among themselves until finally one of them came and asked me who I was. I said I was the son of Béla Rubinstein, who used to live there before the war. They were all very excited about that but seemed a bit nervous as well. Some of them were afraid I had come to reclaim my father's house and flour mill—which had long been nationalized anyway. I felt very, very uncomfortable. It was one of the lousiest feelings I had ever had in my life. It was as if I were a phoenix risen from the ashes and that I should not be there: I should be dead.

"And I think they felt, 'Where did this guy come from? You mean there are still Jews alive somewhere?'

"They were all very solicitous. They asked how my father was doing. Some of them said they had heard that all the Jews who had once lived in this village were alive in America and that they were all wealthy and happy. That was how they soothed their consciences, I guess. They talked among themselves about me, always referring to me as the Jew. I felt like an alien creature in that little village. All during my stay in Hungary I had the feeling of being in the presence of ghosts. It made me feel the events that had been so remote before."

Eli stopped talking for a moment and again no one said anything. I had made the same pilgrimage, only mine had been to Prague. I had wandered for hours in the cobblestoned streets, looking for the house in which my parents had lived, the hospital in which I was born, the grocery store where my mother bought food and the parks in which she had played as a child. Everything was gray in Prague, infused with a great brooding melancholy. I, too, had felt the presence of ghosts.

"You know," Eli continued, "when you live after the fact, you feel an impotent rage. You ask, even though you know the answer: Why didn't anyone do something to stop it? I fantasize about my being there and taking up arms. One of my fantasies today, something I still have at the age of twenty-nine, is getting my hands on a Nazi. I think of all of them as one person who killed my family. I would like to torture him and mutilate him. It scares me when I have thoughts like that. It shocks me because I am not a violent person. In normal circumstances I can't imagine myself doing violence to any other human being.

"There are other things as well. I am in awe of my parents. I often wonder if I could have survived myself and I doubt whether I could have. Being their child has given me a certain depth, a seriousness about life that most people can't possibly have. I'm aware of the evil in the world and I'm not complacent. I feel it requires an active struggle to prevent a revival of the sort of thing that led to the murder of my family. I'm especially sensitive to racism because I identify with the target. That brings out a certain activism in me that wouldn't be there otherwise.

"I'm also uneasy. I can't feel too secure. I can't take it for granted that I will live out my life in peace in Canada. My background has very much influenced my choices in life. Someone who doesn't have that background can't possibly understand me. When I chose my wife, I didn't go out looking for a child of Holocaust survivors, but I do know that my parents-in-law understand me better than native American or Canadian parents could. Also, I've gone into the family business, although I do teach a course in Jewish philosophy. Had I chosen a purely academic career I would have had to move out of Toronto. I want to live where my parents and family are.

"As my parents get older, I'm beginning to sense that everything isn't quite in order, that what they went through just can't be suppressed. I have this fear that it's going to take its toll in a very terrible way. Physically, it's taken its toll on my mother already. She went through some terrible treatment in Auschwitz. She was young and resilient at the time. But the Holocaust is beginning to catch up with her. A few years ago she had an operation for what the doctors diagnosed as bursitis. It turned out when they operated that her shoulder bone was deformed. They questioned her about it and it was something she had blocked out of her memory. A guard had struck her very hard in Auschwitz. There was no care and the cold and the damp damaged it. Now she has trouble with the other arm and her inner ear. I never had the feeling she was maladjusted though. She was always her pleasant, charming self.

"The past comes through in subtle ways now. Uncertainty about the future, when on the surface things would appear very stable and secure. There's a reluctance to accept success and be smug about it. Canada has been very good to us. But my parents feel they can't be too secure, even though they are very rooted here. If you find yourself becoming too secure, you have to shake yourself up, to spare yourself the terrible feeling when someone does it to you."

Eli Rubinstein stopped talking and this time he did not continue. He appeared surprised, as surprised as his friend Irwin Diamond. "As I spoke," he told me later, "I began to realize things on a conscious level that I had known all along but had never put into words. Before, even with Irwin, it was a silent brotherhood. We felt a certain kinship but we had never articulated it before. It was a revelation to him and to me too."

The five of us seated around the tape recorder in Deborah's den did not say much to each other then. We all had retreated into our own thoughts and memories which Eli's long monologue had set into motion. The two men rose to leave. It was late; their families were waiting. As they stood by the door getting into their coats, they appeared to me as different people than those who had come in early that afternoon. Something basic, something I still did not understand, had made us familiar to one another, something that overrode differences in temperament, religious belief, lifestyle, ambition, and personal priorities.

I felt excited. Eli had not only articulated some of his own feelings for the first time, but some of mine as well. A stranger in a strange city had confirmed the reality of my own experience. What Eli had spoken about was only a beginning, but it was a good one. I made arrangements to see Deborah again later on that week. I did not then know where this beginning would take me, that I would be coming back to Toronto, living there for months at a time. All I wanted was to get to a place where I could replay Eli's voice and put on paper what he had said. I wanted to read and reread it.

Esther

Richard Rashke

Using oral and written accounts of survivors,
Richard Rashke wrote *Escape from Sobibor*, from
which the following excerpt is taken. For additional
biographical information on Rashke, see page 109.

Although she escaped from Sobibor (a death
camp in eastern Poland), survived the Holocaust,
and now lives in America, Esther, like so many other
Holocaust survivors, has never entirely escaped her
past. Present-day examples of anti-Semitism also
evoke painful responses from her.

The first time I met Esther Terner-Raab, she was
crying. It was at the International Liberators' Conference, sponsored by the
United States Holocaust Memorial Council and held at the State Department in
October 1981. Esther was a member of a panel discussing uprisings. When she
began to talk about Sobibor, her voice cracked and her emotions took over.

The conference was unusual for many reasons, among them the fact that
Communist-bloc countries had sent to it military delegates who as soldiers had
liberated the camps. Although the Russian and Czech speakers at the conference described the camps and the condition of the prisoners when they freed
them, never once did I hear them say the word *Jew*. If I had not already known
that six million Jews died in the Holocaust, I would have gotten the impression
that the only prisoners in the camps were non-Jewish Russian, Polish, and Czech
civilians. Since I did not attend all the workshops and plenary sessions, I checked
my observation with Jan Karski, the Polish underground courier, who gave a
talk at the conference. He also had thought it both strange and symptomatic of
Communist-bloc attitudes that major participants at a conference on Hitler's
Final Solution avoided saying *Jew*, almost as if they had been coached.

The second time I met Esther, I was angry. It was in her spacious Vineland, New Jersey, home. We were sitting in the kitchen, and my tape recorder was plugged in. Although she had readily agreed to the interview, she wasn't sure whether she would allow me to use her name.

"Why not?" I was surprised and disappointed because, like most writers, I don't like the idea of false names or anonymity. They tend to lessen the credibility of any story.

"I got a letter," she said. "Who needs that?"

The Vineland newspaper had printed a short article about Esther. One of the readers had written her an anti-Semitic diatribe. After the murder of her parents, the months of terror in Sobibor, the uncertainty in Stefan Marcyniuk's barn, the destruction of her Jewish community—after all that—she still felt that she had to hide, not in a straw pile in Poland, but in New Jersey, almost forty years later.

As we sat in her kitchen ("It's cozier in here," she said), Esther was nervous, and her face showed signs of strain. She was not looking forward to dredging up old memories. "Not for a million dollars would I go through this," she said.

But like Tom Blatt and other survivors I had talked to, Esther was anxious that the Sobibor story and her personal story be told with accuracy. Her older son was especially interested. "You ought to see his Holocaust library," she said. "He was one of four children of survivors interviewed on a television show in Chicago."

Esther told me about her three companions in the barn after the escape from Sobibor. Her brother Idel (Jerry Terner) is still alive, Samuel Lerer is a New York City cab driver, and Avram Kohn lives in Australia. She also told me that Wolodia, the Ukrainian guard who supervised her in the armory, fled Sobibor on the night of October 14 with one of the Russian women the Nazis had held as prostitutes (Esther met both of them after liberation in Chelm), and that her close friend Zelda Metz, who had lived near Vineland, died recently. After breaking out of Sobibor, Zelda had bought false identity papers proving she was an Aryan.

Esther missed Zelda. "We used to sleep in the same bunk in Sobibor," she recalled. "Zelda slept on one side of me, and Mrs. Shapiro [chaperone] on the other."

Esther doesn't laugh easily, but her face brightened a little as she recalled a story about her and Zelda. Once they were picking mushrooms in the woods outside the fence at Sobibor. When they had filled a few boxes, they brought them to the canteen. The Nazi in charge told them to wash the mushrooms and put them in the cellar that served as an icebox. When Esther and Zelda walked into the basement, they saw a large pot of soup cooling there. They were delighted.

"We spit in it and washed our hands in it," Esther said. "Don't ask me what else we did to that soup . . . And they *ate* it."

Two of the Jews who had escaped from the forest brigade after the Ukrainian guard was killed—Podchlebnik and a man named Hoenigman—also used to live near Esther. The Nazis had killed all the Polish Jews in the Waldkommando in retaliation.

"Zelda held a grudge against Podchlebnik and Hoenigman until her last breath," Esther told me. "She felt it was too high a price to pay for two lives."

Podchlebnik was dead. Hoenigman, who was very sick, moved to Florida a few years ago. Esther had lost track of him. Unlike Zelda, she wasn't bitter about the two men risking the lives of everyone else in Sobibor to save their own necks. "I don't know what I would have done in their place," she said.

Like the other survivors I had interviewed, Esther had never really escaped from Sobibor. "When Zelda was alive," she told me, "we'd call each other every day and talk about it. I still think about it before I fall asleep, and then I dream."

"About what?" I asked.

"Mainly that I'm running, that the Gestapo is after me, that Wagner is after me, and that I can't run fast enough. Then I start screaming. I see children's heads smashed against wagons, people killed in front of me, people being tortured . . . It has left me so that I can never be happy, and I cannot help it."

Esther had clearly sorted out in her own mind the reasons she survived. At the top of her list is her cousin, Leon Feldhendler. She spoke of him with great pride. "He felt a responsibility toward others," she said. "Very few have that when their own lives are at stake. He never considered escaping to save his own skin. He felt responsible for us—like a father. You fought with almost anyone else at Sobibor, but not with Leon. You listened when he spoke. You felt good when he spoke. He helped a lot of us cope."

Esther also felt she survived because Gustav Wagner was not in the camp on October 14. "He would have sniffed the escape out like a dog," she told me. "He was the smartest Hitler could find. He even knew what you were *thinking*. Shrewd. That man was shrewd."

Esther paused to fish in her memory for a Wagner story. "Once, he gave me two pieces of candy," she recalled. A half-smile crossed her lips. "He probably had it on his conscience for the rest of his life, that he gave a Jew candy."

Esther's unwavering faith in God also saved her. Unlike Shlomo and Tom, she is still an Orthodox Jew. She and her husband own and run a kosher poultry-processing business. When she called my editor to agree to an interview, she added, "Tell him not to call on the Holy Days."

God was Esther's life vest. "I saw so many who didn't believe give up," she told me. "I always believed, but don't ask me why. It helped me. In such danger, you really need something to hang on to—hope. I think religion is hope."

"Others don't believe anymore," I said. "They can't understand how a God would allow all those innocent people to die. Doesn't that bother you?"

"If you're religious, you're not *supposed* to ask those kinds of questions," Esther said. "What did my father do wrong? What did my mother do wrong? What did all the children do wrong?—I really can't answer. And if you believe, you won't even try."

Esther loved talking about the uprising. And when she did, there was disbelief, almost awe, in her voice. "We felt we had no chance of getting out," she said. "But at least, we were doing something. We didn't go like lambs. Even if we killed one Gestapo, it was worth it. We were condemned people anyway. Why not try? If we had only known we'd close the camp down by escaping, it would have been a big thing for those of us who didn't make it."

I didn't feel any strong hatred or thirst for revenge coming through in Esther's voice, so I asked, "Did you hate the Nazis that much, that you'd risk your life to kill just one?"

"Yes. I had feelings of terrible hatred and revenge," she said. "I just couldn't figure out how any human being could do what they were doing. Didn't they think of their own wives and children when they killed us?"

The hatred was there now, in her face, in her eyes, in her strained voice. "What kind of human beings *were* they?" The question seemed wrung out of her, like water from a rock.

When she told me her personal escape story—her dream, her reunion with Idel, her survival in Stefan Marcyniuk's barn—Esther peppered her story with "luck" and "miracle" and "it was meant for us to live."

"I always feel that the dream helped me survive," she said, referring to the night before the escape, when she dreamed that her mother told her to go to the barn. "It was more luck than common sense."

If Esther still hated the Nazis, what she felt for the Poles was not love. "After we were liberated by the Russians," she said with bitterness, "we had to run constantly because the Poles were just as bad as the Germans."

Esther went back to Poland in 1977 to visit the Marcyniuks and to see Sobibor once again. Stefan had died, but Mrs. Marcyniuk was still alive and so were her children. Esther had remained close to them over the years and had helped them financially after they lost most of their wealth during the war. She dragged out a set of drawings of the farm that one of Stefan's sons had made for her. Among them were detailed sketches of the barn where Esther and Idel, Samuel and Avram had lived, including a scale drawing of their house inside the haystack.

"All of Stefan's children were well educated," Esther said, recalling how she had argued with them about the anti-Semitism of the Poles. " 'Why weren't the death camps in any other country but Poland? Why not in Germany—halfway between Holland and Poland?' . . . But they defended Poland."

Esther shook her head in disbelief. "They couldn't see it my way." She paused. "I hope you're not a Polack, are you?"

This time, she really laughed.

Esther said she didn't see Sobibor in 1977 because she became ill while visiting Maidanek, where the barbed-wire fences, watchtowers, and barracks brought back the old feelings of terror. "I got a hundred and two fever," she said. "Next time, I think I'll go to Sobibor first. That may be easier. I feel I should go back again, just as I went back to Poland—to Chelm—my birthplace. I was bitterly disappointed. I knew there was nothing left there for me, but I had to prove it to myself . . . If I see Sobibor, I will not want to go back again. As it is, I still feel there's something I should see."

We talked about the war crimes trials of the Sobibor Nazis. Esther was a witness at each. Hubert Gomerski was the first. He got life in 1948, but in 1978 he asked to be retried on a technicality.

"I saw him walking down the street before the 1978 retrial," Esther recalled. "The old fear came back. I didn't see him as Gomerski, the citizen . . . I saw him as Gomerski, the Gestapo. I was scared stiff. I looked behind me. I was afraid there was another one around to protect him . . . Then I felt anger. 'Look, he's walking down the street and nobody even cares.'"

Gomerski was being retried on yet another technicality in the fall of 1981, and Esther was asked to testify. This time she declined. "What's the use?" she said bitterly.

Erich Bauer was the second Sobibor Nazi to be tried. The German courts had already denazified him; that is, released him, even though they knew he was a Nazi officer, because they had found no evidence of his committing war crimes. The court apparently had not realized that Bauer was the *Badmeister* of Sobibor. Samuel Lerer recognized him later on the street in Kreutzberg, West Germany, and turned him in. Samuel and Esther both testified against Bauer in his 1950 trial in Berlin.

"His wife and daughter said they didn't believe it," Esther recalled. "They said they had never heard about it. But I didn't believe them. I didn't *believe* them. All those suitcases filled with stuff from Sobibor that he brought home every time. They must have asked where he got it all from."

"How did you feel, testifying against Bauer?" I asked. He got life and subsequently died in prison.

"I still felt afraid of him," she said. "Yet I knew he was harmless. 'My God,' I thought to myself. 'This *nothing* had such power?' I also had a sense of revenge.

I knew I was doing something against him. The world would know, and he would be punished."

Twelve more Sobibor Nazis were tried in Hagen, West Germany, in 1965 and 1966, among them Karl Frenzel, Kurt Bolander, Franz Wolf, and Karl Werner Dubois, who had played dead on October 14, 1943, after an escaping Jew had clubbed him. No one seems to know whether SS officers Groth and Poul—both of whom were transferred from Sobibor for raping Jewish women—survived the war or not.

Bolander hanged himself before his sentencing; Frenzel got life, but his sentence was later commuted and he is now free; Wolf got eight years; two Nazis got four years each; two more got three years each; and five others were acquitted for lack of evidence.

Esther was one of the witnesses who got Joseph (the Baker) Kliehr off the hook. She was not unhappy about that. "I don't even know why he was in Sobibor," she told me in defense of Kliehr. "Even the other Nazis picked on him."

She pulled another story from her memory and paused to dust it off. Kliehr was in charge of the barracks where the shoes of the murdered Jews were stored before being sent to Germany for resale, Esther said. He was a soft touch.

"I need some shoes," she told him one day.

"Sit down," he said, waiting on her as if she were his best customer.

"Do you want another pair?" he asked after he had fitted her.

Esther remembers the trial of Karl Frenzel the best. She still can't forget how he killed a baby. "That was the worst thing I saw," she told me. "It just won't leave me."

She described the murder to the court. How she had been working in the Merry Flea when she heard a new transport come in; how she had hidden behind a drape and watched out the window; how she'd seen Frenzel swing a baby by its feet against the boxcar and toss it into the miners' train, as if it were a dead rat.

"You've got to be a *beast!*" she shouted at Frenzel from the witness stand. "There's no word for someone who would do a thing like that."

Frenzel's defense attorney took full advantage of Esther's emotional state. Like a good lawyer, he began to stone her with questions to confuse her and to destroy her credibility. "When did you see it? On which day? At what time? Where did you see it? How far away was it? What color were the drapes? How many centimeters from the window?"

"Listen," Esther interrupted. "I don't have to answer you!"

"Why?" he egged her on.

"It's just one Nazi defending the other."

"How do you know I'm a Nazi?" he asked, hoping to prejudice her testimony.

"If I put an SS hat on you," she said (she was boiling now), "I'm sure I'd recognize that I'd seen you someplace."

Some German university students were observers in the courtroom while Esther sparred with Frenzel's attorney. When she returned to her hotel that evening, she found a card and a bouquet of roses from them. Would she be willing to answer questions in one of their classes?

"They were all so young," Esther recalled. "Afterward, a student came up to me and said, 'My father was a Nazi, but he didn't do anything wrong.' "

"I hate to tell you," she had answered, "but he did."

I didn't have to be very observant to notice how angry and upset Esther was, just talking about the Nazi trials. "Was justice done?" I asked her.

"Not at all," she said without a moment of reflection. "They just took advantage of us witnesses. We didn't keep records at Sobibor. It was our word against theirs. They just tried to confuse the witnesses. I had the feeling that they'd have loved to put *me* on trial.

"It was a joke! They showed no respect. If you met a younger judge, you could expect a little compassion and understanding. I always went by age. If the judge had been a student or judge before the war, I knew he was one of them."

Esther paused, taken aback by the strength of her own emotion. "Now," she said quietly, referring to Sobibor, "it's—nobody saw . . . nobody knew . . . nobody was there."

It would have been hard for me to accept what Esther had just said if I hadn't heard the same things from other survivors who had testified at the Nazi trials—the snickers, the laughter, the disrespect, the anti-Semitism clothed in judges' robes or hiding behind law degrees, the feeling of being on trial oneself, the disbelief at a system that hands out three-, four-, and seven-year sentences for killing Jews like deer out of season.

"I still have the note that came with the flowers," Esther said.

I had forgotten about it. I asked her to get it.

Because of the terrible afternoon [it said], you should have a little pleasure. These flowers are from us.

1988

Valerie Jakober Furth

Valerie Jakober Furth was born in 1926 in the town
of Munkacs in Carpatho-Ruthenia, then part of
Czechoslovakia. She describes her early years as a
protected childhood in a rural and Orthodox Jewish
milieu. When the Nazis occupied Czechoslovakia in
1939, the region where she lived was incorporated
into Hungary. Immediately, her community began
to feel the effects of the anti-Jewish measures already
in place in Hungary. On a personal level, her family
experienced serious economic problems, and Furth's
education was curtailed due to quotas for Jewish
children. More than thirty-six of her family
members were sent to Auschwitz in May 1944. Now
an artist in New York, Furth still feels the influences
of her traumatic experiences during the Holocaust.
She is the author of *Cabbages and Geraniums:
Memories of the Holocaust,* from which the following
recollection is taken.

Nearly forty years after liberation, Furth returned to Auschwitz, where she and her family had
been imprisoned and had suffered. At Auschwitz she
found that she had to confront her painful past again.

This year I returned to Auschwitz. However,
now I stayed only six hours, on a cold and dreary March afternoon. I came with
sixteen other people, including my husband, who were part of a tour sponsored

by the Simon Wiesenthal Center. The tour is a yearly affair, and the center tries on each trip to take at least one survivor of the death camps. Of our group, I was that survivor.

Why had I decided to return? In the months after I finally told the center to include us on the trip, this question flitted in and out of my head. I answered it by saying that my art was at a standstill: on the one hand, when I painted the Holocaust, something was missing. On the other hand, when I tried to escape from my experience, I made pretty pictures. Neither was an acceptable possibility. Perhaps I needed to rekindle my anger at what had happened to me and those I had loved at Auschwitz and the other camps. Lately, I had felt it diminishing, and though in one way this was good, I also felt that there were still too many blanks in my memory. If I were really to come to terms with Auschwitz, then I needed to confront it again.

These were the reasons I gave myself for going in the months before our departure, when I thought at all about what I had embarked on. Most of the time, however, life flowed on comfortably, and what awaited me seemed far away.

On the one-hour bus trip from Cracow to Auschwitz, my feelings changed. I had been asked by Rhonda, the director of the Wiesenthal Center in New York, who accompanied us, to say a few words. Back in the hotel, the speech I had prepared seemed quite satisfactory, but now on the bus I had difficulty speaking because, as we sped through the countryside, pictures of camp life began, like photographs in a darkroom, to enlarge in my mind. And as they succeeded one another in a silent progression, I wanted desperately to feel what I had felt when I first passed through the gates of Auschwitz—as I stood waiting on endless lines to use the latrines, as I lay huddled on my bunk in Barrack C. So, instead of my prepared speech, I said a few words and sat down.

We passed through the gate. Had there been brick buildings in that Auschwitz? All the structures I remembered had been of wood. No, this is not where I had lived and most of my family had died. But there was the crematorium chimney, the look-out towers (but hadn't they been wooden too?), and the barbed wire. Where was I? Meanwhile, the young Polish woman who was our guide had joined us and began talking. She was cool, detached, brisk, and I disliked her immediately. Her voice and manner grated on me. How dare she talk statistics; it was my brother, my nephews, my aunts she was reducing to numbers. (On the night before, I had counted up thirty-six members of my immediate family who had died in the camps.) Impatiently, I broke into the guide's patter.

"Where was C Camp, Barracks 26?" I asked. Her smooth progression interrupted, she became annoyed.

"Camp C was in Birkenau. We'll go there after the museum."

Two other groups were in the dark cool museum with us: a crowd of German tourists and some Hasidim from Israel. A map showed three camps. It was then I recalled that where we had just entered was not the place where I and my family had arrived. The site of the museum had originally housed political prisoners. Until this moment, I had never realized that Camp C, Barracks 26 had been a part of Birkenau.

I asked our guide where the kitchen was on the map. She showed it to me. When I said that I would like to see it, she answered that we would go there after the museum. I had seen many of the pictures on the walls of the museum, but was unprepared for the rush of emotion I felt on looking at the glass cases filled with human hair, toothbrushes, shoes, and suitcases of the camp's inmates. My Aunt Ida's hair, my cousin Nellie's toothbrush, the hiking shoes I had worn at arrival, the backpack my mother carried with her to camp . . . . Were they somewhere in these desolate piles of human debris?

Our last stop in the museum was the small room of eternal light. As I knelt down and lit candles, their flames came up and with them, my life in the Auschwitz inferno rose up too, the flames licking but not burning the images of lost ones from my mind. I felt my husband's hand on my shoulder. Deeply affected, he too was mourning the death of loved ones—the father and stepmother who had vanished in the Nazi night.

After the museum, we got on the bus for our ride to Birkenau. Once again, we entered through an iron gate, but this time I knew where I was. A field, wooden barracks, a brick chimney told me that, after nearly forty years, I had found the way back to my Auschwitz.

Again, I asked the guide, "Where is the kitchen? Where is Camp C?"

She replied that nothing remained of Camp C except some brick chimneys.

"Can we go there anyway?"

"Impossible, the gates are locked. We can, however, see the ruins of the crematorium."

Nothing to be done. As we approached the ruins, the forest, used by the Nazis as a holding place when the crematorium was too full, loomed menacingly. Nearby, I glimpsed a lake, the same lake into which the ashes of the dead had been dumped. But it was Camp C, not them, that holds my attention. I try to zoom in on it with my cam camera.

"Can we go to the barracks in Camp A?" I ask, already anticipating the No that is the answer.

"We don't have time," the guide says. But, after I tell Rhonda I am not leaving until we stand on that ground, and she had a whispered conversation with the guide, it is decided that we will see the barracks after all.

It is not Barracks 26, Camp C, but all the barracks were identical in their arrangement and structure, so I will have to be content, and as I stand on the barracks floor, for the first time since we arrived I am no longer a tourist. I am cold and hungry; my mother is talking to me with a worried look on her face about food, recipes. She is praying, she is crying, "Where are my sisters, my brothers?" Beside her, I am vowing, "I won't die, and I won't let her die."

I came back to reality. Now I know why I have returned to Auschwitz: to make sure that what happened to me forty years ago was not a dream, to renew the pledge I made in my art: to grip those who see my work so that they will remember what happened to us and never let it happen again. I look around me at the wooden slats that once held my shivering body. I am ready to leave.

But that night in the hotel room, my head spins with images. One that recurs is of the ditch where I used to get water to wash after it had rained. There had been a rag. How had I ever acquired it? My possessions had been reduced to zero. This small rag was half the size of a handkerchief. I had used it as my washcloth, towel and pillow case.

Theresienstadt, which we visited three days later, looked civil in contrast to Auschwitz. The sky was blue, and we had a new guide—a middle-aged Czech with a human face. Though we were never shown the part of the camp where the Jews were housed, I was not so angry as I had been with the Polish accountant. By the fake cemetery which the Nazis had built to hide the fact that no bodies slept underneath the headstones—for all that remained of these dead were their ashes—we read aloud poems written by the children of Theresienstadt. In this peaceful setting of death, their clear voices, alive to the world's beauty, were unbearably moving.

It is almost a month since I have returned home. Since then, I have wakened each morning with a great heaviness in my body. One day I identify this feeling: It is how I used to feel lying pressed against my mother on the wooden slats that were our beds in Auschwitz.

I have returned home. Patiently, I wait to see how my art will contain the answers to the questions that set me forth on this painful journey back.

Babi Yar

Yevgeny Yevtushenko

Yevgeny Yevtushenko was born July 18, 1933, in Zima, Russia, a fourth-generation Ukrainian exiled in Siberia. He became a major figure for post-Stalinist writers with his campaigns for greater artistic freedom and for the removal of politics from the arts. His publications include *Early Poems*, *Wild Berries*, and *Collected Poems*.

A ravine on the outskirts of Kiev, Babi Yar was the site of the Nazi massacre of over thirty thousand Russian Jews on September 29–30, 1941. Over the next few months, more Jews, along with Gypsies and Russian POWs, were executed, raising the death toll to close to a hundred thousand people.

There are no monuments on Babi Yar,
A steep ravine is all, a rough memorial.
Fear is my ground—
Old as the Jewish people, a Jew myself it
    seems,
I roam in Egypt in her ancient days,
I perish on the cross, and even now
I bear the red marks of nails.

I am Dreyfus, detested, denounced,
Snared behind prison bars:
Pettiness
Is my betrayer and my judge.
Shrieking ladies in fine ruffled gowns
Brandish their umbrellas in my face.

And now a boy in Bielostok,
I seem to see blood spurt and spread over
    the floor.
The tavern masters celebrate:
Under the smell of vodka and of onions
And of blood.
Kicked by their heavy boots I lie
Begging in vain for pity.
The rampant pogrom roars
"Murder the Jews! Save Russia!"
A man is beating up my mother.

Anne Frank, I am she,
A translucent twig of April
And I am filled with love that needs no
    words.
We are forbidden the sky and the green
    leaves
But in this dark room we can embrace.

Love, do not fear the noise—it is the
  rushing
Of spring itself.
Come, let us kiss . . .
The sounds of thawing ice change to
  pounding on the door.

Wild grasses rustle over Babi Yar,
The trees stare down, stern as my judge,
Silent the air howls.
I bare my head, graying now,
And I am myself an endless soundless howl
Over the buried
Thousands and thousands of thousands,
And I am every old man shot down here
And every child.
In no limb of my body can I forget.

O Russian people,
I know your heart
Lives without bounds
But often men
With dirty hands abuse
The body of your clear name.
Shamelessly,
Without the quiver of a nerve
These pompous anti-Semites call
  themselves
"The union of the Russian people."

Let the Internationale
Be sung
When the last reviler of the Jews is dead.
No Jewish blood is mixed in mine, but let
  me be a Jew
For all anti-Semites to hate, to spit upon.
Only then can I call myself
Russian.

Dedication

Czeslaw Milosz

Czeslaw Milosz, a
naturalized United States
citizen, was born on June
30, 1911, in Szetejnie,
Lithuania. During the
war, he worked as a
literary programmer for
Polish Radio, first in
Wilno and later in
Warsaw. He also was
involved in resistance
activities and in writing,
editing, and translating
anti-Nazi literature. The
best known of these
works was *The Invincible
Song*, an anti-Nazi
anthology. He is the 1980
recipient of the Nobel
Prize for Literature, a
tribute to the entire body
of his literary work. His
publications include
Selected Poems, from
which the accompanying
poem is taken.
  "Dedication" pays
tribute to those who
perished in the
Holocaust.

You whom I could not save
Listen to me.
Try to understand this simple speech as I
  would be ashamed of another.
I swear, there is in me no wizardry of words.
I speak to you with silence like a cloud or a
  tree.

What strengthened me, for you was lethal.
You mixed up farewell to an epoch with the
  beginning of a new one,
Inspiration of hatred with lyrical beauty,
Blind force with accomplished shape.

Here is the valley of shallow Polish rivers. And
  an immense bridge
Going into white fog. Here is a broken city,
And the wind throws screams of gulls on your
  grave
When I am talking with you.

What is poetry which does not save
Nations or people?
A connivance with official lies,
A song of drunkards whose throats will be cut
  in a moment,
Readings for sophomore girls.
That I wanted good poetry without knowing
  it,
That I discovered, late, its salutary aim,
In this and only this I find salvation.

They used to pour on graves millet or poppy
  seeds
To feed the dead who would come disguised
  as birds.

I put this book here for you, who once lived
So that you should visit us no more.

A Shayna Maidel (Act 2, Scene 3)

Barbara Lebow

Barbara Lebow is a prominent American playwright
and director. She has been associated with the
Academy Theater since 1965, when her first play was
produced there. She is currently the Academy's
playwright-in-residence and director of the human
service program. Lebow's plays include *The
Adventures of Homer McGrundy, Cyparis, The Keepers,
Trains,* and *Tiny Tim Is Dead.* The recipient of
numerous awards, Lebow is best known for *A
Shayna Maidel,* which has been staged worldwide
and was produced as a Hallmark Hall of Fame
presentation for television.

   A Shayna Maidel tells the story of Rose Weiss,
who, with her father, Mordechai, escaped from
Poland to New York as a small child, leaving behind
her mother and an older sister, Lusia. Rose grows up
as a typical American child. When Lusia is liberated
and joins Rose and Mordechai in New York in 1946,
the stark contrast between the sisters' lives brings
into focus the difficult task that many survivors
faced—that of rebuilding a devastated life. In this
excerpt, we see Rose, Lusia, and Mordechai
chronicling and mourning their losses, coping with
the guilt of surviving, and learning to live as a family
again. As this scene begins, Lusia is busily cleaning
Rose's apartment.

ROSE.   I wish you'd stop, Lusia, and take it easy. It doesn't need to be *that* clean.

LUSIA.   I like to.

ROSE.   I've never heard of anyone cleaning that way. I'm sure no one's ever done it in here before.

LUSIA.   That's how come I . . . achoom?

ROSE.   (*As she disappears into kitchen.*) Sneeze.

LUSIA.   Sneeze. First time I use that word. Sneeze. For something to be too much clean is impossible. Anyway, if I live here, I do something to help.

ROSE.   (*Coming into living room with dusting cloth.*) But you could stop for a little while and rest. If you will, I will, OK? You could get in the bathtub and soak all day. Go on. I know how you love that bubble bath. Sometimes I think you'll never come out.

LUSIA.   I'm sorry. I'll try to be more faster.

ROSE.   That's not what I meant. You can stay in as long as you like. Only I don't think you should always be working. Half the day at the immigrant office and here the rest of the time. You won't even come to the movies anymore. You deserve some peace. Outside of the bath.

LUSIA.   (*A bit huffy.*) Peace I'll get when this all cleaned up. OK? (*Rose shrugs, goes back to her dusting and polishing with added energy. Lusia and Rose are both working furiously. Each begins singing to herself, Rose a popular song, Lusia a song in Yiddish, softly, not really aware that she is singing. It is the same song she hummed earlier to drown out Hanna. Rose, however, is aware of Lusia's song and listens to it as she continues her work. Then she is still, just watching her sister.*)

ROSE.   That's pretty. (*Lusia stops singing, keeps working.*) No, don't stop. That sounded so nice. It reminds me of something. Lusia, it's one of those times I told you about. Did my—our—mother used to sing that song?

LUSIA.   That song, no. But sing, yes, always when she's working in the house or cooking or sewing something. But not too good, same like me. Maybe this is what reminds you.

ROSE.   No, you have a sweet voice. Sing some more. Teach me. I'd like to learn it. (*Pause.*)

LUSIA.   This song is from the camps.

ROSE.   (*Quickly.*) Oh, I'm sorry. (*She turns away.*)

LUSIA.   (*Watching Rose.*) Rayzel. Rose. It don't matter. Is a good song. Happy. About how the world will be after war is over. Was a song then about future, yes? So now is a song about now. I teach you it. Come. (*Rose sits beside Lusia on the floor. Lusia sings, as a teacher.*)
O, di velt vet verren shayna.
libe greser, sine klayna
You know what this means?

ROSE.   Some of it. Not every word.

LUSIA.   It says the world will be beautiful. Love will get more and hate . . . *(She gestures.)*

ROSE.   Less.

LUSIA.   Less. And that's for everybody. Between women and between men and between one country and the other country. *(Lusia begins the song again. Rose joins in tentatively for the first two lines. When the verse is repeated she joins in again, singing more strongly.)*

LUSIA and ROSE.   *(Singing.)*

> *O, di velt vet verren shayna,*
> *libe greser, sine klayna*
> *tvishn froyen, tvishn mener,*
> *tvishn land un land.*

> *O, di velt vet verren shayna,*
> *(Lusia is singing more strongly, forgetting Rose.)*

> *libe greser, sine klayna*
> *tvishn froyen, tvishn mener,*
> *(Rose, watching Lusia, fades out and Lusia finishes alone.)*

> *tvishn land un land.*
> *(Pause.)*

LUSIA.   Enough for now. Is a longer song. Too much. Enough. Hanna used to sing with me.

ROSE.   Is she a friend of yours? *(Lusia nods, returns to her energetic cleaning.)* From the war?

LUSIA.   And from before. From children together.

ROSE.   *(Treading carefully.)* Was she liberated with you? *(Lusia nods. Rose is relieved.)* You came through it all together?

LUSIA.   Is why I live now. And Duvid.

ROSE.   Well, where is she? We could bring her here, you know. You don't only have to be a family to sponsor someone. If the two of you went through it together and came out of it together . . .

LUSIA.   Hanna was too sick. Tee . . . ty-phus, you know. She was all . . . nothing left of her. I say when I really look for first time in hospital, "But Hanna, we is bones, both of us, nothing but bones. We never be womens again." She say old saying, like Mama. Too sick hardly to talk, she says, "*Bainer on flaish iz do; flaish on bainer iz nito!*" *(She laughs.)* Farshtaist?

ROSE.   I think so.

LUSIA. "Bones without meat you can have; meat without bones, is impossible." This way she makes jokes and was living only one more day. *(Rose turns away and goes off into kitchen.)* But she was free. And clean. And was thinking things for the future. *(Lusia goes back to her brushing. Rose returns shortly, with a full picnic basket.)*

ROSE. I know I can't get you to leave that spot, so I brought a picnic. *(Rose unwraps chicken legs, bread and cheese, etc. laying them on the cloth on the floor near Lusia.)*

LUSIA. For this I can stop.

ROSE. Your appetite is improving.

LUSIA. Mine sister is a good cook. An expert. *(Lusia and Rose eat heartily. Rose takes chocolate milk from basket and gives it to Lusia.)*

ROSE. With chocolate?

LUSIA. With chocolate. *(Enjoys drinking some.)* This chocolate in the milk you learn from your *Tanta* Perla, no?

ROSE. She used to do anything to get me to drink milk. Because she thought she should.

LUSIA. She seems like kind woman when I meet her. Like bird, like you say, but with hurt foot, hop . . . ? *(Rose nods.)* . . . hopping to get seeds, to get a warm.

ROSE. Worm.

LUSIA. Worm. Warm. Worm. *(She considers.)* To get a worm to sing little bird song about bird troubles.

ROSE. You know her perfectly! That's just what she's like. More a sparrow than a hen. *Tanta* Perla could not hatch an egg.

LUSIA. In my house, your house, too, in Chernov, before the war, for long time we got chickens. Many. Eggs every day and some extra makes for more chickens for soup Mama makes delicious. In Brooklyn I see no one got chickens and much . . . hard where you walk, how you say this?

ROSE. Pavement. Sidewalks.

LUSIA. Much pavement sidewalks not good for to grow trees with fruit. We have in the summer baby apples.

ROSE. Crab apples.

LUSIA. And *barnes* . . . pears. Mama can make grow anything and then make for bread jelly, jam, all good, for whole year.

ROSE. That's something I never tasted homemade.

LUSIA. This we have even when trouble begins because is right by house. Until all Jewish got to move to one place. But before—how you say— married, . . . still childrens, me and Duvid, only fifteen, sixteen, we take— steal—from Mama the jam and bread and have . . . like this . . .

ROSE. A picnic.

LUSIA.   By the river in woods. We feel so bad, like thief, so have to eat up all
this jam, the whole bottle, with a spoon—

ROSE.   To hide the evidence!

LUSIA.   And is best pic-nic I ever have. *(Pause.)* Rayzel, yesterday in the
morning a man came into immigrant office. Is very thin, much more than
me. And teeth black and poor clothes, much worser than mine. He has list,
he says, lots of names what happened last six years Poland, even from
beginning of war, like time when Duvid been arrested. He kept list secret in
camps and copied very neat, many pages, who died, who lived, who
escaped, how, where. Of course, this I want to see right away. The man says
no, will not give list to nobody. Only will sell. For money.

ROSE.   How awful!

LUSIA.   No. He needs money for food, clothes, to live. This list is his work,
his talent. He's not a bad man.

ROSE.   Well, what happened? What did you do?

LUSIA.   I can do nothing. I send him to a man more important. Today I'll
see what happens. I think maybe Duvid is on this list.

ROSE.   What makes you think so?

LUSIA.   Is time for Duvid. Is already—*(The doorbell rings. Again. Then
pounding on the door. Rose jumps up in panic.)*

ROSE.   It's Papa! What's he doing here now? In the middle of the day! *(She
calls.)* Papa? *(Rose is answered by more pounding. Tossing the cheese to Lusia.)*
The cheese. Hide the cheese! I'm supposed to keep kosher . . . Coming,
Papa! *(Lusia starts to run off with the cheese as the pounding continues. She runs
back; very serious.)*

LUSIA.   But, Rayzel, is a sin to lie to a papa, no? *(Rose freezes, stares helplessly
at Lusia. Suddenly.)* Di milch! *(Rose and Lusia are both frantic, grabbing the milk
and other offending items. At the same time, they are beginning to laugh very hard.
When Lusia is safely in the kitchen, and the remnants of the picnic are looking
kosher on the floor, Rose goes to open the door. Mordechai enters behind her, wearing
a hat but no scarf. It's a warm spring day. He carries a shoebox tied with a string.)*

MORDECHAI.   It's nice. I got nothing better to do all day than to knock on
a door. *(Lusia returns from kitchen. Both she and Rose are working to control their
laughter. Seeing the picnic.)* What goes on here?

ROSE.   A . . . picnic, Papa.

LUSIA.   Rayzel just cleaned up the table so we been eating on the floor.

MORDECHAI.   So, if I sweep the floor, maybe you'll eat on the table! *(This
is too much. Rose and Lusia burst out laughing, holding onto each other to keep
from falling. Mordechai is amazed at the success of his joke.)* Is good *shvesters*
should laugh together. *(Rose and Lusia recover, aware for a moment of their
physical closeness.)*

ROSE.   I'm sorry, Papa. You want something? A drink, maybe? I've got some delicious chicken.

MORDECHAI.   *(Putting down his hat and cane in the dinette.)* No, no. I got all I need. I want you two should clean up your picnic and come sit down. I'm on important business. *(During the next several lines of dialogue Rose and Lusia pick up and put away the picnic and cleaning things. Mordechai is arranging chairs around the dinette table.)*

ROSE.   How come you left the store? You really surprised us.

MORDECHAI.   Today they're doing inventory. For this, I can leave. For this, Greenspan can manage alone. He can count. He can write down numbers in a book. Especially when I got something more important.

ROSE.   Does it have to do with that box? A surprise, maybe?

MORDECHAI.   That's it. Exactly.

ROSE.   Lusia, you see what your being here has done? Everything's topsy-turvy. Surprises in the middle of the week, yet. Papa taking off early. Amazing!

MORDECHAI.   Enough, already. Sit. Both. *(Rose and Lusia sit. Mordechai, still standing, holds the box.)* This box is the most important thing in the world. In the universe, even, for us. In here is your family, your history, who and where you're coming from. It's proof who you are. *(He puts the box on the table.)* It's proof of people we'll never see no more, parts of them alive still, in you. And better yet, in your children, with God's help. Old pictures I had *fun* mine parents, *fun* aunts and uncles. Some I stopped showing you when you was little, Rayzel, always making you cry too much for your mother, may she rest in peace, or for Lushke, as you used to say.

ROSE.   I don't remember that!

MORDECHAI.   These I showed you again later when they was the same to you like pictures in your schoolbooks and they didn't make you cry no more.

ROSE.   They were just faces. You *were*, Lusia, far away and different.

MORDECHAI.   All these I got. I want Lusia and you should look at them together, remember together. Maybe like that it would mean more. All names and what year, what place, is written on the back. Anything you want to know you write down on a piece paper so you don't forget and next time I'll tell you what's what.

ROSE.   We will, Papa.

MORDECHAI.   Lusia? *(Lusia nods. Pause as Mordechai sits between his daughters. He includes Lusia, but is primarily speaking to Rose, presenting something to her.)* Some months ago came to see me a Polish woman. Nobility. A countess, a friend *fun* your mother—an employer—who your mother made beautiful dresses by hand and she, your mother, would give this rich woman sometimes a present, baked goods or fruit from her garden. *(Lusia looks stricken, turns away.)* This countess, of course, is not a Jew, but, still, a good woman. She came in person. She wouldn't take a chance to send something what it might get lost. In person, only, she wants to see me.

MAMA'S VOICE.   *Ich blayb mit mayn kind . . . (Lusia pulls further away from the others. Mama enters the bedroom area slowly, as Mordechai speaks. She is older, in her late 40's, moving around in the outer edges of the space. She carries a knapsack. Her head is covered by a scarf.)*

MORDECHAI.   She never sat down, didn't take off her coat or take a glass tea. But she gave me a bundle *fun* your mother. *(Rose reaches for the box.)* Wait. *(Mordechai unties the package very slowly. Rose's attention is on the package, too. Unheard by the others, Lusia suddenly gets up, comes forward, paces as she talks to Mama, apart from her.)*

LUSIA.   Mama! *Farvos bistu nit gegangen?* I told you to go!

MAMA.   It was impossible.

LUSIA.   But you would be here now! You'd be here with me and Rayzel and Papa. I told you to go! If only—

MAMA.   If your grandma had a beard, she'd be your grandpa . . .

LUSIA.   Don't do that. It's not funny. Don't be so stubborn!

MORDECHAI.   Come, Lusia, sit. Stop pacing. It makes me so I can't think. *(Mama is signalling Lusia to hush. Lusia sits. Mordechai has the package opened. He puts the box aside and removes a smaller bundle wrapped in a head scarf identical to the one Mama is wearing. Lusia is frozen by it. The Voices begin quietly. Gently beginning to open the bundle.)* This is exactly how she gave it to me. I put it back the same so you could see. She didn't touch it from the way your mother first put it. *(Mama is sitting on the bed. In the dim, cold light, she opens the knapsack and removes an old candlestick, which she holds, barely moving.)* It was many years since I heard anything from *mine* wife. The first thing I found, in here, like this, was a letter for me. It was from over three years before. When I read it the worst already happened, but I didn't know yet. The countess carried this around the world until she came to America. Even if not Jewish, they knew to run from Hitler. Anyway, this from your mother she carried like a holy package, I couldn't believe it. The next is some pictures you never seen of your sister here when she graduated school and this is a wedding . . . *(Mordechai is passing the pictures to Rose, intending her to hand them on to Lusia. Lusia turns away, slowly gets up.)*

ROSE.   Papa, can't we look at these later? I think it's hard for her. It's much too painful. *(Lusia is on her way to the bedroom. Voices fade.)*

MORDECHAI.   *(Touching his head.)* All these pictures she's got here inside, already. This paper don't make the pain, believe me. *(Rose starts to follow*

Lusia. Mordechai holds her back. They continue to look quietly at photos while the scene in the bedroom continues. The lighting emphasis changes.)

LUSIA.   Mama, you've got to go with her and get out of this horrible place!

MAMA.   *(Repacking knapsack.)* Don't argue.

LUSIA.   But she wants to protect you, to take a chance herself because she thinks so much of you.

MAMA.   She's a wonderful woman.

LUSIA.   Then go!

MAMA.   All right. She said they have room for one more. You. But not the baby. Not Sprinze. You want to come, too?

LUSIA.   How dare you! Don't be crazy, Mama!

MAMA.   You stay with your child, I stay with my child.

LUSIA.   But this is different. I'm not helpless like the baby. You have another daughter, too. You could be with Rayzel again. Finally. Mama. And Papa.

MAMA.   When you have a grandchild, you have two children. Here where I am, I have two. There, where I may never arrive, is one I lost long ago. I won't take the chance of losing more.

LUSIA.   But, Mama, then you had no choice. This time you do.

MAMA.   It only looks like a choice. If God wanted us to be in America, you never would have caught scarlet fever. Your father would not have had such business troubles—

LUSIA.   I'll never agree with you, never! About God.

MAMA.   God doesn't care if you agree or not. He does what He does. God doesn't argue and God doesn't change His mind. Besides, maybe where they're sending us this time will be an improvement. In the country somewhere. At least not a ghetto. Trees, maybe, some flowers—

LUSIA.   Mama, listen. Please! Anything the Nazis do will only be worse, never better. You go with the countess. I'm young. I'll do all right. I have the medicine for Sprinze. It puts her to sleep for two days so she won't cry. I'll carry her in my knapsack. Others have done it. They won't even know I have a baby.

MAMA.   I stay with my child. *(She kisses Lusia on the forehead.)* . . . *Ich blayb mit mayn kind.*

ROSE.   *(Standing and moving towards Lusia as lights return to normal in dinette and fade in bedroom.)* Lusia, look! *(Lusia, returning to reality, leaves the bedroom and meets Rose, who is holding a small silver spoon with a sealed letter and a scarf. Mama exits.)* Papa says this is my baby spoon! I used to eat with it. *(Lusia takes the spoon.)*

LUSIA.   Sometimes I feed you with this.

ROSE.   And a letter for me, from Mama! *(Rose is holding the letter out to Lusia. Lusia takes it hands it back, with the spoon. She goes directly, angrily, to Mordechai.)*

LUSIA.   How long ago this countess visits?

MORDECHAI.   November, December, maybe.

LUSIA.   Mama sends these things for Rayzel. Why you don't give them before?

MORDECHAI.   Until I knew for certain—

LUSIA.   And now you already know for a long time!

MORDECHAI.   I was hoping we should all be a family again—

LUSIA.   *(Overlapping.)* Is no more hoping! Mama's dead! We was supposed to come here! Was your promise. I want Rayzel should know this. *(To Rose.)* Mama was all ready we should come here when he sends a letter about the bad money times, saying we should wait. So we wait. Then comes a letter from your *Tanta* Perla. She's asking us why Papa won't take no money. Some group in Brooklyn is giving him the money so we could come and he should pay it back later. But Papa says no. He won't take from no one.

MORDECHAI.   This you should understand. *(Pounding the table.)* Not to owe nothing! *(He rises.)*

ROSE.   But, Papa!

MORDECHAI.   What? I knew was coming the Depression? I knew the doors would be closed here? I had a crystal ball showed ten years ahead to Hitler? *(Pause.)* Every penny I made since went to bring them over myself! *(Rose is looking hard at Mordechai.)*

LUSIA.   Then it don't matter no more. Is too late. *(To Mordechai.)* And now you don't want even to read to her what Mama is saying. Now you don't want even to touch something of Mama's. From shame. From shame!

MORDECHAI.   *(Calmly, quietly.)* Rayzel, who you want should read your Mama's letter, me or your sister? Say only the truth. *(Rose holds out the letter to Lusia.)* It should be better a woman. *Tanta* Perla, maybe. *(Rose holds the letter out again. Lusia takes it, holding it away from herself. She moves slowly into the living room and sits down. Mordechai gets up, goes to get his hat and cane.)* Lusia, read the letter for your sister. I'll wait for you downstairs. When you're finished, you come. I got some new places we should leave word about your husband. *(Mordechai is almost out the door, remembers something. He comes back and removes a photograph from his vest pocket, shows it to Lusia and then Rose. Lusia closes her eyes.)*

ROSE.   A pretty girl.

MORDECHAI.   Age sixteen only.

ROSE.   It's Mama, isn't it?

MORDECHAI.   *(He nods.)* A shayna maidel. *(Mordechai puts the photo back into his pocket and leaves.)*

ROSE.   *(After a moment, amazed, as she sits.)* He must keep that picture with him all the time.

LUSIA.   *(Thrusting envelope out to Rose.)* You open, please. Is your letter. *(Rose opens the envelope carefully.)*

ROSE.   It's very fresh. Like it was just written.

LUSIA.   Mama keeps the paper, I think, for long time before she sends this letter. Was all ready for when someone comes like countess. I never seen her write nothing. *(Rose hands the open letter to Lusia, who hesitates, then smells the scent of the letter. Lusia can hardly speak.)* Is Mama. Before . . . *(She tries to give the letter back to Rose.)* Ich ken nit . . . Ken nit! *(Rose keeps looking at her, waiting. Lusia breathes deeply, composes herself, then slowly sits apart from Rose, begins shakily, relaxes more as she feels and enjoys her recognition of Mama in the words. As she continues Rose stiffens, reacting almost politely, as someone at a tea party. There are no tears.)* Mayn tyereh tuchter, Rayzel . . .

Mine dearest daughter, Rayzel,

I'm not a learned woman. I wish I could be so I could say everything to you the right way. For a long time I have written and I know it could happen you don't get the letters. This one is meant by God's will to reach you. Maybe it is the last one for a time so I want to tell you everything how I feel.

If I could really be with you and put around you mine arms, it would be much better, but that is impossible. It cannot be. If I cannot hold you in mine arms, I hold you anyway in mine heart and this is true for every day in your life since you was born, if you was in Chernov, Poland, or Brooklyn, New York, America.

I want you should have your baby spoon. Your favorite, just your size and you could first feed yourself with it. Every day since you and Papa went away, I keep it in a pocket with me, to touch what you touch. I knew I would give it back to you before you were five years old and now look what happened! Well, who are we to question the plan from God? Now when you have this baby spoon, you must get a feeling from your mother. Sometime you will have a child to use it, too, and she will feel from her grandmother. Or, who knows, maybe the family will be together by then.

You would think I would have more to tell you besides this baby spoon; advice and so forth, but I can't think of anything more important right now. You can't put life on a piece paper. Or love. I am not a smart person with writing down words, but I wish you understand how I am feeling for you, mine pretty little girl.

Your only mother,
Liba Eisenman Weiss
Chernov, Poland, June four, nineteen hundred and forty-two.

(Lusia and Rose sit silently for awhile, then Lusia puts the letter back in the envelope, kisses it, and gives it to Rose.)

ROSE.   Thank you, Lusia. *(Silence again for a time, then Lusia stands up.)*

LUSIA.   Papa's waiting. *(Rose nods. Lusia gets her pocketbook. Rose gives her the scarf in which everything was wrapped. Lusia leans over and kisses Rose on the forehead. Lusia exits. Rose opens the letter again, tries to drink in the scent. Rose clasps the letter and the spoon, which she is still holding, to herself. She sounds at first like the child's voice she heard earlier.)*

ROSE.   Mama. Mama! *(Now the sound that comes from her is a chant, an intoning that is trying to make something happen. Each repetition becomes more intense, almost angry.)*

Mamamamamamamamamama.

Mamamamamamamamamama.

Mamamamamamamamamama!

(The Voices are emerging out of Rose's call. She moves into the bedroom. She puts down the letter and spoon. The Voices are continuous. She gets the pen from the night table. Slowly and deliberately, as if she is carving, she draws a number on her left forearm and stares at it. The sound of the Voices is a comfort to her. As it becomes Mama's lullabye, she sits on the bed, arms outstretched, welcoming it. She embraces the sound and herself, as the lights dim. Slowly, she curls up on the bed as the Voices fade.)

Acknowledgments

Adler, David A.: From *We Remember the Holocaust* by David A. Adler. Copyright © 1989 by David A. Adler. Reprinted by permission of Henry Holt and Co. Inc.

Anielewicz, Mordecai: "The Last Letter from Mordecai Anielewicz" in *Documents on the Holocaust, Selected Sources on the Destruction of the Jews of Germany and Austria, Poland, and the Soviet Union.* Edited by Yitzhak Arad, Yisrael Gutman, and Abraham Margaliot. Jerusalem, Yad Vashem, 1981. Reprinted by permission.

Block, Gay and Malka Drucker: "Arie van Mansum" from *Rescuers: Portraits of Moral Courage in the Holocaust* by Gay Block and Malka Drucker (New York: Holmes & Meier, 1992). Copyright © 1992 by Gay Block and Malka Drucker. Reproduced by permission of the publisher.

Borenstein, Emily: "I Must Tell the Story" by Emily Borenstein, as appeared in *Blood to Remember*, edited by Charles Fishman, 1991. By permission of the author.

Borowski, Tadeusz: "Silence" and "This Way for the Gas, Ladies and Gentlemen / 9-29," from *This Way for the Gas, Ladies and Gentlemen* by Tadeusz Borowski, translated by Barbara Vedder, Translation copyright © 1967 by Penguin Books Ltd. Original text copyright © 1959 by Maria Borowski. Used by permission of Viking Penguin, a division of Penguin Books USA Inc. and Penguin Books Ltd.

Brecher, Elinor: "Introduction," from *Schindler's Legacy* by Elinor Brecher. Copyright © 1994 by Elinor Brecher. Used by permission of Dutton Signet, a division of Penguin Books USA Inc.

Brecht, Bertolt: "I, the Survivor" by Bertolt Brecht (translated by John Willet) from *Holocaust Poetry* by Hilda Schiff. Copyright © 1995 by Hilda Schiff. Reprinted by permission of St. Martin's Press.

Bush, Lawrence: From *Rooftop Secrets and Other Stories of Anti-Semitism* by Lawrence Bush. Copyright © 1986 by the Union of American Hebrew Congregations. Reprinted by permission.

Cohen, Helen Degan: "In Hiding" by Helen Degan Cohen from *Blood to Remember*, edited by Charles Fishman, 1991. Reprinted by permission of the author.

Dambroff, Susan: "There Were Those," from *Memory in Bone*, Susan Dambroff, Black Oyster Press, 1984. Reprinted by permission of the author.

Delbo, Charlotte: From *Days and Memory* by Charlotte Delbo, translated by Rosette Lamont, Marlboro Press, 1990. By permission of Northwestern University Press, Evanston, IL.

Delbo, Charlotte: "Street for Arrivals, Street for Departures" by Charlotte Delbo from *None of Us Will Return.* Copyright © 1965 by Editions Gonthier. Reprinted by permission of Georges Borchardt, Inc.

Dwork, Deborah: From *Children with a Star* by Deborah Dwork. Copyright © 1991 by Deborah Dwork. Reprinted by permission of Yale University Press.

Edelstein, Dov Beril: From *Worlds Torn Asunder* by Dov Beril Edelstein. Copyright © 1985 Dov Beril Edelstein. Reprinted by permission of KTAV Publishing House, Inc.

Eichengreen, Lucille: From "Displaced Persons' Camp" from *Ashes to Life* © 1994 by Lucille Eichengreen. Published by Mercury House, San Francisco, CA, and reprinted by permission.

Eichengreen, Lucille: From "Liberation" from *Ashes to Life* © 1994 by Lucille Eichengreen. Published by Mercury House, San Francisco, CA, and reprinted by permission.

Eliach, Yaffa: "Jews, Go Back to the Grave!," "Stars," and "The Mosaic Artist's Apprentice" from *Hasidic Tales of the Holocaust* by Yaffa Eliach. Copyright © 1982 by Yaffa Eliach. Reprinted by permission of Oxford University Press, Inc.

Epstein, Helen: From *Children of the Holocaust* by Helen Epstein. Copyright © 1979 by Helen Epstein. Reprinted by permission of Curtis Brown Ltd.

Ficowski, Jerzy: "A Girl of Six From The Ghetto Begging in Smolna Street in 1942" by Jerzy Ficowski (translated by Keith Bosley) from *Holocaust Poetry* by Hilda Schiff. Copyright © 1995 by Hilda Schiff. Reprinted by permission of St. Martin's Press.

Fink, Ida: From *A Scrap of Time and Other Stories* by Ida Fink. Translation copyright © 1987 by Random House, Inc. Reprinted by permission of Pantheon Books, a Division of Random House, Inc.

Fishman, Charles: "September 1944" is reprinted with the permission of Charles Fishman from *The Death Mazurka* (Texas Tech University Press, 1989). Copyright 1987 Charles Fishman.

Frankl, Viktor E.: From *Man's Search for Meaning* by Viktor E. Frankl. Copyright © 1959, 1962, 1984, 1992 by Viktor E. Frankl. Reprinted by permission of Beacon Press.

Friedman, Ina R.: Excerpts from *The Other Victims* by Ina R. Friedman. Copyright © 1990 by Ina R. Friedman. Reprinted by permission of Houghton Mifflin Company. All rights reserved.

Furth, Valerie Jakober: From *Cabbages & Geraniums* by Valerie Furth. Copyright © 1989 by Columbia University Press. Reprinted with permission of the publisher.

Gershon, Karen: From *We Came as Children: A Collective Autobiography* by Karen Gershon, Harcourt Brace, 1966. Reprinted by permission.

Glik, Hirsh: "Silence, and a Starry Night" originally titled "Partizaner Lid." from *A Treasury of Jewish Folksong* by Ruth Rubin. Copyright © 1950 by Schocken Books, Inc. Copyright renewed 1978 by Ruth Rubin. Reprinted by permission of Schocken Books, published by Pantheon Books, a division of Random House, Inc.

Gordon, Harry: Reprinted from Harry Gordon, *The Shadow of Death*. Copyright © 1992 by the University Press of Kentucky. By permission of the publishers.

Gotfryd, Bernard: Reprinted with the permission of Pocket Books, a Division of Simon & Schuster from *Anton the Dove Fancier* by Bernard Gotfryd. Copyright © 1990 by Bernard Gotfryd.

Gross, Leonard: Reprinted with permission of Simon & Schuster from *The Last Jews in Berlin* by Leonard Gross. Copyright © 1982 by Magilla, Inc.

Gurdus, Luba Krugman: "What Happened That Day" by Luba Krugman Gurdus, from *Painful Echoes: Poems of the Holocaust*. Reprinted by permission of the United States Holocaust Memorial Museum.

Hachenburg, Hanus: "Terezin" by Hanus Hachenburg in *I Never Saw Another Butterfly*. Reprinted by permission of the Jewish Museum in Prague.

Hallie, Philip: Excerpt from "Burned Shoes and the Quakers" from *Lest Innocent Blood Be Shed* by Philip Hallie. Copyright © 1979 by Philip Hallie. Reprinted by permission of HarperCollins Publishers, Inc.

Hillesum, Etty: From *Letters from Westerbork* by Etty Hillesum. English translation copyright © 1986 by Random House, Inc. Reprinted by permission of Pantheon Books, a division of Random House, Inc.

Holliday, Laurel: Reprinted with the permission of Pocket Books, a Division of Simon & Schuster from *Children in the Holocaust and World War I* by Laurel Holliday. Copyright © 1995 by Laurel Holliday.

Joffo, Joseph: Excerpt from *A Bag of Marbles* by Joseph Joffo, translated by Martin Sokolinskuy. Copyright © 1974 by Joseph Joffo. Reprinted by permission of Houghton Mifflin Company. All rights reserved.

Korwin, Yala: "39 Casimir-the-Great Street," "Noemi," "They Had a System," and "Singing in the Sun" by Yala Korwin, from *To Tell the Story*, 1987. Reprinted by permission of the United States Holocaust Memorial Museum.

Kraus, Joanna Halpert: From *Remember My Name* by Joanna Halpert Kraus. Copyright © 1989 by Joanna Halpert Kraus. CAUTION: Professionals and amateurs are hereby warned that "Remember My Name" being fully protected under the copyright laws of the United States of America, the British Commonwealth countries, including Canada, and the other countries of the Copyright Union, is subject to a royalty. All rights, including professional, amateur, motion picture, recitation, public reading, radio, television and cable broadcasting, and the rights of translation into foreign languages, are strictly reserved. Any inquiry regarding the availability of performance rights, or the purchase of individual copies of the authorized acting edition, must be directed to Samuel French Inc., 45 West 25 Street, NY, NY 10010 with other locations in Hollywood and Toronto, Canada.

Latour, Anny: "The Networks of the Jewish Resistance" by Anny Latour, from *The Jewish Resistance in France, (1940–1944)*, 1981, translated by Irene R. Ilton. Reprinted by permission of the United States Holocaust Memorial Museum.

Lebow, Barbara: From *A Shayna Maidel* by Barbara Lebow. © Copyright, 1988, by Barbara Lebow. © Copyright, 1984, by Barbara Lebow as an unpublished dramatic composition. CAUTION: The reprinting of *A Shayna Maidel* included in this volume is reprinted by permission of the author and Dramatists Play Service, Inc., The stock and amateur performance rights in this play are controlled exclusively by Dramatists Play Service, Inc., 440 Park Avenue South, New York, N.Y. 10016. No stock or amateur production of the play may be given without obtaining in advance, the written permission of the Dramatists Play Service, Inc., and paying the requisite fee. Inquiries regarding all other rights should be addressed to Mary Harden, c/o Bret Adams Limited, 448 West 44th Street, New York, N.Y. 10036.

Leitner, Isabella and Irving Leitner: Reprinted from *Saving the Fragments: From Auschwitz to New York*, published by NAL (pp. 13–16; 25–30; 53–58), with permission of Gelfman Schneider Literary Agents., Inc. on behalf of the Author.

Levi, Primo: From pages 13–27 in *Survival in Auschwitz* by Primo Levi, translated from the Italian by Stuart Woolf. Copyright © 1960 by The Orion Press. Used with permission of Bobbe Siegel Literary Agency.

Levi, Primo: Reprinted with the permission of Simon & Schuster from *If Not Now, When?* by Primo Levi, translated by William Weaver. Copyright © 1982 by Giulio Einaudi editore, s.p.a., Torino. Translation © 1985 by Simon & Schuster.

Levi, Primo: "The Awakening" from pp. 204–208 in *The Reawakening* by Primo Levi, translated from the Italian by Stuart Woolf. Copyright © 1965 by The Bodley Head. Reprinted by permission of Bobbe Siegel Literary Agency.

Levi, Primo: "The Thaw" from pp. 15–21 in *The Reawakening* by Primo Levi, translated from the Italian by Stuart Woolf. Copyright © 1965 by The Bodley Head. Reprinted by permission of Bobbe Siegel Literary Agency.

Lewin, Abraham: From "Part II: Diary of the Great Deportation" by Abraham Lewin in *A Cup of Tears*, edited by A. Polonsky, 1989. Reprinted by permission of Blackwell Publishers.

Lustig, Arnost: "The Lemon" in *Diamonds of the Night*, translated by Jeanne Nemcova (Northwestern University Press, 1986) 90–107. Reprinted by permission.

Lustig, Arnost: "The Return" from *Night and Hope*. Reprinted by permission of Penguin USA.

Marczak-Oborski, Stanislaw: "Warsaw in April 1943" by Stanislaw Marczak-Oborski from *Poems of the Ghetto: A Testament of Lost Men*, edited and translated by Adam Gillon. Copyright 1969 by Adam Gillon. Reprinted by permission.

Marks, Jane: From *The Hidden Children* by Jane Marks. Copyright © 1993 by Jane Marks. Reprinted by permission of Ballantine Books, a Division of Random House Inc.

Meed, Vladka: "Leaving the Ghetto," "The Ghetto in Flames" (retitled "The Warsaw Ghetto Uprising"), and "Volunteers" by Vladka Meed from *On Both Sides of the Wall*, 1979. Reprinted by permission of the United State Holocaust Memorial Museum.

Meltzer, Milton: "Why Remember?" from *Never to Forget* by Milton Meltzer. Copyright © 1976 by Milton Meltzer. Reprinted by permission of HarperCollins Publishers.

Mikofsky, Bernard S.: "1945" by Bernard S. Mikofsky, from *Blood to Remember*, edited by Charles Fishman, 1991. Copyright © 1975 Friday Forum of the Jewish Exponent (Philadelphia). Reprinted by permission of the author.

Milosz, Czeslaw: "Dedication" from *The Collected Poems* by Czeslaw Milosz. Copyright © 1988 by Czeslaw Milosz Royalties, Inc. First published by The Ecco Press in 1988. Reprinted by permission.

Nomberg-Przytyk, Sara: "A Living Torch," "Natasha's Triumph," and "Taut as a String" reprinted from *Auschwitz: True Tales from a Grotesque Land*, by Sara Nomberg-Przytyk. Copyright © 1986 by the University of North Carolina Press. Used by permission of the publisher.

Orenstein, Henry: From *I Shall Live* by Henry Orenstein. New York: Beaufort Books. Copyright © 1987 by Henry Orenstein. Reprinted by permission of the author.

Ozick, Cynthia: From *The Shawl* by Cynthia Ozick. Copyright © 1980, 1983 by Cynithia Ozick. Reprinted by permission of Alfred A. Knopf Inc.

Papanek, Ernst: "Why Me?" from *Out of the Fire*. Reprinted by permission of Sterling Lord Literistic, Inc.

Petrow, Richard: Text pp. 208–212, 215–221 from *The Bitter Years* by Richard Petrow. Copyright © 1974 by Richard Petrow. By permission of William Morrow and Company, Inc.

Pillin, William: "A Poem for Anton Schmidt" by William Pillin. Reprinted by permission of Boris Pillin.

Plant, Richard: "Before the Storm" from *The Pink Triangle* by Richard Plant. Copyright © 1986 by Richard Plant. Reprinted by permission of Henry Holt and Co., Inc.

Rashke, Richard: From *Escape from Sobibor* by Richard Rashke. Copyright © 1982 by Richard Rashke. By permission of the author.

Rich, Adrienne: Part II of "Letters in the Family" from *Time's Power: Poems 1985–1988* by Adrienne Rich. Copyright © 1989 by Adrienne Rich. Reprinted by permission of the author and W. W. Norton & Company, Inc.

Rittner, Carol and Sondra Myers: "Chaim Asa" and "Irene Opydyke" from *The Courage to Care*, edited by Carol Rittner, R.S.M. and Sondra Meyers (New York: New York University Press, 1986). Reprinted by permission.

Rogasky, Barbara: Text copyright © 1988 by Barbara Rogasky. All rights reserved. Reprinted from *Smoke And Ashes: The Story of the Holocaust* by permission of Holiday House, Inc.

Romano, Elio: From "A Prelude to Hell" from *A Generation of Wrath* by Elio Romano. Copyright © 1984 by Elio Romano. Republished with acknowledgement to Severn House Publishers Ltd.

Rosenberg, Maxine B.: "Andy Sterling" from *Hiding to Survive: Stories of Jewish Children Rescued from the Holocaust*. Copyright © 1994 by Maxine B. Rosenberg. Reprinted by permission of Clarion Books/Houghton Mifflin Company. All rights reserved.

Rosenfeld, Harvey: From *Raoul Wallenberg* by Harvey Rosenfeld (New York: Holmes & Meier, 1995). Copyright © 1982, 1995 by Harvey Rosenfeld. Reproduced by permission of the publisher.

Sachs, Nelly: "Chorus of the Rescued" from *O the Chimneys* by Nelly Sachs. Translation copyright © 1967 and renewed © 1995 by Farrar, Straus & Giroux, Inc. Reprinted by permission of Farrar, Straus & Giroux, Inc.

Seiden, Othniel J.: From *The Survivor of Babi Yar* by Dr. Othniel J. Seiden, 1980. Reprinted by permission of the author.

Selzer, Michael: Excerpts as submitted from *Deliverance Day* by Michael Selzer. Copyright © 1978 by Michael Selzer. Reprinted by permission of HarperCollins Publishers, Inc.

Senesh, Hannah: From *Hannah Senesh: Her Life and Diary* by Hannah Senesh, translated by Marta Cohn. Text Copyright © 1971 by Nigel Marsh. Reprinted by permission of Shocken Books, published by Pantheon Books, a division of Random House, Inc. and Vallentine Mitchell & Co. Ltd.

Sierakowiak, Dawid: From "Dawid Sierakowiak's Diary" in *Lodz Ghetto* by Alan Adelson and Robert Lapides. Copyright © 1989 by The Jewish Heritage Writing Project. Used by permission of Viking Penguin, a division of Penguin Books USA Inc. and The Jewish Heritage Project.

Stiffel, Frank: "Treblinka" from *The Tale of the Ring: The Kaddish* by Frank Stiffel. Copyright © 1984, 1994 by Frank Stiffel. Reprinted by permission of Pushcart Press.

Sutzkever, Abraham: "1980" by Abraham Sutzkever, translated by Cynthia Ozick, from *The Penguin Book of Modern Yiddish Verse* by Irving Howe, Ruth R. Wisse and Chone Shmeruk. Copyright © 1987 by Irving Howe, Ruth Wisse, and Chone Shmeruk. Introduction and Notes Copyright © 1987 by Irving Howe. Used by permission of Viking Penguin, a division of Penguin Books USA Inc.

Wasserman, Burton D.: "1945, The Silence" by Burton D. Wasserman. Copyright © 1985 by Burton D. Wasserman. Reprinted by permission of the author.

Weinberg, Werner: "Hannover Happening" by Werner Weinberg from *Self-Portrait of a Holocaust Survivor*, 1985. Reprinted by permission of the author.

Weinberger, Florence: "Survivor" by Florence Weinberger from *Blood to Remember*, edited by Charles Fishman, 1991. Copyright © 1985 by Florence Weinberger. By permission of the author.

Wiesel, Elie and Gerd Korman: "Death Against Life" by Elie Wiesel from *Hunter and Hunted* by Gerd Korman. Published under the auspices of the B'nai B'rith Commission on Adult Jewish Education, 1973. Reprinted by permission.

Wiesel, Elie: Excerpt from *The Accident* by Elie Wiesel, translated by Anne Borchardt. Translation copyright © 1962 and renewed © 1990 by Elie Wiesel. Reprinted by permission of Hill and Wang, a division of Farrar, Straus & Giroux, Inc.

Wiesenthal, Simon: "Steps Beyond the Grave" by Simon Wiesenthal from *Hunter and Hunted* by Gerd Korman. Reprinted by permission of B'nai B'rith Commission on Adult Jewish Education.

Wiesenthal, Simon: "The Sunflower." Published in 1976 by Schocken Books. Reprinted by permission.

Yevtushenko, Yevgeny: "Babi Yar" by Yevgeny Yevtushenko, adapted from the Russian by Rose Styron. Reprinted by permission.

Zable, Arnold: Excerpt from *Jewels and Ashes* by Arnold Zable, copyright © 1993 by Arnold Zable, reprinted by permission of Harcourt Brace & Company.

The publisher has made every effort to contact copyright holders. Any omissions or errors will be corrected upon written notification.

Index of Authors and Titles